D1034134

RICHARD
W.
PEPE

GERONIMO!

Also by William B. Breuer

Bloody Clash at Sadzot
Captain Cool
They Jumped at Midnight
Drop Zone Sicily
Agony at Anzio
Hitler's Fortress Cherbourg
Death of a Nazi Army
Operation Torch
Storming Hitler's Rhine
Retaking the Philippines
Devil Boats
Operation Dragoon
The Secret War with Germany
Sea Wolf
Hitler's Undercover War

356.6
Be46
24 x 15.5

GERONIMO!

American Paratroopers in World War II

WILLIAM B. BREUER

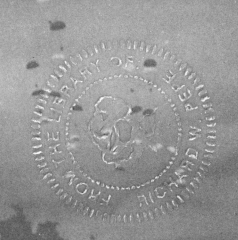

St. Martin's Press
New York

FROM THE LIBRARY OF RICHARD M. PEI...

GERONIMO! AMERICAN PARATROOPERS IN WORLD WAR II.
Copyright © 1989 by William B. Breuer. All rights
reserved. Printed in the United States of America. No part
of this book may be used or reproduced in any manner
whatsoever without written permission except in the case of
brief quotations embodied in critical articles or reviews. For
information, address St. Martin's Press, 175 Fifth Avenue,
New York, N.Y. 10010.

Design by Jaye Zimet

Library of Congress Cataloging-in-Publication Data

Breuer, William B.
    Geronimo! : American paratroopers in World War II.
        p.   cm.
    Includes index.
    ISBN 0-312-03350-8
    1. United States. Army—Parachute troops—History—
World War, 1939–1945. 2. World War, 1939–1945—Aerial
operations, American.
    I. Title.
D769.347.B47 1989 940.54′4973—dc20 89-32763

First Edition

10 9 8 7 6 5 4 3 2 1

Where is the prince who can afford so to cover his country with troops for its defense, as that ten thousand men descending from the clouds, might not, in many places, do an infinite deal of mischief before a force could be brought together to repel them?

—*Benjamin Frankin, 1784*

Dedicated to
Major General William C. Lee
Father of the United States Airborne
and to the
elite legion of gallant young men
who, over five decades, dared
to meet the challenge to
"stand up and hook up"
for America

Maj. Gen. William C. Lee
Father of the United States Airborne

Contents

PART THREE: History's Mightiest Endeavor

PART FOUR: Parachutes Around the World

PART FIVE: The Boys of Winter

PART SIX: Final Operations

MAPS

Author's Note

Since the historic D-Day landings in Normandy, I have been indelibly aware that the American paratrooper was a special breed of warrior, and that his lot was one of extreme peril requiring the highest order of courage, daring, and resourcefulness. Although I had never shared the ordeal of bailing out of an airplane behind or on enemy lines, my mortar platoon was attached to paratroop units—both to the 82nd Airborne and to the 101st Airborne Divisions during fierce fighting in Normandy, and later to the famed 509th Parachute Infantry Battalion during the Battle of the Bulge. I had had ample opportunity to observe what made these bold young men tick.

In recent years, I have tramped many European battlefields that were consecrated by the intrepid deeds and the lifeblood of American paratroopers: Sainte-Mère-Eglise, the La Fière and Carentan causeways in Normandy; Draguignan, LeMuy, and Les Arcs in Southern France; countless locales where Belgium's Battle of the Bulge was fought; Nijmegen, Best, Groesbeek, and Eindhoven in Holland; and Wesel and the Huertgen Forest in Germany. These visits helped me to get the "feel" of the exploits described in these pages.

Geronimo! (the battle cry of American paratroopers) is based overwhelmingly on personal and telephone interviews and contacts with 562 paratrooper participants—from generals to privates—as well as the flood of combat diaries, small-unit journals, personal letters, maps, and related materials that they provided at my request. Because of strict space limitations, this enormous amount of grassroots data resulted in constant decisions by the author about what fascinating events would have to be omitted.

Likewise, in order to keep this book in manageable proportions, America's other airborne men—the glider soldiers—did not receive the complete recognition they had so distinctly earned. More than 30,000 Americans rode into battle in flimsy gliders during World War II, and they performed with great dash and elan. Two glider soldiers were posthumously awarded the Congressional Medal of Honor: Pfc. Charles N. DeGlopper, 325th Glider Infantry, 82nd Airborne Division, and Sgt. Clinton M. Hendrick, 194th Glider Infantry, 17th Airborne Division.

And some day, it is hoped, a monument will be erected to honor the largely unsung heroes of American airborne warfare—the glider pilots and the C-47 and C-46 crews who flew the paratroopers and glider soldiers into battle and who suffered heavy casualties.

Invaluable in the reconstruction of American airborne operations were the highly dedicated historians and activists of the large number of World War II paratrooper alumni associations who performed "over and above" in providing the author with detailed information, who patiently responded to his avalanche of questions, and who helped to locate participants. Some of their names follow:

Richard L. Hoyt and George Doherty, 11th Airborne Division; Charles Beckman and Jack Bauer, 13th Airborne; Edward Siergiej and Joe Quade, 17th Airborne; Virgil Carmichael, Louis Hauptfleisch, Don Lassen, Clarence Hughart, and O. B. Hill, 82nd Airborne; and Elmer Sandeen and William E. King, Jr., 101st Airborne; Robert F. Atkins and William E. Blake, 503rd Parachute Infantry; Thomas J. Dellaca and Charles H. Doyle, 509th Parachute Infantry; Clark Archer, Thomas Cross, Charles LaChaussee, and Dr. Charles Pugh, 517th Parachute Infantry; Dan Morgan, 551st Parachute Infantry; Bradley Biggs, 555th Parachute Infantry; and Doug Wilmer of the glider pilots.

Deep appreciation is expressed to paratrooper combat veteran Lou Varrone, whose superb drawings of many Medal of Honor recipients enrich these pages, and to former paratroopers Keith Rose and Laurence Maxton, both highly knowledgeable paratrooper history buffs.

Most helpful in a variety of ways were Pierre Gosset of Liège, Belgium; Jan Bos of Nijmegen, Holland; Hillary Roberts of the Imperial War Museum, London; officials of the Bastogne Historical Center, Belgium; Jim Phillips of Phillips Publications; Dr. John Duvall and his staff of the 82nd Airborne Museum, Fort Bragg, North Carolina; Dr. Richard J. Sommers and his associates at the U.S. Army Military History Institute, Carlisle, Pennsylvania; Henry I. Shaw, Jr., chief historian, Danny J. Crawford, head, reference section, and their associates at Marine Corps headquarters, Washington, D.C.; Col. Lyman H. Hammond, Jr., director, MacArthur Memorial, Norfolk, Virginia; Benis Frank, distinguished author and World War II Marine; and Dr. William F. Atwater, director, and his staff at the Don F. Pratt Museum, Fort Campbell, Kentucky.

Finally, a tip of my hat to numerous qualified men who read related chapters of *Geronimo!* with the critical eye of participants and provided the author with their expert critiques.

Introduction

Most high-ranking officers in Gen. John J. Pershing's American Expeditionary Force in France considered Col. William P. "Billy" Mitchell to be an agitator, a gadfly, an officer whose head was filled with crackpot schemes. Mitchell did, indeed, march to his own drummer, and his critics were convinced that the 39-year-old pilot was consistently out of step.

His detractors were largely adherents of static trench warfare, in which both adversaries would hurl waves of soldiers (that is, "fresh meat") against the defenses of the other side. This was the doctrine that had slaughtered some 3 million Allied and German soldiers in four years of savage struggle on the western front.

Flamboyant Billy Mitchell was air service adviser to Blackjack Pershing, and on October 17, 1918, he laid out a radical tactical plan before the AEF chief. The proposal was designed to seize a key objective without a bloody, battering-ram approach.

Mitchell wanted to collect all of the available American bomber squadrons, 60 of them, consisting of 1,200 aircraft. Each bomber would be loaded with two machine guns and 1st Infantry Division men wearing parachutes. Then the planes would lift off from fields in France and drop the 12,000 soldiers of the Big Red One at a predesignated target behind German lines. This great sky armada, larger in scope than warfare had known, would be protected by hundreds of swift pursuit planes.

Once the 1st Infantry Division soldiers were dropped, other pursuit planes would buzz around them at low levels until they had formed into units, dug in, and set up machine guns. Meanwhile, the American main attack would have jumped off, presumably against German soldiers already panicky because of the presence of the large American Airborne force behind them.

When Billy Mitchell had completed the briefing, General Pershing sat silently for several moments. Blackjack's career had begun as a horse cavalryman in the Old West, so Mitchell doubted if his revolutionary mass-parachute concept would be well received. To the air officer's astonishment, General Pershing gave him the green light to proceed with detailed planning.

Delighted, Mitchell rushed to his own headquarters and excitedly explained to Maj. Lewis H. Brereton how he had sold Pershing his plan. (Neither air officer had any way of knowing that 26 years later Brereton would command an entire Allied airborne army.)

Mitchell's and Brereton's plan began to take shape. The assault would strike against German forces defending the fort-studded stronghold of Metz, France, in spring 1919. However, before much work had gone into a detailed parachute-assault plan, peace broke out, on November 11, 1918. It would be 21 years before the American military would again focus on the concept of "vertical envelopment"—a surprise strike from the air behind enemy lines.[1]

Colonel Mitchell's scheme had been far ahead of its time. Even the mode of transportation, the airplane, had evolved only in December 1903 when brothers Orville and Wilbur Wright flew the world's first power-driven, heavier-than-air machine on a strip of sand called Kill Devil Hill, near the village of Kitty Hawk, North Carolina. The strange-looking apparatus with the wobbly wings had cost the Wrights $15 to build. With Orville at the controls (he had won a coin toss with Wilbur), the machine traveled 120 feet, at about 6.8 miles per hour, and remained in the air for 12 seconds.

Perhaps building on Billy Mitchell's concept, the Russians were the first to develop the basic techniques for the use of parachute troops as a military weapon. In 1931, Soviet emissaries were sent to the United States to purchase several thousand new-type parachutes made famous by big-name circus attraction Leslie L. "Sky High" Irvin. These chutes had rip-cords (instead of opening by a line attached to an aircraft) and were known as the Model A.

On August 18, 1933, the Red Army had 46 paratroopers jump from two bombers to reportedly break the world's record for mass bailouts. At the same time, a small combat tank was dropped by a giant parachute, probably the first drop of such heavy equipment. And foreign military observers were stunned at Russian maneuvers in 1935 when transports suddenly appeared in formation and dropped two battalions of infantry, which seized an airfield and held it while reinforcements, including 16 artillery pieces, were flown in.

Using intelligence obtained from the Russians by military observers and spies, the Germans expanded and refined airborne techniques. The World War I Treaty of Versailles prohibited Germany from rearming, but on February 23, 1933, rotund Hermann Goering, a fighter-pilot ace in that war and now Minister of the Interior in Adolf Hitler's Third Reich, founded the *Polizeiabteilung Wecke* (Police Detachment Wecke). Under command of Maj. Hans Wecke, the unit's principal function was to root out and arrest Communist cells in the Berlin region. Most of the volunteers were from the Berlin police department.

When preparing to carry out a raid, Major Wecke had aerial photographs taken of the targeted area by his *Luftaufsicht* (air section). After the photos had been studied, a plan of action was drawn up. Stealth and surprise were crucial. An airplane would then fly over the locale where the Communist cell was thought to be located, and the parachuting policemen would bail out and try to collar the suspects.

Within two years, Wecke's police parachute unit had been so successful that Goering, now the Luftwaffe chief, absorbed it into his organization. It mushroomed in strength, until it became the 1st Parachute Rifle Battalion. On July 1, 1938, Maj. Gen. Kurt Student was appointed to command the airborne forces of the Luftwaffe, and the *Fallschirmjaeger* (paratroops) began to expand into regiments, then divisions. It was Student, a World War I pilot, who infused his men with an intense fighting esprit—an elan that would come to be known in all nations as the "paratrooper spirit."[2]

On May 11, 1940, the keenly honed *Wehrmacht* airborne arm finally struck with a mixture of fury and surgeon's skill. The *Falschirm-Pioniere Abteilung* (Parachute Engineer Unit), led by *Oberleutnant* Rudolf Witzig, swooped down by glider on top of Belgium's Fort Emael, reputed to be the strongest fort in the world. The nine-fort complex was fully manned by Belgian troops, but the Germans, blasting away with satchel charges, captured the stronghold at a cost of only six dead and 15 wounded.

At the same time, 30 gliders carrying 350 Germans crash-landed around three vital bridges over the Meuse River, which were soon captured, and 500 paratroopers bailed out over Holland to seize key airports and bridges.

These spearhead operations permitted German panzers to dash through the Low Countries and into France, where the French Army—thought to have been the world's finest—was smashed in only six weeks. (Adolf Hitler and his generals had introduced *Blitzkrieg* [lightning war] to the world.)

During the 1930s, America's military brass in Washington, reflecting the popular "keep-out-of-other-nation's-quarrels" mood of the time, had yawned while Russia and Germany were developing airborne capabilities. "Window dressing" was the general opinion of the new paratroop units in the War Department.

However, there were mavericks with a different view lower down in the U.S. chain of command. These junior officers were mostly disciples of Gen. Billy Mitchell, who had held the nonsensical notion that large bodies of soldiers could be parachuted behind enemy lines. During mid-1930s maneuvers near Fort DuPont, Delaware, Army Air Corps Capt. George C. Kenney had the audacity to violate the static-warfare tactics still in vogue with most U.S. Army brass: He airlanded an infantry platoon behind "enemy" lines. There were screams of "foul!"[3]

It was not until the fall of 1939, when Adolf Hitler's war machine had gobbled up Poland and gone to war with Great Britain and France, that the dozing United States Army brass began to stir. Early in January 1940, Maj. Gen. George A. Lynch, chief of infantry, appointed Maj. William C. Lee to experiment with the transport of foot soldiers by air. A native of Dunn, North Carolina, the 43-year-old Bill Lee had seen combat in World War I as a platoon leader and company commander. For the next four years, Lee would drive himself remorselessly in developing airborne doctrine, in creating equipment, and in activating new units. He would become known as the Father of the American Airborne.

Despite Lee's hammering at the War Department for improved parachutes, a few aircraft, and a handful of men to carry out test experiments, the Army dragged its feet until the stunning success of Gen. Kurt Student's airborne troops in Belgium and Holland in May of 1940 shocked the American high command. A "Parachute Test Platoon" was finally authorized.

Almost at once, a bitter squabble erupted between regular

Army and Army Air Corps leaders over who would control this "glamour" group. The men would be air grenadiers, so they should be commanded by the air corps, the air generals declared. "Nonsense," exclaimed the chief of infantry; the parachutists would be infantry soldiers and should be directed by the Army Infantry Board. (Seldom had so many argued so vehemently over so few.)

The Infantry Board at Fort Benning, Georgia, prevailed, however.

At the morning formation on June 26, 1940, soldiers of the Infantry School's 29th Infantry "Demonstration" Regiment were informed of a golden opportunity to volunteer for the elite Parachute Test Platoon, which would be dedicated to exciting adventure and the creation of airborne equipment and techniques. Many eagerly signed up; others blanched at the thought of falling out of flying airplanes.

Two hundred men volunteered for the Test Platoon, and 39 were selected. Lt. William T. Ryder, who had graduated from West Point four years earlier, was appointed platoon leader, with Lt. James A. Bassett as his second-in-command. Thus was established the paratroop concept "every man a volunteer."[4]

Civilian Conservation Corps cleared an area to the south of Benning's Lawson Field to serve as a landing zone for the Test Platoon (and thousands of paratroopers who would follow). Almost at once, this patch of Georgia landscape was given the name Cactus Field; it seemed as though every prickled plant in Georgia had been brought in to welcome descending paratroopers.

On August 16, 1940, Lt. Bill Ryder made the inaugural jump, from a Douglas B-18 bomber, thus gaining enduring fame as "America's first paratrooper." The enlisted man who, by a drawing, was to leap out behind Ryder, "froze" in the door of the bomber, so the next man, Pvt. William "Red" King, leaped out, thereby becoming the nation's "first enlisted paratrooper."[5]

On the night before the Test Platoon's first mass jump, tall, lanky Pvt. Aubrey Eberhardt and three comrades had taken in a post movie, a standard Western shootout involving the U.S. Cavalry and the Apache chief Geronimo. Before heading back to their barracks, the four soldiers spent a couple of hours at a beer garden, and one crony needled Eberhardt that he would be too frightened before the morrow's jump to even speak. Nonsense,

Eberhardt responded. What's more, he would shout *"Geronimo!"* as soon as he leaped out the door of the Douglas bomber.

Eberhardt kept his pledge, and other Test Platoon men bailed out with Indian war whoops and shouts of *"Geronimo!"*

In the future, Test Platoon men called out the Apache chief's name on each practice jump, and later newly formed parachute units would adopt the yell. "Geronimo!" became the battle cry of American paratroopers, and with a heavy media focus on the yell, much of the civilian population associated the cry "Geronimo!" with the nation's paratroopers.

Maj. William M. Miley. *(U. S. Army)*   Lt. William T. Ryder. *(Lou Varrone)*

Two months after the Parachute Test Platoon was formed, the U.S. Army's first airborne tactical unit was activated—the 501st Parachute Infantry Battalion. Leader of this pioneer formation was Maj. William M. Miley, who for two years had served as Benning's athletic officer. At 42 years of age, "Bud" Miley was old for a parachute battalion commander, but he had been a star gymnast at West Point, he kept himself in superb physical condition, and he would handle the rigors of being a sky soldier without difficulty.[6]

These pioneer American paratroopers were viewed by others

in the army with varying degrees of resentment. Early paratrooper Lou Varrone recalled that era:

> *Almost from the start, we sensed a bureaucratic animosity and*
> *misunderstanding of these newly incubated soldiers. Due to our*
> *distinctive deportment, jump boots, and bloused trousers, we were*
> *considered to be swaggering, cocky, overbearing, and arrogant. But*
> *these views were grossly mistaken, for the qualities of self-esteem, a*
> *strong sense of destiny, supreme confidence, arduous training, a*
> *mystical camaraderie, and the pioneering spirit of a challenging*
> *new frontier, were what we were all about. How were super-elite*
> *troops supposed to act—like we had an inferiority complex?*

Hard on the heels of the army's airborne birth, the Marine Corps
launched its paratroop program; in October 1940, the first group
of "Leathernecks" assembled at the Naval Air Station, Lakehurst,
New Jersey. The parachute trainees included Lt. Walter S. Os-
ipoff, Lt. Robert C. McDonough, and 38 enlisted men. None of
these eager and adventurous Marines knew anything about training paratroopers, but no one else in the Corps did, either.

Back in 1927, Marine brass showed a fleeting interest in the
concept of dropping soldiers behind enemy lines. At that time,
12 Leathernecks had made a mass jump from a transport plane
over Anacostia in Washington, D.C. Ten years later, another airborne spark flickered in the Marine Corps high command when
parachutists were used in 1937 during fleet-landing exercises on
islands off California. However, Corps brass considered the concept of dropping Marines behind enemy lines by parachute to be
a sideshow, a carnival attraction.

Three years later, Secretary of the Navy Frank Knox shared
the shock of most American military leaders at the stunning success of Adolf Hitler's airborne forces, and directed the Marines to
form similar units. It was planned to train a battalion of each
regiment as an air-landing force, including a company of paratroopers for each Marine division to "conduct raids, reconnaissance, and other independent operations."

Lakehurst was a Navy facility, so after several classes of Marine paratroopers graduated, the Corps set up its own parachute
schools at Camp Gillespie, California, and New River, North
Carolina. By early 1941, tiny cadres for Leatherneck companies
and battalions had been formed.

On July 29, 1941, Marine Capt. Robert A. Williams and what the newspapers would describe as "40 heavily armed young gentlemen of the Marine Corps" almost disrupted the activities of 17,000 soldiers at the U. S. Army's new Caroline County maneuver area near Fredericksburg, Virginia. Williams, who had joined the paratroopers after a stint as aide-de-camp to President Franklin D. Roosevelt, and his high-spirited men had hatched a plot to stage a surprise parachute attack on the unknowing Army troops.

At the appointed hour, a Douglas transport plane, marked with the Marine Corps' globe-and-anchor insignia, roared over the Nottingham airport, dead in the center of the Army's maneuver area. Used as a military field, the airport was the Marine paratroopers' objective. At 750 feet, Bob Williams jumped, followed by 10 other paratroopers. A second transport then flew over the field, 10 more Leathernecks jumped, and finally two more Douglases appeared, and 20 other men leaped.

All of the Marine paratroops wore a uniform that had been modeled after the one used by German *Fallschirmjaeger*—knee-length overalls and a new crash helmet. Army men looked up in amazement as these "living bombs" (as the paratroopers would be described by the media covering the maneuvers) suddenly appeared in the sky.

The unexpected touch of airborne *Blitzkreig* created an uproar, for it was the first major employment of parachute troops in United States maneuvers. Staff cars and umpires' vehicles raced to the airport, which had been "captured" by Captain Williams and his Leathernecks. Colonels, majors, and captains scrambled from the vehicles and demanded to know what in the blankety-blank was going on. Army officers were far from happy—especially after they learned that the interlopers were *Marines!*

Not to be outdone, the Army's airborne arm pulled a similar caper a few weeks later at the big Army war games in Louisiana. A force of 127 paratroopers was deposited by the Blue army behind the Red army lines. There were loud cries of "foul!" from Red army commanders, who had been caught with their map cases down. By prior agreement, all the paratroopers were to surrender if not captured within 20 hours of landing. When the time expired, more than half of the parachutists were still on the loose, slashing Red army telephone wires and generally creating havoc—a technique that would be duplicated for real in the battles that were to come.

On December 7, 1941, Japanese bombs at Pearl Harbor sent America's pacifist leaders and unilateral disarmament "experts" scurrying for cover. The United States had literally been blasted into a global war. Along with the rest of the Army, America's airborne units began to mushroom. The Airborne Command was set up at Fort Bragg, North Carolina, with Bill Lee, now a one-star general, as its boss. Five new parachute regiments were rapidly formed—the 503rd, 504th, 505th, 506th, and 507th.

At this point, in late spring 1942, the War Department planned no airborne unit larger than a regiment, but that view changed. In mid-August, the 82nd Motorized Division, based at sun-baked Camp Claiborne, Louisiana, was split in half and became the 82nd "All-American" Airborne Division and the 101st "Screaming Eagles" Airborne Division. Each outfit would have 8,321 men (compared with the 14,000 in a conventional ground division).

Steadily, paratroopers were gaining widespread fame among American civilians, who were curious to know what made these crazy guys tick. At a Washington press conference on paratroopers, Maj. Gen. Lesley J. McNair, commander of Army Ground Forces, remarked:

"They [the paratroopers] . . . are our *problem children*. They make a lot of money, and they know they're good. This makes them a little temperamental, but they're great soldiers." McNair's tone was one of thinly concealed admiration, much like the mood of a doting father whose offspring brings home all A's for achievement on his report card but flunks deportment.

Meanwhile, around the war-torn globe, the Allies were taking a severe licking at the hands of the Japanese, Germans, and Italians. In an effort to stem the tide, American Army and Marine units, many of them half-trained and lacking adequate weapons and equipment, were being rushed overseas. In early June 1942, one U.S. Army parachute battalion was shipped to England, and a day later the Marine 1st Parachute Battalion set sail for the Pacific. They were America's airborne vanguard.

PART I

Paratroop
Pioneers

1
First to Fight

D-DAY, AUGUST 7, 1942, 0300 HOURS Deep in the musty bowels of the transport *Heywood*, men of the Marine 1st Parachute Battalion were being rousted from their bunks. Few had slept that night; most had tossed fitfully. Nine hours from now—at high noon—these Chutes ("paramarines," some called them) would be storming ashore on a tiny, Japanese-held islet that none had heard of until briefings a few days earlier— Gavutu.

Led by Maj. Robert H. Williams, the Marine paratroopers were frustrated and angry. For many months, they had trained arduously to jump behind Japanese lines, create havoc, and strike fear and terror into the hearts of their enemy. The Jumping Gyrenes had lugged their parachutes from the United States to New Zealand in July 1942, and then had been told that they would become amphibious troops for the invasion of the Solomon Islands.

The *Heywood* was part of the invasion fleet that was now sailing past the western tip of a primitive, 90-mile-long island called Guadalcanal. Carried in the convoy were more than 20,000 men of Maj. Gen. Alexander A. Vandegrift's 1st Marine Division and attached units, which included Williams' paratroopers. Code-named Operation Watchtower, the Solomons invasion would be the first American offensive action of the war and the largest amphibious assault ever undertaken by Americans. It was a gamble—no one, from General Vandegrift down to his riflemen, knew quite what would happen.

For 40 years, the United States Marines had conducted countless landing exercises with the fleet, but neither Vandegrift nor other commanders involved with planning or directing Operation Watchtower had ever been involved in a *combat* operation of this scope. In fact, the invasion had been conceived only five weeks earlier, and it was mounted as a crash operation after word had been received that the Japanese had landed on Guadalcanal.

For nine months now the mighty armed forces of Japan had burst southward toward their ultimate goal in the southern Pacific—Australia. The Australians had thought that they had a protective screen in the wild, desolate chain of islands a few hundred miles to the north—the 600-mile-long Solomons. A haunting new specter now emerged: in Japanese hands, the Solomons could turn into a stepping-stone for a bayonet-tipped leap into Australia.

Rounding the western tip of Guadalcanal and steaming eastward through the black waters of Sealark Channel, the convoy split in two parts as planned. Task Force Yoke, led by Brig. Gen. William H. Rupertus, the assistant commander of the 1st Marine Division, would assault and seize Gavutu, Florida, Tanambogo, and Tulagi islands and islets. Yoke consisted of Williams' 1st Parachute Battalion, Lt. Col. Merritt E. "Red Mike" Edson's 1st Raider Battalion, and elements of the 2nd Marine Regiment.

Force X-Ray, built around the bulk of the 1st Division, would invade the northern shore of Guadalcanal and capture one of Operation Watchtower's prized objectives, a partially completed Japanese airfield a short distance inland. (That crude facility would be named Henderson Field.)[1]

Much of Archer Vandegrift's invasion force was only half-trained. His junior officers were of the "Young Breed"—eager, bright, tough, and green. Most of the privates and privates first class were teenagers, adventure-minded youths who had joined the Leathernecks prior to Pearl Harbor. Mixed in with the youngsters were the old salts, largely corporals and sergeants, who had seen jungle fighting in Haiti during a United States expedition to Central America in the early 1930s.

Vandegrift and his battle leaders had another deep concern: the Marines would be landing "blind." Little was known about Guadalcanal or the cluster of islands across Sealark Channel. Maps consisted of rough sketches (they would prove to be woefully inaccurate), drawn from vague recollections obtained hastily by Lt. Col. Frank Goettge, the 1st Division intelligence officer, from men and women in Australia who had once lived or worked in the Solomons.[2]

Now, just before dawn on D-Day, the split invasion armada slipped into positions off Guadalcanal and the islands to the north. On a weather deck of the *Heywood,* at 6:30 A.M., Maj. Bob Williams was peering through binoculars at the hazy silhouette of Gavutu, a tiny patch of sand and coral. Like his men, Williams was deeply disappointed over the invasion role assigned to his finely honed paratroop outfit.

Williams, widely regarded as the "father of the Marine airborne," had graduated from Ohio State University, was commissioned by the Marine Corps, washed out of Navy flight school at Pensacola, Florida, pulled duty with the Fourth Marines in Shanghai, and served as an aide-de-camp to President Roosevelt.[3]

Through his binoculars, Major Williams could view the lone, partly wooded Hill 148 that dominated the islet. Out of view was the wharf where ancient, coal-burning interisland steamers had tied up. There was not a sign of Japanese activity, but Williams suspected (rightly) that large numbers of unseen enemy soldiers were burrowed mole-like into caves on the slopes of the big hill.[4]

Despite landing by sea rather than by air drop, Williams and his men were proud to know not only that they would not only be among the "first to fight" (the Marine Corps motto for more than a century), but they would also be the first American paratroopers in history to engage in combat.

H-Hour for the attack on Tulagi had been set for 8:00 A.M.— one hour before the Marines were to hit Guadalcanal; but at 7:40 A.M., Bill Rupertus radioed Archer Vandegrift offshore. "I know I'm jumping the gun, but we're all ready to go and I'd feel better about going in now," the Yoke Force leader said.

"Take off!" was the brisk reply.[5]

An hour later, Red Mike Edson's Raider Battalion and 2nd Battalion, 5th Marines, stormed ashore on Tulagi against scattered resistance, and quickly fanned out over the island. First ashore on Guadalcanal, at 9:10 A.M. were the 1st and 3rd Battalions of Col. Leroy P. Hunt's 5th Marines. Hardly a shot had been fired at the invaders, and they rapidly pushed inland to seize the partially completed airstrip.

Offshore from Gavutu, Bob Williams' Chutes had to await the

arrival of assault boats that had taken the Marines into Tulagi. The battalion would land in three waves, one company in four boats in each wave. Capt. William McKennan's Company A would hit the beach first. There had been no strategy involved in selecting McKennan's outfit—he had won a coin toss for the "honor" of going in first. ("*Lost* the toss," Company A men quipped grimly.)

Once the 377-man paratroop battalion was ashore (intelligence had predicted little or no opposition), the Chutes would secure Gavutu, then march over the 200-yard crushed-coral causeway to seize the neighboring islet of Tanambogo. No one could foresee that the looming fight on Gavutu would be as fierce as any in the Guadalcanal bloodletting that was to rage for six months.

At about 10:00 A.M. Bill McKennan's Chutes threw legs over the *Heywood*'s railing, slithered down rope ladders, and dropped with thuds into assault boats. Marines, a mass of green uniforms and camouflaged helmets, were silent and nervous—a contrast to the gaiety, songs, and boasting that had filled the few preceding days. Now the moment of truth was at hand.

The Navy coxswain in each craft drew abreast of one another and headed for shore. Halfway to the beach, the light cruiser *San Juan* began pounding the hill and the landing beach on Gavutu with her 14 five-inch guns to "soften" the defenses. The Chutes kept their heads down below the gunwales, and wondered just how soft that would be.

With the *San Juan*'s guns blasting away, the din was ear-splitting. Peeking cautiously from below helmet rims, the Marines saw that Gavutu seemed to be erupting in a cloud of thick black smoke and sheets of orange and yellow. How could a human survive that inferno of explosives?

Nearing the beach, the Chutes felt a new surge of anxiety. Hearts beat faster. Sweat beads grew larger. Despite the excitement of the moment, there was no talking. Then the four boats in the first wave slipped gently onto the soft mud of shore. Bill McKennan leaped out, no doubt hoping to be the first American paratrooper ever to storm a hostile beach.

As the Chutes waded through the surf, only an occasional shot was fired at them. One of these bullets killed Capt. Kermit Mason, the battalion intelligence officer, who had stood up to get a better view of the terrain. Company A began pushing forward.

Four minutes behind McKennan's boys, B Company's boats

approached the beach—and ran into a mass of gunfire. Japanese with machine-guns and rifles, packed in caves on Hill 148, poured heavy bursts of fire into the landing craft. Chutes were killed in the boats; others were shot as they splashed ashore or while on the beach.

American paratroopers were first blooded in the bitter fight for flyspeck Gavutu islet (above). Marine Corps Maj. Robert H. Williams, parachute battalion leader (right). *(Marine Corps photos)*

Hard on the heels of B Company, Capt. Richard Heurth's C Company reached the shore, drawing even more intense fire from the hill. Heurth started to jump from his boat when a bullet tore into his head, killing him instantly. Moving like a well-oiled machine, Bob Williams' entire "airborne" battalion was on Gavutu within 18 minutes of the first ramp touching down.

One of those ducking bullets on the beach was Chaplain James J. Fitzgerald, a Chicago priest, who could have served as a Hollywood casting director's image of a combat padre. The moment he had stepped ashore, the Marine to his front took a bullet through the head. Now the chaplain, under a hail of fire, was crawling and slithering around the beach, administering church rites to the dead and wounded.

Meanwhile, Capt. George R. Stallings, of Augusta, Georgia, the battalion operations officer, was making his way to a spot where he and Bob Williams had agreed to meet to set up a makeshift command post. When Stallings arrived, the battalion commander was not there. Word was that he had either been killed or had taken a contingent across the causeway to attack Tanambogo.

A short time later, Williams showed up at the command post (in a wooden shack), and rapidly organized an assault against Hill 148. Only a few snipers or a machine gun or two were expected to be encountered. The Chutes had no way of knowing that the steep elevation was honey-combed with caves, each a mini-fortress. Each cave was filled with Japanese soldiers, who had no food or water but plenty of weapons, ammunition and grenades, and who intended to fight until death.

Bob Williams himself led the assault up Hill 148 and was immediately shot through the chest. As Chutes tried to drag their leader to relative cover, they were raked by fire from the enemy on the heights. A pair of Chutes were wounded in the process. Williams, ashen faced and coughing spasmodically, ordered his men to leave him be and get on with the assault. Command of the battalion passed to Maj. Charles A. (Tony) Miller.

The Chutes began crawling and scratching up the hill. Many of the caves were connected, and made a sort of labyrinth. Marines would pour fire into one cave, only to have the occupants suddenly appear in another hole.

Capt. Harold L. Torgerson, of Valley Stream, New York, quickly decided that this was a type of warfare that neither the Chutes nor any other Marine had anticipated. So the ingenious officer improvised by tying 30 sticks of dynamite together, then dashing to a cave mouth while a few of his men poured fire into the opening. He then lit the fuse, shoved the TNT in amongst the Japanese—and ran like hell.

Torgerson employed this technique repeatedly, using up 20 cases of dynamite and most of the matches on Gavutu. A bullet shot off his wristwatch and creased his wrist. Another slug creased his buttocks. But nothing stopped his explosive campaign.

On one occasion, Torgerson tried a revised approach. He attached a five-gallon can of gasoline to one of his home-made bombs. That particular bomb went off with an enormous roar that seemed to shake the hill. Not only did it blow in the roof of a cave, but it knocked Torgerson down and blasted away most of his trousers. Undaunted, the Mad Bomber of Gavutu got to his feet and remarked to a Chute: "Boy, that was a pisser, wasn't it?"

In the meantime, Chutes were cleaning up other caves. The Japanese fought with incredible stubbornness—to the death. Cpl. George F. Grady, of New York City, made a solo charge against eight Nipponese. He gunned down two enemy soldiers with his tommy gun and, when the weapon jammed, used it as a club to bash and kill a third Japanese. Then, dropping his gun, he whipped out a trench knife and plunged it into two more of the enemy. Moments later George Grady was killed by the three Japanese who had survived his onslaught.

Cpl. Ralph W. Fordyce, of Conneaut Lake, Pennsylvania, alone wiped out six enemy positions, holding at least six Japanese each. Then he charged into another cave ("dungeons," the Chutes would call them) with tommy gun blazing, and dragged out the bodies of eight of his victims.

Because the Chutes had run head-on into unexpectedly stiff opposition on Gavutu, Capt. Edgar Crane's B Company, 2nd Regiment, was ordered to rush to the tiny island. Earlier that morning, Crane's outfit had waded ashore on nearby Florida island and rapidly secured its objectives—a dominating hill and Haleta village.

Ed Crane reported to the Chutes' Major Miller at about 6:00 P.M. and was ordered to take his reinforced rifle company to adjoining Tanambogo and seize the islet. "What's the opposition there?" Crane asked. "Only a few snipers," Miller replied.

Crane's men reboarded their six landing craft and went ashore after dark on Tanambogo, where they were greeted by such a heavy fusillade of automatic weapons fire that they had to re-embark, bringing along numerous wounded comrades. As on Gavutu, the lone hill on Tanambogo (121 feet high) was honeycombed with fortified caves. A few of Crane's men had inadvertently been left behind, and they swam the few hundred yards to Gavutu.

When word that Captain Crane's company was repulsed on Tanambogo reached Gen. Bill Rupertus, he ordered elements of Lt. Col. Robert G. Hunt's 3rd Battalion, 2nd Regiment, to assault Gavutu's neighboring islet. Hunt's men went ashore on Tanambogo at 4:15 P.M. with two tanks, both of which were knocked out by bands of screaming Japanese who swarmed over the tracked vehicles.

Bitter fighting on Gavutu-Tanambogo raged all that day, but by nightfall both blood-stained islets were in Marine hands. In 48 hours of battle against a clever and tenacious foe, the 1st Parachute Battalion had suffered 27 men killed and 48 wounded—including the unit's leader, Bob Williams—in its baptism of fire. The Chutes, as was often said of a green unit, had been "blooded."

After the fireworks had died down, except for an occasional die-hard sniper, Richard Tregaskis, who was a highly regarded reporter covering Operation Watchtower, scrambled to the peak of Hill 148 on Gavutu. Later he would file his story:

> *I wondered how [the Chutes] had ever succeeded in taking this island. Looking down from this precipitous hill to the dock area where the Marines had landed gave one the feeling of looking into the palm of one's own hand. I thought: If I did not know that the Marines had taken this island hill, I would have said that the job, especially against a well-armed, numerically superior force, was impossible.* [6]

The focus of the Solomons struggle now shifted to Guadalcanal, and on September 4 the 1st Parachute Battalion was shipped to a hellhole of thick, steaming jungles and swamps filled with huge crocodiles, lizards, snakes, rats, leeches, poisonous centipedes, and swarms of mosquitoes, flies, and a wide array of insects. The "Canal" (as the Marines called the island) was a breeding ground for malaria, beriberi, and jungle rot—a fungus that spreads sores over the body.

Archer Vandegrift's Marines had formed a big, fortified half-circle perimeter around the invasion's prize, Henderson Field.

Already, American fighter planes and dive bombers were using the 3,778-foot-long runway to pound Japanese shipping and to lend close support to Leathernecks on the ground.

Meanwhile, on September 6, Maj. Gen. Kiyotake Kawaguchi, the able leader of Japanese troops on the island, was in the jungle about 12 miles from Henderson Field preparing to launch an all-out assault to wipe out the invaders. Kawaguchi, who sported a handlebar mustache, was supremely confident. Before departing Rabaul, a Japanese stronghold 580 miles to the north, he and his superior, Lt. Gen. Harukichi Hyakutake, had pinpointed the spot on the Guadalcanal coast where the Marines' surrender was to take place.

Through "Magic," the code-name for the intelligence gained from the interception and deciphering of secret Japanese messages, General Vandegrift was aware that the *Kawaguchi Butai* (brigade) would strike soon. He concluded that the most likely point to be hit was a ridge about 1,000 yards long and 1,700 yards southeast of Henderson Field. Vandegrift ordered the 1st Parachute Battalion, led by Maj. Tony Miller, and Red Mike Edson's 1st Raider Battalion to take up positions along the ridge, dig in, and hold.

Just before moving forward, the Chutes and Raiders had their first mail call in the Solomons. As they marched off for the ridge they carried packets of letters and boxes of cigars, cigarettes, and candy, along with one Marine's purple-and-red plaid necktie from Mom. Many of these coveted letters from home would never be read.

Reaching the ridge, the Marines heard shouts: "Okay, start digging in!" That order triggered an avalanche of grumbling. "Jesus Christ, you'd think they'd give us a chance to read our mail!" a Chute snarled, summing up the view of comrades.

As the Chutes and Raiders scooped out holes, coordinated artillery and mortar fire, and strung their meager allotment of barbed wire, Archer Vandegrift, an apple-cheeked, extremely affable man from Lynchburgh, Virginia, scrambled onto the ridge. Below in the thick jungle could be heard the movement of large numbers of Japanese, who were chanting constantly like the cheering section at football games back in the States. "What are they saying?" the calm general asked an interpreter.

"What they are chanting, sir," the Japanese-American Marine replied, is 'Marines, you die tonight, Marines, you die tonight!'"

The Chutes and the Raiders were hollering back at their unseen enemies at the bottom of the ridge, mimicking their chantings and throwing in a colorful collection of four-letter words.

Neither Vandegrift nor the Leathernecks had any way of knowing that here, on this rugged ridge split by deep defiles, would be fought one of the most crucial actions of the Pacific war. If the Japanese *Kawaguchi Butai* of some 2,100 men were to break through the thin line of Chutes and Raiders to capture Henderson Field, a monumental debacle would be inflicted upon the Americans.

There were not enough Marines to man a continuous ridge line; rather there was a series of strongpoints, with large, yawning gaps. The Chutes held the left flank, the Raiders were on the right. With nightfall, an eerie hush fell over embattled Guadalcanal.

About 9:00 P.M. the silence was broken by "Louie the Louse," as Marines called the Japanese float planes that roamed over the island at night, which dropped flares on Henderson Field and over the ridge. Thirty minutes later, three Japanese warships began shelling Henderson Field, destroying several planes; they then shifted their fire to the Chutes' and Raiders' foxhole line. Amidst the din of exploding shells, the boys on the ridge could hear the Japanese chants drawing closer . . . and closer: *"Marines you die! Marines you die!"*

Suddenly, red rocket flares broke out in the black sky over the ridge. Nervous Leathernecks tensed. Loud shouts rang out: "Here come the bastards!"

A rash of Japanese knee-mortar shells exploded among the Chutes and Raiders. Silhouetted by the red glow of the flares, hordes of enemy soldiers, led by officers waving swords and screaming *Banzai* and *Totsugeki* (Charge!), scrambled up the ridge. Hundreds of voices were yelling in Japanese, "Blood for the Emperor! Blood for the Emperor!"

The night turned into a cacophony: Marine machine guns chattering, Japanese rifles cracking like long strings of firecrackers, grenades exploding amid shouts and screams.

A bitter hand-to-hand fight erupted. Marine squads were overrun, others were cut off but kept firing. The Leathernecks began to fall back under the human tidal wave. Shortly before dawn, the Japanese broke off the fight and scurried back down the ridge. The Marines had been badly mauled, and their line had bent—but it did not break. Scores of Japanese bodies were sprawled grotesquely among foxholes and on the forward slope of the ridge.

Rapidly, the Chutes and Raiders reorganized. They knew the Japanese would strike again after dark. Grimly, the Marine survivors, wearing the haunted look of those who have journeyed through the valley of the shadow of death, braced for the onslaught. At his command post a few hundred yards behind the ridge, Archer Vandegrift, preparing for the worst, told his operations officer, Lt. Col. Gerald Thomas, to draw up a plan to conduct guerrilla operations if Henderson Field were captured.

At 8:35 P.M. red parachute flares lit up the ridge. Screaming and yelling *Banzai! Banzai!*, the Japanese charged, firing their .25-caliber Arisaka rifles and 7.7-millimeter Nambua light machine guns. Marine artillerymen to the rear fired howitzers until the barrels were red hot, cutting great swaths into the ranks of the oncoming enemy soldiers. The embattled ridge became a grotesque kaleidoscope of color: a red glow from the parachute flares, white from the tracers, and the fiery orange flashes of grenade and shell explosions. Silhouettes, dancing shadows.

The Chutes bore the brunt of the savage assault. Overrun by the charging masses, some Chutes bolted for the rear. They were intercepted by Capt. Harold Torgerson, the Mad Bomber of Gavutu, who turned around and challenged them to "Get the hell back up there and fight." Most of the dazed men did return.

Doggedly, the Marine remnants clung to the ridge through the night. At dawn, the Japanese had vanished and the pockmarked elevation was strangely quiet, except for the chirping of birds and the humming of insects. Unknown to Archer Vandegrift or to the Leatherneck survivors on what was now called Bloody Ridge, the *Kawaguchi Butai* had thrown in the towel at a time when one more full smash no doubt would have broken through the decimated and exhausted Chutes and Raiders.[7]

Burly General Kawaguchi's men had taken a severe beating. More than 600 Japanese corpses were counted on and around Bloody Ridge. Kawaguchi had hurled some 2,100 soldiers against the ridge; perhaps 1,200 were now trudging inland through the thick, steaming jungle, laboriously lugging wounded comrades, many of whom would be abandoned along the way to die in agony.

Victory in war is seldom cheap. A price in blood must always be paid. Eighteen Chutes had been killed and 118 wounded. The Raiders lost 31, with 104 wounded. Scores of Marine engineers, artillerymen, and riflemen from other units had also become casualties.

When the Henderson Field situation had been stabilized, the 1st Parachute Battalion was pulled out and shipped a thousand miles to New Caledonia. At Gavutu and Bloody Ridge, the battalion had lost 212 of its 377 paratroopers. The Chutes set up a tent city, which was named Camp Kiser after a comrade, Lt. Walter W. Kiser, who had been killed in the Gavutu assault.

In late 1942 and early 1943, the battle-tested men of the 1st Parachute Battalion were joined by the Marine 2nd and 3rd Parachute Battalions fresh from the States, and these three outfits were merged into the 1st Parachute Regiment. Its commander would be the newly promoted Lt. Col. Bob Williams, who had recovered from wounds suffered in the Gavutu assault.

Rigorous airborne training was conducted while the Jumping Gyrenes waited eagerly for the call to bail out on or behind Japanese positions. Plans were hatched for parachute assaults on Kolombangara, Bougainville, and New Ireland. Because of a shortage of transport planes—the Pacific war would be fought on a shoestring—and lack of enthusiasm for "airborne sideshows" by some high Marine brass, these missions were scrubbed.

Marine paratroop units would fight with great esprit at Vella Levella, Choiseul, and Bougainville, but would never make a combat jump. By early 1944, the Marine Corps disbanded its parachute program, and its units ceased to exist. It was a bitter pill for the gung ho Leatherneck paratroopers to swallow.

2
Mission
Impossible

On the night of September 12, 1942, less than two years after America's first paratroop battalion had been activated, Maj. William P. Yarborough was in his modest quarters in the heart of blacked-out London, mulling over a seemingly impossible assignment that he had been handed a few hours earlier. Seattle-born, 29-year-old Bill Yarborough was airborne adviser to Maj. Gen. Mark W. Clark, chief planner for "Operation Torch," an Allied invasion of North Africa designed to relieve the pressure on Soviet armies battling against Adolf Hitler's military juggernaut.

Operation Torch would be the first major Allied offensive since the Meuse-Argonne in World War I. It was a hurry-up operation conceived in response to strident clamor by the American and British press on a "Second Front Now" theme. Not knowing that the Anglo-American forces were pitifully weak, the armchair field marshals of the media had fallen prey to relentless pounding by Soviet Premier Josef Stalin's propaganda virtuosos and were clamoring for an assault across the English Channel against German-held France.

Gen. Dwight D. Eisenhower, commander of ETOUSA (European Theater of Operations, United States Army) and Mark Clark's boss, could not inform the press of the truth—that a cross-Channel attack would result in a bloodbath—so the West ern Allies would open a Second Front in North Africa, 1,500 miles from England, where defenses were far less formidable.

The spots along more than 1,000 miles of North African coastline where the Western Task Force would hit were Casablanca, the Center Task Force at Oran, and the Eastern Task Force at Algiers. General Clark had asked Yarborough if the 509th Parachute Infantry Battalion, posted in England, could be dropped inland from Oran and could seize the two airfields called Tafaraoui and La Sénia.[1] Tafaraoui was the only hard-surfaced airfield from the Atlantic all the way to central portions of Algeria. Enemy fighters and bombers taking off from these two fields could wreak havoc both on the Allied invasion fleet and on troops landing at H-Hour. La Sénia was 10 miles south of Oran, and Tafaraoui was five miles below La Sénia.

"Well, can our parachute boys do it?" Clark had asked Yarborough, aware that American paratroopers had never jumped into combat.

"That's difficult to answer on the spot," the major replied.

"Well," Clark responded, "give me your answer early in the morning."

Bill Yarborough had returned to the United States in early 1940 from three years with the famed Philippine Scouts, and his adventurous spirit drew him to the fledgling paratroopers like a moth to a flame. Maj. Bill Miley made him a company commander in the pioneer 501st Parachute Infantry Battalion, and he doubled in brass as a test officer for parachute equipment.

Yarborough quickly put his innovative bent to work and designed both the jump boots and the parachute wings—a paratrooper's most coveted symbols, which would be proof to all that the wearer was one of America's finest soldiers.

Yarborough had also designed a two-piece jumpsuit to replace the standard one-piece mechanic's coveralls, which the pioneer 501st Parachute Infantry battalion had been issued. The new uniform not only identified the wearer as an elite fighting man, but the extra-large pockets on the sides of the trousers and on the jacket would later serve as the paratrooper's combat pack, to be crammed with everything from whiskey bottles to hand grenades.[2]

Mark Clark's proposal appeared to be a classic suicide mission. Bill Yarborough could give numerous reasons why the parachute operation should be scrubbed, but he knew that the airborne concept was on trial. Back in Washington, influential generals, who still clung doggedly to the static-warfare doctrine of World War I, wanted to scrap the new paratroop units and distribute their men among conventional infantry forces.

Generals who were antagonistic to the new concept of dropping armed soldiers behind enemy lines did not include lanky, 46-year-old Mark Clark. Despite his background as an infantry captain in the World War I (he had been wounded in the Vosges mountains), Clark was a tactical visionary who was enthusiastic over the potential of airborne units.

Now in the solitude of his quarters at 2:00 A.M., Major Yarborough began writing down the pluses and minuses involved in the paratroop operation. Tantalizing questions plagued him. Would the men of the 509th Parachute Infantry Battalion be fit to fight after 10 or more hours in flight without oxygen at a 10,000-foot altitude? There were few, if any, fully qualified celestial navigators available; so could the planes hit the pinpoint targets? What if Luftwaffe fighters were to pounce on the unescorted, plodding C-47 armada? It would be a turkey shoot.

Finally, there was the most gut-wrenching uncertainty of all. Despite their eight-year head start over American airborne forces, the Germans had not had the capability, or perhaps the nerve, to fly over 400 miles when their paratroopers bailed out over the Low Countries in 1940 and over Crete the following

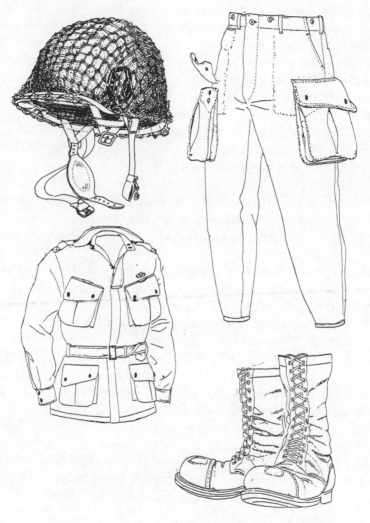

Paratrooper battle dress. *(Courtesy of Clark Archer)*

year. Now the upstart Americans were contemplating a flight of 1,600 miles—four times the maximum distance that Luftwaffe troop transports had flown on combat missions.

However, there were positive factors. Two months remained in which to train navigators, and with newer mechanical navigational aids, finding the DZs (drop zones) would be possible. Because the distance from England to Oran was so great, surprise might be obtained through a possible enemy failure to consider such an operation feasible. And finally, there was an intangible factor: Dropping more than 550 American paratroopers behind enemy lines could create confusion and even panic among the enemy, thereby aiding the seaborne assault on the beaches and subsequent advance inland.

Now global politics, volatile and unpredictable, entered Yarborough's planning process. America would be invading French colonies. How would the defenders react? France had traditionally been a friend of America, so its forces in North Africa might allow landings without a fight. On the other hand, a puppet French government, set up in Vichy after the nation's crushing defeat by the Germans in 1940, had maintained a neutral stance in the war, but it had been far more neutral toward Nazi Germany. Eighty-four-year-old Marshal Henri Pétain, a revered hero in World War I who headed the French regime, might order his armed forces to vigorously resist the American invasion of sovereign territory.

Mark Clark wanted not only one paratroop plan, but two, in order to meet either eventuality. "We're going to try to convince the French that they should come to our side and fight the Germans," Clark had told Yarborough. "But if they refuse, we'll fight the French as we would the Germans."

At 8:30 A.M. a sleepless Bill Yarborough dashed to Norfolk House and briefed Mark Clark. "Plan Peace" was to be implemented if covert negotiations with the French, then under way in North Africa by American envoy Robert Murphy, were successful. In that event, the 509th Parachute Infantry Battalion would land unopposed in C-47s at La Sénia airport. "Plan War" would be followed if Murphy's parley with French generals failed. Then the American paratroopers would bail out near Tafaraoui and La Sénia, seize both airfields, and destroy all French warplanes on the ground.[3]

Clark, who was called "The American Eagle" by Winston Churchill, interjected a few pertinent questions, and, with typical decisiveness, exclaimed, "Let 'er rip!"

When the 509th Parachute Infantry Battalion had crossed the Atlantic on the peacetime British luxury liner *Queen Elizabeth* in June 1942, the troopers wore the plain uniforms of regular soldiers, having been shorn of their coveted jump boots and parachute wings in order to thwart Nazi spies. On landing at Greenock, the port for Glasgow, a friendly Scottish railway official asked a trooper to what kind of outfit did he belong. Deadpanned, the parachutist replied: "Oh, us? Why we're USO entertainers."

Arriving at their new home, Nissen huts on a sprawling estate at Chilton Foliat, near Hungerford in Berkshire, the American paratroopers immediately learned that the cloak-and-dagger masquerade had fooled few—especially Nazi spies in the States and in England.[4]

Archie Birkner, then a lieutenant in the 509th Parachute Infantry Battalion, remembered:

> *We had hardly dropped our bags at Chilton Foliat before Lord Haw-Haw, the Nazi propagandist, broadcast from Berlin: "Welcome to England, you men of the 509th Parachute Infantry Battalion. You are a long way from home, now that you have come to fight in Churchill's war. Please enjoy yourself there in Chilton Foliat before your lives are tossed away to preserve the British Empire." He then gave a "warm welcome" to Colonel Raff and to a few other battalion men, whom he named and gave their ranks. Lord Haw-Haw's startling broadcast caused many of our fellows to suspect that we had a Nazi spy in our outfit.*

D-Day for Operation Torch (November 8, 1942) was rapidly approaching. Major Yarborough was swamped with an avalanche of planning details, most of them secret in nature. Gnawing at him remorselessly was the paramount question: How could the C-47 train find the drop zones at night after a 1,600-mile trek, with no moonlight, and in strange and probably hostile territory? He and every trooper knew by training experience that finding a drop zone at first pass, even in daylight, was often a difficult task.

Yarborough felt that he had the answer in two supersecret radar devices, code-named Rebecca and Eureka. By means of the two electronic aids, a pilot supposedly could guide an airplane to a map coordinate location even though he could not see the ground. There was one catch to their use in the Torch parachute mission, however. Someone had to be on the ground to place Eureka on the spot that the pilot wanted to locate.

The crucial cloak-and-dagger task fell to a young lieutenant named Howard Hapgood (code-named Bantam), who ostensibly belonged to the U.S. Army Signal Corps. Yarborough suspected that Hapgood was actually some sort of an intelligence operative for the Department of State, but was not concerned with the Eureka-placer's *bona fides*.

Bantam looked more like a scientist than he did a man who had volunteered for this dangerous job. He was tall and thin and walked with a slight stoop. His sallow face reflected long stretches in some laboratory, perhaps delving into the theory of electronics as it related to the yet-untested Rebecca and Eureka. Hapgood habitually wore civilian clothes of indifferent tailoring, and he guarded the two brown suitcases containing the Rebecca and Eureka as though they were the crown jewels.

Major Yarborough and the British secret service operatives who worked with him were confronted with a seemingly insolvable problem: how to get Bantam into North Africa. The solution was intricate and devious. Lieutenant Hapgood was given a discharge from the army while still in London—the first step in throwing Nazi agents off the scent. Then, with the proper mixture of security and feigned laxity, the "disgraced" American was hustled onto an airplane and shipped home, a scenario enacted for the benefit of Hitler's snoopers in England.

William Yarborough remembered Bantam's departure from London:

> We bade Lieutenant Hapgood good-bye about three weeks before D-Day (for Torch). Our last glimpse of him was of his tall, stooped figure, bent a little more under the weight of his two suitcases, struggling along Regent Street until he was finally picked up by a taxi. Before he left the office, he had proudly showed us the little devices on each suitcase which, if activated, would blow Eureka to bits. Even the Gestapo could not put the machine together once the destruct mechanisms had done their job.

Back in the States, military intelligence agents took Bantam in tow and commenced an elaborate procedure that resulted in smuggling the American and his suitcase-hidden Eureka device into Algiers. Once there, he and his supersecret Eureka vanished, never to be heard from again.

In the meantime, the Royal Navy had volunteered to furnish another electronic navigational device to help the paratroop sky armada to find the drop zone. A British merchant ship, the *Alynbank*, was to sail around an elliptical course two miles long and one mile wide in the western Mediterranean, and the American airborne planners were given the polar coordinates of this ellipse, with respect to the drop zone. The *Alynbank* would transmit a radio signal that, it was thought, could be picked up by the

C-47s about 250 miles off the African coast, and then ride in. Having passed the radio ship, the airborne officers believed that they could fly on an azimuth that would soon bring the planes under Eureka's influence. Then, Bantam's Algerian "underground" (which would later prove to be nonexistent) would ignite ground flares around Tafaraoui and La Sénia and the 509th Parachute Infantry would bail out.

For the Operation Torch mission, a Paratroop Task Force had been created under the command of Col. William C. Bentley of the Air Corps, with Major Yarborough as his executive officer. Raff's paratroopers and the 60th Troop Carrier Group were placed under Bentley's command. Over in Berkshire, Raff had set up a war room, guarded around the clock by armed sentries. In the room were elaborate scale models of Airport A and Airport B. Created by the British from thousands of high- and low-level air photographs taken by the Royal Air Force and from espionage sources, these scale models were studied for countless hours by revolving knots of paratroopers. Only shortly before takeoff would the highly curious men be told that A and B were Tafaraoui and La Sénia.[5]

Most of Ed Raff's paratroopers were straining at the leash and raring to go, but in the rarified atmosphere of Norfolk House, powerful forces were seeking to skuttle the airborne operation. Colonels Bentley, Raff, and Yarborough were summoned to the Operation Torch planning center, and they listened with solemn faces while British Air Vice Marshal William Welsh, who was head of air operations for Torch, launched into a litany of reasons for canceling the American parachute drop. Some C-47s might be "lost" en route, and troopers and crews could be captured, creating the danger that the enemy might be tipped off to the invasion, Welsh argued. What is more, he declared, it would be better to hold back the three squadrons of the 60th Carrier Group for the rapid movement of conventional ground forces eastward into Tunisia, where the Wehrmacht was expected to rush strong reinforcements from Europe once the Allies had landed in Algeria and Morocco. The tense conference adjourned with the question of whether to include American paratroopers in Operation Torch still hanging in the air—by a thread.

Influential Americans then joined those who wanted to cancel the paratroop operation. Two Air Corps whiz kids, Col. Hoyt S. Vandenberg (who many years later would become Air Force

Parachute pioneers of the 509th
Parachute Infantry Battalion,
Lt. Col. Edson D. Raff (top left),
Capt. Carlos C. "Doc" Alden
(top right), and Maj. William P.
Yarborough (bottom right).
(Author's collection)

chief of staff) and Lt. Col. Lauris Norstadt (who, in time, would
become supreme commander of NATO) argued that the long-
range airborne mission had little chance of success. Worse, the
operation could result in a catastrophe if the C-47 sky train were
pounced on by German fighter planes. Large numbers of paratroopers would be lost, as would cargo planes needed for air
corps supply.

That crucial conference at Norfolk House was remembered
by Yarborough:

> *Our mission, and possibly the future immediate employment of
> American airborne troops, might have gone down the drain had it
> not been for the presence of Jimmy Doolittle. Of course he was
> famous for his daring raid over Tokyo during the darkest days of the
> war. Brigadier General Doolittle was a powerful supporter. He
> thought the idea of a long-range paratroop assault against strategic
> targets in North Africa was a great concept. It was probably Jimmy
> Doolittle's voice that convinced Mark Clark to go ahead with the
> operation when even General Eisenhower thought it was sort of
> harebrained.*

It was chilly and damp at a bleak locale known as Land's End, a
cape in Cornwell in the westernmost point of countryside in England, when grim men of the 509th Parachute Infantry Battalion
arrived at two airfields, Predannack and St. Eval, which were a
short distance inland. These 556 paratroop pioneers would soon
lift off for America's first mass combat drop, flying in 39 C-47s.
The flight route would bring high-level political risks, for it
would take the paratrooper convoy over neutral Spain, whose
dictator, Gen. Francisco Franco, leaned heavily toward Hitler's
Germany. Even if the American intrusion of Spanish air space
brought Spain into the war on Hitler's side, the chance would
have to be taken.

It was November 7, 1942—D-Day minus 1.

3
"Advance Alexis"

Late on the afternoon of November 7, 1942, Paratroop Task
Force commander Col. Bill Bentley, Lt. Col. Ed Raff and Maj.
Bill Yarborough were huddled tensely at the St. Eval airfield ra-

dio tower for word from the powerful British station on Gibraltar. From that huge rock perched in the narrow entrance to the Mediterranean Sea, orders would come setting the airborne expedition in motion.

If the code words "Advance Napoleon" came racing through the ether, it was war. If the American invaders had to fight the French in order to get to the Germans, then so be it. If the words "Advance Alexis" came through, the paratroop flight would take off with the assurance that the French would not oppose the landing.

At 5:10 P.M., with dusk gathering over Land's End, Gibraltar radioed "Advance Alexis." The undercover negotiations with French officials in North Africa had been fruitful. Plan Peace was in effect.

This meant that departure would be delayed for four hours. If Plan War were called for, the 1,600-mile flight, at an average speed of 135 miles per hour, would be timed to permit the paratroopers to bail out over Tafaraoui and La Sénia in darkness. Plan Peace takeoff would permit the 509th Battalion to arrive over North Africa in daylight.

Gathered in little knots around their C-47s, Raff's parachutists were keyed up, their adrenaline pumping furiously. They were ready to go, so the four-hour wait seemed to be interminable. Lt. Hugh G. Hogan of Oswego, New York, commander of the mortar platoon, had removed his jumpsuit and, like the other paratroopers, put on full-length woolen underwear (long johns to the Americans). After pulling his lightweight jumpsuit over the heavy underwear, Hogan taped the legs so that the baggy pants and bulging pockets would not catch in the doorway if he had to bail out.

Nearby, Lt. Sheldon D. Harvey, a native of Portage, Wisconsin, checked the small American flag of the kind each trooper had sewn to the sleeve of his jump jacket. One of the two battalion surgeons, 31-year-old Capt. Carlos C. "Doc" Alden of Buffalo, New York, was seated on his steel helmet under the wing of a C-47. He scribbled a plea in his pocket diary: "Dear God, in Thy wisdom help me to come back. But if I do not, then help me to do my duty as an American and as a man."

Ed Raff's yet untested 509th Parachute Infantry Battalion was a close-knit group. Many were double volunteers. They had volunteered for the Army; then again for the paratroops. Its members were fiercely proud of their outfit and of being history's first American parachute unit to make a combat jump. They were members in good standing of one of the world's most exclusive fraternities—the paratrooper brotherhood. Membership could not be bestowed because of political or social connections or wealth. Rather, entry could be earned only by enduring the most arduous training that diabolical minds could conceive—then by qualifying as a parachutist after five jumps, and eventually by measuring up in the crucible of battle. American paratroopers were tough, resourceful, and cocky. They were the Army's elite, and they knew it.

Suddenly, there was the revving up of powerful engines on St. Eval and Predannack airfields. Shouts rang out, "Next stop, North Africa!" And the troopers, one after the other, filed into the C-47s. At 9:05 P.M., the first airplanes sped down the runways and lifted off. Forming up over Land's End, the sky train set a course for Oran, 1,600 miles away.

With the winged armada flying at 10,000 feet, the paratroopers, wedged in shoulder-to-shoulder in bucket seats, grew increasingly miserable as frigid air began seeping in. Orders forced the men to wear their parachute packs, as well as their cumbersome, inflatable lifebelts (called Mae Wests after the buxom Hollywood movie star) at all times during the flight.

For two hours, the sky train was right on course and in precise formation; but over the Bay of Biscay, strong easterly winds, heavy rains, darkness, and navigators' inexperience all conspired to scatter the aircraft. Most of the troopers, who were expecting a peaceful landing in North Africa after dawn, were dozing, unaware of this alarming development.

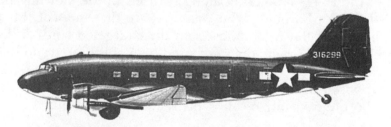

Workhorse of the American airborne—the C-47.

Unbeknownst to the 556 parachutists and the air crews, a second haunting specter had risen its head. In Vichy, France, shortly after the Americans had lifted off from Land's End, aged

Marshal Henri Pétain issued orders for his forces in northwest Africa to "resist the invaders with every means at your disposal."[1]

At his battle headquarters deep in the bowels of the Rock of Gibraltar, Gen. Dwight Eisenhower learned, through electronic interception of coded messages, of Pétain's order. Word was flashed to the mighty naval fleet approaching North Africa: "French prepared to fight!"

On HMS *Alynbank,* circling off the coast, radio operators were frantically sending a message to the paratroop flight: "Play ball! Play ball!" That was the coded phrase to inform Raff's paratroopers that Plan War was now in effect. None of the operators on the C-47s responded; someone had given the *Alynbank* the wrong frequency.[2]

Daylight brought a surge of alarm to the awakening paratroopers. Peering through the small windows, they saw that their C-47s were alone or were with only two or three other aircraft.

Dr. Carlos Alden remembered that occasion:

> It was a little unsettling to see that there were only four C-47s with us. Where in the hell were the other 34 airplanes? Our C-47 was named Shark Bait, *and all of us now thought that to be most appropriate, for all we could see below was endless blue water. Then one of our fellows came back after visiting the pilot's compartment and said, "Here's more good news! The fly boys don't have the faintest notion where we are—and we're nearly out of fuel!" So we began the tedious job of pumping up by hand the inflatable rubber rafts.*

One of the C-47s lumbering along by itself in the morning haze carried Bill Yarborough, who was unaware that most of the aircraft had been flown 50 miles from their targeted landfall. Desperately, the C-47 radio operator used his Rebecca to try to reach Eureka, which the mysterious Bantam (Lieutenant Hapgood) was supposed to be manning on the drop zone.

Yarborough vividly recalled his feelings at that juncture:

> Rebecca was dead as a mackeral. It looked as though we were invading North Africa alone. Suddenly I noticed a speck moving toward us in the sky from a great distance. It was coming fast. Trying to keep my voice calm, I said, "All right, men, take the plugs out of the windows and put the muzzles of your weapons through. If this is an enemy fighter, wait until he's close enough before you fire.

He won't think this flying banana has any armament, so maybe we can fool him!"

Aerial history was about to be made. Perhaps for the first time infantrymen would be engaging in a shootout in the sky with a hostile fighter plane. The speck grew larger. Troopers took aim with Garand rifles and tommy guns. As the unidentified plane drew closer, the tension vanished from the two lines of kneeling sharpshooters. It was one of the C-47s.

"I'll bet that son of a bitch is lost, too!" Sgt. Jack Pogue called out. The cabin shook with laughter.

Joy was short-lived. The pilot of Yarborough's plane, Lt. Col. Thomas Schofield, commander of the 60th Troop Carrier Group, turned east after reaching the coast. Through landmarks, he realized that the C-47 was over Spanish Morocco, some 200 miles from La Sénia and Tafaraoui airports. The airplane pressed on. At about 140 miles from the objectives, a crewman called out: "We're nearly out of gasoline!" Soon a few more wandering C-47s were spotted, and they hooked up with Schofield's plane.

Meanwhile, another group of C-47s that had banded together knifed over the coast near Oran and sped southward to what those onboard thought would be a routine landing at La Sénia. As the first plane neared the airfield, French gunners began blasting away. Puffs of black smoke filled the sky, and explosions rocked the planes.

Nearly out of gasoline, the clutch of C-47s pulled up, lumbered westward for a short distance and landed on the Sebkra D'Oran, a dry salt-water lakebed 32 miles long and seven miles wide. A few minutes later, a second handful of transports circled overhead and came in for a landing. Fuel gauges showed empty. Hopping out of one of the planes was Capt. Doc Alden, relaxed and chipper. Approaching a paratroop officer, the surgeon quipped: "If this is Tafaraoui Airport, where in the hell are the hangars?"

At another point along the coast, Ed Raff was in a C-47 piloted by Colonel Bentley, who was in charge of the airborne operation until the paratroopers were on the ground. Lost, Bentley was flying along the coast seeking some sign of Oran. Behind him were five planes carrying Capt. William J. Morrow's parachute company.

Raff was worried. Where were the other 33 airplanes with his

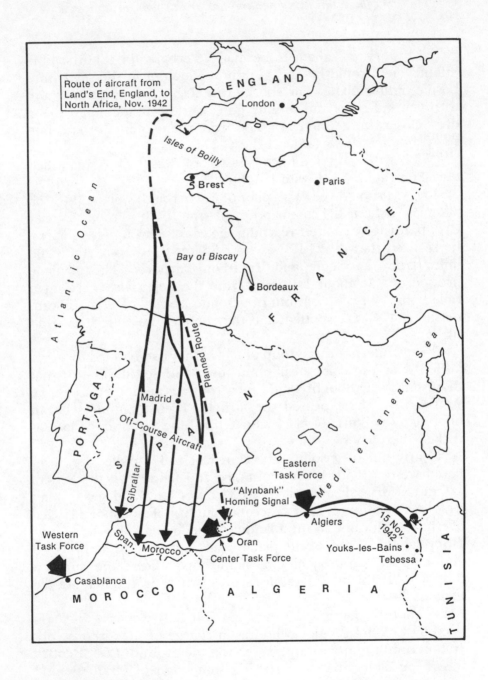

Route of aircraft from Land's End, England, to North Africa, Nov. 1942

paratroopers? Shot down by Luftwaffe night interceptors as British Air Vice Marshal Welsh had warned?

Officers on the Sebkra D'Oran were huddled to discuss their next move when they heard airplane engines. Squinting into the bright sky, they saw Raff's six C-47s. A radio operator on the dry lakebed signaled Bill Bentley that the troopers and airmen on the ground were "under fire" from a force of undetermined size to the north of the parked airplanes. It was a jittery analysis of men in a combat situation for the first time; in fact, there was no "force of undetermined size" and no shooting.

Moments later, Bentley spotted three tanks in the distance moving toward the grounded aircraft. "Those tanks are firing at our guys around the C-47s!" the Air Corps officer called out excitedly.

Raff made an instant decision: He and his six planeloads of paratroopers would bail out and fight the menacing tanks. A signal was radioed to parachutists in the other five planes: "Watch for Raff to jump; then bail out after him."

Raff jumped; the others followed. The colonel struck the earth heavily, smashing his chest into a large, jagged rock, knocking the wind from him and breaking two ribs. But the scrappy Raff was ready to lead his men against the attacking tanks.

Suddenly, a lookout on a knoll shouted, "Colonel, there's big white stars on those goddamned tanks! They're ours!" Actually, the tanks belonged to Lt. Col. John K. Waters' column of the 1st Armored Division, pushing inland from the point near Oran where they had landed.[3]

Minutes later, Bill Yarborough's three C-47s touched down. The major strolled up to Raff and asked the standard question: "What in the hell is going on?"

"Damned if I know," Raff replied, spitting out blood. "But the French are obviously fighting, Plan Peace or no Plan Peace!"

Although relieved to find the planes on the *sebkra*, Raff was still anxious. Nine C-47s with 135 paratroopers were unaccounted for. At the time he could not know that one plane, its gas gauge registering empty, had landed at Gibraltar after having circled over Spain for much of the night after it became lost. Two C-47s had crash-landed near Oran, and two others had touched down at an airfield in French Morocco, where troopers and air crews were captured by the French. The remaining four transports had landed in Spanish Morocco, where those onboard were taken into custody by the Spanish government.

Ed Raff was in so much pain he could hardly walk. So he waited for an armored division jeep to arrive, while 90 paratroopers, with Major Yarborough in the lead, set off on foot toward Tafaraoui, some 38 miles away. Each step across the *sebkra* was a chore. Just under the dry upper crust of the lakebed was a type of plastic mud that would have immobilized a dinosaur. Soon each trooper's foot felt as though it weighed 20 pounds. After the keenly conditioned parachutists had trudged for seven miles, they were nearly exhausted.

As Colonel Raff inched up in his jeep, a communications sergeant handed Yarborough a message he had picked up from Tafaraoui. There were friendly tanks on the airfield, the message stated, but paratroopers were badly needed to wipe out some French machine-gun nests that were still firing. It added that the tankers had rounded up a lot of prisoners and had no one to guard them.

Yarborough showed the message to Raff. "How about it, Ed," the major said, "I can slip a company in there by air."

"The planes are all out of gas."

"Not all of them. A few may have a half hour left even if their gauges register empty."

Raff thought a moment, then said, "Okay, go ahead."

Yarborough thought his old friend looked a little green around the gills from his injuries.

A radio signal was sent to the parked C-47s, and soon Lt. Joseph Beck brought up three transports and landed them on the lakebed next to Yarborough's parachutists. These planes would whisk some of the troopers to Tafaraoui, where a promise of action lay. Everyone wanted to go, but Raff selected Capt. John Berry's company and a few battalion headquarters men. They scrambled aboard in a carefree spirit, unaware that they were bound for disaster.

Soon the three C-47s, packed with paratroopers, were flying at 100 feet toward Tafaraoui. Yarborough was standing behind Joe Beck, the pilot. Suddenly, the major spotted a movement to his right. "What is that, Joe?" he asked evenly.

William Yarborough would have the events that followed etched into his mind for a lifetime:

Joe didn't answer. He became a whirlwind. He slid into a steep bank and cut the engine. The copilot pumped the flaps down, throwing shudders through the whole ship. My heart jumped into my throat

*and stayed there. I could feel the impact as bullets from the French
Dewoitine fighter planes hit our ship broadside. The fuselage began
to leak light as the rounds poured into the defenseless mass of men
seated on the floor. The noise was deafening. We slid into the
ground going 130 miles per hour and slewed around to a violent
halt.*

Most of the troopers leaped from the C-47 wreckage, raced a
short distance and buried noses in the sand. Lt. Dave Kunkle, a
highly popular officer from New York City, remained in the
plane, grabbed a light machine gun, and set it up in the open
door. Before Kunkle could squeeze the trigger, machine gun
slugs from a diving Dewoitine tore into his stomach. Bleeding
profusely, Kunkle fell to the floor and died, the first American
paratrooper to be killed in a combat-jump operation.[4]

Under repeated attacks by the French fighter planes, the
other two C-47s had to make crash landings on the barren terrain. Staccato bursts of machine-gun fire echoed across the
lakebed as the attackers made repeated passes against the helpless troopers and air crews. Then the Dewoitines flew away. In
the silence, the three C-47s lay ghostly, still, and riddled with
bullets.

Lifeless bodies were strewn about the landscape. One dead
paratrooper in Yarborough's plane was hanging face down out of
the cargo door, blood dripping down his fingers to form little
pools of blood in the sand. Yarborough regained his feet and a
trooper, his face a bloody mask, staggered toward him.

"Medic! Medic!" the major called out. No response. The
wounded man fell to the ground and whispered, "I am the medic."
Yarborough knew him, but had not recognized the trooper.

Capt. William Moir, one of the two battalion doctors, was
holding his hand against the side of his head. Blood was oozing
from between his fingers and trickling down his elbow.

"How do you feel, Doc?" Yarborough asked, knowing that the
question was absurd.

"I've been grazed twice in the head and got a slug in the
shoulder. The one in my shoulder stings like hell!"

Paratroop Sgt. Alain Joseph was sitting on the ground, his leg
knicked by a bullet. "Look at Lieutenant Beck," he told a comrade. "He was up on top of that wing trying to check his antenna
even before that last strafing run hit us."

Capt. John Berry, the company commander, was sobbing with

rage and swearing vengeance against anything French. Bill Moir, despite his wounds, was tending to the wounded men. Some of the lightly wounded troopers were trying to make the more seriously injured men comfortable by opening parachutes to block out the fading rays of the sun.

Seven troopers had been killed and 20 wounded. The wounded men were left in the care of Captain Moir (trucks would be sent for them later). Major Yarborough formed up 61 troopers, a few of them walking wounded, and set out on foot toward the 509th Battalion's objective, Tafaraoui. Night had fallen. The men were weary from the day's events—the long flight from England, the arduous march across the *sebkra,* the emotional stress of their baptism of fire. Each man was loaded with weapons and other accoutrements of war. Huffing, wheezing, and cursing, they pressed on.

Meanwhile, back at the parked C-47s on the Sebkra D'Oran, the C-47 named *Shark Bait* was about to lift off for Tafaraoui. *Shark Bait*'s crew had managed to scavenge a few gallons of gasoline by siphoning a quart or two from a number of other parked planes whose gauges registered empty. Capt. Doc Alden, telling comrades that he had no intention of trudging 35 miles "across that damned desert," scrambled on board, taking a seat in the open door with his legs dangling. Riding shotgun, he called it.

The C-47 lifted off, and less than a half hour later, it landed at Tafaraoui. French artillery in the hills saluted the arrival of *Shark Bait* with a salvo of shells that exploded around the plane. The pilot quickly taxied behind a small knoll, and Doc Alden leaped to the ground.

The 509th Parachute Infantry Battalion was on its D-Day objective—with a force of one trooper.

4
Raff's
Ruffians

Shortly after dawn on November 9—D-Day plus 1—Maj. Bill Yarborough and his 61 paratroopers were reeling toward Tafaraoui. They were numb with fatigue. They had trudged along all night, rested a few minutes, then pushed on. Now they could hardly drag one leaden foot after the other. Most had walked in their sleep for the past four hours, but not one man had pitched away his weapon or a single round of ammunition.

At midmorning, after a tortuous 38-mile trek, the Five-O-Niners staggered into Tafaraoui. Yarborough promptly ran into Capt. William A. Medlin of Florence, North Carolina, who had managed to sneak a band of parachutists into the eastern end of the airfield in the early morning darkness.

Yarborough was near exhaustion, but he soon became embroiled in a chaotic situation that had not been covered in his West Point textbooks. American officers were arguing bitterly with those of the captured French garrison. The Frenchmen, with much arm-waving and shouting, were demanding that their tricolored national flag fly over Tafaraoui, even though they were prisoners of war. Wisely, after acrimonious debate, it was agreed that American and French flags would fly side by side over the airport's bullet-riddled operations building.

Meanwhile, Capt. Doc Alden had learned of the wounded troopers back at the site of the strafing, and he rounded up four old trucks and a few medics and set out in that direction. Arriving at the scene without incident, Alden and his medics loaded the dead and wounded onto the trucks and drove off for Tafaraoui.

Suddenly, from out of the sun, a fighter plane zoomed in with all guns blazing and poured bullets toward the trucks. No one was hit. This time, there was a marked difference from the previous day's strafings: The Americans had been attacked by a British Spitfire.

One of the seriously wounded paratroopers brought in was Pvt. John Thomas "Tommy" Mackall, a 22-year-old farm boy from Ohio. Ten months earlier, when he had volunteered for the Army, Mackall had concealed from examining physicians a crippled hand that would have barred him from serving. All through the rigors of paratroop training, he had apparently kept his officers in the dark about his handicap.

Knowing that Tommy Mackall was in need of prompt surgery, Doc Alden arranged for him to be flown to Gibraltar. Four days after his arrival, Mackall died.[1]

That afternoon, an improvised fleet of antiquated buses, trucks, and cars, looking much like a gypsy caravan, chugged into Tafaraoui. Ed Raff was in a jeep at the head of the convoy. The ragtag collection of vehicles had been "requisitioned" along the route and carried the remainder of the 509th Parachute Infantry that had landed back on the Sebkra D'Oran a day earlier.

A few miles north of Tafaraoui, Bill Bentley, the Air Corps officer who had commanded the Paratroop Task Force, sat in the kitchen of an old farmhouse outside Oran, sipping a cup of coffee and chatting with two amiable French officers. Bentley's plight was typical of the frustration felt by many who participated in America's first paratroop operation. After Ed Raff and his stick had jumped, Bentley's plane ran out of gas, crash-landed, and the colonel and his air crew were taken prisoner.[2]

Elsewhere, fighting had been raging at many points across a wide sweep of North Africa, as most French officers honored old Marshal Pétain's order to "resist by all available means." However, American seaborne forces captured the port of Algiers, and there netted the biggest fish of all: Admiral Jean-François Darlan, commander in chief of French forces in northwest Africa.

Two days later, after much jockeying for position in heated sessions with Gen. Mark Clark, Darlan ordered a halt to French resistance and came over on the side of the Allies. But would the French fighting men obey Darlan or Pétain?[3]

By the evening of November 14, Ed Raff had moved his parachute task force 250 miles east of Tafaraoui to the Maison

Blanche airport outside Algiers. The next morning, the colonel reported to Gen. K. A. N. Anderson, commander of the British 1st Army, under whose control the 509th Parachute Infantry would be. Raff found that Mark Clark was also present. Three days hence, on November 18, Raff's paratroopers were to jump and seize Youks les Bains airfield in eastern Algeria, near the Tunisian border.

"German paratroopers may already have moved into the field," Anderson said. "If they have, take it from them."

Once Raff had captured Youks les Bains, he was to send a contingent of his men to seize a smaller airfield nine miles away near the town of Tebessa.

At seven o'clock the next morning, 350 of Raff's troopers filed out from hangers and climbed into waiting C-47s. Two of the men who would make the jump did not belong to the 509th Parachute Infantry. Bill Yarborough was a member of Mark Clark's planning staff, and 34-year-old, bearded John H. "Jack" Thompson was an adventurous, unruffled correspondent for the *Chicago Tribune*.

While Raff's men were marching toward their airplanes, they passed some British paratroops—the "Red Devils"—who were also enplaning. The Americans were curious over where the British were going. Only later would they learn that the Red Devils were on their way to jump at an airport near Bône. (The Germans also had their eyes on Bône, and only a fluke prevented them from getting there before the Red Devils did. A flight of Luftwaffe planes crammed with *Fallschirmjaeger* [paratroopers] turned back to their base in Tunisia while in full view of the Bône airfield and while British parachutes were already descending on the objective.)

At 7:30 A.M., 22 troop transports crammed with American parachutists lifted off, circled while forming up, and set a northeasterly course for the circuitous flight to Youks les Bains. A squadron of British Spitfires hovered around the troop officers, much like mother hens watching over their broods. Soon the C-47s were over mountains, then were forced down into valleys by low-hanging clouds. Troopers craned their necks to peer upward at the towering peaks.

Above the roar of engines and the rush of wind through the open doors came the shouts "Stand up!" Everyone got to his feet. "Hook up!" Metal fasteners on parachute static lines were snapped to overhead anchor cables. Silent and tense, the men waited. And waited some more. Three minutes. Five minutes. Ten. Curses rang out. The pilots were circling, trying to locate the airfield drop zone.

Suddenly, "Go!" rang out, and the men barreled through the doors in piggyback fashion. Soon the bright blue sky was awash with white canopies interspersed with red, yellow, and blue ones carrying equipment bundles. A combination of the relatively low jumping height (365 to 400 feet) and the rarified air (a mile above sea level) resulted in jolting collisions with the hard ground. Around the field, numerous men writhed in agony. Capt. John Berry broke his leg in several places, and the medical officer, Doc Alden, cracked three bones in his foot. Two jumpers suffered compound fractures of legs, and splintered, bloody bones protruded through the flesh. Seventeen men had major injuries, and hardly a man escaped some sort of bruise, cut or scrape.[4]

Reporter Jack Thompson recalled that episode:

> *I was the only parachuting novice in the entire lot. My jump "training" had taken place two days earlier. It consisted of 20 minutes of instruction by an officer who began with, "Now this thing is what is known as a parachute . . ." Yet I was about the only one to jump at Youks les Bains who landed unscathed.*

Thompson, whose beard earned him the nickname "Beaver," had become the first American reporter to jump in a paratrooper combat operation.

Despite the rash of jump injuries—hazards that go with the profession—the 509th Parachute Infantry Battalion dropped in an almost textbook-perfect pattern. Nearly every trooper had landed on the drop zone, and in only 20 minutes, the battalion had formed into battle units and set out at double time for the airfield perimeter to dig in.

All were breathing sighs of relief. Instead of the tough, battle-tested German paratroopers they had expected to encounter, smiling French soldiers, weapons slung over shoulders, greeted the new arrivals from the sky. These were men of the French Zouaves, whose regiment had a long tradition of battlefield gallantry. The Zouaves' motto was *J'y suis, j'y reste* ("I'm here, and here I stay").

According to plan, John Berry's E Company, now under Lt. Archie Birkner, struck out on foot to seize the airport at Tebessa, nine miles away. After occupying the field, Birkner and his men looked up and saw a Luftwaffe plane circling at about 2,000 feet, then zoom down toward an American C-47 sitting in the middle of the runway. No doubt, the German pilot thought that only French ground crews were manning the field, and that he would chalk up an easy kill.

Every paratrooper now within range opened fire on the unlucky Luftwaffe plane. Riddled with bullets, the aircraft fought for altitude, flew on for a short distance, and crashed into a hill within sight of the Americans. Their cheers echoed over the landscape.

Meanwhile back at Youks les Bains, Ed Raff was pacing about like a caged tiger. Passively guarding two remote Algerian airfields was not the scrappy Raff's idea of how American paratroopers should fight a war. He wanted to attack the Axis-held town of Gafsa, 90 miles southeast of Tebessa.

William Yarborough recalled:

> Ed Raff was a human dynamo. "We're going right into Gafsa after the bastards," he said. The fact that his little force was operating without artillery or certain resupply or tanks bothered him not at all. Raff wanted Nazi hides, and he was going after them as fast as he could.

British Gen. K. A. N. Anderson, with whom Ed Raff had clashed frequently, got wind of the bold Gafsa raid and issued direct orders for it to be scrubbed—but Raff had suddenly gone stone deaf. He scrounged up a weird conglomeration of ancient French trucks, buses, and cars, loaded up his paratroopers and elements of the 3d French Zouaves, and, at 2:00 A.M. on a bitterly cold night, charged off for Gafsa. It was a tortuous and perilous trek over narrow, twisting mountain roads and across barren desert.

At dawn, the caravan halted outside Gafsa; the stiff and aching paratroopers and Zouaves jumped out, wincing as their cold feet struck the hard ground. Dashing about like a whirling dervish, Ed Raff formed up his men to attack the town. After a short fight, the Italians and a few German defenders were driven out.

Recognizing a *fait accompli,* General Anderson instructed his rampaging American subordinate not to go beyond Gafsa. Raff ignored the order, and launched a series of daring forays across the Algerian border into Tunisia, where his paratroopers and a platoon of tanks slugged it out with Rommel's Afrika Korps. After an all-day battle at Faid Pass, the Americans collared 130 German and Italian prisoners, and left the pass filled with dead and wounded enemy soldiers.[5]

Meanwhile, the flow of war caught up with the 509th Parachute Infantry, whose men now called themselves "Raff's Ruffians." Operation Torch forces closed up to the western Tunisian border, where the Ruffians had been fighting for two weeks, and Bernard Montgomery's seasoned British Eighth Army pushed up to the southern Tunisian border. There, the "Desert Rats" bumped into Rommel's heavily fortified Mareth Line, and their month-long, 1,000-mile eastward advance ground to a halt.

5
"Blow Up Rommel's Railroad!"

Although Col. Ed Raff's 509th Parachute Infantry Battalion was getting its first real taste of battle at Faid Pass, Field Marshal Erwin Rommel flew to Berlin to plead with Adolf Hitler to pull all Axis forces out of Tunisia. "*Mein Führer*, if our army remains in North Africa, it will be destroyed," the youngest field marshal in Germany history declared.[1]

That remark threw Hitler into a towering rage. Rommel, known to the British as the "Desert Fox" for his bold forays, grew red-faced in anger as the Führer shouted that he was a defeatist, and even cowardly. Not only would Axis forces remain in Tunisia, but they would be heavily reinforced.

In late December 1942, Hitler gained an ally in North Africa—torential winter rains that turned the already inferior roads into quagmires. The Allied drive to "Dunkirk" Rommel bogged down in a sea of mud—and stiff German resistance.

As promised, the Führer began pouring reinforcements, weapons, and supplies into the ports of Tunis and Bizerte in northern Tunisia. At these points, the troops and cargoes were loaded onto trains that ran along the north-south coastal track to the Mareth Line in southern Tunisia.

Seeking to halt this flow to Rommel, the Allies sent bombers to destroy a key railroad bridge near the coastal village of El Djem, but the attacks failed to bring down the span. Then a squadron of American P-40 fighter bombers, led by Lt. Col. Philip Cochran, strafed guard shacks at each end of the bridge and fired rockets into the bridge.[2] When the smoke cleared, the railroad trestle remained standing.

Air Corps photo interpreters were puzzled. Aerial pictures had indicated that the El Djem bridge was of relatively light construction, so a hit by a rocket or two or a bomb should have brought the span crashing down.

In southern Tunisia, Rommel's tough Afrika Korps soldiers, bolstered by ammunition, supplies, and weapons flowing down the north-south railroad, were making battlefield life tough for Bernard Montgomery's Tommies. The El Djem railroad bridge had to go; so the task was assigned to Raff's 509th Parachute Infantry Battalion, which was in the front lines 90 miles west of the crucial trestle.

On December 23, Lt. Dan A. DeLeo, who had pinned on his gold bars for the first time only the previous June, was summoned by Ed Raff. The 24-year-old parachute officer, a Chicago area native, had yet to see hostile action; he had brought a group of 180 paratroop replacements from England to North Africa by boat after Operation Torch forces were ashore.[3]

Dan DeLeo recalled the conference that followed:

> I received a very short briefing from Colonel Raff. He told me that I was to lead a parachute raiding party to the El Djem bridge, blow it up, after which we were to make our way back through enemy territory for 90 miles to friendly lines. Air Corps Lt. Col. Phil Cochran was present. He would lead the C-47s that would fly us to El Djem. Cochran was very cool and confident. He told me that he would drop us at night just north of the bridge, so we would have no problem finding it. All we had to do was to march south until we bumped into it.

Among the men of the 509th Parachute Infantry, DeLeo's job sounded like a classic suicide mission. They conjectured that he—instead of a battle-tested officer—had been chosen to lead the raid because DeLeo and his troopers would possibly never return. This theme gained credence after Doc Alden volunteered to go along and was turned down by Raff, who hinted that he could not risk losing the battalion's only doctor.

Dan DeLeo rapidly began preparations. Thirty-two parachutists, including five demolitions experts and two French Army men, would carry out the raid. Sgt. Jean Guilhenjouan and Cpl. Paul Vullierme, the Frenchmen, had been stationed in Tunisia, supposedly knew the country well, spoke fluent Arabic, and were to guide the raiders back to American lines once the bridge had been blown by hand-set explosives.

At about 9:00 P.M. on Christmas Eve 1942, DeLeo and his raiding party strolled toward a pair of C-47s at Maison Blanche airport outside Algiers. It was a grim group. A few made efforts to joke. "Merry Christmas," one called out. Each trooper was handed an escape kit containing a small saw blade, a few yards of tough fishing line, a waterproof plastic container holding 10 or 12 wooden matches, and a tiny magnetic compass.

Sharply at 10:30 P.M., the two transport planes lifted off and sped through the blackness toward once insignificant El Djem bridge. Inside the cabins, the parachutists huddled silently in their bucket seats. Colonel Raff had tersely summed up their task: "Blow up Rommel's railroad!"

Winging through the night in the black cabins, Dan DeLeo and his men sat largely in silence. No doubt their thoughts drifted back to home and to loved ones who would soon be opening Christmas presents. Suddenly, a glowing red light shook them from reveries, and the troopers got to their feet. It would be only minutes now. Then the green light flashed on and the men, one after the other, leaped into the darkness.

At the same time, Phil Cochran and the other pilot flipped switches, and a pair of 200-pound bundles of explosives, one attached to the belly of each C-47, were released and parachuted to the ground.

Pvt. Roland W. Rondeau, a 22-year-old rifleman from Woonsocket, Rhode Island, tried to glimpse the railroad track while floating downward, but it was so black he could see nothing. Then *crump!* He had hit the earth with jarring impact. Rondeau's head was spinning, but he lay motionless and listened for any indication that the enemy was near. All that he heard were the thuds of comrades hitting the ground around him and the murmur of C-47 engines fading in the distance.[4]

Lieutenant DeLeo had quickly found the railroad, and now he stood on the tracks and wigwagged a muted light to assemble his men. Rondeau saw the dim beam, scrambled to his feet, and trotted toward DeLeo. At almost the same time, other troopers arrived from out of the blackness, and within 20 minutes, the lieutenant had assembled his men. So far, so good.

An immediate search was launched for the two explosives bundles, but only one of them could be found. No one was unduly concerned. It had not been unusual in practice jumps at night for parachuted equipment to be lost. They would have to make do with only the 200 pounds of dynamite. Besides, Dan DeLeo knew that he had an expert demolitions sergeant who would get the job done.

Lt. Dan A. DeLeo. (*Author's collection*)   Pvt. Roland W. Rondeau. (*Author's collection*)

Because the drop zone was supposed to be north of the El Djem bridge, DeLeo and his group began trudging southward, their baggy pockets bulging with blocks of dynamite. Pilot Phil Cochran had told the raid leader that he would bump into the span by walking toward the south, so there would be no problem in locating the objective, even though it was pitch-black. What DeLeo and the troopers did not know was that they had been dropped south of the bridge, not north of it.

Trying to remain as quiet as possible, the raiders marched for an hour. Still no sign of the El Djem bridge. Nagging concern began to tug at the troopers. It was now pushing 2:00 A.M., and they would have only a few more hours of darkness in which to reach the bridge, kill the guards at both ends of the span, plant the blocks of dynamite at strategic points, blow the bridge, and get out of the area.

Dan DeLeo had another worry. Before leaving the drop zone, he had been confronted by two Arabs pushing a cart. He had been in North Africa long enough to know that Arabs were likely to pop up in unexpected places at any time of the day or night. Through his French interpreters, DeLeo told the two natives that if they kept their mouths shut about the raiders' presence, they could have the parachutes scattered about the scene. The Arabs had eagerly collected several of the silk chutes and disappeared into the night. Now DeLeo reflected: Would the two Arabs betray the Americans? He would have his answer soon enough.

When the raiders had marched for more than two hours and there was still no bridge to their front, DeLeo was convinced that the pilots had dropped the group a far greater distance than the targeted five miles to the north of the bridge. So the troopers walked, hoping that a troop or supply train would come along; perhaps they could derail it with explosives.

Faint tinges of gray in the dark sky foretold the imminent arrival of dawn. As it grew lighter, the parachutists, now weary after a night of carrying heavy blocks of dynamite and their battle gear, could see nothing but bleak flatland around them. But as the shimmering morning haze began to dissipate, the contour of a group of hills could be discerned off in the distance.

DeLeo halted his men and pulled out a folded map. Orienting himself by the hills, he took a number of compass readings and sadly said, "Men, we're about 22 miles south of the El Djem bridge."

Retracing their steps would require perhaps five hours to reach the railroad trestle, and the march and blowing of the span would have to be done in broad daylight, making discovery almost a certainty. And since the troopers were already near exhaustion, it would require a near miracle for them to make the 22-mile march. Consequently, DeLeo decided to inflict maximum mayhem where they were.

Nearby was a building beside the tracks, and inspection revealed that it was unoccupied. Inside was electrical equipment that, a trooper indicated, controlled switching operations along the track. The demolitions men rapidly went to work planting explosives in the building and the electrical apparatus. At the same time, other demo troopers were placing dynamite blocks along 100 yards of the track. All the explosives were then joined by a single detonation cord.

When the wiring job was nearly done, Dan DeLeo looked up to see a sentry whom he had sent south of the site running toward him. Nearly out of breath, the trooper blurted, "Lieutenant, there's about a platoon of Krauts coming up the tracks toward us!"

Now a sentry posted to the north dashed up to DeLeo. An even larger German force, about a mile away, was marching toward the Americans.

It had been a profitable night for the two Arabs whom the raiders had encountered earlier, DeLeo realized. Not only had they collected several valuable parachutes from the Americans, but no doubt the Germans had also paid them handsomely for squealing on the paratroop saboteurs.

As the Americans suspected, they had been caught in a trap. German patrols were scouring the countryside; guards were placed on roads to thwart the intruders' escape. After a hasty consultation with his men, DeLeo decided quickly that they would split into small groups and set out cross-country for the American lines—90 miles to the west.

A three-minute fuse was lighted; then the troopers raced off to avoid the explosion. Suddenly, an enormous blast rocked the region, and debris from a hundred yards of Rommel's railroad track and the building full of electrical equipment spiraled into the graying sky.

Dan DeLeo, Sgt. John Betters, Pvt. Roland Rondeau, and Pvt. Frank Romero, along with the two French guides, traveled together. They hid out that day, marched all the next night; then holed up at dawn in a thick woods near a well-traveled road. They noticed that numerous vehicles were randomly heading westward, so DeLeo decided to hijack one of them and drive the raiders hell-bent toward friendly lines. The men concealed themselves at the edge of the woods and waited for just the right vehicle to come along. By fate, the first one to approach was a truck with a canvas over the back—perfect for concealing the escapees.

Without his helmet, DeLeo strolled out into the road, holding a pistol behind him. He flagged down the vehicle and when the driver, an Italian soldier, poked his head out through the open window, he found himself staring into the business end of a .45 Colt.

Scrambling from the bushes, the raiders leaped into the covered back of the truck, and DeLeo climbed in beside the petrified driver. In flawless Italian, DeLeo told the enemy soldier, "Start driving. And no monkey business or I'll blow your head off!"

DeLeo picked up a white scarf lying on the seat and wrapped it around his head, Arab style. A short time later, he saw a chilling sight: Two long columns of German infantrymen, one on each side of the road, were marching toward the truck. "Krauts!" DeLeo called softly to the hidden troopers. "Keep still and have your weapons ready!" The vehicle chugged onward and reached the approaching Germans. The Americans felt their hearts beat faster; nerves were taut. Now the truck was moving along slowly between the two columns. DeLeo tried to look casual; he could have reached out and touched the passing enemy soldiers. Few of the Germans even glanced at the "Arab."

After going a considerable distance, the coughing, wheezing old truck broke down along a muddy trail. What to do with the Italian? If he were turned loose, the alarm would be spread. Some of the raiders suggested shooting the quaking man, but he was taken along. It was still more than 50 miles to American lines.

The raiders and their hostage pushed ahead on foot. They halted only when exhausted; then resumed marching. Most of their food was gone, so they haggled with Arabs for something to eat. DeLeo told the natives that he and his men were Germans, and when Arabs balked over giving them food, the lieutenant menacingly fingered his pistol.

Three weeks after their jump at the El Djem bridge, the hungry and nearly exhausted paratroopers came upon a friendly French farmer who told them how to reach a French army outpost. The farmer supplied the Americans with food and coffee; they handed out chewing gum to the children.

After trudging over a mountain range, the Americans felt a surge of elation. Off in the distance was the French outpost. Walking onward, Roland Rondeau noticed that several French soldiers had come out and were waving their arms frantically. "What in the hell are those crazy Frogs supposed to be doing?" Rondeau said to DeLeo. The lieutenant shrugged. When the raiders reached the French outpost, they learned the reason for

Lt. Dan DeLeo disguised in Arab headgear sits beside petrified Italian soldier as they drive through town filled with German troops. Other raiders peek from beneath canvas. *(Author's collection)*

the wild gesticulating: The paratroopers had been marching across a minefield!

Soon, Dan DeLeo, Rondeau, Betters, Romero and the two French guides were back with the 509th Parachute Infantry Battalion. Only two other men in the raiding party, teenaged Pvt. Charles Doyle and Pvt. Michael P. Underhill, eventually reached friendly forces in Tunisia. Along the way, Doyle and Underhill had been surprised and captured by Italian soldiers, who took away their jump boots to discourage an effort to escape. After being driven for several miles in a dilapidated old truck, the two Americans were herded into a makeshift and flimsy little POW cage.[5]

With only six unarmed Americans—all without boots—to guard, the lone Italian sentry sat down to relax. It was around midnight. While the Italian was busily trying to light a pipe, Underhill, Doyle and the other four paratroopers sneaked up to the wire fence, slipped under it, split up into pairs and melted into the blackness.[6]

For many weeks, bitter fighting raged in Tunisia as Adolf Hitler sought desperately to avert another Stalingrad. Fed into the line in piecemeal packets by British General Anderson, the men of the 509th Parachute Infantry Battalion were in the thick of the bloody slugfest.

On May 13, 1943, the death knell sounded for Axis forces in North Africa. Hitler had pulled out Erwin Rommel to fight another day, so the Desert Fox's successor, Col. Gen. Juergen von Arnim, presided over the final debacle. It *had* been another Stalingrad. More than 240,000 Axis soldiers had been corraled, and 125,000 of them were Germans.[7]

At the conclusion of hostilities, Dan DeLeo took a quick jeep trip to the El Djem bridge. He recalled that event:

> *Ever since our sabotage mission nearly five months earlier, I had been curious over whether we could have blown the bridge with the amount of explosives we had with us. No wonder the air corps bombs and rockets hadn't been able to collapse the span. It had 15 huge stone pillars that must have been 35 feet high, and they held two sets of tracks. I became convinced, on seeing the bridge close up, that we had sabotaged the railroad as effectively by blowing up the tracks and the equipment building as we could have done by blowing up the bridge.*

On May 20, a gala Victory Parade was held in Tunis, with Allied generals beaming and slapping each other on the back. Not present were members of the 509th Parachute Infantry Battalion, who had spearheaded the Operation Torch assault. America's pioneer paratroopers had been shunted off hundreds of miles to the west, to pup tent camps on the sunbaked desert outside Oujda, French Morocco.

In mid-May, a month after the Five-O-Niners reached "The Place That God Forgot" (as the troopers called Oujda), the 82nd Airborne Division—a spirited but untested outfit—arrived from the United States after a 450-mile train trek from the port of Casablanca.

Four months earlier, on January 13, 1943, an Allied summit conference was held at Hotel Anfa, near Casablanca. President Franklin Roosevelt, Prime Minister Winston S. Churchill, and top military brass sought an answer to the following question: After the Tunisian campaign was concluded, where would the Anglo-Americans strike?

Two weeks later, General Eisenhower received a directive from the Combined Chiefs of Staff: "You are to launch an assault against enemy-held Sicily in 1943, with the target date to be the period of the favorable July moon."[8]

6
Feuds and a Crucial Secret

At the time that Gen. Dwight Eisenhower had received the Sicily directive from the Combined Chiefs, he and his Allied Force Headquarters staff at Algiers were immersed in the Tunisian battle. Ike then scraped up an ad hoc group of ground and air planners and sent them to Cairo to rough out an airborne scheme for "Operation Husky," the code name for the looming invasion of Sicily.

As a guide, the Cairo group used two earlier British plans for seizing the large, mountainous island lying two miles off the toe of Italy. "Operation Influx" had been concocted in 1940, and "Operation Whipcord" had been drawn up in 1941. Both of these schemes were based on earlier military thinking, and lacked the airborne finesse developed later, so the Cairo group's initial plan was a disoriented, hodgepodge operation that called for dropping paratroopers into small, isolated pockets.

This concept was rejected out of hand by Eisenhower's staff, and the planners were sent back to the drawing board. Now they proposed that paratroopers be dropped almost on the Sicilian beaches to wipe out enemy defenses before seaborne troops would storm ashore. This suicidal proposal also was rapidly pigeonholed.[1]

Now a simmering controversy erupted within Allied ranks when the American airborne leaders learned that Maj. Gen. G. F.

"Hoppy" Hopkinson's British 1st Airborne Division was slated to carry the ball in Sicily, with the 82nd Airborne in a supporting role.[2] The Red Devils (as they were called due to their maroon berets) had never been involved in a full-scale airborne combat operation. But they had earlier carried out small raids of German-held coasts on the Channel and in Norway, and had fought as straight infantry in Tunisia.

Maj. Gen. Matthew B. Ridgway, the 47-year-old leader of the 82nd Airborne, was furious: He refused to allow his elite outfit to play second fiddle to anyone. Consequently, Ridgway quickly locked horns with Britain's senior airborne officer and Eisenhower's advisor, Maj. Gen. Frederick A. M. "Boy" Browning. Ridgway was convinced that the dapper Browning, who had served with distinction in World War I, was the "culprit" responsible for British dominance in proposed airborne operations in Sicily.

As a counterbalance to Browning's clout at Eisenhower's elbow, Ridgway dispatched Brig. Gen. Maxwell D. Taylor, the 82nd Airborne artillery commander, to take up residence in Algiers. Taylor, known for his diplomacy and keen intellect, would serve as Ridgway's eyes and ears in the rarified atmosphere of supreme headquarters.[3]

Like Ike Eisenhower, Gen. Bernard Montgomery—"Good Old Monty" to his legion of worshippers at home—was appalled when he studied the initial plan for Husky. It called for widely separated seaborne assaults on the northwest and southeast coasts, with paratroopers sprinkled around in helter-skelter fashion. Monty, no shrinking violet, demanded and got dramatic revisions. In the final plan, his British and Canadian Eighth Army would go ashore near Syracuse in the southeastern tip of triangular-shaped Sicily and drive northward to Messina, in the northeastern section. Meanwhile, Lt. Gen. George S. Patton's U. S. Seventh Army would land some 90 miles to the west of Montgomery, near Gela, and push inland to guard Montgomery's flank.

Hardly had this final plan been adopted by Algiers than Matt Ridgway and Boy Browning locked horns over the allocation of transport planes to carry the paratroopers and tow the glidermen into Sicily. There were only 390 transports (360 American C-47s and 30 British Halifaxes and Albermarles), far too few to carry all of Patton's and Montgomery's airborne forces simultaneously.[4]

Maj. Gen. Matthew Ridgway (left) greets Col. Rueben Tucker. Despite the intense heat of the African desert, both men are wearing neckties. *(Courtesy of Virgil Carmichael)*

As D-Day neared, the transport feud grew hotter. For tactical reasons, Patton and Monty, both strong-willed leaders, demanded that they get most of the available aircraft in order to carve out beachheads at the lowest possible cost in blood. But there was a second reason for Ridgway and Browning to arm-wrestle over transports: a spirited rivalry between the All-Americans and the Red Devils. This would be the first major Allied airborne operation in history, so Ridgway and Browning each wanted his own fighting men to outshine those of the other.

When Browning called on Ridgway to unveil airborne plans for Husky, the 82nd Airborne boss grew incensed. Browning, Ridgway felt, was condescending toward the newcomer to war from the colonies. The American general gained the impression that Browning was conniving to seize full control of all airborne forces.[5]

There was more than vanity involved in Ridgway's concern. If his staunch British rival were to be appointed airborne commander for Husky, he would have final say over the allocation of troop transports, in which case, Ridgway was convinced, the Americans would be drastically shortchanged.

In Algiers, Eisenhower got wind of the Ridgway-Browning feud, and on a routine visit to Allied headquarters, the 82nd Airborne commander was sternly scolded by Ike's right-hand man and alter ego, Lt. Gen. Walter B. "Beetle" Smith. No doubt Ridgway had been taken to the woodshed at the instigation of the supreme commander. Smith forcefully reminded Ridgway of Ike's policy of close cooperation between Allied leaders, and that anyone who violated this dictum would find himself on the first slow boat bound for home.

Properly chastised, Matt Ridgway returned to his CP to lick his wounds. Clearly, he was losing his duel with the suave Browning. What Ridgway needed, he concluded, was more clout, so he pleaded with George Patton to leap into the fray. The volatile and profane Patton, who had earned high-command praise for his battlefield prowess in Torch operations, eagerly complied. Already angry over his own secondary role in Husky as guardian of Montgomery's flank, Patton made it known, loud and clear, that he stood behind Ridgway all the way in this bitter dispute over transport planes.[6]

George Patton's broadsides only heated up the altercation, so Eisenhower took it upon himself to allocate the transports. Two hundred and fifty C-47s would go to Patton and 109 to Montgomery (who would also have the 30 Albermarles and Halifaxes). No one was satisfied with the supreme commander's decision. Ridgway swore that Eisenhower had caved in to the British, and the British howled that he had favored his own countrymen.

When the 82nd Airborne had arrived at Oujda in mid-May, the independent 509th Parachute Infantry Battalion had been bivouacked there for a month after the Tunisian fighting. Battle-tough, cocky, mindful of their enduring fame as America's first paratroopers to jump in a combat operation, the Five-O-Niners were angry to learn that their battalion had been attached to the 82nd Airborne Division.

It was downright humiliating, the Five-O-Niners told each other, to have to take orders from an outfit that had never heard a hostile shot. Soon fireworks erupted. In sleazy Oujda dives packed with men from both units, the 509th veterans began to announce in loud voices that the 82nd Airborne Division (12,000 men) was attached to their battalion of 600 men.

One word led to a thousand, and soon fists and bottles were flying, with barroom furniture in supporting roles. Almost every night this same violent scenario unfolded. Dr. Carlos Alden, who had been the 509th Battalion surgeon, remembered those events:

> Each morning I made a routine call to the Oujda encampment's infirmary. I could always tell which side, the 509th or the 82nd, had won the previous night's barroom brawls by counting the number of black eyes and broken noses.

Despite their intramural feuding and fussing and head cracking, troopers in both outfits stood united on one point: Oujda was the hellhole of the universe. Conditions were brutal. Relentless training was held on the rock-hard desert. After all-night marches with weapons and full field packs across the barren landscape, the exhausted troopers crawled into pup tents. But when the fireball sun rose, they were nearly broiled alive, so few got any sleep. Temperatures reached 135 to 140 degrees. Blast furnace gusts of wind scalded the troopers and peppered them with sand and dust. It was impossible to keep clean, so most quit trying. Tempers were frazzled. Rollicking fistfights broke out regularly along the tent rows.

Dysentary was rampant, so entrenching tools were taken on guard duty for sudden emergencies. Flies—millions of flies—were everywhere. Harried cooks did their best, but the food was suspect.

Kenneth R. Shaker, who had been a lieutenant in the 509th Parachute Infantry Battalion, recalled those miserable days at Oujda:

> We usually had our meals while sitting on the ground. Blasts of hot air blew sand into our mess kits and onto our food. It was futile to try to pick out the specks, so we ate sand and all. When we drank coffee, we learned to clench our teeth to strain out the dead flies, and then we would spit them out.

There were no outcries of protest when, in mid-June, it was announced that the 82nd Airborne and the 509th Parachute Infantry would climb into rickety old boxcars (known as 40-and-8s—40 men or eight mules) and trek hundreds of miles eastward to Tunisia. By July 4, all airborne elements were bivouacked in a complex of pup tents in a 30-mile arc around the Moslem holy city of Kairouan.

A few days after the division reached Kairouan, two new men were taken aloft for a night jump. Each of the youths leaped into the blackness, pulled his rip cord, and a white canopy blossomed overhead. Then the newcomers plunged into giant cactus trees whose thick, two-foot needles pierced their bodies. They were suspended in this position, and their screams of agony echoed across the landscape for interminable minutes.

The human pincushions died a horrible death. Too many cactus spines had penetrated them to pull out, so the boys were buried with the needles sticking in their bodies.

This brought the division's practice-jump death toll to four in the past month. One trooper had plunged to earth with a "streamer"—a parachute that failed to open—and another's chute had been caught by heavy gusts of wind after he reached the ground, dragging him over the terrain and bashing his head against a stone wall.

At dawn on July 7, men of the 82nd Airborne Division were given electrifying news: Within 48 hours, large numbers of them would parachute into Sicily. Lean and mean by their own admission, most of the troopers were raring to go, for the rigorous training and tedious boredom would be over. D-Day was July 10.

This was heady stuff. From Matt Ridgway on down, the All-Americans were buoyed by the knowledge that they were on the brink of a historic operation. Not only would American paratroopers be cracking open *Festung Europa* (Fortress Europe), but it would be the initial major combat jump by troops of any nation at night. Not even the Germans, who for 10 years had been developing airborne techniques, had dared to launch *Fallschirmjaeger* operations at night in Hitler's invasion of Belgium and Holland in 1940 and Crete in 1941.[7]

Because of the shortage of C-47s, not all of Ridgway's parachute elements could be dropped in the initial strike (code-named Husky One). Jumping into Sicily shortly before midnight on July 9—D-Day minus 1—would be a combat team of 3,406 paratroopers led by 36-year-old Col. James M. Gavin of Mount Carmel, Pennsylvania, known to his men as "Slim Jim." The force would consist of his own 505th Parachute Infantry Regiment, the 3rd Battalion of Col. Reuben H. Tucker's 504th Parachute Infantry, two batteries of the 456th Parachute Field

Artillery Battalion, Company B of the 307th Engineer Battalion, and signal, medical, and naval-gunfire support units.

Gavin's combat team was to drop on the heights known as Piano Lupo, north and northeast of the coastal town of Gela, where it would block enemy efforts to rush reinforcements to Patton's landing beaches, disrupt enemy communications, and create widespread havoc and confuse and disrupt the defenders.

At the same time, some 90 miles to the east, the British 1st Air Landing Brigade, under Brigadier P. H. W. "Pip" Hicks, would crash-land in gliders to the rear of Montgomery's beaches and capture the key, high-arched Ponte Grande Bridge at Syracuse. That operation was code-named "Ladbroke."

If sufficient Waco gliders became available (most of them had been allotted to the British for Ladbroke), the third major component of the 82nd Airborne, Lt. Col. Harry L. Lewis' 325th Glider Infantry Regiment, would land in daylight on D-Day plus 3 or 4 on airfields captured by Gavin's paratroopers. The 509th Parachute Infantry Battalion was held in reserve in Tunisia to be called on to jump into Sicily if need be, and it was now commanded by Lt. Col. Doyle R. Yardley, a Texas schoolteacher in peacetime, who replaced Edson Raff.[8]

Since his 1929 graduation from West Point, Col. Jim Gavin had never heard a shot fired in anger. But his men had great faith in their young leader. One parachutist summed up the consensus view: "I'd follow Slim Jim into hell—and pay for the coal to keep the fires stoked!"[9]

Just as Gavin was elated to be leading the first parachute assault on Hitler's Europe, 32-year-old Rube Tucker, the firebrand commander of the 504th Parachute Infantry, was frustrated and angry. He and the bulk of his troopers, who had long been keen rivals of Gavin's Five-O-Fives, would jump on the night of D-Day plus 1 on an airfield already captured by Gavin's men.

Known in his younger days as "Tommy" after the Mother Goose character, Tucker had been a four-sport star at Ansonia, Connecticut, high school and a cadet corps leader at West Point. He was not accustomed to what he considered to be a back-up role. It was a bitter pill for Tucker to swallow.[10]

Carrying the American paratroopers into battle would be Brig. Gen. Harold L. Clark's 552nd Troop Carrier Wing, which was based at air strips around Kairouan. Matt Ridgway, Gavin, and Tucker had been and were alarmed over the obvious inex-

Leaders of 505th Parachute Infantry prior to Sicily assault. Front row, left to right: James A. Gray, Arthur F. "Hard Nose" Gorham, James M. "Slim Jim" Gavin (commander), Herbert F. Batcheller, Edward A. Zaj, Edward C. "Cannonball" Krause. Back row, left to right: James P. McGinity, Captain Paliconi, John Norton, Alfred W. Ireland, Captain Wall, Captain Wolfslayer, Walter DeLong. *(Courtesy of Alfred Ireland)*

perience of Hal Clark's pilots. "No one knows that better than Clark himself," Ridgway had told his commanders. There simply had not been time, neither in the States nor in North Africa, for these pilots to be fully trained in the precise flying formations and pinpoint accuracy required of airborne operations.

Meanwhile, at his headquarters south of Rome, Field Marshal Albrecht Kesselring ("Smiling Al" to Allied brass) felt that the main Anglo-American blow would strike Sicily, with the possibility of diversionary attacks at Sardinia, Greece, or elsewhere.[11] Should the Allied forces succeed in surprising the Wehrmacht and disaster ensue, Adolf Hitler would need a scapegoat.

Kesselring, regarded by the Allies as one of the Führer's most capable generals, had no intention of being measured for horns. So he sent a lengthy message to the *Oberkommando der Wehrmacht* (High Command) in Berlin, detailing German and Italian troop dispositions throughout the Mediterranean region.

Kesselring's report had been transmitted in the Enigma code, which German leaders thought to be unbreakable. But the message had been intercepted and deciphered by the supersecret British device that was code-named "Ultra," whose operation was concealed in the sleepy village of Bletchley Park, 40 miles north of London. A translated version of the Kesselring report was on Eisenhower's desk in Algiers at almost the same time that the original message reached Berlin.

The intercepted report struck Eisenhower's headquarters like a bombshell. Instead of the invaders meeting the demoralized, ill-equipped, and poorly led Italian army in Sicily, as Allied intelligence had believed to be the case, they would be confronted by two first-rate German panzer divisions that had secretly been slipped across the two-mile-wide Strait of Messina. One of these units, the veteran Hermann Goering Panzer Division, was bivouacked a short distance inland from where Gavin's lightly armed paratroopers would drop.

Eisenhower was faced with one of his most agonizing dilemmas of the war. His paratroopers would have nothing to defend themselves with against panzers but 2.36-inch bazooka rockets, which had bounced off of German tanks in North Africa. If the panzers drove through Gavin's men, they could reach Patton's landing beaches and rake the seaborne troops at point-blank range as they came ashore.

No doubt Gavin's parachutists would be better prepared to deal with German tanks if they knew in advance of the tracked vehicles' presence. But paratroopers isolated behind enemy lines were likely candidates for capture, and German interrogators would soon learn that the Americans knew that the Hermann Goering Division was nearby. This could cause Berlin to suspect that the Allies had broken the Enigma code; it would be abandoned and a new code would be established, thereby depriving the Allies of the enormous military advantage of knowing enemy plans in advance during the monumental battles that loomed before Hitler was brought to his knees.[12]

So even if Gavin's paratroopers were wiped out, even if the entire invasion were smashed, Eisenhower concluded that the secret of Ultra would have to be protected. Jim Gavin and his troopers would leap into Sicily unaware that swarms of German tanks lurked nearby.[13]

Meanwhile, German officers in Sicily, hoping to discourage civilians from aiding the invaders if that island turned out to be the Allied target, spread the word that American paratroopers were murderers and rapists. At the inland town of Vittoria, wide-eyed citizens were warned that American parachutists were hardened, long-term convicts who President Roosevelt had released to join his airborne troops.

Shortly after noon on July 9—D-Day minus 1—Gavin's paratroopers climbed into trucks and were driven to airfields around Kairouan. Dismounting, the grim men piled their weapons and equipment beneath the wings and under the fuselages of the squat, low-winged C-47s. The moment of truth was at hand.

Many of the parachutists had shaved their heads completely, while others left only a narrow strip of hair running from the nape of the neck to the forehead, giving them the appearance of Indians on the warpath. To embellish their ferocious looks, the men with the Indian haircuts daubed warpaint on their faces.

Each trooper was loaded for bear. He would jump carrying a Garand rifle, a carbine or a tommy gun; a big, nasty-looking trench knife with brass knucks on the handle; and a switchblade knife, honed to razor-blade sharpness, concealed in a secret jumpsuit pocket for use on an unsuspecting enemy soldier in the event of capture. Bandoliers of rifle ammunition crisscrossed their chests, extra tommy-gun ammo hung from clips on belts, grenades stuffed pockets and were hand-carried in canvas bags.

In addition to two parachutes, each man would carry an entrenching tool, a canteen of water, a gas mask, a first-aid packet containing a syringe and morphine, K and D rations (the latter were concentrated chocolate—one bar of which could keep a soldier going for a day), field bag, clothing, jump boots and a steel helmet. Altogether, these accoutrements of war added 80 to 90 pounds to each trooper's jump weight.

At one airfield, a tall, heavyset man with a black, bushy beard was having a difficult time slipping into his parachute harness, no doubt from lack of practice. He was John "Beaver" Thompson, the *Chicago Tribune* correspondent and "instant paratrooper" who had jumped with the 509th Parachute Infantry Battalion at the Youks les Bains airport the previous November.[14]

Now chilling shouts echoed across the airfields: "Load 'em up!" Suddenly, war was no longer an abstract affair to be discussed and trained for or seen in movie theater newsreels. Rather, war had emerged as real, immediate—and extremely personal.

Lining up in single file at the doors of the C-47s, the heavily laden paratroopers waddled crablike up the short ladders, then moved inside the cabins to designated bucket seats. Soon, the collective roar of the engines was ear-splitting. Propellers whipped up thick clouds of dust.

Alfred W. Ireland, who had been the 505th combat team's personnel officer, recalled the takeoff:

> Just as our C-47 was ready to start down the runway, an air corps lieutenant from the field's weather station came charging up. He blurted out excitedly to Jim Gavin, standing in the door, "They told me to tell you that the wind is 35 miles per hour, west to east!" Jim returned to his seat and grumbled to me, "Well, I don't know what in the hell I'm supposed to do about that!"
>
> The news hardly bolstered our morale. In training camp, jumps had been canceled as far too risky when winds reached 20 miles per hour.

Circling over Tunisia to form up, the 266 transports then flew out over the azure Mediterranean. The sky train would fly a dog-leg, 415-miles course, first east to the tiny island of Malta, then generally northward to Sicily, a trek that would take three and a half hours. If all went well, Gavin and his troopers would be on the ground just before midnight, with several hours before the full moon set and daylight arrived in which to assemble into battle units and set up defensive positions.

Wedged shoulder to shoulder in their bucket seats, the men gazed wistfully at the orange glow of the sun as it began to slip into the western horizon. That blast furnace sun had fried their hides for two months, and they had cursed it relentlessly, but now it was beautiful. Many wondered if they would ever see another sunset.

7
Parachute Assault on Fortress Europe

Just as the American paratroop sky train was doglegging to the left near Malta for the final 75-mile run to the drop zone behind Patton's landing beaches, the resolute leader of the Hermann Goering Panzer Division, Maj. Gen. Paul Conrath, received word that an Allied invasion fleet was steaming toward southeastern Sicily. Only a few days earlier, he had been told by Field Marshal Albrecht Kesselring: "If the Allies strike, don't wait for orders from above to attack. There may not be time."

"If you mean to go for them," Conrath replied, "then I'm your man."[1]

Conrath's panzers were concealed around his headquarters at Caltagirone, only 22 miles from where Patton's 1st Infantry Division would storm ashore at Gela and his 45th Infantry Division would land near Scogletti. If the Goering Division leader had been briefed by General Eisenhower on Allied invasion plans, Conrath could not have selected a more perfect locale for holding his panzers in readiness.

Now, at 10:05 P.M., Conrath flashed word to his panzers: Head for the shore at Gela and Scogletti. He was gambling that the Allies would land at those two places. The panzers rumbled southward in two battle groups. One column to the west would go through Niscemi toward the Big Red One beachhead, and the other, or eastern column, in the direction of the 45th Division landing beaches.

About an hour and a half after the panzers started rolling, the point of the paratroop armada knifed over the shore, and a cacophony of noise and fury erupted below. Enemy gunners had opened fire.

Long streamers of white tracers hissed toward the C-47s. Inside the cabins, anxious ears heard tearing noises—bullets ripping through wings and fuselages. Soon the night air was filled with crisscross patterns of tracers and black puffs of smoke left in the wakes of the exploding shells.

The parachutists knew that C-47 fuel tanks were not self-sealing, so a single tracer could turn the airplane into a fiery torch. The tension was nearly unbearable. Some men fought off an urge to rush the open door and bail out. Others vomited.

Standing in the door of a C-47, Col. Jim Gavin could not recognize a single landmark, and became convinced that his entire flight had been blown far off course. However, orders were for everyone to jump, regardless of the situation.

Suddenly, the green light in the cabin (activated by the pilot) flashed on. "Let's go!" Gavin shouted, and he hurtled into space, followed at split-second intervals by the others in the stick.[2] Clearing the C-47, Gavin felt the angry hurricane blasts ripping at his body. Moments later, a sharp jolt—then the white flash of exultation—his parachute had popped open.

The gale force winds were causing his parachute to oscillate and gyrate wildly as the earth rushed toward him. *Crump!* He struck the ground with terrific impact. Shucking his chute harness and getting to his feet, Gavin shook his spinning head to rid it of cobwebs, checked his carbine, and looked around. White canopies should have been coming down on all sides, but the leader of 3,406 paratroopers was alone.

Gavin started walking and had gone but a short distance when he glimpsed two silhouetted figures moving toward him. Troopers? Or enemy soldiers? He leveled his carbine and called out the night's password in a stage whisper: "Halt! George!" There were several moments of silence. Then came the countersign: "Marshall!" Maj. Benjamin H. Vandervoort, the combat team's operations officer, and Capt. Al Ireland stepped forward.[3]

James Gavin recalled that three-man union:

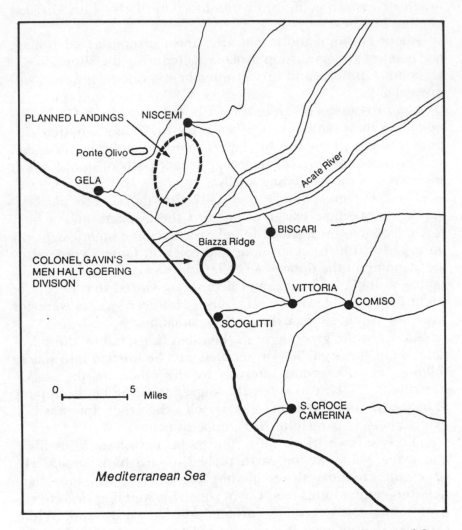

Planned parachute landings. Actually landings were dispersed from Niscemi southeast to S. Croce Camerina. Twenty-three planeloads jumped in the British sector, some 40 miles east of S. Croce Camerina.

I told Ben and Al that we had better take off cross-country toward the DZ. I tried to speak with an assurance that I didn't feel, for I did not know where I was, where the DZ was—or even if I had landed in Sicily. We started walking in what we hoped was the right direction. This was very barren terrain—no roads or road markers to help orient us. As we moved along, we collected other troopers, some of them badly wounded. My total force consisted of Ben, Al, and seven men.

Earlier, Capt. Robert G. Kaufman was standing in a C-47 door, a minute or two from the shore. His men had already hooked up and were waiting nervously for the green light. Suddenly, shells burst outside, and a white-hot jagged piece of shrapnel struck Kaufman in the neck. At that precise moment, the green light flashed on, even though the C-47 was still over water.

Either killed instantly or critically wounded, Captain Kaufman fell forward and plunged into the Mediterranean, 500 feet below. Seeing their leader depart and the green light glowing, the remainder of the stick bailed out. The Number 2 and Number 3 men parachuted into the sea and were dragged under to watery graves. Having a few more seconds for the C-47 to get over land, the others came down directly onto an enemy pillbox complex and a fierce shootout erupted.[4]

Elsewhere over Sicily, the *Chicago Tribune* correspondent, Beaver Thompson, bailed out. He remembered that experience:

As soon as I cleared the door, the sky around me broke out in a brilliant white, just like it was high noon under a blazing sun. A C-47 had apparently been struck by shellfire, bursting into a fiery ball. How many of our boys had gone to their deaths? I wondered. The sight sickened me.

Thompson saw by the light of the full moon that he was going to plunge into an olive grove. Branches crackled and snapped as his body hurtled through the trees before striking the ground with tremendous force. The newsman felt sharp pain: He had suffered two broken ribs, a severely wrenched knee, an ugly gash on one leg, and cuts and bruises on his knuckles.

Thompson struggled to his feet, but could not see anyone or hear a sound. He was convinced that he had made a one-man parachute assault on enemy-held Sicily—a feeling hundreds of American paratroopers felt that night in isolated landings.

The injured reporter stumbled off, clutching a trench knife. He felt a little foolish. "I'm a typewriter jockey, not a fighting man," Thompson had quipped before the jump. Suddenly, he heard a voice calling from the shadows nearby: "Beaver! Beaver! Where in the hell are you?"

A relieved Thompson recognized the voice: it was that of Lt. Col. William T. Ryder, who had come along as an official observer. The two men had chatted together throughout the flight. Ryder was a true paratroop pioneer. Back at Fort Benning's primitive airstrip on August 16, 1940, genial Lt. Bill Ryder had made history by being the first American paratroop officer to jump from a plane.[5]

As the flights continued to approach the coast, Maj. Mark J. Alexander, leader of the 2nd Battalion of the 505th Regiment, was in the door of his C-47. Ahead he could see thick fountains of machine-gun tracers searching the sky for intruders. Although still over water—and unbeknownst to Alexander—the pilot flipped on the red warning light. The troopers struggled to their feet, anxious to jump, for they could see the curtain of fire toward which the C-47 was heading.

Now the green light flashed on and the men scrambled to get out the door. Only Major Alexander realized that they were still over water. They tried to push him out through the opening. However, through shouts and physical strength, Alexander succeeded in calming the troopers, no doubt saving them—and himself—from jumping too soon and drowning.[6]

A short distance inland, Alexander and his battalion bailed out over a complex of huge Italian bunkers, some three stories high, and the defenders opened up withering fusillades of fire at the descending Americans. Lt. Robert Clee, a battalion surgeon, dropped heavily just in front of a pillbox. Stunned, Clee tried desperately to free himself from wire entanglements into which he had fallen. Italians inside the bunker poured fire at the doctor, killing him instantly.

Nearby, Sgt. Harold Freeland was also caught in the barbed wire after landing. Unlike Lieutenant Clee, Freeland did not try to free himself. He feigned death and lay motionless in front of an Italian-manned pillbox for several hours as a savage fight raged all around him. When his comrades captured the bunker, Freeland disengaged himself from the barbed wire and rejoined the fight.

Meanwhile, Capt. John Norton, Alexander's executive officer, had landed alone and was wandering through the night in search of comrades. He spotted the dim outline of a house and edged up to it. Faint voices were heard coming from inside. Some troopers must have holed up there, Norton thought. Cautiously, he called out the password, "George!" Came back a booming voice with a thick Italian accent: "George, hell!"

Captain Norton flopped to the ground and a stream of tracers zipped over his head. He crawled away. Only later would he learn that the "house" had been a pillbox and an Italian command post.[7]

Elsewhere, many miles from the drop zone, 20-year-old Sgt. Buffalo Boy Canoe, an Oglala Sioux Indian, landed in a heap on the boulder-strewn ground. Moments later, he realized that enemy soldiers were on three sides. Tracers began whipping over his head. Lying flat on the ground, he leveled his carbine to return the fire and squeezed the trigger; the weapon jammed. Apprehension gripped him; all Canoe had to fight with was a trench knife and a few grenades.

Slithering along on his stomach and crawling, Canoe edged away. Finally he was able to walk upright, and in about a half mile he detected the contour of a small farmhouse. Silently, he crept up to a faintly illuminated window, peeked inside, and saw three Germans laughing loudly, talking and lifting wine bottles to their lips.

Sgt. Buffalo Boy Canoe.
(Author's collection)

John H. "Beaver" Thompson.
(Jim Phillips)

Sergeant Canoe concealed himself in nearby shadows. Presently one of the Germans staggered out of the house, walked a few yards, and began relieving himself. That would be his last act on earth. Clutching his trench knife, Canoe crept forward; then charged the unwary German. He threw his adversary to the ground and plunged the knife into his stomach. The German gurgled, twitched violently; then lay still.

Soon the remaining two Germans cautiously edged outside. Each was carrying a pistol. They apparently had heard the ruckus and emerged to investigate. One of them called out what apparently was their missing companion's name. Canoe watched from the shadows. Then he pitched a grenade and an orange fireball exploded around the two enemy soldiers. They fell to the ground and Canoe slipped away.

Shortly after midnight on D-Day, Capt. Willard R. "Bill" Follmer, the 25-year-old leader of I Company of the 505th Regiment, was crawling along a hillside on his hands and knees. Plummeting to earth minutes earlier, Follmer had heard a loud snapping sound and felt a sharp pain shoot up his leg. His ankle was broken in three places.

Follmer, like so many other All-Americans that night, was alone. After crawling for 50 yards, he halted abruptly on hearing a faint rustling noise in the dark shadows. He whipped out his .45 Colt and, in a low voice, called out, "George!" Came the response: "Marshall!" Follmer felt a surge of relief when his sergeant aide stepped out of the underbrush.

Captain Follmer, at the urging of the other, climbed onto his husky batman, and in piggyback fashion, the two men set out in search of I Company troopers. As they traipsed along, other men of Follmer's unit emerged from the shadows. Within the hour, nearly all of the company had assembled. Only later would the captain learn that his unit was one of the few companies to land on its designated drop zone, northeast of Gela.

Follmer's mission was to block roads to enemy reinforcements seeking to rush to the landing beaches. But how could the injured and immobile captain direct I Company operations? His men had the answer. They "liberated" an ancient mule from a violently protesting farmer, hoisted the captain aboard, and Follmer rode off at the head of his troopers astride the animal.[8]

Elsewhere, a small band of paratroopers led by 26-year-old Lt. Richard Janney and Sgt. Carl Hearn had landed amidst half a dozen enemy pillboxes. At first, there were only six Americans, but they took the concrete bunkers under attack, and a fierce firefight broke out. Attracted by the sounds of battle, Janney and his men had knocked out all six pillboxes and captured in excess of 250 Italians. Of the 14 paratroopers in the fight, five lay dead and three others were wounded.[9]

Meanwhile, a group of 80 paratroopers of G Company, 505th, was engaged in a bitter firefight with Germans defending the key Ponte Dirillo, a two-lane concrete slab stretching for 200 yards across the bone-dry Acate River. Ponte Dirillo lay in the zone of advance of the seaborne 45th Infantry Division, which would have to cross the span to capture a pair of badly needed airfields.

Maj. Gen. Troy Middleton, leader of the 45th "Thunderbird" Division, had assigned one of his battalions to seize the bridge. However, the 80 parachutists, under Capt. James McGinity, drove the German defenders from the pillboxes guarding the site and seized the objective of a battalion that had not yet come ashore.[10] A price was paid for the feat of arms. Numerous All-Americans were sprawled in death about the dry-river span.

Neither Jim Gavin, who was still tramping across the dark landscape with a handful of troopers, nor others in the parachute force knew what was going on. Actually, the gale force winds of 36 miles per hour, the enemy gunfire along the coast, and the inexperience of the 552nd Troop Carrier Command pilots had resuluted in 3,406 paratroopers being scattered helter-skelter along a 60-mile stretch of southern Sicily.

8
"All Missions Accomplished!"

At his headquarters in the ancient walled city of Enna, in the center of the island, Italian *Generale d'Armata* Alfredo Guzzoni, the 66-year-old commander of the Axis Sixth Army, was swamped with field reports, many of them panicky in tone. American parachute units were said to be dropping all over southern Sicily. Not aware that most of these sightings were individual and tiny bands of parachutists, Guzzoni's staff estimated that three or four airborne divisions (some 45,000 men) had landed.[1]

Meanwhile at 2:45 A.M., the assault waves of the 1st Infantry Division near Gela and the 45th Infantry Division near Scogletti stormed ashore and began pushing inland. Shoreline resistance was spotty—from minimal to moderate. Far to the east, where Brigadier Pip Hicks' British glider brigade had landed and seized the key Ponte Grande bridge, leading elements of Montgomery's Eighth Army waded onto the beaches near Syracuse.

Shortly after dawn, Col. Jim Gavin, Maj. Ben Vandervoort, Capt. Al Ireland, and six troopers were tramping cross-country toward the drop zone on Piano Lupo. Most of the men were limping from wounds or jarring landings. Gavin was deeply disappointed. For 20 years he had prepared himself for the challenge of leading a large body of men into battle. Now he didn't know where the battle was, he was not certain what county he was in, and his force consisted of eight paratroopers.

In the meantime, over the Gulf of Gela, Navy Lt. C. G. Lewis was piloting a spotter plane. At 8:27 A.M., he radioed the following message to the USS *Boise* offshore: "Enemy tanks and vehicles moving south down Niscemi road toward Gela."[2] Lewis was seeing the western column of the Hermann Goering Panzer Division.

Between the oncoming *Kampfgruppe* (battle group) and the 1st Infantry Division's landing beaches were some 100 men of Lt. Col. Arthur "Hard Nose" Gorham's 1st Battalion of the 505th Regiment. Most of Gorham's unit had dropped about 70 miles to the east in the British sector, but these 100 troopers had landed on or near the Piano Lupo drop zone.

Gorham also had seen the German column and deployed his men along a low knoll to either side of the Niscemi road. Nervously fingering triggers, the troopers watched as about 300 grenadiers (infantrymen) fanned out into a skirmish line and moved forward across the barren, open ground. Onward came the Germans to within 200 yards. Neither side fired a shot. One hundred yards. Eighty. Fifty.

"Fire!" Art Gorham shouted, and an earsplitting fusillade of machine-gun and rifle fire riddled the ranks of the grenadiers.

Scores were cut down. Fearful and confused, others milled about, and they, too, were shot. Most flopped to the ground and lay there while the Americans poured lead into the huddled groups. Perhaps half of the German force in the rear managed to crawl away from the carnage.

"Cease firing! Cease firing!"

An eerie silence fell over Piano Lupo. Dug in and concealed, the troopers had only a few wounded men. Out in front of their smoking guns, clumps of Germans were sprawled in death. Interspersed among them, writhing in agony and crying out for help, were large numbers of wounded.

An hour later, the German battle-group leader sent six tanks around the right flank of Gorham's position to attack the paratroopers from the rear. By happenstance, the panzers bumped into a bazooka squad that was heading for the drop zone. The troopers fired several rockets, striking vulnerable points of two tanks and causing them to grind to a halt with their crews dead inside.

Now the remaining four tanks raked the bazookamen with machine guns, and a platoon of German grenadiers moved in and took the All-Americans prisoners. Not knowing what size force they were facing, and apparently fearful of being ambushed, the panzers spun around and rumbled back to their own lines.

Later that morning, Capt. Edwin M. Sayre, commander of Gorham's Company A, and his 44 men, reflected briefly on events of the past 11 hours. Sayre, a 27-year-old farmer from Texas, and 14 of his men had landed near a thick-walled, heavily fortified farmhouse on Piano Lupo. Holding a grenade in his teeth, another in one hand, and firing a pistol, Sayre led a mad charge on the formidable building. Forty-three Italians and 12 German soldiers inside were captured, and 15 others were killed. Four Americans had been cut down.[3]

Now Colonel Gorham instructed Sayre to take his 44 troopers a short distance to the rear and seize a stronghold Allied planners had code-named Objective Y, a complex of large bunkers dug into a hillside and guarding a key road junction. Sayre knew an assault on the pillboxes would be a bloody one, so he sought to hoodwink the Italian defenders into surrendering. Under a white flag, a captured Italian soldier was sent into the stronghold with an ultimatum: Unless the defenders capitulated immediately, Sayre would demolish their bunkers with a massive bombardment by warships offshore. From their hillside perch, the Italians could see the Allied vessels in the Gulf of Gela.

Minutes later, white flags were flying from the concrete stronghold, and Sayre and his troopers became the new landlords without firing a shot. Perhaps the Italian commander would never know that Ed Sayre had pulled a monumental bluff—he had no means whatsoever of contacting the warships.

At 11:32 A.M., Sayre and his troopers linked up with seaborne elements of the 1st Infantry Division at Objective Y, and the parachute captain used a radio belonging to the newcomers to signal to Matt Ridgway at his command post outside Gela: "All missions accomplished." (Ridgway had come in by boat after dawn.)

That may well have been the understatement of the invasion. Hard Nose Gorham, Ed Sayre, and 100 or fewer paratroopers, together with a few men of Lt. Col. William A. Kouns' battalion of the 504th Regiment, had taken the steam out of the Goering Division battle group's headlong rush to the shore at Gela. Gorham and his band had accomplished a task assigned to Jim Gavin's entire regimental combat team, and prevented what could have been an American disaster at the beaches.[4]

Twenty-five miles southeast of Gorham's fight on Piano Lupo, Maj. Mark Alexander counted noses and found that most of his battalion—455 men—had landed together and were assembled. At dawn, the major could see how formidable the pillbox complex was that he and his men had crashed down on. Although he had no high-velocity guns, Alexander ordered the pillboxes to be wiped out. The job would have to be done with rifles, tommy guns, grenades—and paratrooper guts.

Leading off the attack, Lt. Norman Sprinkle and five men charged across open ground toward a three-story bunker. All six troopers were killed by bursts of machine-gun fire. However, the Italians inside had been distracted, and other troopers slipped around to the side of the structure and pitched grenades through the fire ports. The 36 surviving enemy soldiers marched out with hands upraised. Within an hour, Alexander's men had seized all four of the huge bunkers.

Mark Alexander and his battalion now marched southward, bound for the shore two miles away. Lt. Col. Harrison Harden, Jr., commander of the 456th Parachute Field Artillery Battalion, and 21 of his men were dragging a 75-millimeter howitzer and hand-carrying 31 shells. Left behind in the care of Lt. Lester Stein, a paratroop doctor, were 37 wounded men.

Reaching the Mediterranean near the village of Marina di Ragusa, Alexander and his men were confronted by a complex of coastal fortifications whose big guns could fire only seaward. Alexander ordered an attack. Harden's lone howitzer lobbed a few rounds into the minifortress, and white flags began waving in the hot breeze over the ramparts. More than 100 Italians were captured.

That night on Piano Lupo, Capt. Ed Sayre lead a patrol into no-man's land. The night was pitch-black and the troopers edged along cautiously, weapons at the ready, eyes and ears alert. It was deathly still. Suddenly, the quiet was shattered. A machine gun to the front opened up withering bursts of fire at almost point-blank range. Sayre and his men flopped down.

While bullets hissed past their heads, the nine Americans began crawling and slithering toward the rear. After negotiating 200 arduous yards, they reached a dry creek bed with five-foot-high banks and scrambled into its protective confines. Sprawled on the creek bottom to regain their breaths, the troopers heard shuffling sounds, and then 10 dark figures leaped into the defile almost directly on top of them. Presumably, this was a 1st Infantry Division patrol seeking cover from the spurting machine gun.

The new men sat down and one called out in a hushed voice, *"Kompanie zu welcher Einheit gehosen Sie?"* ("What company do you belong to?")

"They're Krauts!" an American shouted, whipping out his trench knife and plunging it into the nearest German. Now the creek bed was a whirling mass of thrashing, grunting, cursing bodies as men fought savagely with daggers, rifle butts, and swinging fists. Presently, surviving Germans wrenched loose and ran toward their own lines, leaving behind in the defile one dead and three wounded *Feldgrau.*

At the headquarters of the Hermann Goering Panzer Division that D-Day night, Gen. Paul Conrath was furious. He had just been blistered from Rome by Field Marshal Kesselring. Conrath's anger focused on his *Kampfgruppe* commander who had failed to break through Hard Nose Gorham's paratroopers on Piano Lupo and reach the shore at Gela. Conrath relieved the colonel and charged him with cowardice.

Now Conrath prepared to strike again in the morning with even greater force. He exhorted his battle leaders: "Throw the Amis back into the sea!"[5]

Shortly after dawn burst over the purple hills of Sicily, 91

Goering Division panzers charged toward Gela. The bulk of the tanks skirted Piano Lupo far to the west and rumbled over the flatlands toward Gela. At the same time, other panzers were clanking toward Hill 41 on Piano Lupo, where Art Gorham's band of paratroopers were dug in.

Trailing plumes of dust, the panzers roared up to Gorham's foxhole line and raked the paratroopers with point-blank machine-gun fire. Gorham saw two of his men out in the open aiming a bazooka at an oncoming tank, then witnessed them being killed by a blast from the tracked vehicle's gun. Rushing forward, the battalion leader picked up the bazooka and kneeled to fire. The tank shot first. Hard-nosed to the end, Art Gorham fell over dead.

Capt. William Comstock, a paratroop medical officer, ran to Gorham's side. A shell exploded nearby, seriously wounding Comstock, who toppled over beside the colonel's body. Then Lt. Dean McCandless left his foxhole and dashed through a hail of fire to where the two officers were sprawled. With the help of other troopers, he managed to drag Captain Comstock back to relative safety and to recover the body of Colonel Gorham.

While the uneven battle of tanks against bare flesh raged on Hill 41, some paratroopers lay flat in deep foxholes and looked up in terror at the wide tracks and undercarriages of panzers passing over. Other troopers, in shallow slit trenches, were crushed to pulp by the thick-plated monsters.

Gorham's men fought back with bazookas, grenades, and by firing rifles into vision slits. A few troopers leaped onto the panzers and tried to pull open the turret covers to drop in grenades, but the tanks pushed on through the paratroopers and headed for Gela.

Meanwhile, on the plains west of Piano Lupo, swarms of German tanks reached the outskirts of Gela, where they were confronted by dogged men of the 1st Infantry Division and Lt. Col. William O. Darby's Rangers. From the roof of a building in the town, George Patton watched the savage fight. To him, the flatlands seemed to be crammed with tread-to-tread panzers.

As the battle raged to within 2,000 yards of shore, the cruisers *Boise* and *Savannah* and six destroyers poured in 3,194 shells, knocking out perhaps 41 panzers. The furious assault on Gela was beaten back. On Piano Lupo, the American paratroopers were still in their foxholes; not a single man had budged under the weight of the panzer assault.

When night fell over bleak Sicily, hundreds of other 82nd Airborne men, alone or in tiny raiding parties, were stalking the countryside, spreading confusion and fear among the enemy. Using Indian warfare tactics of the Old West, the marauders lay in wait along roads and ambushed enemy couriers and patrols. Often survivors of these ambushes told their headquarters that they had been pounced on by scores of blackfaced Americans in baggy pants. Troopers planted mines in roads and cut telephone lines.

At the same time that German panzers were pounding Gela's gates, some 70 miles to the east a band of about 75 American paratroopers had gathered around an old farmhouse outside the coastal town of Avola. These men had been among the 23 planeloads of Gavin's combat team that had been dropped in the British zone. In charge of this hodgepodge band was Lt. Charles E. "Pinkie" Sammon, intelligence officer of Mark Alexander's battalion in the 505th Parachute Infantry.

Inside the farmhouse, Pvt. Harlan Adams, a medical trooper, had set up an aid station and was doing a brisk business. Many parachutists had received injuries from jarring landings and firefights in the darkness. Two new 82nd Airborne arrivals brought in a trooper named Mike Scambelluri, who was from Albany, New York, and of Italian descent. His face and jumpsuit were saturated with blood. Despite excruciating pain, young Mike insisted on telling his story.

Scambelluri had parachuted into a fortified position, where he lay helpless while several Italian soldiers, including a captain, stood over him, pointed weapons at his head, and robbed him of his watch, wallet, and other belongings. Learning that he spoke fluent Italian, the captain became furious. "You're a goddamned traitor!" the officer shouted. "We know how to handle bastards like you!"

Scambelluri's hands were tied behind his back and he was placed against a wall. At 15 feet, the Italian officer fired his pistol, deliberately sending a bullet through the paratrooper's thigh and a second bullet into his other leg. Scambelluri, his face contorted in pain, refused to cry out or beg for mercy. So the Italian officer sent five more bullets ripping into the trooper— one slug into each arm and the calf, and the final pair into his body.

Mike Scambelluri, proud of his Italian ancestry, but more proud to be an American, fell to the ground, semiconscious. His tormentors, tiring of their savage game and believing the paratrooper to be dead, began to leave. In a final display of defiance, Scambelluri pulled himself to his feet. As he did so, the Italians pitched two of the trooper's own grenades at him; and the explosions sent white-hot slivers of metal into Scambelluri's abdomen.

Again the All-American collapsed. His captors, certain that they had finished him off this time, departed. Regaining consciousness some time later, Scambelluri staggered away and reached an orchard, where he was found by two 82nd Airborne men. Later, Mike Scambelluri died. He was not yet old enough to vote.

Meanwhile, Lt. Pinkie Sammon and his officers agreed that the band of 75 paratroopers would attack Avola, a town of 22,000 people, to aid the British seaborne forces. Many of the parachutists were limping or wearing bloodstained bandages, but they formed into a column and, with Sammon in the lead, struck out for Avola.

Against mixed resistance, the troopers fought their way to the square in the center of town, where they were pinned down by the fire of six Italian machine guns. Suddenly, from the other side of the square, a British Bren-gun carrier roared in with guns blazing. Taken by surprise, the Italian machine gunners fled.

Watching paratroopers cheered. But a company of British foot soldiers, unaware that Americans were in the vicinity, were edging up the street. Mistaking the parachutists for Germans, the Tommies opened fire. The Americans dashed for cover and did not shoot back.

When the British force was only 50 yards away, two Americans placed their helmets on the tips of rifles and waggled the weapons out from a doorway. Firing ceased. A British captain advanced cautiously, and when he became certain that the begrimed men were Americans, he blurted out in astonishment: "I say, what the bloody 'ell are you Yanks doing 'ere?"

Thomas W. Graham, who had been an 82nd Airborne Lieutenant, remembered events at Avola:

We American paratroopers moved toward the British landing beach for eventual evacuation back to North Africa. For transportation, we had mules and carts. I was riding a bicycle with no tires—not an easy task. On the way, we passed General [Bernard] Montgomery, beret and all, standing at an intersection and waving his troops inland. He seemed exasperated over our ragtag group cluttering up the narrow road.

Meanwhile, far to the west of Avola, Jim Gavin and his handful of troopers had stumbled onto a 45th Infantry Division machine-gun outpost in the predawn darkness of July 11. For the first time since parachuting to earth 52 hours earlier, the parachute regimental combat team commander learned precisely where he was—five miles southwest of Vittoria, Sicily.

9
Crisis on
Biazza
Ridge

At around 8:30 A.M. on July 11—D-Day plus 1—Pvt. Philip Foley, a paratrooper from Boston, and a tiny band of comrades were trekking across a low elevation named Biazza Ridge. They were trying to reach the true drop zone on Piano Lupo. Suddenly, chilling sounds were heard: the roar of diesel engines. Foley and his mates had bumped into the point of the Hermann Goering Division's eastern column, which was charging toward the 45th "Thunderbird" Infantry Division's beachhead near Scogletti. In addition to the German armor, which included heavy Tiger tanks, there was a battalion of infantry and a company of 120-millimeter mortars.

Unaware that they had collided with such a powerful force, Phil Foley and his fellow troopers flopped down and opened fire. Moments later, a deluge of bullets hissed into and past the Americans. Foley heard a sickening thud followed by a gasp. Glancing to one side, he saw a lifeless comrade with a neat hole in the center of his forehead.

The Germans began dropping mortar rounds, and a shriek echoed above the din to Foley's rear. A trooper was writhing in agony, his arm ripped off at the shoulder by an exploding shell. Foley slithered toward the screaming youth, but knew there was nothing he could do to help. After interminable minutes of excruciating pain, the mutilated trooper died. Fighting back tears of grief and anger, Foley resumed shooting at the Germans.

Meanwhile, at dawn, Jim Gavin reached Vittoria, obtained a jeep from the 45th Infantry Division, and headed in the direction of Gela. He had heard rumors that there were more paratroopers a few miles away. Soon the colonel came onto about 250 men of the 3rd Battalion of the 505th, who were just awakening in foxholes in a field along the road.

Gavin instructed the battalion commander, Maj. Edward C. "Cannonball" Krause, to get his men on their feet and to start marching westward toward Gela and the battalion's objective. Gavin then took a platoon of engineers and struck out on foot along the road to Gela. Just before 9:00 A.M.—a half hour after Private Foley and his comrades had engaged the enemy force—Gavin and his men reached a point where a small railroad crossed the road, a half mile from Biazza Ridge. He heard heavy shooting in that direction, and he knew that a strong enemy force was on the ridge.

Through a mystifying roll of the dice by fate, Colonel Gavin, who had been mistakenly dropped 24 miles southeast of the true drop zone, happened upon the precise point where the eastern column of the Goering Division was barreling toward the shore. If Gavin and most of his combat team had landed as planned, on the drop zones north and northeast of Gela, there would have been no American force to block this onrushing panzer battle group.

Gavin sent back a messenger to tell Cannonball Krause to double-time forward with his men; then he prepared to attack Biazza Ridge with the available troopers. In addition to Lt. Ben Weschler's engineers, who were fighting as infantrymen, Gavin had collected a motley band of other troopers—cooks, orderlies, riggers, clerks, riflemen, and several officers. There would be no artillery or antitank guns—only a few bazookas to fight enemy tanks.

Gavin deployed his men in a skirmish line and took his place in the center of the force, which numbered some 60 to 70 troopers. Fighting as infantrymen in charge of no one but themselves were the following official observers: Lt. Col. Bill Ryder of St. Louis; Lt. Col. Charles Billingslea of San Francisco; the executive officer of the 505th regiment, Lt. Col. Herbert Batcheller; Maj. Ben Vandervoort; and a few captains and lieutenants.[1] The paratroopers thought that they would be attacking an Italian force; Allied brass had told Gavin that the only Germans in Sicily were a few technicians!

Gavin gave the signal to move forward. Almost at once, the Germans on Biazza Ridge opened up withering bursts of automatic weapon fire. Troopers went down here and there, but the All-Americans pressed on.

As the shootout raged, Gavin's force, despite numerous casualties, expanded steadily. Maj. William J. Hagen, the executive officer of Krause's battalion, arrived with elements of his unit, and they joined in the fight. Also hustled into the assault was a lost platoon of the 45th Infantry Division. Paratroopers wandering around the region heard the sound of the guns and rushed to embattled Biazza Ridge. Now probably 250 Americans were fighting for this once-insignificant piece of Sicilian real estate.

By early afternoon, Gavin's mixed bag of fighting men had clawed to the top of the ridge, charged the line of German foxholes, and killed or wounded many occupants. Other German troops fled. Biazza Ridge's new American landlords occupied the premises.

Long ago at West Point, Jim Gavin had learned a military axiom: When the enemy is on the run, keep him on the run. So he ordered his men to pursue the enemy down the back slope, and a savage clash erupted as the All-Americans battled panzers in orchards and vineyards. Kneeling in the open, a trooper fired a bazooka at a Tiger tank that was clanking toward him, but the rocket failed to penetrate the tank's thick four-inch frontal armor. On came the Tiger, crushing the trooper and his loader. Maj. Cannonball Krause bounced two bazooka missiles off a tank; then received a minor wound when German machine gunners opened fire on him.

Parachutists crept up on the sides of the lighter panzers and fired bazooka rockets into the vulnerable points—fuel tanks and ammunition racks. Three Mark IV tanks were knocked out by these tactics and their crews were killed.

Soon wounded troopers were filing back over the ridge past

Jim Gavin's foxhole command post. One of them was Maj. Bill Hagen, who was hobbling badly. One leg was bleeding profusely from a gaping hole torn out by a chunk of shrapnel. Also shuffling past Gavin were the first German prisoners, bareheaded, hands clasped behind necks, and some wearing bloody bandages.

Thick clouds of dirt and smoke clung to Biazza Ridge. The pungent smell of cordite from exploding German shells assaulted the nostrils, and the din of battle was ear splitting. Gavin was blasting away with his Garand rifle from atop the ridge when an alarming sight met his eyes: Some 900 yards in the distance, large numbers of panzers and hundreds of grenadiers were massing to attack the outnumbered and outgunned Americans.

Just then, Capt. Al Ireland, who had been fighting as a rifleman, dashed up and flopped down beside the colonel. A mortar shell exploded nearby, showering the two officers with dirt and debris. Known to fellow officers as "Irish," the captain suggested that he rush back to the beach to get help.

"Irish, that's the best idea I've heard today," Gavin responded.

Ireland had no transportation, so he struck out in a trot. After running for about a mile, he spotted an old bicycle parked next to a farmhouse, and he hopped aboard and rode off. A farmer rushed out of the door, shouting angrily and waving a clenched fist.

Luck was with Captain Ireland. About three miles farther on, he came to a 45th Infantry Division command post and rushed into the tent. Gen. Troy Middleton, leader of the "Thunderbirds," was conferring with Lt. Gen. Omar N. Bradley, the soft-spoken, bespectacled commander of Patton's II Corps. Rapidly, Ireland related how Gavin and his paratroopers were about to be overrun on Biazza Ridge.

Bradley, always unflappable, asked in his high-pitched voice, "What do you need up there, captain?"

"Mainly artillery, sir, but we could use some tanks. There're Kraut tanks swarming all over the place."

Meanwhile, back on Biazza Ridge, the large force of Germans that had been massing a half-mile to the front began moving forward to storm the elevation. A jeep roared up behind the American lines, and out jumped Captain Ireland, with a forward observer for a battery of 155-millimeter "Long Toms" and his radio operator. The three men ran to the crown of the ridge and were greeted by a salvo of shells that sent them sprawling into the dirt.

Alfred Ireland recalled that event:

The forward observer was a fat guy who had never been under fire. But the shelling never fazed him. He leaped up, grabbed the radio transmitter from his operator, and gave map coordinates to his guns back near the beach. I heard the big guy shout into the mouthpiece, "To hell with zeroing in! There's so goddamned many targets out there you can't miss! Fire for effect!"

Two minutes later, heavy shells from the Long Toms swished overhead and exploded among the oncoming German infantry and tanks. Salvo after salvo was poured into enemy ranks. A young American Navy ensign who had parachuted in with Gavin's men radioed warships offshore, and soon their big guns were also pounding the attackers. The German force wavered, then halted, and finally pulled back. The shelling ceased; an eerie silence fell over the battlefield.[2]

James Gavin remembered:

I wanted to destroy the German force and to recover our dead and wounded. So I ordered a counterattack. But before we attacked, six of our Sherman tanks [aid that Captain Ireland had obtained from General Bradley] roared up. Our boys on the ridge cheered loud and long. No doubt the Germans heard the cheering and wondered what was going on.

The six Shermans lined up along the ridge and opened fire. Then the paratroopers moved forward and were raked with machine-gun fire and pounded by artillery and mortars. Many All-Americans were cut down, but their comrades pressed on.

Twenty-five-year-old Lt. Harold H. Swingler, a former intercollegiate boxing champion from St. Louis, and two troopers worked their way along the top of a cut through which ran the road bisecting Biazza Ridge. They were taken under fire by an enemy machine gun, and Swingler's two companions were killed.

Still under fire, Swingler slithered to the lip of the cut, looked down, and was startled—directly below was a Tiger with its crew standing outside. Calmly, the former boxer dropped a grenade and killed the crew. Comrades moved in and captured the Tiger, the first to be taken by American parachutists.

Steadily the Germans were pushed back, leaving behind their dead and wounded. Seized by the 82nd Airborne men were several tons of equipment and supplies, 12 artillery pieces and mortars and large stacks of shells for them, and two trucks.

The violent clash at Biazza Ridge had been an auspicious baptism of fire for the green American paratroopers. Fighting for most of the time without artillery, tanks, or antitank guns, they had driven a veteran panzer *Kampfgruppe* that was far larger from the battlefield, and blocked it from smashing into the vulnerable 45th Infantry Division beachheads. However, a stiff price had been paid for the feat: In addition to scores of wounded troopers, the corpses of 51 men wearing the 82nd Airborne patches were sprawled around Biazza Ridge.

Capt. George B. Wood, Protestant chaplain of the 505th Regiment, arrived at Biazza Ridge the morning after the battle and began preparations to bury the dead troopers, who had been tenderly carried by comrades to a collecting point on the pockmarked elevation. Known to the troopers as "Chappie," Captain Wood may have been history's first American parachute chaplain to jump in a combat operation. A native of Biddeford, Maine, Wood had been ordained in the Episcopal church in 1936. Commissioned by the Army in early 1942, he quickly volunteered for the paratroops.[3]

Rev. George Wood remembered the melancholy events on embattled Biazza Ridge:

> *Our fatalities in the fighting of the day before were lying in the sun. Immediately I organized a detail to dig graves and prepare for the burials. The stench was unbelievable, with corpses rotting from the hot sun. My clerk ran away from the task, and I had to order him to return. It was neither the time nor the place for personal reactions. We had a job to do, and it had to be done quickly.*
>
> *Probably the most horrendous incident was when we pulled a trooper in six pieces from an Italian tankette. He was from the artillery battalion, and he had driven the captured vehicle up on the ridge to draw enemy fire.*
>
> *While the wounded were being tended, I had a shortened burial rite after the bodies were reverently placed in the ground, their dogtags and personal effects having been removed. We had fashioned crude wooden crosses out of K-ration crates.*
>
> *Only when the grisly task on Biazza Ridge was completed, came the recognition of the horror of it all.*

Earlier that same morning, Gen. George Patton ordered Matt Ridgway to bring over Rube Tucker's 504th Parachute Regimental Combat Team from Tunisia. Because of the uncertain battle situation in Sicily, Tucker's mission had been postponed for 24 hours. At 8:40 A.M., Ridgway sent a coded message to Brig. Gen. Charles L. "Bull" Keerans, assistant commander of the 82nd Airborne, in Tunisia: "Mackall tonight. Wear white pajamas."

Keerans, who had been a daredevil motorcycle rider in his youth, informed Tucker that his combat team would be making a routine reinforcement jump that night on Farello, an airfield three miles east of Gela. Farello was already in American hands.

One hundred and forty-four C-47s of Hal Clark's 552nd Troop Carrier Command would carry 2,304 of Rube Tucker's men into Sicily. The combat team consisted of Tucker's own 504th Regiment (minus Kouns' 3rd Battalion, which had jumped with Gavin's team two nights earlier), Lt. Col. Wilbur M. Griffith's 376th Parachute Field Artillery Battalion, Company C of the 307th Airborne Engineer Battalion, plus medical and signal units.[4]

Chaplain George B. "Chappie" Wood. *(Author's collection)*

To avoid the possibility of rattled gunners on Allied ships in the Gulf of Gela opening fire on the low-flying C-47 armada, the flight plan of Gavin's mission had been altered. The final leg of the course to Farello airport would take them 35 miles over the American beachhead.

Late that evening, Tucker's troopers were clustered around

their C-47s at the Kairouan airfields. The mood was grim. Sure, this was a routine flight, they had been told. But anything could happen in a parachute operation—that they knew. Trooper Victor Castillo, for one, was gripped by a curious premonition of disaster.

Staff Sgt. Sam DeCrenzo, however, reflected the view of most. He scribbled in his pocket diary: "Glad to be going. The tension of waiting is over."

Going along for the ride would be Gen. Bull Keerans, a nonjumper. His job was to supervise the movement of 82nd Airborne men and supplies to Sicily, but he succumbed to an overpowering urge to participate in the airborne operation— even though he would be flaunting Ridgway's strict order prohibiting his going. Keerans was a bit of a maverick.

Keerans would ride in an airplane piloted by Capt. John M. Gibson and copiloted by Lt. Ray O. Rousch. The mission was billed as a "milk run," so Keerans expected to be back in Tunisia long before dawn. There was no reason to believe that he would be the first American airborne general to lose his life in a combat operation.[5]

The radio operator in Keerans' aircraft, Sgt. Ray L. Butler, remembered waiting at the field for the signal to take off:

> The night before, we had all hung around the plane and were finally told that the mission had been canceled. We were all disappointed because we had one mission under our belt [Gavin's combat team] and this one would be a "milk run." We were all gung ho.
>
> When the paratroopers arrived, our crew chief, Sgt. Fielding Armstrong, got the slop buckets out and put them in the plane. We had learned back at Pope and Lawson fields in the States that this saved a lot of cleaning up the next day.

Just before 7:00 P.M., the first C-47 lifted off, and 45 minutes later the last of the 144 planes was in the air. Forming up, the sky train headed for the checkpoint at Malta. Soon it began to get dark. The summer night was cloudless, and the dancing waves below reflected the pale light of the moon that had started to ascend into the starlit heavens.

10
Holocaust in
the Sky

Late on the night of July 11, an eerie silence blanketed the
American beachhead and the Gulf of Gela. Junkers bombers had
just flown away after pounding the region for the fourth time
that day. Tension was thick. Ears were cocked for the sound of
approaching Luftwaffe planes. Jittery fingers were on triggers.

At 10:32 A.M., on the heels of the departing German bombers, the first flight of C-47s carrying Rube Tucker's combat team
knifed over the coast on target, near Cape Passero, turned northwest and flew for 35 miles over the bridgehead to the drop zone
at Farello. There the paratroopers bailed out and landed routinely.

Just as the second serial winged over the shore at about 700
feet, a long American machine gun spit a stream of tracers skyward. Almost immediately, a second gun followed suit. Then another. And another. Soon, a wide sweep of the Gela coast was
aglow with a kaleidoscope of color: yellow flares, geometric patterns of red tracers, and the black puffs of exploding antiaircraft
shells. Directly into this hailstorm of friendly fire the C-47s flew.[1]

Angry bursts of tracers whizzed past and into the plane carrying Lt. Col. Bill Yarborough, commander of the 2nd Battalion of
the 504th, and his stick. Stomachs, already churning, twisted into
knots. Palms and foreheads broke out in sweat. Throats went dry.
A shaky voice called out: "Someone try to say something funny!"

Sgt. John Magee, a tough fighting man, held his rosary, and
his lips moved in prayer. Magee would do his duty if he reached
the ground, but right now it seemed certain that he and his comrades would plunge to a fiery death. Next to Magee, a trooper

was vomiting in his helmet. Exploding shells rocked the C-47 and hurled shrapnel against the fuselage. Lt. Lewis Fern had a vagrant thought: "Now I know what is meant by the term 'sitting duck.'"

Peering through the open door, Yarborough could see C-47s, with troopers and aircrews still inside, burst into flames and plummet crazily to earth. Others received direct hits, exploding in midair and disintegrating. Seated next to Yarborough was 25-year-old Lt. John O'Malley, a platoon leader.

O'Malley vividly remembered that holocaust in the sky:

> *Riding in the plane on our left wing was half of my platoon. In its frenzy to escape the lethal inferno, their C-47 veered sharply to its right and almost struck our plane. I watched in horror as their C-47 then tilted and plunged to earth, where it exploded in a huge ball of fire. Those were my boys. That was the most anguishing experience of my life; one that I would never forget.*

Like a covey of quail suddenly fired on by concealed hunters, the flight formation scattered. Some troopers, their C-47s ablaze, leaped without static lines hooked up and plunged to their deaths. Jim Gavin and his troopers on Biazza Ridge heard sickening thuds as a few bodies hurtled into the ground.

Other All-Americans, already hooked up, bailed out pell-mell and descended into a sector held by American units. Nervous ground soldiers thought the dark figures under the white canopies were German paratroopers and shot them in midair or after they landed and were struggling to get out of harness. Pfc. James McNamara and his friend, Pfc. Joseph Hart, landed only 150 yards from the water. Crawling along a ditch, they heard American voices and decided to take a chance. McNamara stood up and called out, "We're American paratroopers." There were a few moments of silence; then bursts of automatic-weapons fire from the bivouac area sent McNamara diving back into the ditch.

At Farello airfield, where they had gone to greet the parachutists, George Patton and Matt Ridgway stood side by side and looked on in shocked disbelief as plane after plane tumbled out of the sky like fiery torches. Two of the United States Army's toughest generals were nearly overcome with grief and frustration, powerless to intervene. "My God! My God!" Patton muttered repeatedly.

After the second serial of the sky train had been pummeled, Rube Tucker's plane, leading the third serial, was raked with bullets. Several men, including Tucker's S-4, Maj. Julian A. Cook, were wounded. Confused by the firestorm, the pilot flew westward along the coast. Recognizing the coastal town of Licata, Tucker ordered the pilot to reverse his course. Despite the blackness and sky pyrotechnics, the Farello drop zone was detected, and the 504th Combat Team leader and his stick jumped. Reaching the ground, Tucker ran to five tanks that were blasting away with .50-caliber machine guns at the C-47s and, banging on the turret and cursing, halted their frantic firing.[2]

Elsewhere, Capt. Mack C. Shelley was standing in the door of a C-47. Before anyone in the plane could jump, it was hit, caught fire, wobbled downward crazily, and crashed. Shelley was flung out of the door and onto a heavy growth of brush that cushioned the impact. Woozy, in pain, he freed himself from his chute harness and crawled back to the burning plane wreckage to rescue his comrades. Edging inside, Shelley began tugging at the limp bodies. Moments later, the plane exploded, blowing him from the wreckage like a rag doll.

An undetermined amount of time later, Shelley regained consciousness and became vaguely aware that two Italian soldiers were hovering over him. He understood the language sufficiently to know that they were engaged in a heated dispute over whether or not to kill him. Again he passed out. Two days later, his wounds and burns wrapped in yards of white gauze, Shelley awoke in a German field hospital on the eastern coast of Sicily.

Meanwhile, in the firestorm over southern Sicily, the airplane carrying Gen. Bull Keerans was rocked by shell explosions, and tracers ripped through the floor. Sgt. Ray Butler, the radio operator, reflected: "God, this is it!"

Suddenly, Sgt. Fielding Armstrong, the crew chief, called out, "The port engine's on fire!" Skillfully handling the controls of the disabled craft, Lt. John Gibson ditched about 400 yards offshore.

Sergeant Butler edged along to the back of the dark cabin and could discern limp bodies draped over the bucket seats. Concluding that the paratroopers were beyond help, Butler scrambled out of the partially submerged door. Frightened because he could not swim, the airman grabbed onto a floating piece of debris and tried to paddle toward shore, but the current kept pushing him back under the tail section. In extricating himself, Butler gulped down a mixture of salt water, gasoline, and oil.

Now machine gunners on shore opened fire on the barely floating plane and the men floundering in the water. Butler saw a couple of heads go under. Finally he and a few paratroopers crawled, exhausted and gasping, onto the beach. Moments later, the same machine gun sent bursts of fire at the little knot of soaked survivors.

In the skies over Gela and Scoglietti, 81 paratroopers were killed, 16 were missing and presumed dead, and 132 were wounded. Hal Clark's troop carrier wing had suffered 60 men killed and 30 wounded. Twenty-three airplanes had been shot down and many others had been badly damaged but limped back to Tunisia. It had been one of the great disasters in American military history.[3]

One of the bullet- and shrapnel-riddled C-47s that had made it through the curtain of fire carried Lt. Col. Bill Yarborough and his stick. Twenty-five miles inland, they bailed out "blind," not knowing where they were. Two wounded men insisted on jumping, although they could have returned to the safety of Tunisia in the airplane.[4]

Shortly after dawn, Sgt. Fielding Armstrong, crew chief of the plane in which General Keerans had been riding, was scouring the shore looking for his pilot, John Gibson, and copilot, Raymond Roush. He could find neither and feared that they had perished. (Both Gibson and Roush had been injured, but survived.)

Fielding Armstrong remembered:

> Along the shore I ran into General Keerans. He apparently had escaped the ditching and subsequent machine-gun shooting unscathed. While we were talking, the general spoke to a number of passing people he apparently knew. He asked me to go inland with him, and I said no, that I was going to try to get back to my outfit [in Tunisia].

Bull Keerans apparently went inland by himself and mysteriously vanished. Later, he would be listed as killed in action, the first American airborne general to die in a combat operation.[5]

Early on the morning of July 12, Col. Jim Gavin drove to Piano Lupo, where Hard Nose Gorham and his paratroopers

Brig. Gen. Charles L. "Bull" Keerans (left), first American airborne general to be killed in action, confers with Maj. Gen. Eldridge G. Chapman at Camp Mackall. (*Author's collection*)

had battled repeated armored assaults for 48 hours. Strolling about the terrain, Gavin was sickened by the sight. Sprawled about grotesquely in death were the bloated bodies of many of his boys. They lay where they had fallen—facing the enemy. Tiny gas bubbles oozed from hideous wounds. Thick swarms of flies hovered over the bodies. Some corpses had turned purple from the unyielding rays of the Mediterranean sun. Laboring mightily to conceal his grief, Gavin climbed into his jeep and told the driver, "Head for Gela."

On a hill, Gavin spotted the imposing figure of George Patton gazing out toward the beehive of activity in Gela harbor. Rifle in hand, the colonel approached the Seventh Army commander. Breaking out in a wide grin, Patton said in his high-pitched voice, "Hello, Gavin. You and your men did one hell of a god-damned great job!"

Reaching into his back pocket, the silver-haired, ramrod-straight general whipped out a large flask and thrust it toward Gavin. "You look like you could use a drink—here, have one," Patton said. The colonel took a healthy gulp. This dramatic occasion called for more than a simple thank you, Gavin concluded. So the colonel, 21 years and three ranks junior to Patton, launched into a short speech, the theme being that it was a high honor for the leader of an American parachute combat team to

Mark Alexander's transportation-shy battalion of the 505th
Parachute Infantry advances through Vittoria on D-Day plus 2.
(U. S. Army)

be drinking out of the same flask with one of history's greatest
generals. "Old Blood and Guts," as Patton came to be known,
beamed.

Back in Tunisia that morning, Col. Harry Lewis, the eldest
(by far) of the 82nd Airborne regimental commanders, was
handed disappointing news. His 325th Glider Infantry was already at the airfields around Kairouan, ready to be towed to Sicily, but the disaster inflicted on Rube Tucker's combat team
during the night caused Lewis' glider mission to be canceled.

Twelve hours later—just before midnight—Brigadier Gerald
Lathbury's British 1st Parachute Brigade lifted off from Sicily on
Operation Fustian. Carried in 135 aircraft, including 105 of the
U.S. 51st Troop Carrier Wing, the 1,836 Red Devils bailed out
seven miles south of Catania, on the east coast, and seized the
key Primasole bridge. Fierce fighting erupted around the span,
but Montgomery's 50th Division rushed over the bridge and captured Catania.

The morning of July 13 found the Allies firmly established in
Sicily, so British Gen. Harold R. L. G. Alexander, the overall
commander, issued orders to clear out Axis troops from the remainder of the island. Montgomery's Eighth Army would attack

northward from Catania and capture Messina, the escape valve to Italy for German and Italian forces. Patton's Seventh Army was to mop up the western two-thirds of Sicily.

Matt Ridgway now had under his control 3,883 of the 5,307 paratroopers who had jumped into Sicily. On the morning of July 18, a provisional corps set up by Patton, with Rube Tucker's decimated 504th Parachute Regiment in the lead, jumped off toward the west. Since the Five-O-Fours had only a few old Italian trucks for transportation, most of the trek would be on foot.[6]

Weighed down by heavy gear, broiled by the sun, Tucker's men trudged along, wheezing and huffing. Soon a strange malady struck their march route. Donkeys, horses, mules, burros, bicycles, carts, and weapons belonging to farmers began to vanish mysteriously, only to reappear in the paratroopers' marching ranks. In some instances, Tucker's men assured protesting Sicilian owners that General Eisenhower himself would be coming to pay for their "borrowed" conveyances.

It was a curious trek. At times, it seemed like a training hike, but suddenly a machine gun would open up; then white flags would appear. A shot had been fired to satisfy an Italian officer's "honor." In a remarkable display of physical stamina, the Five-O-Fours marched 150 grueling miles in five days, then seized the large towns of Alcama and Castellammare del Golfo in the northwest part of the island. "My blisters have developed blisters!" a Five-O-Four trooper moaned.

At the same time, Jim Gavin's 505th Regiment laid seige to the port of Trapani, the 82nd Airborne's main objective, on the westernmost tip of Sicily, where 5,000 Italians were holed up. After an exchange of artillery fire through much of the morning of July 23, Capt. Al Ireland volunteered to jeep into Trapani under a white flag of truce. He returned with Adm. Giuseppe Manfredi, who surrendered the port to Ridgway and Gavin.[7]

Meanwhile, across Sicily on the eastern shore, Canadian troops broke into a German field hospital and freed wounded Allied soldiers, including American paratrooper Capt. Mack Shelley, who had been a patient there for 10 days since being blown out of a crashed C-47. The Canadians moved the American to their aid station, where he was told he would be evacuated to North Africa.

Despite his extensive burns and injuries, Shelley wanted to fight, so he decided to go AWOL. Ripping off his medical evacu-

Paratroopers of the 82nd Airborne with Sicilian and his donkey.
(Ivan Woods)

ation tag, he "liberated" the weapon of a wounded British officer and, swathed in bandages, hobbled off toward the front. En route, he bumped into four Germans and a shootout erupted.

Shelley's right arm was badly burned, so he propped himself against a stone wall and blazed away with his good arm. When the four grenadiers charged firing Schmeisser machine pistols, the paratrooper killed three of them. The fourth hurled a potato-masher grenade, and the explosion sent a fragment tearing into Shelley's shoulder.[8] However, he heaved a grenade that finished off the German.

Canadian medics found Shelley, barely conscious, and loaded him into an ambulance, which joined a road convoy heading for the British evacuation beach. Halfway on the trek, the Luftwaffe attached the convoy, and a bomb exploded next to Shelley's ambulance, blowing him out through the back doors. He sustained yet another injury—a broken arm.

Picked up from the road, the American was placed in a second ambulance, and this time he reached the shore. Mack Shelley, the paratrooper who refused to be killed, finally sailed in a hospital ship to North Africa.[9]

During late July and early August, German and Italian forces, under constant pressure from Patton's and Montgomery's ar-

Eighty-second Airborne paratrooper Linzee Prescott's eyewitness version of the 504th Parachute Infantry's long trek across western Sicily.

mies, conducted a masterful withdrawal into the northeastern port of Messina for evacuation across the Strait to Italy. All the while, the veteran 509th Parachute Infantry Battalion had been bivouacked around Tunisian airfields, waiting for the call to jump into Sicily. Capt. Carlos Alden scribbled the following in his pocket diary: "This has been a tough month for morale in the 509th. Just sitting. Alerted for action. Rescinded. Alerted again. Rescinded. Dry, hot, sandy, dusty, boring." Restless, Doc Alden decided to take an unauthorized jaunt to the battlefront in Sicily, and drafted his fellow surgeon, Capt. A. A. Engleman, in his scheme. The two officers caught a ride on a C-47 to an airstrip behind Patton's lines just west of Messina. They hitchhiked to the front and marched forward, passed American outposts, and found themselves in Axis-held Messina.

Both paratroopers were wearing their jumpsuits with tiny American flags sewn on the sleeves. Dr. Carlos Alden recalled:

No doubt I, in particular, stood out like a beacon, for I was wearing a red beret that General "Boy" Browning, the father of the British airborne, had taken off his own head and given to me a few weeks earlier in North Africa. Why did Engleman and I pull this caper?

Just for the hell of it—and to make certain that American paratroopers were the first to get into Messina.

After nearly bumping into German infantry units marching along the cobblestone streets, Alden and Engleman holed up in an empty building with American and British shells crashing around them during the night.

At dawn on August 17, the two Americans awoke and found the streets empty and silent. They concluded rightly that the last Axis contingents had slipped over to Italy. About an hour later, Patton's leading tanks cautiously poked into Messina and were greeted by a pair of grinning parachute captains named Alden and Engleman.[10]

Troopers of the 82nd Airborne attend a field mass during a lull in the fighting. *(Ivan Woods)*

The Allied victory had been blemished. Under the noses of the powerful Allied air forces and navies, three first-rate German divisions and four mobile Italian divisions had made a clean getaway through Messina.

Once Sicily had been secured, a number of influential American generals let it be known that they had gone sour on the revolutionary new battle concept of vertical envelopment—a surprise attack from the sky. One of the pessimists (who would later reverse his view) was General Eisenhower, who wrote a memo in longhand: "Our losses [in Sicily] were inexcusably high, with blame about equally divided among the several services, and with a large measure falling on me . . ."[11]

The Allied supreme commander followed that gloomy observation with a letter to his boss, Gen. George Marshall, in which he said flatly: "I do not believe in the airborne division."

James Gavin recalled those dark days for the airborne's future:

> *Apparently what Eisenhower wanted to do was to use small packets of paratroopers for special missions. I was puzzled by the fact that no senior officers from a high headquarters came to Sicily during or after our operation. Certainly no high-ranking officer ever discussed our mission with me afterward. So the negative views reaching Washington were impressions gained from Eishenhower's headquarters, hundreds of miles from the action.*

Another staunch opponent of airborne expansion was Gen. Lesley McNair, commander of Army ground forces in Washington, who had cut his military eyeteeth in the static warfare of World War I. McNair had grown disillusioned with paratroop operations after North Africa and Sicily, and he was nearly ready to hand down a verdict: Future airborne operations would be limited to battalion size or smaller.

Clearly, the airborne concept was on trial. Therefore, many eyes in Washington were now focused westward where paratroopers were preparing for the first American combat jump in the Pacific.

11
MacArthur's "Kids" Strike in the Pacific

On the evening of September 5, 1943, Gen. Douglas MacArthur and his chief of air operations, Lt. Gen. George C. Kenney, were immersed in conversation at Port Moresby, New Guinea, across the Coral Sea from northern Australia. Since mid-1942, Mac-Arthur had been conducting what he called a "hit-'em-where-they-ain't" campaign of speed and surprise. For more than a year, the 62-year-old commander of the Southwest Pacific Theater of Operations had been leapfrogging up the spine of primitive, inhospitable New Guinea. He was bypassing Japanese strongholds, constructing air and sea bases, then jumping to the next locale, where the process was repeated.

"General, I've decided to go with our paratroopers in the morning," the diminutive Kenney said in a casual tone. "They're my kids, and I want to see them do their stuff."

MacArthur, typically cool and collected, puffed on his corn-cob and after a thoughtful pause replied, "You're right, George, we'll both go. They're my kids, too."

Kenney was taken aback and protested, "But, General, isn't it foolish to risk having some five-dollar-a-month Jap pilot shoot a hole through you?"[1]

MacArthur shook his head. "I'm not worried about getting shot, George," he replied. "Honestly, the only thing that disturbs me is the possibility that when we hit the rough air over the mountains, my stomach might get upset. I'd hate to throw up and disgrace myself in front of the kids."[2]

The supreme commander added, "Besides, this will be the first taste of combat for my paratroopers, and I want to give them such comfort as my presence might mean to them."[3]

The "kids" being discussed by the two generals were, in terms of age, little more than that. They belonged to the independent 503rd Parachute Infantry Regiment, and on the morrow would leap out over Nadzab, an abandoned New Guinea airfield that had been hacked out of *kunai* grass. It would be America's first combat jump in the Pacific.

Col. Kenneth R. Kinsler's 503rd Parachute Infantry Regiment would jump as part of an intricate tactical plan that MacArthur had conceived for capturing the Japanese stronghold of Lae and destroying some 10,000 enemy troops defending that region. Like a champion boxer, MacArthur would bob and weave. His ground forces on New Guinea would feint with a left jab against the city of Salamaua, which lies 15 miles south of Lae. Then, when the Japanese rushed troops from Lae to block that blow, thereby lowering their guard at Lae, MacArthur would swing a right-hand haymaker by sending the Australian 9th Division on a wide amphibious run up the coast of New Guinea to storm ashore at two points just east of Lae.

While the seaborne Aussies launched an attack against Lae from the east, the 503rd Parachute Infantry would drop on Nadzab, 21 miles northwest of Lae. Once the paratroopers had seized the airfield, Australian engineers, who had been hacking through thick jungle for 45 miles to reach Nadzab, would join Kinsler's men in rehabilitating the landing strip. Then Kenney's transport planes would fly in the Australian 7th Division, which would attack Lae from the west. It would be a classic MacArthur hit-'em-where-they-ain't operation. The Japanese at Lae would be caught in a nutcracker, suddenly under seige from the east and the west.

Kenney was especially enthusiastic over the paratroop mission. Nadzab would give him a forward base for pounding Japanese positions and shipping farther to the west, and a terminus for supplies airlifted from Australia and Port Moresby to support MacArthur's drive up the New Guinea spine.[4]

Most of Ken Kinsler's parachutists were also eager to go into action. The 503th Regiment had arrived in Australia in December 1942, and since then it had been engaged in seemingly endless jungle training. Any ordeal would be an improvement in their lot, the troopers reasoned. D-Day had originally been set for August 1, was moved to August 27, and finally to September 5 in order to allow General Kenney time to scrape up sufficient aircraft to get the job done.

Kenney managed to locate 96 transport planes. It was a modest fleet considering his task—flying a regiment of paratroopers in an assault, then rapidly lifting an entire infantry division and their weapons into battle before the Japanese would have time to react.

Kenney's plight was typical of the "shoestring war" that MacArthur had to fight, which resulted from a strategic decision by President Roosevelt and his joint chiefs of staff to crush Nazi Germany first. MacArthur would never be allocated as much as 15 percent of America's war effort, and he would command but 12 percent of all troops sent overseas.[5]

Six days before the Nadzab operation, Colonel Kinsler briefed his commanders. All three battalions, one after the other, would jump onto the airfield, then rapidly assemble and move off to their designated objectives. Lt. Col. John W. Britten's 1st Battalion would clear the field of Japanese, although Intelligence had indicated that there were no enemy troops in the immediate vicinity. Lt. Col. George M. Jones, a native of Memphis, and his 2nd Battalion would seize the village of Gabsonkek, north of the field. And 26-year-old Lt. Col. John J. Tolson, III, of New Bern, North Carolina, and his 3rd Battalion would capture the village of Gabmatzung, east of the airstrip.

Tolson, known to fellow officers as "Smiling Jack," would be the first to jump from the lead C-47, thereby becoming the first American paratrooper to bail out in a combat operation in the Pacific war. Tolson had already had several eyewitness views of the Nadzab airfield and adjacent terrain. He had hitched rides on Kenney's Fifth Air Force bombers, knowing they would wing over the targeted area on the way to and from their objectives.[6]

Meanwhile, Lt. Robert W. Armstrong, of the 1st Battalion of the 503rd, had a unique task: giving a crash course on parachuting techniques to four officers and 28 men of the Australian field artillery who had never jumped from an airplane, nor had they seen a chute close up. All of the Aussies had volunteered for the Nadzab mission, and their 75-millimeter pack howitzers, which fired 25-pound shells, would provide welcome support for the lightly armed paratroopers. The artillerymen from Down Under would jump two hours after Smiling Jack Tolson bailed out. Their dismantled field pieces and shells would be dropped by parachute.

Ken Kinsler's paratroopers would be getting their baptism of fire in one of the world's harshest locales—New Guinea. Thick jungles were studded with mangrove swamps. Often root-tangled trails were covered with waist-deep slop. The air was putrid with the stench of rotting undergrowth and of stink lilies. Minimal light penetrated the matted screens of *liana* vines overhead, and when torrential rains ceased, a boiling sun emerged and suffocating waves of steam rose from the dank forests. Blades of *kunai* grass, such as those that surrounded Nadzab airfield, were six to eight feet high and could lay a man's face open as quickly as a surgeon's scalpel.

It was into this vile region, one populated by swarms of poisonous snakes, cannibals, and vicious frogs as large as a man's head, that the green 503rd Parachute Infantry—MacArthur's "kids"—would soon be jumping and fighting.[7]

Shortly after dawn on September 5, elements of the Australian 9th Division landed at two beaches 12 and 16 miles east of Lae, tangled briefly with scattered Japanese bands, and marched westward to attack Lae. At the same time, the American paratroopers were huddled in pairs or tiny knots around their C-47s at Jackson and Ward airstrips outside Port Moresby. Seventy-nine of the transports, belonging to Col. Paul H. Prentiss' 54th Troop Carrier Wing, would carry 1,706 of Kinsler's men to Nadzab.

The sky armada was to have lifted off not long after daybreak, but a thick fog blanketed the Ward and Jackson airstrips and clung to passes of the towering Owen Stanley Mountain range through which the C-47s would have to fly. It appeared that America's first Pacific airborne operation would be scubbed.

Strolling around among the nervous paratroopers was their Catholic chaplain, Capt. John J. Powers. Outwardly, Father Powers was a portrait of confidence and serenity; inwardly, his stomach was as queasy as those of the troopers carrying the weapons. The padre, too, would be jumping into the unknown that morning, and he was steeling his own spirit, as were his comrades.

A newspaper reporter who was at the airfield to witness the takeoff asked Captain Powers, a crack pistol shot, how he felt about American paratroopers going into battle on this day, a

Sunday. Powers pondered the question briefly; then replied evenly, "The better the day, the better the deed."[8]

Waiting under the wing of a C-47, Jack Tolson was chatting idly with troopers when out of the corner of an eye, he caught a small group of men striding toward him. Turning, he came face-to-face with Douglas MacArthur, who was wearing his famed gold-braided cap with the scrambled-egg visor.[9]

John Tolson recalled that episode:

> *General MacArthur greeted me warmly and placed his hand on my shoulder in friendly fashion. He made small talk—what's my name, where's my home, what was my job in the regiment? Then he moved on to talk with many of the troopers who were about to board our planes. Of course, he had come to the airfield to lend us encouragement and to wish us well. Said he'd be watching our jump. Everyone was happy over the fact that the supreme commander had come to see us off.*

Just before 8:00 A.M., the fog broke, and a reconnaissance plane that had been sent to probe the Owen Stanley pass radioed back: "All clear!" Loaded with heavy gear and tense, but glad to have the interminable waiting over, the troopers waddled into their aircraft, and at 8:26 A.M., the first C-47s raced down the runways.

Through broken clouds, the sky train climbed steadily and flew into the mountain pass at 9,000 feet (the lowest point in the range). Once through the pass, the flight descended to 3,500 feet and picked up an escort of 102 fighter planes from the strips at Dobadura, Tsili-Tsili, and Marilinan.

Now the armada dipped to almost ground level, and hedgehopped toward Nadzab. The flight had been bumpy, especially while knifing through the mountain pass, and ill troopers began calling for "honey buckets," which were passed up and down the C-47s as needed.

Up ahead, six squadrons of twin-engined B-25 bombers were sprinkling fragmentation bombs on Nadzab airfield, and six A-20 attack bombers zoomed low to lay a curtain of thick smoke.

The C-47 flight climbed to 700 feet and leveled off for its run to the drop zones. Jack Tolson was standing in the door of a C-47, watching the plumes of smoke that towered for a thousand feet over Nadzab. As planned, the artificial fog shielded the field

General MacArthur chats at planeside with Lt. Col. John J. Tolson III, who would be first American paratrooper to jump in a combat operation in the Pacific. *(U. S. Army)*

from Japanese observation on the ground, but left the drop zones open to view by the pilots.

John Tolson remembered the event:

> *I saw the airfield coming up and checked for the green light, but it didn't flash on. Later I learned that the pilot or navigator had gotten excited and forgot to switch it on. So I hesitated for a few moments; then saw we were over the middle of the field, and I jumped. As a result of this delay of a few seconds, a large number of my men landed in the trees on the far end of the DZ.*

Following the jump by Tolson's 3rd Battalion, John Britten's 1st Battalion and George "The Warden" Jones' 2nd Battalion dropped with pinpoint accuracy. All 79 C-47s were cleared of paratroopers in four and one-half minutes.

High overhead, General MacArthur was circling in a B-17 bomber and watching the undulating parachutes, resembling graceful jellyfish, floating to earth. Wave after wave of C-47s roared over, leaving strings of pearly spawn in their wake. Suddenly, one of MacArthur's bomber's engines sputtered; then went dead. His pilot suggested that they turn back to Port Moresby. "Carry on," the supreme commander said. "We're staying."

After the last American paratrooper had touched down, MacArthur departed. At Moresby, he fired off a telegram to his young wife, Jean, in Australia: "It was a honey!"[10]

There was no armed opposition. But a price had been paid—two paratroopers plunged to their deaths with streamers, another was caught in a tall tree and on releasing his chute harness fell to earth and was killed, and 33 men were injured.

Meanwhile, back at Port Moresby, 11 gliders were loaded with engineers and equipment, ready to be towed to Madzab to reinforce the 503rd Parachute Infantry. The airborne operation had been so successful, however, that Lt. Gen. Thomas Blamey—the cheerful, stubby Australian who commanded MacArthur's ground forces—canceled the glider mission.

Early the next morning, D-Day plus 1, the first flight of C-47s, carrying elements of the U.S. 871st Airborne Engineer Battalion, landed routinely at Nadzab, and within hours Maj. Gen. E. A. Vasey's Australian 7th Division was pouring in by air to the field on the banks of the Markham River. Vasey's jungle-toughed soldiers plunged eastward to attack Lae from the rear while the Aussie 9th Division was driving toward the Japanese stronghold from the east.

By September 11, Colonel Prentiss' C-47 crews, flying around-the-clock with virtually no sleep and eating snacks in the air, had carried in 420 planeloads of men and equipment.

Caught in a vise between the two attacking Australian divisions, the 10,000-man Japanese force in the region was splintered, dispersing into the jungles of the Huon Peninsula in small groups. Salamaua fell on September 12, Lae four days later.

Meanwhile, Jack Tolson's battalion of paratroopers was ordered to push from Nadzab toward Lae to intercept and destroy fleeing bands of Japanese. Tolson and his men moved out in single file along a narrow path covered with thick vines that had to be hacked away with machetes. The battalion was strung out for a mile, with Capt. John H. Davis' Company I out in front. Battling suffocating heat, high humidity, and the brutal terrain, the troopers were gasping for breath after a few miles of the grueling march. At a tiny collection of native huts known as Log

Crossing, the point of I Company was suddenly raked with fire by a machine gun dug in along the west bank of the Bambu River. After a firefight, three of the Japanese gunners were killed and the other fled.

Next, a platoon led by Lt. Lyle Murphy was trudging downstream when it collided headlong with a large Japanese force. A fierce shootout erupted. Marching between I and H Companies, Jack Tolson heard the firing, rushed forward, and called up the rest of his battalion. Both sides blazed away for nearly three hours, until darkness engulfed New Guinea.

The paratroopers dug in. Throughout the night there were peridoic cracks of rifle fire, as individual Japanese stragglers tried to break through Tolson's defense. Three Japanese were detected slipping into Log Crossing village and were cut down by tommy guns. Headquarters 1st Sgt. Frank Boganski discovered an enemy soldier hiding near Tolson's command post and shot him. The dead Japanese turned out to be a medical officer, and his expensive leather bags were presented to the 3rd Battalion surgeon, Capt. Thomas Stevens.[11]

During the night, the Japanese contingent, which had been fleeing from Lae, disappeared into the jungle, apparently seeking another escape route. Tranquillity descended upon the Nadzab region, and Tolson was ordered to return his battalion to the airfield. Before pulling out of Log Crossing, Tolson's troopers buried eight comrades. Some of the 12 wounded men had to be carried back to the airfield, where the battalion lifted off for Port Moresby to rejoin the remainder of the 503rd Regiment.

Although carried out in daylight against no antiaircraft fire, the first combat jump in the Pacific had been a masterful example of skilled planning and coordination between paratroop leaders and air corps commanders—an almost textbook-perfect operation. The 503rd Parachute Infantry had been dropped on schedule and right on the button.

In Washington, the Nadzab mission provided heavy ammunition for those seeking an expansion of airborne capabilities in the United States Army. And halfway around the globe, Gen. George Patton praised American paratroopers in Sicily two months earlier. "Despite the original miscarriage, Colonel Gavin's initial parachute assault speeded our ground advance by 48 hours," Patton declared.[12]

Seventy-two-year-old Secretary of War Henry L. Stimson, regarded by many to be one of Washington's keenest minds, took note of the Pacific parachute mission and, in a memo, urged field commanders to give the 503rd Parachute Infantry jump "effective application in prospective operations."

Translation: "Consider using airborne troop forces in future invasions or seaborne assaults."

PART II

Focus on the Mediterranean

12
Giant 2:
Suicide
Mission

Even while the fighting had been raging in Sicily in mid-July, 1943, the Allied Combined Chiefs of Staff were debating over the next target, and they hoped to continue the momentum gained from a smashing victory in Sicily. So on July 23, the Combined Chiefs instructed General Eisenhower to assault the deep-water port of Naples, 100 miles south of Rome and about one-third the way up the Italian boot. Naples was found to be out of fighter-plane range, however, and that plan was hastily junked.

Meanwhile, cagey Field Marshal Albrecht Kesselring had not fallen asleep at the switch. At his headquarters in Frascati, south of Rome, he told his staff that the Allies would not risk landings in Italy outside the range of tactical air cover based in Sicily. That left only three beaches where the invaders might land, and two of the sites had distinct disadvantages for an amphibious force. Pointing to a wall map of Italy, the field marshal concluded that, by default, the Allies would have only one locale where they could land—along the Gulf of Salerno.[1]

At the same time, Eisenhower and his advisers were huddled in the supreme commander's office in Algiers' St. George Hotel to pick a new landing beach. The Italian shoreline was studied intensively, and one site after another was discarded until only

one remained—the Gulf of Salerno, 40 miles south of Naples.
There the Allies would strike.

Forty-eight hours after Eisenhower had received his Italy invasion directive—July 25—mild King Victor Emmanuel III summarily booted out Adolf Hitler's crony, squat, bombastic Benito Mussolini, who had been Italian premier for 21 years, and replaced him with aging Marshal Pietro Badoglio. Mussolini was arrested and locked up.

King Victor's dramatic action did not catch Hitler unprepared. Long anticipating that Italy would covertly seek a separate peace—or even commit the perfidy of going over to the Allies—the Führer rapidly beefed up German forces there. Five infantry and two panzer divisions were rushed into northern Italy, and two more crack outfits—the 2nd Parachute and 3rd Panzer Grenadier divisions—along with a strong panzer force hurried into positions outside Rome. Altogether there were some 45,000 German troops in and near the capital.

Around the Naples-Salerno area were two first-rate Wehrmacht units: the 15th Panzer Grenadier and the Hermann Goering Panzer Division. It was the Goering Division that Col. Jim Gavin's paratroopers had tangled with at Biazza Ridge and on Piano Lupo in Sicily.[2]

Meanwhile, Allied invasion plans were finalized. The assault on mainland Europe would consist of two coordinated operations. Bernard Montgomery's British Eighth Army would leapfrog from Sicily across the narrow Strait of Messina onto the toe of Italy under cover of darkness on September 3. (The maneuver was code-named "Operation Baytown.") Montgomery's mission was to draw off forces from the Salerno area, where Gen. Mark Clark's Fifth Army would storm ashore six days later, on September 9.

Code-named "Operation Avalanche," the Fifth Army assault had as its primary objective the capture of Naples, on D-Day plus 13.

Avalanche would be the Allies' Sunday punch, but Mark Clark's force was woefully weak for the task. It would consist of nine green or largely untested divisions—about equally divided between American and British—and they would be contested by the same number of veteran German divisions deployed around Rome and in southern Italy.

Meanwhile, at the secret site of Bletchley Park, north of London, Ultra was intercepting and deciphering the blizzard of

Enigma-coded messages flowing back and forth between Kesselring in Rome and the *Oberkommando der Wehrmacht* in Berlin. From these intercepts, Eisenhower knew about the divisions that the Führer had rushed into Italy.

This high-grade intelligence caused Eisenhower sleepless nights. To beef up Operation Avalanche forces, the supreme commander made available to Clark either the British 1st Airborne Division or the U. S. 82nd Airborne. There were some 350 troop transports in North Africa and Sicily, only enough to carry two parachute regiments simultaneously. Clark chose the All-American division.

As the days rolled past, the 82nd Airborne commanders anxiously waited for word of their Avalanche mission. Finally, on August 18, orders arrived at Matt Ridgway's headquarters at Trapani, Sicily. News of the operation was greeted by amazement. Code-named "Giant I," the mission called for the 82nd Airborne to strike by air and by sea at the key road hub of Capua, on the Volturno River 20 miles north of Naples and 40 miles from the nearest Allied beach at Salerno.

Two parachute regiments would jump, and some 135 gliders would crash-land with artillery, antitank guns, and ammunition. Lewis' 325th Glider Regiment, still eager for its first combat action, would land by boat at the mouth of the Volturno, march inland for about 16 miles, and join the paratroopers in the airhead. Giant I's objective was to block German forces rushing southward from the Rome area to the Salerno bridgehead.

Jim Gavin was selected to be the airborne task force commander. His job was to hold the line of the Volturno until the British 46th Division would break through from Salerno and link up with the All-Americans. Gavin hoped contact would be made in a maximum of five days.

James Gavin recalled:

> We [on the Volturno] would have needed steady resupply by air for many days. In fact, if the operation had been carried out as planned, it was probable that we would have been on our own for a whole month. Any serious failure in the resupply of the 82nd Airborne task force could have only meant its destruction.

At the same time that Giant I would unfold, the veteran 509th Parachute Infantry Battalion, which had not seen action since tangling with Rommel's Afrika Korps in Tunisia the previous

April, would jump at Avellino, Sarno, Minturno, Nocerna, or Battipaglia, behind the Salerno beachhead. The mission of the 509th would be to block any German forces trying to reach Salerno through those routes.

On August 31, a glittering galaxy of Allied brass congregated at Fifth Army headquarters at Mostaganem, Algeria, for a final briefing on invasion plans. Two-star Matt Ridgway, one of the lesser lights in terms of rank, was given three minutes to discuss Giant I. Ridgway, a West Point classmate and an old friend of Mark Clark's, pulled no punches. Giant I, he declared, was tactically unsound and could result in the destruction of the entire 82nd Airborne Division.

Ridgway's frank analysis touched off a heated round of debate. Finally, on the recommendation of Eisenhower's air adviser, Marshal Arthur Tedder, Giant I was canceled. D-Day for Avalanche was only nine days away, and the All-Americans were still in the unemployment line, much to the consternation of Ridgway, Jim Gavin, Rube Tucker, and others.

All the while, an intricate cloak-and-dagger melodrama had been unfolding behind the scenes. On August 9, while Axis forces were pulling out of Sicily through Messina, *Generale d'Brigata* Giuseppe Castellano, who despised the Germans and saw the probable future for Italy, took matters into his own hands. At the risk of his life if the scheme backfired, Castellano suggested to his boss, *Generale d'Armata* Vittorio Ambrosio, chief of Italian armed forces, that he, Castellano, covertly contact the Allies to seek a separate armistice, after which Italy would join with her former enemies in fighting Hitler.[3]

In an audience with King Victor the next day, Ambrosio broached the subject of a peace emissary, and the monarch approved the proposal. Marshal Badoglio was notified of the king's order, and he appointed Castellano to be the contact with the Allies. Seventy-two hours later, Castellano, garbed in civies and using the *nom de guerre* of Señor Raimondi, took a train from Rome to Portugal.

In the meantime, General Eisenhower received a mysterious telegram from Washington. He was ordered to send a pair of top officers to meet with a certain Señor Raimondi in Lisbon. Clad in ill-fitting civilian clothes borrowed from Italian natives, Gen. Walter B. "Beetle" Smith, Eisenhower's chief of staff, and British Brigadier Kenneth D. Strong, Ike's intelligence head, sneaked into Lisbon.

Smith and Strong rendezvoused with Castellano in a dimly lit room on a Lisbon back street. Castellano had hoped to negotiate a peace favorable to Italy, but his hopes were quickly dashed. Smith sternly told the Italian that he, as Eisenhower's envoy, was not there to negotiate, but to lay down terms that Italy would have to accept unconditionally.

Crestfallen, Castellano listened as the unsmiling Smith described Eisenhower's terms: An armistice between the Allies and Italy would take effect at a time of Ike's choosing, and the supreme commander would announce the cessation of hostilities over Radio Algiers. Smith revealed that the Allies were preparing to invade Italy, and that government authorities in Rome would be given five hours' advance notice of the main landings. Hard on the heels of Eisenhower's Radio Algiers announcement, an Italian government official was to make a similar statement over Radio Rome.

Beetle Smith made it clear that if Eisenhower's headquarters did not hear of acceptance of the terms by the Italian government by August 30, it would be assumed that the Allied proposal had been rejected. Shaken by the unexpected turn of events—Castellano thought that he would be welcomed with open arms—the Italian emissary left for Rome. His luggage concealed a clandestine radio and a code book that Smith and Strong had provided Castellano for contacting Allied headquarters in Algiers.

On August 30, Castellano radioed Algiers that he would fly to Sicily the following day to discuss the armistice terms. Reaching Cassible, outside Syracuse, Castellano dropped a bombshell on Beetle Smith: Because of heavy German reinforcements rushed into Italy and the iron grip that strong German forces had on Rome, King Victor and Marshal Badoglio would be unable to announce an armistice until the Allies were firmly ashore in their country.

An argument raged all day. Smith pleaded, cajoled, and threatened. Castellano countered with a wide array of reasons why the Italians could not comply with Eisenhower's terms. It became clear to General Smith that the Italians were far more frightened of the Germans than they were of flaunting the Allies. Finally, in exasperation, the sharp-tongued Smith blurted: "Well, then just what in the hell will it take to get your government's cooperation?"

Giuseppe Castellano replied that, at a minimum, the Allies

would have to drop at least one airborne division on Rome with a strong armed force to land by sea near the mouth of the Tiber River to link up with the paratroopers and glidermen.

On the evening of September 2, Matt Ridgway listened grimly to a briefing by a British colonel at Gen. Harold Alexander's 15th Army Group headquarters at Cassible. "You will land the strongest airborne force possible on three airfields just north of Rome on the night of September 8–9 and seize control of the city," the colonel explained.

Ridgway was shocked to learn that such an audacious, complex plan would be laid on by Allied brass without even consulting him—the division commander—in advance.

Code-named "Giant 2," the operation called for the entire 82nd Airborne Division to be delivered in and around Rome on two successive nights. Rube Tucker's 504th Parachute Infantry would drop the first night on Fubara airport, just north of the Tiber River, near the Tyrrhenian Sea. Tucker and his parachutists would take off from scattered airfields in Sicily at 6:30 P.M. on the night of September 8. Jim Gavin's 505th Parachute Infantry would bail out the next night over Glidonia, Littoria, and Centrocella airfields, all located about 25 miles northeast of Rome. After Gavin's men had seized the three airfields, Harry Lewis' 325th Glider Infantry regiment would land in C-47s.

Boiled down, Giant 2 was a scheme to drop a few thousand lightly armed paratroopers 250 miles from the nearest Allied soldier, where they would be isolated without heavy artillery, tanks, antitank guns, tactical air cover, or even a reasonably certain method of resupply. The All-Americans would have to slug their way through thick concentrations of German grenadiers and panzers for 20 miles over rugged, mountainous terrain, and then capture Rome—a sprawling city of 3 million people.

There would be a good chance that the 82nd Airborne sky trains would not even reach the drop zones. The Germans had heavy ack-ack along the mouth of the Tiber, and, because Rome was beyond fighter-cover range, the plodding C-47s would have to go the final leg of the flight unescorted—a situation that could result in total disaster if the troop carrier armada were to be intercepted by the Luftwaffe night fighters based around the Rome area.

Giant 2 appeared to have all the ingredients of a classic suicide mission.

A few hours after a disturbed Matt Ridgway departed to begin planning for the airborne assault on Rome, elements of Bernard Montgomery's British Eighth Army slipped across the Strait of Messina in landing barges under cover of darkness and waded ashore on the toe of Italy. Resistance from scattered bands of Italian soldiers was halfhearted, and the Tommies quickly pushed inland.

At his headquarters, Ridgway, Jim Gavin, Rube Tucker, and other 82nd Airborne leaders had grown increasingly pessimistic about an operation that promised to destroy an elite division. Consequently, Ridgway decided to try to get Giant 2 canceled. He called on Harold Alexander, the overall commander, and pleaded his case. His presentation was in vain: The airborne assault on Rome would be launched as planned.

As a result, on September 4 and 5, the 82nd Airborne Division was flown from its encampments in Tunisia to Sicily in order to lift off from airfields closer to Rome.

That night in his barracks, Rube Tucker was briefing his commanders on the operation, now less than 48 hours away. The signal for the 504th Parachute Infantry to take off for Rome would be given on the evening of September 8 at 6:30 P.M., when Eisenhower would be heard telling of the Italian armistice over Radio Algiers.

Despite precautions to prevent others from overhearing his remarks, Tucker became increasingly loud. Richard Tregaskis, a widely known syndicated reporter and author, who was lounging down the hall, picked up everything the firebrand Tucker was saying behind closed doors. The young colonel's booming voice warned his confidants in the barracks room: "Now you fellows know and I know what I'm talking about. But if anyone in this room so much as mentions the name of that goddamned *town*, I'll have him court-martialed!"[4]

Dick Tregaskis and Cy Korman, a *Chicago Tribune* reporter, were let in on the Big Secret the next morning. They were seated under an olive tree and began talking with Lt. Col. George E. Lynch, the son of a former army chief of infantry and now G-2 (intelligence) for the 82nd Airborne. Both correspondents would go with the seaborne 325th Glider Infantry. "According to the latest poop we've obtained," Lynch said in a conspiratorial tone, "the Italians will light the way into the airfields where we will jump. They will also turn on beacons to light the route for our C-47s."

Korman and Tregaskis reflected: "How do we *know* the Italians are going to do all those things—and what if they don't?"

Lynch continued: "The Italians are even going to make a diversion for us with their own airplanes, shooting down any Luftwaffe fighter planes that may try to interfere with our operations."[5] Again, the civilians were dubious. The Italian air force had almost refused to fight the Allies in Sicily two months earlier, so why would they suddenly decide to battle the Germans in the skies over Rome?

Rising to his feet, Lynch grinned. He knew, as did Tregaskis and Korman, that this rosy litany was a recital of Algiers headquarters' wishful thinking, replete with ifs, buts, and maybes.

With hours ticking away and time for Giant 2 nearing, Eisenhower became increasingly concerned that he had a budding catastrophe in the offing. He was especially worried over the true intentions of the Italian government, whose assistance was crucial to the success of the airborne mission. So he decided to sneak two high-ranking officers into Rome to determine firsthand if the Italians could produce all that General Castellano, the armistice emissary, had assured the Allies that they could.

Selected for the cloak-and-dagger mission were Brig. Gen. Maxwell Taylor, the 82nd Airborne's artillery commander, and Col. William T. Gardiner, commander of a troop carrier squadron based in Sicily. Taylor spoke five languages fluently. The burly, 53-year-old Gardiner, a lawyer and a former governor of Maine, had excelled as a college oarsman and learned to fly at age 45.

Taylor, the senior officer of the two-man team, was told by Eisenhower that he had authority to radio back from Rome any changes in the paratroop operation that he felt were vital. He was also empowered to cancel the parachute mission by radioing a single code word—"Innocuous."

Taylor and Gardiner, having removed rank insignias and ribbon decorations, departed by PT boat; then transferred to an Italian navy corvette. They landed at Gaeta and climbed into an Italian ambulance for the 75-mile trek to Rome. The vehicle was halted at several German roadblocks and drove past numerous columns of marching Germans before reaching the Palazzo Caprara in Rome at 8:30 P.M., just as night was falling.

Almost at once, the Americans became convinced that the Italians were stalling. Not Ambrosio nor Castellano nor any high official was at the palace to greet the emissaries. Max Taylor demanded that a general come to the palace immediately, and at

10:30 P.M., *Generale d'Corpo d'Armata* Giacomo Garboni, chief of Italian army intelligence, appeared. Nervously, he told Taylor and Gardiner that the Germans had moved 125 tanks and 24,000 men to the area just south of Rome and 12,000 men to the north of the capital. In addition, the Wehrmacht had 12,000 troops on both sides of the Tiber near Rome, with some one hundred 88-millimeter guns, dual-purpose weapons that were as deadly against aircraft as armor.

It would be only 19 hours until Rube Tucker's Five-O-Fours lifted off for Rome. Already, Mark Clark's invasion fleet was knifing through the Tyrrhenian Sea toward Salerno. Max Taylor picked up his clandestine radio transmitter to contact Algiers. At 8 A.M. the next morning—D-Day minus 1—General Eisenhower put on his horn-rimmed spectacles to read Taylor's decoded message. The airborne landings around Rome would probably meet with disaster, Taylor asserted, because of the failure of the Italians to declare an armistice and to safeguard the drop zone airfields and because of heavy German troop concentrations around Rome. He requested further instructions.

In Rome that morning, Max Taylor and Bill Gardiner waited anxiously for a reply from Allied Force Headquarters. Despite their fiercest glares at the set, the radio remained silent. At 11:55 A.M., only 10 hours before Rube Tucker and his men were to bail out over the airfields outside Rome, Taylor fired off a signal to Algiers—*"Situation innocuous."*

Eisenhower promptly canceled Giant 2. Fearful that the order might get garbled in transmission, he instructed Brig. Gen. Lyman L. Lemnitzer to fly to Sicily and personally hand the cancellation order to Matt Ridgway. Lemnitzer and his pilot lifted off from Bizerte, Tunisia, bound for Licata, on the southern coast of Sicily, but the pilot became disoriented and nearly missed the island altogether. As the pilot tried to orient himself, Lemnitzer nervously fingered the crucial cancellation order.[6]

Finally, Lemnitzer and his pilot recognized towering Mount Etna in northeast Sicily, and they reversed course and headed southward. As the fighter plane raced toward Licata, Eisenhower broadcast the Italian armistice. That was the signal for Rube Tucker's flight to take off. There was a mightly roar as powerful engines revved up. Just then, Lyman Lemnitzer's wandering airplane touched down, and the general dashed up to Tucker and, with a visible sigh of relief, thrust the cancellation order into the other's hand.

Had Lemnitzer remained lost for a few more minutes, 1,700 lightly armed American paratroopers—or what remained of them—would have been on the ground outside Rome and confronted by the 26,000 men of two veteran German divisions supported by panzers, artillery, and the Luftwaffe.[7]

13
Doomsday
Looms at
Salerno

Early on the morning of September 12, 1943, Gen. Mark Clark hauled his angular frame into a jeep and began a tour of the Salerno beachhead. His American and British Fifth Army had stormed ashore in the early morning hours of darkness three days earlier in the first contested Allied invasion of mainland Europe. Reinforcements had poured ashore, and now the bridgehead was 11 miles at its deepest point and stretched in a huge semicircle from Agropoli on the south to Amalfi on the north, with a circumference of 44 miles.

Even as the first Allied soldier had waded ashore, Field Marshal Albrecht Kesselring began rushing troops and panzers to Salerno. Within 72 hours, major elements of seven of the eight German divisions in southern Italy had fashioned a steel noose around the invaders.

Mark Clark had started that morning buoyant and confident, but steadily his optimism faded. Savage fighting had erupted and raged all day. The Allied front crumbled in places, units were cut off, overrun, and wiped out. Clark's dead and wounded piled up. There was little Clark could do—beachhead reserves were nonexistent. As darkness veiled the Gulf of Salerno, the Germans had smashed to within only six miles of the shore at all points. A grave crisis was at hand. The Allies were in danger of being driven into the sea.[1]

At Algiers, Eisenhower and his staff were stunned. None had dreamed that Kesselring, capable as he was, could ring the beachhead with such astonishing speed and power. Recognizing that a debacle was looming at Salerno, Eisenhower ordered his ground, sea, and air commanders to rush aid to the beleaguered Mark Clark.

However, shipping ground reinforcements would require many days. By then, there might not be a Salerno bridgehead. Clark was desperate. What he needed was instant help.

So now, just before midnight on September 12, Mark Clark sent for his airborne adviser, Lt. Col. Bill Yarborough, who hurried into his office trailer. Yarborough had returned to his earlier slot as Clark's airborne adviser after being relieved of his 82nd Airborne battalion command for protesting vocally the events involved with the shooting down of 23 paratroop-laden C-47s by friendly fire.

"Bill, I want to bring in Matt Ridgway's boys as soon as possible," Clark said. "What do you propose?"[2]

Bill Yarborough, at age 32, was confronted with the most crucial challenge of his career. An entire Allied army stood in danger of being wiped out. Fallout from a debacle could severely cripple armed forces and homefront morale, and provide an enormous boost to the spirits of the Wehrmacht and the *Herrenvolk* (civilians) of the Third Reich.

Pondering his boss' question briefly, Yarborough proposed a course of action. Two parachute regiments of the 82nd Airborne would be dropped directly onto the beachhead, behind Allied lines, for "numerical and psychological reinforcement." Since there was an acute shortage of C-47s, the regiments would have to be dropped 24 hours apart, and because of Luftwaffe strength in Italy, the missions would have to be conducted at night.

On a large wall map, the adviser pointed to Avellino, a sleepy, unprententious town 20 miles north of Salerno. "There is the real German bottleneck," Yarborough said. "German rail and road movements from Rome and northwest Italy must pass through Avellino to reach the beachhead. We should stick a cork in that bottleneck."

The adviser suggested dropping a battalion of paratroopers near Avellino. It would be an especially tough mission, he explained, for there were German troop concentrations around the crucial mountain town. However, he felt confident that the parachutists could do the job without undue losses.

Clark was silent for a few moments, then said, "Thanks, Bill, I'll think about it and give you my decision in the morning."

That night in the vineyards, olive groves, and defiles around the bridgehead, German grenadiers and panzers were massing for renewed assaults to drive the invaders into the Tyrrhenian. At dawn, the Germans struck. Bitter fighting raged. Numerous American units were chopped up or sent reeling. Mark Clark called in a secretary and began dictating a letter to old friend, Matt Ridgway, who was in Licata, Sicily, more than 300 miles away.

"The fighting on Salerno has taken a turn for the worse," Clark dictated, "and the situation is touch and go. I realize the time normally needed to prepare for a drop, but this is an exception. I want you to make a drop within our lines on the beachhead, and I want you to make it tonight. *This is a must!*"[3]

Enclosed with Clark's letter was a map, hastily sketched by Bill Yarborough, designating the drop zone, south of the Sele River near Paestum in the American sector, and operational procedures for the two regiments that would bail out behind friendly lines.

Meanwhile, Mark Clark had instructed his 44-year-old chief of staff, Maj. Gen. Alfred M. Gruenther, who had a keen mind and was a world-class bridge player, to send an officer to round up a pilot to carry the message to Ridgway. The aide collared Capt. Jacob R. Hamilton, who had just landed his twin-boomed P-38 on the airstrip near Paestum. Hamilton entered Clark's office trailer, bewildered and unaware that he would be the Paul Revere of the twentieth century.

General Clark handed the large envelope to Hamilton and said grimly: "I want you to leave immediately for Licata, Sicily. This is a matter of the highest priority. You are to deliver this envelope personally to General Ridgway and to no one else. Do you fully understand these instructions?"

"Yes, sir," Captain Hamilton responded crisply. He saluted, turned on his heel and bolted out of the trailer. Fifteen minutes later, Hamilton leaped into his P-38, which had been warmed up and awaiting his arrival, and, with Clark's envelope on his lap, lifted off for Sicily. Shells crashing near the strip punctuated the dire urgency of his mission.

That afternoon, the Allied crisis worsened. Faced by what seemed certain disaster, Clark went forward to rally the troops. Cooks, headquarters clerks, truck drivers, musicians, and the walking wounded were handed guns and thrown into the fray. The massive bombardment by warships offshore was mainly responsible for halting the German tidal wave at sunset.[4]

At his headquarters in the mountain village of Sant'Angelo de Lombardi, Gen. Heinrich von Vietinghoff, the Tenth Army commander, was not discouraged by the failure of his troops to reach the sea that day. In the winner-take-all slugfest, the Allies had been left groggy and hanging on the ropes. At dawn, von Vietinghoff would launch the knockout punch. A staff officer penned in the Tenth Army war diary: "A wonderful present for our beloved Führer. The battle for Salerno appears to be about over."

Early on the afternoon of September 13, Capt. Jacob Hamilton's P-38 touched down on the Licata airfield and the pilot jumped out. He glanced at his watch: It was 1:35 P.M. By coincidence, Col. Jim Gavin was at the field, and he told Hamilton that Ridgway had taken off from the same airport 30 minutes earlier, bound for Termini, Sicily. Gavin offered to deliver Clark's letter when Ridgway returned. The air corps officer refused, explaining Mark Clark's strict order to give the envelope to no one but Ridgway.

Aware that the message was of deep significance, Gavin contacted the 82nd Airborne's chief of staff, Col. Ralph P. "Doc" Eaton, who, at age 41, was ancient for an airborne officer. Eaton and Ridgway had served together in the prewar army, and were an odd couple. Ridgway was a stickler for military regulations; Eaton was a disciple of throwing the book away and getting the job done. However, they hit it off well together.[5]

Doc Eaton promptly radioed Ridgway and urged him to return to Licata. Even while the 82nd Airborne commander was winging back, word that "an urgent job" was on tap spread through the ranks of the All-Americans, who were bivouacked in olive groves around the airfield. "Yeah, Old Matt's been out looking for work—and he's found it, sure as hell!" a crewcut corporal mused to his tentmate.

Matt Ridgway's feet had barely touched the dusty runway than Captain Hamilton thrust out Mark Clark's envelope. Ridgway moved to one side, tore open the envelope, and read the documents. "Let's get going, boys," the division commander said. "We've got a rush job. Mark Clark's in big trouble."

At his command post, Ridgway hastily wrote a reply to Clark and handed it to Jacob Hamilton, who flew back to the beachhead. While speeding toward Clark's trailer in a jeep, the messenger was strafed by four Luftwaffe fighters. Clutching Ridgway's letter, he leaped out and into a ditch, and was jolted by an agonizing surge of pain. Only later would he learn that his shoulder had been dislocated.

Reaching the trailer, the courier handed over Matt Ridgway's letter. Clark eagerly read it and his face glowed with relief and out of admiration for the airborne men who would soon ride to the rescue like the horse cavalry of the Old West. Ridgway's first two words were *"Can do!"*

Ridgway, no doubt still haunted by the specter of the friendly fire catastrophe in Sicily, also wrote: "Rigid control of antiaircraft fire is absolutely essential."

Clark couldn't have agreed more. He promptly conferred with Vice Adm. H. Kent Hewitt, commander of naval forces off Salerno, and Maj. Gen. Ernest J. "Mike" Dawley, leader of the U.S. VI Corps into whose sector the paratroopers would drop. Clark also fired off an order to all of his units: "At precisely twenty-one hundred [9:00 P.M.] tonight, and until further notice from me personally, not a single aircraft gun on this beachhead or offshore is to fire for any reason . . . repeat, for any reason." As a secondary precaution, officers were dispatched to each anti-aircraft gun battery to make certain that these don't-shoot orders had been received and understood.

Meanwhile, back at Licata, airborne and troop carrier officers were putting the finishing touches on plans for that night's mission. In only four hours since Jacob Hamilton had appeared in Sicily like a bolt out of the blue, parachute and C-47 commanders had been briefed.

Ridgway selected Rube Tucker's 504th Parachute Infantry Regiment, less its 3rd Battalion, to jump that night. The 3rd Battalion, led by its executive officer, Maj. William R. Beall, was going to Salerno by landing craft along with Lewis' 325th Glider Infantry Regiment. Other elements in Tucker's 1,300-man flight would be the 376th Parachute Field Artillery Battalion and Company C, 307th Airborne Engineer Battalion.

The plan was for Maj. Dan Danielson's 2nd Battalion, flown by the 313th Troop Carrier Group, to take off from Trapani, in far western Sicily. At about the same time, the 61st and 314th Troop Carrier Groups would lift off from Comiso airfield with

Lt. Col. Warren Williams' 1st Battalion and the engineers. Danielson's and Williams' flights would rendezvous over Cape Rasocolmo on the northeast tip of Sicily, then head generally north to the bridgehead drop zone.[6]

At 6:15 P.M., men of Williams' 1st Battalion had gathered around their C-47s at Comiso. Junior officers gave quick briefings. One platoon leader explained the "crash" mission:

> *Men, here's the poop. Those goddamned Krauts are kicking hell out of our straight-legs [nonparatroopers] over at Salerno. Mark Clark wants us to rescue his boys. When the green light comes on, jump. When you hit the ground, be ready for anything. We're supposed to drop behind our own lines—but the Krauts might be on the DZ when we get there. Any questions?*

While waiting for orders to go, S. Sgt. Sam DeCrenzo, the 1st Battalion's graybeard at age 31, jotted in his pocket diary: "Fifth Army in precarious position. They need our help. Briefing in fast time—two minutes. Dust all over field. Colonel Tucker dashing about."

At an airfield outside Agrigento, near the southern coast of Sicily, Lt. Col. Joel Crouch, a former United Airlines pilot and now operations officer of Hal Clark's 52nd Troop Carrier Wing, climbed into the cockpit of a C-47. He would lead a three-man flight carrying 50 pathfinders, who would jump on the drop zone 15 minutes in advance of the main body and, with electronic homing devices, guide the C-47 pilots to the tiny drop zone in the vast blackness.[7]

Less than three weeks earlier, a limited number of 82nd Airborne troopers and C-47 crews had taken a brief experimental course in pathfinder techniques. Tonight, each of the three teams would jump with a 33-pound radio beacon known as a 5G; Krypton lights to be used to assemble the troopers on the drop zone; and a Eureka, Mark II, which would send out pulses to the Rebecca in the first C-47 in each serial, permitting the operator to tell the direction of the beacon.

Now there was the raucous revving of engines, and the three pathfinder planes sped down the dark, dusty runway and headed for the Salerno beachhead. It was 8:40 P.M.—10 hours since Mark Clark handed the crucial letter to Captain Hamilton for delivery to Matt Ridgway. The fire-alarm mission to save Fifth Army had been launched.

14
Bailouts to Save an Army

Standing on the black drop zone on Salerno beachhead, Bill Yarborough peeked at the luminous face of his watch. It was 10:55 P.M. His ears were cocked toward the south, listening for the first faint purr of engines that would foretell the arrival of Joel Crouch's pathfinder C-47s.

Mark Clark's airborne adviser labored to banish haunting thoughts from his mind. Would this mission be another Sicily, with the paratroopers scattered to the four winds or their winged convoy blasted by friendly guns? Many of the pilots were inexperienced, so if their planes came under fire from Germans ringing the beachhead would they become rattled and drop their troopers to watery graves in the nearby Tyrrhenian Sea? Would Luftwaffe night fighters suddenly appear and enjoy a turkey shoot with the plodding, unescorted C-47s?

Along the heights overlooking the drop zone like a huge theater balcony were German artillery observers who would have choice seats for the parachute extravaganza that would unfold on the stage below. Once Tucker's men began to bail out, would the drop zone be pounded with murderous barrages? That risk had to be accepted—this was the only site on the shrinking bridgehead suitable for a mass parachute landing. It was 1,200 yards long and 800 yards wide.[1]

Throughout the day, Yarborough had been heavily occupied, supervising an innovative procedure that his fertile mind had hatched to guide the sky trains to the drop zone. Jerry cans filled with gasoline-soaked sand were placed every fifty yards, and a soldier stood next to each container. When Yarborough would hear the C-47s, he would fire a Very pistol, an instrument designed to shoot a brilliant green flare into the dark sky. That would be the signal for each soldier to light his jerry can, and a fiery T, each leg a half-mile long, would suddenly appear.[2]

At about 11:05 P.M., Joel Crouch's pathfinder flight was approaching from the south, after having flown at an 800-foot altitude over a few miles of bridgehead without a friendly shot being fired from below. In the open door of the lead airplane was Lt. William B. Jones, a New Jersey native, who would become the first American pathfinder to jump in a combat situation.

Hooked up behind Jones were Sgt. Milton "Fuzzy" Knight, Sgt. Regis J. Pahler, and the rest of the stick. Pahler would bail out lugging the large homing beacon, an assignment he had drawn because he was the biggest and strongest man in the group. The others also would parachute carrying parts of homing devices.

Just as Crouch called out, "The DZ should be right ahead," brilliant pyrotechnics erupted in the sky and on the ground—a green flare and then a huge flaming T.

"Let's go!" Lieutenant Jones yelled, and he leaped out, followed in split-second fashion by the stick. Most of the 50 pathfinders in the three planes landed in a tight pattern on the drop zone, and within minutes set up their homing devices. So skilled were these pathfinders that they were capable of assembling and operating the equipment while blindfolded.

The burning T was extinguished. So far, so good.

At 11:25 P.M., about 14 minutes after the first pathfinder had landed, lead C-47s carrying Dan Danielson's 2nd Battalion neared the target. Again the iridescent green flare and the fiery T. In moments, the dark sky blossomed with scores of white parachutes, floating down majestically over the center of the drop zone.

With hundreds of paratroopers on the ground and others descending, Bill Yarborough was struck by a puzzling thought. Why hadn't the Germans, perched on the hills and no doubt watching the spectacle, rained shells on the drop zone? It was one of those illogical battlefield mysteries that would never be solved.

As the minutes and then hours ticked past, Yarborough grew

concerned over the absence of the flight carrying Warren Williams' 1st Battalion and Rube Tucker's headquarters group. Major Danielson could shed no light on the riddle. When Tucker's C-47s had failed to arrive at the Sicily rendezvous point, Danielson's flight continued on to the beachhead. Radio silence was being observed, so Tucker could not be contacted.

Eighty-second Airborne dropping on Salerno beachhead. *(Courtesy of Keith Rose)*

Tucker and most of this troopers were, in fact, winging toward the drop zone, but the flight was strung out for 300 miles. Back at Comiso airfield, Tucker's 51 C-47s had been ready to depart on schedule at 9:00 P.M., but the flight was delayed because of a few balky engines that had to be repaired. Tucker paced about like a tiger in a cage, became impatient, and ordered his C-47s to lift off solo, in pairs, and in small groups.

At about 2:30 A.M., Tucker's first planes reached the drop zone, and the troopers started jumping onto the flaming T. When 1st Battalion commander Warren Williams bailed out, the reserve chute on his chest struck him a blow in the mouth, dazing him and knocking loose several teeth. Then he crashed hard into the ground and was belted groggy once more. Slowly, Williams became aware that a shadowy figure was helping him to his feet, and he recognized Lt. Col. Charles J. Denholm, a West Point classmate and old friend. Denholm was now on Gen. Mike Dawley's staff at VI Corps.

"Damn, are we ever glad to see you fellows!" Denholm exclaimed.

"Where're the Krauts?" Williams asked.

Denholm pointed inland and replied: "See those hills over there? Well, if it was daylight, the Krauts would be watching you and me talking!"

Williams' battalion and Tucker's command group had landed routinely, but 76 men had been injured, one of them seriously. Using the pathfinders' Krypton lamps as rallying points, Williams rapidly assembled his men and counted noses. Eight planeloads of Company B men—some 120 troopers—were missing. Williams feared that they had jumped over the nearby sea and been drowned. (Actually, the absent men had been misdropped on land and would rejoin the battalion later.)

At 4:05 A.M., Rube Tucker, typically full of fight, reported to General Dawley. "How soon can you assemble your regiment?" the corps commander asked. "They're assembled now and ready for action," the colonel replied.

Dawley attached the 504th Parachute Infantry to the 36th Infantry Division, a National Guard outfit known as the "Texas Army." Tucker's men would defend the front in the Monte Soprana sector, on the heights overlooking the American portion of the beachhead, where the Texas Army had suffered heavy casualties in fierce fighting. By dawn, the Five-O-Fours were in the line and spoiling for a fight.

With daylight, a curious phenomenon swept through the ranks of the beleaguered and weary GIs and Tommies on the fireswept and shrinking bridgehead. Scores of them had stood in their foxholes and cheered lustily when they had seen Tucker's men bailing out. Word that 1,300 tough American paratroopers had leaped onto the battlefield, like lightning from the black sky, infected haggard and demoralized men with a new sense of confidence, even buoyancy. The spiraling boost to sagging Allied spirits was grossly disproportionate to the relatively small number of parachutists involved. This was the "psychological reinforcement" about which Bill Yarborough had spoken to General Clark.

Cheering and morale-boosting alone would not ward off the surging tide of Germans, Mark Clark knew. So that night of September 14th, with the issue at Salerno still much in doubt, Jim Gavin's 505th Parachute Infantry was winging toward the bridgehead. This would be a much larger drop than Rube Tucker's had been. Slightly more than 2,100 Five-O-Fives were being carried by 131 C-47s. It was an encore of the previous night's premiere parachute performance.

With the peripatetic Joel Crouch once again at the controls of the lead C-47, the 505th pathfinders leaped out and landed almost on top of the fiery T. Fifteen minutes later—at 1:10 A.M.— the first of 54 planes carrying Cannonball Krause's 3rd Battalion, along with Gavin and his regimental staff, flew over the T and troopers began spilling out.

Bill Yarborough's orders were to promptly bring Gavin to Mark Clark's headquarters. But Gavin might land anywhere on the drop zone—or far from it. Locating the 505th leader among hundreds of descending troopers could be a time-consuming task. One parachutist crashed down almost on top of Yarborough and began rolling up his chute. Walking over to the tall, shadowy figure, the airborne adviser was astonished to find that this was Jim Gavin himself.

Behind Krause's battalion were 38 C-47s with Lt. Col. Mark Alexander's 2nd Battalion on board. Just before 1:30 A.M., Alexander and his men dropped, right on the bull's-eye. Perhaps the battalion commander wished the jump had not been so precise: Alexander slammed down hard on his back after frantic last-moment efforts to avoid plunging directly onto a flaming jerry can.

It was nearly two hours later before the final flight of 38 C-47s, carrying Lt. Col. Walter F. Winton's 1st Battalion, soared over the drop zone and the troopers tumbled out. However, three of Winton's planes had become lost, and the pilots found themselves over German-held Naples. They quickly reversed course. One C-47 located the drop zone, and its troopers jumped. The other pair of planes flew back to Sicily without unloading their passengers.

Less than an hour after the last Five-O-Fiver landed, the regiment climbed into trucks and headed for an assembly area. Yarborough took his old friend Gavin to Clark's headquarters, but the Fifth Army commander, who had been awake and on the go for 72 hours, was snatching a few winks of sleep.

Al Gruenther, Clark's chief of staff, gave Gavin his orders. The 505th Parachute Infantry was to defend the southern sector, which Clark had to virtually denude of troops in order to strengthen the center of the beachhead where the Germans had been threatening to smash through to the shore and split American and British forces. "You will tie in with Tucker near Albanella, and your line will extend to the sea near Agropoli," Gruenther explained.

Before the sun peeked over the rugged Apennines, elements of the 505th Parachute Infantry were in the line.

The two fire-alarm parachute missions to "psychologically and numerically reinforce" the beachhead had been masterpieces of planning, logistics, and execution by Colonel Yarborough and the officers and men of the 82nd Airborne Division and the 52nd Wing. In 24 hours, some 3,400 superb fighting men had been airlifted from scattered bases more than 300 miles away, dropped directly on target, and were at the front and fighting. All this had been attained with only a few hours' advance notice.

American paratroopers had plugged the badly leaking dike at bloody Salerno. But the German floodtide still threatened to inundate the Allied bridgehead. Now it was up to the bottleneck corkers to come through at Avellino in the third—and by far, most perilous—of the three crash paratroop missions.

It was not until 3 P.M. on the afternoon of September 14 that Lt. Col. Doyle Yardley and his men in the 509th Parachute Infantry Battalion learned from a visit by Matt Ridgway that they were going to jump that very night 20 miles behind German lines to seize a crossroads at the village of Santa Lucia di Sorino, three miles south of Avellino. "This is a mission of the gravest urgency," Ridgway declared.

For six hours after Ridgway jeeped away in a cloud of dust, the 509th Battalion's olive-grove bivouac area and command post at Licata were beehives of activity. As the purple shadows began to fall, Yardley's 640 paratroopers were huddled in tiny knots near to their C-47s at Comiso airfield.

Each Five-O-Niner recognized the mission for what it was: a desperate effort to help save a large Allied force hanging on by its fingernails at Salerno. Ridgway had told them that they were to hold the key crossroads "until relieved by the Fifth Army." But how could Fifth Army, which was in a defensive situation and battling for its life, suddenly lunge forward through strong German forces for 20 miles to link up with the Avellino paratroopers?

There were unique perils for the 509th other than the risks of being isolated and chopped to pieces. Fifth Army G-2 knew nothing of what German units might be in the Avellino area. And the towering mountains surrounding Avellino meant that the Five-O-Niners would have to bail out from around 4,000 feet, almost assuring a wide dispersal pattern. At Avellino, tricky air currents swirled through the mountain passes, so billowing parachutes might be carried for miles from the drop zone.

Now, in the gloaming, Doc Alden, the battalion surgeon, scribbled in his pocket diary the unspoken sentiment of most Five-O-Niners: "If we don't come back, there are thousands to take our places and win this war. I hope I make it. But more important, I hope I can do my duty as an American paratrooper."[3]

At 9:21 P.M., a lone C-47 roared down the dark runway and lifted off for the 325-mile trek to the drop zone at Santa Lucia di Sorino. On board were two lieutenants, Fred Perry and Henry F. Rouse, and nine troopers. They were the battalion's pathfinder team that had been experimenting with techniques for locating a drop zone.

Fifteen minutes later, 39 C-47s of Brig. Gen. Roy Dunn's 51st Troop Carrier Wing, loaded with 640 paratroopers, followed from Comiso airfield. The flight route would be the same as that of the two 82nd Airborne regiments, only instead of veering out to sea after the beachhead was reached, the Avellino sky convoy would continue northward to Montecorvino and on through mountain valleys to the drop zone.

Passing over German lines north of the bridgehead, the pathfinder plane was rocked by shell explosion, but flew onward. A short time later, Lieutenant Perry was standing in the door, searching intently for landmarks on the moonlit landscape. He saw none. One mountain looked just like any other mountain. There had been no time for aerial photos—the trailblazers would jump blind.

Suddenly, a crossroads loomed below, the green light flashed on, and out Perry went—the first American pathfinder to leap into enemy territory. Hard on his heels, the stick jumped, landing in a neat cluster. Hastily reconnoitering the terrain, Perry and Rouse discovered that they had dropped on the wrong crossroads, this one a mile south of the true drop zone. There would not be time to march the one mile before the main C-47 serial arrived, so the electronic homing devices were rapidly set up on the spot.

Perry and his team were equipped with only a 5G radio beacon and two Aldis lamps. There was no Eureka, because Dunn's 51st Wing had no Rebeccas. Only much later would Perry and his team learn that their equipment had been useless. The mountains deflected electronic signals aimed at the approaching C-47 caravan, and the narrow-beam Aldis lamps were nearly impossible for a pilot to pick up unless he was flying a precise course.

Meanwhile, Five-O-Niners in the main body were riding largely in silence. Time and time again their thoughts centered on their parachutes. For months they had been using their parachute packs for pillows in the desert of North Africa and in Sicily, expecting that new chutes would be issued for any combat jump. But the crash nature of the current mission had not permitted bringing in new parachutes, so the leery troopers would jump with what they had. Would the chutes open or would the silk canopy be full of holes?

Yardley's men recalled that one of their own, an old Army sergeant, had quipped that afternoon when informed of the mission 20 miles behind German lines: "Our brass are throwing the Krauts a bone. The 509th Parachute Infantry Battalion is going to be a nice, juicy, 640-man bone to take Hitler's mind off our guys on the beachhead!"

Here and there a grim face in the dark C-47 cast an eerie glow, lighted by the fire of a cigarette. A sergeant traced semaphorelike patterns with his hands as he checked his harness straps and gear—then checked them again. A teenager chanted a few words from the old training camp song, which nightly had echoed across the bars around Fort Bragg, North Carolina: "Gory, gory, what a helluva way to die . . ." Sensing the icy glare of comrades, he fell into silence. The song's title: *Blood on the Risers.*[4]

The sky train burrowed on through the night toward the unknown fate that awaited the 509th Parachute Infantry Battalion.

15
The Lost
Battalion of
Avellino

A C-47 carrying 18 members of a 509th Parachute Infantry bazooka team flew down a valley that the pilot thought would lead to Avellino and the drop zone. Crouched in the door was S. Sgt. William W. Sullivan, of Galesburg, Illinois, the jumpmaster. The red light was on; the troopers were hooked up. It would be only minutes before bailout. Sullivan sensed the throttling of the engines, the lifting of the tail. The plane was slowing. He tensed to jump.

Then . . . suddenly the engines revved, speed increased, tail dropped. No green light. It was much like a foot race, a brutal, gut-wrenching foot race. Ready . . . set . . . but no go.

The C-47 crew chief worked his way back from the cockpit. "The pilot didn't like what he saw down there," the airman explained in a shout above the roar of engines and rushing wind. "He's going to take another pass at locating the DZ." Sullivan admired the pilot's spunk: He could have flashed the green light, dumped his paratroopers and hightailed it home.

Turning sharply, the C-47 reversed its course. Standing in the door, Bill Sullivan had a unique sight; his plane was going in the opposite direction from that of other C-47s carrying his comrades. "Like two ships passing in the night," he reflected. Sullivan rightly suspected that the Avellino mission was already "royally screwed up."[1]

Indeed it was. The battalion's 640 paratroopers were being

sprinkled over a 1,000-square-mile area of central Italy, all the way to Caserta, 40 miles to the north of the drop zone near Avellino.

Presently, Sergeant Sullivan's plane made another run at the drop zone, and the stick bailed out. When his chute popped open, Sullivan was showered with a cloud of North African insects and dust.

A few miles south of Avellino, Capt. Doc Alden was floating to earth and unable to discern other parachutes around him. Suddenly, only 100 feet below, loomed an open well about five feet wide. Frantically, he tugged on the risers to sideslip, but plunged into the well. At the last split second, his blossoming canopy caught on a large overhanging tree, jerking him to a halt in water up to his chest. Had he descended three more feet he would have drowned, unable to extricate himself from his chute harness.

Taking stock of his predicament, the doctor, using his suspended parachute risers, hand-over-hand pulled himself from the well. Shucking the harness of the parachute that had saved his life, Alden stole off into the night.

A mile from Doc Alden's well, Doyle Yardley, the battalion commander, walked up to a shadowy figure in a field. It was Lt. Fred Perry, his pathfinder-team leader. Told that they were not on the true drop zone but one mile south of it, Yardley replied, "That's close enough."

Not far away, 21-year-old Pvt. Edward W. Pawloski was coming down in his chute—directly onto German-held Avellino. From high above he could hear the loud pealing of church bells from within the maze of dark buildings. Pawloski managed to miss the town and sideslip to a landing in a cabbage patch just north of Avellino.

Pawloski listened and watched. He was alone. No enemy. No comrades. He headed for nearby woods, and there bumped into Pvt. J. J. O'Brien. Cautiously, the two men slipped out of the forest and headed for the drop zone. Shortly, they encountered three more troopers, Pvt. Frank Stanovich, Sgt. Walter Cherry, and a man from another company. As the road to the drop zone ran directly through Avellino, the five troopers decided to try to sneak through the town.

Just as Pawloski and the others reached the edge of Avellino, the silence was shattered. A German machine gun erupted with heavy bursts of fire. Sergeant Cherry was struck in the chest, collapsing in a bloody heap. O'Brien was killed by the same fusillade that had seriously wounded Cherry.

Before Pawloski could flop to the ground, he felt a heavy blow against the side of his body. Startled, he glanced down and saw smoke pouring from a jacket pocket. With bullets whipping past his head, Pawloski rapidly opened his pocket, pulled out the smoking hand grenade that had been hit by a German slug, and gave it a pitch. While blasting away at the enemy with his rifle, Pawloski offered a silent prayer. Had not the grenade been in his pocket, the bullet would probably have killed him.

Firing as they went, the three remaining Five-O-Niners pulled back into the mountains.

Miles away, Sgt. Robert Akers descended onto a hornet's nest. White tracer bullets fired from the ground hissed around him, resulting in a brightness by which he could have read a newspaper. Crashing to the ground, Akers felt a sharp pain in the head. Vegetation stubble had struck him in the left eye, causing tears to flow profusely. He was temporarily blinded. Firing was going on all around him. Clutching his tommy gun, Akers got to his haunches to dash off, but German machine gunners were raking the terrain in search of paratroopers. Perhaps 30 minutes later, his blurred vision returned, Akers decided against fighting a one-man war against machine guns and slipped away.

About a half-mile onward, Akers came upon his company commander, Capt. Casper E. "Pappy" Curtis, who had rounded up 17 troopers. The little band located railroad tracks and began walking along them, a trek that, it was hoped, would take them into Avellino. There were no landmarks to orient them. After nearly an hour of marching, Pappy Curtis saw the shadowy contours of a town and, with weapons at the ready, the troopers began moving in single file down the dark and silent main street.

It was an eerie sensation. House shutters were tightly closed. The old buildings stood mute and gaunt in the moonlight. A black cat, its back arched in fear of the unknown intruders, scampered across the cobbled street in front of the troopers. Where are we? each wondered. Are we walking into a trap?

Reaching a street intersection, deserted and foreboding, the moon's beams flashed onto a crudely painted sign along the front of a rickety building—*Avellino!*

Stealthily pressing onward, Captain Curtis and his band arrived at a large square. Halfway across the square, Curtis halted. A dim light, barely discernible, could be seen inside a store. Outside the building, a German weapons carrier was parked. A trooper was sent forward to investigate. He reported back and whispered to Curtis, "There're five or six Krauts inside looting. The weapons carrier is loaded with radios, electric appliances, and other stuff."

The troopers melted into the shadows and waited. A few minutes later, the Germans, arms loaded with merchandise, emerged from the store to be greeted with bursts of tommy gun and rifle fire. It was over in seconds. Five *Feldgrau* (for field gray, or the uniform of the average German soldier) lay sprawled in the street—dead.

Minutes later, Pappy Curtis and his men heard the ominous sounds of tanks approaching from the north. No doubt, the fusillade of fire had alerted other Germans in and around Avellino. Rifles and tommy guns would be no match for the firepower of thick-plated panzers, so the paratroopers rapidly pulled back out of town.

Elsewhere, Lt. Lloyd G. Wilson, a platoon leader, and George Fontanesi, his platoon sergeant, were huddled under a poncho on the side of a hill and, by the beam of a tiny flashlight, were trying to orient themselves on a map. They concluded that they were some 10 miles east of the drop zone. At the bottom of the hill could be heard the rumble of traffic—German convoys of troops and weapons bound for Avellino and then on to the Salerno bridgehead.

"That road leads to Avellino, I'm sure," Wilson said. "If we're going to reach the DZ before dawn, we've got to shake a leg."

Wilson and Fontanesi, along with troopers William Herb, George Gately, James Ray, Samuel Callahan, and six others headed cross-country parallel to the German-traveled road. The terrain was sliced by deep gorges and clogged by thickets. The moon had vanished; the night was inky black, and the troopers stumbled, fell, got up, fell again. Muffled curses signified a man plunging down a ravine or sprawling headlong into a thicket.

While crossing a level field, the lead trooper stumbled onto a small tent and fell heavily on top of two sleeping forms inside. One of the rudely awakened occupants shouted at the unknown bumbling intruder: *"Schweinehund!"* (Son of a bitch!) There was a squirming of tangled bodies as the American sought to disengage himself from the hostile forms under the canvas.

Soon dark figures were stirring about and calling out in German. Wilson and his men had blundered into the center of a

large enemy bivouac. Masked by darkness and German confusion, the paratroopers withdrew hastily and trudged on toward
the drop zone.

Just as the sun rose, Lloyd Wilson and his troopers halted,
and the lieutenant pulled out his grimy map. He made an en-
couraging discovery: the little band was right on the true drop
zone, south of Avellino. But where were the other 627 men of
the 509th Parachute Infantry Battalion?

Exhausted, the troopers crawled into thick bushes and tried
to sleep. But sleep would not come. There was the steady sound
of enemy activity on all sides—the grinding of panzer treads and
the rumble of trucks on the nearby road, an occasional shout by
a German officer presumably directing his men in search of the
American paratroopers who had landed during the night.[2]

Elsewhere, Lt. Dan DeLeo, who had led the bold raid on the
El Djem bridge in Tunisia the previous winter, and his stick
dropped almost directly onto the headquarters of a German panzer force. Machine gunners poured tracers toward DeLeo and
other descending parachutists. Two troopers' chutes caught on
tall trees just inside the large walled enclosure that was a water
pumping station for Naples but now was serving as the German
command post. As the two Americans dangled helplessly, several
Germans dashed up and riddled them with Schmeisser machine
pistols.

Nearby, DeLeo and a few of his men landed in a cluster and
were raked by machine-gun fire from a woods as they tried to
shuck their chutes. Flopped on the ground, the Americans fired
back, but within seconds four of the paratroopers were wounded.
Sgt. Fred Miller was struck by a dum-dum bullet that tore a gaping hole in his buttock, and bloody slivers of bone protruded
through the flesh of his leg.

Dragging and half carrying wounded comrades while continuing to fire at the German machine gunners, DeLeo and his
handful of men slipped away and reached the relative security of
a rugged, heavily wooded hill. Marching to the drop zone with
four wounded troopers was out of the question, so DeLeo decided to stay put and, along with able-bodied men, sneak out at
night to wreak havoc on the Germans.[3]

Meanwhile, Doc Alden, his jumpsuit still wet from the plunge
into the well, came upon the field where Doyle Yardley had assembled 25 to 30 troopers. Alden was not the stereotypical battalion surgeon. He went into combat a walking arsenal, although

the Geneva Convention, which laid down rules for civilized killing and maiming, forbade medical soldiers from toting weapons. But Alden lived in the real world. In North Africa, he had seen his unarmed medics shot down by the enemy, and concluded that the Germans respected the Geneva Convention only when it suited their purpose.

In combat Alden carried a tommy gun or rifle, a .45 Colt pistol on his hip and a .38-caliber pistol in a shoulder holster, a nasty-looking trench knife in a boot, and grenades crammed in one large pocket. None of these weapons was for show: Alden was an expert in their use. He would quip that he lugged this arsenal to ward off wild animal attacks while treating wounded men in the field.

Alden had in tow an Italian calling himself Roger, whom the surgeon had bumped into along the road to the drop zone. Edging up to Yardley, Alden said, "Roger here says the Krauts have 250 trucks parked a short distance from here. He's willing to lead us there without using a main road."

"Okay," Yardley responded. "We can knock out the trucks, then go on and grab the crossroads at Santa Lucia." Alden reflected that 640 paratroopers had been assigned to seize and hold the crossroads; now Yardley was going to try to do the job with only 30 or so men.

Roger moved onto the narrow dirt road and, walking at a brisk pace, headed for the enemy truck park. Yardley and his troopers followed at about 15 yards' distance from the guide. Trudging through the night for a mile, Roger turned off into a narrow path. Yardley and Alden, at the head of the column, thought it was curious that Roger would suddenly veer off the road when the hikers were making such good time. No doubt Roger was taking a short cut, they reflected.

Marching for another half-mile, the column rounded a sharp curve in the path and Yardley noticed with alarm that Roger had vanished. The column halted for a hasty conference.

Suddenly the stillness was shattered. Machine guns to the front had begun to chatter, and the Americans scattered into ditches and behind trees. Streams of white tracers zipped overhead. Clearly, the Italian had led the troopers into an ambush.[4]

Brilliant iridescence broke out as the Germans fired flares into the ebony sky. Peeking from beneath helmet rims, the prostrate Americans saw the shadowy silhouettes of several German panzers. Then . . . *swissshhh, crack! Swissshhh, crack!* Flat-trajectory

88-millimeter shells from German artillery were exploding around the paratroopers.

Cries of "Medic! Medic!" pierced the din of battle. Now enemy flakwagons—vehicles mounted with multiple machine guns—raked the Americans. Paratroopers who had not been hit fired back at their tormentors. Then, as if on cue, the trapped men began to crawl and creep out of the direct line of fire.

Slithering away, S. Sgt. Leon Maenhout glanced to one side and saw Doc Alden, bathed in the light of German flares, blasting away with a pistol in each hand. Then the doctor also crawled off. Sprawled on the ground and writhing in agony was Doyle Yardley. A jagged shell fragment had chewed a large chunk of flesh from the battalion commander's buttocks.

Lt. Jack Pogue, the battalion communications chief, and a few troopers crawled to an adjacent field and took refuge behind a large shock of corn. By now, the moon had fled and it was black. Pogue and the others dashed toward a woods, but were raked by machine-gun fire. One trooper was carrying a Hawkins mine strapped to his waist and had the detonator in his pocket. A bullet struck the detonator, causing an explosion that ripped off the man's leg. Conscious and in excruciating agony, the American rolled about with blood pumping from the leg stump. His comrades were powerless to help him.

Lt. Jack Pogue was flat on his stomach firing his carbine when an exploding grenade sent a steel fragment ripping into his elbow. Using his good arm, the lieutenant continued to fire at the machine guns. Then a brilliant orange flash erupted, and a sliver of metal plunged into Pogue's left eyeball. A few seconds later, he lost consciousness. After dawn, Pogue awakened in the back of a German ambulance, vaguely aware of a wounded comrade on a stretcher beside him. It was Col. Doyle Yardley.[5]

As the morning of September 15 wore on, continuous efforts by Mark Clark's Fifth Army headquarters on the beachhead to contact Yardley at the crossroads south of Avellino proved to be fruitless. No one had any way of knowing that Yardley had been seriously wounded and captured or that the 509th Parachute Battalion had been dropped helter-skelter over a vast area. Clark, beset by deep concerns—the Germans were still attacking the beachhead violently—hoped for the best, but the worst kept gnawing at his mind: had the crack 509th Parachute Infantry Battalion been wiped out?

For Gen. Heinrich von Vietinghoff, the Salerno beachhead

situation had taken on a new dimension, one whose impact on the main German effort was difficult for him to assess. Field reports from a wide area poured into Tenth Army. These told of American paratroopers dropping in the night and marauding about the countryside, ambushing German patrols, shooting up vehicle convoys, cutting telephone lines, and attaching isolated outposts. But how many paratroopers had dropped? A battalion? A regiment? A division?

That afternoon at a field hospital, two German officers and a few enlisted men dragged a weak Lt. Jack Pogue from his cot and threw him in the back of a command car. A one-inch steel sliver still protruded from one eyeball, and he was in enormous pain. Pogue was driven to a remote, heavily wooded area and half-carried out of the vehicle.

"Kneel, you bastard!" a German officer rasped to the nearly blind Pogue.

The American complied. In his woozy condition, he was aware that a pistol was cocked, and he felt the muzzle pressing against the side of his head. "All right, you bastard, start talking or I'm going to blow your goddamned head off," the German barked in English. "What's your unit? How many of you jumped last night? What's your mission? Are any more *Fallschirmjaeger* going to jump tonight? Talk, you bastard!"

Pogue concluded that his life would end in seconds. Would his body ever be found? Would his family ever learn what had become of him? These thoughts raced through Pogue's mind.

The Germans hammered away with questions. Pogue remained silent. Finally, he blurted out: "Go ahead and shoot me and put me out of my misery. I won't tell you sons of bitches anything!"

Moments later, the parachutist felt the gun muzzle leave his head, and heard the angry German officer mumble, "Stubborn pig!"

Back on his hospital cot, the "stubborn pig" relished his triumph, despite his extreme pain.

In the days and nights ahead, tiny bands of Five-O-Niners roamed the countryside and harassed the Germans. Many troopers were surprised and captured, including Doc Alden, who had been alone in a cornfield and surrounded.[6] Far to the northwest of the drop zone—some 40 miles behind German lines at the beachhead—a group of 20 paratroopers deployed in the darkness around a small bridge over which Wehrmacht convoys were rolling toward Salerno. Included among the marauders were Capt. Edmund J. Tomasik, Lt. Justin T. McCarthy, Lt. William Sherman, and Sgt. Sol Weber.

Explosives had been planted on the bridge. One man was to plunge down on a detonator when the first German truck reached the middle of the span. Bill Sherman was in charge of riflemen concealed on a knoll overlooking the bridge. "Shoot any damned Kraut who tries to cross over!" Sherman told the marksmen.

Soon the rumble of approaching truck motors was heard to the north. The Five-O-Niners tensed. Now the first German truck, its slitted cat's eyes splitting the darkness, rounded a curve. Several other trucks, a few loaded with infantry, followed closely. As the first unsuspecting driver wheeled his big vehicle onto the bridge and rolled onward, a mighty blast erupted. The truck seemed to rise into the air. Now the concealed paratroopers poured small-arms fire into the stalled convoy. Bewildered *Feldgrau* piled out of their trucks and scrambled for cover.

Knowing that the Americans were far outnumbered, a parachute officer shouted above the earsplitting din: "Let's get the hell out of here!" The band of marauders melted into the night.

Elsewhere, far from the drop zone, Capt. Archie Birkner had collected 15 troopers. They tried an Indian-warfare technique. Instead of stalking the countryside in search of German targets, Birkner and his men would let the targets come to them.

For several days, the troopers had been positioned along a secondary road periodically used by the Germans. Lookouts posted at high points signaled the approach of enemy vehicles, and the parachutists rapidly hid in ditches and behind trees and boulders on each side of the road. When the Wehrmacht vehicle and its occupants reached the ambush site, it was raked by withering bursts of fire.

Birkner's troopers disposed of staff cars, motorcycles, and trucks of the unlucky Germans. The enemy corpses were dragged inside a nearby woods and buried in shallow graves. Soon there were 14 telltale mounds of earth. However, the mysterious disappearance of numerous comrades focused German attention on the locale. Strong patrols probed the region, and Archie Birkner and a few of his troopers were taken by surprise and captured.[7]

Early on the morning of September 18—D-Day plus 9—Allied reconnaissance planes reported heavy German traffic moving northward. Vietinghoff's 175,000-man Tenth Army had conceded the savage struggle for Salerno beachhead.

Mark Clark recalled:

> Remarkable courage and sacrifice by every American and British soldier on the beachhead helped win this victory. But it had been touch and go all the way. When victory or defeat hung in the balance, the 82nd Airborne reinforcement drops behind our lines and the 509th Parachute Infantry operation around Avellino tilted the scales in our favor.[8]

Shortly after dawn on September 23, Fifth Army struck toward Naples, 30 miles to the north. Fighting on some of Europe's most rugged terrain and battling cold, rains, demolitions and a tenacious rear guard, the attack by the British X Corps bogged down. Mark Clark rushed in the 82nd Airborne Division, along with Bill Darby's Rangers, and on the evening of September 29, patrols of Gavin's 505th Parachute Infantry probed into the outskirts of Naples and found the Germans gone. By October 1, the All-Americans of the 82nd Airborne had taken over the first major European city to be captured by the Allies.

Meanwhile, individually, in pairs and in small bands, the men of the 509th—the "Lost Battalion of Avellino"—infiltrated back toward the advancing Fifth Army from deep behind German lines. It would be three weeks before most of the Five-O-Niners were accounted for. Of the 641 men who had jumped, 532 made it back. Many had been killed. Others would survive the war in German prison camps or escape and make their way to friendly forces.[9]

Now the retreating German Tenth Army dug in along the Volturno River, north of Naples. There, the Wehrmacht would make its stand.

16
On to
Rome!

Naples, the third-largest metropolis in Italy with a population of around 1 million persons, could have been renamed Airborne City, U.S.A. For the sprawling city in the shadow of volcanic Mount Vesuvius was alive with American paratroopers and gliders. While Mark Clark's long-suffering dogfaces, as American foot soldiers called themselves, and armored units hounded the retreating Germans northward, the 82nd Airborne Division was ordered to police Naples.

Matt Ridgway set up headquarters in the Naples police chief's building and divided the city into three sectors, each assigned to a regiment. Mark Clark's Fifth Army command post opened for business in a comfortable complex of buildings, and the 509th Parachute Infantry returned to a spit-and-polish routine in the role of palace guard for the installation.

Naughty Naples, one of Europe's most notorious sin cities, was in chaos. Shots rang out in the night as revenge-minded Neopolitans gunned down "Nazi collaborators," who, for the most part, were actually business competitors, love rivals, or longtime blood-feud enemies. Italian gangsters set up brothels and black-market operations, and hijacked American supply trucks. Murders were frequent. So were robberies. No paratrooper would dare venture alone or without a gun into the sleazy back-alley saloons.

German demolitions and Allied bombings had destroyed much of the dock areas, communications systems, and water and electrical facilities. Time-bombs and booby traps, devious devices that were nearly impossible to locate, were plentiful. On October

7, the main post-office building was blown up by a bomb hidden in the basement, causing in excess of 75 casualties, about half of them 82nd Airborne men. Four days later, a time-bomb exploded in a barracks occupied by men of the 307th Airborne Engineers, killing 18 and wounding 56 of them.

In the meantime, the depleted ranks of the 509th Parachute Infantry Battalion were filled with eager young men fresh from the jump school at Fort Benning, Georgia. And Lt. Col. Bill Yarborough, an old friend of the pioneer parachute outfit, replaced the captured Doyle Yardley as battalion commander. Almost at once, Yarborough became aware of a situation that gnawed at his battle-tested veterans. Several hundred paratroop replacements were sauntering around Naples, and there was no way to distinguish between those who had made combat jumps and those who had not.

So Yarborough, who had designed the paratroop jump boots and wings and had helped develop the jumpsuit, noticed that his veterans had begun wearing tiny stars (one for each combat jump) on their jackets, positioned about one inch above the parachute wings. Yarborough, a bit of a maverick, liked the idea and decided to improve on it—without official sanction. He allowed Five-O-Niners to place the small stars directly upon the coveted wings (a practice that other veteran outfits would adopt).[1]

Paratroopers in Naples were furious over the fact that rear-area service soldiers had confiscated hundreds of prized jump boots and were strolling around Naples in them. Rear-echelon brass had also taken a fancy to the boots.

There was little that enraged combat paratroopers could do when passing a sharply dressed desk-borne officer with general's stars on his shoulders and highly polished jump boots on his feet. But when a rear-area GI was caught wearing the boots, the paratroopers took matters into their own hands—they grabbed the offender and forcibly removed his footware.[2]

In mid-October, Matt Ridgway wrote to the War Department in Washington that the airborne warriors in Naples were "the gentlest of conquerors." Neapolitan saloon owners and American military police would have been astonished over that analysis. With no Germans for the troopers to fight, Naples bars became the new battlegrounds. There the parachutists took on the MPs, merchant seamen, service troops, British soldiers, and members of rival airborne units. Almost nightly, one or more saloons were left in shambles after fierce brawls with fists, bottles, and chairs.

Eventually, the harried military cops became the paratroopers' favorite targets. The men, wearing black armbands emblazoned with the letters MP, often had to take the rap for what the fighting men called the "chicken feathers" regulations conceived by some rear-echelon commander.

Soon, the MPs began making their rounds in pairs; then in trios. Under orders, the MPs executed a new tactic against the pugnacious paratroopers—crack heads and ask questions later.

Meanwhile, there was a war being fought against the Germans in Italy. Through the magic of Ultra, Gen. Harold Alexander had been reading Field Marshal Kesselring's orders almost as rapidly as were Smiling Al's subordinate commanders. It was Kesselring's plan, Alexander knew, to make a fighting withdrawal from Naples to the Volturno River; then to defend that waterline tenaciously in order for German engineers to complete the Gustav Line, a fortified belt stretching across Italy, about halfway between Rome and Naples. Adolf Hitler's scheme was to deny the Allies the glittering propaganda prize of Rome for as long as possible.[3]

As a result of this irrefutable intelligence, Alexander's strategy was to send Mark Clark's Fifth Army up the western coast and Bernard Montgomery's Eighth Army northward along the eastern half of the boot. Both armies were to try to leap the Volturno on the run and pierce the Gustav Line before it could be completed and fully manned. The Allied battle cry was *"On to Rome!"*

Clark's staff drew up a plan that called for one parachute regiment of the 82nd Airborne to drop at Sessa, behind German lines along the Volturno, while at the same time an amphibious force would "skirt left end" and go ashore at Mondragone. Paratroopers and seaborne soldiers were to link up, raise merry hell in the German rear, and cause Tenth Army to pull back from the Volturno. However, the operation was scrubbed when Fifth Army intelligence learned that the proposed drop zone was "crawling with Krauts."[4]

Meanwhile, Fifth Army's two corps had pressed up to the Volturno, so Clark's planners conceived another task for the 82nd Airborne: It would fight as conventional infantry to spearhead Maj. Gen. John P. Lucas' VI Corps assault across the rushing river that flowed to the sea through a deep and treacherous gorge.

Matt Ridgway, Jim Gavin, and Rube Tucker promptly drove

to a hill overlooking the crossing site. On the far side of the river gorge, the Hermann Goering Panzer Division was dug in along a series of hills. A suicide mission, the parachute officers agreed. If undertaken, the 82nd Airborne, a keenly honed outfit whose function was to drop behind enemy lines, would be cut to pieces and destroyed.

Ridgway went to Mark Clark and protested the looming sacrifice of the 82nd Airborne while engaged as assault infantry. Ridgway heard nothing more about the plan, but did learn that Maj. Gen. Lucian K. Truscott's 3rd "Rock of the Marne" Infantry Division, heavily reinforced, had been designated to force the Volturno.[5]

In the meantime, on Sunday, October 10, a brief ceremony was held in front of the Questura, the Naples police station, which was being used as 82nd Airborne headquarters. Matt Ridgway pinned on Jim Gavin the one star of a brigadier general, after Gavin had been appointed assistant division commander. That post had been vacant since Bull Keerans mysteriously vanished the previous July in Sicily after his C-47 was shot down in the friendly fire disaster. At age 36, Jim Gavin became the youngest general in the United States Army. He was replaced as leader of the 505th Regiment by Lt. Col. Herbert Batcheller, the executive officer.[6]

Since his arrival in Naples on what amounted to garrison duty, Gavin had been giving renewed attention to the crucial need for developing improved techniques for aiding C-47 convoys to find tiny drop zones, especially at night. So in mid-October, Lt. Col. Whitfield Jack—a gung ho bundle of energy who was division G-3 (operations officer)—announced that a pathfinder experimental team of 125 officers and men was being formed. The team would return to Comiso, Sicily to conduct tests. Jack had two pages of questions that General Gavin wanted answered.

Capt. Jack Norton, a veteran of the Sicily and Salerno jumps, was put in charge of conducting the experiments. Capt. Frank Boyd of the 376th Parachute Field Artillery Battalion flew with the test group from Naples to Comiso.

The only equipment the pathfinder experimenters had were the 90-pound British-made Rebeccas, a backbreaking load for a paratrooper to jump with along with his personal combat gear. (Later American adaptations would reduce Rebecca's weight to around 30 pounds.) Two 82nd Airborne riggers were brought over from Oran, and they were armed with an ancient sewing machine and a supply of canvas and webbing. Lights for marking glider landing zones at night were made from Delta lanterns.

Cpl. Danny Bost and Cpl. Robert Shirley, the riggers, promptly put their sewing machine to use and created a canvas pack for the Rebecca's transmitter that a pathfinder would wear strapped to his leg, and pouches for the landing lights.[7]

Frank Boyd recalled:

> *The entire group performed beautifully together. We had assigned eight C-47s and eight CG4A gliders, and the pilots entered right into the spirit of things. The glider pilots happily smashed up their gliders. At the end of two weeks, top brass came for a demonstration, including a mass jump by the 456th Parachute Artillery Battalion. We got most of General Gavin's questions answered.*

Meanwhile, elements of the 82nd Airborne had been sucked into the fight along the Volturno. Mark Alexander's 2nd Battalion and Walter Winton's 1st Battalion, both of Batcheller's 505th Parachute Infantry, were attached to the British X Corps. On the night of october 13, Alexander's troops, in the face of murderous German artillery fire, spearheaded an X Corps assault across the Volturno River and carved out a bridgehead on the north bank. Alexander's outfit had suffered heavy casualties, but the next day, remnants of the battalion attacked again and seized crossings over three canals. By the night of October 14, most of Fifth Army's assault divsions had poured over the Volturno. However, the Gustav line was now fortified, and the Germans pulled back to occupy it.[8]

In early November, preparations began for shipping the 82nd Airborne to England to get ready for "Operation Overlord," the massive cross-Channel assault on Nazi-held France. Mark Clark protested bitterly. Faced with an acute manpower shortage, confronted by a tenacious German army and the most hostile terrain in Europe, the Fifth Army leader wanted the 82nd Airborne to bypass the dug-in enemy by conducting amphibious leapfrog operations up the boot.

Clark's request triggered a howl from Matt Ridgway. His division had been created specifically to help lead the Overlord assault, and he didn't want his outfit bogged down in the treacherous mountains of Italy, slugging it out yard by yard as straight infantry and being bled white. Heated discussions erupted in high Allied councils, and a compromise was hammered out. Clark would temporarily keep Tucker's 504th, returning the regiment to Ridgway in plenty of time for Overlord, and also hang onto Bill Yarborough's 509th Parachute Infantry Battalion.

Mark Clark, possibly leery that the controversial decision might be rescinded, promptly committed Rube Tucker's regiment to help plug the yawning gap on the rugged north-south spine of the Appenines between Fifth Army and Montgomery's Eighth Army. Weather conditions were brutal—heavy rains, sleet and oceans of gummy, freezing mud . . . mud . . . and more mud. Trucks, jeeps, and halftracks bogged down. Supply vehicles in the valley had to move at night, for the enemy had zeroed in on roads and other approaches.

There was no continuous front line. Both Germans and Tucker's Five-O-Fours clung to the peaks. Patrols from each side roamed behind the other's "line." The November 5 entry in Dan Danielson's 2nd Battalion Unit Journal stated:

> *Yesterday one of the Bn messengers, Private Dates, on the way to F Company, was captured by 8 Germans. He had the presence of mind to swallow the message, which was of importance, carbon paper and all. The Germans took Dates' jump jacket, inspected his rifle, and let him go. The only explanation for this action was that they must have been stragglers left behind by the retreating army. Private Dates is cold without his jacket . . . but happy.*

On November 18, the 82nd Airborne Division, less the 504th Regimental Combat Team (which included the 376th Parachute Field Artillery Battalion and a company of the 307th Airborne Engineers) sailed for England. Before departing, Matt Ridgway was still fuming over Clark's "stealing" his regiment. He knew from long experience that units loaned on a "temporary" basis often become permanent. So Ridgway penned a letter to old friend Mark Clark: "I know I can count, as you have assured me I may, upon your assistance in securing the prompt return of (my) troops to Division control as soon as the temporary need for their services in your Army shall have ceased . . ."[9]

Clark responded that he would do his best to comply.

Because of the manpower crunch, the Fifth Army leader had to send three other elite outfits onto the bony spine of the peninsula at the Gustav Line to slug it out with the Germans as straight infantry: Bill Yarborough's 509th Parachute Infantry Battalion; Brig. Gen. Robert T. Frederick's American-Canadian 1st Special Service Force, and a contingent of Bill Darby's Rangers.

Lucian Truscott, the tough old cavalryman who commanded the 3rd Infantry Division, which was hammering its head against the Gustav Line north of Venafro, briefed war correspondents:

> *This is by far the strongest defense we've run into so far in Italy. The Krauts have the mountaintops fortified with pillboxes blasted out of rock and reinforced with concrete. Along the lower features, the Germans have very deep entrenchments, wired in, and extensive mine fields. In a great many places they have machine gun nests in concrete bunkers.*[10]

The war in "Sunny Italy," as the peacetime travel posters called it, would be cold, brutal, and bloody.

17
Mountains, Mud, and Mules

The cold, rainy autumn of 1943 in Italy turned into a biting, miserable winter. Entrenched on mountain peaks, a handful of Germans with a few machine guns and mortars could stall an entire attacking battalion for days, exacting a heavy toll in blood, then falling back to the next mountain to repeat the process.

On November 11—Armistice Day—Bill Yarborough's 509th Parachute Infantry, attached to Truscott's 3rd Division, marched out of shell-battered Venafro to assault the frowning, barren elevation to the front, Mount Croce. Like surrounding mountains, the 3,205-foot peak was steep and composed of tricky masses of rotten stone given to sudden landslides of boulders. Seizing Croce was a crucial mission. On its bald crown, German artillery observers were bringing down devastating fire on convoys, troop concentrations, and command posts in the valley around Venafro.

It would be a tortuous, seven-hour cllmb to the top where the German troops were dug in. Burdened by heavy combat gear, perspiring heavily despite the cold weather, the Five-O-Niners advanced in single file over a narrow, twisting goat path, the only avenue to the top. When the troopers' legs and lungs gave out, they halted for five-minute breaks.

By late afternoon, the huffing and wheezing paratroopers had reached a point some 300 yards from the crown. This would be the toughest haul of all, for the climb would be almost perpendicular. Here the path ended; not even mountain goats could go any higher. But the Five-O-Niners struggled onto the crown, and after a brief but fierce shootout in the clouds, chased surviving Germans off the peak.

The Germans reacted violently. The Americans were pounded by artillery and mortar barrages night and day, and enemy mountain troops launched repeated attacks against the summit. Steadily dwindling in numbers, the parachutists clung doggedly to the peak, now pockmarked with craters and stinking with the acrid odor of cordite from exploding shells.

Medics were under enormous pressure. Constantly, like Sisyphus, they clawed their way up Mount Croce from the aid station in Venafro, dodging shells, then made 12-hour treks back down the goat path while lugging wounded comrades on stretchers. A medic quipped grimly: "I've grown goat hooves where my feet used to be."

Boulders along the trail became spattered with dried blood where lone wounded men staggered down the sharp incline or those being carried on stretchers stopped briefly to rest. Discarded bandages saturated with blood and mud were strewn along the rocky trail. Often, a seriously wounded trooper failed to survive the jolting stretcher trek to the bottom.

Forty-eight hours after his battalion had seized Mount Croce's peak, Bill Yarborough and his executive officer, Capt. Edmund Tomasik of New Bedford, Massachusetts, negotiated the haul to the top. Yarborough sought out Doc Alden, who was in a foxhole with his tommy gun, wearing the ever-present maroon beret that he had been given by British Gen. Roy Browning back in North Africa. Alden had shrugged off suggestions by comrades that the Germans would single out his bright headgear as a target.

"I've got bad news for you, Doc," Yarborough said solemnly. "Your medical detachment was displacing forward up the mountain, and they've been wiped out. Stumbled into a minefield— 'Bouncing Bettys' got them."

Alden was thunderstruck and fought back tears. These were his boys. He had handpicked each one. Now, in one fell swoop, many of them were dead or wounded: Pfc. Al Petzold, born in Berlin, killed . . . Sgt. Gordon Hahn, seriously wounded . . . Cpl. Royal Maynard, seriously wounded . . . Osborne, wounded . . . Cyr, wounded. There were others.

Among those seriously wounded was the other 509th surgeon, Dr. Bill Engleman, the free spirit who had accompanied Doc Alden into Axis-held Messina, Sicily, the previous August. As a civilian in his native Midwest, Engleman had been a promising young surgeon. The blast had mangled his right arm, and Army doctors feared that he would never be able to perform surgery on his return to civilian life.[1]

Arctic weather gripped Mount Croce. Pelted by sleet, blanketed by snow, blasted by icy wind gusts of 50 miles per hour or more, Five-O-Niners with heavy colds, deep coughing, pneumonia, and limb-threatening trench foot were coming down the mountain in larger numbers than were those being evacuated due to bullet and shrapnel wounds.[2]

Supplying the isolated men on Mount Croce had become a nightmarish problem. Mules had been lugging ammunition, food, and water up to the peak until the last few hundred yards, where the loads were transferred to the backs of paratroopers for the final straight-up leg to the top. But the rocky surface had become so icy that the beasts of burden—four-legged or two— could not tote the heavy containers.

Many of the men on the peak had been there for 16 interminable days and nights, and now their ammo was nearly depleted and they had been without food for 36 hours. (Snow filled their need for water.)

Capt. Charles C. W. Howland, a 25-year-old parachute officer from Royersford, Pennsylvania, was determined to relieve the mountaintop supply crunch, even if it cost him his life. Down in the valley, he jeeped to a landing strip for artillery spotter planes, borrowed a Piper Cub, and filled it with containers of ammo and food. Howland, a licensed pilot as a civilian, would fly the aircraft himself and seek to drop the supply bundles to his comrades on the peak.

The venture would be fraught with peril. Tricky air currents could grab his light plane and smash it against the mountain. German ack-ack guns in the valley in front of Mount Croce could blast the slow-moving Cub into splinters, and enemy infantry dug in along the slope could riddle the craft with automatic weapons.

Howland flew a circuitous course to the peak, and at a height of only 100 feet, dropped a few containers next to the troopers' foxholes. Then he banked, came back, and unloaded the remainder of his cargo. His frail little craft was promptly dubbed the "509th Parachute Infantry Battalion Air Force."[3]

Meanwhile, on a craggy saddle that connected Mount Croce with an adjoining peak to the east, a company of the 509th Parachute Infantry was dug in. Privates Wesley Coombs and Charles Doyle were told to help a pair of seriously wounded comrades down the steep incline where goats feared to tread in the arctic winter. Lt. Henry F. Rouse had been shot through the neck and was bleeding profusely, and Sgt. Robert Akers' face had been cut up by an exploding shell.

Akers in particular would have a difficult time getting down the steep and icy mountain—the blast had popped out his eyeball and he was cupping it, still attached to its cords, against his cheek.

Twelve hours later, Akers was in a field hospital, where doctors popped his eye back in place. Eventually, he would recover his sight.

Doc Alden was treating the wounded and ill in his Venafro aid station on the night of November 26. Large caliber shells were crashing into the town. The surgeon fished out his dogeared little diary and wrote:

> Here's a tribute to the wounded and dead of the 509th Parachute Infantry Battalion. Not one has complained, cried, or carried on in any way. They are tops! A straight-leg artillery observer got a sniper's bullet in the thigh today. Superficial. Cried and moaned and had to be carried down the mountain. Our guys, much more seriously wounded, walked down without a word.

On December 13, more than 34 days after the 509th Parachute Infantry had become the new landlords of Mount Croce, the men on the peak were relieved by an infantry regiment. In single file, feet numb from the bitter cold, many running high temperatures, some wearing bloody bandages, the frozen zombies staggered back down the goat path. All the time on the mountaintop, the troopers had never washed their hands or shaved or taken off their mud-caked boots.

Two days earlier, not far from embattled Mount Croce, Rube Tucker's 504th Parachute Combat Team had been clawing and scratching their way up ice-coated, 3,950-foot Mount Sammucro. Loaded with rifles, tommy guns, BARs (Browning automatic rifles), grenades, bazookas, mortars, shells, machine guns, and extra ammunition, the Five-O-Fours slipped on the narrow, crooked goat paths, swore muffled curses, got up, struggled onward, fell again. During most of the arduous ascent, Tucker's men were regulary sent sprawling face down by the heaviest shellings they had endured in Italy to date.

It was even harder going for Wilbur Griffith's 376th Parachute Field Artillery Battalion. Griffith's cannoneers, in tandem with a few platoons of mules, had to lug their 12-pack howitzers and shells far up Mount Sammucro in order to provide fire support for the infantry.

Ironically, the 75-millimeter pack howitzers had first been conceived for mountain fighting, in which each weapon would be broken down into nine major components and lugged by mules, one piece to a mule. An assembled howitzer weighed some 1,300 pounds, and had wooden or hard rubber wheels, permitting it to be rolled into new firing positions.

Back in the 1940–41 pioneer era of American airborne experimentation, the bright young officers creating doctrine and equipment could foresee no need for mules to haul howitzers, so the long-eared beasts vanished from the airborne artillery picture. Each of the nine pieces of a howitzer would be parachuted to battle in a separate bundle attached to the bottom of C-47s. Now, in the rugged Appenines of central Italy, the C-47s had vanished and the mules were back in the artillery business.

A. E. "Ernie" Milloy, who had been a captain and commander of the 504th Parachute Infantry's Company C, recalled those wretched days in frozen Italy:

The 1st Battalion went into position along the crest of Hill 1205 [Mount Sammucro]. My C Company was sent out about 1,000 yards to establish an outpost line. The position may have looked good on a higher headquarters situation map, but on the ground, it was nearly untenable.

The ground was barren and too rocky to dig in, and we were literally under the gun muzzles of the Germans. Any movement on our part immediately drew heavy fire. Suffice it to say, living conditions were miserable. We were sent up there for "about a week" but two weeks later, we were still there.

On a bitterly cold Christmas morning, I heard rocks rolling down the hill and the unmistakable sounds of someone walking along the goat path which meandered by the company CP—a small natural cave in the hillside. In loud and extremely uncomplimentary language, I inquired as to "who in hell" was stumbling around so noisily in the daylight.

"It's only your battalion commander coming to wish you fellows a merry Christmas," was the reply. As Warren Williams came abreast of us, he bent over, ostensibly to tie his boot lace, and rolled a bottle of Old Granddad into the cave entrance. "Merry Christmas and have a bit of holiday cheer," Warren said as he trod on down the path, as though he were on a Sunday outing in the park.[4]

In their ice-lined slit trenches on Mount Sammucro, troopers of the 504th Combat Team spent the birthday of the Prince of Peace ducking artillery and mortar shells and nibbling on frozen K rations. Two days later, Tucker's troopers were relieved. The infantry companies had been reduced to half-strength, and Griffith's "mule-borne" cannoneers and C Company of the 307th Engineers had also suffered their shares of dead, wounded, and sick.

Heavily bombed Pignatoro, a bleak town in the heart of the Volturno River valley, was the rest center for the combat team. Shower baths were available, so was clean clothing; movies were being shown in a ramshackle theater with part of the roof missing, and Hollywood tough guy Humphrey Bogart and his troupe put on a show from the bed of a six-by-six GI truck.

Rumor mills were grinding furiously. One report held that the Five-O-Fours would sail soon to rejoin the 82nd Airborne in England. Another rumor had the unit going to the States to train new paratroopers. No one mentioned or had even heard of an old pirates' lair up the Tyrrhenian coast named Anzio.

18
Devil's
Cauldron

Anzio (population 7,493) had sat for hundreds of years quietly on the Tyrrhenian seacoast, 33 miles south of Rome. Before the war, the charming little port had been a pleasant resort to which Romans would drive on holidays to escape the hustle and bustle of the teeming capital. Anzio was built on a low promontory, with smooth, sandy beaches on each side. Holiday villas snuggled in the pine woods behind the beaches.

Barren flatlands stretch for miles along the Anzio coast, but off in the distance is a line of low hills from which a sightseer can gain a breathtaking view of a wide sweep of the shoreline and the azure beauty of the blue Tyrrhenian Sea. Farther inland, only 10 miles south of Rome, are the Alban Hills, the dominating terrain feature.

On Christmas Day 1943, the hardworking, deeply devout citizens of Anzio were attending Mass, unaware that at that very moment in Tunis, North Africa, Allied leaders were approving a military operation that would bring a holocaust to the once-peaceful Italian resort.

In the huge drawing room of a stately mansion in Tunis, 69-year-old Prime Minister Winston Churchill, in his self-appointed role as super supreme commander in the Mediterranean, was regaling Dwight Eisenhower and top land, sea, and air commanders with the military wonders that would accrue if the Allies adopted his pet scheme to break the bloody logjam at the Gustav Line and capture Rome on the cheap.

The "Prime," as he was called by American brass, declared that it would be folly to invade northern France (Operation

Overlord) in spring 1944 with Rome still in German hands. Then he sprung the bold plan he had concocted. A force of at least two divisions would land at Anzio, 58 miles behind German lines. Jabbing his long, black cigar for emphasis, Churchill declared that Kesselring would panic and hastily pull back from the Gustav Line, leaving the door to Rome wide open.

"We will be hurling a raging wildcat onto the beaches to rip the bowels out of the Boches!" the Prime trumpeted.[1] Eisenhower, for one, was not buying. Except for a couple of British generals who remained silent, nearly everyone expressed concerns over the "left hook" gamble.

As usual, the forceful Churchill carried the day. Anzio would be his "baby." He signaled President Roosevelt: "Unanimous agreement reached on 'Shingle' (code name for Anzio operation) and everyone here is in good heart."

Picked to lead the audacious foray to the German rear was mild-mannered, white-haired Gen. John Lucas, who had performed capably at Salerno. Known to his troops as "Foxy Grandpa," Lucas was seldom found without his corncob pipe.

Lucas' VI Corps would go ashore with an initial force of 40,000 men—about half the size of Mark Clark's assault unit at Salerno. Once again, the manpower crunch in the Mediterranean would dictate the employment of three elite formations, this time functioning as amphibious assault troops: Yarborough's 509th Parachute Infantry, Darby's three Ranger battalions, and Tucker's 504th Parachute Infantry.

As hasty planning progressed, Foxy Grandpa began to fret, scribbling in his diary: "They plan to put me ashore with inadequate forces and could get me in a serious jam. Then, who will take the blame?"[2]

Operation Shingle called for Tucker's 504th Parachute Regimental Combat Team to jump on the southern outskirts of Rome, but that mission was quickly scuttled as being suicidal. On January 12, Tucker was handed another plan, code-named "Sun Assault." Paced by three planeloads of pathfinders, Tucker's combat team would lift off from airfields near Naples in 178 C-47s of Hal Clark's 52nd Troop Carrier Wing and bail out over two drop zones about eight miles north of Anzio town. Once there, the All-Americans would block the road and rail line that skirted the Alban Hills and ran between Rome and Anzio.

D-Day for Operation Shingle had been set for January 22, 1944. On January 19, nine new pathfinder planes, equipped with the latest Rebeccas, arrived in Naples. However, the aircraft would not be used in Shingle, for early on the morning of January 20, General Clark canceled Sun Assault. Instead, the 504th combat team would land at Anzio by sea. Rube Tucker was far from happy over the turn of events. "Hell, we're paratroopers, not sailors!" he snorted.

Reasons for the cancellation of Sun Assault would remain a mystery. It was rumored that Mark Clark had grown concerned that the lightly armed paratroopers would be "cut to pieces" by German tanks. Reports had it that Clark had learned that Sun Assault's security had been pierced, and that a large force of Germans would be on the drop zones to riddle Tucker's parachutists as they were descending.[3]

Neither Harold Alexander, Mark Clark, nor the planners could foresee that when the landing struck, there would be only about 1,000 German troops anywhere near Anzio.

The Shingle landings would take place at 2:00 A.M. during darkness. The British 1st Division and a commando force would land on Peter Beach, north of Anzio. Truscott's 3rd Infantry Division would storm ashore on X-Ray Beach, four miles below Anzio, and the 509th Parachute Infantry Battalion and Bill Darby's Rangers would land directly in Anzio town. After daybreak, Tucker's Five-O-Fours, 376th Parachute Artillery, and a company of the 307th Airborne Engineers would come in by sea.

In perfect weather on January 21, the 375 vessels in the Shingle fleet set sail from the Bay of Naples under a cloud of barrage balloons. Hoping to deceive German spies and recon planes, the armada plowed southward toward Africa until nightfall; then it reversed its course and steamed toward Anzio.

On HMS *Winchester Castle*, the presence of pipe-smoking Capt. Harry Stone was conceived by men of the 509th Parachute Infantry to be a bad omen. Stone was a straight-leg who had been brought along as assistant surgeon of the 509th. "If we need a second doctor, then the brass must think we're going to run into a meat-grinder at Anzio!" a Five-O-Niner declared, neatly summing up the view of comrades.

A prayer service was held on the *Winchester Castle* and was well attended. Before going into battle, many Five-O-Niners, like most other soldiers, were stricken with acute attacks of religious ferver. Leaving for the prayer service, Pfc. Leon F. Mimms, a good old Georgia boy and a machine gunner in the 509th, noticed that a teenaged comrade was not going to attend and asked why.

"Aw, I don't go for all that religion stuff," was the reply.

"Maybe not," Mimms observed in his southern drawl. "But if you and I are still alive 10 days from now, and we probably won't be, you'll come to me and tell me you've been praying."

"Aw, like hell I will. Someone else can do the prayin'."

Leon Mimms would prove to be wrong. The boy would not come to him in 10 days after the landing and admit that he had been praying—it would be only three days.

Bill Yarborough's men on the British transport had it a little more comfortable than did Rube Tucker's parachutists, who were crammed into 13 landing craft for the trek to Anzio.

Now, shortly before midnight, 10 to 12 miles off the coastline at Anzio, the ghostly hulks of scores of Allied ships were anchored and rolling gently in the calm waters of the Tyrrhenian. Presently, loudspeakers called out, "Away all boats!" and the first wave headed for the dark, eerily silent shore. Hoping to gain total surprise, there was no thunderous naval bombardment, and the assault troops hit the beach without a shot being fired at them.

In Anzio town, Bill Darby's 1st and 4th Ranger Battalions landed abreast and began to fan out in and around the resort city. The only "action" was when four German officers, returning from a gala night in Rome and roaring drunk, drove their Volkswagen into the open doors of a landing craft that was unloading supplies on the beach, thinking that they were heading into a garage. Gleeful Rangers promptly collared the four befuddled Germans who, no doubt, wondered what all these Americans were doing 60 miles behind the Italian front.

At Truscott's X-Ray Beach, the only contact with the enemy was when 190 German service soldiers were captured en masse— caught in bed in their underwear.

Immediately after landing Darby's two battalions, the assault craft returned to the anchorage and picked up the 509th Parachute Infantry Battalion and the Ranger 3rd Battalion, putting them ashore in Anzio town. The paratroopers began rapidly marching southward along the tree-lined coastal road, bound for their objective of Nettuno, a mile away.

In the meantime, Ranger Lt. Louis Martin was leading a column of men through the black streets of Anzio. Suddenly, a heavy burst of small-arms fire erupted a considerable distance to the south where, Martin knew, the 509th Parachute Infantry was to seize Nettuno.

"What in the hell is that firing all about, Lieutenant?" a Ranger called out in a stage whisper. "Might mean trouble," the bespectacled Martin replied softly. "But then again, those hopheads in the 509th parachutes would shoot up a storm in any situation. Hell, anyone who would join hands and jump out of airplanes. . . ."

Offshore, Foxy Grandpa Lucas, who had been expecting a bloodbath, could hardly believe his good fortune. Elated, he fired off a message to Mark Clark in Naples: "Paris–Bordeaux–Turin–Tangiers—Bari–Albany," which were code words meaning "weather fine, sea calm, little wind, force's presence not discovered, landings in progress, no resistance on shore yet."

Shortly after 3:00 A.M.—one hour after the Allied soldiers had hit Anzio beach—Field Marshal Albrecht Kesselring was awakened at his headquarters at Monte Soratte near Rome. Quickly poring over reports that were arriving from the Tyrrhenian coast, the unflappable Smiling Al remarked calmly to a staff officer, Maj. Wolfgang Hageman, "Better pack your bags, Wolfgang. We have nothing between Anzio and Rome."[4]

By 5:00 A.M., Kesselring was certain that Anzio was an all-out assault and not a decoy raid to mask a major landing elsewhere. So he flashed the signal: *Code Richard.* That launched the 4th Parachute Division, near Rome, and the Hermann Goering Panzer Division, in reserve at the Gustav Line, and other units in southern Italy hurtling toward Anzio. Within hours, battle-tested divisions from France and the Balkans were in movement toward the Allied beachhead.

As the sun came up over the bleak Appenines, Rube Tucker was pacing about an LCI (Land Craft, Infantry) like a tiger in a cage. They were holding a war on shore, and he was idling on a navy vessel out to sea. Finally, at about 10:00 A.M., the landing craft carrying his parachute combat team headed for the beach. All was quiet, and it looked like a good deal. But the veteran Five-O-Fours knew that good deals were often what got men killed and maimed, so they felt nervous.

About 300 yards offshore, the paratroopers were waiting to unload and wade through the ice-cold water. Suddenly, from out of the sun, a few Luftwaffe dive bombers screamed down and unloaded their cargoes. Bombs barely missed several landing craft, sending up towering columns of oily water which fell back onto the vessels and left some of the Five-O-Fours coated with oil.

One bomb scored a direct hit on an LCI carrying C Company of the 3rd Battalion, and an entire platoon was wiped out, leaving the craft a burning, twisted wreckage. However, unloading continued, and Tucker's troopers, cold, wet, mad, miserable, disgusted, and oil-coated, marched two miles inland and bivouacked in the Padiglione Woods.

Rube Tucker's Five-O-Fours scramble ashore at Anzio from dive-bombed and burning landing craft. (*U. S. Army*)

For two days, Anzio was as peaceful as an Iowa cornfield. Lucas was content to dig in, build up his supplies, and await the arrival of reinforcements before jumping off toward Rome in a full-blooded offensive. His lines remained fairly static, seven to eight miles deep at points and stretching in a semicircle around Anzio town, from the Mussolini Canal on the south to the Moletta River on the north.

In far-off London, Winston Churchill was enraged over the failure of Lucas to exploit the surprise stroke behind German lines. "I thought we were throwing a wildcat onto the beach," he rasped to confidants. "Instead, we have a stranded whale."[5]

In the meantime, the 504th Parachute Infantry, along with Robert Frederick's American-Canadian First Special Service Force, had been given the job of protecting the bridgehead's right flank, and the troopers went underground along the *Canale Mussolini.* None of the Five-O-Fours had any way of knowing that they would fight their hardest battle on the Anzio beachhead.

The canal's channel was about 20 feet wide, but the banks were some 30 feet high and at least 100 yards apart. It was an ideal barrier against tank and infantry assaults, and Tucker's boys would come to both hate and love it.

Cpl. Fred J. Baldino. *(Author's collection)*

Fred J. Baldino, who had been a 20-year-old corporal in Company A, recalled those early days:

> *Things were relatively quiet at first along the canal, and we thought for sure that we'd be in Rome within a week, so we dug only shallow slit trenches. None of us could know that this mud would be our "home" for more than three grueling months, a time that none of us who were there will ever forget.*

On D-Day plus 3, the Anzio commanders wanted to know what the Germans were up to, so they sent two battalions of the 504th

Parachute Infantry across the Mussolini Canal that night. The last trooper had hardly cleared the murky stream when the battalions were raked by murderous fire from several German flak wagons mounted with 20-millimeter automatic guns.

Caught in the open, the parachutists hit the deck. They felt naked and helpless. Bullets from the multibarreled wagons hissed and sang just over their heads. Here and there a cry told that a projectile had torn into human flesh. Lt. Col. Warren Williams, the 1st Battalion leader, leaped to his feet and, under a hail of fire, raced to a Sherman tank that had crossed the canal with the troopers. Beating on the turret, Williams shouted to the tankers, "Put a few rounds on that bastard [the flak wagon]!" Moments later, the parachutists, peeking out from under helmet rims, felt like cheering; the Sherman had scored a bull's-eye, and the flak wagon disintegrated in a fiery orange ball.

In the morning, the Anzio brass got the alarming word that the Germans had built up their strength with astonishing speed.

German artillery fire began pounding American and British positions with ever increasing intensity. The enemy had even moved in an enormous 280-millimeter railroad gun, which was later called the Anzio Express because its shell sounded like a train rushing through a tunnel when it approached the bridgehead.[6]

Fred Baldino recalled:

> Our foxholes along the Mussolini Canal got deeper and deeper. We were like moles. Because we had to stay down in our holes constantly, the wax boxes that the K rations came in were very useful. They served us urinals, and if you tore them up into small strips and put a match to it, it made just enough heat to warm up a canteen cup of water to be used for coffee or bullion.

On the morning of January 30, there were 70,000 Allied troops, in excess of 500 guns, and 238 tanks ashore. At his damp, dark and dingy command post in an underground wine cellar in Nettuno, General Lucas decided to launch a major attack to enlarge the bridgehead. When American and British forces jumped off at 1:00 A.M., they ran into heavy fire. Caught in the open by swarms of panzers and artillery bombardments, the Allies suffered heavy casualties.

Bill Darby's Ranger force, which was spearheading a 3rd Infantry Division drive to seize the key road junction of Cisterna, was ambushed. Within 12 hours, two of Darby's battalions were wiped out, and the third was badly mauled. Lucas called off the attack and braced for a German counterstroke.

Meanwhile, Kesselring had rushed in Col. Gen. Eberhard von Mackensen, a shrewd and resolute Prussian aristocrat, to take charge at Anzio. Smiling Al's instructions had been terse: Throw the Allies back into the Tyrrhenian Sea.

Based on intercepted wireless messages, Lucas knew that von Mackensen would strike down the Albano-Anzio road into the British 1st Division, so he ordered Lt. Col. Leslie Freeman's 3rd Battalion of the 504th Parachute Infantry to move from the Mussolini Canal to the beachhead's left flank and then to attach to the British 1st Division.

On reporting to Col. Andrew Scott, commander of the Irish Guards regiment, Freeman charmed his new battlefield comrades with his opening words: "Those goddamned Krauts, I sure hate their guts!"

Les Freeman, a tall, first-rate fighting man from Virginia with a slow drawl and a winning manner, and his troopers the Irish Guards, took to the word "Kraut." Never again would they describe the hated foe as "Heinies," "Boches," or "Jerries" as they had through two world wars—it would be "Krauts" from then on.

Freeman's parachutists were put into a backup position across the Albano-Anzio road in front of the village of Carroceto. There were wide gaps in the British lines, so the Five-O-Fours might be called on to attack or defend at any point.

It was cold and wet on the night of February 3 when von Mackensen struck. At 11:00 P.M., the barren flatlands erupted with the roar of scores of German guns. The heaviest shelling yet encountered in the war poured into Freeman's troopers and the Irish Guards as they lay huddled miserably in water-filled slit trenches.

Out of the darkness German grenadiers, shouting *Seig Heil! Gott mit Uns!* (All hail! God is with us!), charged forward. A hectic hand-to-hand fight broke out. Streams of tracers zipped through the black night. Orange fireballs flashed where grenades exploded. Artillery and mortars on both sides pounded the same area, killing friend and foe indiscriminately. Screams pierced the din. Throughout the night, the Irish Guards and Freeman's American paratroopers slugged it out with the German 65th Division.

Icy rain beat down in sheets and the wind howled. At dawn, panzers were rushed forward, and they began raking the Irish Guards and Les Freeman's troopers at point-blank range. During the onslaught, the able-bodied Americans pulled back several hundred yards to the village of Aprilia. German artillery—including the Anzio Express—now pounded Aprilia, and Luftwaffe dive bombers unloaded on Freeman's paratroopers. Then swarms of *Feldgrau,* their ankle-length greatcoats flapping at their heels, charged into the village and a bitter fight erupted with knives, bayonets, rifles, and grenades before the Germans were finally driven out.

Freeman's companies were reduced to 20 to 30 men each, so the battalion remnant fell back a short distance to a railroad overpass. For nearly a week, the beleaguered paratroopers beat off panzer and grenadier assaults, stood their ground, and eventually forced the Germans to abandon all-out efforts to smash through the overpass and on to the sea.

Meanwhile, Bill Yarborough's 509th Parachute Infantry Battalion was spread thinly in an exposed position between the 36th and 45th Infantry Divisions. For a week, Lt. Kenneth Shaker's platoon had been pelted by sleet and pounded night and day by the heaviest shelling Shaker had been under during the war. One by one, the 27-year-old Californian's men were being killed and wounded.

Ken Shaker, who had fought as a teenaged mercenary in the Spanish Civil War in the late 1930s, recalled those dreadful days:

> *Another day or two in that barren, exposed position and every last one of our platoon would be killed. So at twilight, I sent a runner back to the company CP to find out when we would be relieved. It was dark when the runner returned. "Well, what did Captain Winsko say?" I asked. "Nothing," he replied. "Then what did the XO [executive officer] say?" I said. "Nothing," he responded. I asked, "You mean neither one of them said anything?" "They couldn't, Lieutenant," the messenger responded. "They were both killed in the same foxhole—a shell came right in after them."*

Anzio beachhead had turned into a slaughterhouse. After one month of violent conflict, each adversary had lost about 20,000 men, or 20 percent of the combined 200,000 soldiers engaged in the death struggle. The brutalities and rigors of Anzio would forever be seared in each survivor's brain as if from a blowtorch.

19
Death
Struggle

Paratroopers on Anzio knew their ultimate destiny in the war and accepted it. They had been set aside to die if need be. And death was a bitter pill to swallow, especially for youths in their teens and twenties. Those who had seen heavy fighting in North Africa, Sicily, Salerno or in the Appenines knew that they were fugitives from the law of averages, that, sooner or later, their battlefield number would be called—although perhaps they would be the lucky ones who would survive honorably through serious wounds or capture.

Many of these parachutists had grown up not knowing violence any more severe than junior high school playground shoving matches. Now, they had become trained killers. And existing under the constant threat of violent death and hoping to stay alive and sane, they had turned brutal. Mind-numbing fear, and the rage that goes with it, were the front-line emotions that those at home would never be able to comprehend.

After a firefight or two, soldiers were not the same. They changed. Scared, they fell into fitful sleep at night and they awakened pierced by one gnawing question: "Will I be alive tonight?" Their goal was to survive another day, another hour, another minute. They stopped being nice kids and became brutal because that was the only way they could continue breathing. They killed anything that threatened them, looked down at the corpses and thought: "We're alive, and you're nothing!"

Patrolling out in front of the lines at Anzio was a vital and extremely hazardous function because commanders on either side had to know if the other side was building up for an attack.

In mid-February, Cpl. Paul B. Huff of Company A, 509th Parachute Infantry Battalion, volunteered to lead a patrol into no-man's land.

As a youth growing up in Cleveland, Tennessee, Huff had been an admirer of Sgt. Alvin C. York, the famed World War I hero who lived only a short distance from Huff, at Pell Mell. Young Huff had always hoped that, if the occasion arose, he would conduct himself on the battlefield in the same manner as did his fellow Tennessee mountaineer in the previous war. Unbeknownst to the parachute corporal, that time was at hand.

At 7:30 A.M., Paul Huff and his six-man patrol slipped into no-man's land and advanced up a draw. Suddenly, the troopers were raked by machine-gun fire and flopped down in the defile. Here was almost the same situation that had confronted Sergeant York 26 years earlier. Huff told his men to remain under cover while he dealt with the chattering machine gun.[1]

Lt. John R. Martin. (*Author's collection*)   Cpl. Paul B. Huff. (*Lou Varrone*)

Huff had wriggled forward for about 100 yards when two other machine guns and a 20-millimeter flak gun began pouring fusillades toward him. Then Huff discovered that he was in the middle of a minefield, but he continued to slither ahead as bullets whipped past his head and thudded into the ground around him. Grasping his tommy gun tightly, Huff nearly reached the spitting German weapon. Then he leaped up, charged, poked the tommy gun's muzzle into the machine-gun nest and riddled the five-man crew.

Huff and his patrol reported back to their company commander and gave detailed information on Germans to the front. A larger patrol, led by Sgt. Kelly C. Bath, was formed, and at 1:00 P.M., it shoved off toward enemy lines, about 500 yards away. Paul Huff went along.

Nearing the enemy positions pinpointed by Huff's earlier patrol, Sergeant Bath and his troopers got into a fierce firefight with about 125 Germans, and after an hour's shootout, drove the *Feldgrau* force away. Bath, Huff, and the others captured 21 grenadiers, and 21 Germans lay sprawled in death. Three Americans had been killed.[2]

Along the Mussolini Canal, Rube Tucker was sending out Five-O-Four patrols nearly every night. Cpl. Fred Baldino went along on one 12-man probe. While the patrol was stalking slowly and cautiously through the hushed blackness, a new replacement whispered, "We must be in a German cemetery, there are a lot of crosses on the ground." "Those aren't crosses, you stupid bastard," Baldino whispered back. "Each one has lettering saying '*Achtung, Mienen.*'" Finally, the new trooper caught on: The patrol had stumbled into a German minefield.

At night, no-man's-land on Anzio was an eerie montage of ghostly shadows, silhouetted human figures, flares, muffled noises, occasional streams of tracers—and sudden death. Fred Baldino was on another night patrol when, on the way home, the troopers were caught in a heavy American artillery barrage. Being pounded by "friendly" shells was an especially unnerving experience.

Perhaps miraculously, none of the troopers was killed or wounded, but a few had holes in their jump suits. While returning, the Five-O-Fours plopped into a ditch beside the road to wait for two lagging troopers to catch up.

Fred Baldino remembered:

> *About nine of us laid there, panting, scared, tired, and shook-up. It was a black night. Suddenly, we heard footsteps coming down the road. Probably our two trailing comrades. But then we could make out the shape of a German helmet and its dark figure carrying a*

machine pistol. It turned out that he was a noncom, and probably checking on his outposts.

We planned to let him walk on past, for we'd had enough trouble for one night. But just as the Kraut got even with us in the ditch, only about 10 feet from us, one of our troopers got excited and took the safety off his rifle with a loud snap. The Kraut looked right down on us and called out, "Vas ist?"

With that, all nine of us blasted the poor bastard. I'm glad I didn't have to look at his body the next day.

During this period, a tall, thin, curly-haired member of the 504th Parachute Infantry, Pvt. Ted Bachenheimer, became a legend on the beachhead. He was 20 years of age, spoke flawless German, had the facial features of a choir boy, and aspired to be an opera singer. Soft-spoken, friendly, held in awe by his comrades, Bachenheimer was something of a mystery man in the regiment. It was only known that when Ted was about 10 years old, his parents had fled their native Germany to escape Nazi oppression, eventually settling in California.

Bachenheimer made no outward display of his hatred for Nazi Germany, but the few troopers close to the thin youngster knew that he was pledged to conducting a one-man war against Hitler. His specialty was solo raids into and behind German lines—before long his foes at Anzio knew Bachenheimer by name. He had become an irritating—and often deadly—menace.

Bachenheimer's commander, Lt. Col. Warren Williams, a resolute fighting man himself, remembered the "Lone Raider of Anzio":

Watching Ted apply soot and dirt to his face before departing for a trek behind German lines one night, I asked, "Tell the truth, Ted, aren't you sort of scared of these missions?" He pondered that question, then replied softly, "Well, I'm a little nervous when I leave friendly lines, and have to piss a few times, out in no-man's-land. But after that, I'm not bothered."

One night, Bachenheimer was persuaded to take along three comrades on a particularly perilous mission. Out between the lines, a flare shot into the sky and the four-man patrol was raked with machine-gun fire. Three of the troopers, reasoning that their task was to locate German positions, headed back toward friendly lines. Bachenheimer continued onward.

Minutes later, automatic weapons chattered angrily in the direction that Bachenheimer had taken. Then silence. Ted's comrades speculated that the "Lone Raider" had been killed. A half hour after the three troopers returned, an outpost telephoned the Five-O-Four lines: "Bachenheimer just passed here on the way back. He's got a Kraut sergeant in tow."

When Bachenheimer and his captive reached the light of battalion headquarters, the German sergeant was mortified to see that he had been taken prisoner by, as he termed it, "a kid 10 years younger than me." The *Feldgrau* insisted on telling Five-O-Four intelligence officers how it had happened. He said that his men had become nervous because American paratroopers had been infiltrating German lines almost nightly, and that one of his outposts had opened fire at a "movement." The sergeant went forward to investigate and heard a voice call out in German: "Here are the Amis [Americans]. We've got them!" So when he walked toward the voice, an American (Bachenheimer) with a pistol pointed at the German's stomach, instructed him to "come with me or you're dead!"

On another dark night, Ted Bachenheimer was prowling around German lines when he came upon an enemy soldier in a slit trench. The paratrooper sat down nearby and the two engaged in casual conversation; men on outpost duty get lonely. Ted told the German that he was from an adjacent Wehrmacht unit. Finally, tiring of his cat-and-mouse game, the American shoved a pistol in the startled *Feldgrau*'s stomach and ordered him to come along quietly.

A German who had been laying quietly overheard the conversation, raised up and shot Bachenheimer through the left hand. The paratrooper killed both Germans; then returned to his own lines, disappointed that his prisoner-for-the-night had eluded him via a sudden case of lead poisoning.

On the way back, Bachenheimer stuffed dirt into his hand wound to stem the bleeding. Reaching 1st Battalion headquarters, the "Long Raider" was told by Warren Williams that he would be evacuated to Naples, but the soft-spoken youth protested so vigorously that the battalion commander reluctantly changed his mind.[3]

The war along the *Canale Mussolini* was brutal and bizarre. A few miles away was Colli Lazuali, a steep mountain with an extinct crater on the summit. From it, the Germans could observe nearly every movement the Five-O-Fours made. So the troopers along the canal had to suffer through seemingly endless days and nights in water-logged, frigid, cramped holes while buffeted by thick sheets of rain and howling winds.

Each day, paratroopers along the canal died in an unspectacular manner: by artillery and mortar shells while huddled miserably in holes. Feet and legs were blown off when men on night patrols stepped on *Schu* mines.[4] In a major probe of enemy lines, 50 troopers of the 1st Battalion were cut off, surrounded by panzers and had to surrender. A huge shell made a direct hit on a shed where 14 replacements sought protection from the cold and rain, blowing bits and pieces of bodies to the four winds.

A few weeks after the Anzio landings, Rube Tucker and his staff were looking at a translation of an entry in a diary taken from a dead German officer:

> *American parachutists—devils in baggy pants—are less than 100 meters from my outpost. I can't sleep at night: they pop up from nowhere and we never know when or how they will strike next. Seems like the black-hearted devils are everywhere.*[5]

Meanwhile, in the early morning blackness of February 29, Lt. John Martin's Company B of the 509th Parachute Infantry was spread thinly along a barren knoll between the 3rd and 45th Infantry Divisions. Behind Martin's outfit was another company of the parachute battalion in a second line of defense, and a third company was in reserve.

Martin's exposed hill protruded like a sore thumb out from the main line of resistance, and troopers were forced to lie in icy water in shallow slit trenches, to urinate in K-ration boxes, and to pitch out the contents after dark. None dared to sit upright even briefly for fear of attracting a heavy artillery barrage. At night the Germans watched by flare light, and shells shrieked in steadily. The psychological impact of being incessantly under the gaze of Germans in the hills was gut-wrenching, knowing that one brief, careless moment might be fatal.

At about 3:30 A.M., John Martin received a telephone call at his slit trench command post from Bill Yarborough. "John, corps has intercepted a Kraut message," the 509th Battalion commander said. "They're going to hit your hill at oh-five-thirty [5:30 A.M.]."

Martin fully understood the significance of the call. For five weeks, the Germans had been launching violent attacks in an

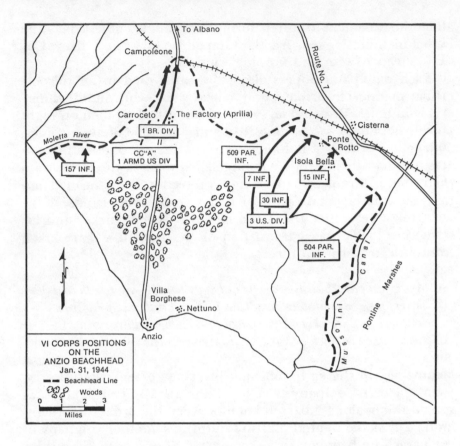

effort to hurl the invaders back into the sea. Steadily, the Americans and British had been pushed back to what the Allied high command called "the final beachhead line." Orders came down: "Don't give up another inch of ground. Hold at all costs." Martin knew that his company's job was to stand firm, to die if need be.

"Good luck, John," Yarborough said as he rang off.

It was against this thin line of American paratroopers that General von Mackensen would make an all-out effort to break through to the sea. Just before 5:30 A.M., a tremendous artillery barrage caused the knoll to shake and quiver as though an earthquake were in progress. Thick clouds of black smoke covered the hill, and the pungent odor of cordite fumes filled nostrils. The Five-O-Niners clung to the bottom of their holes, mouths dry, hearts pounding, minds gripped by fear. Many prayed, some out loud. Above the enormous din came pitiful screams of mutilated men.

Suddenly, the thunderous bombardment lifted. The moaning and cries of seriously wounded troopers were drowned out by the roar of panzers rumbling toward John Martin's company. Behind the thick-plated monsters were hundreds of grenadiers. From his foxhole command post, Martin put in an urgent radio call for artillery fire to his front. But German voices were on his frequency, so his desperate appeal never got through.

Onward came the gray-green wave. When less than 100 yards from the paratroopers, the *Feldgrau* broke into a trot, shouting oaths and battle cries, and firing rifles and Schmeisser machine pistols into Martin's men. The parachutists fired back, and dead Germans began to pile up at the mouths of their machine guns.

Outnumbered four to one, the Five-O-Niners ran out of ammunition; then hurled their weapons at Germans leaping toward their foxholes. A savage hand-to-hand fight erupted. Fists flailed, and bodies thrashed about. Grenades exploded. There were grunts as trench knives ripped into flesh. Curses, shots, and screams rang out. Through sheer weight of numbers and concentrated firepower, the grenadiers swept on past the knoll.

Minutes later, a second wave of Germans, shouting curses in broken English, charged up the gentle slope with machine-pistols burping and pounced on the few remaining paratroopers. Again hand-to-hand combat ensued. The second wave continued onward.

Now elements of the 1028th Panzer Grenadier Regiment, which had smashed through John Martin's company, crossed open fields and were on their way to Nettuno and Anzio town. But the German force bumped into 96 of Lt. Dan DeLeo's Company A paratroopers, who were lying in waterlogged slit trenches alnog a road some 600 yards to the rear of John Martin's hotly contested knoll.

Dan DeLeo recalled that episode:

> *I peeked out from my hole and was astonished by what I saw. The battalion or so of Germans were coming at us in close formation as if they were on parade back in Berlin. Apparently, they thought there was nothing out in front of them.*

And paratrooper Nick DeGaeta remembered what happened then:

> *We quickly rolled up a German antiaircraft gun, a high velocity baby that we had captured and were keeping for just such a situation. We had plenty of ammo for it. Our first shell plowed into the closely packed German ranks and cut them down like a bowling ball spilling ten-pins.*

Raked by the antiaircraft gun and automatic weapons, pounded by American artillery fire, the German force wavered, halted, then pulled back over the little knoll where Martin's parachutists had made their stand—literally to the last man. The *Feldgrau* took the seriously wounded John Martin with them to their own lines.[6]

Shortly afterward, Capt. Doc Alden, along with several medics, rushed out of the aid station and to the site of that day's bloody disaster on the knoll. Many dead paratroopers were strewn about. Some had heads blown off. Others had been bayonetted in their holes. A shell fragment had sliced off the face of a trooper. One Five-O-Niner lay dead with stumps for legs. Two trails of blood, one from each leg stump, indicated that he had tried to carry on the fight. A few badly wounded survivors, their faces ashen, were gasping for breath; they had been shot through the lungs.

Late that night at his aid station, after administering to wounded Five-O-Niners, an exhausted Doc Alden scrawled in his pocket diary:

> *It has been the saddest day ever for me. A gruesome day. We brought out bits and pieces of bodies all afternoon and evening. Our men were greatly outnumbered, pinned down by artillery, assaulted by infantry, then tanks. But our guys stopped the German attack! They didn't budge an inch.*

All through March, violent fighting raged on Anzio and along the Gustav Line. Near to the end of the month, Rube Tucker's combat team was pulled out of the beachhead and shipped to England to rejoin the 82nd Airborne Division, which had been training arduously for the mightiest amphibious endeavor in the history of warfare—Operation Overlord. After 73 days of continuous fighting in the Anzio inferno, Yarborough's Five-O-Niners also were withdrawn to prepare for "Operation Dragoon," the invasion of Nazi-held southern France.

Then in May, the Allies broke out of Anzio and through the Gustav Line, and the two forces linked up and raced for Rome, the glittering prize that Winston Churchill had hoped to grab on the cheap six months earlier. Rome fell on June 4. The world's focus now shifted to the English Channel, where history's mightiest invasion force was about to be launched.

PART III

History's Mightiest Endeavor

20
Threshold
of Overlord

In November 1943, Brig. Gen. Jim Gavin, the 36-year old assistant commander of the 82nd Airborne Division, arrived in London on temporary assignment as senior airborne adviser to COSSAC (Chief of Staff Supreme Allied Command). COSSAC had been established in mid-1943 to do the initial planning for Operation Overlord, the massive cross-Channel invasion of northwest France.

COSSAC's boss was British Lt. Gen. Frederick E. Morgan, a scholarly, 49-year-old artillery and tank officer, who was noted for his jolly courtesy, keen mind, and his like for, and admiration of, Americans. Gavin hit it off with Morgan from the beginning.

Before leaving Naples, Gavin had been warned by Matt Ridgway to be on guard against the "machinations and scheming" of Gen. Frederick Boy Browning, Ridgway's bitter foe from the controversy of the Sicily days. Hardly had Gavin reached London than he tangled with Browning, who was two ranks senior to the American and Britain's foremost airborne officer.[1]

Gavin reported to Frederick Morgan for the first time when, minutes later, the dapper Browning, wearing his maroon beret at a jaunty angle, strolled into the COSSAC chief's office. Browning promptly let loose with a cutting remark about Ridgway for not parachuting into Sicily with his men, implying that Ridgway lacked guts. Gavin bristled, but kept his composure. Ridgway had had far more responsibility than just the Sicily parachute assault,

Gavin retorted, and had handled the division precisely as it should have been handled.

James Gavin remembered those early days with COSSAC:

Although the Americans would provide most of the troops and airlift [for Overlord], the British seemed determined to take control of the total Allied airborne effort. Browning had never been in a command position so far, but had been promoted to three-star general; thus, due to his rank, he might automatically be named to command the combined American-British airborne force.

Jim Gavin held a unique spot in the hearts of the troopers of the 82nd Airborne. Veterans who had been with him in Sicily and Italy spoke of his battlefield daring, how he was the first to jump on combat missions, how he could always be found up front where the shooting was the hottest. They knew that Slim Jim had lied about his age to join the army when still in his mid-teens, and they loved to regale each other with often outlandish tales of Gavin's childhood. In endless bull sessions, the troopers claimed that Gavin had actually joined the army as a teenager because a juvenile judge had let him choose between becoming a soldier or serving six months in jail at hard labor.

Gavin always chuckled when hearing that story and others that his men told. "I've been accused by the boys of using the army as a dodge from every charge from arson to kidnapping," the one-star general laughingly told a reporter for *Yank* magazine. "When I was a kid, I just wanted to play soldier."

However, Gavin did admit to being the tactician and leader of a Mount Carmel, Pennsylvania, gang of boys that "played soldier" by making raids on such places as Mr. Heiglemann's fruit stand. And he also confessed that one such raid had ended in a "battlefield disaster" that resulted in a severe scolding by a judge.[2]

Now, 23 years after that judicial rebuke, Jim Gavin was studying a draft of COSSAC's initial plan for Overlord. It called for an assault against a single beach on the Normandy coast between LeHavre on the east and the Cherbourg Peninsula on the west. D-Day was set for May 1, 1944.

COSSAC had estimated that there would be available for the invasion one American airborne division, five parachute regiments, and one airborne tank battalion; the British would have available one airborne division. The expected shortage of transport aircraft meant that only about one-third of the available Allied airborne force would be simultaneously dropped or landed in Normandy.

Two of the three first-priority missions would go to the British—the capture of the cathedral city of Caen, the capital of Normandy, and the seizure of the Orne River bridges between the Channel and Caen. A battalion of American paratroops would destroy a battery of powerful coastal guns perched on Pointe du Hoc, on the western edge of the landing beach.

If sufficient aircraft could be scraped up, there would be a number of secondary missions. Six American parachute battalions would drop inland from the beach (code-named "Omaha") to seize and hold crossings over the Aure River and to block crossings over the Vire River to keep German panzers from rushing to the landing beach. If planes were available, American paratroopers would make an assault on Carentan, well to the west of Omaha Beach and below the neck of the Cherbourg Peninsula, and would capture the Vire River bridge at Insigny.

Gavin was appalled by the operational plan for Overlord. Both the airborne and seaborne forces were grossly inadequate for the task, he felt. "This is nothing more than an oversize Dieppe," Gavin told a fellow American.[3]

The young general hurried to Omar Bradley's headquarters in Bryanston Square to voice his deep concerns. Typically, Omar the Tentmaker, as the reporters called the professorial leader of American ground forces for the invasion, was sympathetic to Gavin's views. Indeed, Bradley declared in his high-pitched voice, the invasion force would have to be beefed up and more airborne troops should be employed in the initial assault.

On January 16, 1944, while Allied brass were wrangling over plans for Overlord, the newly appointed supreme commander, 54-year-old Dwight Eisenhower, arrived in London aboard his private railroad coach, *Bayonet,* which had whisked him through the thick fog from Prestwick airport in Scotland. From that moment, Overlord began to dominate every aspect of the war against Hitler. Within a few days of arriving at Supreme Headquarters Allied Expeditionary Force (SHAEF) on Grosvenor Square, the affable, chain-smoking general with the mule-skinner's vocabulary was staggering under a tremendous burden.

On January 21, Eisenhower unveiled a revised Overlord plan. A new beach had been added—"Utah"—at the eastern base of the Cherbourg Peninsula, and airborne operations had been greatly beefed up. D-Day was set ahead a month, to May 31.

The American part of "Operation Neptune" (the assault phase of Overlord) called for Maj. Gen. J. Lawton "Lightning Joe" Collins' VII Corps, spearheaded by the green 4th (Ivy) Infantry Division, to storm ashore at Utah Beach, then attack northward to seize the crucial port of Cherbourg at the tip of the peninsula. Behind Utah Beach, to help Collins get ashore, the battle-tested 82nd Airborne and the untried 101st Airborne Divisions would drop and land.

Maj. Gen. William Lee's "Screaming Eagles" would jump first and capture four causeways leading inland from Utah over a marshy region, seize a pair of bridges over the Merderet River west of Sainte-Mère-Eglise, then drive southward a few miles to take Carentan. Matt Ridgway's All-Americans would jump and glide a considerable distance to the west of Utah, in the vicinity of Saint-Sauveur-le-Vicompte to cut off the peninsula. At the same time, the British 6th Airborne Division would jump and glide behind Bernard Montgomery's British and Canadian beaches on the invasion's eastern sector.

One of those present at the Eisenhower unveiling of the Neptune assault plan was the "father of the American airborne," Bill Lee. The plan had proved Lee to be an astute prognosticator. Back at Camp Claiborne, in August 1943, after formation of the two airborne divisions, Lee had pointed out to Matt Ridgway's map and said, "If our divisions are ever called on to spearhead a cross-Channel attack, we will come down right here"—and he designated the precise drop and landing zones that SHAEF planners would pick.

Lee's Screaming Eagles were billeted in villages and towns in the counties (shires) of Berkshire and Wiltshire in the south of England. Lee and his assistant division commander, diminutive 51-year-old Brig. Gen. Donald F. Pratt, opened a command post at Greenham Lodge, just outside Newbury.

Lee's division had been crossing the Atlantic piecemeal for several months, and the last unit to arrive was the 501st Parachute Regiment, led by the flamboyant Col. Howard R. "Jumpy" Johnson. A graduate of the United States Naval Academy, Johnson had taken a commission in the infantry, and he was one of the few officers or men in the division who had made more than 100 parachute jumps. Hence, the nickname Jumpy.

Johnson had activated the 501st Regiment at Camp Toccoa, Georgia, in November 1942. There, beneath Currahee Mountain, Jumpy began to build one of the most spirited regiments in the army, one molded after his own dynamic and aggressive personality.

Monsignor Francis L. Sampson, a wartime chaplain in the 501st Parachute Infantry, recalled his first encounter with Johnson:

> *I had been looking forward with great interest plus a certain degree of trepidation to meeting Colonel Johnson. He had left a reputation at jump school for being the roughest and noisiest officer ever to hit the silk. When the colonel walked into the room, the atmosphere was immediately changed by his forceful and domineering personality. "Hi ya, fella," Colonel Johnson said breezily to me. "Who in the hell are you?"*
>
> *He was carrying a long bowie knife in one hand. This was overplaying his character a bit, I thought, but he explained that he practiced knife-throwing for an hour each day. We went into his office and had a long talk. Colonel Johnson concluded it by barking, "I'm the pappy of every mother's son in this regiment. I'm your pappy, too. Understand?"[4]*

Indeed, Jumpy did practice his knife-throwing daily. He used a six-foot plywood board for a target. On one side, he had Hitler's life-size picture and on the other side, that of Hideki Tojo, the diminutive, owl-faced Japanese warlord. "I hate those two bastards!" he would snarl.

When he sent his bowie knife through the Führer's throat, Johnson would yell like a wild ape. On two occasions, his knife rebounded and cut him rather severely, once on the arm and once on the leg. He refused to let medics even look at the gashes.

Johnson was good with his "dukes," and would boast that he could flatten any officer or man in the regiment—few doubted that he could. Jumpy had his eccentricities, but he had color, lots of it, and his men idolized him.

Col. George Van Horn Moseley, Jr., a third-generation Army man who commanded the 502nd Parachute Infantry, was another tough, zany character. His regiment came to be known as the "Five-O-Deuce" or "Five-O-Duck," and after taking over back in the States in 1942, he had quickly put his unique stamp on the entire outfit. Moseley was a curious blend of intellect and earthiness, and he made enormous demands on those who served under him as well as on himself.

"Sure, Old Moe is kind of crazy," an admiring trooper said of the colonel. "But, what the hell; so are the rest of us or we wouldn't have volunteered for the paratroops."

Along with Jumpy and Old Moe, Col. Robert F. Sink, or "Bounding Bob," was the leader of the 506th Parachute Infantry—"the Five-O-Sinks," as his men proudly called themselves. Sink, who had been in charge of the regiment since formation in 1942, was dynamic, flamboyant, and for years had been the subject of countless barracks-room yarns—many of them false. Other outfits in the 101st Airborne swore that Sink's regiment marched to its own drummer, a colorful, rugged bunch that had gained wide publicity by taking their training camp reviews on the double—while wearing blue trunks.

Earlier, on December 9, 1943, the 82nd Airborne Division— less Rube Tucker's 504th Parachute Regimental Combat Team— landed in Northern Ireland after being brought up from the Mediterranean. Then, in early February, the All-Americans closed in on the Midlands of England, and on February 14, Matt Ridgway established a command post at Braunstone Parke, at Leicester.

Meanwhile, Jim Gavin, his work finished at COSSAC, returned to his post with the 82nd Airborne. On February 18, Matt Ridgway rushed him to London for an urgent discussion with the British on the Operation Neptune airborne operations. The session was held at Bentley Priory, headquarters of British Air Chief Marshal Trafford Leigh-Mallory, air commander for Overlord. Leigh-Mallory had distinguished himself on the ground directing Royal Air Force fighters in the crucial 1940 Battle of Britain, but his grasp of parachute and glider operations was virtually nil, Gavin felt.

The conference droned on for hours, and grew heated at times. Leigh-Mallory was highly skeptical that the American airborne arm could do what its leaders were confident it could do. When the lengthy session broke up, Gavin was a worried man, convinced that Leigh-Mallory would use his clout at SHAEF to skuttle American airborne participation in Neptune.

Now fate dealt a cruel blow to Bill Lee. Command of a crack airborne division in a major combat operation had been his dream for four years. While with his troops in the field, however, on February 9, the Screaming Eagles commander suffered a major heart attack and was rushed to the hospital. Ten days later, Lee's doctors gave him crushing news: He would have to be sent to the States for treatment. His dream would never be fulfilled.[5]

No doubt Don Pratt, as assistant division commander, felt that he was the heir apparent to succeed Lee. But for whatever their reasons, Eisenhower and Bradley turned thumbs down on Pratt and brought in highly regarded Brig. Gen. Maxwell Taylor, the 82nd Airborne artillery commander, to lead the Screaming Eagles. Taylor flew to England from Italy, and on March 14, formally took over.

No one knew better than the astute Taylor that anyone who tried to fill the enormous shoes of the idolized Bill Lee would be confronted by thinly veiled resentment. Not only was Taylor an "outsider," but, worse perhaps, in the eyes of his parachutists, he was not a bona fide paratrooper, having made only one practice jump.

21 Forecast: Airborne Bloodbath

As the countdown to D-Day for Overlord moved inexorably forward, General Eisenhower, his planners, and airborne commanders were haunted by a frightening possibility: What if the bulk of the parachute and glider elements that were to pave the way for the seaborne forces would be scattered to the four winds because of failure of navigational techniques? In that event, the entire invasion could be smashed.[1]

In late December 1943, Bill Lee, commander of the 101st Airborne, had called in one of his highly regarded young officers, Capt. Frank L. Lillyman, and ordered him to train and command a group of pathfinders, those who would jump first and direct the main bodies to their drop zones and landing zone. "You'll have the total support of my staff and every commander in the 101st," Lee told Lillyman. A call went out to the regiments and battalions for "volunteers" to take part in a highly secret mission. Candidates were to have a background in communications and be able to send and receive in Morse code.

Lillyman was appalled by his initial difficulties in trying to whip into shape a keenly honed pathfinder group. Far from the cooperation that General Lee had promised, his unit leaders, like those from the dawn of military history, leaped at this opportunity to jettison their deadwood.

Frank Lillyman recalled:

> *Many commanders figured that here was an excellent opportunity to get rid of their eight balls by sending them to my pathfinder group. I had no TO [table of organization] so there was no rank among the enlisted men. I inherited former first sergeants and other NCOs who were excellent men, but who had been busted to private because they had disciplinary problems. A few didn't even know what the Morse code was.*

It took Lillyman 72 hours to screen his batch of recruits, then he rushed to see Bill Lee. Stoicly, Lee listened while the captain explained that a gang of misfits had been dumped on him. Without a word, Lee turned to his chief of staff, carrot-topped, 34-year-old Gerald Higgins, and said, "Gerry, see to it that this situation comes to a halt!" Lillyman sent about 75 percent of his first recruits back to their units, much to the dismay of company commanders and platoon leaders who hadn't expected their prodigal sons to return.

Again the call went out for "volunteers," and the pathfinder trainee ranks were once more filled. Charles R. Malley of the 506th Parachute Infantry, a "busted" private who was Lillyman's acting first sergeant, remembered his pathfinder protégés:

> *We had a bunch of good guys who had screwed up in one way or another. Our pathfinder unit was stationed just outside Nottingham, home of Robin Hood, and the famous bastille where good ol' Robin had been incarcerated. Many were the times that I received calls from the sheriff of Nottingham to come and get our present day Hoods out of his jail. The good thing about English justice—no fines, no nothing—just get 'em the hell out of there.*

When I returned from Robin Hood's jail with the bodies,
Captain Lillyman made inquiries as to the seriousness of the offenses
or any damages inflicted upon the English citizenry. If the situation
seemed bad, he gave the guy company punishment, thereby
forestalling a possible court-martial. He saved me once that way.

Meanwhile in early 1944, air crews and C-47s of the new IX Troop
Carrier command of Lew Brereton's Ninth Air Force were arriv-
ing and settling into seven airfields in the Midlands, where they
would be close to the 82nd and 101st Airborne Divisions. It was
the IX Carrier Command that would lift the All-Americans and
Screaming Eagles to Normandy. Then, on February 25, 1944,
Maj. Gen. Paul Williams and his staff were rushed up from the
Mediterranean to take over the IX Carrier Command.

Williams seemed to be an ideal choice. He had gained wide
experience directing troop carrier operations in Sicily and Italy,
and he was tuned to the same wavelength as the often temperamental airborne leaders. Williams' command would consist of
Hal Clark's veteran 52nd Carrier Wing from the Mediterranean,
and two wings fresh from the United States, the 50th and 53rd.
On D-Day, Clark's wing would carry all of the American parachute elements, and the 50th and 53rd would tow the 82nd and
101st Division gliders.

With Paul Williams' carrier command now open for business
in the Midlands, a pathfinder school was established at a brand-
new airfield at North Witham. Boyish-faced Col. Joel Crouch,
the pathfinder pioneer who had flown the lead C-47 plane for
the airborne trailblazers in the Salerno beachhead and Avellino
drops, had come up from the Mediterranean and was in command of the North Witham school.[2] Pathfinder candidates from
both the 82nd and 101st Division would hone their techniques
here.

The password at North Witham was "Teamwork." Each stick
of pathfinders was assigned to a particular C-47 and a specific
crew. They worked, ate, and lived together. Colonel Crouch and
his air corps officers lived at one end of a barracks; parachute
officers resided at the other end.

All of the pathfinder officers were put through an orientation
course so that each man could better understand the problems of
the other. Paratroop officers and most of the enlisted men
learned how to start, and taxi, a C-47, and they were taught the
principles of aerial navigation. Some of the more gung ho air

corps officers were given a crash course and became qualified parachutists.

The student pathfinders jumped five to seven times each week, at least two of them being bailouts at night. Because the trailblazers would drop at night in Normandy, they were put on a special high-caloric diet, which air corp flight surgeons, who hovered over their North Witham brood like mother hens, claimed enhanced night vision.

Meanwhile, the paratroopers were experimenting in the use of radar (Eureka-Rebecca), lights, smoke, and luminous panels, all or some of which would be used for marking drop zones and landing zones. For their part, Joel Crouch's pilots, navigators, and crewmen were honing their abilities to navigate at night and to locate a certain point with a particular Eureka-Rebecca set.

Elsewhere in the Midlands in March and early April, training was rigorous (even diabolical, the troopers swore) for the men of the 82nd and 101st Airborne Divisions. It seemed to the troopers that it was always raining. "Maybe we ought to build an ark!" they would quip.

In the meantime, on April 22, Col. Rube Tucker and his 504th Parachute Regimental Combat Team reached England, four weeks after being pulled out of the devil's cauldron of Anzio. Typically, the fiery Tucker was anxious to get in on the Normandy invasion, as were an undetermined number of his officers and men. But the Five-O-Four leader's hopes were quickly dashed: He and his troopers would sit this one out in England.

When Jim Gavin, who would be in command of all 82nd Airborne parachute elements in the assault, learned of Matt Ridgway's decision to bench one of his stars (the 504th) on the eve of the "Big Game," he was both puzzled and angry. Gavin pleaded with Ridgway to substitute the battle-tested 504th for the unblooded 507th or 508th Regiments, but his boss turned down the request.

Ridgway's explanation was that Rube Tucker's outfit had been too severely chewed up at Anzio (590 men had been killed, wounded, or missing) to be ready in time for Operation Neptune, now only six weeks away. However, Jim Gavin had visited the Five-O-Fours after their arrival and found them to be high-spirited and, in most cases, raring to go.

Louis Hauptfleisch, who was S-1 (personnel officer) of the 504th Parachute Infantry at the time, remembered his team's "benching":

*True, the 504th [including the 376th Parachute Field Artillery
Battalion and C Company of the 307th Airborne Engineers] was
short of officers and enlisted men. But how often had we enjoyed the
luxury of having our ranks filled during our overseas actions? That
should not have been construed as an impediment [to taking part in
Neptune] since, at that time, the majority of Os and EMs in the
504th Combat Team represented a valuable base of combat-
experienced troopers. Replacements were flowing in regularly, so the
504th seemed to be adequate and ready.*

*But let's face it. After lucking out in Sicily, Salerno and Anzio,
perhaps many of the veteran Five-O-Fours were not gung ho about
going in on D-Day.*

Whatever may have been the feelings of the Five-O-Fours—and
no doubt sentiment was mixed, for some 45 officers and men
answered a call for special D-Day missions—the dye was cast. Jim
Gavin, as leader of the 82nd Airborne's Task Force A, would
parachute into Normandy with Col. William E. Ekman's 505th
Regiment, Col. George V. "Zip" Millett's 507th, and Col. Roy E.
Lindquist's 508th.

Not long after Rube Tucker's outfit reached England, an
American paratroop officer browsing through the bookstalls of a
London store spotted a volume entitled *Paratroopers*. His professional curiosity aroused, the officer picked up the book and saw
that its author was Maj. F. O. Miksche, a Czechoslovakian belonging to a unit of Gen. Charles de Gaulle's Free French forces
in England.

Leafing through the pages, the American noticed that the
book contained a summary of German airborne operations in the
war. Then he felt his heart skip a beat as he stared intently at
a full-page map that the author had drawn to illustrate a story on
a hypothetical Allied airborne assault that would spearhead a
cross-Channel invasion of France. The hypothetical plan, as dra-
matized by the map, showed the airborne divisions landing in
three zones, two of which were almost precisely where the 82nd
and 101st Airborne Divisions would touch down on D-Day. The
third zone was only a few miles off the true Allied target.

The chilling discovery sent shockwaves of concern through
the American airborne staffs in the Midlands as well as the
rarified atmosphere of SHAEF in Grosvenor Square in London.
There was little doubt that Major Miksche's book *Paratroopers* was
in the hands of the German high command. The question was

whether Hitler and his generals would consider the theoretical Cherbourg Peninsula plan to be an incredible Allied security leak and pack the region with troops and antiaircraft guns.

Maxwell Taylor, who led the 101st Airborne Division into Normandy, vividly remembered his feelings at that time:

> There was nothing we could do about the book Paratroopers except to hope that the German high command did not take it seriously. But I had never gotten the book entirely out of mind, and when flying with my division to Normandy a few weeks later, the book crept back into my thoughts.

As high-level planning and low-level troop training continued at a constantly accelerated pace, a violent dispute erupted at the headquarters of Bernard Montgomery's 21st Army Group, which would command all ground forces in Overlord, and which served as a planning center for the invasion. The argument was between two top commanders, one American and the other British, and it threatened to shake the foundation of Allied solidarity.

Touching off the heated debate at an airborne planning session was a proposal by Air Chief Marshal Trafford Leigh-Mallory to cancel the parachute and glider assault by the 82nd and 101st Divisions.

"I cannot approve your plans," Leigh-Mallory, the SHAEF air chief, told Omar Bradley. "Your losses will be far more than what your gains are worth. I cannot go along with you."

Bradley was stunned—and furious. "Very well, sir," the American general replied, "If you insist on cutting out the airborne attack, then I must ask that we eliminate the Utah assault. I am not going to land on that beach without making sure we've seized the exits behind it."

Now it was Leigh-Mallory's turn to be shocked. After a moment's silence, he responded, "Then let me make it clear. If you insist upon the airborne operation, you'll do it in spite of my opposition."

Turning to Bernard Montgomery, the man who was third in the command pecking order at SHAEF said, "If General Bradley insists upon going ahead he will have to accept full responsibility for the airborne operation."

Bradley quickly cut in. "That's perfectly okay. I'm in the habit of accepting full responsibility for all my operations."[3]

The controversial Montgomery, finding himself in the curious role of inter-Allied peacemaker, rapped for order. "That's not at all necessary, gentlemen," he said. "I'll accept the responsibility."

The American airborne assault was still on—at least for the present.

A short time later, Eisenhower summoned his old friend Omar Bradley. Leigh-Mallory had gone to the harried supreme commander to pursue his crusade to get the American parachute and glider assault canceled, and now Eisenhower sought Bradley's view.

Hearing of Leigh-Mallory's refusal to accept the conference table defeat at Montgomery's headquarters, the normally mild Bradley exploded. "Of course the airborne attack is risky," the First Army commander agreed, "but not half so risky as a seaborne landing at Utah without it!"[4]

Bradley concurred with Leigh-Mallory's view that the lumbering low-flying C-47s, packed with American paratroopers and towing American gliders, would be fired on from the ground the moment they knifed over the Cherbourg Peninsula. And he agreed with the air chief marshal that the Normandy countryside, a patchwork of tiny fields, each bordered by thick earthen embankments crowned by hedgerows, would make glider landings costly. But, Bradley stressed, those risks must be subordinated to the primary objective of the invasion—the early capture of the crucial port of Cherbourg.

"If we could accomplish the mission without them [the American airborne divisions], I certainly would not gamble the lives of 17,000 paratroopers and glidermen," Bradley declared. "But I will willingly risk them to insure against failure for Overlord."[5]

Eisenhower, confronted with divergent views from top air and ground commanders, later pondered the issue and ruled in favor of Bradley—the American airborne assault would go on as planned. That ended the bitter dispute—or so Bradley thought.

Overlord planners had known that American paratroopers and glidermen would be greeted, at least on the initial strike, by two German divisions, the 243rd and 709th, plus an assortment of smaller units. Then SHAEF, on May 25, was thrown into a near panic: The Centurie underground network on the Cherbourg Peninsula smuggled word to London that Maj. Gen. Wilhelm Falley's first-rate 91st *Luftlande* (Air Landing) Division had suddenly rushed into the Carentan Saint-Sauveur-le-Vicomte Valognes area, between the 82nd and 101st drop and landing zones.

Did the Germans know something? Had they concluded from the Czech captain's book *Paratroopers* that here was where the Allied airborne divisions would strike? Had intense SHAEF security measures broken down?

Whatever the reason for the 91st Luftlande Division's appearance, it was far too late to drastically revise the Utah Beach plan. So two days after this bombshell had struck SHAEF, the 82nd and 101st Airborne Divisions created a new plan. The ambitious original plan of cutting the Cherbourg Peninsula by dropping and landing Matt Ridgway's division on the western side was discarded. Under the new plan, the 82nd Airborne would land farther to the east on both sides of the Merderet River, then secure the area of Neuville-au-Plain, Sainte-Mère-Eglise, Chef-du-Pont, Etienville and Amfreville. The mission of Max Taylor's division remained generally unchanged.

Despite the handwringing at SHAEF, the 82nd Airborne commanders and staff took the new division mission in stride. They simply slid the regimental drop zones the necessary number of miles to the east, and left unchanged the relative location of the drop zones.

As preparations for the mammoth invasion continued at a feverish pitch in the British Isles, across the Channel on the Cherbourg Peninsula, the head of the underground Centurie network had more than 1,100 part-time spies working for him. One of Centurie's most active cells was at Saint-Lô, an important rail and road center at the base of the Cherbourg Peninsula. There a male schoolteacher had 103 amateur agents spying out German secrets under his direction.

In mid-May, the Saint-Lô underground cell pulled off its greatest coup: stealing plans for the nearby La Barquette locks, which controlled the tidal flow of the Douve River for 25 miles northward into the Cherbourg Peninsula and behind Utah Beach.

The La Barquette locks would be a priority objective of Max Taylor's 101st Airborne on D-Day. Prompt seizure of the locks would be vital to Neptune by keeping the Germans from flooding the eastern half of the Cherbourg Peninsula where American seaborne forces were to storm ashore. The stolen plans, which Centurie quickly smuggled to London, would permit Max Taylor's airborne engineers to rapidly manipulate the locks to keep flooding to a minimum.

Late in May, the gargantuan Overlord time bomb was activated. All over southern England, the dusty roads and narrow-gauge railroads heaved and groaned under the weight of the mighty army edging toward the coastal ports. Seaborne assault troops, grim and tight-lipped, marched into 17 assembly areas called "sausages" because of their oval shapes on high-level military maps.

At the same time, men of the 82nd and 101st Airborne Divisions were sealed into encampments of long rows of pyramidal tents at airfields in the Midlands. There they were briefed on their missions and feasted on such luxuries as fried chicken, fruit cocktail, and white bread with butter. "Fattening the lambs for the slaughter," the troopers told each other.

One who took the "slaughter" of American airborne troops seriously was Trafford Leigh-Mallory. On May 30, he called on Eisenhower to protest a final time the "futile destruction of two fine American airborne divisions." The tune was the same; only the words were different.

"You can expect 70 percent casualties among American glider troops and 50 percent among parachute troops," Leigh-Mallory forecast. It was a heavy load to be dumped on Eisenhower's already sagging shoulders on virtually the eve of the mighty endeavor.[6]

Grim-faced and worried, Eisenhower went to his tent to ponder. It was his decision to make, and his alone. Eisenhower agonized for more than an hour, reviewing over and over each step in the Neptune plan. If Leigh-Mallory turned out to be accurate in his prediction, Eisenhower would one day go to his grave still burdened with the guilt of having disregarded the warning and sending thousands of paratroopers and glidermen to their deaths. But if he canceled the American airborne attack, the seaborne assault on Utah Beach might fail, Cherbourg would not be captured, and the entire invasion would be in most serious peril.

Eisenhower rose from his chair, extinguished the tenth cigarette he had smoked during the past hour, returned to his combat headquarters at Southwick House, perched on heights overlooking Portsmouth, and placed a call to Air Chief Marshal Leigh-Mallory. The American airborne attack was on as planned.[7]

22
Blazing the Trail

With the approach of D-Day, General Eisenhower and airborne commanders were gripped by a gnawing question: Had *Reichsmarschal* Hermann Goering craftily hoarded Luftwaffe aircraft and fuel supplies in order to pounce on the lumbering, unarmed paratroop and glider sky trains when they were crossing the Channel? It was known by Allied intelligence that the German air force had been badly beaten in the great air battles of the winter and spring of 1944. But how badly? No one in the Allied camp knew. Ultra, for once, failed at this crucial point to provide an accurate appraisal of the Luftwaffe order of battle. Estimates among various intelligence branches varied so widely that they might have been drawn from a hat.[1]

Meanwhile, Allied cloak-and-dagger agencies had been working to confound the German Y service—a large, experienced, and capable electronic monitoring branch—in order to mask the approach of the paratroop armada on the night of D-Day minus 1. Through long study of Allied air force wireless traffic, the Y service experts could anticipate that a major strike was in the offing.

So the Allies' principal stratagem was to produce such a vast amount of bogus radio traffic as D-Day grew closer that the German wireless intelligence technicians would be swamped and unable to analyze the significance of the heavy wireless traffic patterns across the Channel. As part of the Allied decoy plan, this same technique had been employed during two large-scale training exercises held in England earlier, so it was hoped that the Wehrmacht would conclude that the rash of pre-D-Day wireless activity signified only another exercise and not *Der Grossinvasion*.[2]

While Eisenhower was being burdened with the torments of the damned, elsewhere in London, Capt. Barney Oldfield was immersed in his own little corner of Hades. Outgoing and congenial, Oldfield was an Army public relations officer who had been saddled with the preposterous task of keeping 58 American media reporters—many of them prima donnas—happy and informed. These were the men and women who wanted, or professed to want, to be in the "first wave" of the invasion. Their lure was looming front-page byline stories and established reputations that would endure for all time.

Before being commissioned in 1941, Oldfield had been a Hollywood press agent, and his clients included a child star named Elizabeth Taylor and a promising young actor, Ronald Reagan. The PR officer was also a bona fide paratrooper, having graduated in Class 23 from the Parachute School at Fort Benning. His mentor in his first jump had been a young airborne officer named Jim Gavin.

There were not enough available spaces on landing craft for all of the reporters to go ashore with the seaborne vanguard, so Oldfield was handed the toughest of all sales tasks: Persuade reporters that the surest way to get to the enemy shore first was to go with the paratroopers. How Oldfield did it was up to him.

A few correspondents approached by Oldfield turned pale after it was suggested that they parachute into Fortress Europe. However, he managed to coerce a number of reporters into agreeing that going in with the paratroopers was the only way to go. Then the airborne commanders balked: These novices might freeze in the C-47 door, endanger the stick, and even jeopardize operations. Undaunted, the resourceful Oldfield came up with a scheme to appease airborne leaders: he would prepare the reporter candidates for their task by qualifying them as paratroopers.

Barney Oldfield recalled the reaction:

> There was no whirlwind of enthusiasm for the honor of emulating Beaver Thompson of the Chicago Tribune *who had jumped earlier in North Africa and in Sicily, or for the distinction of being among the first Americans to touch down behind Hitler's Atlantic Wall.*

*Perhaps there had been too many of those aerial photographs
showing the pointed stakes and rugged posts that stood in every
Normandy field, ready to impale jumpers.*

Captain Oldfield persevered, and arranged for a small number
of correspondents to take a two-week crash course at a parachute
school near Hungerford. But then a new hitch developed. Word
got back to the plush London hotels and the bars that the parachute school was being run by brutes and bonecrushers, most
notably the tough Sgt. Bill "Red" King, a one-time professional
boxer from Nashville. King had been the first enlisted American
paratrooper to jump from a plane, back in 1940.

Barney Oldfield remembered the buzz in the reporters'
London haunts:

> *The two-week parachute-school course would be one of unrelenting
> physical torture for the candidates, it was rumored with only a slight
> degree of exaggeration. The curriculum was not for those who felt
> any aversion to exercise or to muscular aches compounded by
> shooting pains and extreme fatigue. The picture painted by these
> reports suggested that Heinrich Himmler himself and his Gestapo
> thugs were planning on crossing the English Channel and enrolling
> in Red King's parachute school in order to learn the latest
> techniques on sadism.*

Oldfield badgered, coerced, telephoned, and treed in bars likely
reporter candidates for parachuting into Europe. His bulldog
efforts paid off, and a handful of newsmen volunteered for Red
King's course. Joseph Dearing, a *Collier's* photographer, was especially eager, making all five of his qualifying jumps in one day.
On the final one, he crashed into a tree and knocked himself out
cold. William Walton of *Time,* a Wisconsin boy eager for hazardous ventures, and corpulent Phil Bucknell of *Stars and Stripes,*
breezed through the course.

Other scribes who had agreed to take the parachute-school
course found reasons for postponing action—London had been
hit by a sudden rash of reporters spraining ankles while stepping
off curbs in the blackout. Finally, most of them backed out entirely—they would go in by landing craft or a few days later by
boat. However, Barney Oldfield had accomplished his mission;
reporters would bail out over Europe with American paratroop-

ers, and several others would take their typewriters—and their chances—by glider.

Hardly had Oldfield set up shop for this special parachute-training project than a seemingly insolvable problem raised its head. Women reporters, charged up by professional pride and an understandable desire for equal treatment for their sex, demanded that they be allowed to take Red King's course and to jump behind the Atlantic Wall with the paratroopers. The most tenacious petitioners were petite Betty Gaskill, who worked for *Liberty* magazine; Dixie Tighe, an attractive lady of some years who labored for the International News Service; and Judy Barden, a British girl who reported for the *New York Sun*.

Captain Oldfield tried to shadowbox with the three ladies, neatly sidestepping their inquiries and hoping that they would tire of the sport. Instead, they continued to take large bites out of a certain portion of the PR officer's anatomy. Oldfield sought out friends of the ladies in an effort to get them to call off the dogs. All in vain.

Oldfield was skewered on the horns of a dilemma: If he didn't grant the lady reporters' demands, he would be accused of discrimination. If the women were to be killed parachuting into France, he would be charged with a cruel, callous, insensitive brute who had stupidly sent three members of the so-called weaker sex to their deaths. Finally, only a week before D-Day, Oldfield's thrust and parry tactics paid off. With a reasonable degree of grace, Betty Gaskill, Dixie Tighe, and Judy Barden agreed to go in by boat after D-Day.

During these tension-packed days in late May, Western Europe was gripped by miserable weather: rain, fog, cold. Gale-force winds howled, and the Channel churned furiously. At his advance-invasion command post at Southwick House, Eisenhower postponed D-Day to Monday, June 5.

At North Witham airfield on the evening of June 4, Frank Lillyman and his Screaming Eagle pathfinders ate supper at the consolidated air corps-paratrooper mess hall. They had been warned not to even drop a hint that the Neptune trailblazers would take off for France in a few hours. Then the troopers returned to their barracks, drew out all of their equipment, painted faces with charcoal and linseed oil and marched to their waiting C-47s.

It was still daylight, and scores of air corps men saw the pathfinders and now knew that the invasion was on. Lillyman and his men sat tensely beneath the wings and waited for word to load up and lift off. They sat . . . and sat . . . and sat some more. Finally, a messenger was rushed to an area headquarters. No one had thought to inform the point of the Neptune airborne javelin that the invasion had once more been postponed for 24 hours because of the continuing gales and angry Channel waves.

Early on the morning of June 5, the tentacles of the gigantic invasion that extended to hundreds of crowded ships, airfields, harbors, estuaries, encampments, and towns—began slowly to edge toward the coast of France. So enormous was this operation that it was now beyond the capability of Eisenhower or other mere mortals to postpone or cancel Neptune. The Plan itself had now taken over.

That evening, while 6,939 Allied vessels were plowing through the heavy swells of the Channel, Dwight Eisenhower was having dinner with Maxwell Taylor at an airfield near Greenham Common. In a few hours, Taylor and the Screaming Eagles of the 101st Airborne would be making their first combat jump.[3]

Outwardly buoyant and confident, Eisenhower drove after dinner with Taylor to nearyby airfields where hundreds of para-troopoers were donning combat gear, smearing Apache-style warpaint on their faces, and steeling themselves for the looming ordeal. Many troopers had shaved their heads and cropped the remaining strips of hair into freakish "warpath" designs. Grinning, Eisenhower whispered to Max Taylor, "I don't know if your boys will scare the Germans, but they sure as hell scare me!"[4]

Strolling from plane to plane and talking with troopers in his friendly, man-to-man style, the supreme commander concealed the torment that seared his mind: Leigh-Mallory's haunting warning, "Your American paratroopers and glidermen will be slaughtered." Was he stupidly sending these cheerful, bright-eyed youths to their deaths in wholesale numbers?

Ike's inner spirits soared when the parachutists told him repeatedly, "Now don't you worry about a goddamned thing, general. The 101st Airborne is on the job."

Monsignor Francis Sampson, the Catholic chaplain of the 501st Parachute Infantry, was one of those with whom Eisenhower shook hands, and he vividly remembered the occasion:

Gen. Dwight Eisenhower chats with "Screaming Eagles" of the 101st Airborne minutes before they boarded C-47s for Normandy. *(Jim Phillips)*

> *As General Eisenhower passed among the troopers with his friendly grin and informal chats, it was difficult to say whether he gave them more confidence than they gave him as they grinned back at him. He was the soldiers' "right guy," and he refused to show in his face the terrific burden of the airborne decision for which he had accepted full responsibility. He had gambled with the lives of these fine young men; he knew it, but it was okay with them. They were ready and willing to vindicate his judgment.*

Eisenhower, his round of visits to the paratroopers completed, shook hands with Taylor. "Well, good luck, Max," he said softly. As Ike walked to his waiting staff limousine to return to invasion headquarters at Portsmouth, an aide cast a fleeting glance at the supreme commander. There was a tear in Eisenhower's eye.

At one 101st Airborne field, Col. Howard Johnson, the firebrand leader of the 501st Parachute Infantry, was standing on the hood of a jeep, his men assembled around him. He was delivering a spirited pep talk—that no doubt he had been looking forward to giving since America went to war, and one he had rehearsed for months. Jumpy was a *fighter*—nothing else. And he never pretended to be anything else.

At the emotional peak of his exhortation, Jumpy reached for a trench knife strapped to his boot. He pulled and tugged at it, but could not get it out of its sheath. Getting red in the face, he whipped out a bowie knife from his waist belt and brandished it overhead. "I swear to you," he screamed, "that before the dawn of another day this knife will be stuck in the foulest Nazi belly in France! *Are you with me?*"

Pathfinders of the 2nd Battalion of the 505th Parachute Infantry and C-47 crew prior to liftoff for Normandy. *(Robert Anderson, Jim Phillips)*

Cheers and screams echoed over the landscape: *"We're with you! We're with you!"*

Elsewhere in the Midlands at an 82nd Airborne field, Lt. Col. Edward "Cannonball" Krause, leader of the 3rd Battalion, 505th Parachute Infantry, was also atop the hood of a jeep with his men around him. Holding Old Glory over his head, Krause shouted: "This was the first American flag to fly over Naples when we captured it. Tonight we're going to march on Sainte Mère Eglise in Normandy and fly this flag from the tallest building in town!" Robust cheers and shouts rocked the airfield.

Now the seemingly interminable, tension-racked wait began.

8:00 P.M. Troopers check their weapons; then check them again. They test dime-store metal crickets that each was issued for identification purposes in the blackness on the ground: One squeeze (*click-clack*) to be answered by two (*click-clack . . . click-clack*). American flags, about three by five inches, are fastened to

the right sleeves of jump jackets. Strips of green and brown bur-
lap are woven into helmet nets for camouflage.

8:30 P.M. Seasick pills taken by each trooper. "Puke bags" issued in the event pills do not work. Nervousness intensifies. Men
get up continuously to relieve themselves. A few planes roar,
testing engines. (Troopers hate grating sounds.)

9:00 P.M. Small, solemn groups sit under plane wings, and
watch the sun start its downward journey.

9:30 P.M. Scores of airplane engines howl. Final checkup. Entire airfield seems to be shaking. Some men feel like vomiting the
stew they ate for supper. Heavy equipment is put on. Troopers
waddle toward C-47 doors. Nobody sings. Nobody cheers.

10:00 P.M. Crammed shoulder to shoulder in bucket seats,
troopers crane their necks to get a look at the pilot. Standard
procedure. If he is an "old man" of 30, everyone feels better; he's
probably been through "Flak Alley" before. If pilot is a fuzzy-
cheeked youth of 21, troopers mutter, "Good God, we're being
chauffeured by a choir boy!"

Max Taylor was among the last of the Screaming Eagles to
hop aboard. Burdened with parachute packs and combat gear,
Taylor made a hurried final inspection of his equipment. He felt
his leg bag for assurance. Yes, it was there—a bottle of Irish whiskey he had prudently stored.

One by one the trooper-laden C-47s began speeding down
runways, and by 11:30 P.M., all of the 101st Airborne's 6,638
parachutists were winging toward Normandy—and their baptism
of fire—in 490 planes of Hal Clark's 52nd Troop Carrier Wing.

Riding with Lt. Col. Robert G. Cole's battalion of the 502nd
Parachute Infantry was Wright Bryan, who was covering the airborne assault for the NBC radio network, but would return to
England without jumping. Bryan sought to record the precise
feelings of the paratroopers electronically as they winged toward
their unknown destiny. Thrusting out his hand microphone, the
reporter approached Pvt. Robert C. Hillman of Manchester,
Connecticut.

Hillman held his hand on his reserve parachute. "I know my
chute is okay," he said into Bryan's mike, "because my mother
checked it." The reporter thought the remark was a typical fighting man's quip, but the paratrooper continued: "My mother
works for the Pioneer Parachute Company in our town, and her

job is giving the final once-over to all the chutes they manufacture."

Hillman's mother, in her own way, had given a final touch to her son's safety. Thousands of other mothers, if they sensed the impending danger, could only pray.

Much of the region at the base of the Cherbourg Peninsula onto which the American airborne elements would drop and glide was better suited for scuba divers than for descending paratroopers. Back of Utah Beach, the area was flooded for anywhere from a mile to two miles, and over this inundated pasture land ran four parallel roads (built-up causeways) from the dry sand dunes of the shore to the solid ground inland.

The dominant terrain feature farther to the west of this flooded area is the Douve River which, with its tributary, the Merderet, drains the major part of the Cherbourg Peninsula. Both rivers are narrow—20 to 40 feet—but deep. The Douve and Merederet flow in a southeasterly direction, merge ten miles inland from Utah Beach, and continue southeast another seven miles to the vicinity of Carentan. There the Douve makes a rounded L turn to the northeast and empties into the English Channel a mile below Utah Beach.

Along the lower course of the Douve are swamps, marshes, and water meadows. Additional areas in that region are below sea level at high tide, and could be flooded by the manipulation of La Barquette locks at the bend of the Douve, locks built about a hundred years earlier to hold back the sea at high tide. They were now closely guarded by the Germans.

A half hour out in front of the main body of Screaming Eagles, Col. Joel Crouch was at the controls of the lead C-47 carrying Capt. Frank Lillyman and a stick of his pathfinders toward drop zone A. Altogether, 11 sticks of trailblazers would mark out with Rebeccas and lights three drop zones and one landing zone behind Utah Beach, extending from the vicinity of Saint-Germain-de-Varreville on the north for eight miles to the south near La Barquette locks.

Lillyman was suffering intensely, and had been for three days. In order not to miss the "Big Show," he had concealed the fact that he had badly torn leg ligaments in a jump four days earlier, an injury that can take weeks to heal.

Standing in the open door and shivering from the chilly blasts

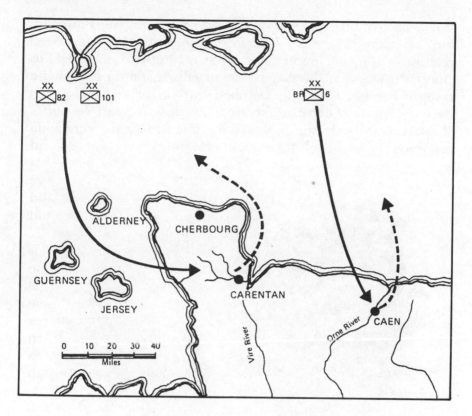

Normandy Flight Routes

of air, Lillyman could see every detail on the Norman ground, which was bathed in the rays of the brilliant moon. Up in the cockpit, Capt. William Culp, the radar operator, notified Crouch and his copilot, Capt. Vito Pedone, that the plane was approaching the village of Saint-Germain-de-Varreville. Moments later, the green light flashed on in the cabin, and out of the door went Lillyman, a big, black cigar clenched in his teeth. On his heels were his number 2 man, Lt. Samuel McCarter, and the remainder of the stick. In the C-47, Culp and Pedone recorded the time: 0015, June 6, 1944.[5]

The invasion was under way.

At almost the same time over the British zone to the east, the leader of the Red Devils pathfinders, Capt. Ian A. Tate, led his stick out of the airplane door.

Even while Frank Lillyman and Ian Tate were parachuting to earth, the duty officer at the Luftwaffe Y service in France had

grown uneasy. His concern was based on the previous interception of many American Mercury broadcasts. Mercurys were
weather intelligence flights, and what made the Y service office
concerned was that the Americans usually made these flights in
daylight because they only bombed during the day. Why were
Mercury flights being made at night during the past 48 hours?
There could be only one explanation: The Americans were about
to launch a major nighttime air operation.

Capt. Frank Lillyman. (*Lou
Varrone*)

So suspicious did these circumstances look to the Y service
officer that he scrambled a few Luftwaffe night fighters, and they
were airborne by 0034. Fortunately for the Allies, the German
night fighters were being vectored between Amiens in France
and Deelen in Holland. Had they patrolled to the west, they
would have stumbled onto the massive sky armadas carrying two
American and one British airborne divisions to Normandy. No
doubt large numbers of hungry Luftwaffe fighters would then
have risen to feast on the plodding C-47s, and the resulting carnage would have made the shooting down of 23 American troop
transports in Sicily look like a sideshow.

Captain Lillyman crashed down hard on his already painfully
aching leg. Like most troopers that night, he was scared, and his
imagination ran wild. Over in the far corner of the field the tall

poplars were swaying and casting eerie shadows, and in the shadows, he could discern something moving. Had the entire German army in Normandy gathered there to pounce on him? Lillyman loaded his tommy gun; it made a sharp noise that he was sure could be heard all the way to Berlin.[6]

Shakily, the pathfinder chief edged toward the moving figures and challenged them with his cricket. No answer. He was about to loose a tommy gun blast when loud moos came from the herd of cows he had challenged. Lillyman laughed. His jitters were gone.

The captain quickly rounded up seven of his men. They had jumped from only 450 feet, and landed near each other. The troopers did a map reconnaissance and realized they were north of their true drop zone, but because of the time pinch, this was close enough, they concluded.

Nearby could be seen the contours of a church, and the pathfinders headed toward it. Lillyman decided to set up his Eureka in the steeple.

The troopers banged hard on the rectory door, and a sleepy-eyed priest holding a lantern responded. When he saw this collection of black-faced, heavily armed creatures confronting him, the village priest's eyes bulged out in surprise and fear. Lieutenant Lavally, who spoke French fluently, said, "*Bonsoir* [good evening], padre. You have just been liberated!"

Lavally explained the mission to the excited priest, and Trooper Owen Council put the Eureka in the steeple. A second radar was set up in a large field, where light patterns were laid out.

Minutes before the main body of C-47s was to arrive, two troopers rushed up to Lillyman and said that a pair of Germans were pedaling bicycles along the road toward the drop zone. Rapidly, a length of piano wire was stretched across the road at neck level to a standing man, and secured tautly to a pair of large trees. Soon the pair of Germans came along on their bicycles, and they flipped over backward when the piano wire caught their necks. Nearly decapitated, the two *Feldgrau* died instantly.

Now the first flight of C-47s roared over, and Screaming Eagles began dropping around Lillyman. He became aware that the troopers, in combat for the first time, were freezing in their tracks or taking refuge in ditches, even though there was no firing on the drop zone. The pathfinder chief shouted at the men to get up and head for their assembly areas, and they scampered off into the night.

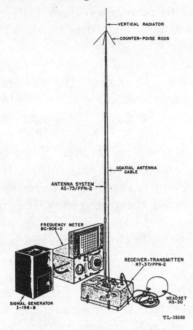

Eureka set up for transmitting.
(Courtesy of Keith Rose)

With his radar set in place and operating, Lillyman took Pfc. Fred Wilhelm and four other men and struck out in the direction of a battery of four large guns near Saint-Martin-de-Varreville. These weapons covered Utah Beach and its sea approaches, and were an urgent objective of Lt. Col. Steve A. Chappuis' Screaming Eagle battalion. On arrival, Lillyman and his men found that there were no German guns on the site—only a cluster of curious cows.

Behind Lillyman's plane came another team of pathfinders led by Lt. Gordon C. Rothwell, heading for drop zone C near Hiesville. Nearing the target, the three-plane flight ran into a barrage of ack-ack shells that exploded around the C-47s, and streams of tracer bullets ripped through wings and fuselages. Rothwell's pilot quickly took evasive action, and zoomed down almost onto the deck.

In acting 1st Sergeant Malley's plane, the men were hooked up and anxious to jump, and then the green light flashed on. But the aircraft was so low that the troopers felt they could grab the treetops. The excited copilot stuck his head back and shouted, "Prepare to jump!"

"Prepare to jump, hell!" a pathfinder roared, "We're only five feet off the ground!"

Now a new danger: an engine caught fire. The pilot headed for the nearby English Channel, off Utah Beach. "We're going down! Get ready to ditch!" the copilot shouted.

Rapidly, the troopers hacked and sawed their way out of their parachute packs and gear until they were down to jump suits and inflated Mae Wests. Eurekas were pitched overboard. Calmly, the pilot fired a red flare to light up the black waters; then pancaked the plane on top of one of the waves that were running high. Water rose to the parachutists' knees, and the copilot bellowed: "Everybody the hell out! This baby's going under!"

There was a mad scramble. Pathfinders who couldn't swim were helped into rubber dinghies. Others swam and tred water

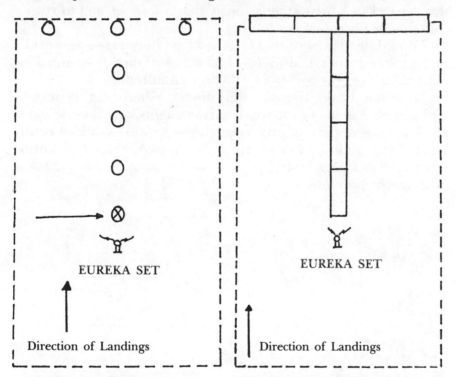

EUREKA SET

Direction of Landings

EUREKA SET

Direction of Landings

Night drop zone set up by pathfinders. Circles are Halifax type lights, which were color-coded for each drop zone. Code letter for drop zone was blinked out in Morse code by light marked with X.

Day drop zone. Rectangles are orange panel markers. (Courtesy of Keith Rose)

for 30 minutes until nearly exhausted. Suddenly someone called out, "There's a ship!"

It was a British vessel, and as it came close to the floundering Screaming Eagles, they could hear the sailors shouting, "Shoot the bastards! They're Jerries (German)!"

"We're American paratroopers! We're American paratroopers!"

That did the trick. One by one the pathfinders were fished out of the water, taken below, and given rum to help thaw their frozen bones.

With Rothwell's C-47 down in the Channel, the burden of marking drop zone C fell upon Lt. Roy H. Kessler's stick, which bailed out dead center onto the target and set up a Eureka and lights. However, they encountered an unexpected obstacle that threatened to give away their presence—a leather-lunged dog that barked so long and tenaciously that a trooper had to cut its throat with his trench knife.

Frank Lillyman and his 11 sticks of pathfinders—the world's finest soldiers, he called them—had accomplished their mission, even though many had been killed or captured.

However, heavy German flak on the Cherbourg Peninsula had scattered many of the troop carrier flights, and now Screaming Eagles were parachuting to earth over a wide swath of countryside and landing in or on rivers, swamps, orchards, pastures, trees, canals, bogs, ditches, rooftops, towns, roads—and on Wehrmacht positions.

23
Dark
Intruders

German Pvt. Erwin Mueller and a comrade, both of the 919th Grenadier Regiment, were peering nervously into the moonlit sky where Allied air activity seemed to be especially heavy on this night. Mueller glanced at his watch: It was 22 minutes after midnight. Only a half hour earlier, his platoon had been rousted out of their bunks by shouting sergeants and hastily deployed around the village of Azeville, three miles northwest of Utah Beach. "Keep on the alert!" the troopers had been warned.

Keep on the alert for what? Hadn't the *Oberleutnant* told them only the previous evening that the weather and Channel tide were not right for an invasion? But Mueller, who had a Danish wife, kept his thoughts to himself. When called up by the German army, he had gone quietly, for fear of getting his wife and children in trouble with the Nazis. But he had never approved of the war, or of Adolf Hitler.

However, Private Mueller expected to fight—and to fight hard, for that would be the only way to survive. He and his company had been told many times that they would find themselves up against American or British paratroopers, and that these parachutists never took prisoners.

Mueller and his comrade, from their post at a hedgerow gate, were entirely ignorant of what to expect, but suddenly their eyes bulged out at the spectacle that was unfolding in the sky to the south and west: scores of white parachutes were floating to earth. The two *Feldgrau* stood mesmerized in awe and a reluctant sense of admiration for an army and air force that could launch such a precision assault. Some of the paratroopers drifting earthward were within rifle shot; but the Germans, who were "elderly" (38 years old), had never been in combat and, knowing nothing of total war, failed to fire. To them, it seemed unfair to shoot a man coming down in a parachute.

All hell soon broke out around Azeville. A band of American paratroopers got into a farmyard opposite Mueller's gate, and when his section advanced to wipe out the dark intruders, a single shot rang out and Mueller's close friend, Friedrich Busch, went down—a bullet through his head. Mueller was shocked by the first death he had seen in battle. Busch was to go on leave the next day to visit his wife and the infant daughter he had never seen.

Fierce firefights raged in the blackness in and around Azeville. There was mass confusion. Erwin Mueller was nearly paralyzed by fear and the belief that none of his officers knew what they were doing. His blood curdled when a *Feldgrau* ran through the village shouting that his squad had been killed. Out in a dark orchard, a man—American or German—screamed incessantly. Along a street, Mueller saw a figure writhing on the ground and went to help. It was an American paratrooper. His light brown uniform was saturated with blood, and on the sleeve of his jacket was the insignia of a fierce eagle. Moments later, the 101st Airborne parachutists shuddered violently and died.

All through the night, Erwin Mueller, Hitler's reluctant warrior, fought the best he could—for there seemed to be no alternative.

Eight miles south of Azeville, Col. Howard Johnson and his stick bailed out almost directly over the 501st Parachute Infantry's drop zone, a short distance north of La Barquette locks. As Johnson neared the ground, a German popped up only 25 yards away and fired at him, the bullet whizzing just past his head. Setting out in search of his men, the colonel stumbled into a German command post, but the enemy soldiers were preoccupied and did not even notice the dark intruder, who quickly withdrew. Jumpy's luck was holding—so far.

Moving along hedgerows and ditches, Johnson collected about 150 men and by dawn was within a few hundred yards of La Barquette locks. His 1st Battalion had the mission of seizing the locks, but the unit had been scattered badly in the drop. Its commander, Lt. Col. Robert G. Carroll, had been killed, and the executive officer, Maj. Philip S. Gage, Jr., had been wounded and captured. All of the company commanders were missing. So Jumpy Johnson attacked and captured the locks with his pickup force.

Several miles to the north of Johnson and his band, not a single planeload of Col. George Moseley's Five-O-Deuce had landed in the regiment's drop zone. His main objective was seizing causeways 3 and 4 at the northern stretch of Utah Beach, but his troopers had been sprinkled around the plush Norman countryside and were groping to locate assembly areas. Among Moseley's men who were lost was 22-year-old Schuyler Jackson of Washington, D.C. Along with another Screaming Eagle, Jackson came upon a German antiaircraft gun, whose crew was blasting away at C-47s winging overhead. The troopers crept up to the site, pitched a few grenades, and the gun fell silent, its crew dead.

Jackson and his comrade melted into the night. Presently, they discerned a form laying in the middle of a field, and went to investigate. It was Old Moe—Col. George Moseley—who was in excruciating pain, having suffered a broken leg on the jump.

Jackson and his comrade started to carry Old Moe to the cover of a hedgerow when they were fired on. They dropped Moseley where he was and gave chase to a German who they spotted dashing along a hedgerow. Jackson halted, lifted his tommy gun and fired a blast into the hedgerow. Much to his astonishment, he heard screams and groans; then a white handkerchief poked through the upper branches. A dozen or so *Feldgrau,* who had been concealed along the hedgerow, came out with hands up.

New to lethal violence, Jackson was shocked by the carnage that he had caused by one squeeze of his trigger finger. One German, supported by two others, was clasping his stomach in agony. Others were drenched with blood. A boy, who looked no more than 15, had been shot through both wrists, and when he tried to put up his hands to surrender, both hung down limply.

Seeing the Germans in such distress, Jackson found he could not hate them as he had expected to hate "The Enemy." They merely looked like pitiful humans. The corporal's comrade took charge of the prisoners, and Jackson went to a nearby deserted farmhouse, where he found a wheelbarrow and returned to George Moseley. The regimental commander was loaded into the conveyance and Jackson pushed the injured officer two miles to an aid station.[1]

Meanwhile, many Screaming Eagles were dropping directly onto German positions. Two parachutists came down in Sainte-Marie-du-Mont, a few miles behind Utah Beach, and were promptly captured, badly beaten by enemy soldiers, and put against a wall to be shot. The intervention of a German officer prevented the troopers' execution.

S. Sgt. Charles R. Ryan landed iniside a barbed-wire entanglement in Foucarville, and before he could shuck his chute, he heard a groan. Cpl. Howard Baker, who belonged to Ryan's company, had badly injured his knee. Ryan helped his comrade to a ditch, and moments later, they were pounced on by six Germans.

Ryan and Baker were taken to a nearby dugout, where seven other Screaming Eagles were being held prisoners. One trooper, his face ashen, was suffering intensely, having been hit in the chest by a fiendish wooden bullet. A German sergeant in the dugout played a harmonica almost continuously; the troopers conjectured whether it was their funeral march.

Later, more chaos erupted. American paratroopers were attacking the strongpoint with bazookas and automatic weapons fire. The captives' nervousness heightened. Would they be cut down unknowingly by their comrades? Finally, the attackers rushed the strongpoint, and the German major in command tried to run. Sergeant Ryan tackled the German, wrested away his pistol, and shot him to death.[2]

Elsewhere, Chaplain Sampson—Father Sam to the troopers—parachuted into a stream with water over his head, dropping his Mass kit. The canopy of his chute stayed open, and the strong wind blew him downstream. Father Sam thought he was a goner, and said a quick Act of Contrition. Only later would it dawn on him that in this moment of extreme danger, he had said the grace before meals!

About a hundred yards downstream, the chaplain reached shallow water, and he lay there a few minutes, exhausted and securely pinned by his harness and equipment. Heavy firing was raging on all sides. Inspired, Sampson hacked his way free with his knife, crawled back upstream to where he had landed, and began diving in search of his Mass kit. After six tries, he located the container.

Then Sampson spotted a figure struggling to get out of the water. Hurrying to help, the chaplain found that the trooper was his assistant, a corporal. Together they took refuge along a hedgerow, and in moments, a fiery ball—a burning C-47—hurtled toward them. The plane crashed about 100 yards away and threw flaming pieces over the two men's heads. Father Sam prayed for the men in the C-47; then watched in horror as two more flaming airplanes plunged to earth about a half-mile away.

Maxwell Taylor, commander of 14,000 Screaming Eagles, recalled vividly his entry into Normandy:

> *I floated down in my parachute toward the top of a tall tree. Not eager to become hung up in it and an easy target for a German rifleman, I made every effort to avoid the branches and succeeded in landing inside a small field enclosed by an impenetrable hedgerow. While there was considerable firing in the neighborhood, I was all alone except for three cows that were casting suspicious glances at this man from Mars.*

For 10 minutes, Taylor hacked at his confining parachute harness with a trench knife, freed himself, drew and cocked his pistol, readied his metal cricket, and headed cautiously toward a gate. Suddenly, the general heard the sound of a cricket, and he responded with two snaps. There in the moonlight stood a 501st Parachute Infantry trooper, bareheaded and bayonet-tipped rifle at the ready. General and private hugged each other.

Taylor and his one-man force struck out in a direction they hoped would lead to Utah Beach and soon linked up with Brig. Gen. Anthony C. "Tony" McAuliffe, the division artillery commander, seven other officers, and a handful of troopers. Neither general knew at the time where they were, a short distance from Sainte-Marie-du-Mont and the two lower causeways at Utah Beach.

In the meantime, Bob Sink, leader of the 506th Parachute Infantry, dropped routinely onto a meadow west of Culoville, not far from his regiment's assembly point. Sink could tell by the shooting that there were "hostile boys," as he called the Germans, on all sides. Efforts to contact his battalions by radio were futile, for the regiment had been widely scattered. His 3rd Battalion, lead by Lt. Col. Robert W. Wolverton, in essence had run into an enemy ambush even before bailing out.

Wolverton's drop zone was a number of large open meadows, and the Wehrmacht commander in the region had concluded that this site would be picked for any landing by an Allied airborne force. So the drop zone was ringed with machine guns. When Wolverton's flight approached, the Germans set fire to a large, oil-soaked barn, and the flaming torch lit up the surrounding countryside, sharply illuminating the descending paratroopers.

There was a raucous chattering of machine guns, and streams of tracers were poured into the Americans dangling helplessly under their undulating canopies. Twenty Screaming Eagles were killed in less than one minute, among them Colonel Wolverton and his executive officer, Maj. George S. Grant.

Just before 2:00 A.M., the field telephone rang on the desk of Gen. Erich Marcks, commander of the German MXXXIV Corps at Saint-Lô. The scholarly Marcks, who had left a leg on the Russian front, himself picked up the receiver. Col. Wolfgang Hamann, acting commander of the 709th Division, was calling from Valognes, some 20 miles to the north.

"There are enemy parachutists south of Saint-Germain-de-Varreville and at Sainte-Marie-du-Mont," Hamann reported. "A second group is west of the Carentan-Valognes road on both sides of the Merderet River, and on the road at Sainte Mère Eglise. The 3rd Battalion, 919th Grenadier Regiment, is holding prisoners from the U.S.A. 101st Airborne Division."[3]

Erich Marcks hung up the receiver. Now there was no doubt in his mind: "*Der Grossinvasion* was on." The Allies would never waste a crack airborne division in some marginal or diversionary operation.

At about the same time, Lt. Arthur Jahnke, commander of strongpoint Number 5—W5 for short—received a telephone call at his bunker on the eastern shore of the Cherbourg Peninsula. Jahnke, who had won the Knight's Cross on the Russian front and was recuperating from wounds, was happy to be in France where things were peaceful. He had no way of knowing that W5 was in the dead center of a beach marked Utah on Allied invasion maps.

"*Herr Lieutnant*," an excited voice exclaimed, "enemy parachutists are dropping behind your position!"

Probably a raid to help the French underground, Jahnke conjectured, and he sent out a patrol to investigate. There would be no invasion that day, Jahnke knew. Field Marshal Rommel himself had told Jahnke at a recent inspection of W5 that the Allies would come at high tide. And the tide had already begun running out.

Thirty minutes later, Jahnke heard machine-gun and rifle fire among the flooded fields to his rear. His patrol had run into 10 American paratroopers who were trying to work their way across the swamp through water up to their waists. The German bursts hit a few Americans, who disappeared under the water. Trapped, the other paratroopers raised their hands.

With eight prisoners, the patrol leader returned to the W5 bunker. The black-faced Americans were lined up against a wall, frisked, and their belongings were closely inspected. Two wounded parachutists, carried in by their comrades, were taken to the aid station in the bunker.

Lieutenant Jahnke called his battalion headquarters. "Eight prisoners of the American 2nd Battalion, 506th Parachute Regiment." The line clicked and went dead.[4]

The underground cable, which had only recently been laid by French "volunteer" workers under the direction of Wehrmacht engineers, had been cut by a band of Screaming Eagles. Jahnke was out of contact with higher headquarters and with strongpoints on either side.

About 2:45 P.M., a *Feldwebel* (corporal) came up to Jahnke.

"Lieutenant, the prisoners are curiously restless. They keep wanting to know the time. Two of the officers are demanding that they be moved—right now."[5] Arthur Jahnke shrugged, unaware that at dawn W5 would be at ground zero in a savagely fierce hurricane of man-made steel and explosives.

Several miles north of Strongpoint 5, a company of Germans was guarding a coastal battery at Saint-Marcouf. Shortly after 1:30 A.M., *Oberleutnant* Hermann Grieg dashed excitedly into the company CP after returning from a patrol. *"Herr Kapitaen,"* Grieg blurted out, "we came under fire, I presume from enemy paratroopers!"

"Paratroopers!" the captain scoffed. "There can't be any paratroopers." He, too, had been told that the weather conditions and tide would not allow an invasion for at least two weeks. However, like any competent commander, the captain would play it safe. He sent out a 22-man patrol, heavily armed with Schmeisser machine pistols and hand grenades, to scour the surrounding swamps. Cautiously, the *Feldrgau* picked their way through the darkness. There was only an eerie silence. As they stole along, the Germans heard an occasional frog croaking from the swamps. Curious, Lieutenant Grieg reflected. He hadn't realized that there were so many frogs in the vicinity of the gun battery.

Suddenly, a German at the end of the skirmish line shouted, "Halt!" There was a crashing sound in the underbrush, and the *Feldgrau* fired. Then a groan. Grieg rushed to where his man was kneeling over a motionless form. "What's going on?" he asked. "An American, probably a paratrooper," the other replied.

Searching the dead soldier's pockets, the *Feldgrau* found a curious gadget—a child's cricket. He pressed it. *Croak!* Again. *Croak!* From the surrounding darkness, they heard *Croak! Croak!* Now the Germans knew the secret. Those weren't frogs they had been hearing, but the metal crickets—and the Americans were using the toys to identify each other.

Lieutenant Grieg's patrol pushed onward, stopping periodically to snap the cricket. When they heard two snaps in reply, they closed in on the unknowing American paratrooper and either killed or captured him. At about 2:00 A.M., the patrol returned to its base with 20 prisoners. Interrogation revealed that they belonged to the 502nd Parchute Infantry Regiment, and that their unit's mission was to capture gun battery 1/1261 near Saint-Martin-de-Varreville. (This was the gun site that Capt. Frank Lillyman had found to be abandoned.)

The German officers were astonished when they inspected the equipment taken from the American parachutists: compasses as jacket buttons, silk scarves with maps printed on them. Even the fields where *Rommelspargel* (Rommel's asparagus, antiglider poles) had been planted only a few days earlier were accurately marked. The German captain had never computed the exact map coordinates of his machine-gun posts, yet these sites were precisely plotted on the Americans' maps.[6]

With all of the 101st Airborne's paratroopers on the ground, dead or alive, the division's 52 gliders making the initial assault were winging through the moonlight toward landing zone E, two miles west of Sainte-Marie-du-Mont. Piloting the lead glider (named the *Fighting Falcon*) was Lt. Col. Mike Murphy, who had been one of the nation's best-known stunt pilots before the war. He had been asked by Gen. Hap Arnold to reorganize the training of glider pilots, whose development had been bogged down in red tape and incompetency.

Seated beside Murphy was Gen. Don Pratt, the assistant division commander. Pratt had been designated to command the division's tail—a water lift—which was an ignominious fate for an airborne soldier. So he had been elated when it was decided to permit him to go into combat in a glider.

Right at 4:00 A.M., Mike Murphy spotted the landing zone, which Screaming Eagle pathfinders had marked with light patterns. Zooming down, Murphy made a perfect textbook landing, locking the brakes, and the glider skidded across the wet pasture for more than 700 feet; then smashed with enormous impact into tall poplar trees. If a glider pilot were to survive the Russian-roulette chances involved in landing, his body usually paid a heavy price. Murphy broke both legs. Don Pratt was crushed to death when a chained jeep broke loose on collision with the sturdy trees. Pratt became the second American airborne general to be killed in action. (Charles Keerans of the 82nd Airborne had lost his life in Sicily.)

On hearing of Pratt's death, Max Taylor would bypass two regimental commanders senior in age and grade, Bob Sink and Howard Johnson, and name his 34-year-old chief of staff, Gerry Higgins, to be the 101st Airborne's assistant commander.[7]

Fortunately for Neptune, some 300 C-47s—70 percent of the 101st Airborne lift—had dropped their paratroopers in an area of eight square miles, in the Sainte Mère Eglise/Carentan region behind Utah Beach. However, some 1,500 paratroopers had

Brig. Gen. Don F. Pratt. *(Don F. Pratt Museum)*

Pfc. Clarence Hughart. *(Author's collection)*

jumped outside that rectangle, all the way from Graignes, six miles south of Carentan, to the outskirts of heavily fortified Cherbourg, 25 miles above Carentan, and most of them would be killed or captured.

24
Swamps and More Swamps

A half hour after the lead aircraft of the 101st Airborne Division had lifted off from England, the first of 377 C-47s carrying 6,418 paratroopers of the 82nd Airborne struck out for Normandy. On board, in order of flight, were Bill Ekman's 505th, Roy Lind-quist's 508th, and Zip Millett's 507th Regiments, along with a pair of howitzers of Lt. Col. Wagner J. D'Allessio's 456th Parachute Artillery Battalion and a contingent of engineers.

The flight hauling the 505th was heading for drop zone O, located about halfway between the flooded Merderet and Sainte Mère Eglise. Ekman's outfit was to seize bridges over the river— one at Chef-du-Pont and one at La Fière—and to capture the road junction town of Sainte Mère Eglise.

Thirty minutes out in front of the main body of the 505th, 18-year-old Robert M. Murphy, a pathfinder, bailed out, and at 1:21 A.M. he landed with a thud, not on drop zone O, but in a garden dead in the center of German-garrisoned Sainte Mère Eglise. The lanky Murphy began hacking away at his harness with a trench knife, and in his excitement also cut away pouches holding a few hundred rounds of crucially needed ammunition. Lugging a bag carrying a Eureka, the teenager struck out for the drop zone.[1]

At about 1:50 A.M., Five-O-Fives in the first serial began bailing out. One of them was Sgt. Buffalo Boy Canoe, the Oglala Sioux Indian veteran of the Sicily and Salerno jumps. Canoe was not listed on his plane's roster, for he was an AWOL-in-reverse. He had been assigned to a job in England that would have left him behind, but after hearing that his comrades were about to lift off for the Big Show, he dashed to the airfield and hopped aboard a C-47 without a weapon. Now he was jumping into hostile Normandy armed with only a grenade that a trooper had given him.

Bill Ekman and his executive officer, Mark Alexander, jumped with the regiment's last serial. Ekman was jolted violently when his chute opened, then crashed hard onto the ground. His head spinning, the 505th leader wandered around lost for two hours before stumbling onto a tiny knot of All-Americans.

A 505th Regiment surgeon, Maj. Daniel B. McIlvoy, Jr., landed near a German artillery position. Back before the Sicily jump, "Doc" McIlvoy had won the gleeful admiration of the troopers when he had been overserved at an officers' cocktail reception and booted a pompous Army Air Corps general in the rear end before conducting a rapid strategic withdrawal.

McIlvoy quickly collected a group of ablebodied and injured Five-O-Fives and they moved into a farmhouse near a road. Lt. Steven Wasecka, whose ankles had been broken in the jump, remained outside as a guard. At McIlvoy's suggestion, Wasecka dug a deep foxhole and cut in sideways, so he could sit in the excavation with his legs outstretched in order to keep weight off of them.

Maj. Daniel B. McIlvoy, Jr.
(Author's collection)

Later, Wasecka yelled that a column of trucks was approaching. Thinking that these were American seaborne troops, the Five-O-Fives dashed excitedly outside, only to be greeted by a torrent of rifle fire from Germans in the passing convoy. As McIlvoy and the others scrambled back inside, the enemy trucks continued onward.

A short time afterward, Doc McIlvoy was treating a close friend, Capt. Matthew Connelly, who was in agony with a fracture of the spine sustained in a jolting parachute landing. Connelly, the Catholic chaplain of the 505th Regiment, vehemently refused evacuation, and would remain in action for 33 days. (Eventually, both of Father Connelly's legs had to be amputated.)

Matt Ridgway, making only his fifth parachute jump and first one in combat, came down softly in a pasture and, after shucking his chute, whipped out his .45 Colt. As with Max Taylor of the 101st Airborne, the commander of 14,000 troops was alone in a strange and hostile environment.

Slipping silently along the hedgerows, Ridgway came upon a trooper who led him to the command post of Lt. Col. Ben Vandervoort, leader of the 505th's 2nd Battalion, who had broken an ankle in the jump and was in agonizing pain. Undaunted, Vandervoort tightly laced his boot, used a rifle as a crutch, and would continue to fight for 33 days.

Next in the line of flight was Lindquist's 508th Regiment, whose drop zone N was on the west side of the swollen Merderet, about halfway between the key bridges at Chef-du-Pont and LaFière. Unbeknownst to Linquist (or anyone else in the Allied camp), the headquarters of Gen. Wilhelm Falley's 91st Air Landing Division had recently been established in a chateau only 2,500 feet south of drop zone N.

Lindquist was greeted by long fingers of tracers when he jumped, and the fire followed him to the ground, where he landed in two feet of water. Shucking his chute, the colonel took but a few steps and was greeted by a sharp: "Halt!" It was his orderly. Together they trudged through the swamp, and twice their trek was broken when they fell into water over their heads. They cursed the antigas jumpsuits that allowed water to enter but wouldn't let it back out.

Eventually, Linquist spotted a blue light—his regiment's assembly beacon. Reaching the site, he was crestfallen; only 20 of his troopers were there, and 1,980 of them were not.

The jump-boot journalists took their lumps with the bona fide paratroopers. Phil Bucknell of *Stars and Stripes* bailed out with Ekman's men and came down swinging on his shroud lines. Crashing hard not far from Sainte-Mère-Eglise, he broke his leg to become the first reporter casualty in Normandy. A paratrooper propped Bucknell against a tree, and the correspondent asked not to be left behind. The parachutist was curt, whispering, "Look, Mac, if I was you I'd just stay here and keep my trap shut. If you make any noise, you might attract someone you don't want to see." And he disappeared into the night.

William Walton, the gusty, 22-year-old reporter for *Time*, landed in a pear tree—a rather good shock-absorber, he thought. Dangling, he was unable to touch anything. Fingers of tracers were zipping through the night. "Knife! Get out your knife!" he thought. But his chute harness had slipped up around his neck, effectively straight-jacketing him. He was a perfect target for snipers, there in the moonlight—and he knew it.

Now Walton heard footsteps and the rustling of underbrush. In a stage whisper, he called out the password, "Flash," and waited in vain for the countersign—"Thunder." From a nearby hedge, he heard voices. German or American? Breathless, he listened intently. Now a voice became clear—someone with a midwestern America accent. Walton resumed breathing. Then a big figure stole catlike out of the bushes, tugged at the tree branches, and with his pigsticker, cut Walton's suspension cords. Falling like an overripe pear, the reporter felt like hugging his rescuer, Sergeant Auge.[2]

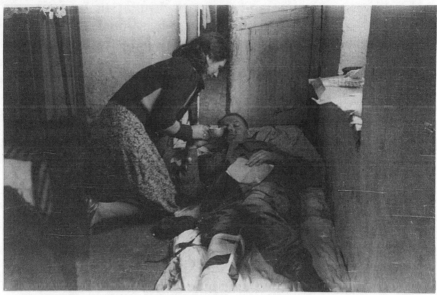

Jump-boot journalist William Walton of *Time* magazine is cared for by a French woman after being injured in Normandy parachute assault. *(Daniel B. McIlvoy, M.D.)*

M. G. Thomas, who had been a private with the 508th Regiment, remembered his introduction to Normandy—and the subsequent combat:

> *I was scared—but not as much as I thought I'd be. The jumpmaster shouted, "Let's go!" Just then the plane was hit by ack-ack. Half the stick got out, but the ninth man was hit just as he got to the door. The rest of us were knocked down. We got up except for the wounded trooper, who was bleeding badly. When the last man had jumped,*

the wounded man somehow got to his feet and leaped out.

I didn't like seeing our boys shot in the air, while they were still in their chutes. I stayed in a ditch for a while; then some troopers came along and we moved on. Suddenly we were boxed in by enemy fire. The Germans raked the ditch where we had dived. It looked like the end. One of our boys asked us to say a prayer, but I didn't know any prayer. All I could say was: "God, if you ever do anything for me, please do it now 'cause I need it."

Eighteen-year-old Pvt. Tony Vickery landed routinely—except for flak and a few ambitious German machine gunners. The men in his company called Vickery the "Milk Bar Commando"—milk shakes being his favorite and strongest drink. (His heaviest epithet was "Gosh dern.") Although he was handsome, Tony had no girlfriends; his mom, back in Georgia, was his best girl. In an outfit of hard-fighting, hard-drinking, hard-cussing soldiers, there had been much talk about whether the well-liked youth would hold up in combat.

Now, in hostile Normandy, Vickery and a comrade moved off toward the drop zone, picking up 15 strays along the way. With daylight approaching, the little band dug into an earthen hedgerow. Suddenly, a skirmish line of *Feldgrau* charged the Americans, and a fierce firefight raged for 30 minutes. When the smoke had cleared, Tony Vickery, still clutching his tommy gun, lay dead, four machine-pistol slugs in his throat. On the other side of the hedgerow from him sprawled 12 dead Germans. The Milk Bar Commando had gotten every one of them.

South of Saint Lô, two American parachutists collapsed in the front garden of a home in Saint-Jean-de-Savigney. One man, his jumpsuit soaked with blood, was gasping and choking; he had been shot in the chest. His comrade had broken a leg when he landed in a tree.

Thomas Porcella, who had jumped into Normandy with Lindquist's 508th Regiment, recalled the two All-Americans' plight:

Across the street lived a French woman named Mrs. Robine. She and another lady moved the two troopers across the street and put them in a small building. The French ladies took care of the troopers, gave them food, and tried to make them comfortable. But another French woman tipped off the Germans and they came and carried off the troopers in a horse-cart.

Meanwhile, some 40 miles deep into France from the nearest American drop zone, 23-year-old 1st Sgt. Leonard A. Funk of the 508th Regiment knew that he and his stick were in trouble. They had dropped so far to the enemy's rear that German vehicles were driving on occasion at night with headlights blazing, and *Feldgrau* were sauntering around villages without weapons.

Leonard Funk, a native of Pittsburgh who would become America's most decorated paratrooper, recalled his predicament:

> *At first, we didn't know where in the hell we were. All we knew was that we had been flying a long time after we'd seen others bailing out. I told my men that, come hell or high water, I would never be taken prisoner, that we were going to fight our way back to friendly forces—even if it took us the rest of the war. It damned near did. We holed up by day, and marched by night. When possible, we avoided enemy contact, but got mixed up in all sorts of shootouts and scrapes. Three of our scouts were killed; so I took the point.*
>
> *Several times, we ambushed Kraut vehicles and small groups, and we blew up one panzer by putting a landmine in the road. Much of the time we were starving and thirsty—didn't dare to approach a house. Hardly ever took our boots off. The closer we got to American lines, the thicker were the Germans. Now it was touch-and-go every yard of the way, and we had several brushes with disaster. Finally, after 21 days, we reached an outpost of our 90th Infantry Division—and we were so filthy and disheveled that the straight-legs thought we were Krauts and damned near shot us.[3]*

Gen. Jim Gavin jumped with the Five-O-Eights, and landed not far from Colonel Lindquist, but on solid ground in an apple orchard. On hand for his arrival was the customary reception committee of mildly curious cows. Almost before Gavin could get out of the orchard, he had collected most of his support staff who had jumped from his C-47: Lt. Hugo V. Olsen, his aide; Cpl. Walker E. Wood, his orderly; Capt. Willard E. Harrison; Lt. Thomas Graham, a liaison officer in the division G-3 (operations); and a few others.

Gavin also had a watchful eye for his bodyguard, a rough-looking warrior who seemed to be scowling all the time, seldom spoke, and wore a gold earring. He belonged to the 504th Regiment, which was sitting this one out in England. A few days earlier, Rube Tucker had told his friend Gavin: "This guy's the toughest bastard in my regiment. You've got to take him along as

Paratrooper patrol of 101st Airborne cautiously edges past dead Germans in Normandy. *(U. S. Army)*

your bodyguard." The trooper with the gold earring had bailed out on Gavin's heels, never to be heard from or seen again.

A short distance from Gavin's apple orchard, 22-year-old Pfc. Orville A. Amorose was descending in his parachute. He vividly recalled the episode:

> *Halfway down, I saw that I was over water. Before, I had been merely scared; now I was petrified—for I didn't know how to swim. I knew I was about to die, that I'd never get out of my harness and the 90 pounds of gear to even inflate the Mae West I was wearing. When I hit, I went clear under the water. That's the end, I thought. But my legs hit the muddy bottom and I stood up—in water up to*

my neck. Miraculously, I had beaten the odds, for many places in that swamp were ten feet or more deep. I thanked God.

Amorose started to struggle through the swamp, and moments later spotted a group of dark figures on dry land—Jim Gavin and his men who had landed a few minutes earlier. The commander of Task Force A (all the 82nd Airborne's parachute elements) told Amorose and two other men to go back into the swamp and try to locate other parachutists. Again, nonswimmer Amorose was petrified, not knowing when he might drop off into deep water and drown. The mission achieved minimal results: Only three paratroopers were brought back, not nearly as many as had been seen parachuting into the swamp.

A glider had crash-landed a quarter of a mile away in the swamp. Because nearly all of the gliders in the night assault carried heavy weapons and equipment, Gavin felt that there might be a .57-millimeter antitank gun in the glider, one that could come in handy if panzers were to attack the lightly armed paratroopers after dawn.

Thomas Graham recalled that episode:

General Jim told me to take four men and go to the glider and see if there was a gun, and could it be salvaged. As we approached the glider, the bullets zipping around us became intense. The glider was mired in the thick grass and mud, as was its unlocking mechanism. The crew had apparently escaped through the canvas sides, which were ripped open. All the while the Germans were peppering us with fire. It was a hopeless case, and we returned to shore.

Slim Jim wouldn't take no for an answer, so he waded into the slimy water up to his chest and led us in a second attempt to salvage the gun. This time, the automatic weapons fire was so heavy that we had to pull back to the shore without reaching the glider. We brought with us a wounded soldier, who was placed along a hedgerow with other troopers who were injured or wounded.

Meanwhile, fate had been frowning on Zip Millett's 507th Regiment. When Millett's pathfinders jumped on drop zone T just west of the Merderet, they were greeted by heavy bursts of machine-gun fire and had to fight for their lives from the moment they crashed to earth. Two officers broke their legs. Several troopers were killed. Capt. John T. Joseph, the 507th Regimental

Smashed American glider and occupants. *(U. S. Army)*

pathfinder leader, could locate only two men, but one of them was a Eureka technician. At 2:20 A.M., the Eureka was operating, and a short time later, Joseph looked up to see 20 of the 83 C-47s hauling the Five-O-Sevens directly over his head, then go on and unload their human cargoes far from the drop zone. Eureka had malfunctioned.

Joseph and his two pathfinders remained in place for 30 minutes, until the German tracer streams zipping past forced a withdrawal. Many of the sticks that he had expected to drop and form up on him were now crawling and gasping half-drowned in the swamps. Others, trapped underwater by their harnesses and bulky gear, drowned—sometimes in three feet of water. Some 507th planes far overshot their mark, and their troopers came down isolated in enemy country, where their problem became one of evasion and survival.

Far from his drop zone, Sgt. Frank P. Costa, a 25-year-old New Yorker who was a communications sergeant in the 3rd Battalion of the 507th, plunged into a swamp with water up to his neck, and nearly drowned before he could hack himself free of his harness. In the excitement of his first combat jump and the imminent threat of death, Costa lost his rifle and helmet, and was left armed only with a trench knife. To the north, perhaps five or six miles away, he could see ack-ack shells exploding in the sky.

Alone, scared, and lost, Costa waded in the cold, waist- to chest-deep water for 30 minutes before contacting a comrade, Cpl. Leo Smith, and then another lost trooper, Ed Stranko. For two hours, the three Five-O-Sevens struggled through the swamps until, nearly exhausted, they crawled onto dry land. But where were they? "Mars," Smith suggested.

Costa noticed that Stranko had a handkerchief wrapped around his wrist and asked, "What happened to you?" Sheepishly, Stranko explained that he had frantically cut himself out of his harness and gear and, in his excitement, was not aware that he was also hacking his wrist.

Frank Costa remembered what happened next:

> *When we had regained our breath, we approached a small house, knocked on the door and called to the folks. They peeked out of a first-floor window and their eyes bulged out as though we were from another planet. Our faces were streaked with black; our jumpsuits were wet and wrinkled and torn, and our hair was matted and unruly. But when we convinced them that we were Americans, they got excited and opened the door.*
>
> *We told them: "This is D-Day! American soldiers have landed in France!"*

From their French hosts, the three paratroopers finally learned where they were: in Graignes, a sleepy little town perched on a patch of dry ground and surrounded by swamps, six miles below Carentan and 15 miles south of Saint Mère Eglise. These isolated Americans had no way of knowing that insignificant Graignes would soon be the site of one of the worst Nazi atrocities in the West.

Some distance from Graignes, another 507th trooper, 22-

year-old Pfc. Clarence Hughart of Morgantown, West Virginia, landed on his back. Stunned, he managed to cut himself free; then sat down to contemplate his next move. Suddenly, there were loud cracks, and Hughart felt a searing pain in one leg. He had been shot. Dimly, the paratrooper saw several Germans hovering over him and pointing weapons at his head. This is the end, he reflected.

Even while the Germans were pilfering Hughart's watch, bill-fold, and other personal belongings, they spoke to him in friendly fashion, wanting to know if he was an American. Hughart tried to rise, but the leg in which he had been shot would not function. Solicitously, the Germans found a sturdy stick, tied it to his leg, and carried him across a field. By the rays of the moon, the American saw that a few of his captors were perhaps 50 years old and the others appeared to be mere boys, hardly the cream of the Wehrmacht.

Clarence Hughart recalled the episode:

> War was a strange thing, I thought. We were supposed to kill each other, but now these enemy soldiers were looking after me. They could have killed me, and my corpse might not have been found for weeks—if ever.
>
> They carried me to a vehicle—a Volkswagen, I think it was—and gently laid me in the back seat on a few parachutes they had collected. I was driven to a company CP and laid on a bed of straw on the floor, only a few feet from where a German captain was working at a desk. He paid no attention to me, apparently not surprised to have an American paratrooper suddenly dumped at his feet.

On this calamitous night, fate also had its eye on Wehrmacht Gen. Wilhelm Falley, the tough, battle-tested leader of the 91st Air Landing Division. Not long after midnight, Falley left his head-quarters in the Chateau Haut, just north of Picauville, and drove southward toward Rennes, in Brittany. Falley would participate in the German Seventh Army's *Kriegspiel* (war games talks), to which all commanders in Normandy had been summoned.

Falley soon grew worried. There was heavy air activity, and pathfinder markers were being dropped. "This is no routine action," Falley told his aide, Maj. Helmuth Bartuzat. "Something big is going on." Then to his driver: "Turn around and head back."[4]

Its cat's-eye headlights marking the way, the powerful Horch roared off for Picauville. Behind Falley, Allied bombers were pounding the Carentan region, and the skyline there was shrouded in smoke and dust. Not far from the Chateau Haut, the driver turned off the main road. Unseen along the road were Lt. Malcomb D. Brennan of the 3rd battalion, 508th Regiment, and three troopers, who opened fire at the speeding Horch.

Bullets ripped into the front of the car and shattered the windshield. Major Bartuzat slumped over, dead. The Horch swerved and weaved; then smashed into a wall. Doors flew open from the impact, and General Falley was hurled into the road. His pistol slithered out in front of him and he began crawling toward it. Falley kept shouting, "Don't kill, don't kill!" but he continued to edge toward his pistol. A shot rang out; the commander of the 91st Air Landing Division collapsed on the road, killed instantly.

At about the same time that Falley was gunned down, four miles to the northeast, Lt. Col. Cannonball Krause was marching at the head of 108 of his men toward his battalion's objective, Sainte Mère Eglise, five miles inland from Utah Beach. Sainte Mère was the district headquarters of the German army, hub of a network of hard-surfaced roads, and midway station of a trunk cable linking Cherbourg with Carentan and other towns in the lower peninsula. Neptune planners had projected that Krause's battalion would be isolated for at least a day and have a fierce fight to seize the town.

But Krause's luck seemed to be holding. He had jumped lucky, and landed routinely in a small garden patch in the corner of a field that he had earlier chosen for his first command post. Then Krause had quickly collected his force of over a hundred men—plus one thoroughly drunk Frenchman who had been hauled in by a few troopers when he was staggering homeward.

The violent shock of suddenly finding himself in the clutches of a large band of blackfaced, heavily armed cutthroats rapidly sobered up the native, and he told Krause everything he needed to know. There was only one German company in Sainte Mère, service troops at that. However, an infantry battalion was bivouacked south of the town.

When the Frenchman volunteered to lead his captors into town by way of little-known paths, in order to avoid the German infantry battalion, Krause leaped at the chance. Thirty minutes later, the troopers were on the outskirts of Sainte Mère, where they halted and Krause told his men, "I want no rifle firing—use only grenades, knives and bayonets!" (There was no reason not to fire weapons—apparently knives and bayonets seemed to be more gung ho.)

Krause and his troopers stole into the dark village and down the main street. The small German garrison had pulled out, but not before it had wreaked havoc on several 82nd Airborne men whose misfortune it had been to parachute directly into the town. Dead troopers, still in their harnesses, hung from trees, shot before they reached the ground. Krause and his troopers stared at the corpses in jump boots and vowed revenge.

Then Krause pulled out the American flag that had flown over Naples. Strolling to the village hall, he ran Old Glory up a flagpole—just as he had sworn to do ten hours earlier in England. Americans had liberated the first town in France. The time was 4:27 A.M.

Eighteen minutes later, 600 assault troops of the 4th Infantry Division, jammed into 20 landing craft, started their run to Utah Beach, 11 miles away. Most of these soldiers were grim and fearful. For two weeks, reports had swept their encampment that the Allied brass expected up to 90 percent casualties among the first waves to hit Hitler's Atlantic Wall.

25
Death Stalks
the
Hedgerows

Dawn of D-Day broke on thousands of lost American paratroopers still roaming the Cherbourg Peninsula. Resourceful by nature and by training, they quickly adapted. Side by side in pairs and in packs, Screaming Eagles and All-Americans fought furiously for objectives they had never heard of. Men of the 82nd Airborne were led by officers of the 101st Airborne and vice versa.

Stalking through the *bocage* (hedgerow) country, was much like wandering around through a maze. Main roads had to be avoided, and the twisting hedgerows and sunken roads between them conformed to no sensible pattern. Death lurked at every hedgerow.

For centuries, the flatlands of the lower peninsula had been divided and subdivided into small pastures by means of thick earthern fences. Many of these barriers were eight to ten feet high, and long snakelike roots packed the dirt together much as reinforcing steel would strengthen concrete. A thorny growth of trees, bushes, and brambles crowned the mounds. Each pasture was a minifortress, for the earthen walls and tangled vegetation provided ideal protection and natural concealment. Paratroopers (and later foot soldiers and tankers) could see ahead for only 50 to 100 yards.

Sounds of a firefight a few fields away might be heard, but conveyed nothing as to distance or direction. It was possible for little packs of American paratroopers to remain lost to one another while roaming the same area, separated by only a few pastures. When the individual parachutist or pairs or tiny bands came to realize that they were lost, the sense of isolation grew overpowering. Then survival became their paramount drive; the desire to reach their units a secondary objective. Often, the adversaries in this lethal game of hide-and-seek collided violently.

Screaming Eagle Lt. Wallace A. Swanson and a band of troopers were dug in at a roadblock outside Foucarville. They were armed to the teeth with rifles, two machine guns, a few bazookas, and 12 pounds of explosives. Soon a German artillery convoy came barreling down the road toward Swanson and his men. The lead truck struck a mine that the troopers had planted and blew sky-high. Four trailing trucks, all loaded with artillerymen, crunched to a halt. Even before the startled *Feldgrau* could scramble out, bazooka rockets tore into all four trucks, and the roadblock machine gunners blasted away at the juicy targets. Only a few Germans managed to escape into nearby woods.

Two miles inland from Foucarville, Lt. Morton J. Smit of the 101st Airborne led a 25-man patrol into the village of Haut Fornel. It appeared to be abandoned, so Smit and Pvt. Harold F. Boone slipped into a building that had been occupied by a Wehrmacht unit and began loading *souvenirs de guerre* into a large

American paratroopers in Normandy stalk enemy machine gun past dead comrades. *(U. S. Army)*

bag. Minutes later, the two men heard shots and running footsteps.

Smit and Boone edged outside the door and almost ran into the arms of about 12 *Feldgrau* who were climbing out of a truck. Smit blasted them with his tommy gun, and cut down most of them. A firefight now broke out in Haut Fornel, and a squad of Germans pitching potato-masher grenades forced Smit and Boone to dash out the back of the building. Running through the courtyard, they spotted a muddy hog wallow and dived in headfirst. Laying flat on their backs below the surface with only their mouths and noses exposed, Boone and Smit stayed for an hour while Germans hunted for them.

Then a band of American parachutists attacked and drove the Germans out of the village. Pfc. John Leviski, a bayonet fixed to the tip of his rifle, caught a glimpse of a humanlike apparition, caked from head to foot with gobs of gooey mud, suddenly rise from an adjacent hog wallow. By instinct, Leviski whirled to bayonet the figure before recognizing that it was Lieutenant Smit.

Meanwhile, on the sands of Utah Beach at 6:39 A.M., a battalion of 4th Infantry Division shock troops, led by 57-year-old Brig. Gen. Theodore Roosevelt, Jr., stormed ashore after a gargantuan pounding of German defense by 17 warships and 276 Marauder bombers. Because of the courage and skill of American paratroopers, and because of the air and sea bombardments, hardly a shot had been fired at the first seaborne invaders.

Roosevelt, son of the 26th president of the United States, was short in physical stature, but extremely long in heart. His son, Quentin, within the hour, would be going ashore at Omaha, the other American beach. Free-spirited Teddy had begged for this job, quipping to his boss: "If the boys in the first wave see a general on the beach, they'll think it's a pretty damned safe place to be."

Now, hunkered down behind a seawall, Roosevelt intently studied his map. "I'm convinced that we're about a mile and a quarter south of where we're supposed to be," he told the battalion commander. "I think we ought to push inland, anyhow. There don't seem to be many live Germans around here."[1]

A cool, veteran campaigner who was armed only with a walking cane, the little general rapidly improvised an attack over nearby Causeway 2. "Okay, let's move out," he rasped, leading the way. "If those German bastards want war, this is a damned good place to start it!"[2]

On the heels of Teddy Roosevelt, wave after wave of 4th Infantry Division troops poured over Utah Beach and pushed inland, contested only by isolated snipers and sporadic shells. By contrast, at Omaha Beach, the 1st and 29th Infantry Divisions ran into a meat grinder. German machine gunners, perched on heights overlooking the shore, raked the invaders with withering fire even before many had gotten out of their landing craft.

A few thousand Americans were pinned to the beach, unable to move or hardly lift their heads. At midmorning, scores of dead GIs were sprawled about and washing back and forth in the heavy surf, now red with blood. One of those lying flat with his nose pressed in the wet sand with men being killed on all sides was pioneer jump-boot journalist, Jack Beaver Thompson of the *Chicago Tribune*.

Jack Thompson recalled that morning on Omaha Beach:

I wanted to parachute in with our troops, but a few weeks earlier, I had received a telegram from my publisher, Robert McCormick. It said, "No more jumping out of airplanes into battles. It's too dangerous. We don't want to lose you." So I picked a nice, "safe" assignment—landing with the Omaha assault waves. When I had a chance to file my story back to the Trib, *I resisted an urge to include a note to McCormick. "Dear Boss, you were right—Omaha was very safe!"*

Only through the courage and individual initiative of junior officers and men was disaster of enormous magnitude averted. Late that afternoon, the Americans clawed their way up the cliff and drove off the Germans.

Three miles southwest of Utah Beach that morning, Maxwell Taylor, leader of the 101st Airborne, was in the primitive hamlet of Pouppeville and desperately trying to make radio contact with elements of the 4th Infantry Division. A hodgepodge collection of Screaming Eagle officers, artillerymen, clerks, military policemen, and a handful of riflemen, led by lanky Lt. Col. Julian L. Ewell, had just killed or captured the German garrison in Pouppeville.

Now, Taylor sent a patrol down the road leading from the hamlet to the beach, and the troopers returned with Capt. George Mabry of the 4th Division. It was the first linkup of airborne and seaborne forces. Taylor and his parachutists gawked at Mabry as though he were from another planet—he had come in by sea. It was 11:02 A.M.

At the same time, a collection of 101st Airborne parachutists under Lt. Col. Bob Cole of San Antonio, Texas, seized the exit of Causeway 4. Leaving a detachment there, Cole and the other troopers moved down to the exit of Causeway 3, where they dug in.

Minutes later, two columns of Germans, pushed back from the beach by the advancing 4th Infantry Division, were trudging along the causeway directly toward the muzzles of Cole's concealed machine gunners and riflemen. As the colonial militia did at Bunker Hill a few wars earlier, Bob Cole waited until he saw the "whites of their eyes," then ordered, "Fire!" Within minutes, the ambushed *Feldgrau* were wiped out to a man.

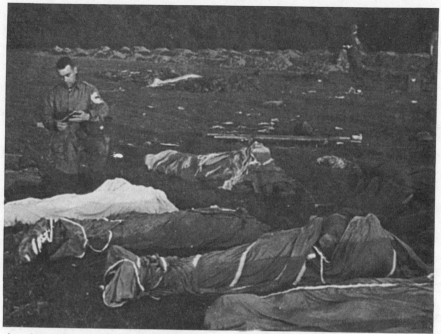

An American parachute padre prays over troopers killed in D-Day airborne assault. (*U. S. Army*)

With all four of the crucial causeway exits held by his Screaming Eagles, Max Taylor sought to satisfy his intense curiosity over a riddle that had puzzled him for weeks. Back in England, he (and other American airborne leaders) had been pouring over countless air photos of heavy poles (*Rommelspargel*) being planted irregularly in Norman fields with the obvious intention of disrupting an airborne assault. By studying nightly the irregular pattern of the poles, Taylor and others had tried to learn how the wily Erwin Rommel expected airborne forces to land and modify their plans accordingly. After countless hours of study, right up to takeoff time, the American brass never discerned a pattern that would reveal a German plan of defense.

Now, Taylor asked a Norman farmer why he had poled one of the fields near his house and left untouched another nearby. His reply was simple: "The Germans ordered us to pole our fields by June 15, but I never poled that field yonder because my cows always liked to graze there."

Taylor felt a twinge of embarrassment. All along it had been the eating preferences of local cows, not a brilliant plan by Rommel, that American airborne leaders had been trying to decipher.

*   *   *

More than 100 miles across the English Channel from fire-swept Cherbourg Peninsula, Dwight Eisenhower had spent a seemingly interminable night at Southwick House, chain-smoking and trying to read pulp-magazine Westerns. About 9:00 A.M., the anxious supreme commander received a telephone call from Air Chief Marshal Trafford Leigh-Mallory, a man of personal courage who said exactly what was on his mind. The SHAEF air chief reported that the 82nd and 101st Airborne Divisions had landed, apparently without heavy losses, and were in action. He voiced his delight over this "good news" and expressed regret that he had found it necessary to add to Ike's personal burden during the final tense period before D-Day.[3]

Capt. Ignatius "Matty" Maternowski, the Catholic chaplain of Lindquist's 508th Parachute Infantry, was a tough and energetic little Pole, who was greatly admired by the troopers in his regiment. Back in the United States, the parachuting padre had on occasion offered to put on the gloves with officers who interfered with his pastoral work or made wisecracks about his church. His jump-booted flock liked a chaplain who could handle his fists.

Now, Father Matty was wandering through the Norman fields in search of his unit when he came across a group trying to pry injured soldiers out of a wrecked glider. Typically, the padre joined in the rescue effort. Moments later, a shot rang out from a hedgerow, and the pugilist-priest went down for the final 10-count.

Meanwhile at Sainte Mère Eglise, the Germans that Cannonball Krause and his band of refined cutthroats had evicted in the hours of blackness decided that they wanted the vacated property back. That morning, a force of about 200 *Feldgrau* attacked the dairy center from the south, but Krause's Five-O-Fives, in their first real battle action, sent the Germans reeling back into a thick forest.

One of those killed by machine-gun fire was Capt. Harold H. Swingler, the former intercollegiate boxing champion, who had single-handedly captured the 82nd Airborne's first Tiger tank at bloody Biazza Ridge in Sicily. Another survivor of Biazza Ridge, Cannonball Krause, was hit three times in this scrap at Sainte Mère. He was grazed by a bullet, nicked by a shell fragment, and finally a slug ripped through his leg. Maj. Bill Hagen, the battalion's exec who had also been wounded at Biazza Ridge, took over.

Meanwhile, that morning, Ben Vandervoort, the broken-legged leader of the 2nd Battalion of Ekman's 505th Regiment, rushed a 41-man platoon northward a mile from Sainte-Mère to the hamlet of Neuville-au-Plain. Led by a scrappy lieutenant named Turner B. Turnbull, the platoon's mission was to disrupt any German threat toward Sainte Mère. Half Cherokee, Turnbull was aces-high with his troopers—he spoke and acted like a fighting man.

Astride the main road leading south from Cherbourg through Sainte Mère to Carentan and beyond, Turnbull deployed his men along a thick-bottomed hedgerow—and not five minutes too soon. Lt. Isaac Michaelman, Turnbull's number 2 man, looked up the road and was mesmerized by the sight. A company of *Feldgrau*, marching along the road toward the dug-in Americans, was in a column of twos, singing, whistling, with helmets off and carrying weapons as though bound for a picnic in Berlin's *Tiergarten*.

Lt. Col. Benjamin Vandervoort, who broke his leg in jump, at Sainte Mère Eglise in Normandy. *(Author's collection)*

All along Turnbull's hedgerow, the riflemen, bazookamen and machine gunners braced, tense yet excited. They had no way of knowing that this carefree collection of Germans was only the vanguard of a 1,000-man *Kampfgruppe* that had hastily been scraped together and rushed southward from Montebourg to recapture Sainte Mère Eglise.

Suddenly, American machine guns chattered and rifles barked. Diving headlong into ditches and crawling into hedgerows, the Germans, many of them veterans of the Russian front, rapidly began returning the fire. One of the first German bullets struck Isaac Michaelman. Above the raucous din, a trooper yelled, "They got the lieutenant—right in the ass!" Using his carbine as a cane, Michaelman hobbled off for medical attention.

While the action was raging, Ben Vandervoort, on crutches he had borrowed from a crippled French housewife and riding in a jeep salvaged from a wrecked glider, raced up to Turnbull's hedgerow. Towed behind the jeep were two 57-millimeter anti-tank guns he thought the beleaguered All-Americans would need.

Vandervoot asked Turnbull, "How are you doing? Do you need help?" Replied the spunky lieutenant, "Everything's under control. Don't worry about me."

At that moment, the Germans were rushing up more troops, and artillery and mortar fire began pounding Turnbull and his men. Then a couple of Mark IV tanks were spotted. At the same time, scores of German grenadiers were working their way along the hedgerows to either side of Turnbull's position. The noose was tightening. Now the Germans were sniping from the Americans' rear. Turnbull's force had dwindled to 23 men, some of them wounded but still firing. Between rounds, the All-Americans were trying to care for 11 badly wounded comrades.

Every man knew that the platoon was trapped. "What do you want to do?" Turnbull asked his troopers. They'd better get out to fight another hour or another day, was the consensus. So the troopers got set to depart. "We'll have to leave our wounded guys," Turnbull stated evenly, concealing the torment that racked him. Now the *Feldgrau* started to rush the position. Cpl. James Kelly, the medical trooper, spoke up: "I'll stay with the wounded and surrender them to the Germans—if I don't get killed first."

A few of the parachutists refused to abandon their wounded comrades. Pvt. Joseph Sebastian said he would cover medic Kelly and his patients with a Browning automatic rifle (BAR), and crawled to the top of the hedgerow to resume fighting. Word-lessly, Sgt. Robert Niland took his place behind a machine gun. But before Niland could squeeze the trigger, a bullet caught him right between the eyes.

"Let's go!" someone yelled. "For Christ's sake, let's go!" Six-teen survivors took out in a run, expecting to be gunned down at any moment, for German grenadiers were swarming all over the vacated hedgerow.

Gutsy Turner Turnbull and his little pack had accomplished their mission—slowing down any enemy rush from the north to-ward Sainte Mère Eglise.

And Lieutenant Turnbull would live to fight again—but only for a few more hours.

Meanwhile outside of Saint-Martin-de-Varreville, about two and one half miles due east of where Turner Turnbull and his men were making their last stand, 28-year-old Lt. Col. Patrick J. Cassidy, leader of the 1st Battalion of "Iron Mike" Michaelis' 502nd Parachute Infantry, received orders to seize several closely grouped farm buildings that were serving as barracks for a Ger-man artillery unit. Since Causeway 4 ran through the vicinity, gaining control of the building complex was of special signifi-cance. Staff Sgt. Harrison Summers was told to take 15 troopers, a mixed bag that had not worked together before, and kill or drive out the *Feldgrau*.

Since Sergeant Summers, slender, almost bashful, hardly the warrior type, didn't know the name of a single trooper, he launched the assault alone; hopefully, the others would follow. Summers sneaked up to the first building, kicked open the door, and sprayed the room with his tommy gun, killing four Germans and causing 10 or 12 others to scramble out through the back.

Summers then charged the second building, and the occu-pants fled. While covering paratroopers poured machine-gun and rifle fire into the windows, the sergeant and Lt. Elmer F. Brandenberger rushed the third structure. A German hand gre-nade knocked Brandenberger down, leaving his arm shredded and bloody, but Summers smashed in the door and hosed down the interior, killing all six troopers.

Now the Screaming Eagles one-man army headed for yet an-other building, and this time an 82nd Airborne captain joined in the rush, but before the All-American had taken 10 steps, a Ger-man rifleman shot him through the head. Undaunted, Harrison Summers pressed on. As he reflected on his next foray, Pvt. John

F. Camien, Jr., armed with a carbine, crawled up to him. "Why are you doing this?" Camien asked. Summers shrugged and replied: "I don't know."

"Well," the young private said, "I'm joining you."

For the next two hours, Summers and Camien killed 30 *Feldgrau* in five buildings, not taking a single prisoner. Their teamwork was flawless, although neither had laid eyes on the other until four hours earlier. One covered a building with the carbine; then the other charged the door and raked the interior with tommy gun bursts.

A covering paratrooper fired tracers into a nearby haystack, setting it ablaze, and the fire spread to a nearby ammunition shack. As the ammo exploded, 30 Germans charged out of the structure and all were shot down by Summers, Camien and supporting parachutists.

At this point, the two wildmen attacked the last and largest structure. Staff Sgt. Roy Nickrent arrived with a bazooka, and he fired seven rounds into the two-story building. The remnants of the German garrison, some 90 to 100 men, dashed from the building—and directly into the withering bursts of fire poured out by Summers' troopers, concealed in a hedgerow, and by a company of 4th Infantry Division dogfaces that had just arrived over the causeway from the beach. Every one of the fleeing Germans was cut down or surrendered.

Soft-spoken Harrison Summers sat down and lit a Lucky Strike. His rampage had been going on for five hours, and he felt a little tired.[4]

With dusk closing in, Chaplain Francis Sampson, who was jolly and deeply loved by men of Johnson's 501st Parachute Infantry, was in an aid station in the village of Addeville. All day, a force of 200 Screaming Eagles, under Maj. R. J. Allen, had been engaged in a bitter fight with a German battalion. Wounded troopers now sprawled about the filthy floor of the dilapidated house serving as the medical center.

A mile or so to the south, Jumpy Johnson and his band of 250 parachutists had been under heavy attack by a large enemy force seeking desperately to recapture the key La Barquette locks on the Douve River. Johnson's pack had been steadily whittled down and now was in danger of being overwhelmed. Over an *SCR* 300 radio, Johnson ordered Allen to disengage at Addeville and to rush to La Barquette locks.

Allen approached Sampson. "We've got to pull out," he said evenly. "You and the walking wounded will go with us. We've got to move in a hurry, 'cause the Krauts will close right in."

What Allen was saying was that the seriously wounded would have to be left behind to be captured. It was one of those agonizing decisions that leaders sometimes have to make in combat. Father Sam's eyes swept the aid-station floor. The trooper in the corner would not live; a grenade had blown off his leg and chewed him up inside. A Screaming Eagle on a cot had a large hole in his back, but he could pull through with enough plasma in him. Two parachutists had compound leg fractures, and bone splinters protruded through the flesh. A trooper with a head wound had been blinded.

Maj. Francis E. Carrel, a Screaming Eagle surgeon, and able-bodied medics had been ordered to pull out with Allen's group, so the chaplain volunteered to stay behind with the 14 seriously wounded troopers. Carrel told him: "There's also a psycho locked up in the shed outside. Better keep him away from the others." The deranged youth could be heard shrieking and pounding on the door of the shed.

Carrel gave a final glance at the wounded parachutists. "This is a bad time to leave them," he said. "Neither side is taking many prisoners, and the Krauts will consider them a liability."[5]

Within 20 minutes, the last of Allen's men had left Addeville. Suddenly, all firing ceased. It was deathly still. Sampson made a white flag from a sheet and hung it outside the door. All night long, the padre tended to the wounded. The boy with the hideous grenade wounds died in Father Sam's arms, clutching a crucifix taken from the wall. All the boys joined in a prayer for the dead trooper.

Sampson looked out and spotted Germans setting up a machine gun in the front yard. He grabbed the white flag and went out to protest. A German lunged at him and stuck a Schmeisser machine pistol in the padre's stomach. Sampson could tell by their insignia that these were tough *Fallschirmjaeger* (paratroopers) and could sense that they were in a nasty mood. His pleas that he was a chaplain taking care of wounded men fell on deaf ears. Two of the surly Germans motioned Sampson toward the road; then, prodding him with their weapons, ordered him to start walking.

After about a quarter of a mile, Sampson was shoved against

a hedgerow, and both Germans pulled the bolts of their weapons and took aim. Father Sam said a hurried Act of Contrition— which again turned out to be the grace before meals!

At that moment, shots were heard and bullets zipped past just overhead. A German sergeant had fired to attract the attention of the two executioners. He came running down the road, a good-looking, tough soldier of about 25 years of age. In German, the sergeant spoke harshly to the pair of captors; then told Sampson in broken English to come with him.

Monsignor Sampson recalled what happened next:

I told the German sergeant that I was a Catholic priest and showed him my credentials. To my real amazement, he snapped to attention, saluted, made a slight bow, and showed me a Catholic religious medal pinned inside his uniform. I was so glad of the universality of the church. The Germans permitted me to return to my wounded men.

Meanwhile, the wounded Screaming Eagles had been terrorized by the *Fallschirmjaeger* who entered the house. One German put a gun to a trooper's head and pulled back the bolt; the other Americans looked away. Another German had fired bullets just over the heads of the prostrate men; then laughed uproariously. When Father Sam returned, the wounded men were even weaker with fear.

Now American artillery—or was it German?—began pounding Addeville. Three shells struck the aid station house. Half of the house collapsed on the two troopers lying in the kitchen. One called out, "Father Sam! Father Sam!" Just as the padre reached the kitchen door, the rest of the ceiling crashed down on the two wounded men.

Frantically, the chaplain cleared away the debris, and cradled one boy's head in his arms. The trooper's heart beat furiously for a minute; then stopped. Sampson dug through the debris until he found the other Screaming Eagle. He was dead.

Throughout the night, artillery plastered Addeville. Father Sam had the wounded men take turns in leading the others in the Lord's Prayer. He noticed that it had a calming effect on them, even as exploding shells rocked the house.

Before dawn, a violent firefight erupted. Americans were trying to recapture Addeville. A tracer bullet zipped through a window and grazed Sampson, setting his trousers on fire. After an hour or so of intense shooting, an eerie silence descended over the village. Then a band of Screaming Eagles moved in and took over Addeville once more.

At midnight on D-Day, Operation Neptune seemed to have been a success. Hitler's "impregnable" Atlantic Wall had been breached; 57,506 American and 75,215 British and Canadian soldiers had established themselves ashore, and 15,500 Americans and 7,900 British airborne men were battling or harassing the Germans inland.

Over Utah Beach that day, 20,000 men and 1,700 vehicles had come ashore, and leading elements of the 4th Infantry Division had driven inland to points but a short distance from Sainte Mère Eglise, now held by elements of the 82nd Airborne Division. Casualties in the 4th Division had been astonishingly minimal—12 dead and 46 wounded.

By contrast, on Omaha Beach, where no airborne soldiers had been dropped or landed, the seaborne invaders suffered 2,374 men killed, wounded or missing, and penetrated only a mile and a half inland at the deepest point.

26
"Fluid" Situations

Even while the seaborne soldiers of the 4th Infantry Division and attached armor were steadily pushing inland on the morning of D-Day plus 1, the situation within the American airhead remained confused and fraught with uncertainty. At his command post in Heisville, Max Taylor was worried about the fluid situation along the Douve River in the south. Securing the line of the Douve was now the 101st Airborne's primary mission, yet a highway bridge and a rail span over the stream had not been blown up as planned, so there remained the clear danger that German armor could pour over these two bridges and drive north toward Utah Beach.

In an apple orchard a half-mile west of Sainte Mère Eglise, Matt Ridgway was also racked with torment. The 82nd Airborne leader had only 2,500 men under his control; the Germans were threatening to overrun Sainte Mère from the north; three large groups of All-Americans were isolated on the west bank of the flooded Merderet; vicious fighting had been raging at La Fière and Chef-du-Pont where German battle groups were trying to cross the causeways and reach Sainte Mère from the west.

At dawn, German guns to the north began pounding Sainte Mère, and one salvo demolished the water pump that serviced the block where wounded paratroopers had been collected. A few were delirious, and began calling for water. Pvt. Dominick DiTullio volunteered to venture outside. "I'll make a good water boy," he quipped to a fellow patient, Cannonball Krause. Dodging the shells, diTullio, an American Gunga Din, was heading back to the aid station with a jerry can of water when a shell exploded at his feet, killing him instantly.

The *Kampfgruppe* that Turner Turnbull's platoon had disrupted the previous afternoon, struck again with renewed fury in an all-out effort to recapture Sainte Mère. Bearing the brunt of the assault was a thin battle line that Ben Vandervoort had established as a shield north of the town. Along with Vandy's troopers were strays from the 101st Airborne and the 507th and 508th Parachute Regiments, as well as a group of glider pilots armed with pistols.[1]

Shells screamed into the All-Americans; then hordes of Germans—no longer singing and whistling—moved forward. Supported by a pair of self-propelled guns, the *Feldgrau* far outnumbered Vandervoort's men, and when the grenadiers began slipping around the flanks to get in behind the Americans, a breakthrough to Saint Mère seemed certain. At this critical juncture, Lt. Waverly Wray was sent back to explain the crisis to Colonel Vandervoort.

Wray was a "good ol' boy" from Batesville, Mississippi, who had honed a woodsman's skills as a boy, including mastery of a rifle. He claimed that he had "nevah missed a shot in mah life that ah didn't mean to," and those who fought with him in Sicily and Italy agreed with the assertion.

Wray was deeply devout, and some troopers called him "The Deacon"—but never to his face. Husky, ruggedly handsome, he did not drink, swear, or chase women. Now 24 years old, Wray had once been his high school's class valedictorian.

Lieutenant Wray rapidly explained to Vandervoort his company's dire situation, that heavy casualties had been suffered, and that swarms of Germans were slipping along the hedgerows on either side. "Okay," the colonel said evenly, "then go back to your company and attack the Germans on your flank."

Back on the firing line, Wray told his injured company commander, Capt. T. G. Smith, about Vandervoort's orders. Then the lieutenant loaded his pockets with grenades, grabbed a rifle and stuck a 38-caliber revolver in his jump boot, and struck out alone to reconnoiter the terrain on his flank. Slipping along hedgerows, Wray advanced about 300 yards while dodging isolated German bands; then headed back to his own lines.

Suddenly, while creeping along a ditch, Wray heard German

voices behind a hedgerow. Stepping up and peeking over the barrier, he saw eight *Feldgrau* gathered around a field radio. Leveling his rifle, Wray barked, *"Hande hoch!"* (Hands up!) Germans thrust arms into the air, except for one man who whipped out his pistol. Wray shot him through the head.

Lt. Thomas W. Graham. *(Author's collection)*

Lt. Waverly Wray. *(Lou Varrone drawing)*

Hearing the shot, two Germans popped out of a hole and tried to take off the American's head with bursts of Schmeisser machine pistols, but managed only to clip off a dime-sized chunk of his ear. Then the seven German captives dropped their arms and went for their guns. The Mississippi woodsman pumped a bullet into each man. One of the Germans cut down by Wray was the commander of the headquarters staff, 1st Battalion, 1058th Grenadier Regiment.

Lieutenant Wray was bleeding profusely from his ear, but had no intention of closing up shop. Reloading his rifle, he stalked cautiously toward the main body of Germans, scouted out their positions, then stole back to his company.

Rapidly, Wray positioned a few 60-millimeter mortars, climbed atop a hedgerow and directed shells onto the enemy hedgerows he had reconnoitered. The firing was deadly and accurate. Then Wray's company moved forward, and pumped heavy fire into German troops fleeing from their foxholes where mortar rounds were exploding.

Suddenly, just as the men in the baggy pants were closing in, a German medical officer popped up waving a white flag. Approaching Lieutenant Wray, the German asked in flawless English, "May we have a truce to carry out our wounded?"

Wray shrugged, "Sure, why not?"

So the Americans halted in place. Sgt. Charles Swan, who had overheard the German's request, slipped down a hedgerow to a point 30 yards from an enemy platoon that was loading up its weapons to pull back under the phony mercy truce. Swan lifted his tommy gun. He could have cut down 10 or 12 of the unsuspecting *Feldgrau*, who had their backs turned to him. Still a novice to war, Swan lowered his weapon. It just didn't seem sportsmanlike to shoot armed soldiers from behind.

While Waverly Wray and his men waited along a hedgerow for the hour of nonfiring to expire, nearly the entire German unit, except for 40 to 50 dead comrades, escaped northward. Left behind was a large number of wounded the Germans had not bothered to take with them.

Benjamin Vandervoort remembered what occurred next:

> *Waverly returned to my CP to tell me that his company's position was now secure. There he was—minus part of one ear. Blood had dried down his neck and shoulder of his jump jacket fore and aft. I said, "The Krauts were getting kind of close to you, weren't they, Waverly?" With just the trace of a grin, he replied, "Not as close as ah've bin gettin' to them, Suh!"*

Once again, the dogged determination of paratroopers guarding the northern approaches to Sainte Mère had prevented a disastrous breakthrough to the town. The smash against Waverly Wray's company had been the gray-green tidal wave's high-water mark.[2]

After two days of bitter fighting, the *Kampfgruppe* had been virtually wiped out. Vandervoort's understrength battalion collared 342 German prisoners, counting more than 400 dead.

Early that afternoon, elements of the seaborne 8th Regiment poked into Sainte Mère from the south, and a short time later, the 746th Tank Battalion, led by Lt. Col. D. G. Hupfer, clanked into town. Minutes afterward, a column of 21 Sherman tanks, paced by their commander, Col. Edson Raff, in a jeep, roared up Sainte Mère's debris-strewn main street. Now, any chance the Wehrmacht had to recapture the key road hub vanished.

Tank commander was a curious role for the scrappy Ed Raff, a pioneer paratrooper who had led the 509th Parachute Infantry Battalion in America's first airborne assault at Tafaraoui airfield to spearhead the invasion of North Africa, back in November of 1942. Raff had reached near-celebrity status in the States in late 1943 after publication of his quickie book, *We Jumped to Fight*. With the mighty cross-Channel endeavor looming in early 1944, Raff, one of the army's youngest colonels, yearned to command a parachute regiment. But there were no openings in that slot, so his boss, Matt Ridgway, assigned him a less spectacular role: command of a seaborne armored task force whose mission was to dash from Utah Beach to Sainte Mère Eglise to provide the lightly armed parachutists with more clout.

Right behind Edson Raff's noisy task force, a command half-track, tightly buttoned up, clanked into Sainte Mère at open throttle. Inside were the scrappy Lightning Joe Collins, the VII Corps leader, and Col. James M. Van Fleet, the 52-year-old commander of the 8th Infantry Regiment. The arrival of the half-track was saluted by the Germans—with a salvo of heavy artillery fire.[3]

After their initial surprise on the night of the drop, German commanders reacted rapidly against the American airhead in Normandy. Vicious fighting raged at La Fière and at Chef-du-Pont where the 1057 Grenadier Regiment was trying to reach Sainte Mère across the two Mederet causeways. On the east bank of the Merderet at La Fière, Lt. Col. Francis Caesar Augustus Kellam's 1st Battalion of the 505th was being chopped to pieces by murderous artillery and automatic weapons fire.

While leading an attack, Kellam, along with his operations officer, Maj. Dale A. Royston, were killed by a shell burst. Maj. Jim McGinity, a veteran of Sicily (where his little band had seized the key Ponte Dirillo bridge) and of Italy, succeeded Kellam. Only a few hours later, an 88-millimeter projectile exploded next to McGinity, killing him instantly. Now Mark Alexander, another 82nd Airborne "old pro," who was exec of the 505th, was rushed in to replace McGinity.

The gods of war had been especially harsh with American parachute battalion commanders Bob Wolverton, riddled by bullets while descending in a chute; Herbert Batcheller, shot and killed on D-Day; Kellam and McGinity, killed by artillery bursts; Cannonball Krause, shot in the leg; Ben Vandervoort, leg broken on landing; and Edwin J. Ostberg, seriously wounded while leading an attack at Chef-du-Pont.

For 35 hours—with time out for a catnap or two—lanky Jim Gavin, his trademark rifle clutched in one hand, had been tramping up and down the east bank of the Merderet, directing the fierce battles at La Fière and Chef-du-Pont. Typically, the commander of all 82nd Airborne parachute elements traveled light: with him were only an aide, an orderly, and a pair of staff officers who had won their spurs in combat. Gavin and all paratroopers battling for their lives along the fireswept Merderet did not know if the seaborne landings at Utah had even taken place. Perhaps the 4th Infantry Division had been repulsed and both American airborne divisions were now ensnared in a gigantic trap on the Cherbourg Peninsula.

James Gavin remembered that haunting and distinct possibility:

> About noon on D-Day plus 1, I met Matt Ridgway at the point where the Sainte Mère Eglise road crosses the railroad just east of the Merderet. As far as we knew, we were on our own. Matt and I decided right then that if the seaborne assault had been called off or beaten back, then we would continue to fight to the end.

One of the parachute officers who accompanied Jim Gavin was Thomas Graham, who recalled an incident that typified the young general's style of command:

> A paratrooper came stumbling and running toward us, shouting, "They're coming! They're coming!" He was nearly hysterical. As he approached, we could see that he was one of our younger troopers, probably only 18 years old.
>
> Suddenly, the boy halted—I'm sure he recognized General Gavin. In a soft voice Slim Jim asked, "What is the matter, son?" The trooper burst into tears and answered: "I thought they were coming!"
>
> Despite his countless burdens, Slim Jim spent a few minutes talking to the boy and assured him he would get some rest. Then the general told his orderly, Cpl. Walker Wood, to accompany the distraught boy back to his unit and relay his rest orders to the trooper's company commander.

While the Merderet was aflame along the western sector of the airhead, savage fighting was raging in the south along the Douve River. Col. Howard Johnson, the flamboyant leader of the 501st Parachute Infantry, and about 250 of his troopers were clinging doggedly to La Barquette locks, which now had become known as "Hell's Corner." Johnson's Screaming Eagles were being plagued relentlessly by artillery and mortars, and sniped at by *Feldgrau* sharpshooters.

The situation around the locks was what the military refers to as "fluid"—meaning that neither adversary knew precisely what was going on, and opposing units were intermingled. What Johnson did know was that he was hemmed in on three sides and running low on ammo. Suddenly, a trooper pointed toward the rear and called out, "Look back there!" Even the stalwart colonel was shocked: struggling through a swamp, slowly and laboriously, directly toward Hell's Corner, was a force of about 500 Germans.

Disaster loomed. Then Johnson noticed that the approaching grenadiers did not have out a point or flank security, and their lackadaisical formation indicated that the Germans felt confident that there were no Americans in the vicinity.

Johnson prepared a warm reception. His machine gunners and riflemen faced the rear, kept concealed, and waited for the signal to fire—a burst from one machine gun on the flank. Onward came the perspiring but relaxed grenadiers. When they were 300 yards away, Johnson shouted to the men on the signaling machine gun: "Now! Let the bastards have it!"

A torrent of fire erupted all along the parachutists' line. Swarms of soldiers could be seen going down, and within 90 seconds the entire German force had vanished, as if by magic. But had the Germans been hit or had they dived for cover behind the hedges and hummocks of the swamp? It soon became apparent that much of the quarry had escaped Jumpy's trap—at least for the time being—because German bullets began whistling into the Screaming Eagles' positions.

For 30 minutes the firefight raged. Then Johnson ordered a cease-fire—the ammo supply was dwindling. His men, transformed within 40 hours from training-camp soldiers to a pack of jackals, ignored the order and continued to blast away.

Suddenly, above the earsplitting din, cries of *"Kamerad! Kamerad!"* were heard from the swamp. Johnson, aware of his ammo pinch, exclaimed, "Maybe we can work out a surrender of

Maj. David E. Thomas. (*Author's collection*)

Col. Howard R. "Jumpy" Johnson. (*Don F. Pratt Museum*)

the whole goddamned force." A trooper, already in a snarling rage, replied, "To hell with that, Colonel, we're going to kill every one of the bastards!"

No one had ever accused Jumpy Johnson of being cowardly—or stupid. If there was the possibility that he might bag the larger German force without heavy casualties to his troopers, then he intended to do just that. So he told his officers to pass the word to cease fire, and, taking along a pair of enlisted men, he set out toward the German lines. Beside him, Pvt. Leo F. Runge and Cpl. William F. Lenz carried orange cloth on rifles held high overhead. As the three men walked onward, rifle fire erupted and bullets whizzed past their heads—Johnson's angry troopers had opened fire again toward the concealed Germans.

Johnson quipped to his companions: "Are our boys trigger-happy—or do they think this is their chance to get me?" Runge and Lenz grinned weakly; somehow, they failed to see much humor in their present predicament.

Then, Johnson turned serious: "If this keeps up, the Krauts are going to start shooting, and we'll be dodging bullets from both directions." However, Lenz and Runge acted as if they were calm and collected—just another Sunday walk in the park. So Johnson continued onward.[4]

After the men had gone about 150 yards, all firing ceased.

From the swamp, a few German troopers arose and advanced toward the Americans with arms overhead in surrender. Suddenly, the advancing Germans went flat and a blistering fusillade of fire erupted all along the enemy line. Leo Runge was knocked down, and felt a searing pain where a bullet had ripped into his arm. Another slug tore into Colonel Johnson's hand. In seconds, the boys in Hell's Corner opened up again.

Caught in no-man's-land with bullets whistling past from fore and aft, the three Screaming Eagles flopped down; then arduously crawled and slithered back to their own lines. All through the odyssey, neither Lenz nor Runge had spoken a word. After a 30-minute firefight, the scene quieted once more. Johnson, his hand wrapped in a bloody bandage, was determined to try again. He called for two volunteers—Lenz and Runge insisted on going with the colonel.

This time, the surrender appeal worked, and the Germans rose from the swamp after pitching away weapons and helmets, and filed into the Hell's Corner lines. The foot-dragging procession went on for a few hours, until almost dusk. At that point, the German lieutenant colonel commanding the battalion came in. Approaching Colonel Johnson, he declared, "I am not a prisoner. You will not search me or take my weapon. Under the Geneva Convention, I have a right to parlay; then I will decide if I wish to surrender."

Jumpy made no reply. He turned to his own adjutant, Capt. Altus F. McReynolds, jerked his thumb toward the German colonel, and snarled, "Just treat this bastard the way you've been handling his boys!" Minutes later, an 88-millimeter shell screamed in and McReynolds and 19 German prisoners were killed.

The boys in the baggy pants at Hell's Corner had made quite a haul: 353 POWs were in the bag. Perhaps another 150 were laying face down in the murky waters of the swamp—all dead. A handful had escaped in the direction of Carentan.

Elsewhere in the airhead, a small group of airborne officers gathered solemnly around a fresh, deep excavation in a pasture. Wrapped in a parachute, Screaming Eagle Gen. Don Pratt was buried. There was no official salute of guns; it was not necessary. All during the service, artillery pounded away and rifles cracked in the background.

Late that afternoon, a smashed American landing craft, riddled by gunfire, washed up onto land near the point where the

Vire River empties into the English Channel. Nearby, Germans went to investigate and found on board five dead American naval officers, one a beachmaster responsible for directing landing traffic on shore. In his dead hands, the beachmaster clutched a case containing maps and documents, apparently of a top secret nature. The waterlogged case was rushed to LXXXIV Corps headquarters at Saint-Lô, 25 miles southwest of Utah Beach.

Early the next morning, interpreters and analysts at Saint-Lô hurried into the bunker office of Maj. Friedrich Hayn, the corps intelligence officer. "Good news, *Herr Major*," one analyst blurted out. "This is the entire operations plan of the Allied forces in the invasion!"

Minutes later, Gen. Erich Marcks, the scholarly, capable corps commander, was staring in disbelief at the plan. Peering through rimless glasses, Marcks noted that the first planned step for the invaders, now that they were ashore in strength, was to link up Utah and Omaha Beaches at Carentan to establish a continuous perimeter around the bridgehead.

The bustling little town of Carentan, at the base of the Cherbourg Peninsula, suddenly became of utmost significance. Through Carentan ran the railroad and Route Nationale 13, the highway running between Paris and Cherbourg. General Marcks had no way of knowing it, but Allied brass also had their focus on Carentan. They feared that Field Marshal Rommel would spot the yawning gap between Utah and Omaha and rush an armored force through Carentan to the Channel coast.

At almost the same time that Erich Marcks was scrutinizing the intelligence bonanza that had fallen into his hands, Gen. Omar Bradley and Lightning Joe Collins were conferring at First Army CP in an apple orchard behind Omaha Beach. Bradley told the other that General Eisenhower had wanted to know why Carentan had not been seized on D-Day plus 1 as planned in order to link up Utah and Omaha forces.

"Joe, you've got to grab Carentan as quickly as possible," Bradley declared. "If it becomes necessary to save time, put 500 or even 1,000 tons of air on Carentan and take the town apart. Then rush in like hell, and you'll get it."[5]

Tapped to "rush in like hell" would be elements of the 101st Airborne, which that day seized the town of Saint-Côme-du-Mont, four miles northwest of Carentan. The looming attack on Carentan could be a bloody one because the Germans had flooded vast areas of marshland leading to the town.

At the same time, the 82nd Airborne was getting ready for a similar and equally nasty job. Allied brass had hoped that the 4th Infantry Division, after landing at Utah, could dash directly to Cherbourg. Because of heavy German opposition, these plans were revised. Joe Collins was ordered to drive westward to the coast in order to cut off the peninsula, then to turn his VII Corps northward to seize Cherbourg.

Collins would need a secure jumping-off locale for his westward attack—a bridgehead on the west bank of the Merderet, where the 91st Air Landing Division had been holding tenaciously for three days.

27
Carnage at
La Fière
Causeway

On the morning of D-Day plus 3, Jim Gavin was under heavy pressure from on high to carve out a bridgehead on the west side of the Merderet, where the 1057th Grenadier Regiment was dug in. There was only one course of action—a rush across the 500-yard-long La Fière causeway, directly into the teeth of murderous firepower that the Germans had clustered at the other end. H-Hour was set for 10:45 A.M.

Because Harry Lewis' largely untested 325th Glider Infantry Regiment was on the scene, it would make the attack. One hour prior to jump-off, the 2nd Battalion of glidermen, which had been designated by Lewis to lead the charge, approached the line of departure near the causeway entrance. Gavin sent word for the battalion commander to report to him for last-minute instructions.

"I can't lead the attack," he told Gavin.

"Why not?" the general demanded.

"I'm ill," was the reply.

Knowing the high stakes involved in the Merderet operation, Gavin promptly sacked the battalion commander, and he was replaced by Maj. Arthur W. Gardner, Lewis' operations officer, who was largely unknown to the men he was about to command.

This hitch did nothing to relieve Gavin's apprehension about how the glidermen might react to their first taste of combat—a terrifying baptism of fire that would have sorely tested a veteran force. He sought out Capt. Robert D. Rae, leader of a company of 507th Regiment paratroopers who were near the causeway entrance. "The glidermen are green and might bog down or break when the shooting gets hot," Gavin told Rae. "If they start to straggle back, I'll signal you to charge over with your boys."

Minutes before H-Hour, Capt. John B. Sauls, whose G Company had been picked to brave the blast first, moved forward to where seven dead 507th paratroopers were strewn around the causeway entrance. Sauls called to a pair of Rae's sergeants, "Help me move these bodies so my men won't see them when we start to go."

As the grim glidermen crouched in ditches, an earsplitting roar erupted as 12 Sherman tanks, lined up hull-down along the river bank, mortars, machine guns, BARs, rifles, carbines—anything that would shoot—plastered the far side. In the rear, a battery of 90th Infantry Division "Long Toms" barked stridently and sent shells whistling over the Merderet.

John Sauls leaped to his feet, made a forward motion with an arm, and shouted, "Follow me!" His men scrambled out of ditches and, with Sauls in the lead, began running at full speed across the narrow strip.

Heavy boots clomping on the macadam surface, weapons flopping about from the bouncing gait, Sauls and his men—wheezing and grunting from the exertion—had nearly reached a bridge at the halfway mark when the Germans at the far end of the causeway opened fire. Bullets, thick and hissing, flew past the running men's heads. Mortar shells began to plop down along the road, exploding in sharp blasts and sending shrapnel into the bodies of the exposed men, many of whom staggered and fell wounded into the ugly brown marsh water and drowned.

There was no place to hide; no place to take cover. The All-Americans were naked in the gunsights of the enemy. Men continued to go down like flies showered with an insecticide, and soon scores of bodies, dead and wounded, were strewn along the causeway.

Bullets were beating on the bridge like hail, and other pellets ricocheted off the hard surface of the road, casting gigantic fire-fly-like sparks into the air. Screams came from the mutilated and the dying. A few men faltered, then more halted, confused, terrified, uncertain. A jam developed as more glidermen joining in the rush piled up behind.

The chaos mounted when a Sherman tank, sent across to support the beleaguered All-Americans, struck a mine and skidded sideways, grinding to a halt along the bullet and fire-swept causeway. Seven men near to the tank were seriously wounded by the explosion.

Now Capt. Charles F. Murphy, skipper of E Company, led his men in a mad scramble over the causeway. A mortar round exploded, shredding Murphy's face and felling four of his men. Murphy struggled to his feet and staggered on toward the far shore before collapsing. His executive, Lt. Bruce H. Booker, took over and near the midway bridge, halted to prod faltering men to push onward. Machine gun bullets tore through both of Booker's legs, and he crawled to one side of the road. Sitting there in extreme pain, he kept waving his arm and shouting, "Come on, you bastards! Get up there! Goddamn it, get on up there!" A few halted men moved onward. Then Booker saw a knot of men coming back toward him, quitting the fight. Pulling out his Colt .45, the lieutenant shot six rounds just above their heads and yelled, "Keep coming toward me and you'll see what happens!" They turned around.

A medic dressed both of Bruce Booker's legs. He tried to rise, but his legs gave out. So, crawling, he went forward, begging other men to follow him. Up and down the blood-soaked causeway, he struggled—cursing, shouting, begging, cajoling.

Meanwhile, Captain Sauls and a handful of his men, who had filtered through the point-blank hailstorm of fire, rushed onto the far shore, where they plopped to the ground, exhausted. Sauls counted noses: In his forlorn group was one squad and a BAR man. They composed the American bridgehead west of the Merderet.

Sauls' "bridgehead" failed to halt the causeway inferno. The scene of carnage resembled an escalator—streams of men on one side trying to get forward, and on the other side, irregular columns of wounded men and stragglers trickling back. Fearing that the stragglers might trigger mass panic, Jim Gavin signaled to Captain Rae and his 91 paratroopers in foxholes behind a stone wall.

Rae jumped to his feet and waved his men forward. Yelling at the top of their lungs, the company set out in a run, weaving in and out of bodies, discarded and smashed equipment and weapons, the disabled tank, as well as hundreds of glidermen milling about. Just past the bridge, Rae and his troopers were blocked by a barrier of massed humanity—wounded men and stragglers.

Finally, Rae and others bulled their way through the pack, but not all of the paratroopers wanted to die as heroes. When the captain charged on forward, only 35 to 40 of his men followed. But parachute Lt. James D. Orwin, whose slender build and choirboy face belied the steel in his makeup, set out to dislodge the human logjam at the bridge. Orwin felt lucky. Twenty minutes earlier on the east bank, a mortar shell exploded at his feet and blew his steel helmet apart without breaking his skin—or even stunning him.

Now Orwin, a free spirit, strolled the causeway in a knitted cap, and stuck under the headgear on each side was a red rose that he had plucked before running onto the causeway. Head held high, grinning broadly, Orwin went from floundering group to group. Without raising his voice, he said, "Now, fellows, we're all going to the other side. Things are good over there. Walk with me—for I'm a lucky bastard!"

Strangely, perhaps, most of those listening got up and trailed the fuzzy-cheeked parachute officer. Said a nearby glider sergeant in amazement, "You'd think they're following Jesus Christ!"

Meanwhile, Matt Ridgway arrived on the east bank and spotted the blown Sherman that was blocking the causeway. Clutching his trademark .30-06 rifle, he picked his way around dead bodies and, with the help of a few enlisted men, began attaching a cable to the wrecked vehicle. Suddenly, an explosion rocked the site. Less than 40 feet from Ridgway, a man was killed and four others were wounded by the blast. Unscathed, the 82nd Airborne commander resumed his mechanic's task and the tank was shunted over the embankment.[1]

Just past noon, Jim Gavin, who had been feeding men and weapons into the assault, sent three Shermans clanking over the causeway. The medium tanks fired their machine guns to each flank to flush out the remaining Germans from their nests in the swamp. Then the young brigadier ran the obstacle course to the west bank, where he joined Rae and his paratroopers who had survived the gauntlet, John Sauls and his fragmented company, and elements of two glider battalions.[2]

Mass confusion reigned. Communications failed. The All-Americans were splintered into scattered little bands. German artillery and mortars pounded them, and the *Feldgrau* continued to resist tenaciously.

Tramping along a narrow road cluttered with litter, abandoned and destroyed German vehicles, self-propelled guns, and other debris of war, Gavin came upon a German mortar crew, all dead and sprawled in a ditch. A German lieutenant clutched a map of the La Fière region. Gavin took it from him, turned it over, and, to his astonishment, there was a map of England with the locale clearly marked from which the 82nd Airborne had taken off for the D-Day drop.[3]

As the afternoon wore on, the All-Americans and the Germans slugged it out amidst the hedgerows, and by 3:45 P.M., a patrol pushed 1,000 yards north of the causeway to forge a slender linkup with a force of 50 paratroopers who had been surrounded since the night of the drop. The leader of the force, Lt. Col. Charles J. Timmes, commander of the 2nd Battalion of the 507th Parachute Infantry, had been slightly wounded twice, but steadfastly refused to surrender his band.[4]

At 6:00 P.M. that day, the Germans struck back, the major blows hitting elements of the 325th Glider Infantry, which was in disarray and its ranks riddled after the causeway charge. Within 30 minutes, the glider units began to show signs of disintegrating, and stragglers were pulling back over the causeway.

Jim Gavin heard of the looming debacle and rushed to the glider regiment's command post in an old stone farmhouse on the west bank. A few hours earlier, Harry Lewis had been evacuated with combat fatigue, and his exec, Lt. Col. Herbert G. Sitler, had taken over. Now Sitler and his staff were hastily preparing to pull the fragmented regiment back over the causeway.

Gavin was livid. Elements of the 82nd Airborne had been battling for three days to establish a bridgehead and had paid a heavy price in blood. He had no intention of vacating the premises.

"We're going to counterattack with every resource we have,"

the general declared. "That includes clerks, headquarters people, jeep drivers, anyone with a weapon—including yourself!"

Sitler looked startled; then replied simply, "Yes, sir."

Fierce fighting raged along the banks of the Merderet, and there was gradual reduction in firing. By 8:45 P.M., the harsh sounds of violent conflict had dwindled away altogether.

Seizing the German-held real estate had been costly. In their first day of battle, the two participating glider battalions had 60 men killed, 283 wounded, and 246 missing, presumably captured or drowned—a 50 percent casualty rate.

With the Merderet bridgehead reasonably secure, Roy Lindquist took his 508th Parachute Infantry over the La Fière causeway, marched southward, wiped out or drove off bands of *Feldgrau,* and rescued a 90-man force of his paratroopers that had been hemmed in for nearly four days and nights on Hill 30. This mixed bag of troopers was under Lt. Col. Thomas J. B. Shanley, leader of the 2nd Battalion, and Maj. Shields Warren, Jr., exec of the 1st Battalion.

After dark on the night that the Merderet bridgehead was forged, 200 paratroopers, who were commanded by "Zip" Millett, leader of the 507th Parachute Infantry, prepared to break out of the locale near Amfreville where they had been surrounded since the drop. Leaving the wounded behind to be captured, Millett and his men walked eastward toward the Merderet, some three miles away.

Most of these Five-O-Sevens had been without real sleep for four days, and they staggered along in a column like zombies. A teenaged trooper, carrying a Gammon grenade in one hand, dropped it, and the explosion blew off his left leg at the hip and his left arm at the shoulder.[5] Maj. David E. Thomas of Cleveland, Ohio, the regimental surgeon could do little for the mutilated boy. He was tagged and left there as the column stumbled on through the night. Steadily, the formation fragmented into tiny groups and pairs.

At dawn, Major Thomas was with a pack of 20 troopers on the western edge of the Merderet, a short distance from the La Fière causeway. Again they were trapped, with German machine guns raking them from both flanks. Several troopers tried to wade through the swamp to get to the east bank, but were cut down by bullets or drowned.

David E. Thomas recalled subsequent events:

> *While digging in along a hedgerow, red crosses on my helmet and*
> *all, a rifle shot just missed me and plowed into the ground in front of*
> *me. I noticed that the bullet barked the trunk of a hedge. Staring at*
> *a tree from which, by back azimuth, it had to come, I could make out*
> *a pair of German boots. So I borrowed a carbine, Geneva*
> *convention or no, and shot the dude out of the tree.*

By afternoon, Dave Thomas and S. Sgt. Roy Perkins, a medic, were the only ones left. They struck off cross-country; while sauntering along a narrow dirt road, they spotted a German patrol approaching and dived into a ditch where a few dead American paratroopers were sprawled. Thomas was face down and breathing shallowly, feigning death. A *Feldgrau* stopped, put his booted foot under the major's ankle, lifted the leg and let it fall. Thomas braced for a bullet in the head, but in moments, the Germans moved on.

Lost and roaming around through the blackness that night, Thomas and Perkins entered a town and were shaken to discover that it was Amfreville, a German strongpoint. Getting onto all fours and crawling, the two men tried to sneak out of the enemy hotbed.

David Thomas continued with his story:

> *Roy Perkins and I decided there was no future in our method, and*
> *the best thing to do was to walk out of Amfreville as we had walked*
> *in—after pitching our weapons. Unfortunately, we met a Kraut*
> *who had listened in basic training, and he challenged us from under*
> *a tree, where he could not be seen. We* hande hoched *and were*
> *bagged.*

The captured paratroopers were split up. Sergeant Perkins was taken to a POW camp in Cherbourg, and Major Thomas to a *Kampfgruppe* command post where he was put to work treating both wounded Germans and Americans. On D-Day plus 7, artillery plastered the command post; while the *Feldgrau* scrambled for foxholes, Dave Thomas slipped through a hedgerow opening, dived into a ditch, and rapidly creeped and crawled away.

Perhaps 30 minutes later, the surgeon saw a troop of German bicyclists pedaling toward him, and he quickly concealed himself in a thick hedgerow. It was here that the Germans decided to take a break, and while Thomas remained motionless in the hedge, the enemy soldiers, smoking and chatting, were close enough for him to reach out and touch them. Finally, the Germans rode away.

For four nights (he holed up during the day), Thomas roamed the dark countryside. Once he found himself in a hedgerow with German soldiers who were blasting away with Schmeissers at an American machine gun that was spitting bullets toward Thomas' hedgerow. Another time, he stumbled into a German command post tent bristling with radio antennae.

Then, while stealing through the night, the surgeon heard a loud voice with an Arkansas twang: "Halt, you son of a bitch!" Dave Thomas was back with friends.

Col. Zip Millett was not as fortunate. While trying to get through German lines, the leader of the 507th Parachute Infantry was captured.[6]

28
Death Alley
at Carentan

At the same time that the All-Americans were making their epic crossing of the Merderet, a strikingly similar scenario was unfolding at German-held Carentan, six miles southeast of La Fière. At dawn on June 10, Max Taylor's Screaming Eagles would jump off to capture the key road and rail center, thereby linking up Utah and Omaha Beaches.

Defending Carentan was the resolute Lt. Col. August Frieherr Baron von der Heydte, a peacetime college professor, and his crack 6th Parachute Regiment, made up of youths whose average age was 17.5 years. They were keenly trained and tough, had exceptional esprit, and would willingly die for their Führer.

Baron von der Heydte was encouraged by the horrendous terrain over which Americans would have to cross to get to his men's strong-points north and east of Carentan. For nearly two miles to the north of the town, the ground was a marshland, impassable to tanks and vehicles. Stretching over this swamp was the asphalt Route Nationale 13, which ran straight as an arrow, its crown some six to nine feet above the dingy brown water and clusters of ugly reeds protruding upward. To come to grips with the German paratroopers, the Americans would have to advance for long distances across this exposed causeway. There the Screaming Eagles would be open targets, with nowhere to dig in, take cover, or pause to regroup.

The 101st Airborne's plan of attack called for two crossings of the flooded Douve River to close in on Carentan from the north and east. One force would make a frontal rush down the 30-foot-wide elevated road from the north, bypass Carentan, and seize a dominant hill southwest of the town. Chosen for the "honor" of spearheading this attack was Iron Mike Michaelis' 502nd Parachute Infantry. Simultaneously, George Wear's 327th Glider Infantry would cross the Douve River three miles northeast of Carentan, then slam into the town from the east.

About 9:30 P.M. on June 9, Capt. Henry G. Plitt, S-3 of the 502nd Parachute Infantry, was cruising in a Piper Cub high over Carentan, where the purple shadows of dusk were starting to enfold the ancient town. For 30 minutes, Plitt flew back and forth, but his plane was never fired on nor did he see any indication of German presence in or around the town. Plitt reported to Michaelis that Carentan had been evacuated.

Pacing the causeway assault would be the 3rd Battalion, led by Lt. Col. Bob Cole, who had seized the two northern causeways at Utah Beach four days earlier. Physically rugged, seeming to others the personification of confident courage, Cole was haunted by an unshakable nightmare that somewhere, sometime, he would fail his troops in a battle crisis.

At 12:30 A.M. on the 10th, Cole led his paratroopers onto the causeway, but after the column had marched for about a half mile, it was blocked by a wide gap in what was called Bridge 2. Michaelis radioed to call off the attack and return to the jumping-off spot. It was a bad omen. An entire battalion had already been stymied in a major operation without a shot being fired.

About 3:00 P.M. that day, Cole's battalion set out again, reached and crossed the now-repaired bridge, and continued to march forward along the causeway. With each step, the troopers became increasingly hopeful that the Germans had pulled out and that they could leisurely stroll into Carentan. Leading elements in the battalion reached Bridge 4, where they were forced to halt by a Belgian Gate that the Germans had dragged across the road. (A Belgian Gate was a heavy iron fence, about 30 feet long, with a gate in the center, used by the Germans for defensive purposes.) The point of the parachute battalion was now only 600 yards from the outskirts of Carentan, and still not a shot had been fired.

Troopers could muscle open the ponderous gate only 18 inches, and through this narrow gap the lead scouts began squeezing, one at a time. This snail-like process caused the remainder of the battalion, strung out for a mile behind, to stop on the causeway as each man waited his turn to wriggle through the obstacle.

Suddenly, all thought of a peaceful cakewalk into Carentan vanished. From higher ground to the front and a group of farmhouses surrounded by thick hedgerows to the right, German paratroopers began pouring withering bursts of machine gun and rifle fire into the exposed Americans on the causeway. With no place to take cover, Cole's men flattened themselves on the asphalt as swarms of bullets buzzed past them. Here and there was a sickening thud as a slug found its mark.

Above the grinding chatter of German machine guns, a series of sharp cracks engulfed the Americans who were on the enemy side of Bridge 4 as mortar shells exploded, sending white-hot chunks of metal whizzing over the causeway. Troopers at the point of the attack saw enemy machine guns spitting at them from 100 yards ahead, but could do nothing but cling to the asphalt or press up against the wet mud of the embankments.

Nineteen-year-old Pvt. Elmer Sandeen, a Minnesota native, and his squad were at the battalion point. Orders were shouted from the rear: "Keep advancing, goddamn it! Keep advancing!"

Elmer Sandeen vividly recalled subsequent events:

> The first scout, Carl Deyak, ran across Bridge 4 and I heard a tremendous machine gun crossfire and saw Carl dive for the ditch on the right side of the causeway. Second scout Ed White did the same thing, with the exact same results. I ran across the bridge third and when I dived in, I landed on Carl and Ed. They were both dead.
>
> Moments later, Pvt. William Mashburn came barreling in on top of me. It was immediately evident that if we were to survive, we couldn't raise any part of our bodies as much as an inch, for a

torrent of bullets were flying past just over our heads. We laid there
motionless for hours, until dusk, trying hard all the time to make
ourselves smaller and lower.

Another trooper at the point, Pvt. Tony De Leon, felt a sharp
pain as though a red hot poker had been thrust into his arm.
Frightened, he called out over the din, "Hurry, I'm hit! I'm going
to bleed to death!" A comrade slithered through a hail of bullets
and put a tourniquet on the arm. De Leon passed out.

Baron von der Heydte's boys had sprung their death trap.
Cole's men, strung out for a great distance along the causeway,
could not budge. Ignoring the hailstorm of fire, Bob Cole
crawled forward, stood over a group of troopers and shouted,
"Goddamn it, start firing and keep firing!" His exhortations
achieved nothing.

Minutes after Cole crawled away, Lt. George A. Larish was
shot through the heart, Lt. John P. Painschlab and Cpl. Earl
Butz were killed, and medic Pfc. Stanley W. Tkaczyk was hit in
the head and died instantly, while going to the aid of a shrieking
comrade.

Dusk was gathering and German machine gun and mortar
fire dwindled. Suddenly, the roar of an airplane engine was
heard, and the Americans sprawled out on the asphalt looked up
to see the craft, flying at about 400 feet, coming directly along
the causeway.

Elmer Sandeen recalled his feelings at that moment:

> *For the first time, I experienced the meaning of absolute terror. We*
> *were trapped. No place to take cover. The Luftwaffe dive-bomber*
> *dropped its cargo on us—antipersonnel bombs—and they exploded*
> *all along the causeway. Then the enemy plane returned and heavily*
> *strafed our long line of paratroopers. That one 90-second episode*
> *cost us more than 40 casualties.*
>
> *It was a strange thing, maybe because we had spent many hours*
> *waiting for instant death, but when the Kraut plane flew away, some*
> *of us broke out laughing hilariously until we cried, because of the*
> *way some of the guys reacted in trying to get away from the bombs*
> *and bullets.*

Many of Cole's troopers were stricken by a curious phenomenon
that often is a shock by-product of sudden disaster. Showing no
interest in their perilous predicament or curiosity about which of

their comrades had been hit, the men began falling asleep on the causeway. A platoon leader, Lt. Robert G. Burns, tried to awaken his men, but with darkness at hand his task was extremely difficult—he could not tell who was asleep and who was dead.

Burns saw bodies roll off of the causeway and tumble partly submerged into the swamp. Scrambling down the embankment, Burns heard loud snoring from each helmeted figure. Efforts to rouse the sleepers, who were in danger of drowning, were to no avail.

Nineteen-year-old Pfc. Kenneth E. Cordry of Hannibal, Missouri, was assigned to a litter detail to lug the wounded back along the causeway to the aid station. He recalled that experience:

> It was a nightmare for me and another trooper. It was pitch-black there on the causeway. We tried to assure the fellows, the ones still conscious, that their wounds weren't too serious, even though in many cases we could tell they would die soon—probably before we got to the aid station. Most of the conscious ones were moaning and delirious. We packed wounded comrades back and forth all night, until we were exhausted and in a state of shock ourselves.

Cordry, whose regular job was rifleman, was back at the tip of the advance after daylight, his nose burrowed into the muck on the side of the causeway. He lay motionless; perhaps the Germans would think he was dead and not shoot at his exposed figure.

Kenneth Cordry remembered that morning:

> Looking up from the ditch, I could see troopers who were wounded but able to walk or hobble, making their way to the rear on top of the causeway. A few were hit again. One I recognized as a jump-school instructor at Fort Benning. Most of his leg had been shot off, but he was somehow getting along on the one leg.

About 4:00 A.M., Capt. Cecil L. Simmons took advantage of the lull to squeeze his H Company troopers, one at a time, through the narrow gap in the Belgian Gate at Bridge 4. G Company followed, and by dawn, half of Cole's understrength battalion was on the German side of the roadblock.

When Simmons' men started advancing, Baron von der Heydte's *Fallschirmjaeger*, dug in around the group of farm buildings just west of the causeway, unleashed a torrent of machine gun fire. Troopers near the front collapsed in bloody heaps. While bullets whistled overhead, Bob Cole slithered forward to the pinned-down company.

It was now 5:30 A.M.; Cole radioed for artillery fire, and for 30 minutes, American shells exploded around the farm buildings. Yet, there was no slackening of the heavy bursts of German machine-gun fire. Bullets continued to whine past Cole and other Screaming Eagles who were huddled in ditches and behind trees.

At this point, Cole had to reach a crucial decision. He could either order his men to start crawling toward the rear—in effect, abandon the ground purchased with so much Screaming Eagle blood—or he could charge the tenacious Germans dug in around the farmhouse complex and risk getting H and G Companies wiped out.

Sgt. Harrison Summers. *(U. S. Army)*   Lt. Col. Robert G. Cole. *(Don F. Pratt Museum)*

Cole shouted to Maj. John P. Stopka, his second in command, who was pinned down to Cole's left a short distance across a dirt road: "We're going to get some artillery smoke on that goddamned farmhouse; then we're going to make a bayonet charge!"

Bayonet charge? Stopka thought bayonet charges had gone out with the First World War. But he shouted back, "Okay." On the other side of the dirt road from Cole were the remnants of G

Company and Headquarters Company. The battalion leader thought that all of these units had received word to fix bayonets, reload with full clips; then wait for his signal to charge.

Minutes later, smoke shells from a 4.2-inch mortar platoon began dropping around the German-held farmhouse and adjacent buildings, and soon the enemy position was shrouded. At 6:15 A.M., Bob Cole leaped to his feet, brandished his .45 Colt overhead, blew his whistle, waved his arm forward, and dashed toward the spitting German machine guns. Twenty men followed. Across the road, Major Stopka yelled, "Let's go!" and some 50 troopers took out after him.

Halfway along the 200-yard distance to the farmhouse strong-point, a huffing Bob Cole dropped to one knee and looked back. He was shocked—only a trickle of his men had joined in the charge. The thought flashed through Cole's head: "Why have my boys let me down?"[1]

The fog of war had interceded. Cole's troopers had been scattered over a wide expanse of meadowland, and in the cacophony of battlefield noise, some did not get the order to charge. Others had vaguely heard something about "bayonets."

But the die had been cast. Cole, waving his men onward, was firing with his Colt in the direction of the farmhouse. "Goddamn it, I don't know what in the hell I'm shooting at, but I've got to keep shooting!" he roared.[2] Despite the peril of their situation, a few men nearby laughed at the remark. "Our colonel is really gung ho," one shouted.

Dashing onward, Cole leaped a hedgerow—and plunged into a ditch with water almost up to his neck. John Stopka, yelling relentlessly to his group, "Let's go! Let's go!" jumped over the same hedgerow, but missed the water-filled ditch. He saw Bob Cole, his jumpsuit soaking wet, clambering out.

Now the smokescreen began to dissolve, and the charging Americans were exposed in the sights of the Germans' weapons. A few troopers reached and passed Stopka. One of them, Pvt. Edwin S. Pastouris, was cut down by a machine-gun burst. As blood gushed from the trooper's chest and stomach, he heard a faint voice: "How are you, Pastouris?" It was Major Stopka hovering over him.

"I'm okay," the grievously wounded youth replied weakly. "Keep going. Keep going." Stopka patted the trooper's shoulder; then resumed the run for the farmhouse.

Pvt. Bernard Sterno was dashing across a field when he felt a dull thump in one hand. But his gloves were on, so he saw nothing amiss until blood began pouring out. A medic hastily bandaged the finger stump, and Sterno resumed the attack.

Moving past a hedgerow, Pvt. Sterno heard a plaintive call, "Help me. Help me." It was a sergeant from his company who had been shot in the stomach and leg. Blood had saturated his jumpsuit and his face was ashen. Sprawled next to him was the medic who had just treated Sterno's finger stump—dead with a bullet through his head. Sterno knew the wounded sergeant was a goner, but he patted him on the shoulder, told him he would be in good shape as soon as he was evacuated, picked up his rifle, and ran forward.

Now, Bob Cole and John Stopka and a few troopers reached the farmhouse. Cole was waving his Colt and shouting, "Keep going! Keep going! The bastards are on the run!"

Strewn around the premises were the dead bodies of a few score of Germans, clad in their round, bowl-like paratrooper helmets and camouflage smocks. They had not budged an inch. These were von der Heydte's high school boys, who only a few weeks earlier had been singing and laughing and worrying if the war would end before they had a chance to get into it. Now their names would appear in black-bordered Berlin newspaper columns headed "Fell for the Führer."

Savage fighting continued to rage around the farmhouse complex. Lt. Edward A. Provost, who had started the bayonet charge with nine men and reached the farmhouse with four, crept up silently to a hedge on the far side of which a German machine gun was spitting bullets. With him was Cpl. James O. Brune, who pitched a grenade over the hedgerow.

Five German paratroopers were at the gun and in an adjoining trench. The grenade exploded in the middle of them. None of the enemy soldiers were killed; they lay stunned or stood upright screaming. Provost and Brune, quick to press their advantage, leaped the hedgerow and charged. Brune started to fire at the dazed Germans, but Provost shouted, "Don't waste your bullets—stick the bastards!" The two troopers bayonetted the five enemy soldiers.

White-hot fury had been aroused on both sides during the bloody struggle along Carentan's Death Alley. Cole sent a 10-man patrol to probe toward the front. As they reached a crossroad, four Germans holding weapons emerged from a thick woods calling, *"Kamerad! Kamerad!"* (Literally "comrade," but commonly used for "We surrender!")

A few hours previously, two Screaming Eagles had been shot down under identical circumstances when they dropped their guard and moved forward to accept a "surrender."

Now, without a word, Cole's patrol opened fire on the four Germans, cutting down two of them, and the other pair fled back into the woods. Only a few days earlier, the Screaming Eagles had parachuted into Normandy, green and naive—now they were learning harsh lessons fast in the crucible of Carentan.

Despite heavy losses, von der Heydte's paratroopers continued to assault American positions. Pfc. Charles L. Roderick and Pfc. Franklin E. Cathon had been firing their machine guns for six hours, and dead bodies in front of the smoking muzzle were hampering German efforts to reach and wipe out the American machine gun. Roderick was firing the automatic weapon when a bullet hit the operating handle, driving a metal chunk deep into his shoulder. Blood flowed freely. Roderick refused to be evacuated, and continued to squeeze the trigger with his good arm, his other arm hanging limply at his side.

Near the road leading back to the causeway, Sgt. Charles R. Derose fell into a hole and broke his leg. He declined evacuation, and stood in the hole for four hours directing the flow of ammunition from the rear to the front. Derose constantly gritted his teeth; the pain was nearly unbearable. Suddenly, his suffering ended—a mortar shell came right in the hole after him.

At his farmhouse command post, Bob Cole was deeply concerned. Von der Heydte's paratroopers were attacking the farmhouse complex in considerable numbers; Cole could hear the nearby heavy bursts of Schmeisser fire as the Germans closed in. He was convinced that the remnants of his battalion were about to be overrun and wiped out.

Maj. John Stopka, who had been moving from window to window and firing at bobbing targets, called out, "The bastards are all around us. It's getting goddamned hot!"

No doubt Cole was again racked by the specter that had haunted him for months: Would he fail his boys in a battle crisis? Now he knew there was only one last chance to hold the position—and save most of his men. He called for a heavy concentration of artillery fire—almost directly on top of his command post and his troopers. Outside, there was the angry *b-r-r-r* of a

Schmeisser, and a stream of bullets stitched the wall over Cole's head.

At this crucial point, the radio of the artillery forward observer, Captain Rosemond, balked. He shook it violently and cursed it. Finally, the radio crackled and Capt. Charles Aldrich at the artillery fire-control center came on the air. Cole sighed with relief and grabbed the transmitter: "Give 'em all you've got—right in front of our farmhouse!"

"But we're almost out of ammo!" was the reply.

"Then for God's sake, get some—or we're dead ducks!"

Twelve minutes later, above the rattle of Schmeissers and the crash of grenades, Cole could hear the approaching sound from behind that brought renewed hope to his heart—the rustle of American shells, large clusters of them, heading toward the advancing German paratroopers, only a hedgerow or two away.

Shells exploded among the hedgerows, giving off geysers of flame and thick black smoke. Every gun or mortar within range was pounding the *Fallschirmjaeger*. "Hot damn, they're giving those Krauts holy hell!" a trooper in the command post shouted jubilantly. Moments later, he and the others flopped to the floor when a salvo crashed outside, rocking the house.

When the barrage lifted, the German fire from the front had diminished to only an occasional rifle shot. Cole sent patrols forward, but the enemy had abandoned the battlefield, leaving behind scores of dead and seriously wounded comrades. The back of Baron von der Heydte's 6th Parachute Regiment had been broken.

At 2:00 P.M. the following day, another Screaming Eagle battalion relieved Bob Cole's exhausted and depleted unit. In an orchard, the colonel ordered a roll call. Some 640 of his troopers had entered the death struggle for the Carentan causeway two days earlier—now only 132 answered "present," and many of them were wounded.[3]

Meanwhile, the 327th Glider Infantry, now led by Col. Joseph H. Harper, stormed across the Douve as planned, linked up with the 2nd Battalion of Bob Sink's 506th Parachute Infantry (which had been hurled into the assault), and on June 12, Carentan was in Allied hands.

That night at his Berchtesgaden chalet perched high in the Bavarian Alps, Adolf Hitler flew into a towering rage after learning that the Screaming Eagles were the new landlords of Carentan. On June 9, he had ordered Baron von der Heydte to "fight to the last man and the last bullet." The Führer now felt that he had been betrayed. In fact, the German 6th Parachute Regiment had been cut to pieces, and von der Heydte had withdrawn his tattered and bloody remnants to the flatlands a mile south of Carentan to continue the fight.

So upset was the Führer over the loss of Carentan that only a few hours later, he issued a directive to all Wehrmacht commanders in Normandy:

> *Explicit orders demand that everyone in strongpoints, points of resistance and other defensive positions surrounded by enemy units must defend the position to the last man and the last bullet, in order to allow time for preparation for the counterattack and the reconquest of the [Normandy] coast. No orders to retreat will be issued [by any commander].*

Even while Utah and Omaha Beaches were being linked at Carentan into one continuous Allied line, some six miles south of that road and rail hub a shocking scenario was unfolding in the once sleepy little town of Graignes.

29
Mass
Murder at
Graignes

For eight centuries, the belfry in the old Roman Catholic Church in Graignes had benignly watched over the God-fearing, hardworking citizens who had endured life without the slightest hint of excitement. Suddenly, on the morning of June 6, 1944, the community six miles south of Carentan was electrified: scores of young Americans clad in waterlogged jump boots and baggy pants had appeared in their midst.

Most of these newcomers had parachuted from the black sky into the swamps that ringed Graignes on three sides, in water ranging from one to five feet deep. Entangled in their parachute canopies and suspension lines and weighted with 100 pounds of combat gear, many drowned. Aided by bright moonlight, survivors discerned the church belfry outlined against the sky, and instinctively began wading toward the landmark.

Paratroopers drop into swamp outside Graignes. *(Courtesy Adolph Coors Co., George Skypeck, artist)*

All during the day and for the next 48 hours, paratroopers straggled into Graignes until the force totaled 14 officers and 168 men. Dropped from eight to 15 miles south of their true drop zone, they were mainly from the 82nd Airborne's 507th Parachute Infantry, but also included 18 to 20 men of the 101st Airborne Division, along with a glider pilot, a C-47 pilot (whose plane had been shot down), and two 29th Infantry Division soldiers who had landed at Omaha Beach.[1]

Early on the morning of June 7—D-Day plus 1—Alphonse Voydie, the mayor of Graignes, held a town meeting in the church. Nearly every man, woman and child was present. Emotions ran high—Mother France was being liberated. Amid tears and applause, the Graignai agreed unanimously to give every possible help to their "guests," the young fighting men from across the ocean.

Adults in the assemblage knew the risks involved for aiding the enemies of the Third Reich—summary execution if caught. There were no Germans in Graignes, but they were posted in several adjacent villages. Under the leadership of Mayor Voydie and their priest, Abbé Leblastier, the civilians began combing the swamps for the weapons, ammunition, and supplies that had been dropped by parachute in bundles. So successful were these scavenger hunts that the Americans were soon heavily armed with machine guns, mortars, and ammunition.

Maj. Charles D. Johnson, executive officer of the 3rd Battalion, 507th Parachute Infantry, took command of the isolated force, set up a command post, and organized strong-points all around Graignes, for a German attack could hit from any direction.

On D-Day plus 2, Johnson and his crew of parachutists were confronted with a crisis: They had run out of rations. Madame Germaine Boursier, the 50-year-old greengrocer who ran a small café, leaped into the breech. In effect, she became the Americans' "mess sergeant." Together with her two daughters and other women and older girls, Madame Boursier foraged for food and milk, prepared two meals daily and hand-carried them to the paratroopers at their observation and gun positions. Bread was nonexistent, but as the days passed, the café-and-grocery owner and some of her neighbors made periodic trips by horse cart to German-held Sainte-Jean-de-Daye, five miles away, to bring back bread, which was hidden under hay or straw.

The trek to Sainte-Jean-de-Daye was fraught with peril. Madame Boursier, her daughter, Madame Odette Lelavechet, and other women traveled over poorly marked mined roads and through German roadblocks and past foot patrols. Once, a German group searched Madame Boursier's cart and found the bread. Her heart beat furiously, but outwardly, she was a portrait of serenity, explaining that the bread was merely for the villagers of Graignes.[2]

Meanwhile, 25-year-old Joseph Folliot and his younger brother, Charles Gosselin, risked their lives repeatedly to guide the reconnaissance patrols that Major Johnson was dispatching steadily. So much did Folliot and Gosselin hate the *Boches* that they had to be restrained from carrying weapons. (If captured with weapons, the Frenchmen would have been executed.)

Other eager young Graignai—mainly Gustav Rigault, André Yvres and Albert Maugier, Sr.—also risked their necks by fanning out into the countryside and bringing back valuable intelligence on German patrols, movements, and dispositions. Although Rigault was seriously ill, when not going on one-man reconnaissance patrols, he often waded through the murky swamps in search of more parachuted bundles.

On the afternoon of D-Day plus 2, the paratroopers of Graignes had their first clash with the Germans. A patrol was trekking along a dirt road a half mile from the Graignes church, when the men heard the sound of an approaching vehicle. Quickly, they took cover in a hedgerow, just in time to spot the oncoming German truck filled with grenadiers. On cue, the Americans fired, killing several of the *Feldgrau*. But others took cover and began shooting back with Schmeissers. Outgunned, the paratroopers hauled out and returned to Graignes.

While dashing away, S. Sgt. Fredric D. Boyle dropped a few clips of valuable BAR ammunition he had been assigned to carry, and the patrol leader sent him back to retrieve the lost items.

Fredric Boyle recalled what happened next:

> *I had in my pocket a Gammon grenade that contained a half pound of a substance called Composition C, a puttylike mixture with great explosive properties. As soon as I reached the ambush site, I saw about 20 or so Germans in two files coming along the road. They were only about 50 feet from me, but could not see me because I was behind a hedge. I got out my Gammon grenade to blow hell out of them, but I did not know that the Composition C was still damp. I pitched the Gammon, expecting to see pieces of Germans flying skyward. Instead, there was only silence—it did not go off and I had given away my presence. Bullets started whistling into the hedgerow around me, so I hightailed it back to Graignes—without the ammo clips.*

That afternoon, a 12-man patrol led by Lt. Lowell Maxwell was probing north of Graignes along the road leading to Carentan, when it collided with a German field artillery unit, and a fierce but brief firefight erupted. Far outgunned and outnumbered, the Americans scattered and each trooper made his way back to Graignes on his own.[3]

Major Johnson was concerned that the enemy artillery outfit was part of a force that was going to attack Graignes from the north, so he sent Lt. Francis E. Naughton and a patrol to blow up a bridge on the Carentan road. Reaching the span, the demolitions men began setting charges. Suddenly, a 12-year-old French girl watching the activity called out, *"Boches! Boches!"* A German force was coming down the road directly toward the bridge.

Frank Costa recalled subsequent events:

> *Lieutenant Naughton told David Purcell and me to get to the other end of the bridge (the German end) and hold off the enemy until the charges were ready. We double-timed to the other end and set up my BAR, and Purcell was armed with a carbine.*
>
> *Moments later, about 30 Krauts rounded a bend a couple of hundred yards away. I let loose a blast with my BAR. They scattered, but kept coming. When the charges were readied, I ran back over the bridge, with the Germans not far behind. Lieutenant Naughton shouted, "The bridge is ready to go!" I suggested that we wait until some Krauts were on the bridge. Sure enough, when the Germans started to cross, firing as they came, Naughton turned the switch, and the bridge—and the Krauts—blew sky-high. We got the hell out of there.*

On the morning of June 10, Trooper Frank P. Juliano and a few comrades were concealed along a hedgerow covering one of the approaches to Graignes. Suddenly, they heard the sound of engines and saw a German motorcycle patrol coming down the road. When the first vehicle was abreast, the troopers opened fire. All the German cyclists were killed except the man in the rear, and he spun around and raced away, no doubt spreading the word that an American force was in Graignes.

Meanwhile, Capt. Abraham Sophian, Jr., a paratrooper medic, had set up an aid station in the old church and was treating the wounded and those injured in the drop. His supplies and medicine were almost nonexistent. Women and teenaged girls were serving as nurses, and Abbé Leblastier and Mayor Voydie, both outwardly relaxed and cheerful, were a calming influence on the casualties.

Sunday morning, June 11, was peaceful in Graignes. Dressed in their Sunday best—threadbare but immaculately clean suits and dresses—the Graignai were worshipping at 10:00 A.M. Mass, at which Abbé Leblastier was officiating. Suddenly, Madame Joseph Rerrete burst inside and yelled excitedly, *"The Germans are coming!"*

The Americans attending the services dashed outside and to their assigned defensive positions. An hour later, German artillery and mortars began pounding Graignes; then grenadiers edged forward along the hedgerows. A spirited firefight broke out around the paratroopers' perimeter, and after 30 minutes, the *Feldgrau* pulled back, leaving behind a few score of dead comrades.

What the paratroopers did not know was that this had been but a probing attack, a reconnaissance in force to sniff out American strong-points. At 7:00 P.M., the Germans opened up with every gun and mortar they had. Shells screamed into Graignes, exploding in sheets of orange flame and black smoke. Lt. Elmer Farnham, leader of the 507th Regiment's mortar platoon, started to climb into the church steeple to observe fire for his mortars, which were emplaced in the churchyard.

"Better not go up there," Farnham had been warned by his close friend, Lt. Ercle R. "Pip" Reed. "That steeple will be a prime target." Farnham shrugged and Reed departed for his machine-gun position. Minutes later, a high velocity shell tore into the steeple, killing Elmer Farnham and an assistant.

Then Maj. Charles Johnson, the Graignes force leader, was killed by a shell, and Capt. Leroy D. Brummitt took command.

For two hours, the Germans bombarded the village and points around it. Then an eerie silence fell. Around the defensive circle, the Americans were praying that friendly forces would soon break through to them, for ammunition was running low and it was obvious that strong German formations, backed by artillery, mortars and armored cars, were on all sides.

The lull was ominous. Tense Americans fingered triggers and could hear the sound of vehicles moving about to the west and southwest, activity masked by the hedgerows. Now enemy movements were discerned to the north; the troopers were unaware that these were German units pulling back from Carentan.

Just before dusk on this Sunday evening, swarms of *Feldgrau* charged Graignes from several directions. Having no other place to go, the paratroopers stood and fought. The harsh sounds of automatic weapons and rifle fire echoed across the shadowy hedgerows and swamplands.

Ercle R. Reed recalled events:

> *One of our machine guns caught a platoon of Krauts in the open and cut down every one of them. But the Germans, who far outnumbered our force, came on, and it seemed that every enemy soldier was firing a machine pistol. They were numerous, so numerous that some of our men crouched into deep foxholes and let a wave pass; then opened up on the Germans from behind.*

Through the blackness, the conflict raged. German infantrymen were pouring into the village. Near midnight, the Americans were virtually out of ammunition and the word was passed, "We're pulling out! It's every man for himself!"

Huddled along a hedgerow near the church, Sgt. Fredric Boyle and another trooper had only about five rounds of carbine ammo remaining. Nearby, a German voice was calling out orders. Then the grenadiers charged. Boyle and the other man were lying facedown, and several Germans stomped on the Americans' backs as they ran forward.

Fredric Boyle remembered:

> *There were Krauts swarming all over the place, but in the darkness and confusion, I and my comrade slipped out of Graignes and promptly bumped into a column of parked trucks, and heard the Germans standing beside them talking. We crept off in another direction and scrambled over a hedgerow. Suddenly, a dark figure a few yards away popped up in front of us and yelled: "Halt!" In the moonlight, we could see his coal-bucket helmet. My comrade pumped his last three bullets into the German's belly.*

Not all of the surviving defenders of Graignes got the word to pull out. Until they had exhausted their ammo, Frank Costa, 19-year-old Pvt. James Klingman, and 20-year-old Edward Page blasted away at the Germans from their six-foot-by-six-foot foxhole at the edge of the swamps south of town.

At dawn, Costa was on watch and saw an alarming development: 10 or 12 Germans were digging in at the end of his field,

Sgt. Fredric D. Boyle. *(Author's collection)*

Cpl. Edward Page. *(Author's collection)*

only 70 yards away. Quickly, he awakened Page and Klingman. Costa recalled:

> *We were on the far side of the hedge from Graignes. I asked Ed Page to get to the other side and see what he could in the village. Ed returned and said evenly, "The town is filled with Krauts—there must be a thousand of them there!"*

A hasty council of war was convened. The three troopers agreed that they should depart immediately and try to infiltrate to American lines in the north, but their plans would be postponed for 24 hours—the Germans at the end of the field revealed no inclination to move on.

Meanwhile in the night, most of Graignes' frightened civilians had fled into the swamps, although Madame Boursier (the paratroopers' "mess sergeant"), Abbé Leblastier, a young priest, and two women nursing wounded Americans in the church refused to leave.

That morning, the German occupants were in a vicious mood. They knew that the invading Allies had secured a firm foothold in Normandy, and here in Graignes, behind German lines, surrounded American paratroopers had taken a heavy toll in dead and wounded *Feldgrau*. Worse perhaps, most of the trapped parachutists had evaded their clutches.

A Frenchman who survived the Graignes ordeal told what happened:

> *The triumphant Germans dragged to the village square 12 American paratroopers, most of whom were wounded. The Graignes people were filled with anxiety, seeing these boys they had been aiding huddled there and waiting to be murdered. We wondered if the Boches would take revenge on them, right before our eyes. Were they going to murder them like they murdered in front of his parsonage Abbé Leblastier and the young Franciscan priest, Father Charles Lebarbarchon?*
>
> *The Germans loaded the Americans into a truck and took them to Mesnil-Angot (a few miles to the southeast) and into a field, where they shot or bayoneted them. Later, their bodies were found covered only with a small layer of dirt, their arms and heads protruding, in a common grave.*

On the following day, 12 more captured paratroopers were murdered in Graignes and thrown into a pond near the church. Two French women who had been nursing the wounded Americans in the church were also executed for "aiding the enemy."

Later, after American forces reached the Graignes region, only 12 of the murdered paratroopers were identifiable: George Baragona, Benton J. Broussard, Jesus Casas, Walter J. Chouquette, Ray M. Callahan, William Love, Arnold J. Martinez, James Noff, Leo P. Parklom, Edward J. Pittis, Robert R. Rockwell, and Joseph Stachowiak. Also killed were the parachute surgeon, Captain Sophian, and Capt. Loyal Bogart, among others.[4]

Mayor Voydie was in hiding, but 44 Graignai, including Madame Boursier, were arrested and threatened with death unless they revealed the identity of neighbors who had "collaborated." None talked.[5]

Sixty-six homes were destroyed and 139 were partially demolished, leaving only two houses unscathed from the fighting and the razing by the Germans. The stately old church, which had stood for eight centuries and loomed as a symbol of the patriotic steadfastness of the Graignai, was the special target of their fury. The edifice was blown up.[6]

When the Germans had overrun Graignes, the American

paratroopers—alone, in pairs, and in small bands—armed only with trench knives and bayonets, slipped into the murky swamps and tried to evade capture. One 82nd Airborne trooper remained in Graignes for two days, however, hidden in the ruins of the old church. Despite the certain threat of execution if detected, Madame Meuriet guided the American out of town at night, right under the noses of the Wehrmacht, and to a bridge north of the village. There she gave him directions, and he eventually reached American lines at Carentan.

Capt. Leroy Brummitt, the Graignes force commander, led one group of 20 evaders to the hamlet of L'Port Saint-Pierre, a short distance to the northwest, where it hooked up with another pack under Lt. Francis Naughton, who had blown the bridge north of Graignes four days earlier. Picking their way northward through the swamps and hedgerows, this group of 50 to 60 parachutists eventually made contact with an American armored patrol south of Carentan.

On the evening of June 14, Frank Costa, Ed Page, and Jim Klingman, the troopers who had been manning the large foxhole south of Graignes, were holed up in the hayloft of a barn on the farm of Gustave Rigault, outside L'Port Saint-Pierre. Below, they heard rustling sounds and, clutching their weapons, glanced down onto the heads of two Germans who were searching for paratrooper evaders. Had the two started up the hayloft ladder, they would have been blasted. But they quickly lost interest in the barn and departed. Breathing a sigh of relief—rifle blasts would have alerted the Germans on the premises—Ed Page whispered, "It's a good thing that the Krauts goldbrick sometimes; just like we do!"

After dark, the three troopers and a band of other evaders holed up nearby, climbed into a few flat-bottomed boats that would, if all went well, take them up the Carentan Canal, right through German lines, for nearly five miles to American positions. The tiny flotilla was shepherded by Joseph Folliot, the young Frenchman who had guided numerous paratrooper patrols from Graignes during the past week.

Folliot told the Americans to lie flat, and the flotilla moved out. Passing through German lines, flares went up regularly and machine-gun bursts could be heard off in the distance. The leaky old boats were one-third filled with water. Everyone remained deathly still and silent, and then a trooper, Carlos Hurtado, called out in a rather loud voice, "I'm getting all wet." Frank Costa replied in a stage whisper, "And where in the hell do you think the rest of us have been for the past hour? If you don't shut your trap, you'll get us all killed!" Thirty minutes later, the Frenchman said, "Okay, you can get off here and follow this path into Carentan, a few hundred yards away."

At Carentan, the evaders, totally exhausted, were put in trucks and driven to 82nd Airborne headquarters in Sainte Mère Eglise. They dismounted, lay down on the concrete street, and slept for 18 hours. Altogether, about 100 (the precise total will never be known) of the 182 Americans who held Graignes for six days reached friendly lines. Most of them now gorged themselves on food, took showers, were issued clean uniforms, and in 24 hours were back with their units and in the thick of the fighting that was raging in Normandy.[7]

On June 27—D-Day plus 21—three American infantry divisions captured Cherbourg, the Neptune objective. The Allies were on the Continent to stay. Among the numerous 82nd Airborne and 101st Airborne troopers liberated from a Cherbourg POW camp were Clarence Hughart, who had been shot after dropping, then treated kindly by a group of German soldiers, and Roy Perkins, the medic who had been with Maj. Dave Thomas, the Screaming Eagle surgeon, when they were captured in Amfreville.[8]

The capture of one of Europe's finest commercial ports had exacted a heavy toll in American lives. Battle casualties sustained by Lightning Joe Collins' VII Corps since D-Day totaled 22,119, including 2,811 killed, 13,564 wounded and 5,665 missing (most captured, many drowned). Best estimates available for German losses in the Cherbourg campaign were 47,000 killed, wounded, or captured, including six generals.

The 82nd and 101st Airborne Divisions suffered particularly—their losses comprised 41 percent of VII Corps' total casualties. The All-Americans sustained 4,480 men killed, wounded, missing or captured, and the Screaming Eagles had an almost identical total—4,670 casualties. In addition, in the airborne assault in the early hours of D-Day, 60 percent of all supplies and heavy equipment dropped by parachute or landed by glider were destroyed, damaged, or missing.

Following his capture in the Cap de la Hague west of Cherbourg where he was one of the final German commanders to hold out on the peninsula, Lt. Col. Günther Kiel told his captors that the speed with which the 4th Infantry Division assaulted Utah Beach and drove inland had been far greater than Wehrmacht commanders had anticipated. Kiel had a complaint: "Each time we tried to assemble behind Utah Beach on D-Day, we were disrupted by bands of American paratroopers."

PART IV

Parachutes Around the World

30
Jungle War
on
Noemfoor

The Allies focused their avid gaze on Normandy, where the war's largest and most spectacular invasion had taken place, but savagery continued to rage in the Pacific part of the world conflict. For two years, Gen. Douglas MacArthur had been leapfrogging almost 1,300 miles up the rugged spine of New Guinea in a masterful campaign. By June 1944, his forces had nearly clawed their way to the Vogelkop Peninsula at the western tip of New Guinea, the world's second largest island.[1]

In early May 1944, MacArthur set his sights on Biak, a tiny island perched in the mouth of Geelvink Bay, which bordered the eastern shores of the Vogelkop peninsula. This would be another of the supreme commander's "hit-'em-where-they-ain't" leapfrogging operations. His intelligence had reported little indication of Japanese presence on Biak. However, the enemy was there in strength—nearly 10,000 warriors who were dedicated to dying for the emperor, supported by tanks and heavy guns.

On May 27, a task force built around the 41st Infantry Division assaulted Biak—and ran headlong into a stiff defense. The Japanese infantry were dug in along cliffs overlooking the American landing beaches, concealed in countless caves, and huddled in underground "spider" holes and bunkers. GIs wielding rifles, tommy guns, BARs, machine guns, flame throwers, bayonets, trench knives, and bazookas had to advance foot by foot, rooting out their tenacious enemies. Huge amounts of gasoline were poured into caves and bunkers and set afire, incinerating the Japanese holed up there. Burned and mutilated Japanese corpses were strewn everywhere, and the stench on the island was sickening. Still, the Japanese fought on.

While the Biak holocaust raged, MacArthur's intelligence learned that the Japanese were using Noemfoor Island, 75 miles west of Biak in Geelvink Bay, as a staging area to slip reinforcements and supplies at night into beleaguered Biak. So the Cyclone Task Force, led by Brig. Gen. Edward D. Patrick and centering on the 158th Infantry Regimental Combat Team, was hurriedly thrown together and given the mission of seizing Noemfoor (code-named "Operation Table Tennis").

Late in June, Col. George Jones, leader of the independent 503rd Parachute Infantry Regiment, was alerted that his outfit might be called on to jump onto Noemfoor. The 503rd had made its last combat drop on Nadzab airfield back in September 1943, but in recent weeks, had been patrolling the jungles around Hollandia, some 500 miles to the east of Noemfoor.

Noemfoor was the typical Pacific island: primitive, hostile, thick with jungle growth, and surrounded by jagged coral reefs. Fifteen miles long and 11 miles wide, the circular-shaped island had provided for centuries a peaceful habitat for up to 4,500 natives, but all that changed in November 1943, when a large Japanese force suddenly descended on Noemfoor and began building three airstrips, two in the north and one in the south.

Memphis-born Col. George Jones, known to his men as the "Tennessee Walking Horse," recalling his native state and the rapid rate he set on training marches, had replaced Col. Kenneth Kinsler, who had killed himself after the Nadzab operation. Now Jones immediately launched his key officers in a series of reconnaissance flights over Noemfoor.

The 503rd officers flew as observers in regular air corps bombing and strafing runs against the island. Those making the flights in separate aircraft included Jones, his three battalion commanders—Maj. Cameron Knox, Lt. Col. John Britten, and Maj. John Erickson—and Capt. Harris T. Mitchell, Lt. William T. "Wild Bill" Bossert, Capt. John R. Richmond, and Capt. John B. Pratt.

Harris Mitchell, operations officer of the 503rd Parachute Infantry, made his run over the target on June 29. Like the other observers, he was wedged tightly in a narrow space in an A-20A attack bomber, lying flat on his stomach and looking over the shoulders of the pilot and copilot. It had taken a great deal of pushing and shoving to get Mitchell into place for the long flight to Noemfoor.

Kamiri Airfield, hacked out of north shore jungles by hundreds of imported Formosan slave laborers using little more than basic hand tools, was the target of the flight carrying Mitchell. Wasting no time, the twin-engined A-20As began bombing and strafing the runway and adjoining facilities. Mitchell's plane, zooming along at deck level, caught a large group of Japanese in the open and riddled them with bullets. While pulling up, the bomber grazed the top of a tall tree, neatly shearing off much of its right wing.

The pilot gave the ship an extra thrust of power, preventing an immediate crash, but he was unable to gain higher than 500 feet altitude. Realizing that the mutilated bomber was in trouble, Japanese on the ground raked it with heavy machine gun fire, and bullets ventilated the fuselage.

Heading out to sea, the pilot turned to Mitchell and said, "Our best chance to get out of this mess is to crash-land in the water by one of our vessels and let them pick us up." The Navy was offshore shelling Noemfoor.

Harris Mitchell vividly recalled the ensuing episode:

I wasn't too thrilled with this suggestion. As tightly as I was shoehorned in, I wouldn't have stood much chance of getting out before the plane went under. All the time, the pilot was fighting the controls to keep us airborne. Finally, he said we would try to make it to Biak. The 75-mile flight seemed to take forever. The pilot radioed ahead that we were coming, and as we approached the coral landing strip which was not very long, I could see the fire trucks, ambulances, people of all kinds dashing about. Obviously, they expected a gruesome scene, which did nothing to improve my morale.

Unable to fully control the aircraft, the pilot had to land at a high rate of speed, and he immediately applied the brakes, put the flaps down and skidded along the runway. As the bomber neared the palm trees at the end of the strip, the pilot swerved the aircraft and the plane flipped over, eventually skidding to a halt off the runway. Fearful of a fire or explosion, the crew scrambled out of the wreckage—but Harris Mitchell remained stuck in his straightjacket.

Despite the clear peril, rescue workers reached the parachute officer and after extensive prying, pushing, pulling, and shoving, Mitchell was freed and rushed to a nearby aid station.[2]

Harris Mitchell remembered:

> *They asked me if I was all right. I told them I was okay. I thought to myself that I must I must really be a "cool customer" to feel so calm after what I had gone through. The medical officer gave me a shot of bourbon, but then reaction set in and I got to shaking so badly that I could hardly hold the glass. But I got that drink down—and several more. Finally, I settled down.*

Capt. Harris T. Mitchell.
(*Author's collection*)

Sgt. Ray E. Eubanks. (*U. S. Army*)

Earlier, on June 21, a pair of PT boats landed a squad of Alamo Scouts on Noemfoor, and these specially trained supersleuths prowled around Kamiri airstrip and other parts of Noemfoor for two days before being picked up by the same speedy little craft. They reported that there were more than 3,000 Japanese soldiers on the island, and that most of the enemy's defenses were concentrated around Kamiri.

At dawn on D-Day—July 2—warships began shelling suspected Japanese positions around Kamiri, and bombers pounded the airstrip and an adjacent ridge. Cyclone Task Force assault troops waded ashore at 8:00 A.M. without firing a shot—or having a shot fired at them. Kamiri airstrip was quickly seized, and by sundown, some 7,000 American and Australian soldiers were ashore.

A Japanese soldier who had been dazed by an exploding shell and captured reported that 3,000 additional Nipponese had landed on Noemfoor a week earlier, which would have made a combined enemy force in excess of 6,000 men. (Actually, there were fewer than 2,000 Japanese soldiers on the island, and only 1,000 of them were combat troops.)

Alarmed by this report, even though the captured soldier had said he had not seen the supposed reinforcements, General Patrick contacted Gen. Walter Krueger's Sixth Army headquarters with a request that the 503rd Parachute Infantry drop on Kamiri the next morning to reinforce his Cyclone Task Force. Within the hour, Krueger ordered George Jones to launch the parachute operation.

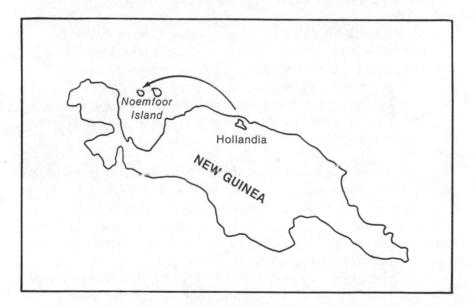

Leapfrog to Noemfoor

Typical of the shoestring style in which Douglas MacArthur had to operate in the Southwest Pacific, there were not sufficient

C-47s to haul the entire parachute regiment at one time, so one battalion would be dropped on three successive days.

At 6:30 A.M. on July 3, George Jones, jumpmaster in the lead aircraft, his regimental staff, and Major Knox's 1st Battalion lifted off in 41 aircraft of the 54th Troop Carrier Wing from Cyclops airfield at Hollandia. The men were to bail out along the narrow Kamari strip, so the C-47s flew in a column of twos.

Approaching Noemfoor, Jones was standing in the open door of his C-47 and behind him, ready to jump, was Capt. Harris Mitchell, now bounced back from his harrowing ordeal in the Noemfoor recon flight. Jones and Mitchell were concerned. The jump was to be made at 500 feet—a common height for a combat operation. But the airplane seemed to be much lower. However, both officers dismissed this nagging worry—heights over water can be misleading. Neither man knew that the altimeters in the first two C-47s were out of kilter, and that they were indeed flying low—only 300 feet. Succeeding planes were at less than 400 feet.

Over Kamiri the green light flashed on in Jones's plane, and out he went. Jones recalled that particular jump:

> My chute had barely opened when I crashed hard on the coral runway, and took a terrific blow on the head. I thanked God for my steel helmet, otherwise, my brains would have been splattered around. I staggered to my feet; my head was spinning and it throbbed like someone was using a jackhammer on it. For a week, I had such a violent headache that I thought for certain that my skull had been cracked.

Harris Mitchell also landed—*hard!* He too was dazed, but went to help others. Jones' radio operator had broken both legs. Major Knox had broken a foot. Mitchell looked up at other planes coming in, and they seemed far too low. Men landed on Japanese construction equipment sitting on the runway, and others were jolted when they crashed onto the rock-hard surface.

There had been a heavy toll, considering that no enemy action was involved. A total of 739 troopers had jumped; 72 of them had been injured, 31 of whom had sustained severe broken bones.

Hardly had the last trooper slammed into the ground than General Patrick ordered the construction equipment and assorted debris cleared from the runway in preparation for the next morning's drop by John Erickson's 3rd Battalion—much like locking the barn after the proverbial horse had been pilfered. The runway housecleaning did little good. When Erickson's 685 troopers, jumping from the prescribed 500 feet, crunched onto the hard-packed runway and into bordering trees, 56 of them were soon writhing in agony with broken bones and other injuries.

A stick of the 503rd Parachute Infantry drops on Noemfoor. *(U. S. Army)*

So far, a total of 1,424 men had bailed out, and 128 of them were casualties. George Jones had lost a battalion commander, his communications officer, three company commanders, and many key junior officers and noncoms. There were now two drops down and one to go. However, the Tennessee Walking Horse urgently requested that another means be found for bringing in John Britten's 2nd Battalion, and General Krueger agreed. So Britten's men were flown to Biak, where they were loaded onto LCIs for the 75-mile water trek to Noemfoor, landing on July 11.

After Jones' entire regiment had assembled around Kamiri,

patrols fanned out to try to locate the main body of Japanese, which had yet to be heard from. Contact was not long in coming, and a violent series of clashes erupted. It was brutal warfare. Men on both sides lived and died in the sweltering heat, tangled vegetation, snake-infested swamps and thick jungles. Plagued by typhus, malaria, dysentery and other tropical diseases, the paratroops steadily had their strength sapped.

There were no roads, few paths. Dead, wounded, and ill paratroopers were laboriously carried on ponchos stretched between poles through the jungle for many miles to reach the field hospital at Kamiri. Two-man teams had to rotate in lugging the casualty, while others served as guards. Because these mercy treks took up to 12 hours, the wounded trooper, who would have been saved under ordinary battlefield conditions, often succumbed due to shock or loss of blood.

George Jones' patrols and small battle units were scattered all over Noemfoor while trying to root out the Japanese. Field telephones were impractical, and radios were virtually useless because of the thick jungle and hills. So the regimental leader concocted a unique scheme for maintaining at least partial control of his units. He flew in a light plane over the jungle and watched for colored smoke released from grenades at previously designated locales. That would inform him that the patrol or unit was still operational. Light planes were also used to drop messages and limited amounts of blood plasma and food to remote jungle sites.

On July 23, patrols of Britten's 2nd Battalion collided with the main Japanese force led by a fire-eating colonel, Itsugi Shimizu, who, troopers knew from captured enemy documents, carried a samurai sword that was said to have been in his family for 300 years. Shimizu had sworn to fight to the death on Noemfoor, and the American paratroopers were eager to accommodate him—and "liberate" his coveted samurai sword.

A savage firefight erupted, and one platoon of D Company was cut off and isolated. Sgt. Ray E. Eubanks of Snow Hill, North Carolina, a squad leader in another platoon, was ordered to attack the Japanese position with his unit in order to lessen the enemy firing against the isolated platoon. Creeping and crawling forward under heavy rifle and machine-gun fire, Eubanks maneuvered his squad to within 30 yards of the dug-in Japanese.

Shouting above the din for his squad to pour bullets into the Japanese position, Eubanks and two scouts slithered forward to within 20 yards of spitting enemy machine guns. Directing the scouts to remain in a shallow depression, Eubanks wriggled over the ground to within 30 feet of the foe, then began blasting away with his automatic rifle. The Japanese now concentrated their fire on the sergeant, wounding him and rendering his weapon useless.

While blood saturated his combat fatigues and his teeth gnashed from the enormous pain, Eubanks grabbed his rifle by the barrel, charged forward, and clubbed to death four of the Japanese machine gunners. He had just finished off the last one, when an enemy bullet ended his one-man rampage. Eubanks died while draped over the Japanese machine gun.[3] Ray Eubanks' bull-like rush had so distracted the enemy that the separated platoon was able to maneuver back to its company.

It was not until August 17, after countless hide-and-seek skirmishes with die-hard but elusive bands of Japanese, that the 503rd Parachute Infantry and other units trapped and wiped out the last of the Japanese garrison on Noemfoor. An extensive search was launched in caves, spider-holes, and among Japanese corpses for the elusive Colonel Shimizu, but no trace of him was ever uncovered. Apparently, he had chosen to welch on his vow to fight to the death for his emperor and had taken advantage of darkness to steal away from Noemfoor in a small boat.

Noemfoor was officially declared secure on August 31. The 158th Infantry Regiment had killed 641 Japanese, at a relatively moderate cost of six men killed and 41 wounded. George Jones' 503rd paratroopers had counted 1,087 dead Nipponese and freed 312 Formosan slave laborers. Piled on top of the 128 casualties in the drops, the 503rd lost an additional 39 men killed, 72 wounded, and more than 400 laid low and hospitalized from an assortment of tropical diseases.

Douglas MacArthur wasted no time in his island leapfrog campaign on the long road to Tokyo. Supported by fighters and bombers based at Kamiri airfield, the 6th Infantry Division stormed ashore at Sansapor on the Vogelkop Peninsula on July 30, even while the series of nasty little clashes were raging on Noemfoor. Vogelkop, except for the customary mop-up of die-hard Japanese bands, was soon secured.

MacArthur now turned his gaze northward—to Corregidor and the Philippines.

31
The War's Worst-Kept Secret

Some Allied generals called Bob Frederick a "crazy bastard." But the slender, soft-spoken 37-year-old brigadier general's men in the crack First Special Service Force didn't mind the description. "Left-handed praise," his hard-bitten American-Canadian fighters assured each other, or just "jealousy." Generals were not supposed to be up front where the shooting was heavy, but Bob Frederick already had a fistful of Purple Hearts from North Africa and Italy by mid-1944.

Frederick's First Special Service Force, many of whom were qualified parachutists, had been known as the "Black Devils of Anzio," a sobriquet pinned on them by the Germans, who grew to fear their nighttime raids behind their lines.[1] His men paid Robert Tyson Frederick their highest accolade. They called him the "Head Devil."

Early in July, after Frederick had turned over command of his beloved First Special Service Force to his executive officer, the young general was ordered to report at once to Lt. Gen. Jacob L. "Jakie" Devers, Allied deputy supreme commander in the Mediterranean, at Algiers, North Africa. Devers got right to the point: "Bob, you're going to command our airborne troops in an invasion of southern France."

Frederick never changed expression, but his mind was in a whirl. Although a qualified paratrooper, he had no experience in planning or leading a strictly parachute and glider force. "How long will we have to get ready for the operation," Frederick asked evenly.

"Five weeks—D-Day is August 15," Devers replied.

Bob Frederick showed no sign of his shock. Only 35 days to plan, organize and carry out an airborne attack destined to be one of the largest in the war! A few minutes later, Frederick asked, "Well, where are my airborne troops?"

Devers looked the younger general directly in the eye and replied in measured tones: "So far, *you* are our airborne force."

Code-named "Operation Dragoon," the massive invasion of southern France, second in scope only to Overlord in Normandy, would involve a force of 300,000 men, 1,000 vessels and nearly 2,000 aircraft. Bob Frederick's paratroopers would spearhead the assault in the predawn darkness. The invasion would hit along a 37-mile stretch of the fabled Riviera and was designed to seize the vitally needed major ports of Marseilles and Toulon to the west, to liberate the southern two-thirds of France, and to form the lower pincer to link up with Overlord armies in the North.

Brig. Gen. Robert Frederick. *(William S. Story)*

Col. Rupert D. Graves. *(Clark Archer)*

Typically, Bob Frederick wasted no time in handwringing or soul-searching over the enormity of the endeavor suddenly thrust upon him, and he promptly set up headquarters for his 1st Airborne Task Force (FABTF) at Lido di Roma airfield outside the Italian capital. There were shortages of almost everything. Thirty-six officers from the green 13th Airborne Division in the States and a few from the Airborne Center, camp Mackall, North Carolina, were rushed to Italy to become Frederick's staff. There was an alarming shortage of cargo parachutes and air delivery equipment for resupply operations, and an urgent request resulted in 600,000 pounds of these crucial items reaching Rome by air and sea as late as D-Day minus 4.

Meanwhile, a hodgepodge of airborne units had been scraped up from throughout the Mediterranean and assembled in scattered airfields in west-central Italy. The FABTF would be of airborne-division size (9,732 officers and men), but there would be one notable difference in Frederick's command: Unlike American and British airborne divisions that had trained and later fought together as cohesive units, the FABTF was a collection of independent paratrooper and glider regiments, battalions, companies, and even platoons, which would have to be welded together with unprecedented swiftness.

The stakes were gargantuan. If Frederick's airborne force were to fail in its Dragoon mission to block German efforts to rush reinforcements to the Riviera landing beaches, then the entire invasion might falter or even become a debacle.

Code-named "Rugby Force," Frederick's command included these elements: the 517th Parachute Infantry Regiment (Lt. Col. Rupert D. Graves) and attached 460th Parachute Field Artillery Battalion (Lt. Col. Raymond Cato); the 596th Airborne Engineer Company, and Company D of the 83rd Mortar Battalion (4.2-inch mortars); the 509th Parachute Infantry Battalion (Lt. Col. William Yarborough) and attached 463rd Parachute Field Artillery Battalion (Lt. Col. John Cooper); the 551st Parachute Infantry Battalion (Lt. Col. Wood G. Joerg) and attached platoon of the 887th Airborne Engineer Company; and the British 2nd Independent Parachute Brigade (Brigadier C. H. V. Pritchard) and attached 2nd Mortar Battalion (4.2-inch mortars).

Some of Bob Frederick's units, while keenly trained, tough, and spirited, had never heard a shot fired in anger. Although blooded in brief skirmishing in Italy a few weeks earlier, Graves' 517th Parachute Infantry regiment, the largest unit in the FABTF, would be making its first combat jump.

Paratroop outfits were short of jeeps, so frequent nocturnal reconnaissance patrols were made into Rome, where American rear-echelon outfits were surfeited with the vehicles. Suddenly, the Eternal City was stricken with an epidemic of vanishing jeeps, which, curiously, reappeared in FABTF areas.

A 517th "patrol" of Cpl. Bill Frieze, Barney Gossen, and Ray "Pop" Boyce, was speeding back to friendly lines one night in a liberated jeep when an MP jeep took out in hot pursuit. Apparently acting under previous orders, the MPs began shooting at the fleeing "felons." Riding in back, Frieze noted a knapsack filled with smoke grenades, and he began tossing them out at intervals, allowing the troopers to escape. Later, Frieze told comrades: "Those damned MPs really went up in smoke!"

Hardly had Bob Frederick opened his command post than he received yet another jolt: A Dragoon airborne plan, drawn up at the U.S. Seventh Army headquarters in Naples, had totally ignored a cardinal principle in airborne doctrine—landing troops in a concentrated mass.

"For Chrissake," one of Frederick's officers exploded, "they've got us sprinkled all over southern France in tiny bands!"

Promptly, Frederick dispatched Bill Yarborough, who had already planned three major parachute operations and had jumped in two of them, to Naples to work with Seventh Army planners in drastically revising the airborne plan. Finishing his task, Yarborough hurried back with the new plan (which was largely his creation).

"Now, that's more like it!" Frederick exclaimed.

Twenty-four hours later, Frederick briefed his unit leaders. Pointing to a large wall map of the Riviera region, Frederick said, "See that town of Le Muy, about 15 miles inland from the coastal town of Fréjus? All roads leading from the west, north and east go through Le Muy. If we seize that town, the Krauts will not be able to rush more troops to the coast and attack our amphibious forces while they are coming ashore. We will drop on and capture Le Muy."

Bill Yarborough then explained the airborne plan. "My 509th Battalion will jump at oh-four-fifteen (4:15 A.M.) on D-Day, land to the south and southeast of Le Muy, and capture the high ground overlooking the town," the veteran parachute officer stated. "Colonel Graves' 517th Parachute Regimental Combat Team will jump 15 minutes later and seize the high ground west and north of Le Muy and block the main roads leading west to Toulon and to Draguignan, where a Kraut corps headquarters is located."

Yarborough added prophetically: "Maybe with a little luck,

we'll be able to personally invite a Wehrmacht general at Draguignan to be a guest of the United States government."

At 6:00 A.M., Pritchard's British 2nd Independent Parachute
Brigade would jump and capture Le Muy itself. A glider force
would bring in artillery and mortars to support the Red Devils'
assault against Le Muy, and at around 6:00 P.M., Joerg's 551st
Parachute Infantry Battalion would jump. Fifteen minutes later,
Sachs' 550th Glider Infantry Battalion would land.

"Hopefully, and I repeat, hopefully, the seaborne forces will
link up with us not later than D-Day plus 4," Yarborough concluded.

In closely guarded war rooms, the wide-eyed paratroops studied large maps labeled Top Secret and memorized terrain features in the Riviera region, particularly those on and around
their drop zones. Towns in southern France were given code
names to keep objectives and the locale of the invasion from
enemy eyes and ears. "Chicago," "Galveston," "Milwaukee,"
"Houston," and "Dallas" were among the code names. A platoon
sergeant in the 517th Parachute Infantry was given his platoon's
objective—Dallas. As he and his men were leaving the briefing
test, the sergeant asked a comrade, "I wonder what the population of Dallas is?"

"Oh, I'd guess about a half-million," the other replied, refer-
ring to the real Dallas, Texas.

The sergeant was silent for several seconds; then declared solemnly, "That's going to be a goddamned big job for only my one
platoon!"

Operation Dragoon was the worst kept secret of the war—
perhaps of any war. It was the subject of widespread gossip on
the streets and in the sleazy waterfront bars of Naples, Rome,
Salerno, and in the towns of Sardinia, Sicily, and Corsica.

Nineteen-year-old Cpl. Charles E. Pugh of the 596th Parachute Engineer Company, was listening to Axis Sally on Radio
Berlin, playing a record of a popular American ballad called
"Sentimental Journey," after which she said testily: "Our courageous German boys in southern France know how to deal with
you vicious gangsters from Chicago." To the Nazis, those American paratroopers who were not murderous ex-convicts were
gangsters from Chicago.

Not all the Wehrmacht defending the 300-mile Mediterranean coast of southern France between Italy and Spain were
"German boys," courageous or otherwise. Commanded by the ca-

pable General of Infantry Friedrich Wiese, the German Nineteenth Army, composed of seven infantry divisions and one panzer, was liberally sprinkled with non-German "volunteers"—Orientals, Poles, and Russians who had been dragooned into the Wehrmacht.

Information gained from the French underground and through Ultra intercepts indicated that there were some 3,000 German troops in the Le Muy area, including 1,000 zealous Wehrmacht officer candidates who could be counted on to resist fiercely.

On the afternoon of August 14—D-Day minus 1—a mighty armada of 1,000 Allied ships departed from many Mediterranean ports and knifed through the calm blue waters toward the French Riviera. Among those on board were men of the veteran 3rd, 36th, and 45th Infantry Divisions who would storm ashore at beaches code-named "Alpha," "Camel," and "Delta." It would be the job of Bob Frederick's airborne boys to keep Friedrich Wiese, whose command post was in the stately Dominion Hotel at inland Avignon, from rushing his scattered units to the Riviera.

At the same time, paratroopers had been trucked to 10 airfields carved out of the flatlands in the vicinity of Rome. Swarms of squat, camouflaged C-47s—526 in all—of Gen. Paul Williams' 50th, 51st, and 53rd Troop Carrier Wings sat along dirt and hard-surfaced runways. Also waiting to lift off for France were 452 Waco and 51 Horsa gliders.

At an airfield near Grosetto, Capt. Ernest T. "Bud" Siegel, who had been a member of the New York State police and now was a company commander in the 509th Parachute Infantry Battalion, decided to while away the tense hours before takeoff by attending a final briefing for the C-47 pilots who would haul his unit to France. With Siegel were his three platoon leaders, Lts. Hoyt Livingston, William Pahl, and Kenneth Shaker.

Ernest Siegel recalled that briefing:

> We were surprised at the extreme youth of the pilots. I don't think some of them had shaved yet. When the air corps colonel concluded his briefing, he asked the customary, "Any questions?" A rosy-cheeked young pilot from the South drawled, "When the plane is throttled back on the left side to lessen the parachutists' opening shock, is the tail up or down?"
>
> We were shocked. A tail-down position for a C-47 would result

in disaster for the paratroopers as they bailed out, for parachutes would become entangled on the tail surface. A real confidence builder. We didn't know if the pilot was serious or was just pulling the colonel's leg.

Most of the departure airfields were simply dusty cow pastures, and at one of them, Col. Rupert Graves, was preparing for his first combat jump. At age 43, the leader of the 517th Parachute Regiment was in advanced years for a paratrooper, and on occasion, he reflected dryly, "Good God, I'm two decades older than my battalion commanders." His graying hair and a moustache to match made him look "goddamned ancient" to his teenaged troopers. Highly regarded by nearly all the regiment, Graves was known as the "Gray Eagle." But when someone got angry at him over a real or imagined grievance, the Gray Eagle became "Old Hose Nose."[2]

Now, on the eve of battle, Graves was amused over a letter he had been handed a few hours earlier. It was a stern rebuke from a desk-borne general who commanded the Rome Area Base region. The letter ordered Graves to report to the rear area general headquarters at 2:00 P.M. on August 15 to explain why there were so many vehicles with other units' markings in the 517th Regiment's area. At the designated time, Rupert Graves and his troopers would be fighting behind the French Riviera. "That's one chewing out I won't get," the Gray Eagle mused.

It was a few minutes after midnight on D-Day when three airplanes carrying Pathfinder teams of the 509th, 517th, and 551st parachute outfits lifted off from a dark and dusty airstrip at Marcigiliana. Once they had touched down after the 500-mile flight, these vanguard soldiers, all picked men, would have less than 60 minutes to reconnoiter the ground and plant portable beacon signals on the various drop zones to guide in the original flight of 396 troop carriers.

William W. Lumsden, who was a 1st sergeant with the 551st Battalion Pathfinders, remembered that mission:

Everything went wrong that could possibly have gone wrong. They jumped us way off where we were supposed to be, we lost our equipment bundles, and it was cowboys and Indians for quite a while.

There was moonlight and I could see that I was coming down right into an electrified railroad yard. I landed onto some wires that

American paratrooper on right forces a smile shortly before his stick bailed out along the French Riviera. *(U. S. Army)*

sent electrical flashes and sparks flying; then fell hard on my back across the tracks. It was chaos with people shouting and running about—shooting. A Kraut came running up to me with a Schmeisser and fired a burst at me from 10 feet away. I was still in my harness and lying flat on my back. He must have thought I was dead, so he turned and ran back. I got out my .45, just by reflex, and shot him in the back. I felt blood running down one arm—one of the shots had gone through my left elbow. A couple of us slipped off into some woods. When I took off my [parachute] reserve pack, there were four holes where the German's other shots had been stopped. Otherwise, his bullets would have ripped into me.

Elsewhere in the blackness, another 517th pathfinder, Sgt. Jack Burns, was shot as he struggled to get out of his chute. But he recovered quickly, whipped out his .45, and put a slug through his antagonist's head. Yet another 517th trailblazer, Pvt. Joe Gavin, landed in a German position and was promptly captured while in his harness. He was hustled to a Wehrmacht command post, where a German intelligence officer grilled him, demanding to know details of the airborne landings. For the next few hours, Gavin insisted that the operation had been launched from Brooklyn, New York. (Two days later, seaborne forces would rescue the young paratrooper.)

Lt. Dan DeLeo, who had led the bold raid on Rommel's railroad in Tunisia in December 1942, was now in charge of the 509th Parachute Battalion's pathfinders. The entire region was shrouded in a thick blanket of fog, and after DeLeo's pilot circled out to sea and came back three times, the crew chief yelled, "We can't find the goddamned DZ. You'll have to jump now!" All the while, German gunners had been firing at the C-47.

DeLeo, followed by his stick, bailed out. He felt a searing pain and lost consciousness. A chunk of ack-ack shrapnel had grazed his head and ripped off his helmet. An undetermined amount of time later, DeLeo slowly recovered his senses and became aware that his parachute had caught in a tall tree and he was dangling in his harness far off the ground.

Then the lieutenant heard a rustling noise in the brush. It grew louder. Now he spotted a dim helmeted figure, holding an automatic weapon, stalking toward him. "This is the end!" DeLeo reflected. Only 30 feet away, the shadowy form halted. For moments, the other man stood motionless. Then he called out in a stage whisper, "Lafayette!" DeLeo heaved a sigh of relief on hearing the American password, and responded with the countersign, "Democracy!"

Charles McDonald, one of DeLeo's pathfinders, quickly cut him down. Seeing the lieutenant's hair, face and jumpsuit saturated with blood, McDonald remarked in a low voice, "Damn, you're a hell-of-a-looking mess!"

Meanwhile, pathfinders from all the 1st Airborne Task Force units were wandering lost through the black night and the murky forests and over the rugged hills, lugging heavy beacons and desperately seeking their drop zones. Bedeviled by the darkness and the thick fogbank, pilots had dropped their trailblazers, in most instances, as far as 18 miles from their targeted areas. None of the American pathfinders was able to reach the Le Muy region in time to set up beacons to guide the approaching C-47 flights loaded with the main body of paratroopers.

32
Thunder
Along the
Riviera

A C-47 sky train, stretching out for more than 100 miles, was nearing the Côte d'Azur of southern France. On board were 5,607 infantry, engineer and artillery paratroopers of the 1st Airborne Task Force. The balance of Frederick's outfit, 3,400 men, would jump and glide later in the day. These warriors from the sky would bail out at altitudes ranging from 1,500 to 1,800 feet, three or four times as high as the ideal combat jump elevation, so that the C-47s did not smash into adjacent mountains.

It was nearly 3:00 A.M. on D-Day. So far all had gone well. The sliver of a crescent moon had been shining, the Luftwaffe had not appeared, the armada had not been fired on by Allied vessels below, and the 396-plane flight was precisely on course.

At the very point of the sky javelin, Capt. Bud Siegel of the 509th Parachute Infantry, who, except for the pathfinders, would be the first paratrooper to jump was approached by an excited crew chief. "Guess our good luck couldn't last forever," the sergeant shouted above the roar of engines. "The entire coast and far inland are blanketed with thick fog!"

Pilots of the 442nd Troop Carrier Group were facing a dilemma. They had on board the entire 509th Parachute Infantry Battalion that would spearhead the invasion. Yet the drop zone was invisible. No beacon signal was received from DeLeo's pathfinders. Off in the hazy distance, projecting above the blanket of fog, the pilots spotted the dim outlines of jagged peaks, resembling those surrounding the drop zone on the sand-table mock-ups of the region that the air crews and troopers had studied diligently for countless hours.

An instant crucial decision was reached: The paratroopers would be dropped based on estimates by the air crews of their flight position as suggested by the peaks.

Bud Siegel glanced at his luminous watch—4:18 A.M. The green light flashed on and out went Siegel, followed by his stick and those of other C-47s hauling the 509th Battalion. "Operation Albatross," the parachute assault against Hitler's Riviera, was under way.

Like countless others on this night in the thick forests of southern France, Siegel's parachute caught on a tall tree, leaving him swinging 15 feet off the ground. He managed to cut the harness strands with a trench knife and scrambled down the tree.

One of Siegel's fellow officers, Capt. Ralph Miller, who had recently been promoted and given command of a 509th company, and his stick bailed out into the fog. Neither Miller nor his stick were heard from again. They had jumped over the Mediterranean Sea far offshore.

Hard on the heels of the 509th drop, Rupert Graves and his

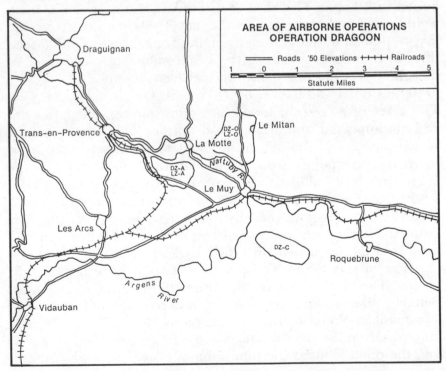

517th Parachute Regimental Combat Team jumped. The Gray Eagle himself landed hard, his carbine, which was tucked under his reserve chute on his chest, smashed him violently across the face, stunning him. His canopy collapsed over him, so Graves pulled his pistol and laid it carefully on the ground in case he should be pounced on by lurking Germans while getting untangled. Hacking at the tough cords with a knife, Graves finally cut himself free, then began feeling around on the ground for his pistol—and could not find it. After 10 minutes he gave up the search and struck out through the blackness to find his men.

Eventually, the 517th leader came upon a pair of troopers he heard thrashing about. "Where are we, colonel?" one asked. "I feel reasonably certain that we're somewhere in France," Graves replied dryly. "Other than that, I haven't the faintest notion where we are."[1]

Roger and Richard Tallakson of Cato's 460th Parachute Field Artillery Battalion were identical twins who had asked to jump from separate airplanes, no doubt so that Mom and Pop wouldn't get a double jolt in a single telegram from the War Department. When they jumped on this night, Roger landed some 25 miles from the drop zone, and Richard came down 30 miles from the targeted field.

(After daylight, each twin began asking other troopers for information on the missing brother. Roger heard that Richard had been evacuated with a broken leg. Richard heard that the other had been evacuated with a broken back. Actually, neither twin had been injured, and two days later, they were reunited in an assembly area.)

Another of Cato's cannoneers, Thomas Mehler, had been an artillery observer with the 1st Armored Division and volunteered for the paratroopers, but his four practice jumps were one short of qualifying him. Mehler insisted on going along to southern France, so his combat jump also qualified him as a bona fide paratrooper.

Sgt. Leo Turco of Rochester, New York, also a Cato cannoneer, came to grips with the enemy much sooner than anticipated—he parachuted into a tree directly behind a building occupied by a squad or so of *Feldgrau*. Dangling in his harness, Turco could hear the Germans talking inside. As quietly as possible—he felt the noise could be heard in Berlin—Turco cut himself loose, dropped to the ground and took refuge in a garden. Now the enemy soldiers came out of the building, deployed, and began raking the garden with small-arms fire. Under a hail of bullets, Turco slipped away and stumbled off in search of comrades.

Cpl. Donald Barry of the 517th was one of those rare troopers who had actually fallen asleep on the flight. Suddenly, someone shook him awake, and he saw a glowing red light and comrades hooked up, ready to jump. Rapidly, he got on his leg and chest straps and part of his equipment, just in time for the green light to flash on. Out went the stick and Barry.

Moments later, Barry was hurtling a long distance through black space—in his drowsiness he had forgotten to hook up his static line. Frantically, he pulled the rip cord on his reserve chute, and heaved a sigh of relief when a white canopy blossomed—just in time. His life had been saved by the fact that the jump had been made from 1,500 feet—not the customary 450 to 600 feet—and he thus had the time to open the reserve chute.

Shortly before dawn, Maj. Thomas R. Cross of Graves' 2nd Battalion was hobbling along in severe pain, having parachuted into a ditch and broken his leg. He longed to remove the heavy pressure of his jump boot from his throbbing leg but he did not dare do so for fear he could not get it back on again and then would not be able to join in the fight.

Cross was leading a company-size group of paratroopers who, alone and in pairs, had joined the major's column. The battalion executive officer was trying to reach his drop zone, but he was hopelessly lost. In the gray light, Cross saw a Frenchman approaching on a bicycle and tried to get directions. The farmer remained mute. Cross pulled his pistol, placed the muzzle against the Frenchman's head, and barked: "Now talk! Which way to Le Muy?"

Now the ashen-faced Frenchman began to shake uncontrollably but still made no reply. Thomas Cross remembered that episode:

> Suddenly I realized the reason for the Frenchman's silence, even after I threatened to blow off his head. He was too petrified to speak. Not only was a gun being pointed at his head, but he was in shock from unexpectedly being confronted by what appeared to him to be a sinister group of blackfaced cutthroats with Mohican Indian hair styles, and loaded with dangling hand grenades, nasty-looking daggers, and all kinds of weapons.

Major Cross replaced his pistol and began to move onward with his column. "Hell, you can't blame Pierre," he exclaimed. "The way we look I'd be speechless, too!"

Not far from the confrontation with the petrified Frenchman, curious doings were taking place in Trans en Provence. Daylight found the Germans holding one end of the town, men of the 517th Regiment were barricaded in the other end, and Pvt. Jack Mann held the middle. Seated calmly in a chair with a rifle across his lap, Mann was being given a shave and a haircut by a nervous French barber who had "volunteered" the service.

In another part of Trans en Provence, Pfc. "Red" Daigh captured a German captain, took over his car, Luger, and the equivalent to three hundred dollars, and breezily drove off in search of the 517th regimental command post.

Around Trans en Provence in the gray light of early dawn, an assortment of 18 troopers under Lt. Loren S. James had been engaged in several successful skirmishes with groups of *Feldgrau*. After one brief shootout, James spotted a long column of men marching toward Les Arcs. Not wanting fellow troopers to waste their time feeling out terrain his pack had already cleared, James sent Cpl. David Robertson to inform the other column of the situation.

Robertson ran at full speed to some 50 yards of the marching group, waving his arms and yelling, "Hey, wait a minute!" His reply was a withering burst of fire from German Schmeissers. Robertson hit the dirt, and began crawling back to his comrades. Rapidly, the Germans deployed and headed for James' band, but Pfc. Arthur Purser, sizing up the situation, set up his machine gun in an open field and pumped lead until the others could withdraw.

Many miles from the skirmishes around Les Arcs and Trans en Provence, 28-year-old Lt. Col. Melvin Zais, Graves' 3rd Battalion leader, was conferring with Capt. Martin J. Fastaia, commander of his headquarters company, in an old farmhouse outside the village of Seillans. Zais, a University of Massachusetts graduate, was both agitated and concerned.

His battalion was to have landed near Le Muy and blocked Route Nationale 7, the main highway leading to Saint-Raphael and Fréjus on the Riviera coast. But Zais, much of Fastaia's company, and a few stragglers—105 troopers in all—had dropped so far from the drop zone that the area did not appear on Zais' maps. Finally, two Frenchmen were brought in and Zais learned where he was—25 miles northeast of his drop zone.[2]

Leaving behind 19 men badly injured in the jump, Zais and the other 86 troopers struck out cross-country for the drop zone. Suddenly the gray early dawn was pierced by the roar of low-flying airplanes. The parachutists hit the ground as a flight of four American twin-boomed P-38s zoomed along the stretched-out column and dropped their bombs. Then Capt. William Pencak threw a yellow smoke grenade—the recognition signal.

The P-38 flight had banked and was coming back at treetop level for a strafing run. At the last moment, the aircraft zipped upward and flew off in search of other prey. Miraculously, perhaps, none of the paratroopers had been hit.

Meantime, near La Motte, Lt. Albert W. Robinson, leader of the 517th Regiment's machine-gun platoon, and a few of his men were searching in the dark for equipment bundles. Robinson was so weak that his legs wobbled. Only two days earlier, he had sneaked out of a Naples hospital to join his comrades in the jump. It was chilly in the predawn Mediterranean air, but the young officer was perspiring freely with a high fever.

Suddenly streams of Schmeisser tracers tore through the blackness. Robinson toppled over, dead. A few slugs ripped into Pvt. Pat Clark. Under a hail of bullets, a comrade slithered to Clark's aid, but the grievously wounded youth called out weakly, "I'm okay—you guys get the hell out of here while you can."

At dawn, several troopers returned to the site of the ambush and recovered Robinson's body.[3] Nearby, was the lifeless form of Pat Clark, a pool of blood under him. His rifle was lying beside his stiff hands. Clark, although in excruciating pain and his life ebbing away, apparently had shot it out with the German force to permit his surviving comrades to get away. The ammo clip in his rifle was empty.

Not far from Le Muy, Pvt. Frederic Johns and a few troopers were stalking through the night toward their drop zone when a German machine gun opened fire. Three bullets tore into Johns, and he collapsed. After an intense but brief firefight, the enemy machine gunners melted into the darkness. Frederic Johns lay quietly. Blood was streaming from his wounds, saturating the jumpsuit in which he took such deep pride. He softly uttered a few words, and a comrade knelt down and placed his ear to the youth's mouth. "What did you say, Frederic?" the comrade asked. "I'm sorry I let you fellows down," was the whispered reply.

Moments later, Frederic Johns was dead.

Elsewhere, Lt. James A. Reith, a 517th platoon leader, was relieved to see the dark sky dissolving into gray; whatever dawn might bring, it would be better than continuing to stumble along virtually blind in the darkness and fog. Reith had urgent matters in mind: He and 15 of his troopers had been assigned a special mission. They were to have dropped just outside Draguignan, slip into that German stronghold before the enemy realized that southern France was under parachute attack, and kidnap Gen. Ferdinand Neuling, commander of the German LXII Corps. If kidnapping the enemy general alive was not possible, then Neuling was to be killed and the paratroopers were to get out of Draguignan as best they could—if they could.

Now Reith glanced at his watch. It was 5:35 A.M. How could he conceivably hope to carry out the kidnapping mission? Reith was alone, he had no idea of his location, and the Wehrmacht in Draguignan and at points in between was certain to be on full alert by now, aware that large numbers of American paratroopers were roaming the countryside.

A short time later, Reith's faintest hope of perpetrating the Neuling snatch was dashed. He ran into his mortar sergeant, Joseph Blackwell, who told the platoon leader, "We're at least 20 miles from Draguignan."

In the meantime, the C-47 carrying Bob Frederick was winging through the night toward France. Wearing a white scarf made of parachute silk, the taciturn leader of the 1st Airborne Task Force had had little to say on the long flight. As the aircraft neared the Riviera, there were flashes of light from German ack-ack guns. "It looks like they're expecting us," Frederick said calmly.

Seated next to the general was his bodyguard, 20-year-old Cpl. Duffield W. Matson, Jr., who often described himself as "one mean son of a bitch." No one had challenged that description. Matson was carrying a Sicilian dagger and four other razor-sharp knives, his pockets were full of grenades, and he would bail out loaded with several blocks of TNT. Like scores of others carrying explosives, Duff Matson tried not to dwell upon the nasty mess that would ensue if German machine-gun bullets ripped into the TNT on his way down.

Frederick bailed out carrying a blue-lensed flashlight for signaling on the ground, and made a routine landing. Duff Matson crashed down hard nearby, landing on a tree stump or stake and "messing up" his left leg. Peering through the darkness, the corporal detected a parachute draped over a pole in a vineyard and concluded that it had to be Frederick: The general's blue-beamed flashlight was glowing there.

Matson hobbled toward the general, recalling the stern words of an officer who had assigned the youth to be Frederick's bodyguard: "You are to protect the general from harm—even if it costs you your life!"

Matson spotted five or six figures edging toward the task force commander, and then he discerned the silhouettes of their coalbucket-shaped helmets—*Germans!* He shouted a warning to Frederick, who was poring over a map by the blue flashlight, then squeezed off several quick rifle shots in the direction of the dark figures. Two of the Germans toppled over, and the others fled.[4]

General Frederick casually looked up, then returned to his map.[5]

In the vast sweep of landscape behind Hitler's so-called South Wall, American paratroopers, picking their way through the night toward their drop zones, pounced on the enemy at every opportunity. They blew up small bridges, cut telephone lines linking German CPs and defensive positions, planted mines in roads, and created widespread havoc.

Three of these black-faced marauders, Sgt. Clark Archer, and Troopers Forrest Sutton, Steve Weirzba, and Joe Kellogg—all of the 517th Regiment—were concealed in a drainage ditch along Route Internationale 7. Soon they heard the purr of an approaching vehicle, and as it raced toward them, the four parachutists opened fire. Weirzba's antitank grenade failed to explode, but it struck the driver in the head. The stylish civilian convertible careened to a halt, and later would be turned over to Colonel Graves—after splatterings from the unfortunate German officer's cranium were scoured from the floor.

Twelve miles south of Le Muy, Capt. Jess H. Walls, a company commander in Yarborough's 509th Parachute Battalion, had collected a force of some 250 paratroopers around his hilltop command post near the coast outside the exotic peacetime resort of Saint-Tropez. Most of the men belonged to Walls' Company C, but there were 19 men from Company B of the 509th and elements of Cooper's 463rd Parachute Field Artillery Battalion. It was 5:45 A.M.

Added to the normal concern he felt over his company being

dropped far off target, Walls was beset by an even more haunting predicament: He and his men were directly on the coastline impact area, which would soon be heavily bombed from the air and pounded by the guns of warships.

As Walls was discussing the situation with officers, two Frenchmen who lived in Saint-Tropez were brought before him. They claimed to belong to the French underground, and said they had expected the Allies, having heard code phrases broadcast over BBC in London advising Côte d'Azur resistance fighters that the invasion was at hand. Excitedly, the two natives told Jess Walls that the Germans were getting ready to blow up the facilities in Saint-Tropez to deny them to the invaders. Hardly had the words been spoken than a tremendous explosion shook Saint-Tropez and adjacent areas: The Germans had begun demolition of the docks, the electrical and water systems, and other key facilities.

Captain Walls' mind was made up. He would attack Saint-Tropez and try to keep the docks from being destroyed. But before the paratroopers could attack, they had to cling to the ground for two hours—while being pounded by their own shells and bombs. Then the seaborne assault troops came ashore at Alpha, Camel, and Delta beaches. Only the 45th Infantry Division in the center met heavy resistance.

Now Jess Walls and his good-size band of parachutists charged into Saint-Tropez and, with the help of elements of the seaborne 45th Infantry Division, chased the Germans out.

Outside Draguignan shortly after daybreak, Gen. Ferdinand Neuling, typically calm and collected, was poring over field reports that had arrived during the past three hours. Most of the messages of paratrooper sightings were grossly exaggerated; the fog and blackness and widespread dropping abetted the Wehrmacht's confusion. However, the reports caused Neuling to believe that a far greater number of parachutists had landed than had actually been the case.

33
Objectives
Secured

At daybreak on D-Day, German commanders in and around the key road hub of Le Muy were apparently unaware that a large portion of the 509th Parachute Infantry Battalion was perched on heights overlooking the town and was also dug in just to the north of its outskirts. Soon a German column of infantry entered Le Muy from the south, marched through the town, and was heading along the road where Lt. Kenneth Shaker's platoon had deployed. Shaker's boss, Capt. Bud Siegel, had been watching this German contingent from a hilltop, and now he moved his other two platoons into ambush positions along the road leading out of Le Muy. Siegel ordered his platoons to hold their fire until he gave the order: He wanted to make certain the entire Wehrmacht column had entered his iron trap before his men began blasting away.

As the enemy contingent neared the concealed Five-O-Niners, it suddenly halted, its commanders apparently sensing that they were plunging into an ambush. Quickly deploying, the Germans opened a fusillade of machine-gun and rifle fire into the woods where Siegel's men were waiting. All hell broke loose as the troopers opened up.

For nearly two hours, the Five-O-Niners and the *Feldgrau* slugged it out before the enemy force pulled back into Le Muy, leaving scores of dead and wounded comrades sprawled about the fields. Sixty Germans were taken prisoners.

Despite the small victory by the American paratroopers, the key initial objective of the 1st Airborne Task Force, Le Muy, remained in German hands.

Meanwhile, Maj. Forest Paxton, operations officer of Graves' 517th Regiment, was leading 75 troopers toward the drop zone by way of the village of La Motte when the faint purr of approaching motors was heard. Paxton waved his men into ambush on both sides of the road, and moments later a pair of Germans on speeding motorcycles were blasted by small-arms fire from the brush. After dragging the corpses and the motorcycles into some woods, Paxton and his men marched onward and entered La Motte unopposed at 8:55 A.M. La Motte may have been the first town in the southern two-thirds of France to be liberated from the Wehrmacht.

At the same time, Maj. William J. "Wild Bill" Boyle, leader of the 1st Battalion of the 517th Regiment, and five troopers, who had been misdropped nine miles southwest of their drop zone, were trudging over the rough terrain toward Le Muy. Even before enhancing his Wild Bill monicker during brief fighting in Italy, Boyle had gained a reputation as a free-spirited paratrooper.

Back in the United States, 517th officers had been holding a boisterous "Prop Blast" (booze party) when Boyle volunteered to go fetch a resupply of the dwindling liquor. A few officers climbed into Wild Bill's antiquated Ford to join in the procurement mission. While returning to the Prop Blast after a productive patrol, Boyle and his cronies decided that the regiment's pet, a feisty lion cub, would enjoy the festivities. So the old Ford detoured to the animal's den, and after much heaving and shoving, the officers got the reluctant lion in the back seat of the car, then squeezed in around the beast.

Lions don't like to be awakened—especially in the middle of the night nor do they take a fancy to crowded automobiles. So the grumpy feline apparently singled out Bill Boyle as the chief culprit, and took a couple of hefty swipes with her paw at the major's head.

Boyle was taken to the post hospital for embroidery work, and after daylight he appeared on the rifle range looking like an Arabian sultan—his head swathed in yards of white gauze.

Now in France, the danger was not from irritated lions, but from the Germans. When Boyle arrived at the crossroads town of Les Arcs at 1:00 P.M., he found 50 of his troopers fighting for their lives against a large German force he would learn later numbered in excess of 300 men. Apparently, the enemy unit was trying to break through to the landing beaches.

All that morning, firefights had erupted as the Germans probed into Les Arcs. Meanwhile, paratroopers, alone and in pairs, had filtered into the town and joined their comrades. One of them was Sgt. Paul Vukovich, a burly football player, who was limping with a badly injured leg while carrying a 60-millimeter mortar, a BAR, and 30 pounds of ammo.

On his arrival, Wild Bill Boyle went to the point of the action. Standing tall and refusing to duck when bursts of machine-gun fire hissed past, Boyle could see Germans—plenty of them. Soon the fire of enemy automatic weapons grew intense, and swarms of *Feldgrau* could be seen advancing toward the Americans and fanning out into side streets. A savage firefight raged for an hour as Boyle's besieged band struggled to prevent the much larger enemy force from surrounding them.

Boyle realized that he and his men were about to be trapped. Heavy firing could be heard on three sides. "Okay, we've got to pull out," the major shouted. "But make goddamned sure that not a single wounded man is left behind!"

Leaving a couple of BAR men to cover the withdrawal, Boyle's force, one by one, began slipping out of Les Arcs to the rear. Boyle was the last man to depart. When nearly all of his men had crawled away under a hail of bullets from three sides, the major strode around the abandoned positions, making certain that no wounded trooper would be left behind. Again he stood upright, his tall figure making an ideal target, as bullets whizzed past his head.

"Fer Chrissake, Major!" one of the last men to leave shouted. "Get down or you'll get your head shot off!" Boyle shrugged and spat in the direction of the Germans.

Satisfied that all of his men were accounted for, Boyle led his column out of Les Arcs. Wounded troopers were being carried over the shoulders of ablebodied men, and those injured more seriously were being hauled on improvised stretchers. Just outside the town, the column was greeted by heavy machine-gun fire from the front. A few men were hit; a couple of wounded troopers once again had slugs rip into their bodies. The Germans were now on all sides; Boyle and his band of 50 able-bodied troopers were trapped by a force perhaps eight times larger.

Meanwhile, just before 6:00 P.M., the second American paratroop mission of the day—"Operation Bluebird"—was approaching the Côte d'Azur. On board the sky train were Lt. Col. Wood G. Joerg and the 46 officers and 796 men of his 551st Parachute

Infantry Battalion, all combat green, but eager. (Joerg was a native of Eufala, Alabama, but he claimed Texas as his home state, and "The Yellow Rose of Texas" was his favorite song.) At West Point, where he had been a hard-hitting welterweight on the varsity boxing team, the 29-year-old officer had been known as "Tiger." With him on this flight to France, Joerg carried a Confederate flag, which would be the rallying point for the 551st Battalion.

Cheerful and personable, Wood Joerg was an enigma to his officers; they respected and admired him, yet thought him to be slightly withdrawn. Long before, the battalion commander had won the hearts of his enlisted men, because they considered him to be especially sensitive to their needs.

The 551st flight of 47 carriers flashed green lights, and the sky two miles southeast of Le Muy was soon awash with billowing white parachutes. Sgt. Bill Dean of the light machine-gun platoon landed in a tree, scrambled down to the ground and took a bullet in the hip. A short time later, comrades heard him howling and cursing: "Some son of a bitch shot me!" Comrades lugged Dean and five other wounded or injured troopers to an old barn where they would remain for two days and nights while Germans prowled around outside.

Lt. Andy Titko, the 551st Battalion communications officer, bailed out in a foul mood. Before leaving Italy, Titko had lost his wallet containing two months' pay, his identification card, and his dog tags. Then, in the final mail call, he received a "Dear John" letter. Now, things continued to go sour. When Titko's parachute opened, his foot caught in the suspension line, but he broke loose before reaching the ground. There he smashed into a large tree, which ripped a nasty gash under one eye. Now his canopy caught in the upper branches, and he dangled several feet off the ground. Blood streamed down his face, temporarily blinding him. He could hear rustling noises on all sides, and did not know if they were German or American. Finally, a trooper came along and cut the lieutenant down.[1]

As Wood Joerg wriggled out of his harness, a figure dashed up to him. It was Capt. Tims Quinn, the battalion operations officer, who had jumped earlier with the 509th Parachute Infantry in order to be on the drop zone when the 551st jumped.

"A beautiful job, Colonel!" Quinn said. "I think the entire battalion dropped right on the button!" Indeed, it had been an almost textbook-perfect operation.

Joerg smiled and hurried off to plant the Confederate flag and assemble his troopers. Time was crucial: Ed Sachs' 550th Glider Infantry Battalion was to land within minutes on the precise drop zone that Joerg's parachutists had dropped onto.

Soon the Riviera sky, from horizon to horizon, was blanketed with Uncle Sam's aircraft. There was a seemingly endless umbrella of C-47s, with gliders trailing each tug at 300-foot distances. Then the gliders cut loose and, dangling heavy nylon ropes, began weaving, darting, and floating to crash landings on landing zones spiked with *Rommelspargel.*

Many of Wood Joerg's parachutists were still on the landing zone when Sachs' gliders began swooping in. Maj. Ray "Pappy" Hermann (so nicknamed because the youthful paratroopers considered him "old"—at all of 34) was dashing across a wide pasture to reach the 551st assembly area. All the time, he was dodging and bobbing about like a halfback on a long open-field run, seeking desperately to avoid being struck or decapitated. Gliders were ripped into kindling as they smashed into trees, boulders, ditches, and Rommel's poles at speeds of up to 90 miles per hour.

From the wreckage of some Wacos there was only silence; all aboard had been killed. From others came hideous shrieks and wails of mutilated men pinned where they lay. Hard-bitten Pappy Hermann uttered to a companion: "I'll stick to parachutes!"[2]

Harry Renick, who had been a communications corporal in the 551st Parachute Battalion, recalled the glider landings:

> *I had parachuted onto my back hard and was laying on the DZ. I couldn't even get up, much less stand, and thought I'd broken my hip, so I was told to wait right there for medics. Then the gliders started crashing all around me. Inspired, I got up and hobbled the hell out of their LZ.*

Late that D-Day afternoon, Bob Frederick was engaged in a heated dispute with Brigadier Pritchard at a bridge outside Le Muy. Frederick demanded to know why the British Red Devils had not taken Le Muy as planned, and he was told by Pritchard that there were too many Germans in the town. Returning to his command post in an old farmhouse outside the village of Le Mitan, Frederick contacted Ed Sachs, the 550th Glider Infantry leader, who had collected much of his outfit despite the carnage on the landing zone.[3]

Typically, Frederick's order was crisp and clear: "Ed, go into Le Muy in the morning and run the Krauts out of there!"

At a villa a half mile outside Le Muy, Ed Sachs hastily drew up a battle plan. This would be the first real action for the "Five-and-a-Half," as the battalion called itself. Jump-off time for the assault was 2:30 A.M., under the cover of darkness. Almost at once, the glidermen were greeted by heavy bursts of fire; clearly, the key town was strongly defended. Under a hail of bullets, the green Americans pulled back, and Sachs quickly organized a new attack.

At 11:40 A.M., the glidermen again moved forward across open fields and fought their way into Le Muy, where a house-to-house battle erupted and raged for four hours. By late afternoon, the road hub was solidly in American hands. More than 700 Germans were captured in and around the town, and perhaps 300 more were killed or wounded. It had been an auspicious baptism of fire for Ed Sachs and his glider soldiers.

Elsewhere, Wild Bill Boyle of the 517th Regiment and his men were still trapped outside Les Arcs by a far superior German force. In addition, Rupert Graves was concerned by the fact that Les Arcs was still in enemy hands. Now, the Gray Eagle contacted Lt. Col. Richard J. Seitz, the 25-year-old commander of the 1st Battalion, who had assembled most of his troopers north of Les Arcs. Graves told Seitz: "Get on down there right away and give Wild Bill a hand. We've got to grab Les Arcs!"

Within minutes of receiving the urgent order, Dick Seitz of Kansas City had his battalion marching toward Les Arcs, three miles away. To Seitz, this was more than just a military mission— his good friend Bill Boyle and his band were in danger of being wiped out.[4]

When Seitz's battalion reached the outskirts of Les Arcs, it received heavy machine-gun fire from within the town. Patrols were sent ahead to probe German defenses, but by the time they returned, it was nearly dark, so Seitz, wanting to avoid the inevitable confusion of a night attack, decided to jump off at dawn.

All the while, Lt. Col. Mel Zais, commander of Graves' 3rd Battalion, and a column of his men, had been marching toward the 517th Regiment command post in the Château Sainte-Rosseline, three miles west of Le Muy. On his 25- to 30-mile trek from where he had been misdropped, Zais steadily picked up his troopers, who had been strewn along an eight-mile swath from Seillans (where Zais had landed) toward the drop zone.

Just after 4:00 P.M. on D-Day plus 1, Zais and his men wearily trudged into the yard of the Château Sainte-Rosseline, after their two-day march up one mountain and down the other. They had stopped periodically to battle Germans, and the several wounded and injured troopers who had to be carried slowed the pace. Zais and his men, all robust specimens, were exhausted.

Thirty minutes after they had sprawled on the ground to sleep, Rupert Graves told Zais that General Frederick had ordered Zais' battalion to strike out immediately, despite the men's extreme fatigue, to link up with Dick Seitz's troopers in the assault on Les Arcs.

In action are men of Raymond Cato's 460th Parachute Field Artillery Battalion. (*Drawing by Chris Graves*)

Zais' awakened men, cursing and ranting, struggled to their feet, put on their combat gear, and attacked down a valley toward Les Arcs against sporadic opposition. By nightfall, Zais was on his objective, the high ground looking down on the town.

Early on the morning of D-Day plus 2, Dick Seitz's battalion advanced on Les Arcs. Stalking through vineyards and open, green fields, the parachutists reached the first houses without being fired on—then German automatic weapons opened up and shells began screaming into the Americans' ranks. As the fight raged inside the town, Mel Zais' paratroopers pushed into Les Arcs from the south.

Caught between converging attacks by Seitz's men from the east and Zais' troopers from the south, the defenders began to pull back, then abandoned the town. By withdrawing, the Germans also released their steel noose from around Bill Boyle's Little Alamo pack. "Hell, we didn't need any help," Wild Bill exclaimed with tongue partially in cheek. "The Krauts outnumbered us only 10 to one. In my book, 10 Krauts against one American paratrooper is an even match!"

Five miles north of Les Arcs during the previous night, Wood Joerg's 551st Parachute Infantry Battalion was picking its way toward the German stronghold of Draguignan. Two hours earlier, Bob Frederick had issued Joerg a customarily concise order: "Attack and seize Draguignan."

Leading the attack, along with Capt. Marshall Dalton of A Company, was Capt. James "Jungle Jim" Evans, leader of B Company. Evans had lost his helmet and had a piece of a parachute tied around his head which, with his handlebar mustache, gave him a ferocious appearance. He was not wearing his jump jacket, and had an olive drab undershirt and suspenders. One of his platoon leaders, Lt. Richard Mascuch, whispered to Evans: "You look like a damned pirate!"

Looming through the darkness was the dim silhouette of a large cluster of houses—the outskirts of Draguignan. Now was the moment of truth for Wood Joerg and his 551st Battalion—their first real taste of combat as an organized unit. Out in front were three French Resistance fighters who had volunteered to serve as guides. As the ghostly figures stalked into deathly silent Draguignan, the Frenchmen's hard leather heels striking the cobblestones sent chills up the troopers' spines—the noise seemed to echo for miles.

Crraaaccckkk! A lone rifle shot rang out. Then heavy shooting erupted in the shadowy streets. At his command post in the center of town, Gen. Ludwig Bieringer, the Wehrmacht's district commander, looked up from his desk as rifle, machine gun, and submachine gun fire rattled over and around the buildings. Obviously, an American force of undetermined size had infiltrated the town.

Capt. James "Jungle Jim" Evans.
(Dan Morgan)

Bieringer, an officer reared by the Prussian code of courage and determination, was appalled by what he witnessed. A large number of his headquarters soldiers nearly trampled each other while scrambling into the air raid shelter.

Bieringer tried to telephone his superior, Gen. Ferdinand Neuling, at LXII Corps headquarters on a mountainside outside Draguignan. The effort was futile; American paratroopers or French underground fighters had cut the wires between the two headquarters.

Meanwhile, Pfc. Joe Cicchinelli, a young, former boxer, was lead scout for Dalton's A Company, and was guiding his outfit along the black streets while Evans' B Company was advancing nearby. Suddenly, Cicchinelli held up his arm, and the column halted in the shadows of the houses. Slipping back to the nearest troopers, the scout whispered, "I don't know what's inside of that big building there, but there's a huge Nazi flag flying over the front door. Must be some Kraut bigwigs inside."

"Let's take the bastards!" Sgt. Donald M. Thompson exclaimed.

Joseph Cicchinelli recalled storming the building:

I was in the lead and Don Thompson, Ed Schultz, and Bud Hook were right on my heels as we dashed through the huge front doorway with tommy guns and rifles at the ready. We broke down the first door to the right and rushed into the room. There we were startled to come face-to-face with a middle-aged Kraut wearing a monocle. He was seated at a large desk with a few German officers around him, and he slowly arose but said nothing as we aimed our weapons at him. One of our guys said, "Look at all those decorations and the monocle on the old Kraut—he must be a colonel or something!" At the same time, we did not know that we had captured Gen. Ludwig Bieringer, district commander of the Wehrmacht, and most of his staff.

Bieringer was probably the only German general captured by American paratroopers during the war, until the final days when the Wehrmacht was surrendering in wholesale lots.

When the Nazi general was marched away, Joe Cicchinelli shinnied up the flagpole reaching out horizontally over the front door of the headquarters building and confiscated the huge black and red, swastika-emblazoned Nazi flag that had flown there for nearly two years.[5]

As a hot, muggy dawn of D-Day plus 2 broke out over southern France, the battle situation inside Draguignan was still fluid. Joerg's troopers had control of about half of the town, the Germans the other half. Fighting raged all that day, but by late afternoon, the echo of gunfire in Draguignan diminished, then faded entirely. At 5:15 P.M. Wood Joerg, at his command post in the Hotel Madeline, radioed Bob Frederick: "Mission accomplished. Draguignan secured."

With the capture of Les Arcs and Draguignan, the final pieces of the gigantic jigsaw puzzle code-named Operation Rugby, the airborne assault, had fallen into place. All 1st Airborne Task Force objectives had been seized within 61 hours of the first paratrooper bailing out, mass confusion had been created behind German coastal defenses, communications had been cut and roads blocked to prevent enemy reinforcements from rushing to the Riviera landing beaches. However, Frederick's paratroopers and glidermen had paid a heavy price: one third of them had been killed, wounded, injured, or were missing.

Four hundred miles to the north on August 25, the U.S. 4th Infantry and French 2nd Armored Divisions liberated Paris, touching off one of history's most frenzied civilian celebrations. GIs were wined, dined, hugged, kissed, squeezed, and romanced by eager and joyous mademoiselles. An unofficial representative of the American paratrooper brotherhood in the tumultuous Paris jubilee was Cpl. Bill Walton, the jump-boot journalist who had bailed out with Gen. Jim Gavin in Normandy.

Walton established a beachhead at the Royal Fromentin Hotel in Montmartre, the bailiwick of shabbier elements of the Paris population. After a night of wild rejoicing, Walton awakened in his hotel room to the sounds of raucous cheering outside. Prying open one eye, then the other, he stumbled out onto the second-floor balcony, where, like a conquering Roman emperor, Walton bowed and waved regally to the screaming multitude of hookers, pimps, pickpockets, petty thieves, and other Montmartre habitués.

Bill Walton's fellow paratroopers everywhere would have been proud.

Meanwhile, Frederick's American airborne units (509, 517, 550, 551, artillery battalions, and the parachute-trained 1st Special Service Force) attacked eastward along the Côte d'Azur and established defensive positions in the rugged, towering Maritime Alps at the Italian border. Their mission was to block efforts by Wehrmacht forces in northern Italy to lunge into the long, extended columns of the U.S. Seventh Army, which were driving up the Rhone Valley to link up with Overlord forces near the French town of Dijon, southeast of Paris.

These were heady days in the ivory towers of SHAEF. Hotly pursued by five Dragoon and Overlord armies, the Wehrmacht was retreating rapidly to the borders of the Third Reich. Eisenhower's chief of staff, Beetle Smith, on September 2, told reporters: "Militarily, the war in Europe is won."

Nevertheless, someone had neglected to inform Adolf Hitler and his fighting men of that fact.

34
War Among the Windmills

Just prior to 7:00 P.M. on September 8, 1944, while many Londoners were eating dinner, a terrific explosion rocked the suburb of Chiswick. It sounded like a thunderclap but the sky was clear. Terrified citizens dashed for basements, unaware that Adolf Hitler's first V-2 missile had arrived. The blast demolished 19 Chiswick homes and gouged out a 30-foot-deep crater in the ground. Scores of dead and injured were dug out of the ruins. More V-2s rained down on London with equally disastrous results.

Shaped like a cigar, the V-2 was 47 feet long (as tall as a six-story building when erect on its launching pad), and carried a one-ton warhead capable of leveling an entire block of buildings. The huge missile could attain a height of 90 miles and such an enormous speed (990 miles per hour) that those on the receiving end would not even see or hear it approaching.

London was in deadly peril. But no one in the sprawling metropolis knew that the Chiswick explosion would trigger the mightiest airborne operation that history had known.

Allied Intelligence ferreted out the fact that V-2s were being launched against London from sites along the Channel coast of Holland, where they were emplaced in the hearts of cities, including The Hague, a city of 400,000 population. If the Allies tried to carpet-bomb missile-launching sites in the hope that an occasional bomb might hit a target, they would slaughter thousands of Dutch civilians.

Forty-eight hours after the first V-2 exploded in Chiswick, Field Marshal Bernard Montgomery (he had just been promoted and now outranked his boss, Eisenhower) called on the supreme commander to present a bold plan of action to bring the European war to a quick end. Eisenhower was astonished by the audacity of the plan, code-named "Operation Market-Garden."

Customarily cautious and methodical in battle, Montgomery now proposed dropping huge numbers of paratroopers and landing gliders behind German units, like pieces on a checkerboard hopping over their opposition, to seize a number of key bridges over the multitude of waterways that crisscrossed Holland.[1]

But in war, unlike checkers, the enemy pieces that have been hopped over are not thereby swept from the board. They have to be removed by force. So it would be the job of Brian Horrocks' British XXX Corps, paced by the crack Guards Armored Division, to dash through the 60-mile-long dotted line traced by the airborne troops and bolt over the Rhine (known in this region as the Neder Rijn) on the big bridge at Arnhem. Then spearheads would wheel eastward and head toward Berlin.

Market-Garden, Monty stressed, would not only eliminate the V-2 launching sites on the Dutch coast, but also permit the Allies to skirt the Siegfried line (which ended at the German city of Cleve) and avoid the heavy bloodshed that would result if that menacing concrete-and-steel fortified belt had to be pierced.

Bernard Montgomery never drank, smoked, or cursed, and he went to bed each night promptly at 10:00 P.M. And he had never gambled. But now the peppery little field marshal was proposing one of the war's greatest toss-ups. However, Eisenhower, who also had one eye on the secret V-2 missile sites in Holland, bought Monty's plan.

Despite his seeming switch from caution to extreme boldness, Montgomery had not acted impetuously: He knew that he would have at his disposal the First Allied Airborne Army (FAAA), which had been activated only a month earlier (on August 8) amidst a storm of controversy.

The First Triple A, as the new command was called, consisted of the U.S. XVIII Corps (the yet-to-arrive 17th Airborne Division and the 82nd and 101st Airborne Divisions); and the British 1st Airborne Corps (comprising the 1st and 6th Airborne Divisions,

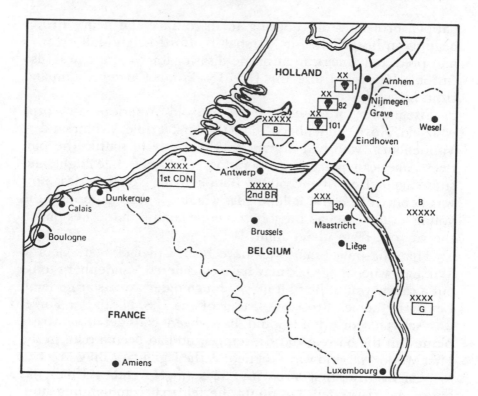

Operation Market-Garden

a Polish Brigade, and miscellaneous smaller units). Also integrated into the First Triple A would be the U. S. IX Troop Carrier Command (50th, 52nd, and 53rd Wings) and the British Troop Carrier Command (38th and 46th Groups).

Creation of the new command had gained a unanimity of opinion among both American and British brass—absolutely all concerned were angry. Omar Bradley, commander of most United States ground forces in northern France, felt that this was an unneeded layer of authority insulating him from his airborne divisions. Eisenhower indicated that the top FAAA command should go to an American, a proposal that triggered howls of indignation from the chief of the Imperial General Staff, Field Marshal Alan Brooke. Sure, the Americans would have far more troops, aircraft, and air crews than would the British, but the British were far more experienced, Brooke argued.

Brooke, a World War I hero and Britain's most decorated soldier since Marlborough, had the ideal candidate to command the First Triple A—his protégé, Boy Browning. For his part, the dapper Browning did nothing to discourage the heavy drum-beating on his behalf. Air Marshal Trafford Leigh-Mallory, who had predicted American airborne disaster for Neptune, was also furious. He would lose the U.S. IX Troop Carrier Command from his air force.

Eisenhower proposed the 34-year-old American air corps whiz-kid, Hoyt Vandenberg, to be the First Triple A commander. Vandenburg, who had argued so vigorously to scuttle the pioneer American parachute operation (the 1,600-mile flight and subsequent drop of the 509th Battalion) in North Africa, now was deputy of Leigh-Mallory. Just when it looked as though the young air general had the job, someone behind the scenes pulled the rug out from under him.

That rug-puller may well have been Chief of Staff George Marshall, who, at age 63, may have considered Vandenberg to be but a callow youth. Be as it may, a much older three-star general, Lewis H. "Looie" Brereton, leader of the U.S. Ninth Air Force, was selected for what should have been considered a career plum. But the 55-year-old Brereton, who had been a pilot in the First World War and was assigned by the legendary Billy Mitchell to plan history's first airborne attack (in November 1918) was angry and frustrated. No doubt, he felt that commanding lumbering transport planes and the soldiers they hauled or towed in relatively infrequent missions was a distinct comedown from his prestigious post as leader of the powerful Ninth Air Force, whose hundreds of swift fighter planes roamed the skies of Europe daily.[2]

Brereton, five-foot-six, hard-boiled, and relentlessly driven, was not the only one displeased over his appointment as First Triple A chief. Omar Bradley was also; he had clashed frequently with the bespectacled air corps general during the Normandy campaign. Bradley felt that Brereton's flyers were not providing effective close-support for hard-pressed infantrymen in Normandy.

Eisenhower, seeking to soothe frayed British tempers, named Boy Browning to be Brereton's deputy. Not overburdened with humility, Browning was unhappy with his second-banana role. He barely concealed his disdain over having to work under an *air corps* officer, especially one who was four months' junior to him in rank.

In one respect, Matt Ridgway agreed with his longtime, bitter foe. He, too, felt that the First Triple A command should have gone to an American airborne leader with experience in planning and leading parachute and glider operations. Possibly, Ridgway's ideal candidate for the top post could have been—Matt Ridgway.

Ridgway's ruffled feathers were smoothed to an extent when Eisenhower named him to command the new XVIII Airborne Corps, an appointment that left a vacancy at the helm of the 82nd Airborne Division. In part because of a highly laudatory endorsement sent to the supreme commander, Jim Gavin took over the helm of the All-Americans and would later be promoted to major general—at age 37, he became the youngest two-star officer in the U.S. Army since the Civil War.[3]

By early September, rough-and-ready Looie Brereton had fidgeted in frustration for weeks. Seventeen times since the Normandy breakout he had drawn up plans for a historic strike: the landing of all or a major part of an Allied airborne army, a force capable of fighting on its own behind German lines. Seventeen times he had had to scrap the plans. The Allied ground forces had advanced so swiftly across France and into Belgium and Holland that the First Triple A was not needed. Now, with Montgomery's audacious proposal, Brereton's eighteenth plan would go through.

Operation Market (code-named for the airborne half of the plan) would employ some 45,000 men—20,000 paratroopers, 15,000 glider soldiers, and 10,000 infantrymen landed by air. This airborne army would lay down a slender carpet northward for 60 miles along a single road, all the way to Arnhem on the Rhine. Maj. Gen. Robert L. "Roy" Urquhart's British 1st Airborne Division, reinforced by Stanislaw Sosabowski's 1st Polish Parachute Brigade, would have the toughest—and most perilous—task. The 42-year-old, jumbo-sized Urquhart was to seize the massive bridge over the Rhine at Arnhem, and scrape out airstrips to receive the British 52nd Airlanding Division.

Jim Gavin's 82nd Airborne would jump and land near Nijmegen, 11 miles below Arnhem, capture the 1,100-foot bridge over the Mass River at Grave, grab at least one of the four bridges over the Mass-Waal Canal, and finally seize the huge bridge over the Waal River in the heart of Nijmegen, a city of 100,000.

The job of Max Taylor's 101st Airborne was to secure the 16-

mile stretch of road that began behind the German positions, at Eindhoven, and ran north through Zon, St. Oedenrode, Vechel, and Uden.

A shortage of C-47s meant that the airlift would be carried out over a period of several days, because Brereton had decreed that air crews could fly but one mission each day. The airborne army leader also reached another crucial decision: His troopers would jump and glide in broad daylight in order to avoid the mass confusion that had resulted in the D-Day blackness of Normandy. Brereton was counting on Allied bombers to neutralize the string of Luftwaffe airfields that lay a short distance behind the Third Reich border and for dive bombers to wipe out flak guns on and around the drop zones and landing zones.

Finally, the First Triple A chief made a controversial command decision that rankled Matt Ridgway and other American leaders: Boy Browning would have airborne field command in Holland.

At this crucial point, Allied Intelligence suffered a sinking spell. Ultra, the beacon that had cast light for so long upon the secrets of the Wehrmacht, began to dim. Possibly, the Germans may have come to realize that their "unbreakable" Enigma code had been penetrated and ceased using it. Montgomery had expected to meet only rag-tag, disorganized German units in Holland, but under the noses of Ultra and the powerful Allied air forces the first-rate Fifteenth Army, which for months had been manning the Atlantic Wall along the Pas de Calais in France, had slipped undetected into The Netherlands. And the 9th and 10th SS Panzer Divisions, full of fight, were concealed in the forests and villages in the vicinity of Arnhem and its key bridge. Also helping lull Montgomery (and SHAEF) to sleep was the absence of warnings from the Dutch underground, which, for many months, had been keeping the Allies abreast of Wehrmacht movements in Holland. Unbeknownst to SHAEF, an energetic and astute *Abwehr* (counterintelligence) major, Hermann Giskes, had wiped out the Dutch resistance network in one fell swoop.

Sunday, September 17, dawned bright and clear—perfect weather for an airborne operation. At 24 airfields in England, thousands of Allied airborne men were steeling themselves for the looming ordeal. Unlike the rookies, most veterans were especially tense. Flying in plodding transport planes within a stone's throw of Luftwaffe airfields in broad daylight was a haunting specter.

The big parade started. More than 1,500 transports were crammed with paratroopers and accompanied by towed gliders that hauled the field pieces, jeeps, munitions, food, and all the thousands of things a self-contained army needed. By 11:30 A.M., all of the transports were aloft. For 90 minutes, the sky train roared over various sections of London at 1,500 feet. It was noon on this Sabbath and tens of thousands of worshippers emerged from churches to gawk at and to cheer for the awesome winged war machine.

Two parallel routes would be taken: Gavin's 82nd and Urquhart's British 1st Airborne would fly the northern course; Max Taylor's 101st Airborne would take the southern lane. Leading off in the northern flight were two British outfits, Brigadier P. H. W. Pip Hicks' 1st Airlanding Brigade and Brigadier Gerald W. Lathbury's 1st Parachute Brigade, consisting of some 3,800 men in all. Between 1:00 and 3:00 P.M., the two units, along with Roy Urquhart, dropped and glided to perfect landings on their drop zones and landing zones eight miles west of Arnhem.

Hard on the heels of the British was a transport stream hauling 7,250 paratroopers of Gavin's 82nd Airborne. Bill Ekman's 505th Parachute Infantry was in the lead, followed by Edwin Bedell's 307th Parachute Engineer Battalion, Rube Tucker's 504th Roy Lindquist's 508th, and finally, Wilbur Griffith's 376th Parachute Field Artillery.

Piloting one of the C-47s of the 440th Troop Carrier Group was 22-year-old Capt. Donald M. Orcutt of Palisades Park, New Jersey. This group was carrying elements of the 508th and the 376th cannoneers. Casting quick glances at either side, Orcutt was comforted by the sight of dozens of Spitfires, Typhoons, P-47s, and Mosquitos bobbing and weaving about the transport train.

As Orcutt's flight neared the Dutch coast at Schouwen Island, German flak batteries opened fire, and before they were silenced by Typhoons, a C-47 ahead of Orcutt was hit and spiraled downward. The Wehrmacht was now fully alerted, and it seemed to Orcutt that every German who could fire a weapon was taking aim at his C-47. Like most others in the sky armada, Orcutt's mind flashed to the 1,800 pounds of grenades, bazooka shells, ammunition, and TNT that was slung below the fuselage in six bundles. One lucky shot could ignite an explosion that would blow the airplane into confetti and the occupants into dust.

Donald Orcutt recalled that flight over German-controlled real estate:

As we approached our I. P. [initial point] at s'Hertogenbosch, Holland, from where we would make a bee-line to the DZ, the flak got so heavy it formed a veritable cloud layer of black smoke at our flight level. The lead airplanes in our serial disappeared from view as they flew into this black cloud. I thought they couldn't possibly survive this hail of enemy fire, and I tried to make myself as small as possible in the hope that I could pass through without being shot down.

Amazingly, the lead airplanes emerged on the other side just as my squadron was entering the black cloud. My navigator, Lt. Michael Whitfill, shouted that he could hear hits being scored on us. Indeed he had. When we got back to England, we counted more than 100 bullet and shell-splinter holes in our C-47.

Although the one C-47 had been shot down, the remaining 479 dropped their All-American paratroopers onto three drop zones, four miles southeast and southwest of Nijmegen. This was an almost perfect drop, the kind that Gavin and other pioneer parachute officers had been striving for since the early days at Fort Benning's Lawson Field, but had rarely been able to achieve during combat missions.

Pilot Capt. Donald M. Orcutt stands by his bullet- and shrapnel-riddled airplane after return from dropping 82nd Airborne paratroopers in Holland. *(Donald M. Orcutt)*

Behind Gavin's paratroopers came a flight of 88 gliders hauling elements of Tex Singleton's 80th Antiaircraft Battalion, most of the 82nd Airborne division staff, and Browning and his British 1st Airborne Corps staff. Although 38 Wacos glided down a mile from their landing zone, it had been a successful operation: only seven glider soldiers had been injured and only two Wacos destroyed.

At the same time that the All-Americans and the Red Devils were winging to battle, Max Taylor's 101st Airborne was flying the southern course. On board 424 C-47s were 6,769 paratroopers of Jumpy Johnson's 501st, Iron Mike Michaelis' 502nd, and Bob Sink's 506th regiments. Shortly after the Screaming Eagles' sky armada knifed over the Dutch coast, it ran into flak thick enough to walk on, five minutes from the green light.

Engines caught fire and wing strips broke loose, but the C-47 pilots refused to take evasive action and held steadfastly to their course, thereby giving the Eagles the chance to bail out right over the drop zone. Standing in the open door of one C-47, Lt. Col. Patrick Cassidy, leader of the 502nd's 1st Battalion, was mesmerized by the gut-wrenching sight of a nearby airplane in flames, and failed to see the green light flash on. Max Taylor, who would jump behind Cassidy, leaned forward and said calmly, "Patrick, the green light is on."

Minutes after landing in Holland, James Gavin (center) issues orders to an officer. At the left is Alfred Ireland. (*James M. Gavin*)

"Yes, sir," Cassidy responded, and out he went.

Despite the intense flak, it had been the most successful jump of the 101st Airborne, in either training or combat. Within an hour, most of the battalions had formed up and moved out to secure their objectives. Jump casualties were minimal: less than 2 percent.

An hour behind Taylor's paratroopers came 70 of the division's gliders, but only 53 of them landed routinely on the landing zone. Three of the motorless craft crashed on the landing zone, seven came down behind German lines, two missed the drop zone, nine came down at scattered locales on the Continent, two aborted in England, and one plunged into the English Channel.

By 3:00 P.M. on D-Day, the entire American and British airborne force in the initial lift was on the ground—five hours after the first troop transport had taken off from England—and preparing for war among the windmills.[4]

35
Hell's
Highway

Like well-oiled machines, the 82nd and 101st Airborne Divisions began seizing or moving toward their Operation Market objectives with astonishing speed and efficiency. In the All-Americans sector, Rube Tucker's Five-O-Fours captured intact the long, low bridge over the Maas River at Grave, which would allow British armor to cross and rush on northward to Nijmegen and Arnhem.

Twenty-one-year-old, soft-spoken Ted Bachenheimer, still a private although he had become a division legend as the "Lone Raider of Anzio," had been the first trooper over the bridge. His job had been to draw enemy fire. (Bachenheimer had turned down sergeant's stripes several times because the rank would, he said, "interfere with my activities"—that is, prowling behind German lines.)

Once over the bridge, the free spirit continued onward and slipped alone into German-held Nijmegen. In the railroad station, he got into a shootout with eight or nine German soldiers, and was called on through the loudspeaker, which announced the arrival and departure of trains, to surrender. While the ultimatum was being "broadcast," Bachenheimer slipped out of the station.[1]

Along with the Grave bridge, Tucker's troopers seized two canal bridges, and Lindquist's 508th and Ekman's 505th were dug in and facing west toward the Reichswald, a thick forest across the German border that held untold dangers for Gavin's airhead because any panzers or grenadiers concealed in the Reichswald could not be seen in aerial photos. Only the towering, steel-girdered Waal (Rhine) span at Nijmegen was still in enemy hands.

Shortly after dropping, Jim Gavin was at the point of a small column of engineers and marching rapidly toward the site he had earlier chosen as division headquarters, a mile from where he had landed. At the young general's side was a fabled Dutch underground fighter, Capt. Arie Bestebreurtje—known to the Americans as "Captain Harry."[2] Halting briefly to wipe out a German machine-gun post, the column reached the outskirts of Groesbeek.

Captain Harry went into a house, picked up the civilian telephone, and through a code, talked to the Dutch Underground in Nijmegen and in Arnhem, the latter in the British airhead some 25 miles to the north. Captain Harry emerged in a high state of excitement: Dutch resistance fighters inside Arnhem reported that the Red Devils had landed and that all seemed to be going well.

Nothing could have been further from the truth: Roy Urquhart's airborne men were in big trouble. Much to the amazement of Gavin, Taylor, and other American parachute leaders while back in England, the British had elected to bail out eight miles west of Arnhem, instead of dropping near the critical Rhine River bridge.

John D. Frost's 2nd Battalion of Lathbury's 1st Parachute Brigade had rapidly marched to Arnhem and established an isolated beachhead at the northern end of the bridge in the heart of the city. But Lathbury's two supporting battalions were attacked violently while heading for Arnhem and got bogged down in house-to-house fighting. Making a difficult situation even worse, Roy Urquhart and his driver got cut off in residential Arnhem, and the commanding general was out of contact with his division for 36 critical hours.

By late afternoon, Gavin had a jeep, and he set out to call on his units. The first outfit he encountered was the 376th Parachute Field Artillery Battalion, where he was approached by Lt. Col. Wilbur Griffith, who had broken his ankle in the jump and was being pushed about in a wheelbarrow. Laughing and saluting, Griffith said, "General, the 376th Field Artillery is in position with all guns ready to fire!"

That night was pitch black, and a 505th Regiment outpost in Groesbeek heard the plaintive wail of a locomotive whistle. Not anticipating the approach of a train, the troopers made no effort to fire on it, and the locomotive chugged on through Groesbeek toward Nijmegen. It may have been the only time in World War II when an enemy locomotive broke through American defensive positions.

A short time later, the embarrassed parachutists in Groesbeek got their revenge. Another train came through bound for Nijmegen, and a happy trooper later chortled over the radio network: "We shot the hell out of the Iron Kraut!"

That same night, Shields Warren's 1st Battalion of the 508th was ordered to head for the south end of the Nijmegen bridge. Just before moving out, the commander of the leading company was introduced to a Dutchman who claimed to be a resistance leader. He assured the captain that he could not only guide the parachute outfit through the dark maze of streets, but also take it to the control center that contained the mechanism for blowing up the Waal bridge.

With the Dutchman in the lead, two of Warren's companies reached a crossroads a short distance south of the bridge. "I'll be back shortly," the guide explained before slipping off down a sidestreet. He would never return.

After waiting for a short time, the two companies pushed forward. Everything was black and silent—and eerie. Reaching a traffic circle just below the bridge, Warren's troopers were raked by fire and were ordered to hold up. No doubt the Dutch "patriot" would earn a handsome fee: the All-Americans were

Gen. James Gavin (right) confers with Gen. "Boy" Browning in Holland. (*U. S. Army*)

Gen. Lewis Brereton, commander, First Allied Airborne Army. (*Imperial War Museum*)

hemmed in by German grenadiers, armored cars with machine guns, and self-propelled 88s. In the face of this fusillade of fire, Shields Warren tried to pull back his battalion, but he and his troopers would be cut off for two days.

Meanwhile, Max Taylor's Screaming Eagles—some of them pushing on ahead on bicycles and in cars grabbed from unsuspecting *Feldgrau*—rapidly seized their D-Day objectives. Jumpy Johnson's 501st Regiment took intact a bridge over the Williams Canal and another one over the Aa River. Mike Michaelis' 502nd landed south of Johnson, then dispatched a force north to link up with the 501st at St. Oedenrode and a reinforced company led by Capt. Robert E. Jones to seize a bridge at Best. And Bob Sink's 506th, south of the 502nd, quickly captured Zon and had a force pushing south toward the division's main objective, Eindhoven.

During the fighting around Zon, Capt. Melvin C. Davis, leader of Company A of the 1st Battalion, was felled by heavy fire from a group of flak guns. Medics dashed up to give Davis first aid, and while they were going about their work, the badly wounded captain was hit by a bullet.

"You medics had better hurry up," Davis quipped through clenched teeth. "The Krauts are gaining on you!"

At the base of the 60-mile-long Allied javelin, there was a worrisome development. Hardly had the Guards Armored Division tanks clanked forward than they were slowed by elements of Baron von der Heydte's crack 6th Parachute Regiment, the teenagers who had fought the Screaming Eagles so tenaciously at Carentan three months earlier. Market-Garden called for the Guards to reach Eindhoven on D-Day, but its spearheads advanced only eight miles, halfway to Eindhoven.

Diminutive, monocled Field Marshal Walther Model, commander of Army Group B, had watched the Allied parachute spectacle from his headquarters at Oosterbeek two miles west of Arnhem. Even though the Wehrmacht had been caught totally off guard, within hours Model and his two senior battle leaders, Lt. Gen. Willi Bittrich of the II SS Panzer Korps and Gen. Kurt Student of the First Parachute Army, evaluated the Market-Garden plan with incredible accuracy.[3]

Clearly the huge highway bridges over the Waal at Nijmegen and the Rhine at Arnhem were the sky invaders' primary targets. Already panzers and grenadiers had bottled up John Frost's Red Devil battalion at the northern end of the Arnhem bridge, and now Bittrich rushed the 9th SS Panzer Division's reconnaissance battalion southward with orders to cross the Nijmegen bridge and hold onto it. By 9:00 P.M. on D-Day, elements of the SS battalion, under an aggressive captain named Fritz Euling, were in Nijmegen at the south end of the river span. These were the Germans that Shields Warren's paratroopers had unexpectedly collided with in the blackness.

Far south of the Nijmegen bridge at dawn on D-Day plus 1, flamboyant Bob Sink of the 506th Parachute Infantry was briefing his battalion commanders at his command post in Zon. "We've got to get to Eindhoven this morning, and we can't waste time killing Krauts," Sink exclaimed. "So if you run onto any Germans, just let them filter on through you, and the Ducks [502nd] will take good care of them."

When troopers of the Five-O-Sink jumped off, they overran or drove off scattered bands of *Feldgrau,* then pushed into

Eindhoven. There a stubborn force of Germans, armed with automatic weapons and a few 88s, battled back, but by noon Eindhoven's new landlords wore baggy pants and jump boots.

It was not until 6:30 P.M. that Bob Sink's boys detected the sounds they had been straining to hear: the clanking and rumbling of tanks of the Guards Armored Division coming up from the south. Hardly pausing—the Guards were already 24 hours behind schedule in the race to Arnhem—the British drove through Eindhoven and on northward to Zon, where a blown bridge forced the tanks to pause for the night.

The Screaming Eagles inside Eindhoven, now finding themselves temporarily in the backwash of war, accepted the applause and cheers of a delirious citizenry, along with the offered beer, schnapps, and a variety of favors from the grateful young ladies. But only four miles northwest of Eindhoven's frenzied multitudes that day, other Eagles were engaged in a bloody struggle for the bridge over the Wilhelmina Canal at Best, the span that Capt. Bob Jones's reinforced company had been sent to the afternoon of D-Day.

When Mike Michaelis learned that the Germans were putting up a savage fight for the Best bridge, he sent two battalions to join in the fight against an estimated 1,000 Germans backed by heavy artillery. During one brief lull in the shooting, Lt. Col. Bob Cole, leader of the 3rd Battalion, strolled out in front of his troopers to get a better look at the terrain. For several seconds Cole stood there, his upraised hand shielding his eyes from the sun. Suddenly a rifle shot rang out. A German concealed in a house a hundred yards away put a bullet through Cole's head, killing him instantly. Cole would never know that he had already been awarded the Congressional Medal of Honor for leading the bayonet charge at Carentan shortly after D-Day in Normandy.

Moments later, a *Feldgrau* dashed from the house, and one of the battalion's machine guns cut him down. No one would ever know for sure if this was the German who had killed Bob Cole, but the troopers assured each other that they had gotten the perpetrator of the black deed.

Men of the 2nd Battalion were thunderstruck: Their "indestructible" leader had been killed. Lt. Ralph A. Watson was with Cole at the time, but could not bring himself to send back the words: "Colonel Cole is dead." Instead, Watson radioed Maj. John Stopka, Cole's executive officer: "You are in command of the battalion." Thinking that he was functioning as commanding officer on a temporary basis until Bob Cole again took over the reins, Stopka issued orders for the attack to be resumed.[4]

Meanwhile, fate had frowned on Capt. Bob Jones's company from the moment it struck out for the Best bridge, a single-lane concrete span about 100 feet long. First, the company got lost in thick woods; then, it ran into a large German force near the Best bridge. Under withering bursts of fire, Jones had to pull back his company for perhaps 600 yards. Colonel Cole had radioed Jones to rush a reinforced platoon to the bridge at once.

Lt. Edward L. Wierzbowski and his platoon, augmented by a few engineers, were given the unenviable task. Only when he started to move out at dusk did Wierzbowski realize how much the fighting had decimated his platoon—only 18 troopers remained. Almost at once the little band was raked by German machine-gun fire, but for the next several hours, Pfc. Joe E. Mann, the lead scout, guided the tiny band through the pitch blackness of the woods and to the Wilhelmina Canal. Slipping and stumbling, Wierzbowski and his men began picking their way westward along the banks toward the targeted bridge, when the Americans were suddenly caught in the middle of a rainstorm.

Wierzbowski felt that he was near the bridge, so he and Joe Mann slithered forward and soon discovered that they were at the end of the span. But they were not alone; only a few feet away the two troopers could discern the dark silhouette of a German sentry. Wierzbowski and Mann were in a quandary: If they knifed this *Feldgrau,* the German sentry at the other end of the bridge might hear the commotion and spread the alarm.

For what seemed to be an eternity, Wierzbowski and Mann, their hearts furiously pounding and perspiration beads dotting their foreheads, lay flat and motionless—staring at the *Feldgrau*'s jackboots almost in front of their noses. Thirty minutes ticked past.

The remainder of the platoon had grown nervous over Wierzbowski's prolonged absence. Suddenly, from across the canal, a flurry of potato-masher grenades was hurled at the troopers; then machine-gun and rifle fire from both sides of the canal split the silence of the night. Bullets hissed past. Seeking better cover, the troopers scrambled behind the embankment, and the outburst of firing allowed Wierzbowski and Mann to slip away and rejoin the platoon. Artillery and mortar shells now burst

Pfc. Joe E. Mann. *(Don F. Pratt Museum)*

Lt. Edward L. Wierzbowski. *(Don F. Pratt Museum)*

around the Americans, and they pulled back up the canal for 100 yards and dug in.

At 3:10 A.M. the Germans ceased firing. Sheets of heavy rain continued to deluge the miserable, hungry, and anxious little band of troopers trapped far in front of their lines.

As dawn broke over embattled Holland, Ed Wierzbowski and his men got their first good look at the once-insignificant concrete span for whose control so much American and German blood had already been spilled. The sentries were gone, but on the far side of the one-lane span a large number of Germans were dug in. Each time the Screaming Eagles raised up to charge the bridge, they were raked by intensive fire.

At precisely 11:00 A.M., a tremendous explosion rocked the region: The Germans had blown the bridge, and pieces of concrete and steel rained down on the parachutists' foxholes. However, Wierzbowski had no way of getting word of the demolition back to his battalion.

Joe Mann, the quiet, unassuming lead scout, and a comrade named Hoyle spotted a German ammunition dump about 100 yards away. Grabbing a bazooka, they started crawling toward it, and Mann blew up the explosives with a few rockets from the launcher. Suddenly six infantrymen charged the pair of troopers, and Mann and Hoyle shot all of them. In the shootout, Mann was grazed twice by bullets. Sneaking back to their platoon, the men saw an 88-millimeter gun along the canal, and Hoyle wiped it out with a single well-placed bazooka round.

Not knowing that the Best bridge had been demolished, Michaelis' two battalions in the woods behind Wierzbowski and his men were battling the Germans, trying to break through. At the same time, a contingent of *Feldgrau* attacked the isolated little band, but Wierzbowski's men drove them off. Lt. James B. Watson of the 326th Engineers got out of his hole to look around and was struck by a bullet in his lower body.

A medic, Pfc. James Orvac, rushed to Watson's side, as did Ed Wierzbowski. Writhing in agony and bleeding extensively, Watson thought his private parts had been shot off and begged Wierzbowski to take his 45 Colt and kill him. But Wierzbowski replied, "Jim, your family jewels are still intact."

Minutes later, the heaviest German fire yet hissed into the beleaguered and decimated platoon. One man was killed, another shot in the spine and paralyzed in agony. Two bullets ripped into Joe Mann, and both of his arms had to be bandaged by medic Orvac. That made four Wehrmacht slugs that Mann had taken.

Now the platoon's medical supplies had been exhausted. So three troopers set out to prowl the canal banks, and an hour later returned with four German prisoners—a wounded lieutenant and, incredibly, three medics with crucially needed medical supplies. Wierzbowski ordered the enemy medics to go to work on Jim Watson and the other wounded men.

That night, the cut-off platoon fell into an exhausted sleep, almost to a man. At first light, Ed Wierzbowski rose from his hole to have a look and saw a squad or two of *Feldgrau* charging toward him. The lieutenant shouted a warning, and several of his men pitched grenades, but German potato-mashers were already hurtling through the air toward the Americans.

One enemy grenade hit the machine gun and exploded next to Trooper Laino, blowing out an eye, blinding him in the other, and leaving him bloody pulp for a face. A bullet went through Trooper Koller's head. A grenade flew past Wierzbowski and bounced into the hole of the blinded Laino, who heard the thud, groped for the lethal object and pitched it out, a split-second before it exploded.

Nearby, Joe Mann was sitting in a large excavation with six

other troopers. Both of his arms were bound tightly because of his four wounds. Suddenly, he heard or saw the potato-masher as it thudded into the hole behind him. Shouting "Grenade!" to his comrades, he quickly lay back on the potato-masher and the explosion seemed to lift him into the air.

Two men in the hole received fragment wounds, but none were killed. Ed Wierzbowski rushed to the excavation. Mann whispered to the platoon leader: "My back's gone." Two minutes later, without a cry, whimper or moan, Joe Mann was dead.

Sensing the annihilation of the little cluster of Americans that had become a thorn in their side, the Germans rushed toward the foxholes. Only three of the paratroopers were not wounded and they were out of ammunition and grenades. Reluctantly, Ed Wierzbowski had to surrender.

Meanwhile, Maj. John Stopka's 3rd Battalion and Steve Chappuis' 2nd Battalion, supported by Guards tanks, were slugging their way toward the site of the Best bridge, which was thought to be intact. What had started out as a reinforced platoon mission to grab the span had now turned into a fight involving much of the 101st Airborne and a large number of British tanks.

Stopka sensed the tide was turning after he ran forward to give orders to one of his companies and 75 Germans dashed out of the woods toward him—to surrender. In his sector, Chappuis saw a band of *Feldgrau* leave their positions and move forward to give up, only to be mowed down from behind by machine guns triggered by fellow Germans.

Sweeping through fields littered with dead enemy soldiers, Stopka's and Chappuis' battalions closed up to the Wilhelmina Canal. Stopka ordered a body count, and over 600 Germans were sprawled in death in his 3rd Battalion area alone. Both battalions had collared in excess of 1,100 prisoners.

There was a bright footnote to the Screaming Eagles' smashing victory at Best—the paratroopers freed Ed Wierzbowski and the other survivors of the "Lost Platoon."

Elsewhere in the Allied airhead on the afternoon of D-Day plus 1, the First Triple A poured in more troops and firepower. On the Arnhem drop zones, far west of the town where John Frost and his men were bottled up, John "Shan" Hackett's British 4th Parachute Brigade and the remaining half of Pip Hick's 1st Airlanding Brigade dropped and glided amidst a torrent of machine-gun and antiaircraft fire. This mission landed some 4,000 Red Devils.

Some 15 miles to the south, 450 C-47s towing gliders brought in the 82nd Airborne's 319th and 320th Glider Field Artillery Battalions and the 456th Parachute Field Artillery Battalion—1,906 cannoneers in all—along with elements of the 80th Airborne Antiaircraft Battalion and the division signal and medical contingents. While the gliders were swooping down onto landing zones protected by Gavin's paratroopers, they were raked by heavy bursts of fire from Germans concealed in the nearby Reichswald.

Even while enemy machine-gun fire continued to sweep the landing zones, the All-American glidermen dashed about and were able to collect and assemble 30 of the 35 howitzers brought in by the three artillery battalions, and all eight 57-millimeter antitank guns.

Almost simultaneously, 428 gliders tugged by C-47s brought in a total of 2,579 men to beef up Max Taylor's 101st Airborne Division around Zon and Eindhoven. On board were two battalions of Col. Joseph Harper's 327th Glider Infantry, and medical and engineer detachments. Except for one glider that was hit by flak in midair and blown to pieces, and 10 others that had to abort or cut loose early, the Screaming Eagle gliders landed in relatively routine fashion. Also in the glider flight were C-47s carrying a battery of the 377th Parachute Artillery Battalion, which jumped into action.

These three D-Day plus 1 reinforcement missions had landed more than 9,000 "Triple A" men, bringing the total number of American and British paratroopers and glider soldiers on the ground in Holland to nearly 29,000—and making Market-Garden history's largest airborne operation.

Late on the afternoon of D-Day plus 1, German Field Marshal Model and his subordinate, Willi Bittrich, were engaged in a heated argument. Bittrich declared that the Waal bridge at Nijmegen was the key to the entire Allied thrust into Holland. Blow it up, the II SS Panzer Korps chief exclaimed, and the entire British 1st Airborne Division would be cut off and destroyed at Arnhem.

"No, *Herr General*, absolutely no!" Model retorted, glaring through his monocle. The little field marshal demanded that Horrocks' tank thrust be halted long before it reached the Nijmegen bridge.[5]

36
Epic
Crossing of
the Waal

By dawn of D-Day plus 2 (September 19) the Allied thrust into Holland was under heavy assault. Along both sides of the slender salient the Germans launched fierce attacks in an effort to seize back key bridges and to cut the lone road over which British tanks would have to rumble in order to reach the beleaguered Red Devils at Arnhem.

Just past 8:30 A.M., Jim Gavin and Boy Browning met leading elements of Maj. Gen. Allan Adair's Guards Armored Division at the Grave bridge that Rube Tucker's paratroopers had grabbed shortly after jumping on D-Day. Gavin's elation over the linkup of his division with the British tanks was tempered by a grim possibility: Roy Urquhart's Red Devils had been cut off for three days at Arnhem, and unless the Guards' tanks reached that city— and soon—the entire British 1st Airborne Division would be doomed.

However, the armored relief column would first have to roll over the Waal, and the bridge at Nijmegen was still in German hands. Gavin had been trying for two days to seize the Nijmegen bridge, and at noon on this day he sent Ben Vandervoort and his 505th battalion into the city to try to get the crucial job done.

Vandy and his men had their work cut out for them in Nijmegen. Working hand in glove with Lt. Col. Edward Goulburn's Guards tanks, the parachutists were deployed on both sides of the tree-lined Hell's Highway leading through the heart of Nijmegen to the Waal bridge and on to Arnhem. The goal was to hack out a two-block corridor to the river span. Going against the advice of West Point tactics textbooks, Vandervoort ignored the security of his flanks. Time was crucial: He had to reach the bridge at the earliest possible moment and could not get bogged down in widespread and time-consuming street fighting in this city of 100,000 inhabitants.

Whatever may have been the clash of towering egos at the pinnacle of the First Allied Airborne Army, at the foxhole- and gun-barrel-level Yankees and Tommies fought side by side in a spirit of comradeship and close cooperation.

Ben Vandervoort recalled that relationship at Nijmegen:

For soldiers of different Allied armies, ones who had never fought together until this day, it was amazing how beautifully the Brits and the paratroopers teamed together. When the tanks got in trouble our boys came running to their aid; when we got in hot water, the tanks quickly rumbled to our side.

The savage fighting deteriorated into Indian warfare—confusing face-to-face, kill-or-be-killed showdowns between tiny, momentarily isolated groups and individual soldiers. Friend and foe mixed in deadly proximity. Germans suddenly popped up where least expected—a trooper fired fast and straight, or he was dead.

There was no complicated tactical plan. This was a brawl directed by American lieutenants, platoon sergeants, and squad leaders, many of whom were cut down in the wild melee. For his part, Ed Goulburn, a perceptive commander, more or less turned loose individual tanks and let them go—up the alleys, through the once-immaculate gardens, and along the cobblestone streets.

Much of the fighting was done in a residential neighborhood of two-story brick and stone row houses. Some were topped with attics and flat roofs. Since the German 88s and antitank guns were positioned to cover the streets, Vandervoort's resourceful warriors launched a technique for skirting these menacing enemy weapons. The troopers fought from roof to roof, scrambled through bedroom windows to get to the next row house, punched or blew holes in attics to scramble to the adjoining attic, then dropped to alleys and backyards.

Meanwhile, Goulburn's tanks were dueling with the 88s and blasting German strongpoints on the ground to cover the rooftop warriors of Nijmegen. The Churchills also served as battering rams to smash through garden walls, after which Vandervoort's footsloggers would dash to the next house. When the SS troops were especially stubborn, poking a 76-millimeter barrel through a kitchen window inevitably triggered a stampede of German soldiers out of the house.

Finally, Ben Vandervoort's men occupied the residential row of houses facing Huner Park, an open ornamental interchange for all roads crossing the Waal. Only 400 yards ahead was the superbly engineered bridge whose owners could determine the success or failure of Market-Garden.

Commanding the sweep of Huner Park was a red brick tower: old Fort Belvedere, whose foundation was a relic of Charlemagne's reign. The lower floors of Belvedere had in peacetime housed a tea room, and its tower had been a tourist lookout. Now Belvedere had reverted to a fort once more: Out of its doors and windows stuck the snouts of German guns.

Huner Park was congested with SS troops, concealed in air-raid shelters and huddled in foxholes and trenches. Vandervoort's troopers would have to dig out these Germans in order to reach the bridge. It promised to be an especially bloody affair.

Meanwhile, paratrooper mortars were lobbing rounds onto the roadbed of the massive stone-pierced and steel-arched bridge. "What if a shell hit a charge causing the bridge to blow sky-high?" someone asked Ben Vandervoort. "Then we'd know for sure that the damned thing was booby-trapped!" the colonel replied.

It was now late afternoon. Vandervoort was itching to unleash his men to wipe out the SS men in Huner Park, rush the bridge entrance, and race on over the bridge to the north side. The momentum was his, he felt, and casualties would be less now before the enemy got reorganized.

Ben Vandervoort remembered his disappointment:

> I radioed the generals that my battalion was ready to take Huner Park and put the Brit tanks over the bridge. Instead, I was ordered to consolidate our positions for the night. That was a strange night, there near the big bridge. It was quiet, even eerie. Our boys felt that it was the lull before the storm.

Late that afternoon, at about the same time that Vandervoort reached Huner Park, Boy Browning, Jim Gavin, and Alan Adair met in a small schoolhouse in the village of Malden. All three generals realized that the hour of desperation had been reached—the lightly armed Red Devils at Arnhem could not survive much longer against the swarms of panzers that were blasting them from three directions. Browning, in command of the airborne corps, told Gavin, "The Nijmegen bridge must be taken today—tomorrow at the latest."[1]

The entire Market-Garden monkey had now been put on Jim Gavin's back: If he and his All-Americans failed to seize the Nijmegen bridge, the entire operation could meet with disaster.

Rushing back to his command post, Gavin mulled over the battle situation. A tough SS unit, backed by heavy mortars and 88s, was dug in at the southern approach to the bridge over the Waal. If Gavin did nothing but hurl his paratroopers and British tanks against this tenacious group of Germans, it might take days to root out the last defender. By that time, the Red Devils to the north would be out of ammo, food, and medical supplies and be forced to capitulate. In that event, the SS outfit defending the Nijmegen bridge would pull back over the span and blow it, thereby blocking any advance by Allan Adair's tanks. Already, Horrocks' XXX Corps vehicles were backed up, tank tread to tank tread, bumper to bumper, along the narrow, two-lane road nearly all the way to Eindhoven. Hell's Highway had become the world's longest parking lot.

It was nearly dark when the 82nd Airborne commander reached his command post. At once, he and his staff plunged feverishly into drawing up a scheme to grab the big Waal bridge. Simultaneous attacks would have to be launched in order to seize both the south and the north ends of the span. (Only 56 hours later would Gavin learn that the Germans had planted demolitions in the structure years earlier and painted them over to give the appearance of being part of the bridge.)

Both Browning and Horrocks approved Gavin's final plan, in which Ben Vandervoort's battalion and the Guard's tanks would attack through Nijmegen's Huner Park and capture the south ends of both the highway bridge and a parallel railroad span. At the same time a battalion of the 504th, selected by Rube Tucker, would cross the Waal two miles downstream in hand-paddled boats, then attack eastward and gain control of the north end of the highway bridge before the Germans could demolish it with explosives.

James Gavin recalled the agonizing dilemma with which he was faced:

Ideally, I would have preferred to delay the [Waal] crossing for 24 hours to give us time to reconnoiter the riverbank and to go over under the cover of darkness. But every moment counted. Sending the 504th battalion across the river in daylight was one of the most difficult decisions I had to make during the war. However, I could not conceive sitting at the south end of the bridge with one of my regiments and a large number of Guards' tanks while Urquhart was destroyed 11 miles to the north.

Meanwhile that night, Ted Bachenheimer, the Lone Raider, was ensconced in a candlelit basement headquarters of the Dutch Underground in German-held part of Nijmegen. Two days earlier, his 504th comrades saw him start to peddle an old bicycle toward the town, and when they cautioned him that the enemy was there, Bachenheimer shrugged and replied, "Aw, I'm just going over there to see what the score is."

Slipping into Nijmegen, he had made contact with the Underground, and its leaders urged him to take charge of their operations. Much like a field marshal directing his army's operations, Bachenheimer sent out his "troops"—a motley but eager band of Dutchmen wearing orange armbands and armed with a strange assortment of weapons—to ambush Wehrmacht patrols and to attack isolated outposts and sentries. Other patrols were dispatched to collect information on German positions around the Waal bridge, intelligence he would send back to his regiment.

A few miles south of Bachenheimer's Nijmegen basement that night, it was drizzling rain on the bivouac area of 27-year-old Maj. Julian Cook's 3rd Battalion of the 504th. Cook, who had been wounded in the Sicily friendly fire disaster in which 23 C-47s filled with paratroopers had been shot down, was conferring with his S-2, Lt. Virgil F. Carmichael. Just before 11:00 P.M., a jeep careened up to the 3rd Battalion command post with orders for Cook to report immediately to division headquarters.

Virgil Carmichael remembered that episode:

Julian [Cook] returned to the CP about midnight, and said that General Gavin had told him the battalion was to cross the Waal

River in boats the next day. Cook, a courageous and loyal soldier, had asked Gavin about the boats to be used in the assault crossing, and Gavin told him that he [Cook] would have to collect small boats from the natives along the river bank. It was all very uncertain. At that time, Gavin either did not know, or had no assurance, that the British would supply collapsible canvas boats for the crossing.

Anyway, we were all frustrated. The Krauts were still along our side of the river at places, so we didn't know if we could even get to the bank where we had been told to cross.

September 20, 1944, would be one of the cataclysmic days of the war in the West. Allied fortunes would hinge on whether American paratroopers could seize the mile-long Nijmegen bridge before the Wehrmacht could blow it; German Field Marshal Model also considered it the day of decision. With customary efficiency, Model launched full-blooded attacks against the Allied javelin all the way from Arnhem southward to Zon. His order to Gen. Kurt Student had been terse: "Wipe out the Allied airborne force!"

At dawn that day two miles west of Nijmegen, Julian Cook, Virgil Carmichael, Capt. Henry Keep (Cook's operations officer) and the company commanders went to the top of Nijmegen's power plant, overlooking the Waal crossing site. Henry Keep remembered that event:

As soon as we learned that our battalion was to be the guinea pig, we wanted to see what we'd be up against. The scene that greeted us from the top of the power plant was indelibly imprinted on my mind forever. It seemed like ours would be a classic suicide mission. No one spoke a word—just gawked.

On our [south] side of the Waal the ground was flat and bare for 300 yards. There was a rapid current and the bridge was discernible in the morning haze up the river, which was broad— maybe 500 yards.

Across the Waal on the German side was a broad, flat plain, void of cover or concealment for 400 yards, where there was a built-up highway that would give us our first protection—if we got that far. We could see a formidable line of defenses on the German side of the river—pillboxes, machine-gun emplacements, and a wicked-looking old Dutch fort loomed at a point about midway from where we would reach the far bank and the bridge.

Even before Julian Cook and his boys could jump off for the far bank, the fortunes of war created new woes for the Allies in Market-Garden. Turbulent weather forced cancellation of a drop by Major General Sosabowski's 1st Polish Parachute Brigade to reinforce the beleaguered Red Devils at Arnhem, and a flight of 167 planes dropped nearly 400 tons of ammo and other supplies to Urquhart's men, only to have nearly all of this crucial cargo fall onto or behind German lines.

At the same time, Jim Gavin was struck a similar blow. A flight to bring in Chuck Billingslea's 325th Glider Infantry also had to be scrubbed. Gavin had planned to use Billingslea's men to relieve the 504th, which basically had a defensive mission, to release Tucker's troopers for the Waal crossing. A second C-47 mission to drop crucial supplies to the 82nd Airborne also aborted, leaving Gavin desperately short of ammo.

Meanwhile, Julian Cook and his battalion of paratroopers were huddled behind an embankment at the Waal crossing site and waiting for the arrival of the British boats. H-hour was set for 3:00 P.M. The minutes ticked past. They waited . . . and waited some more. Still no boats. In a way, the lull before the river-crossing storm was even more gut-wrenching than the anxiety-packed interlude before taking off for a combat jump into the ominous unknown. At least in combat jumps, paratroopers knew the precise time of liftoff. Now Cook's warriors had to undergo their nagging uncertainties as of the interminable morning dragged into the afternoon.

Nerves taut to the breaking point, a few men made feeble efforts to joke. "I'm going to stand in the prow of the boat like George Washington crossing the Delaware," Julian Cook said with a trace of a grim smile. "Then I'll clench my fist, push it forward, and yell, 'Onward, men, onward!'"

Others seemed resigned to their fate. Few thought that any of the battalion would survive and reach the far shore. Lt. Harry F. "Pappy" Busby pulled out a pack of Chesterfields, lit one of the cigarettes, then tossed the nearly full pack away. "I won't need those any more," Busby said calmly. Then he pitched the Zippo lighter he had used. "Won't be needing that, either," he added.

(As it happened, an hour later, Pappy Busby, riddled by machine-gun bullets, would be lying dead on the far bank of the Waal River.)

Also waiting nervously for the word to go was Capt. Delbert

Kuehl, Protestant chaplain of the 504th Regiment and a veteran of combat jumps in Sicily and at Salerno. Without Rube Tucker's knowledge, the padre had volunteered to join with the assault battalion. Kuehl had been reared in the lake area of Minnesota, and since receiving his first rifle at age nine had been an expert marksman.[2] Chaplains are not supposed to be in the forefront of infantry attacks—especially in one that had all the earmarks of a suicide mission. But Kuehl told Julian Cook: "If our boys ever needed me, that time is now."

Fifteen minutes before the 3:00 P.M. H-hour, the British trucks with the collapsible canvas boats rumbled up to the Waal bank. Seven hours late, the convoy had got caught in the massive traffic tangle back on Hell's Highway. There was a rush to unload and assemble the boats.

At H-hour minus five minutes, a flight of fighter planes strafed and rocketed German positions on the far side, then 82nd Airborne howitzers laid a smoke screen along the north shore to "blind" enemy gunners.

Now the gripping tension mounted. Cook's paratroopers, stomach churning, stood by their boats. There would be 13 men to a boat, and each craft would also hold three troopers from the 307th Parachute Engineers whose job it was to paddle the craft to the far shore, then return to pick up the second wave—Lt. Col. Willard E. Harrison's 1st Battalion of the 504th.

Suddenly, an earsplitting roar erupted. Howitzers of the 82nd Airborne and Rube Tucker's mortars began bombarding the Germans across the Waal, and some 30 Churchill tanks of the Guards Armored Division, deployed track to track along the south bank, poured direct fire from their 76-millimeter guns into enemy ranks and over the heads of the All-Americans who would cross the river.

At the same time, elements of Lt. Col. Edward M. Wellems' 2nd Battalion of the 504th stretched out in exposed positions along the south shore and blistered the north bank with automatic weapons and rifle fire. There was no reaction from the German side—perhaps the resistance would be far less than had been anticipated.

Above the tumultuous racket, a whistle shrieked. Each crossing team hoisted its 200-pound boat onto shoulders already burdened with weapons and combat gear and staggered out toward the river. Feet sank deep into the mud and wet sand; each boat seemed to weigh a ton. Finally, the craft were flipped over and placed in the water; the paratroopers scrambled aboard and began paddling toward the far shore. So far, so good.

There was ample reason for the failure of the Germans to immediately open fire: They had been taken by total surprise. Unbeknownst to the Americans, Gen. Heinz Harmel, Wehrmacht commander in the Nijmegen region, had discounted the possibility that anyone would attempt to cross the Rhine River (Waal) by boat in broad daylight and against an entrenched enemy without lengthy and elaborate preparations, including saturation bombing by swarms of heavies and an enormous bombardment by hundreds of big guns, lasting for several hours. Harmel's focus was on keeping Ben Vandervoort's paratroopers, battling the SS force in the streets of Nijmegen, from seizing the south end of the highway bridge.

Henry Keep, who had been paddling furiously, remembered vividly what happened after the boats had advanced for 100 yards:

> Suddenly, all hell broke loose. The Germans opened up with everything they had—machine guns, mortars, artillery. The racket was terrific. They fired at us from the far shore, from down the river on our side, and from the railroad bridge a short distance to the east. It was as though the Krauts were enraged at us for trying something so drastic. By now, the smoke screen had dissolved, and I felt as naked as the day I was born.
>
> On occasion, I sneaked a glance to the boats on each side, and saw our fellows falling right and left—but not a single boat faltered.
>
> Had it not been for the horrible situation, the sight of the troopers trying to paddle and keep the boats straight would have been ludicrous. Those without paddles used rifle butts, and even though everyone was paddling mightily, we seemed to be working against each other.
>
> We lunged forward and sideways in fits and jerks. Suddenly I was struck by an incongruous vision—that of our coxswain at Princeton on Lake Carnegie, pounding rhythmically on the sides of our flimsy shell to keep us oarsmen in unison. So now, in the middle of the fireswept Waal, I began counting loudly—"one, two, three, four"—then repeating it over and over. Finally, out of breath, achieving nothing and feeling silly, I shut up.

By now, the broad expanse of the Waal was covered with small canvas craft, all crammed with frantically paddling men striving desperately to get to the far shore as quickly as possible. There they could at least shoot back. Large numbers of troopers were hit in all boats, and the bottoms of these craft were littered with dead and wounded men, and a mixture of blood and water flowed around these inert forms. Troopers used helmets and canteen cups to bail out the bullet-riddled boats and keep them from sinking. Some men plugged holes in the craft with handkerchiefs. All of the troopers were soaked to the skin. They became a pack of animals, devoid of anything resembling dignity and normality in their frantic efforts to get through the hailstorm of fire.

Maj. Julian A. Cook. *(Author's collection)*

Lt. Virgil F. Carmichael. *(Author's collection)*

Troopers, hit by bullets, toppled overboard. Some men sank, others were grabbed by comrades and hauled back in. Virgil Carmichael, the battalion S-2, was in the boat next to Julian Cook's. Carmichael vividly recalled that haunting experience:

> *Bullets were flying everywhere. Our boat started going around in circles. When I was young I had paddled a canoe quite a bit on the Tennessee River, and knew how it was supposed to be done. So I slipped over to the left rear of the craft, took a paddle from one of the men, and kept the boat steered straight for the other shore.*

One of my men, Pvt. Paul Katonik, had just joined us in England before the Holland jump. He was kneeling next to me when he was hit badly by what appeared to be a 20-millimeter bullet. Gasping, "Give me my [sulfa] pills," Katonik fell over. That's the way it went—we lived or died by a distance of a few inches.

Chaplain Delbert Kuehl was in Cook's boat, and he kept repeating aloud over and over again, "Lord, Thy will be done. Lord, Thy will be done." Reverend Kuehl recalled ensuing events:

Enemy fire was so intense that it reminded me of rain hitting the water. Major Cook was praying in a loud voice, "Hail, Mary, full of Grace. Hail, Mary, full of Grace." He told me later that he had been trying to say the rosary, but those words were all that came out. I heard a thud and glanced over and saw that the trooper sitting shoulder to shoulder with me had evidently been hit by a 20-millimeter shell, because the top of his head had been sheared off and you could see inside his skull.

I paddled until I was gasping for breath, and the paddle slipped from my hands. It seemed ages until we finally reached the opposite river bank.

One or two at a time, the shot-up, fragile craft beached. Climbing over dead and wounded comrades, Cook's boys, exhausted and emotionally spent, more dead than alive, staggered zombielike through knee-deep water and onto the bank, where they sprawled behind an unexpected, but welcome, low embankment. A torrent of German bullets continued to whistle overhead. Some troopers made it out of the boats and onto the bank; then keeled over from wounds received during the crossing. Reverend Kuehl remembered:

There were dead and wounded in every boat. Only 11 or 12 boats out of the 26 made it—the others had been sunk or the engineers killed and the craft drifted aimlessly downstream laden with their human cargo of dead and wounded troopers. One boat reaching the bank had four dead troopers draped across each other. I carried an aid kit, so immediately began working on the wounded, as did Captain Shapiro, our battalion doctor, and carrying them to the boats to be taken back. While leaning over one trooper, who had three bullet holes in his abdomen, a mortar shell exploded behind me, and a piece of shrapnel hit me in the back, knocking me prostrate over the man I was helping. Despite his being so seriously wounded, he called out, "Chaplain, did they get you, too?"

My wound did not prevent me from continuing to treat the wounded and helping with their evacuation. All the while we were receiving small-arms fire from the Germans. Later, when Colonel [Rube] Tucker came across with Harrison's second wave, he saw me and barked: "Chaplain Kuehl, what in the hell are you doing over here?"

What had gathered on the north bank of the Waal was a group of American fanatics, men rendered crazy by rage over the fiendish ordeal which they had had to helplessly endure and the sight of comrades being killed and mutilated in midstream. Now these troopers had a lust to kill.

Cook's surviving warriors were beside themselves, their only desire being to get to the Germans along the road embankment who had been and were spewing bullets toward them. Temporarily, ingrained fear vanished. All along the bank, rallied by junior officers and noncoms, the All-Americans deployed as skirmishers and headed for the big embankment, some 400 yards away over barren flatland. Now the German fire became even more murderous, but the troopers, cursing and yelling, trudged

Chaplain Delbert A. Kuehl.
(Louis Hauptfleisch)

Pfc. John R. Towle. *(Lou Varrone)*

onward, firing their BARs and rifles from the hip. Here and there, men grunted and dropped in their tracks.

All the while, the Churchill tanks and Ed Wellem's paratroopers on the other shore were blasting the *Feldgrau* ensconced along the embankment. Finally, the troopers charged the enemy's line of foxholes, and with savage cries began bayonetting and pitching grenades. No prisoners were taken. Those Germans who survived fled amidst a hail of American bullets. The menacing road embankment now belonged to Julian Cook's troopers— or what remained of them. But the death struggle for the Waal was only at its halfway mark: The north end of the Nijmegen bridge was still two miles to the east—and in German hands.

37
Triumph at Nijmegen

It was 4:45 P.M. Crouching in a ditch, Rube Tucker radioed a message to the 82nd Airborne command post: "Regiment across river. Advancing [eastward] toward bridge." Gavin was not at home. Earlier in the afternoon he had placed the Waal crossing in the hands of Tucker and had rushed to Beek, two miles southeast of Nijmegen, and to Mook; seven miles south of the Waal bridge, where Lindquist's 508th and the remainder of Ekman's 505th regiments were under fierce attack. If those towns fell, disaster could ensue for the All-Americans struggling to capture the Waal bridge.

Meanwhile, Julian Cook's parachutists, led by Capts. Thomas M. Burriss and Carl W. Kappel, battled the *Feldgrau* through orchards, down ditches, and from one house to the next one. There had been no time to reorganize, so there was little semblance to company formations. Rather, the All-Americans bounced ahead in small, mixed groups. Bullets were whizzing past as the Germans turned their attention first to one pack, then to another.

Julian Cook and Henry Keep were leading one band of about 30 men in a dash across an open field when enemy machine gunners opened up on them. A private leaped for a nearby foxhole, Cook plopped in on top of him, and then Keep dived in. There were three layers of bodies in a foxhole built for one. On the bottom, the smothered trooper was yelling for the other two to get off of him, an act that wild horses could not force them to perform. German lead was still zipping past the hole. Despite the clear peril, Cook and Keep broke out in gales of laughter over their curious predicament.

When the ambitious *Feldgrau* machine gunners let up, Cook, Keep and the squashed private wriggled out of the excavation and resumed the advance. All around could be heard the sounds of fierce skirmishes. One group of troopers was pinned down by Germans, armed with Schmeissers, who were holed up in the draw-bridged medieval Fort Hof van Holland. A sergeant swam the stinking moat, surprised and seized the Germans at the entrance, and waved his comrades on over the drawbridge. They rapidly mopped up the fortification.

By late afternoon, Cook's paratroopers had bottled up some 260 *Feldgrau* at the north end of the big highway bridge and accounted for them to a man. Cook radioed Rube Tucker that the "German side" of the bridge had been seized and the tanks could start rolling over the span—the lifeline to Arnhem.

At about the same time that Cook sent his signal, Ben Vandervoort in Nijmegen got the word: "Go for the bridge!" From a vantage point in a second-story window 20 feet above ground, Vandervoort and his company commanders looked down on Huner Park and its network of German dugouts bristling with automatic weapons and antitank guns. Roughly one-quarter mile square, the park was relatively barren and covered with well-kept, close- cropped grass. "A bare-assed prospect!" one captain muttered.

Again, there was no tactical plan, no time for flanking maneuvers and decoy operations. Rather two companies of paratroopers and Goulburn's tanks would simply rush the bridge—right through Huner Park. Just before 6:00 P.M., under the cover of a blistering fusillade of fire from troopers in second story windows, 280 All-Americans, along with Churchill tanks—four abreast—

charged the German positions, shooting and yelling. This was the moment of truth. Should Vandervoort's men fail, Market-Garden would fail—and Rube Tucker's Five-O-Fours would be cut off on the German side of the Waal.

Capt. Fritz Euling's resolute SS men never budged, but loosed withering bursts of machine-gun and rifle fire, most of it directed at the oncoming iron monsters. Sparks from ricocheting bullets bounced off the Churchill like fireflies. Huner Park became a cacophony. The Germans kept firing full bore until they were killed or overrun. Tanks rolled over foxholes and trenches, grinding SS men into pulp, and fired point-blank into air raid shelters. Amidst the earsplitting din of small-arms and tank fire came the sharp cracks of exploding grenades. Here and there, the noise was pierced by the screams of wounded Americans or Germans.

Scrappy Lt. John Dodd, the most beloved young officer in F Company, was leading his men in a charge against a German strong-point when he was caught in the stomach by an exploding 20-millimeter shell. That should have killed Dodd instantly, but the boyish-faced lieutenant died hard. The platoon medic rushed to his stricken leader and, with tears in his eyes, gave him a double shot of morphine to ease the excruciating pain. A few minutes later John Dodd, barely old enough to vote, was dead. Infuriated, his platoon charged and overran the SS gun that had killed the lieutenant. The troopers took no prisoners.

It was a fight to the death, dog-eat-dog, a bloody clash of elite adversaries—SS troops against American paratroopers supported by British tanks. In the slaughterhouse, men on both sides became crazed. One SS man dashed from his foxhole and knifed an American paratrooper who was bending over and giving first aid to a badly wounded German.

Ben Vandervoort, who was in the thick of the action, recalled that savage fight in once peaceful and pristine Huner Park:

> No quarter was asked by either side and none was given. The fight was so close and intense that individual Germans were either too brave or too scared to surrender. They seemed indifferent to death. Our paratroopers reacted with ice-cold ruthlessness in a gladiatorial test of wills. Finally, the SS troops broke, and those who could, ran east and west and some actually jumped into the Waal River. Thirty minutes after the jumpoff, resistance at the south end of the bridge had been neutralized.

Now the first few British tanks rumbled onto the bridge and started to cross. Would the span blow up with the Churchills and their crews on it? That was precisely what Gen. Heinz Harmel planned to do, and through binoculars he observed the bridge from a half-mile away. With him was an engineer with a detonator box connected by wires to demolitions on the bridge.

"Let it blow!" Harmel shouted. The engineer slammed down the plunger. No explosion. The British tanks rolled onward. "Hit it again!" Harmel roared. Down went the plunger. No gigantic explosion. No British tanks plunging into the Waal amidst twisted girders. Nothing. In Harmel's mind, German disaster loomed: There was little to keep the Guard's Armoured Division from barreling on the 11 miles to Arnhem.[1]

Fred Baldino, a Five-O-Four veteran, recalled those dramatic moments:

> I was crouched in a foxhole at the north end of the bridge. It has been reported many times that we waved an American flag to our comrades [Ben Vandervoort's troopers] on the south side of the bridge for the tanks to come across. Actually, some of our fellows had wigwagged whatever pieces of cloth they could get their hands on. We greeted the first British tanks enthusiastically, and one trooper actually kissed the leading tank.

At about the same time that Julian Cook's paratroopers had been paddling over the fire-swept Waal, the final curtain was falling on a melodrama of high courage and devotion to duty that had been unfolding at the Arnhem bridge. John Frost and his decimated battalion of Red Devils, whose mission was to hold for 48 hours, had been surrounded and battered relentlessly since the evening of D-Day.

After four horrible days and nights, Frost had only about 100 men remaining—exhausted, nerve-shattered men, many burned and many wounded, including Frost himself. They had been through possibly more concentrated hell than any Allied unit had yet endured on the Western Front. There had been day-long, night-long fights against swarms of panzers and far larger numbers of Germans.

Frost and his Red Devils were barricaded in a few buildings at the bridge entrance. Basements were jammed with mutilated and bloody men. Shells and "Screaming Meemies" (multibarreled

Vehicles roll across bitterly contested Nijmegen bridge. *(U. S. Army)*

mortars the Germans called *Nebelwerfers*) exploded almost constantly.[2]

Finally, the British enclave buildings were set afire, and the burning timbers crashed down onto the wounded Red Devils. Ammo and food were exhausted. Blood-covered, ashen-faced, racked with pain, John Frost surrendered the bruised remnant of his battalion.[3]

John Frost recalled Field Marshal Walther Model's rapid response to the gigantic Allied airborne assault:

> *Since the war there has been endless conjecture that the Germans had been tipped off in advance by a spy, and that the Germans had found the entire plan for Operation Market in the wreckage of a glider on D-Day, and therefore, knew where and when we were coming.*
>
> *For many years after the war, I had conversations and exchanged letters with two of the German commanders on the scene, Gen. Heinz Harmel of the 10th SS Panzer Division and Col. Walter Harzer of the 9th SS Panzer Division. Each one declared that the first the Germans had known about the [Market] operation was when the Holland skies were filled with parachutes. Nor have I*

ever talked to any German commander in Holland who knew anything about our operational plan being found in a wrecked glider.

Back at the Nijmegen bridge, dawn of September 21 broke over a grotesque scene that could have come from Dante's inferno. Perhaps 200 Germans had been trapped in the center of the massive structure when both ends had been secured by American paratroopers. Like animals in a tangled jungle seeking to escape approaching hunters, German soldiers had scrambled high into the steel girders of the great bridge. From these vantage points, they continued to pepper with rifles and Schmeissers the tanks and vehicles crossing the bridge.

All through the night, American paratroopers at both ends of the bridge sprayed the upper girders with bullets and heard occasional sickening thuds when an unseen German plunged 100 feet to the span's roadway. In daylight, it was a grotesque and gruesome sight. Intertwined throughout the girders dangled scores of corpses in gray-green uniforms, looking for all the world like hideous gargoyles, glaring menacingly at passersby far below.

Early that morning, Jim Gavin jeeped over the bridge and on to Rube Tucker's command post in a small schoolhouse 1,000 yards north of the river. The 504th leader was belching fire when Gavin walked through the door. "What in the hell are they doing?" Tucker barked. "We've been here for 12 hours, and all they seem to be doing is brewing tea! Why in the hell don't they get to Arnhem?"[4]

Gavin had never seen his old pal Rube so furious. The young general merely shrugged, then departed to recross the Waal and try to find out the reason why the British tanks were sitting idle north of the bridge.

Meanwhile that morning, German forces struck back at Tucker's defensive positions in an effort to recapture the bridge. One company of Five-O-Fours, still exhausted from their ordeal of the previous 48 hours, heard ominous sounds and from their shallow holes on the flatlands saw two Mark VI tanks and an armored halftrack rumbling toward them. Eyes riveted to the menacing gun barrels that any split second could blow them to bits, the parachutists watched in terrified helplessness. Perhaps most or all of them would be dead in minutes.

Conjecture raced along the line of American foxholes: Would

the enemy tankers, no doubt furious over the loss of the Waal bridge, wipe out the depleted company of parachutists or give them a chance to surrender? At that point, teenaged Pvt. John R. Towle came dashing up with his bazooka. A native of Cleveland, the dark-haired, slender Towle was deeply devout and mild mannered—the type that battle-hardened veterans had doubted could hold up in the crucible of combat.

Towle had joined the 504th in Italy, and now it was both his fate and luck to be the only bazooka man in Company F with any ammunition. The youth quickly climbed a road embankment and peeked at the panzers, then slid back down and prophetically quipped: "Well, I see I'm going to get the Congressional Medal of Honor today!" Then the boy crawled back up with his bazooka to confront the panzers.

Now a new menace reared its head: About 100 grenadiers broke out of the woods behind the German tanks and headed for Company F positions. An enemy breakthrough could result in the loss of the Nijmegen bridge and disastrous consequences.

Johnny Towle fired his bazooka, slid down the embankment to reload, then crawled up to another point and let loose a couple of more rounds. Meanwhile, the panzers, like prehistoric monsters swatting at an irritating bee, concentrated their 88 and machine-gun fire on this pesky paratrooper. Whenever he stuck his metal pipe over, the tanks sniped at him at point-blank range. However, Towle's rockets struck both panzers, disabling them, and they limped away like wounded beasts.

Then Towle, fully exposed and peppered by small-arms fire, moved to one flank and began dueling with nine Germans holed up in a house. With one bazooka round, he killed all of the *Feldgrau*. Meanwhile, other F Company men had been blasting the oncoming grenadiers.

Now the one-man army hurriedly replenished his ammunition, and rushed for 100 yards through enemy fire to a point where he could take on the enemy halftrack with his rocket launcher. Out in the open, Towle kneeled to fire. A mortar shell exploded next to him, and the boy fell over dead. Had he lived for a few more minutes, Johnny Towle would have seen the surviving grenadiers pulling back from the battlefield.[5]

Finally, on Friday (D-Day plus 5), after a delay of nearly two days, Guards Armored Division tanks, in tandem with foot soldiers of the British 43rd Division, clanked off for Arnhem. A short distance up Hell's Highway, German tanks and self-propelled guns were awaiting them. The British advance ground to a halt.

Benjamin Vandervoort recalled his feelings at the time:

Whomever was to blame for failure of the Guards to barrel on to Arnhem as soon as the Nijmegen bridge was in our hands, it sure as hell was not the Tommy tanker nor the battalion-level and junior officers. The Guards were grand soldiers and proud of their role in the Nijmegen show, and rightly so. They were the only tanks we [paratroopers] ever worked with in the war that we did not have to give an occasional goose.

Some 15 miles south of the Nijmegen bridge that same day, a vicious fight erupted along Hell's Highway in the thin corridor defended by Max Taylor's 101st Airborne Division. When the Germans struck near Veghel in an all-out effort to cut the lifeline road, Iron Mike Michaelis and a group of key officers were discussing the situation under a large tree. A lone shell screamed in, and when the smoke had cleared, all of the Screaming Eagles were sprawled on the ground.

Michaelis had been seriously wounded, and his orderly, Pfc. Garland E. Mills, was dead beside him. Other wounded officers included three of Michaelis' staff, the division G-2 and G-3, the commander of the 377th Parachute Field Artillery Battalion and a forward observer, and the leader of the 1st Battalion of the 501st Regiment, Lt. Col. Patrick Cassidy.

It had been a devastating blow to the Screaming Eagle leadership. Replacing Michaelis as commander of the 502nd was Lt. Col. Steve Chappuis, the battle-tested leader of the 2nd Battalion. Chappuis and the Five-O-Deuce would have their hands full. The Germans succeeded in cutting Hell's Highway for nearly five days before being evicted.[6]

On September 25, the British tragedy at Arnhem began its final act before an admiring worldwide audience kept informed by a clutch of United Kingdom reporters who had landed with the Red Devils. Out of ammunition, food, and medical supplies, the remainder of Roy Urquhart's 1st Airborne Division men were bottled up in and around Oosterbeek, two miles west of Arnhem, with their backs to the Rhine.

Urquhart radioed: "All will be ordered to break out in small groups rather than surrender. We have done our best. We will continue to do our best."[7]

Under cover of darkness that night, the Red Devils began crossing the Rhine to the south bank in small boats. Out of Urquhart's total force of 8,905 officers and men and about 1,100 glider pilots (who had been fighting as infantrymen), 2,163 of them got to the south bank. It had, simultaneously, been one of British history's most stunning battlefield debacles and glorious epics of courage.[8]

Operation Market-Garden crunched to a halt just short of the Arnhem bridge. A high price had been paid for the 55-mile salient into Holland. In addition to Urquhart's losses, Sosabowski's 1st Polish Parachute Brigade (which had jumped south of the Rhine opposite Oosterbeek) lost in excess of 1,000 men, and Gavin's 82nd Airborne and Taylor's 101st Airborne Divisions had, respectively, 1,669 and 2,074 men killed, wounded, or missing. Altogether, between September 17 and 30, about one-third of the 34,876 Allied airborne men who had descended on Holland from Eindhoven to Arnhem were casualties.

Outside Paris at Versailles, where hundreds of impeccably tailored SHAEF officers were ensconced in a palace complex, the mood was one of disbelief and shock. How could this setback in Holland have happened? The Germans apparently did not know that for several weeks now high-ranking SHAEF officers had been telling the press that the Wehrmacht was nearly ready to collapse.

In the days ahead, the British steadily widened the Hell's Highway corridor, so early in October, Taylor's 101st Airborne and Gavin's 82nd Airborne were leapfrogged northward and into defensive positions between the Waal River at Nijmegen and the Rhine at Arnhem. There, until the crucially needed Belgian port of Antwerp were to be seized by British armor and infantry, the two elite American divisions would fight as straight infantry.

The first few days of fighting in "The Island" (as the paratroopers named it) was heavy and quite costly, especially for the men of the 101st Airborne. Late on the afternoon of October 6, Col. Howard Jumpy Johnson, the flamboyant leader of the 501st Parachute Infantry, was inspecting frontline positions. With him was Lt. Richard O. Snodgrass, a company commander. Soon the familiar rustling sound was heard of a large-caliber incoming shell. Everyone scrambled for ditches and holes—except for Johnson.

Looking down on the others, who had used the good sense gained in heavy combat, Jumpy laughed and kidded them, not knowing that racing his way was a second shell with his name on it. A loud explosion, then a white-hot jagged fragment ripped into the colonel's spine. Johnson was rushed to a hospital at Nijmegen, and en route he whispered hoarsely to one of his officers: "Take care of my boys!" Moments later, the seemingly indestructible Howard Johnson died.

Replacing the officer who had trained and led the 501st since its birth was 28-year-old, lanky Lt. Col. Julian Ewell, an officer of keen mind and droll wit who commanded the 3rd Battalion.[9]

Fighting on The Island was nasty—Anzio all over again. Static warfare. Freezing weather, sheets of rain, foxholes half-filled with cold water, endless night patrols, feet and legs blown off by fiendish *Schu* mines, cold C rations—and always the specter of sudden death. Relentlessly, shells screamed into the troopers' foxhole line, and soon men began to duck and cringe at even the slightest sound.

It was during this period that the 82nd Airborne's Lone Raider, Ted Bachenheimer, vanished while behind German lines. Later, his body would be recovered. The curly haired youngster would never know that his commission as a second lieutenant had come through. Bachenheimer's death spread a pall of gloom over the entire division.[10]

The Island held no favorites, regardless of rank. On November 9, a shell burst near Max Taylor, the head Screaming Eagle, and fragments were imbedded in his posterior, hospitalizing him for a week. Like any wound, it was painful, but Taylor would quip that the main injury was to his dignity.

Bitter skirmishing on The Island dragged on into mid-November, when the 82nd Airborne was relieved after 57 days of unrelenting violence since D-Day for Market. However, the 101st Airborne men had to remain in position until November 27—D-Day plus 71. By truck and by train, the All-Americans and the Screaming Eagles were pulled back to billets around historic Rheims, France.

Airborne officers there had the opportunity to add up the heavy casualties that each division had suffered on The Island. Max Taylor's unit had taken 1,682 casualties of all types, while Jim Gavin's outfit was jolted with 1,912 men killed, wounded, and missing.

Just before leaving Holland, Julian Ewell conducted a memorial ceremony on the outskirts of Nijmegen where men of the 501st Parachute Infantry Regiment who had been killed in Holland were buried. There were row after row of white crosses, each one representing a youth who had once been so anxious to get home to his loved ones.

Catholic and Protestant chaplains said brief prayers, and Ewell spoke a few words of sincere appreciation for those who had made the supreme sacrifice. Then he called out each of their names, and taps echoed in the distance.

Julian Ewell had arranged for a wreath of flowers to be placed on each grave. After the ceremony, he walked to Col. Howard Johnson's grave and picked up a carnation from it. Seeing that a few officers were watching, he walked over to them and said: "I guess I'm getting a little soft, but I thought Howard's wife might like to have it."[11]

38
America's First Black Paratroopers

In November 1944, while battle-weary men of the 82nd and 101st Airborne Divisions were enduring the brutality and miserable weather of The Island in Holland, back in Camp Mackall, North Carolina, a group of American paratroopers known as the "Triple Nickels" were eagerly anticipating an early crack at Hitler's legions. Superbly conditioned and tough (most of them were athletes), these men were pioneers, blazing the trail for countless others. They belonged to the just-activated 555th Parachute Infantry Company—America's first all-black paratroop unit.

So far during the global conflict, the War Department had been reflecting the deep-seated racial prejudices among citizens in a large part of the nation and segregating white and black soldiers. Many senior officers in Washington clung to the lingering view that blacks could not or would not fight for their country—and most certainly, they would be unwilling to jump out of airplanes.

With mobilization, the number of blacks in the army had grown to some 700,000 by mid-1944—an army in itself. Most of the blacks were draftees, who had no more liking for military discipline and the flea bites of army life than did white soldiers. One black wore a star (Brig. Gen. Benjamin O. Davis), and 5,000 black officers had been commissioned—none of whom would command white troops.[1] Proportionately few blacks had been put in combat units; most had been relegated to other chores (labor, kitchen, laundry, trucks, stevedores). The exceptions to this had good combat records: the 99th Pursuit Squadron in Tunisia and Sicily; the 93rd Infantry Division, fighting on Bougainville, and now the 555th Parachute Infantry Company.

It had been mellow Gen. Ben Davis, a respected regular of 43 years, who unswervingly insisted that blacks be given the chance to fight, which had tilted (at least partially) War Department thinking in that direction. The Army had never wanted or hoped to solve America's race problem. That was a job for the nation as a whole. All the Army hoped to do was to make and keep its civilians in uniform good soldiers for the duration.

Toward that end, the War Department in 1942 had set up an Advisory Committee on Special Troops Policies (special troops was a term meaning "blacks"). Among committee members were Assistant Secretary of War John McCloy, General Davis, and William Henry Hastie, a black former U.S. district judge and head of Howard University School of Law. Later, Hastie would resign, claiming that the Army had not lived up to its promise to give blacks more vital jobs to perform.

One of the Advisory Committee's recommendations was that qualified black soldiers be assigned to combat units previously restricted to whites. Another was a recommendation that "an all-Negro parachute battalion be formed." Chief of Staff George Marshall ordered activation of the "555th Parachute Infantry Company (colored)," as it was officially designated, but it was not until December 30, 1943, that the all-black paratroop unit actually became a reality. At that time, its members began jump training at Fort Benning. These black pioneers were all handpicked, exceptional men: college graduates, outstanding athletes, top-notch noncoms from the regular army.

In January 1944, 1st Sgt. Walter Morris, a tall, muscular athlete, earned his coveted parachute wings, and became the first black paratrooper. At about the same time, 15 other enlisted men won their wings. It was not until March 4 that the first six officers qualified as jumpers, and they received their wings at a review before Brig. Gen. Ridgley Gaither, commandant of the Parachute School.[2]

Among the first black paratroop officers was Lt. Bradley Biggs, who had grown up in a Newark, New Jersey ghetto, and later played professional football with the New York Brown Bombers. As it developed, that stint on the gridiron may have been a stepping stone to the paratroopers for Biggs. In late 1943, the executive officer at the Parachute School was Lt. Col. Harvey "Jabo" Jablonsky, a former All-American football player at West Point, and Biggs felt that the unspoken gridiron kinship played a role in Jablonsky's accepting the applicant in the paratroops.[3]

During the rugged parachute training at Benning, what rankled the black paratrooper most was to find that he was in a Jim Crow Army. To a man, the Triple Nickels were deeply imbued with black pride, but also with a grim determination to be the best paratroop unit in the army.

Bradley Biggs recalled:

> It wasn't easy. A proud black lieutenant, sergeant, or private with polished boots and paratrooper wings, still had to sit in the back of the bus, use the "colored" toilets and drinking fountains in the railroad stations and theaters, and go out of our way to avoid confrontations with rednecked police in the towns. Black captains and lieutenants found post officers' clubs closed to them. Black sergeants and privates couldn't sit down for a drink in many bars. But we endured it to prove ourselves as paratroopers.

When the 555th Battalion training had been concluded at Benning, a number of black paratroopers went to the post library where they got into a fight with a few straight-legs. A black military policeman appeared, and then the altercation focused on him and the troopers. One word led to a thousand, the MP was backed into a corner and pulled out his .45 Colt, threatening to use it if the parachutists did not stop. His warning went unheeded, so he fired, the bullet striking Trooper Adolph Crisp in the stomach.

Crisp was rushed to the hospital where he lay in serious condition for several days. The night after the shooting, Bradley Biggs and a fellow officer, Lt. Warren C. "Cal" Cornelius, who had been a sergeant in the New Jersey National Guard and a talented light-heavyweight boxer, received word that a potentially nasty episode was brewing.[4] The paratroopers were going to assault the black MP barracks in retaliation for the shooting of Crisp.

Lt. Bradley Biggs, first black paratrooper officer. (*Author's collection*)

Biggs and Cornelius were highly alarmed. This could be precisely the kind of explosive episode that some high-ranking officers in the War Department would use as a reason to scuttle the 555th Parachute Infantry Company and the training of black paratroopers in the foreseeable future.

Bradley Biggs remembered developments:

Cal and I rushed to a big tree where the "raiding party" was to assemble at 8:00 P.M. About 30 or 35 troopers arrived, dressed in fatigues and armed with trench knives, ready for a brawl. Cal and I tried to reason with them. Such an attack would do Crisp no good, and the MP who shot him is being investigated, we pointed out. "If you do this, we're going to be 'dead,'" I told them. "There are people out there just waiting for us to make a mistake. The blacks in the nation are looking for us to succeed. Do you want to let them down?"

The troopers were unconvinced and started toward the MP barracks. Cal and I quickly stepped in front of them. Cal said, "The first one of you to set foot on this sidewalk will get his jaw broken— and anything else Lieutenant Biggs and I can get our hands on." The crowd just kind of melted away. Crisp recovered completely and returned to duty.

By mid-1944, the 555th Parachute Infantry Company (colored) was shifted to the Airborne Center at Camp Mackall and redesignated the 555th Parachute Infantry Battalion. In the official orders, the "colored" had been replaced by an asterisk, and at the bottom of each page, beside an asterisk, were the words: "Negro personnel." Triple Nickel strength was now 11 officers and 165 enlisted men, hardly battalion size. The commanding officer was a captain, James H. Porter of New York City, who had previously been a lieutenant and platoon leader when the Triple Nickels were a company.[5]

At Mackall, the 555th engaged in intensive unit combat training, and its strength grew to over 400 men. Some of the new arrivals had seen combat in Europe and the Pacific, and before reaching Mackall had qualified as paratroopers at Benning. Like their white counterparts, the Triple Nickels were a close-knit outfit with enormous paratrooper pride. Even though public recognition was largely limited to the civilian black press and the post newspapers, the Triple Nickels gained considerable attention in towns around Mackall. Most people there had never heard of, much less seen, a black paratrooper.

Since D-Day in Normandy, the Triple Nickels had been closely monitoring the fierce and bloody battles that had been raging in Europe, and they were aware that by November 1944, General Eisenhower had grown desperate for replacements for his depleted ranks. Now, the Triple Nickels were convinced, they were going to get to tangle with Adolf Hitler, whose snubbing of the great black American track star, Jesse Owens, in the 1936 Olympics was still fresh in their minds.

Jim Porter and Bradley Biggs and Cal Cornelius and "Killer" Kane and "Tiger Ted" Lowry were ready to take on all Axis com-

ers. But that was not to be the Triple Nickels' destiny. Orders
were received for the battalion to report to Pendleton Air Base,
Pendleton, Oregon, for a "highly classified mission" with the U.S.
Ninth Service Command. No one in the 555th was aware that the
paratroopers would be a major component in an operation code-
named "Firefly."

Captain Porter and his troopers would be called on to fight
forest fires that were raging in the heavily timbered Northwest.
Teams of paratroopers, equipped with special firefighting equipment, would drop near the blazes and try to extinguish them. It
would be a hazardous mission, for small bands of paratroopers
could easily become trapped in the center of the conflagration.

Official Washington gave no reason for the forest fires that
were destroying tens of thousands of acres of land in Oregon,
Idaho, Washington, and northern California. Privately, a handful
of government men in the capital knew the true reason: Since
November 3, 1944, the Japanese had been launching balloon-
borne bombs into the high altitude winds of the jet stream across
the Pacific. A unique mechanism caused the balloons to land in
America's Northwest and triggered incendiary bombs. Japanese
military officers hoped that the balloon-borne bombs would
create widespread panic.

Made of paper stuck together with paste made from potatoes,
the balloons were 30 feet across, 70 feet high and filled with hy-
drogen. One bomb was found in a Detroit suburb, another fell
on a street in Medford, Oregon. Near Bly, Oregon, a woman and
five children on a picnic were killed when they apparently tam-
pered with a fallen balloon loaded with bombs.

Japanese warlords in far-off Tokyo would have been delighted had they known how close one of their balloon-borne
bombs had come to inflicting a calamity on the United States. A
balloon loaded with explosives got tangled in power lines just
outside a supersecret plant near Hanford, Washington, where
fuel was being refined for a revolutionary device known as an
atomic bomb. A short-circuit in the power for the nuclear reactor
cooling pumps ensued, but backup devices restored power
rapidly. Had the cooling system been off much longer, a reactor
might have collapsed or exploded.

When the 555th Parachute Battalion reached Pendleton, its
dynamic operations officer, Lt. Edwin H. Wills of Zacata, Virginia, set up a crash three-week course in forest-fire fighting by
parachute. It included demolitions training, tree-climbing tech-

niques, handling fire equipment, jumping into pocket-size drop zones studded with rocks and tree stumps, and survival in heavily timbered and mountainous locales far from civilization.

Then the Triple Nickels began work with bomb disposal experts of the Ninth Service Command, learning the touchy business of dismantling live explosives. Several paratroopers with infantry bomb training and graduates of the parachute demolitions school at Benning served as assistant instructors.

Soon the entire battalion had qualified as parachute firefighters and gained the temporary nickname "Smoke Jumpers." In the weeks ahead, the black paratroopers jumped into tiny clearings in dense, mountainous forest of the Pacific Northwest to bring under control roaring conflagrations. It was dangerous, exhausting, but vital work. However, the Triple Nickels, to a man, were deeply disappointed that they would never have a chance to tangle with the Germans or the Japanese. Not until five years later, when Uncle Sam would go to war in a country called Korea, would black American paratroopers be able to demonstrate to the world that they could perform with great esprit and distinction on the battlefield.[6]

PART V

The Boys of Winter

39
A Mad Rush
to Belgium

Early in November 1944, paratrooper James W. Collins was lounging on his cot in a brick barracks in a German prisoner of war compound at Furstenberg, near Frankfurt. Kentuckian Collins, one of 13 children, had been captured back in Tunisia while fighting with the pioneer 509th Parachute Infantry Battalion against Rommel's Afrika Korps. Furtively, a fellow POW slipped up to Collins and whispered: "Just got word over the grapevine—the Krauts are going to demand we give 'em our uniforms."

As had been forecast by the clandestine American intelligence unit in Stalag 3B, a Nazi officer entered Collins' barracks 18 hours later and announced that uniforms were to be deposited in a pile on the floor. Forewarned, the POWs, one by one, walked to the designated spot and put down their garments, which, a day earlier, they had slashed into ribbons.

The red-faced German *Hauptmann* (captain) stared at the stack of countless bits and pieces of olive-drab material, then turned on his heel and stomped out of the barracks. Jim Collins and his comrades broke out in wide smiles of triumph, aware only that they had thwarted some devious German machination. But the POWs had no way of knowing that the Nazis had planned to use their uniforms to garb bona fide German soldiers who would infiltrate American lines to create mass havoc and confusion in a gigantic offensive code-named *Wacht am Rein* (Watch on the Rhine).

Wacht am Rein would be Adolf Hitler's final roll of the dice to snatch victory out of the jaws of defeat from the Western Allies. Speed and surprise would be crucial, so the Führer would strike at the most unlikely sector on the 500-mile front—the Ardennes region of Belgium and Luxembourg.

The picturesque Ardennes had been so tranquil in recent weeks that it had gained the label "Ghost Front." Both sides used the Ghost Front to rest exhausted and depleted divisions and to get new outfits blooded.

Sparsely populated, hilly, heavily timbered, and crisscrossed with deep gorges, the Ardennes had few roads capable of supporting the tanks and vehicles of a modern army. Aside from the "impassable" terrain, the fact that the Ardennes did not hold a single major military objective had caused Allied brass to largely discount a German threat in this region.

However, Hitler's focus was not on the Ardennes, but on Antwerp, some 90 miles to the northwest. If the Führer's legions could capture Antwerp, it would be a debacle of enormous proportions for the overconfident Western Allies, the Führer told his generals. The front would be split between the Americans and the British to the north, the Allies would be deprived of their principal supply port, and the bloodshed and carnage would be so immense that there would be cries in the United States and in England for a negotiated peace with the Nazi warlord.[1]

Feverish planning under the tightest security measures continued in Berlin into early December. Meanwhile, Eisenhower had moved SHAEF forward to the historic cathedral city of Rheims, northeast of Paris. Nearby Epernay was home base for Matt Ridgway's XVIII Airborne Corps, and billeted for the winter in villages and towns in the locale were nearly all of the American airborne outfits in the ETO.

After three months of fighting in the Maritime Alps following the August invasion of southern France, the 509th and 551st Parachute Infantry Battalions, the 517th Parachute Regimental Combat Team, and the 463rd Parachute Field Artillery had been brought northward by rail and vehicle. A short time later, they were joined by Gavin's 82nd Airborne and Taylor's 101st Airborne from Holland.

Perhaps the many thousands of paratroopers had seen their last battle in Europe, for the *Stars and Stripes* regularly carried hints from SHAEF bigwigs that Hitler had squandered his last pool of reserves and the Wehrmacht was on the verge of collapse.

With no foreseeable mission, American airborne brass fled the Continent. In early December, Max Taylor flew to Washington, Matt Ridgway was spending most of his time at the XVIII Airborne Corps rear command post at Wiltshire, England, and Taylor's number 2 man, Gerry Higgins, and five senior officers went to Great Britain for a series of lectures on lessons learned in the Holland operation.

East of the Rhine River on December 12, the Führer gathered all of his field marshals and generals on the Western Front at *Adlerhorst* (Eagle's Nest), his bunker command post near Frankfurt, and dropped his bombshell on them. Three great armies, totaling more than 250,000 men and nearly 1,000 panzers, would strike at the thin American line in the Ardennes along an 80-mile sector between Monschau, Germany, on the north, and Echternach, Luxembourg on the south. *O-Tag* (D-Day) would be December 16.

SS Col. Gen. Josef "Sepp" Dietrich, a burly one-time bullyboy in Hitler's Brownshirts, would lead the Sixth Panzer Army in the north, and the Fifth Panzer Army would be commanded by able Baron Hasso von Manteuffel in the center. In the south would be Gen. Erich Brandenberger's Seventh Army, consisting mainly of infantry units.

Spearheading the *coup de main* by Sepp Dietrich's army would be the 1st SS Panzer Division, known as the *Leibstandarte Adolf Hitler*. Its leading battle group would be commanded by 29-year-old SS Col. Jochen Peiper, a hard- nosed, driving officer who had gained the Führer's admiration and wide renown in the Third Reich for his daring panzer forays in Russia.

Peiper's mission was to bolt through a hole torn into American lines near Monschau, reach Liège (some 30 miles to the northwest) at the end of O-Tag, cross the Meuse near Liège on the following morning, and race on to Antwerp.

Breathing the fire of bygone days of heady German victories, Hitler exhorted his commanders to give their all for the Fatherland. Said the Führer:

> *This battle is to decide whether we shall live or die. I want all my soldiers to fight hard and without pity. The battle must be fought with brutality and all resistance must be broken in a wave of terror. . . . The enemy must be beaten—now or never!*

Meanwhile, the citizens of Bastogne, a quiet little town in the Ardennes whose origins go back to medieval times, had been growing apprehensive, convinced that a calamity was about to strike them. In the marketplace and around the countryside, frightened neighbors whispered that the dreaded Hun was coming back—and soon.

Bastogne knew what it was like to be trampled by armies from the east. German legions pounded through Bastogne in 1870, again in 1914, and for the third time in 1940. Now the villagers were telling of seeing "strange lights" in the fields around Bastogne in the stillness of the night, and of sinister-looking men in civilian garb who, the townspeople were convinced, were German agents.

In desperation, a delegation of Bastogne citizens called at Troy Middleton's VIII Corps headquarters, located in the town, and relayed their fears to two polite, but bored staff captains. Assured that their suspicions would be investigated, the partly relieved group departed. As the Belgians closed the door behind them, one of the American captains pointed to his head, winked at his fellow officer, and said: "Spy mania." The two men went back to playing cards.

Early in the evening of December 17, 82nd Airborne commander Jim Gavin (recently promoted to major general) was enjoying a leisurely meal with his staff and a few guests at his quarters in Sissonne. An urgent radio call came from Doc Eaton, XVIII Corps chief of staff: The Germans had made a massive breakthrough, and the 82nd and 101st Airborne Divisions had been ordered by SHAEF to move out for Belgium within 24 hours of daylight the next day, December 18th.

Then Eaton threw in a shocker: Matt Ridgway was in England and Max Taylor in the States, so Gavin was now the acting corps commander.[2]

It troubled the young general that no one had informed him that both Ridgway and Taylor were gone. But he was even more disturbed by the fact that there were no existing plans for the airborne corps' movement.

At 9:30 P.M., Doc Eaton called again: SHAEF now directed that the 82nd and 101st move without delay in the direction of Bastogne, where further orders would be issued. Gavin decided that his All-Americans would lead the long, frigid trek to Belgium, followed by the Screaming Eagles, who were now commanded by Tony McAuliffe in the absence of Taylor and Gerry Higgins.

Eaton's order had been sent in the clear, and Wehrmacht wireless intercept services picked it up. A short time later, Lt. Gen. Heinrich von Lüttwitz, leader of the XXXXVII Korps of Manteuffel's Fifth Panzer Army, returned from a tour of the front east of Bastogne and was handed a translation of the Gavin-Eaton discussion.

Large, paunchy, and seldom seen without his monocle, Lüttwitz was delighted. His crack Panzer Lehr Division was only 10 miles from Bastogne and clanking onward, impeded only by a German infantry division that was clogging the same road. "We will beat them to Bastogne," Lüttwitz declared.

A daring battle leader, Lüttwitz was euphoric over other crucial factors. "If the Americans have to use two elite airborne divisions as regular ground soldiers, that means they cannot have reserves left," he told his staff. "And it means we won't have to worry about paratroop drops in our rear."[3]

Hard on the heels of Doc Eaton's call to Gavin, a frantic scramble to leave for Belgium erupted among the airborne units. The independent parachute outfits—the 509th and 551st Battalions and the 517th Regimental Combat Team—were alerted to move out on two hours' notice as soon as trucks could be scraped up.

At Mourmelon, the entire 501st regimental band descended upon the unit's Catholic chaplain, Capt. Francis Sampson. These frustrated paratrooper musicians had been the constant butt of jibes for having been left out of both the Normandy and the Holland operations. "Father," their spokesman said, "we've been ordered to stay behind again. We joined the paratroopers to fight." Sampson, suspecting he was supposed to give them the green light to disobey orders, replied with an inquisitive, "So?"

"Well, how about our jumping on some trucks when they pull out?" Sympathetic to their views, the chaplain shrugged. But at least he didn't say no.

Later, each 501st rifle company would find that one or two band members had mysteriously appeared in its frontline positions in Belgium, where several of the parachute musicians would be wounded. And all of them would gain what they sought most—the respect of their comrades.

With no combat action in sight, large numbers of paratroopers were on pass, in Paris, Rheims, Mourmelon, Laon, Sissonne, Suippes, and other cities. Military police were ordered to round up the parachutists—some of whom had to be poured onto trucks—and rush them back to their camps.

Lt. Ralph Allison of Graves' 517th Parachute Infantry was in Paris on a vital mission: collecting the regiment's liquor ration. Stranded, Allison promptly "requisitioned" a large, open-top staff car from the Seine Base Area motor pool and sped off for Belgium—liquor and all.

A few hundred miles to the south, Trooper Virgil Dorr of Joerg's 551st Parachute Infantry Battalion was enjoying the winter on the French Riviera. When his outfit had moved north in early December, Dorr had been left behind in a Nice hospital, recuperating from broken ribs. Learning that his comrades were heading into a desperate fight in Belgium, Dorr stole a pass from the hospital and filled it in, showing that he had been discharged (although his torso was still tightly bandaged). Then he caught rides on trains and trucks to Dijon, Lyon, Paris, and finally to Rheims, where he was outfitted and armed.

Not long before the Wehrmacht struck in the Ardennes, Maj. Gen. Bud Miley's 17th ("Thunder from Heaven") Airborne Division had arrived in England, and the troopers settled down for a peaceful and cozy Christmas. Miley, the paratrooper pioneer and one-time star gymnast at West Point, had commanded the 17th Airborne since its activation on April 17, 1943, at Camp Mackall. Now Miley's eager but green parachutists and glider soldiers were rousted from warm beds and began feverish preparations to fly to the Continent. But fate intervened on the side of the Führer: fog and thick clouds would ground aircraft in England for a week.

Chaos reigned among Americans in the Ardennes. From generals to privates, no one knew what was going on. Some officers and men had fled in panic on the approach of German tanks. But other bands of GIs, cut off, outnumbered and bewildered, stood and fought and died, often without even knowing where they were. In many cases, military discipline had vanished, and mass hysteria had taken control.

Hitler had gained total surprise. Baron von Manteuffel's Fifth Panzer Army in the center plunged deep into Belgium. But in the north, Sepp Dietrich, upon whom the Führer had bestowed the honor of raising the Nazi flag over Antwerp, bogged down on O-Tag at Elsenhorn Ridge, only a few miles from jump-off.

All through that long day, Jochen Peiper and his *Kampfgruppe* had waited impatiently for Dietrich's infantry to punch a hole in the thin American line. Peiper fretted and cursed. Why had the *Amis* not collapsed as predicted?

Despite his youth and relatively modest rank, Peiper had been given almost total authority to carry out his mission, upon whose success or failure could rest the destiny of Nazi Germany—and the Führer's neck. By midafternoon of O-Tag, Peiper could wait no longer, so he switched routes and moved southward behind the 3rd Parachute Division, which seemed to be making progress.[4]

At midnight, the German paratroopers climbed onto Peiper's panzers and the combined force lunged forward. Soon, the SS colonel's spearhead scored a complete breakthrough and was racing westward into Belgium, seeking a route to turn northward and cross the Meuse, then roar on to Antwerp.

Peiper's force for the *coup de main* was powerful: some 5,000 men; 72 medium tanks (Mark IVs and Mark Vs); five flak tanks; a battalion with 20 self-propelled, multiple 20-millimeter guns (flakwagons); some 24 self-propelled assault guns; an artillery battalion of 105-millimeter howitzers; 80 halftracks; a battalion of panzer grenadiers; two companies of engineers; a reconnaissance company; and 30 huge, plodding 68-ton Mark VI ("King Tiger") heavy tanks.

Also in Peiper's force were 12 Panther tanks disguised to look like American Shermans, and three jeeploads of Germans dressed as American soldiers, carrying American weapons and riding in American vehicles.

Only five hours after he had been alerted by Doc Eaton at Sissonne, Jim Gavin and two aides climbed into an open jeep and raced into the black, sleeting night toward the famous watering town of Spa, Belgium, where the acting corps commander had been ordered to report to Courtney Hodges, leader of First Army. Within the hour of Gavin's departure, Tony McAuliffe headed for the Ardennes.

Hard on the heels of the two airborne generals, the 82nd Airborne troopers, pawns on the chessboard of high-level strategy, were riding in open cattle trucks toward the unknown in Belgium. All they knew was that they were to be hurled into the path of stampeding German spearheads. Through the black night, they jolted along like herds of sheep bound for the slaughterhouse. They were pelted by icy sheets of rain, and their bones ached from the bitter cold and howling gusts of winter gales.

Finally, the All-Americans reached a grim, moody Belgian crossroads hamlet called Werbomont, 12 miles southeast of Spa, on the cold, foggy and rainy day of December 19. Feet and muscles were numb. Then the troopers began trudging for miles through piles of watery snow. Rube Tucker's Five-O-Fours moved northeasterly toward Rahier and Cheneux, and Bill Ekman's Five-O-Fives hiked eastward in the direction of Trois Ponts on the Salm River. Roy Lindquist's Five-O-Eights headed southeasterly toward Bra and Vielsalm, while Charles Billingslea's 325th Glider Infantry remained at Werbomont in reserve.

In the meantime, after their discussion at First Army headquarters in Spa, Courtney Hodges, and Jim Gavin routed the trailing 101st Airborne Division to Bastogne, 25 miles south of Werbomont. From Bastogne radiated several roads that seemed essential to the advance of the German spearhead.

Julian Ewell and his 501st Parachute Infantry were the first Screaming Eagles to roll into Bastogne, where they were greeted by Tony McAuliffe. Chaplain Francis Sampson asked the droll Ewell: "What's the situation, Colonel?" Replied the lanky Ewell with a poker face: "If I knew anything, I'd merely be confused."

Bastogne was a formidable obstacle in the path of Hasso von Manteuffel's surging Fifth Panzer Army. In the hours and days ahead, vicious fighting raged, and the Screaming Eagles suffered heavy casualties. Among those killed was Lt. Col. James L. LaPrade, leader of Bob Sink's 1st Battalion and one of the more highly regarded young officers in the division.

On the afternoon of December 19, eight GIs in two mud-spattered jeeps bearing the markings of the 28th Infantry Division pulled up before the command post of Rube Tucker's 504th Parachute Infantry in the village of Rahier, eight miles east of Werbomont. Capt. Fordyce Gorham, the regimental S-2, was just coming out of the house, and a captain in the first jeep called to him: "What's the situation around here?"

"Snafu'd as hell!" Gorham replied quite accurately.

The captain in the jeep, wearing a mackinaw and toting an M-1 rifle, asked Gorham how a certain village could be reached. "Can't get there," the Five-O-Four replied. "Bridge's been blown."

The 28th Division officer then bummed a cigarette from Gor-

Men of the 82nd Airborne arrive at Werbomont. (*Pierre Gosset*)

ham, and with a cheery, "Well, good luck, Captain!" drove away.

A short time later, these same two jeeps arrived at a battalion command post along the road to Cheneux, three miles to the northeast. Paratroopers S. Sgt. Edward Lauritsen of Limestone, Maine, and medic Pfc. Theodore Watson of New York watched casually as the newcomers parked their jeeps and struck out on foot in the direction of the oncoming Germans.

Lauritsen hollered a warning, but the men in the GI topcoats paid no heed. Lauritsen and Watson grew suspicious. "Halt!" they yelled. With that, the eight strangers broke into a run, and Lauritsen opened fire with his rifle. A shot apparently struck the captain, for he staggered. But his companions grabbed him and hurried toward a nearby woods.

The shooting attracted the attention of the Five-O-Fours in the command post. "Christ, Lauritsen's gone psycho and is shooting our own guys!" one called out. Lauritsen's comrades were ready to drill him, but held back when the perceptive shooter shouted: "They're Krauts wearing our uniforms!"

In the meantime, Jochen Peiper's *Kampfgruppe,* the spearhead of Sepp Dietrich's Sixth Panzer Army, had fallen far behind its timetable. By now, Peiper was to have been over the Meuse and be roaring hell-bent for Antwerp. But stubborn bands of GIs had thwarted his efforts to swing northward at Malmedy, at Stoumont, and at Stavelot, so he had been forced to continue galloping westward, ever deeper into Belgium, in the hope of finding a route to the Meuse.

40
Collision
with
Kampfgruppe
Peiper

Shortly after daybreak on December 20, Jim Gavin arrived at the 504th Regiment's command post in Rahier. Now he had to be concerned only with the 82nd Airborne because Matt Ridgway had rushed to Belgium from England and established an XVIII Airborne Corps command post in a two-story farmhouse in Werbomont. Rube Tucker told Gavin that he had learned from civilians that a large force of German grenadiers, panzers, and vehicles were in Cheneux, and the two officers concluded that this must be one of Jochen Peiper's spearheads.

Even though Tucker's regiment had no tank support, the colonel was eager to go after the German force in Cheneux. In Holland, the Five-O-Fours had captured a truckload of German *panzerfausts* (bazookas), and with these weapons Tucker felt confident that his troopers could handle the enemy armor. (The panzerfausts were far more powerful than the often ineffective American 2.36-inch bazooka; the German device had six-inch warheads, and could penetrate the front armor of any known tank).

Gavin gave the green light to attack Cheneux, and Tucker designated Lt. Col. Willard Harrison's 1st Battalion to lead the assault.

Just past 1:00 P.M. that day, Cpl. George D. Graves, Jr., of the 504th Regiment's headquarters, was standing beside the road in Rahier and watching Harrison's boys file past on the way to German-held Cheneux. Outwardly, the troopers were in high spirits, talking loudly and laughing to stifle their tensions and to provide saliva for their dry throats. "Only four more shopping days until Christmas—pass it back!" Graves heard one man shout. That seemed like a hell of a good joke, and the marching parachutists roared with hollow laughter. But with each step closer to battle, talk diminished, jokes faded away.

Lt. Robert Magruda, who had just come back from the hospital after having been wounded in Holland, stuck his head in the 504th CP before heading for Cheneux and quipped: "I'm still full of good old penicillin—which is a hell of a way to go into battle!"[1]

Two hours later, forward elements of Harrison's battalion were advancing cautiously down a hilly road that went into Cheneux. Many of the perspiring troopers were veterans, and they didn't like the silence. It looked like a good deal, they knew, not a shot being fired at them—but good deals were what got men killed.

Suddenly, an enormous cacophony erupted from in front of Cheneux where 600 SS grenadiers were dug in and supported by several flakwagons (each mounting a cluster of 20-millimeter

Gen. James Gavin, leader of 82nd Airborne, discusses situation with an officer near Habiemont. *(Pierre Gosset)*

guns), mortars, artillery, and machine guns. Streams of German tracers raced over the landscape, and mortar and artillery shells exploded around and on Harrison's boys. They deployed to each side of the road and began returning the fire.

While the uneven shootout raged (the Americans were only

Troopers of 2nd Battalion, 504th Parachute Infantry, are briefed before attack on Cheneux, Belgium. *(Pierre Gosset)*

lightly armed) somebody hit on the idea of turning a captured German halftrack and its 77-millimeter gun against the enemy force. A call went out for volunteers, and the first trooper to stick his neck out was Pfc. Russell P. Snow of Burbank, California, who was undaunted by an ominous fact: He had never handled any halftrack before, much less a German one. Two members of the 82nd Airborne's antitank unit—Pfc. Harold Kelly of Chicago, and Pfc. Harry Koprowski of Erie, Pennsylvania—agreed to fire the 77.

After a three-minute briefing on driving the German halftrack and firing its gun, Snow maneuvered the vehicle onto the frost-hardened, rutted road, and for two hours the troopers operated their one-vehicle armored force, firing in the direction of the flak wagons and machine guns concealed in thick underbrush and a heavy ground fog. Once the "mechanized parachutists" spotted a column of Germans coming down the road toward B Company. Harold Kelly, at the sight of the weapon, raked the SS troops with shells, forcing them to scatter, then pull back.

Shortly afterward, the Americans' luck ran out. A 20-millimeter shell hit the brace of Kelly's gun, and fragments tore into his face. Racked with pain, his jumpsuit saturated with blood, Kelly collapsed on the bed of the halftrack. At that point, Russ Snow maneuvered his vehicle to get into position against the flakwagon that had hit Kelly, then moved back to take Kelly's place on the gun. Just then, a German halftrack popped up, and Snow fired; the enemy vehicle exploded in a fiery ball.

Meanwhile, their comrades had been engaged in a fierce fight, often at grenade range or closer. Leading a charge against a German flakwagon, a lieutenant was cut down, leaving the group without an officer. Cpl. Curtis Aydelot of Clarksville, Tennessee, leaped into the gap, although he belonged to an intelligence section, and his job was to roll dead Germans for identification papers.

Taking a bazooka man with him, Aydelot skirted the spitting flakwagon and slipped up to it from the flank. Then the two troopers were spotted, and in the shoot-out that followed, Aydelot's helmet was shot off of his head. But the bazooka man fired a rocket into the multiple-weapon vehicle, setting it afire, and the bare-headed Aydelot sprayed it with his tommy gun. None of the German crew survived the encounter.

All along the outskirts of Cheneux, the fighting was vicious. A German firing a flakwagon was wounded, but, leaning over his weapons, he continued to blaze away. Suddenly, a paratrooper charged the flakwagon, yelling, "You Kraut sons of bitches!" jumped onto the vehicle and plunged his trench knife into the SS soldier.

At the 504th Regiment forward command post in Rahier, Capt. Louis A. Hauptfleisch, Tucker's adjutant, looked up as a bloody apparition burst into the house. It was Lt. Bob Magruda, wounded twice more, who had been joking about being full of penicillin only a few hours earlier. "We've been catching hell!" Magruda gasped. "Get some ambulances up there in a hurry!" A few minutes later, Capt. Charles W. Duncan, the 1st Battalion operations officer, entered. An old soldier who had seen much heavy fighting during the war and was noted for his coolness in the heat of battle, said grimly: "We've been cut to pieces!"

As night fell, an eerie silence gripped the scene of bloody strife. Willard Harrison's boys were near exhaustion from the long fight, but now the battalion commander received an order from Tucker: Jump off again at 7:30 P.M. and seize Cheneux.

Harrison's troopers had seen enough that afternoon to know

that this night attack could be a deathtrap. They would have to cross 400 yards of flat, barren terrain—directly into the teeth of spitting flakwagons, dug-in machine guns, and large numbers of rifles. At 50-yard intervals, the fields, devoid of cover or concealment, were crisscrossed with three-strand barbed wire fences.

Waiting for H-hour, the troopers lay immobile in the darkness of a woods, smoking and hiding the glow of cigarettes under blankets. Quietly and with little display of emotion, old comrades clasped hands and whispered good-byes.

Inexorably the seconds ticked past. Then came the order, as orders always will. "Okay, let's go!" As noiselessly as possible in the ominous stillness, the paratroopers got to their feet. Unavoidable crackling of twigs underfoot seemed to echo all the way to Cheneux. Methodically, Harrison's assault companies formed into long skirmish lines. There would be four waves, each about 50 yards apart.

Now the troopers pressed forward. Despite the cold, beads of sweat dotted foreheads. Senses were numbed. Jump boots weighed a ton. Out there in the hush of night, every trooper knew, SS troops had anxious fingers on machine-gun triggers, waiting to commence the slaughter. Now the first skirmish line was halfway across the bald terrain. Neither side had fired a shot.

Suddenly, a terrific racket erupted from the direction of Cheneux, and swarms of 20-millimeter shells, each casting a yellowish glow, raked the naked lines of advancing Americans. Thousands of red tracer bullets hissed angrily across the landscape. Mortar and artillery shells exploded in orange flashes, sending death-dealing chunks of white-hot metal racing in all directions. Scores of Five-O-Fours were cut down as though some supernatural force had swung a gigantic scythe.

German flares burst overhead, turning night into day and sharply silhouetting the Americans into targets. Clumps of bodies were draped over the barbed wire fences, where they were riddled while trying to climb over the obstacles. Above the shattering din came the piercing cries of mutilated paratroopers.

Steadily, Harrison's boys pressed onward into the jaws of death. Technical Sgt. William Walsh of Waunakee, Wisconsin, shouted for his men to keep going, not realizing that most of them were dead or seriously wounded. A short distance ahead, "Knobby" (as comrades called Walsh) discerned a flakwagon spitting out flame. Slithering over the ground to within 30 feet of the vehicle, Walsh was ready to pitch a grenade, when bullets tore into his arm and side. Desperately, the sergeant tried to pull the grenade pin, but could not do so.

Dragging his bloody and useless arm beside him, Walsh crawled back to another trooper and had him remove the pin, then wriggled forward to his former position. In a final burst of strength, Walsh pitched the grenade. Shrieks erupted from the flakwagon, and its gun fell silent. Moments later Bill Walsh blacked out.[2]

Most of the American officers and noncoms had been killed or badly wounded in the face of the murderous fire, and, in many cases, privates were leading decimated squads and mixed packs. Somehow, small bands reached the German main line of resistance. Then, in a scenario reminiscent of a Hollywood war movie, surviving Five-O-Fours, half-crazed from their brutal ordeal, leaped up, let out wild Indian war cries, and charged.

Nearly out of ammo, the paratroopers pounced on the SS troops with trench knives and swinging rifle butts. A private leaped onto a flakwagon that was spurting long lethal fingers of flame and slit the gunner's throat. By 11:00 P.M., Willard Harrison's boys had clawed and scratched their way into the outskirts of Cheneux, and an hour later, they had control of the town.

Reported to have numbered five companies, the SS force had been destroyed or driven off, and a large number of flakwagons, a Mark VI tank, six halftracks, a 105-millimeter howitzer, and a score of machine guns had been captured.

But the savage fight to halt one of Jochen Peiper's columns in its dash for the Meuse had badly mauled Harrison's 1st Battalion. Company B had all of its eight officers and first sergeant killed or wounded, and only 18 troopers survived. Company C had 38 men and three officers left. Altogether, the 504th Regiment had 225 men killed or wounded.

Shortly after dawn, Willard Harrison sat propped against a bale of hay in a barn within Cheneux. Sprawled outside were scores of corpses of American paratroopers and German SS soldiers. A veteran of countless actions, Harrison was staring at the floor and absentmindedly fingering a straw. "You know," he said to a few of his men, "that attack over the open fields and the barbed wire fences was far worse than any nightmare I had ever imagined."

In the wake of the bloodbath, Lt. Vincent E. Voss and Cpl. George Graves, both of the 504th personnel section, struck out on foot for Cheneux to get an estimate of casualties and arrange to remove dead comrades. After walking a mile, they came upon a road junction where five German vehicles had been knocked out.

George Graves remembered the scene:

The surrounding terrain was the worst example I had ever seen of what results when a large number of men are out to kill each other. Broken rifles, loose ammunition, countless helmets, bloody GI clothes and bandages, belts of machine-gun ammo, mortar shells, all sort of miscellaneous items were strewn about the bald hill and ditches along the sides of the road. Dead bodies were everywhere. Living troopers, glassy-eyed and expressionless, were hugging holes scraped out of the banks bordering the road. The overall scene was so sickening that it made you want to shout out to God: "Why was all this necessary?"

At noon on December 22, Julian Cook's 3rd Battalion relieved the tattered remnants of Harrison's outfit. Back they came, bearded, red-eyed, stumbling along listlessly. Only 48 hours earlier, they had gone up this same road, joking and laughing and full of fight. Now the mud-spattered paratroopers had the haunting stare of survivors who had passed through the shadow of the Valley of Death.

While Rube Tucker's troopers were slugging it out with Peiper's SS task forced at Cheneux, 10 miles to the southeast Ben Vandervoort's 2nd Battalion of the 505th marched into nearly deserted Trois Ponts, a rural town of two-story stone houses and small shops. Unbeknownst to Vandervoort, Jochen Peiper also had his eye on Trois Ponts. Through Trois Ponts flows the north-south Salm River, which, north of the town, suddenly takes the name Ambleve. There were two bridges over the Salm and one across the Ambleve. Once Peiper had seized these bridges, it would be clear sailing to the Meuse, and beyond to Antwerp.

However, elements of the 51st Engineer Combat Battalion had earlier blown the span over the Ambleve in the face of a probing Peiper armored patrol, so the bridge over the Salm in Trois Ponts had become crucial to the SS colonel's ambitions. Across the river from Trois Ponts to the east were the Wanne Heights, whose sheer bluffs drop down to the river bank. So vehicles from the east could not enter Trois Ponts except by coming down the steep road carved into the side of the bluff and crossing the Salm bridge.

Sizing up the situation, Vandervoort promptly sent Lt. William J. Meddaugh's E Company over the Salm and onto the 400-foot Wanne Heights bluff to block the road. Rapidly digging in and sowing antitank mines along their front, Meddaugh and his boys knew that their work was cut out for them: The battalion had no tanks, tank-destroyers, or heavy artillery.

Meanwhile, Vandervoort had deployed the remainder of his outfit, together with a platoon of the 307th Airborne Engineers and a group of GI engineers, in the houses on the west bank of the Salm.

Up on the bluff that night, it was eerily silent. Suddenly, just before 3:00 A.M., Meddaugh's boys heard the faint purr of an approaching vehicle, and prepared an ambush. When the scout car neared the American foxhole line, a concealed bazooka team bushwhacked it. The dead Germans and the wreckage were hidden in the woods.

Less than an hour later, a second German armored vehicle, apparently searching for the scout car, blew itself up on a mine in the road.

After daybreak, Ben Vandervoort climbed to an observation post on a high hill, from where he could see the road net to the east and the open fields in front of Meddaugh's company. He saw an alarming sight: panzers and grenadiers were massing in the distance.

Benjamin Vandervoort recalled that episode:

> Prudence dictated that we pull Bill Meddaugh and his company of about 140 officers and men back to more favorable positions on the west bank of the Salm. There the clambake would be on a more equal footing. But [Brigadier] General [Ira P.] Swift, the assistant commander of the 82nd Airborne and new to the paratroops, did not concur. Meddaugh and his men were proud, tough, battle-seasoned soldiers—unless ordered out, they would have stayed until they went down under the treads of Tiger tanks.

Now four or five panzers and flakwagons began pouring lead into Easy Company's positions, and skirmish lines of grenadiers pushed forward. Soon the dull winter sky over the bluffs of Trois

Ponts echoed the harsh clatter of machine-gun fire, the cracks of rifles, and the explosion of shells. The first wave of Germans charged up to Meddaugh's foxhole line and was wiped out to a man.

All that morning heavy fighting raged. Far outnumbered and outgunned, the parachute company was being badly chewed up. As the situation grew from serious to desperate, Vandervoort radioed Bill Ekman, the 505th commander, for permission to send F Company across the Salm below Trois Ponts to smash into the Germans' flank, thereby taking some of the heat off of Meddaugh. "Hell, I don't give a damn on which side of the Salm you keep F Company," Ekman bellowed. "Just keep those goddamned Krauts from getting across the river!"

F Company waded through the icy, shallow water of the Salm to the far side, but understrength and lightly armed, it could do little more than harass Meddaugh's tormentors.

As the battle on the bluff swirled into the afternoon, Vandervoort sent his executive officer, Capt. T. G. Smith, to the Easy Company CP to send back an eyewitness report on conditions. A seasoned combat veteran known for his coolness under fire, Smith radioed: "Situation desperate." Easy Company was teetering on the brink of extinction.

Vandervoort leaped into his jeep and raced over the Salm and up the steep, shell-torn bluff road. Dismounting, he ran through a gauntlet of bullets and exploding shells to Meddaugh's foxhole command post and shouted: "Bill, get your boys to hell out of here—*now!*"

Meddaugh passed the word, and the troopers, with thousands of bullets whistling past them, started pulling back, firing all the while. Sensing a kill, a force of grenadiers pushed into one flank, and some of them shouted in cracked English: "Halt, Americans! You are surrounded!"

Reaching the edge of the 400-foot bluff, Meddaugh's boys began to scramble down its sheer face, jumping the final 20 feet or so. Several men suffered sprains and breaks from the leap, but comrades dragged them along over the bridge and into Trois Ponts. All the while, Vandervoort's men on the west bank of the Salm were blasting away at Germans on top of the bluff. As soon as Meddaugh's last trooper had recrossed the Salm, the bridge was blown, leaving Peiper's panzers marooned on the far side.

Donald Lassen, who had been involved in heavy fighting in

Normandy and in Holland with Vandervoort's battalion and at Trois Ponts, served as the unit's correspondent, recalled these events:

> The Easy Company survivors were a tired, ragged, rugged looking bunch when they assembled in Trois Ponts after dropping off their wounded and injured at the aid station. What I saw was inspiring. About 75 weary troopers, with weapons and ammunition, still ready to fight. The company had suffered about 50 percent casualties on the bluff and during the pullback, but they had inflicted heavy losses on the SS troops.[3]

That night, while German tanks on the bluff poured shells into Trois Ponts, a large force of grenadiers tried to shoot their way over the Salm, but the Germans were driven back in midstream after heavy fighting that lasted until dawn.

Confronted by Vandervoort's stubborn paratroopers and blown bridges, Jochen Peiper knew that the main road to the Meuse had been closed, so he changed his route and headed northward up a narrow, mountainous road in the direction of La Gleize.

That afternoon, Jim Gavin, an M-1 rifle slung over his shoulder, walked down Trois Ponts' main street and into Vandervoort's command post. At this point, German intentions were unknown. Gavin's reputation for being at the most threatened spot during a battle had long been well known, so Vandy grinned and quipped: "Well, I guess we're in a hell of a lot more trouble than I thought!"

"Can you hold?" Gavin asked. "Hell, yes!" Ben Vandervoort replied.

41
Ardennes
Meat
Grinder

Since two days after Adolf Hitler struck in the Ardennes and SHAEF finally concluded that it was a full-blooded offensive, American units had been disengaged from the front to the north and rushed to Belgium. As they arrived, piecemeal battalions, companies, and even platoon were fed into the meat grinder along the 60-mile northern battle line in a desperate effort to stem the German juggernaut from crashing through to Antwerp.

At his Werbomont command post, Matt Ridgway was mildly disappointed. He had hoped to gather all of the American airborne forces into a truly XVIII Airborne Corps, but the exigencies of the battlefield dictated differently. The 101st Airborne at Bastogne was under Troy Middleton's VIII Corps, and the 17th Airborne, when it arrived from England, would also go to Middleton. Now Ridgway's corps included Gavin's 82nd Airborne, Maj. Gen. Leland S. Hobbs' 30th ("Old Hickory") Infantry Division and Maj. Gen. Maurice Rose's 3rd ("Spearhead") Armored Division, all solid, battle-tested outfits.

However, three independent airborne outfits, packed shoulder to shoulder in the cattle trucks and flatbed trailers, were rushing to Werbomont from the Rheims region: Rupert Graves' 517th Parachute Combat Team, Wood Joerg's 551st, and Edmund Tomasik's 509th Parachute Infantry Battalions.

Driving an ammo truck at the tail of the 551st convoy was Pfc. Milo C. Huempfner. When highballing through Leignon,

Men of Wood Joerg's 551st Parachute Infantry Battalion move up during early days of the Bulge. *(Dan Morgan)*

Belgium, on the night of December 20, his truck skidded on ice, careened into a ditch, and was badly damaged. Rapidly, the ammo was shifted to another vehicle, and Huempfner was told to stay until a wrecker could be sent back.

Armed with a rifle, two bandoliers of bullets, a .45 Colt and four clips, Huempfner heard a mighty roar, and in the gathering dawn saw a column of 14 panzers, with 60 to 70 grenadiers riding on them, rumbling down the street toward him. Quickly dousing the truck with gasoline, the paratrooper set it afire.

Milo Huempfner recalled subsequent events:

> *I really took off. Couldn't understand why the Krauts didn't see me, for it was nearly light. I ran into the railroad station and Victor DeVeille, the stationmaster, quickly hid me in a tiny waiting room. There were Germans all over the place, and I could see them out of the small window.*
>
> *Then two German officers came in, and I heard them ask DeVeille if there were any Americans in town. I was only a few feet away. At the risk of his life and that of his wife and children, DeVeille assured them there were none. Fortunately, the Germans left without searching the station.[1]*

Feeling like a trapped animal, aware of reports that SS troops were shooting prisoners, Huempfner remained in hiding for an hour, then stole out of the back door. Spotting a pair of parked German halftracks, he disabled them with hand grenades placed on their engines. Then Huempfner set fire to a barn, and had the satisfaction of seeing a large number of SS troops, thinking that they were under attack, bolt outside and begin firing wildly in all directions.

After dark, a Belgian civilian told the paratrooper that there was a *Boche* tank, guarded by a lone sentry, parked by the big church. When Huempfner sneaked up to the huge iron vehicle, he was seen by the guard who, apparently, thought that the American was a comrade and called out, "Hi!" in German. Huempfner put a bullet through the SS man's head, then high-tailed it into the darkness. After daylight, Belgians, at the risk of their lives, concealed the paratrooper in their homes.

Meanwhile, the three independent parachute units, totaling 4,200 men, arrived in the Werbomont region, and Matt Ridgway split them into "fire brigades" to be rushed from one threatened locale to another. Tomasik's 509th Battalion and Bill Boyle's 1st Battalion of Graves' 517th were rushed off to Maurice Rose, the son of a Jewish rabbi, whose 3rd Armored Division was stretched thinly along a 15-mile east-west line between Hotton on the west and the key road junction of Manhay on the east. Joerg's 551st Battalion was hurried to Leland Hobbs' 30th Infantry Division. Graves' other two battalions (Seitz's 2nd and Paxton's 3rd) were kept in XVIII Airborne Corps reserve near Werbomont.

Richard Seitz recalled being ushered into the XVIII Airborne Corps operations room in an old barn after his battalion reached Werbomont:

> General Ridgway was engaged in a calm, low-key discussion with his chief of staff, Doc Eaton. I was deeply impressed over how cool and organized Ridgway was, sitting there at midnight, completely at ease, no outward show of concern, directing the combat deployment of his troops. Out of all that chaos we had endured, here was the first sign that someone was confident, in charge, and knew what he was doing.

As soon as the 551st Parachute Infantry reached its assembly area in the black of night, the troopers realized that the battle situation was tangled: for instance, American artillery batteries around them were firing in three directions. Pfc. Roger Car-

Pfc. Milo C. Huempfner. *(Dan Morgan)*

Capt. Charles LaChausee. *(Author's collection)*

queville and Pfc. James Coletti were sent out to establish a road-block.

Roger Carqueville recounted that episode:

> *There we were, hunkered down in a ditch, just the two of us. I don't know how we were supposed to halt panzers with our M-1 rifles. It was quiet as hell. Finally, a blacked-out American jeep with a Red Cross flag crawled past us. A few minutes later, it came back again in the other direction, but we didn't challenge it. Then in a couple more minutes, here it came again. We jumped up, and the driver slams on his brakes and I stick my M-1 in the passenger's ear and called out, "What's the password?" Hell, I didn't even know if there was a password. But I was ready to squeeze the trigger.*
>
> *Well, he was a priest, a Catholic chaplain from another parachute outfit. Lost as hell. I said to Coletti, "Since neither of us is going to make it through this scrap, we'd better go to confession—now." So while each of us walked away, the other went to confession—right in the middle of the road.*
>
> *Later I heard that we had scared the hell out of the padre. He thought we were Krauts in American uniforms and were going to blow his head off.*

Twenty-five miles south of Werbomont, Tony McAuliffe was not unduly alarmed over the fact that his 101st Airborne Division was surrounded. Airborne warriors were trained for being hemmed in behind enemy lines. After all of his units had reached Bastogne just before the Germans snapped the trap shut behind them, McAuliffe established a circular airhead, some five to seven miles in diameter, around the town. Facing the main pressure from the enemy on the east were Bob Sink's 506th and Julian Ewell's 501st Parachute Infantry Regiments, while Steve Chappuis' 502nd was generally on the north and northeast portions of the circle. Sprinkled thinly along the northwest, west and south and covering nearly half of the circle was Bud Harper's 327th Glider Infantry.

Part of Tony McAuliffe's cocky confidence may have come from the massive artillery firepower he had at his disposal in the center of the "doughnut." There were four airborne battalions of howitzers: Carmichael's 321st Glider, Elkins' 377th Parachute, Cooper's 463rd Parachute, and Nelson's 907th Glider. In all, there were 12 battalions of artillery, firing pieces from 75-millimeter to 155-millimeter Long Toms.

Intermixed with the paratroopers were Combat Command R of the 9th Armored Division, Combat Command B of the 10th Armored Division, and the 705th Tank Destroyer Battalion.

On the German side, five-foot, three-inch Hasso von Manteuffel, the aggressive leader of Fifth Panzer Army (who Hitler had said was his best field marshal), had no intention of getting bogged down in a lengthy siege of Bastogne, so he ordered the town to be contained and bypassed. Maj. Gen. Heinz Kokott's 26th Volksgrenadier Division, reinforced by one of the Panzer Lehr's regiments, was left behind to deal with Bastogne. Then the bulk of the Panzer Lehr and the 2nd Panzer Division skirted the town to the north and to the south and rumbled on westward largely unopposed.

Just past noon on December 22, Maj. Alvin Jones, operations officer of the 327th Glider Infantry, burst excitedly into Tony McAuliffe's command post in an old Belgian army barracks in Bastogne. Forty minutes earlier, a German major and captain of Kokott's 26th Volksgrenadier Division had driven up the Arlon road from the south under cover of a white flag, and on reaching an outpost of F Company of the glider regiment announced that they were *parlementaires*. No doubt the Germans had come to surrender their division, the bearded glider soldiers conjectured.

Jones handed the typewritten surrender demand to McAuliffe, who read it, muttered, "Nuts!" and flipped it aside. Clearly, the ultimatum would be refused. Twenty-seven-year-old Col. Harry W. O. Kinnard, a gung ho type whose choirboy face belied his ferocity on earlier battlefields as a battalion commander, insisted that the response be brief and defiant.[2]

Harry Kinnard remembered the concluding conversation:

> *Finally Tony McAuliffe said, "Well, what are we going to say?"*
> *And being a brash young paratrooper I answered, "Well, what you said when you got the German message would be hard to beat."*
> *Then Tony said, "What did I say?" And I answered: "You said 'Nuts!'"*

Gleefully, McAuliffe wrote out the single word on a sheet of paper, and Bud Harper carried it back to the waiting, blindfolded German officers. The *parlementaires* read McAuliffe's note and were puzzled. "In plain English," Harper barked, "it means go to hell!"

Joseph Harper recalled the parting exchange of words:

> *The two Germans were red-faced in anger, but they saluted and said, "We will kill many Americans. This is war." And I told them*

Main square in Bastogne in early days of siege. *(U. S. Army)*

that we'd kill every damned Kraut who tried to break into Bastogne.
"On your way, Bud," I told them. To this day, I don't know why I
made a slip of the tongue, but I added ". . . and good luck to you!"[3]

That night, Screaming Eagles in command posts and in frozen foxholes braced for the massive artillery bombardment that the Germans had promised would "annihilate" the Americans if they refused to surrender. Not a shell arrived.

Far north of encircled Bastogne, Jochen Peiper was in his candlelit cellar command post in the battered village of La Gleize, his dreams of raising the Nazi banner over Antwerp evaporated like wisps of smoke. Peiper, 800 of his exhausted and hungry men, and a large number of panzers had been trapped in a cul-de-sac by elements of the 82nd Airborne and 30th Infantry Divisions, with help from the 740th Tank Battalion.

Peiper radioed his headquarters: "Almost all Hermann [ammunition] is gone. We have no Otto [fuel]. Just a question of time before we're completely destroyed. Can we break out?"

Came the reply: "Six *Koenigstigers* [King Tigers] ready for action east of Stavelot. Where do you want them sent?"

Furious over the unrealistic response, Peiper fired back: "Send them via air mail to La Gleize."[4]

Despite Jochen Peiper's hopeless situation, Adolf Hitler remained confident of inflicting a monumental debacle on the Americans. He ordered the *coup de main* in the Ardennes to be shifted from Peiper to Lt. Gen. Willi Bittrich's powerful II SS Panzer Korps in the Manhay sector, southwest of La Gleize. Bittrich's command consisted of the 2nd SS (*Das Reich*) Panzer Division, the 12th SS (*Hitler Jugend*) Panzer Division, elements of the 9th SS Panzer Division, the 3rd Panzer Grenadier Regiment, and the elite *Führer Begleit* (Hitler's Bodyguard) Brigade.

With this crucial tactical decision by Hitler, two-lane blacktopped Route N-15 emerged as the focus of the Führer's ambitions in *Wacht am Rhein*—and possibly for his hopes for a negotiated peace with the Western Allies. N-15 stretched northward from Bastogne through Manhay and on to the Meuse River at Liege.

Spearheading the thrust up the Bastogne-Liege road would be Maj. Gen. Heinz Lammerding's 2nd SS Panzer Division, waiting near Houffalize, 12 miles below Manhay. Bittrich, not Peiper, would now carry the Nazi ball toward the Antwerp goal line.[5]

Defending the Manhay sector east of N-15 was Gavin's 82nd Airborne Division, which was dispersed thinly in a huge arc all the way from Trois Ponts southward along the Salm River and then bending back to the west nearly to the N-15 crossroads of Baraque-de-Fraiture, eight miles south of Manhay. Gavin's All-Americans were defending 25 miles, a fantastic assignment, with foxholes often 200 yards apart.

Responsibility for halting the German blows west of the Bastogne-Liege road fell to Rose's 3rd Armored, particularly Combat Command R, led by Col. Robert L. Howze, Jr., and attached parachute outfits. CCR was so overextended that Howze formed three tank-infantry task forces—Kane, Orr, and Hogan—and sent them southward along separate roads into paths of German spearheads.

Just after dawn on December 21, a jeep roared up to Bob Howze's command post in Soy, eight miles west of Manhay, and an excited officer bolted into the office of the CCR commander. Breathlessly, the visitor reported that he had heard heavy firing in Hotton, three miles southwest of Soy. How could that be? Howze reflected. Hotton was his rear area. Be as it may, this was an alarming situation. Hotton's garrison consisted only of a few clerks, ordnance men, engineers, and signalmen. If this unexpected German thrust from the south behind his back were to break through Hotton, untold havoc could result.

Unbeknownst to Howze, Baron von Manteuffel of Fifth Panzer Army had ordered his 116th Panzer Division to force a crossing of the Ourthe River at Hotton, a stream that was the last major obstacle this side of the Meuse. Howze quickly called in Bill Boyle, whose 1st Battalion of Graves' 517th Parachute Infantry, had been attached to CCR. Boyle was given a terse order: "Attack immediately [to the rear] and clear the area between Soy and Hotton."

One hour later, Boyle's troopers dropped bedrolls, overcoats, and overshoes and marched westward out of Soy through frozen, hilly, thick-timbered countryside. Almost at once Boyle's leading elements collided with German tanks and grenadiers, and a confused shootout raged for the rest of the day and throughout the night.

At dawn, Boyle had to make a crucial decision. His primary mission was to rescue the trapped service troops in Hotton or to seize that town if the Germans occupied it. Now he was bogged down before a strong enemy force. So he ordered his B Company and a platoon of C Company to continue slugging it out with the German force while A Company circled the locale and attacked Hotton from the north.

While A Company disengaged, bitter fighting resumed along the Soy-Hotton road. Lt. Harry Allingham, a platoon leader, was advancing up a ditch in front of his own scout when a German machine gun sent a burst of bullets into him. Collapsing in the ditch and bleeding profusely, Allingham called back to Pfc. Nolan L. Powell: "Bring up the platoon!" Then the lieutenant crawled toward the spitting machine gun, and a second fusillade killed him and set off a WP (white phosphorous) grenade in his pocket.

Disregarding the swarms of German bullets hissing past, Powell stood upright in the road, in plain sight of the enemy, and coolly walked back and forth, deploying his platoon into firing positions. All the while, the Germans, standing up between long bursts, shouted: "Merry Christmas *Amis*. Come and get it, you *Schweinehund* [sons of bitches]*!*"

"Go to hell, you goddamned Kraut bastards!" Powell's paratroopers yelled back.

Meanwhile, Pfc. Melvin Biddle of Anderson, Indiana, a B Company scout, was advancing across a field when a few Germans concealed in the brush opened fire on him. Biddle flopped

Lt. Col. William "Wild Bill" Boyle. *(Clark Archer)*

Pfc. Melvin Biddle. *(Lou Varrone)*

down, then crawled ahead through snow drifts and killed his three tormentors with his rifle. Biddle reloaded and crawled forward for 150 yards where he shot and killed two Germans acting as an outpost for a machine gun, then wiped out the three-man machine gun crew with two grenades.

Now the 21-year-old "Hoosier" scout signaled for his company to move up, and 200 yards onward he was taken under fire by three riflemen to his front and machine guns on both flanks. Crawling and slithering over the frozen ground, Biddle shot the riflemen, then turned his attention to one machine gun on his flank. Slipping up to within 50 feet of the weapon, Biddle hurled his last grenade, then charged and pumped bullets into the crew.

Again the scout waved his company forward. Then, while in a wooded area, Biddle went far forward to investigate the sound of a tank, but was driven to cover by withering bursts of small-arms fire.

Darkness fell. But Biddle was not ready to call it a day. For several hours he prowled around German positions to obtain information. Unable to speak German, the paratrooper could not answer the challenges of sentries and several times had to dash away under a hail of bullets. Once a small German patrol tried to trap the dark intruder, but Biddle eluded them by laying motionless face down—even though one *Feldgrau* stepped on his hand with a hobnailed boot and the trooper had to stifle an outcry that would have doomed him.

Mel Biddle finally returned to his company shortly before daybreak, and was able to furnish a detailed report on the positions of German machine gun and infantry and those of two panzers. This intelligence permitted the Americans to flank the German strong-points when the attack was resumed after dawn, and for two Shermans to knock out the pair of panzers.

Biddle had no intention of letting someone else carry the ball, and he was again out in front when the assault jumped off. Soon, yet another German machine gun raked him with bullets, but he alternately crawled and rushed forward to within 50 yards of the angry weapon, then picked off the crew, one at a time, with his M-1.[6]

In the meantime, Bill Boyle's A Company, after an arduous circular trek cross-country, entered Hotton with only sporadic shots fired at it. Now the situation in Hotton was typical of the mass confusion in the Ardennes: The town had three landlords simultaneously. Boyle's paratroopers occupied the northern part of Hotton; the Germans had the southern portion; and across the Ourthe River to the west, elements of the U.S. 83rd Infantry Division were holding out.

A few hours later, an armored unit sergeant entered Boyle's command post in Hotton. He had four tank destroyers—and was lost. "I'm looking for some outfit—any outfit—to tie in with," the sergeant declared. "Well, you've found a home," Boyle replied. "We're going to clean the Krauts out of the other part of this town, and we sure as hell can use your TDs." After a heavy shoot-out, Boyle's boys held all of Hotton east of the Ourthe.

Past midnight, Boyle received an urgent call from 3rd Armored headquarters in Manhay. It had been learned (probably through wireless intercepts) that a powerful German force was going to smash against Hotton at dawn in the hope of breaking through to the Meuse. "You will hold Hotten at all costs!" the grim voice on the line told Boyle.

The expected attack never came. Hasso von Manteuffel had called it off when told by Maj. Gen. Siegfried von Waldenburg of the 116th Panzer Division that he was opposed by a "strong American force" (Boyle's company and the four TDs) in Hotton. Manteuffel would probe elsewhere for a soft spot that would permit a breakthrough toward Antwerp.[7]

In the early night of December 22, Capt. Charles E. LaChaussee, leader of C Company in Boyle's battalion of the 517th Parachute Infantry, was leading six officers and 87 men through dark and forbidding woods to the village of Freyneux, four miles below Manhay. A few trucks carrying one of his rifle platoons had gotten lost in the fog and darkness during the trek from Soissons.

LaChaussee was totally disoriented. He had no maps. When he had reported to 3rd Armored headquarters in Manhay only a few hours earlier, Maurice Rose could tell him only that he was going to "one of the hottest spots" to join Task Force Kane at Freyneux. That afternoon, TF Kane had run into a powerful German response at Dochamps, two miles south of Freyneux, and had to pull back. Lt. Col. Matthew W. Kane, the lanky task force leader, now ordered LaChaussee to attack at once and seize Dochamps.

It seemed to be a tall order for five rifle squads, but at 8:45 P.M., C Company jumped off. A mile south of Freyneux, the lead scout at the far end of a field near some woods signaled a halt. It was deathly still. The scout had sensed something ahead in the brush. Clutching his tommy gun at the ready, he whispered, "Coleman." (The password and countersign for the night was Coleman/Burner.) There was no reply. Again the scout whispered: "Coleman."

Eyewitness sketch of men of Capt. Charles LaChaussee's 517th Parachute Infantry company in a night fight in Dochamps. *(Drawing by Charles LaChaussee)*

From the black brush came a voice: *"Vas ist?"* (What is it?) Evidently, the German's name had been Kohlman or something similar. With that, the scout emptied his tommy gun into the brush, killing all three of the machine-gun crew.

After an hour-long shoot-out with a German force in the woods behind the ill-fated machine-gun post, LaChaussee's company trudged on to the outskirts of Dochamps, where the troopers were greeted with a murderous fusillade of automatic-weapon and rifle fire. Clearly, five rifle squads were not going to wrest Dochamps from the Germans, so the Five-Seventeens withdrew a half-mile and dug in.

Shortly after a dull daybreak, Charles LaChaussee looked out of a window in the farmhouse that was serving as his command post. Through the heavy fog, he discerned a double column of men carrying rifles and fixed bayonets approaching from the rear. No doubt Matt Kane had sent welcome reinforcements. When the column was only 100 feet away, LaChaussee felt a surge of alarm: these soldiers were wearing ankle-length greatcoats—Americans did not have garments like that.

In a nearby house, Lt. Roland Beaudoin had also spotted the German columns, stuck a machine gun out of the window and held down the trigger. Caught by surprise at point-blank range, the grenadier company was cut to pieces. (Later count would reveal that Beaudoin had killed 23 Germans.)

Both sides had been stunned by the unexpected confrontation. Then pandemonium erupted. Grenades exploded and automatic weapons chattered angrily. Now swarms of Germans began crowding in on the Americans from three directions, and the paratroopers had to pull back rapidly, firing as they ran, a few hundred yards to the village of Lamormenil. The much larger German force was right on their heels.

LaChaussee, followed by a machine-gun team, charged into a house, where a family—father, mother and two children—were eating breakfast despite the uproar. Without a word, the paratroopers dashed upstairs and fired out of a window.

For more than two hours face-to-face mayhem raged in Lamormenil. Just when it appeared that the lightly armed paratroopers would be overwhelmed by sheer numbers, four Sherman tanks roared into the hamlet and charge down the street, firing their .50-caliber machine guns as they came. It was like the U.S. cavalry of the Old West riding to the rescue at the last minute. Within a half hour, surviving Germans scrambled out of Lamormenil, leaving behind piles of dead comrades.

42
A Violent Christmas Eve

Nine miles west of Manhay, the village of Erezee sits on a hill astride the east-west arterial road between Manhay and Hotton. Since Erezee was the 3rd Armored Division's rear area, numerous command posts, aid stations, and supply dumps were crammed into its confines. On the morning of December 24, Doc Alden, surgeon of the 509th Parachute Infantry Battalion, was routinely bandaging wounded troopers when he glanced out of a window and saw an American halftrack rattling down the Erezee street.

Starting to turn back to his work, Alden did a double take. Driving the vehicle and piled into its bed were 12 to 14 heavily armed SS troops. In the confusion of the Ardennes, the Germans had apparently not realized that they were barreling into the center of an American-held town.

Alden shouted to his medics to grab their weapons (the 509th medics went into combat fully armed), and troopers rushed into the street and began blasting away at the halftrack. Other GIs joined in the shooting. Leaping down from the vehicle, the Germans scattered, took cover behind buildings, and fired back with Schmeissers and rifles. One parachute medic sent a rifle grenade into the halftrack, making certain that any Germans who got out of Erezee would have to escape on foot. After a brisk but brief firefight, most of the grenadiers were killed and the remainder were taken prisoners.

Thirty minutes later, with the specter of Germans prowling about the Ardennes in authentic American vehicles fresh in their minds, Alden and his medics spotted a Sherman tank clanking into the village from the same direction that the halftrack filled with SS troops had taken. The approaching tank was buttoned up (meaning its hatch and driver's armored visors were closed) and ready for battle.

Again the parachute medics grabbed weapons and dashed outside. One medic fired a bazooka rocket into the tank's treads, causing the vehicle to spin around crazily and grind to a halt. Slowly, the disabled tank's hatch opened and out hopped three furious occupants—genuine members of the 3rd Armored Division.

"Just what in the hell do you crazy bastards think you're doing?" the tank commander bellowed. "Who in the hell's side are you on?"

"Well, what in the hell do you think you're doing charging in here all buttoned up?" a Five-O-Niner exclaimed. "How'd we know who's inside?"

Calmed down to a degree, the 3rd Armored sergeant ex-

Finally, a meal—tepid to frozen—reaches the front. *(Pierre Gosset)*

plained that his tank had been sent on a special mission that took it through Erezee, and he thought that the village might be held by Germans.

Early that afternoon, Jim Gavin, Brig. Gen. William M. Hoge, leader of CCB of the 9th Armored Division, and Brig. Gen. Robert Hasbrouck, commander of the 7th Armored Division, crowded into Matt Ridgway's farmhouse in Werbomont. Field Marshal Bernard Montgomery, who Eisenhower had put in charge of all troops in the northern battleground, insisted that Ridgway straighten his serpentine "lines."

"Starting at nightfall," Ridgway said solemnly, "the 82nd Airborne will pull back to the Trois Ponts region and 7th Armored [on its right] will pull back to Manhay."

Ridgway, an advocate of constant attack, was far from happy with Montgomery's order, but he understood the reasoning behind it. Gavin's 82nd Airborne was stretched almost to the breaking point and stuck out like a sore thumb. The All-Americans' new sector would run as directly as possible from Trois Ponts westward almost to Manhay.

Engineers of the 508th Parachute Infantry prepare a railroad bridge for demolition, near Vielsalm on December 23, 1944. (*Pierre Gosset*)

Jim Gavin remembered receiving Ridgway's orders:

> *I made a mild protest, the only one of the commanders to do so. I realized that the tactical situation confronting us called for withdrawal. It shortened our defensive sector by half, and the new position assigned to us was far superior in fields of fire and cover than our old positions. However, the 82nd Airborne had always been proud of the fact that we had never given up one inch of ground, so the morale factor of withdrawing in the face of the enemy had to be considered. But orders were orders.*

Christmas Eve was bitterly cold, and the winter moon was shining brightly, causing eerie shadows on fields blanketed with glistening snow. Gavin's boys, the packed snow crunching under their boots, began trudging to the rear in order to "tidy up the battlefield," as Montgomery had phrased it. Covering the withdrawal, scattered squads and platoons were left in place until 4:00 A.M., and the 307th Airborne Engineer Battalion blew bridges over the Salm and sewed minefields to impede pursuing German forces.

At the same time that the All-Americans had started to pull back, Jochen Peiper and 800 survivors of his original 5,000 SS men struck out southward on foot to escape their cul-de-sac at Le Gleize, three miles north of Trois Ponts. Left behind was a 50-man suicide squad (which would fight to the death as ordered), scores of seriously wounded SS men, and 131 prisoners. Also remaining in La Gleize were large numbers of smoldering panzers and other vehicles—mute epitaphs of *Kampfgruppe* Peiper's ill-starred odyssey to Antwerp.

In a rare battlefield development, Peiper's force withdrawing to the south passed Gavin's division pulling back to the north, with neither side becoming aware of what was happening.[1]

Four miles south of Manhay at the Belle Haie crossroads that day, a 3rd Armored task force, built around a platoon of tanks and a few tank destroyers, and led by Maj. Olin F. Brewster, a Texan, and Bud Siegel's A Company of the 509th Parachute Infantry Battalion, were fighting desperately to halt the 2nd SS Panzer Division's thrust up N-15 to Manhay. With the help of P-47 fighter-bombers, the Belle Haie defenders had knocked out nine panzers and gave supporting grenadiers a bloody nose.

Stymied by the stubborn Americans at Belle Haie, Heinz Lammerding, leader of the 2nd SS Panzer, sent his tanks and grenadiers to circle the roadblock. If they couldn't smash straight up the highway, they would take Manhay from the southwest.

Three miles west of Belle Haie, 2nd SS Panzer spearheads collided with Matt Kane's task force of a few tanks, halftracks, and Charles LaChaussee's C Company of Graves' 517th Parachute Infantry at Lamormenil and Freyneux. All day Task Force Kane, outnumbered and outgunned, battled for its life against repeated German assaults, but at dusk Lammerding pulled back to regroup, leaving behind scores of German and American corpses strewn around the snowy fields and in Lamormenil and Freyneux.

That evening, a 3rd Armored lieutenant brought a marked map into LaChaussee's command post in a cellar in battered Lamormenil. The villages of Odiegne, Le Batty, Grandmenil and La Fosse—on LaChaussee's east, north, and northwest—were all in German hands. Manhay had not been heard from. Task Force Kane was trapped.

LaChaussee and his troopers settled down for the night to make the best of an ominous situation. A radio was tuned to London's BBC, and a chorus was singing *"Stille Nacht"* ("Silent Night")—of all things, in German. "Hey," a trooper called out, "it's Christmas Eve!"

Then General Eisenhower came on the air and began reading a (recorded) message to the troops, an exhortation that no doubt had been written by a SHAEF public-relations officer from the rarefied confines of Paris. In part, Ike said over the air: ". . . Congratulations. At last the German has come out of his fortification to fight in the open . . . Good luck and good hunting!"

Cornered, hungry, exhausted, cold, confused and bitter, the paratroopers in LaChaussee's cellar turned the air blue with their curses. Who was doing the hunting—the Americans or the Germans? "Goddamned," an exasperated voice called out, "even Ike doesn't know what the hell's going on up here!"

On Christmas Eve, Tony McAuliffe and an aide were striding briskly past the Bastogne police station when they heard German voices inside singing *"Stille Nacht."* Out of curiosity, the general went into the station, where one of the German POWs shouted at him in English: "We'll be in Antwerp soon!" Another yelled: "We'll soon be free—and you'll be *our* prisoners!" When the ruckus ceased, McAuliffe said: "I came by to wish you a Merry Christmas."[2]

McAuliffe's boys were now calling themselves "the Battered Bastards of the Bastion of Bastogne." Even though their destiny was fraught with peril, artillery ammo was running low, large numbers of wounded troopers were unable to receive proper medical care, and the Germans were attacking incessantly at points around the perimeter, the Screaming Eagles had grown even more cocky after the "Nuts!" scenario.

However, Tony McAuliffe was confronted by battlefield realities. That afternoon, he had been talking on the radio with his boss, Troy Middleton. "The finest Christmas present the 101st Airborne could get," the Screaming Eagle leader said solemnly, "would be relief tomorrow." For three days, spearheads of Patton's Third Army, hampered by miserable weather, hostile terrain and stubborn Germans, had been inching northward to reach Bastogne.

"I know," replied the VIII Corps commander somberly, "I know."[3]

That night the drone of airplanes was heard over Bastogne, then the eerie whistling of falling bomb clusters and ground-shaking explosions. Finally, Hitler was punishing the Screaming Eagles—and 3,500 terrified civilians huddled in freezing basements—for the insolence of the "Nuts!" reply and the failure of his own Wehrmacht to seize the town. Dozens of buildings burst into flames. The improvised military hospital received a direct hit, and timbers and stones crashed down on wounded Americans. Even while the bombs were dropping, soldiers and civilians were digging frantically for the dead and dying patients.

Far to the east, Capt. Francis Sampson, the 101st Airborne chaplain, who had been captured at Bastogne six days earlier when he went looking for wounded paratroopers, and 800 other bedraggled American prisoners were herded into the auditorium of a school near the railroad station in Pruem, Germany.

For five days, the exhausted, hungry and freezing POWs had been tramping through the snow across Belgium and Luxembourg and into the Third Reich. Each had had but one meal per day—a boiled potato and a small green apple. Now Father Sam and the others felt that even the Nazis might note that this was Christmas Eve and feed them a decent meal. But supper consisted of a boiled turnip, a half-slice of brown bread, and a cup of warm water.[4]

American bombers were plastering Pruem. It was pitch black in the windowless auditorium. While explosions rocked the old school, Father Sam led 800 shaky voices in singing "Silent Night."[5]

Not long after nightfall on Christmas Eve, Capt. Ernest Bud Siegel and his jeep driver were creeping southward from Manhay along slippery N-15 toward the Belle Haie crossroads, where Siegel's A Company of the 509th Parachute Infantry Battalion, along with Task Force Brewster of the 3rd Armored Division, had been slugging it out with the 2nd SS Panzer. Suddenly Siegel saw a shadowy figure beside the road about 30 yards ahead, and moments later a hail of automatic weapon bullets riddled the jeep. Both men bailed out, one to each side, and made belly flop landings. (The driver was never heard from again.)

Siegel, miraculously, had escaped death. Because of the bitter cold, he had been holding his hands inside his web belt, which had a pistol clip on it. One bullet had gone through the metal

1st Sgt. Leonard A. Funk, America's most-decorated paratrooper. *(Sketch by Lou Varrone)*

Father Francis L. Sampson as POW.

brace of the windshield, then penetrated the pistol clip, striking him in the hand. The metal brace and the clip had slowed the bullet and kept it from piercing him.

Now the jeep slid onto its side in the middle of the road, and, inexplicably, the headlights came on, illuminating Siegel who was laying in front of the vehicle with a bullet wound in the hand, another in the leg, and a few cracked ribs.

Ernest Siegel recalled subsequent events:

> *The Germans quit firing, and three or four SS men walked up to where I was laying in the glare of the headlights. I felt certain that they would kill me, and that my only hope was in quickly convincing them that I would be a valuable prisoner for German Intelligence. So I called out in German—I speak fluent German—"Ich bin ein offizier!" [I am an officer.] This worked, although there was no way any German interrogator was going to get any info out of me.*

Siegel was disarmed, and an SS man struck him a heavy blow in the face with the butt of a rifle, causing blood to spurt from his nose. Shoving the American in front of them, the Germans began walking back down the road. Soon a tank was heard coming from the direction of Manhay, and the captors shoved Siegel facedown in a snow bank. He thought they were going to shoot him, but the Germans flopped beside him while the tank clanked to within 30 yards of them and halted.

"Get that goddamned jeep off the road!" an American voice boomed from the Sherman. In the darkness, the tanker apparently could not see that Siegel's jeep had been riddled. Assured that the tank was manned by Americans, the SS men sprang to their feet and began shooting, and the armored vehicle's machine gun fired back.

Aware that he would be killed by fellow Americans if he could not silence the tank's chattering weapon, and not knowing the password, Siegel shouted: "Babe Ruth . . . Frank Sinatra . . . Betty Grable. I'm an American!"

Finally, the SS men fled into the woods, leaving behind a wounded comrade. Clutching a tommy gun, the Sherman commander leaped down and slowly approached Siegel. The tanker was furious: In the exchange of fire, a bullet had shot off his finger, so he began beating the wounded German, a boy of 17 or 18, on the head with the butt of his gun. "*Hilf mir* [Help me]!" the teenager pleaded to Siegel, crying profusely.

"Cut it out!" Siegel ordered. "He's just a goddamned kid."

Bud Siegel hobbled onward and reached the command post of his company in a farmhouse near Belle Haie crossroads. When the pain became excruciating, the captain turned over command to his exec, 24-year-old Hoyt Livingston, and limped back four tortuous miles to Manhay for medical treatment.

Hardly had Siegel departed, than the freezing Americans at Belle Haie heard the ominous roar of swarms of diesel engines coming from the darkness to the south. Heinz Lammerding's 2nd SS Panzer had jumped off in a final, full-scale smash up N-15 to seize Manhay. Deployed abreast on both sides of the highway were two regiments of white-sheeted grenadiers.

For the small American force at the Belle Haie roadblock, it was a hold-at-all-costs mission. After two days of warding off sledgehammer blows, Maj. Olin Brewster's task force had lost all but three tanks and was nearly out of ammunition and fuel. And the 100 paratroopers had been suffering casualties while fighting German tanks with only small arms and a few bazookas.

Rumbling up the highway, one tightly behind the other, the panzers blasted the little band of Americans with withering fusillades of cannon and machine-gun fire. Cpl. Clyde Baker, a parachute squad leader, was sent to the stone and timber farmhouse command post with an urgent message, and just after he had entered, a high velocity tank shell ripped into the structure, showering the occupants with debris. Twelve slivers of rock tore into Baker's left eye and six pieces into his right, leaving him blind.

It was a terrifying ordeal for Clyde Baker. For two hours he lay on the floor, sightless and in pain, as a savage fight raged around him and explosions repeatedly rocked the farmhouse. Then the panzer force steamrollered the Belle Haie defenders and clanked on up the highway toward Manhay. On either side of N-15, the grenadiers skirted the crossroads and surged on northward, trapping the paratroopers and the remnants of Task Force Brewster at Belle Haie.

Just before midnight, the men of A Company got the word: They were going to infiltrate back to American "lines" in the Manhay locale, not as stragglers, but as an organized unit ready to fight. Twelve seriously wounded paratroopers, including the sightless Clyde Baker, were placed in a truck. But it soon became clear that the vehicle could not be taken cross-country, so an agonizing decision was reached: The wounded Five-O-Niners would have to be left behind in the hope that the Germans would give them medical treatment.

Meanwhile, Matt Ridgway's order for the 7th Armored Division to pull back that Christmas Eve had failed to reach Col. Dwight A. Rosebaum, whose Combat Command A was blocking N-15 south of Manhay. With all guns blazing, the onrushing 2nd SS Panzer crashed into Rosebaum's force, destroying 19 tanks and inflicting heavy casualties on supporting infantrymen. The remainder of Rosebaum's tanks and tank destroyers then turned and rumbled back up the highway.[6]

At this time, about 10:00 P.M., Doc Alden was walking rapidly up N-15 and nearing the outskirts of Manhay. That afternoon, he had taken his ambulance southward to the Belle Haie crossroads, sent it back with wounded men of the 509th Parachute Infantry, and at dusk begun heading on foot back to Manhay. There he hoped to catch a ride to his aid station in Erezee, eight miles to the west.

Dr. Carlos Alden remembered ensuing events:

> I heard this loud roar behind me, and jumped to take cover alongside the road. I was greatly relieved to see that these were American Sherman tanks, but they were barreling along to the

*"rear" at full throttle. Then right on their heels was another group
of tanks—German panzers. Suddenly all hell broke loose, and I
found myself there in Manhay with a full-fledged fight going on
between American and German tanks. Flat-trajectory shells were
whistling past me, going in both directions.*

Rosebaum's tankers continued their flight northward, leaving
Manhay wide open. Then swarms of German grenadiers poured
into the town and also quickly seized the adjoining village of
Grandmenil on the west. Doc Alden, in the meantime, had
slipped out of Manhay to Grandmenil, where he caught a ride
just as the first panzers were charging into the village.

A gaping hole had been torn into Ridgway's "lines," and now
Liège and Meuse beckoned to the 2nd SS Panzer Division.

43
The
Floodtide
Ebbs

At 9:00 A.M. on Christmas Day, two machine gunners at an outpost of Rube Tucker's 504th Parachute Infantry were gazing
over the landscape east of Manhay, alert for any sign of an expected German attack. Off in the distance could be seen a column of dark figures marching directly toward them. The Five-O-
Fours cocked their machine gun.

A few minutes later, as the column drew closer, the tense
gunner relaxed his trigger finger. These were friends, Hoyt
Livingston's company of the 509th Parachute Infantry Battalion,
who were escaping from their trap at the Belle Haie crossroads.

*   *   *

Back at Belle Haie shortly after that Christmas dawn, the blinded Five-O-Niner Clyde Baker and his eleven seriously wounded comrades heard shouts around the truck in which they had spent six miserable hours in the darkness and freezing cold: *"Heraus! Heraus!* [Come out]" Hauling the paratroopers from the vehicle, the SS grenadiers herded their captives into a barn, where they would remain for two days and nights without food, water, or medical attention.

Then the wounded paratroopers were put into German field ambulances and driven for a considerable distance over rough roads. Suddenly, Baker heard the chilling roar of airplanes—American planes—diving on the vehicles, then the angry rattle of machine guns. Two ambulances were badly shot up and had to be abandoned, but, miraculously, none of the wounded Americans had been hit.

Clyde Baker recalled ensuing events:

Our German guards, already surly, were mad as hell about the strafings. They got another couple of ambulances, however, and we paratroopers, along with a large number of other American and German wounded, were put on a hospital train. Since I couldn't see, I don't know where in the hell we were.

Then more American warplanes came over and dive-bombed and strafed the train, damaging the engine and causing it to halt. Now the Krauts were really furious. They took me and an American pilot in a leather air corps jacket (I learned later that was what he was wearing) to one side, handed us shovels, and told us to start digging our graves. They were going to kill us—me because I was a "murdering" paratrooper and the pilot because he was a "terror bomber."

The pilot was a real smooth cookie. He spoke fluent German, and began lying, telling the Krauts that he was an engineer on a C-47 cargo plane and had never bombed anyone, and that I was merely a rear-area soldier and not a paratrooper, and that I had put on a paratrooper's uniform to try to keep warm. The Krauts bought the yarn. Nine days after I had been hit, I started gaining partial eyesight.

Some 35 miles west of Manhay that Christmas morning, Milo Huempfner of Joerg's 551st Parachute Infantry Battalion, who had been holed up in Leignon amidst Germans since his truck was damaged on the night of December 20, emerged to greet the tanks of Maj. Gen. Ernest N. "Gravel Voice" Harmon's spirited 2nd ("Hell on Wheels") Armored Division. Harmon was engaged in virtually destroying the 2nd Panzer Division, which had nearly run out of fuel.[1]

Huempfner's elation over being rescued was soon tempered. Because he didn't know the current password, the paratrooper was taken into custody by a 2nd Armored MP lieutenant, who suspected that he was a German straggler who had donned an American uniform to escape. Otherwise, what would Huempfner have been doing for six days inside a town swarming with panzer troops?

In Bastogne that morning, Tony McAuliffe left his command post in the Belgian barracks compound and walked to the nearby town cemetery. On all sides could be seen the rising smoke of battle. German prisoners were digging holes in the frozen ground into which the frozen bodies of youths wearing Screaming Eagle shoulder patches would be carefully placed.

"Are the Germans being fed?" the general asked a guard. "Yes, sir, the same as us," was the reply. "Be sure not to neglect them," McAuliffe said as he turned to leave.[2]

Around the flaming Bastogne perimeter, spirits remained high, even though shelling and German attacks took their daily toll in dead and wounded. Grim humor was the hallmark. On Christmas Day, troopers shivering in ice-lined foxholes passed from hand to hand and chuckled over a "social note" in the *Para-Dice Minor*, a mimeographed news sheet put out by paratrooper Pfc. David J. Phillips:

> *Miss Champagne Belcher, your society editor, offers the following tips on where to go for dinner and dancing on your night out.*
>
> *"The Bastogne Bar and Grill" is featuring a tasty little luncheon consisting mainly of* Ratione de Kay avec Café GI *[K-rations with GI coffee]. Gerald Kraut and his 88-piece band furnish lively entertainment during cocktail hour. After sundown, the club occasionally bills Mr. Looft Waffe and his famous "Flare Dance."*
>
> *"The Blue Boche" up the street furnishes a clever program of native folk dances. The most entertaining of these is the renowned German War Waltz, in which the chorus performs in intricate circles*

*with hands high overhead while singing the hit number of the show,
as popularized by the Wehrmacht playboys, entitled, "I'm Forever
Shouting Kamerad!"*

On this birthday of the Prince of Peace, Tony McAuliffe and
his troopers had much to be thankful for. A day earlier, the
murky skies that had grounded most aircraft for nine days finally
cleared. From foxholes on the perimeter and from the streets of
Bastogne, Screaming Eagles gazed in awe at the brilliant blue sky.
Swarms of C-47s swooped over low and filled the air with
brightly colored parachutes, each carrying a bundle of crucially
needed supplies. Down below, the troopers cheered wildly,
clapped their grimy hands and slapped each other on the back as
tears rolled down weather-beaten cheeks.

During the next three days, 962 transport planes would parachute in 850 tons of supplies, and on the twenty-sixth, 11 gliders
would land with several doctors and badly needed fuel. Each
flight was raked from four sides by German ack-ack fire, and
American "fly boys" would pay a stiff price to resupply Bastogne.
Altogether, 102 air corps men would be killed, 19 C-47s would
be shot down, and 51 more aircraft badly damaged. Not a single
flight would turn back because of the intense German antiaircraft
fusillades.

Supplies drop onto surrounded Bastogne. *(U. S. Army)*

*   *   *

Twenty-five miles north of Bastogne that Christmas morning, Matt Ridgway was furious over the night's debacle at Manhay. Only a day earlier, he had assured Courtney Hodges at First Army that the XVIII Airborne Corps was in good shape and could hold off the powerful attacks that were being hurled at it. Ridgway's ire was directed at the 7th Armored Division, mainly Dwight Rosebaum of CCA, who had lost 19 tanks within a few minutes in the wild flight northward through Manhay.

If Ridgway was angry, First Army headquarters was in near panic. Hodges, at Chaudfontaine 23 miles north of Manhay, sent repeated messages to Ridgway, demanding that Manhay be re-taken at once. Liège and the Meuse were in grave danger. Ridg-way issued a stern order to 7th Armored commander Bob Hasbrouck: "Retake Manhay whatever the cost!"

Early in the afternoon of December 25, a hastily scraped-up task force of 7th Armored tanks and elements of the 424th Regi-ment of the 106th Infantry Division, struck at Manhay from the north. It was met by murderous fire, and driven back with hor-rendous losses—one-third of the attacking force.

That night, four miles southwest of Manhay in the gutted vil-lages of Lamormenil and Freyneux, Charles LaChaussee's iso-lated company of the 517th Parachute Infantry climbed onto the tanks of Task Force Kane. A few hours earlier, a paratrooper, Sgt. Jack Burns, and a patrol had discovered an old logging trail that was not defended by Germans and that would hold vehicles. Up that tenuous route, the remnants of Task Force Kane hoped to escape.

Troopers rode on the frigid metal of the tanks with weapons at the ready, expecting to be ambushed at any moment while clanking through the black and forbidding woods. A few hours later, the task force made contact with an outpost of the newly arrived 75th Infantry Division along the Manhay-Hotton road. Only one man failed to survive the trip: an SS officer who had been captured at Freyneux "met with a fatal accident along the way."

On Christmas night and through the morning of December 26, planes and artillery plastered the Germans holed up in the rubble of Manhay. Then Matt Ridgway ordered Rupert Graves' 517th Parachute Infantry to recapture the town "at all costs."

The Gray Eagle gave the nasty job to Lt. Col. Forest Paxton's 3rd Battalion. It would be one of the most crucial attacks in the Ardennes holocaust.

After an arduous two-mile approach march through deep snow in the bitter cold, Paxton's battalion reached its jump-off position 1,000 yards northeast of Manhay at 1:45 A.M. on December 27. The Five Seventeens were in an especially vicious mood. They had just returned from the Malmedy area where Jochen Peiper's SS men had massacred 90 American POWs. The SS men in Manhay would find it difficult to surrender.

Fifteen minutes later, eight American artillery battalions opened fire and drenched Manhay and its southern approaches with 5,000 shells, a murderous barrage that literally caused the ground to tremble where Paxton's boys were waiting.

On the heels of the bombardment, the battalion shoved off for Manhay, with Capt. James Birder's I Company in the lead and Lt. Richard Jackson's H Company close behind. Concerned that the reinforced battalion of SS grenadiers defending Manhay would have time to recover before Birder's boys hit them, Paxton ordered another heavy artillery concentration.

Spearheading the attack was the platoon led by Lt. Floyd A. Stott, one of the battalion's most popular officers. Suddenly Stott and his men heard the chilling sound of shells—American shells—rushing toward them. The errant salvo exploded in their midst, killing Stott and nine others and wounding several troopers.

Despite this demoralizing blow, Capt. Jim Birder, barely 21 years old and a recent Notre Dame graduate, quickly rallied I Company, and with Jackson's H Company on its heels, charged into Manhay. Paxton's boys fired bazookas at tanks and vehicles, pitched grenades into the rubble that had once been houses, and shot at anything that moved. By 3:30 A.M., Manhay had been cleared of Germans. Strewn about were 50 dead SS men; 29 others had been captured.

In the meantime, elements of three German divisions had been launching repeated trip-hammer blows against the 82nd Airborne east of N-15. On the moonlit night of December 26, the 19th Grenadier Regiment, one of the Wehrmacht's best, smashed at the lines of Lindquist's 508th Parachute Infantry in front of Erria. After a bloody fight lasting for three hours, the 19th Grenadiers pulled back.

After the battle: the Manhay crossroads. *(Pierre Gosset)*

Twenty-four hours later, the 9th SS Panzer Division launched an all-out assault against Tucker's 504th Parachute Infantry in front of Bra, and the 508th was hit again. Screaming and yelling, the grenadiers charged shoulder to shoulder toward the American foxholes, much like Japanese *banzai* assaults in the Pacific. Smoking American machine guns mowed them down, and piles of German corpses littered the snowy fields.

Because of sheer numbers—"Never saw so goddamned many Krauts in one place!" an 82nd veteran would exclaim—the Germans overran Lt. Col. Louis G. Mendez's 3rd Battalion of the 508th, but the troopers stuck to their foxholes. Undaunted, Mendez borrowed a company from an adjoining battalion and before daybreak cleaned out a large force of SS men behind his positions. In Erria, Mendez's boys captured several Germans sleeping soundly in bedrolls.

Just as dusk was settling over the embattled Ardennes on December 26, three tanks commanded by 33-year-old Lt. Charles P. Boggess of Patton's 4th Armored Division were clanking toward the outskirts of Bastogne. Boggess spotted colored supply parachutes draped over trees and detected a line of foxholes. American or German?

"Screaming Eagles" on the Marche road outside Bastogne jump with joy on hearing that Patton's spearheads had forged a linkup with the "Battered Bastards." *(Pierre Gosset)*

Taking the risk of having his head shot off, Boggess stood up in the turret and shouted: "Come here! This is the 4th Armored Division!" Silence. Boggess repeated the call. More silence. A third time, and no response. Now he was ready to fire. Then a lone figure climbed out of a snow-covered foxhole and came forward.

"I'm Lieutenant [Duane J.] Webster of the 326th Engineers, 101st Airborne Division. Glad to see you!" he said, beaming broadly and extending a cold hand to Boggess up in the tank turret. The linkup of Third Army and Bastogne was shaky at best; the corridor into the besieged town was not much wider than a Sherman tank.[3]

Since learning in Washington that his division had been surrounded at Bastogne, Maxwell Taylor had been rushing back to Europe. Reaching Paris, he told Beetle Smith, General

Eisenhower's right-hand man, that he planned to parachute into Bastogne. Smith promptly squelched that notion. So Taylor drove to a point south of Bastogne, and on December 27, he and his jeep driver ran the narrow gauntlet into town. "My scariest hour of the war," the driver, S. Sgt. Charles Kartus, would exclaim.

Reaching the 101st Airborne command post, Taylor shook hands warmly with his pinch hitter, Tony McAuliffe, and congratulated him. "What are the situation and condition of the division?" Taylor asked.

Maxwell Taylor (left) after his arrival in Bastogne congratulates Tony McAuliffe. (*U. S. Army*)

"Sir," the spunky McAuliffe, a man of few words, replied, "we're ready to attack!"

On the northern battlefront, Willi Bittrich, leader of the II SS Panzer Korps, had grown desperate. Gavin's 82nd Airborne east of N-15 had not budged under repeated heavy blows, and Paxton's battalion of the 517th Parachute Infantry was standing

Gibraltar-like astride N-15 in Manhay. So Bittrich would make one final effort to break through by smashing at Sadzot, a cluster of 19 farmhouses seven miles west of Manhay.

Spearheading the 2nd SS Panzer's assault would be Maj. Horst Krag's *Kampfgruppe* of grenadiers and artillery. (His tanks could not penetrate this hilly, thickly timbered terrain to reach Sadzot.)

At 1:30 A.M. on December 28, *Kampfgruppe* Krag struck with total surprise. Swarms of grenadiers charged out of the woods that surrounded tiny Sadzot on three sides, pounced on the 70-man Company B of the 87th Mortar Battalion, and after a fierce but brief melee, virtually wiped out the small unit.[4]

Exhausted, famished, and frozen to the bone, Krag's men set up machine-gun posts along the village's outskirts, but most of the Germans shoehorned themselves into the bullet-pocked houses for a degree of protection against the freezing weather. In the meantime, Krag was bringing up his other two grenadier battalions and his artillery batteries, which had lagged far behind.

At his farmhouse command post outside Erezee, three-fourths of a mile northwest of Sadzot, Ed Tomasik was awakened by the harsh sounds of battle. He had no idea which American unit was fighting in Sadzot, but it was clear that a large German force was threatening to break through toward the Meuse.

Edmund Tomasik recalled his dilemma:

> General Rose had warned me the previous afternoon that under no circumstances was I to commit my battalion without his personal approval, for we were the 3rd Armored's only reserve. I tried repeatedly to radio Rose at his CP in Barvaux, but apparently the Germans had jammed the airwaves.
>
> I knew that something had to be done to prevent a breakthrough at Sadzot, so on my own initiative I ordered my battalion to recapture the village in order to blunt the German drive. One of my staff told me that if our attack was successful, my court-martial sentence might be reduced.

Rapidly, Tomasik drew up an attack plan. Capt. Jess Walls' C Company on the right and Hoyt Livingston's A Company on the left would jump off at dawn from the Hotton-Manhay road, a half-mile north of Sadzot. In support would be six 3rd Armored

tank destroyers. Paratroopers of B Company would be in reserve.
Hoyt Livingston recalled waiting to assault Sadzot:

> *This looked like a sure-fire suicide mission. We would have to trudge across 800 yards of flat, barren, frozen fields, with hardly anyplace to take cover, directly into the teeth of SS machine guns. I told my exec, Ken Shaker, "It'll be a miracle if we even get there."*

Less than five hours after the 4.2-inch mortar unit had been engulfed in Sadzot, Tomasik's paratroopers pushed forward. It was eerily quiet. After the Americans had advanced 600 yards without either side firing a shot, all hell broke loose. German machine guns fired withering fusillades, and the parachutists flopped down and responded with rifles and BARs.

With the six tank destroyers clanking forward and madly firing their cannon, the Five-O-Niners charged into Sadzot and bitter hand-to-hand melee ensued. Most of the SS men resisted fiercely until killed or seriously wounded, but others came out of houses to surrender when their ammo had been exhausted.

By 8:15 A.M., Sadzot had new owners. The speed and fury of the paratroopers' assault, as well as the firepower provided by the tank destroyers, had caused American casualties to be amazingly light.

In the lull that ensued, Pvt. Pat Moser, a teenaged paratrooper, found that he was hungry. So he opened a K-ration box and looked around for a dry spot to sit and eat. A German was lying on his back nearby, frozen in death. The teenager glanced at the German's eyes, which were wide open and appeared to be staring back at the American seated on his chest. The ice-coated eyeballs seemed to Moser to be mocking him by way of saying: "It's all over for me, American. But you, you poor bastard, you've got to keep going for a while longer, and then you'll end up dead just like me, anyhow." Pat Moser lost his appetite. He pitched away the remainder of his food, picked up his rifle and moved off.

Back at the 509th Parachute Infantry's command post at noon that day, Cpl. Ted Fina was reporting to a staff officer. Fina had been given the task of counting German bodies in and around Sadzot.

"Well, how many did you count?" the officer asked.

"Sir, 189 Krauts died suddenly of lead poisoning," Fina replied.

"Bloody Sadzot!" the other exclaimed.

In the meantime, the 509th Battalion received orders to establish defensive positions a couple of hundred yards south of Sadzot. Hardly had 22-year-old Lt. Jack Darden and his platoon edged inside the murky forest than a large group of SS troops charged them, shooting wildly and yelling: *"Paree! Paree! Paree!* [Paris]" For 20 minutes, a shootout raged, then the Germans pulled back, leaving behind a score of dead comrades.

By now, Horst Krag's other two grenadier battalions had arrived, and they also joined the death struggle. The woods around Sadzot echoed incessantly with the whine of bullets, the raucous chatter of machine guns, the crump of mortar shells, the swish of bazooka rockets, and the sharp explosions of grenades. Mingled with this earsplitting din were the shrieks of men—American and German—pierced by bullets or mutilated by shells and grenades.

In the midst of this uproar, 25-year-old Richard Fisco of New York was stalking through the thick, snow-thatched forest as lead scout for Jess Walls' C Company. Often, a lead scout's longevity is measured in days or hours, sometimes minutes. But Fisco, who had gained a wildman's reputation for his deeds on countless battlefields, had volunteered for the job. His comrades had always said that Dick Fisco was an ideal scout, that he could "smell out" lurking Germans at 50 yards.

Now Fisco felt a twinge of foreboding. Just before the 509th had rushed to the Ardennes, his beautiful French bride of a few weeks, Louise, had had a haunting dream that her husband would be wounded seriously in the left elbow. Fisco had brushed off her fears.

Suddenly staccato bursts of German machine-gun fire erupted from the woods, and C Company became immersed in a rousing shootout. Fisco crawled to a clump of 10 paratroopers, told them to follow him, and began slithering toward three spitting machine guns. Moments later, a mortar shell exploded and a jagged chunk of hot metal tore into Fisco's left elbow—just as his wife Louise had dreamed.

Dazed, bleeding profusely, his arm hanging in shreds, Fisco continued to lead his 10 troopers forward until every German at the machine guns had been killed. Then he staggered back out of the woods toward Sadzot and collapsed in the snow.[5]

For three days and nights, Tomasik's paratroopers and the SS men engaged in an orgy of bloodletting in the woods around

Sadzot. Finally, *Kampfgruppe* Krag, bruised and battered, broke off its relentless efforts to break through the 509th Parachute Infantry Battalion.

No one in American ranks, from four-star general to private, knew it at the time, but this brutal clash at Sadzot had been Hitler's final gasp to plunge to the Meuse and then on to Antwerp—and a possible negotiated peace. On the morning of December 31, an eerie hush fell along the entire northern battlefront, from Monschau on the east for 60 miles to Celles on the west.

Late in the afternoon of the 30th, the 509th Parachute Battalion, now but a shell of its former self, was relieved. Tomasik's boys had done their job. Against a numerically superior force, the Five-O-Nines had not only halted *Kampfgruppe* Krag, but had chopped it to pieces.

In turn, the pioneer 509th had also been badly chewed up. Paratroop rifle companies had an authorized strength of 148 officers and men. Now A Company had two officers and 20 men, B Company one officer and seven men; C Company three officers and 30 men.[6]

In the south, the three days following the December 27 linkup between the encircled 101st Airborne Division and the 4th Armored were relatively quiet in Bastogne. So quiet, in fact, that Tony McAuliffe found time to pen a testy letter to the one source used by generals and privates alike to let off pent-up steam—the B-Bag (or Gripe Bag) of the *Stars and Stripes*: "Our situation was never desperate, and I know of no man inside Bastogne who ever doubted [the 101st Airborne's] ability to hold the town." Even though the fighting bantam rooster McAuliffe had been regularly calling for aid during the siege, he and other Screaming Eagles had always considered this help to be relief, not "rescue." In another written statement to the GI press, McAuliffe declared: "We resent any implication we were rescued or needed rescue. The whole thing was just our dish."

Be as it may, Bastogne had lapsed into such relative tranquillity that on the morning of December 28, orders were sent down for all Screaming Eagle artillery batteries to police their areas (that is, to pick up debris) and for all men to be cleanshaven for an inspection by McAuliffe. "Jesus Christ," a parachute artilleryman howled, "the brass thinks we're back in garrison!"

Again reflecting the lack of enemy action at Bastogne, the G-2 of Bob Sink's 506th Parachute Infantry wrote in the daily diary: "A German police dog was reported operating against us last night."[7]

It would be the lull before the hurricane.

Now that the German floodtide in the Ardennes had run its course, General Eisenhower was ready to strike back by hacking through the base of the bulge from top to bottom. On the north, Lightning Joe Collins' VII Corps of four divisions would smash directly down the bitterly contested Manhay-Bastogne road (N-15). Attacking on Collins' left would be Matt Ridgway's XVIII Airborne Corps, consisting of Hobbs' 30th Infantry Division and Gavin's 82nd Airborne. At the same time, Patton's Third Army, spearheaded by Troy Middleton's VIII Corps, would lunge northward from Bastogne, and the converging forces would link up about halfway, at Houffalize.

Ebullient George Patton described the situation in vintage Pattonese: "The Kraut has stuck his prick in a meat grinder— and I've got hold of the handle!"

44
Battle of the Billets

At dawn on January 3, 1945, Gavin's reinforced 82nd Airborne Division and Collins' VII Corps on its right jumped off in a howling blizzard along a 23-mile sector in the middle of the northern battleground. Gavin had three regiments abreast: Bill Ekman's 505th Parachute Infantry, Charles Billingslea's 325th Glider Infantry, and Rupert Graves' attached 517th Parachute Infantry. Held in reserve were Tucker's 504th and Linquist's 508th Parachute regiments.

Weather conditions were horrible—Europe's coldest winter in

a quarter of a century. At night, wind-chill factors hit 50 to 60 degrees below zero, and snow drifts—already up to a man's waist—became even deeper. This stage of the fighting had been labeled by the GIs: "The Battle of the Billets." Each morning many men had to leave relatively warm and dry houses or cellars to attack, then once out in the cold they fought like savages, not for God or glory or country, but for the next billets to get warm. For their part, the Germans in the villages resisted like trapped beasts, not for the Führer nor for the Fatherland, but to keep from getting kicked out into the bitter cold.

On the far left of the 82nd Airborne's front, 25-year-old Dick Seitz's 2nd Battalion, spearheading the 517th assault, was attacking blind, not having had a chance to reconnoiter the terrain to be crossed. Late on the previous afternoon, Maj. Tom Cross, Seitz's exec, had jeeped up to the battalion's farmhouse command post after a mad dash from Paris where he was supposed to be recuperating from a broken ankle suffered in the jump in Southern France.

Seitz had told Cross to collect a few men and go forward to reconnoiter the ground to be crossed in the attack. The major had just taken his men behind the command post to brief them and handed his map case to Cpl. Archie Brown when a lone shell screamed in and exploded. Brown was killed and all the others were hit. Tom Cross was bleeding heavily from a head wound and had two shattered legs. Nearby in the snow, lay the shredded helmet that had probably saved his life.[1] Dick Seitz himself rushed forward to reconnoiter, but by then it was too dark to see the ground to be crossed.

Now Seitz's boys quickly seized Trois Ponts on the Salm River, and without pause, trudged on toward their next objective, Mont de Fosse, a half-mile to the south. There were interested spectators to the 517th's advance—Germans perched on Wanne Heights, across the Salm to the east. They bided their time until the unsuspecting paratroopers were marching over open fields and nearing Mont de Fosse. Then, from the bluffs, the Germans opened up with murderous machine-gun fire into the flank and rear of the Americans.

At the same time, 200 Germans dug in at Mont de Fosse raked the parachutists with leveling bursts of automatic-weapons fire, following this with deadly accurate mortar and artillery salvos began exploding among the pinned-down Americans, who were caught in a lethal cul-de-sac.

An hour later a new threat to Seitz's battalion emerged. A large force of German grenadiers waded the shallow Salm and tore into the paratroopers. Heavy fighting raged all day, but in early afternoon, the enemy broke off the attack and pulled back over the river.

For the remainder of the day, the Five-Seventeens lay with noses pressed into the snow while a rain of shells exploded on and around them. It was not until the arrival of the early winter darkness that wounded men could be evacuated.

Sietz's battalion had been hit hard—its worst encounter of the war. Within a few hours, more than 100 troopers had been killed or wounded. All of the rifle company commanders and half of the platoon leaders had become casualties.

Just before dusk, Jim Gavin and Rupert Graves, the leader of the 517th, were walking down a road south of Trois Ponts. Perhaps unaware that Seitz's troopers had been caught in a steel noose and were battling for their lives, Gavin was unhappy over what he considered to be lack of progress by the Five-Seventeens. Rupert Graves recalled that episode:

> Gavin and I jumped into a ditch to escape a salvo of mortar shells. "Your men have gone only a few hundred yards," Gavin said. "I want these towns tonight." He pointed at his map to St. Jacques and Bergeval [about two miles south of Trois Ponts]. With that, Gavin departed, leaving us to figure out how to get Seitz's battalion out of its trap.

Back at his command post at Basse Bodeaux, Graves and Wild Bill Boyle, whose 1st Battalion was in reserve, hastily hatched a plan to seize St. Jacques and Bergeval. Boyle and his men would circle to the west of Seitz's battalion, which was pinned down in front of Mont de Fosse, march southward, then turn to the east and smash into St. Jacques and Bergeval from that direction. Seitz's F Company had been in reserve, and it would go with Boyle's column. When St. Jacques was captured, F Company would pivot northward and attack Mont de Fosse from the rear.

Night was falling when Bill Boyle led his troopers out of Basse Bodeaux. Just before departing, the long-anticipated Christmas dinner arrived, so the men had to eat half-frozen turkey on the march. The night was black; the woods and underbrush thick. Each man had to hang onto the belt of the man in front, and there were frequent halts as the column broke contact.

Although St. Jacques was only a mile and a half away as the crow flies, it took five hours to reach the outskirts.

Hardly pausing, troopers of Capt. Dean Robbins' B Company charged into St. Jacques, whooping and yelling, and with rifles, tommy guns and grenades, mopped up the Germans in 30 minutes.

At once, Charles LaChaussee's C Company pushed on to Bergeval and stormed the village. In less than an hour, resistance ceased. It had been a stunning feat of arms for LaChaussee and his boys. Without the loss of a single trooper, they had killed 12 to 15 Germans and captured 121. Unwittingly, the *Feldgrau* in Bergeval had been gracious hosts. The famished paratroopers devoured the breakfasts that the Germans had been preparing in the houses when violence erupted.

In the meantime, Lt. George Giuchici's F Company had marched northward from St. Jacques, and rushed into Mont de Fosse. Surprised by this unexpected assault from their rear, the Germans milled about in confusion and the town soon belonged to F Company.

Rupert Graves recalled his feelings that morning of January 4:

> *We were all quite elated at the success of our night operations, and hoped to catch our breath. But General Gavin wanted us to keep moving [eastward] until we could, as he put it, dabble our feet in the waters of the Salm River. At any rate, our night attacks prevented at least myself and perhaps General Gavin from having a nervous breakdown.*

In the early hours of darkness, Bill Boyle led his battalion eastward out of Bergeval to occupy the heavily timbered high ground that dominated the crossings of the Salm. Once his companies were dug in, Boyle and three troopers headed back to his command post in Bergeval. While trudging across a snow-covered field in the moonlight, the tiny band heard a German shout: "Halt!" From a few feet away, a burst of automatic weapons fire erupted, and Boyle took five bullets—in the neck, chest, shoulders and arm. Racked with intense pain and bleeding profusely, Wild Bill Boyle uttered a simple prayer: "Oh, God, please don't let me die. I'm not ready."

Opening fire, the other troopers drove off the Germans (apparently a patrol) and returned to where Boyle was stretched out in the snow. Now heavy firing broke out on the ridge where

Boyle's battalion had dug in. "Get on back to Bergeval," the seriously wounded colonel instructed Robert Steele, his intelligence sergeant. "Tell [Maj. Donald] Fraser that all hell's broken loose up there, and that I'm hurt and for him to take command."

"I'm not leaving without you," Steele replied.

"Goddamn it, get on to Bergeval," Boyle grunted through clenched teeth. "There's nothing you can do for me—I'm dying."

Steele knew that the husky Boyle was too heavy to carry. So he decided to get him angry, to puncture his pride.

"The trouble with you, Colonel," Steele said, "is that you don't have enough guts to try to help yourself."

Boyle was furious. *No one* talked to him like that. "Damn it, Steele, give me a hand," Boyle muttered. He struggled painfully to his feet and, leaning on Steele, hobbled almost a mile to Bergeval. Before consenting to go to an aid station, the Wild One insisted on briefing his exec, Don Fraser.[2]

Back on the ridge overlooking the Salm, a wild melee raged throughout the night. A large force of Germans, trying to escape over the river to the east, had collided with Boyle's battalion in the pitch-black Bois L'Enfant (ironically, Children's Woods). With the arrival of the morning fog, all was silent. Clumps of German dead were scattered over the ridge, but Boyle's boys had paid a heavy price, too. One platoon had only seven troopers left.

When the 82nd Airborne jumped off on the morning of January 3,793 officers and men of Wood Joerg's attached 551st Parachute Infantry Battalion were at the line of departure to the right of Graves' 517th Regiment. Off to the south, across open fields, Joerg's assault companies could see large numbers of white-caped Germans manning machine guns at the edge of a woods. Veteran Five-Fifty-Ones knew that they would be marching into much danger.

Four American artillery shells rustled overhead and crashed into enemy positions. Capt. Tims Quinn, the C Company commander, turned to his forward observer and exclaimed: "Great! Right on target! Now give the bastards the full concentration!" Replied the other: "That *is* the concentration." At this crucial juncture in the Ardennes death struggle, there was an ammunition shortage.

Forming into long skirmish lines, the Five-Fifty-Ones began trudging forward. Without white camouflage suits, the paratroopers were starkly outlined targets against the snowy backdrop. It was eerily quiet. When the Americans reached a point 200 yards from the woods, four panzers on their flank began pouring in flat-trajectory shells and German machine gunners and rifleman raked the attackers. Then artillery and mortar shells crashed onto Joerg's boys, who could only lie facedown and take the deadly pounding.

Within 15 minutes, Quinn's C Company lost 45 men, Capt. Marshall Dalton's A Company was badly chewed up. Disaster loomed.

Then, as though on cue, large numbers of paratroopers leaped to their feet and charged through a torrent of bullets and explosions.

Bill Hatcher, who had been a battalion communications sergeant, recalled his astonishment:

> I couldn't believe my ears. Our boys were running toward the Krauts through the deep snow as fast as they could and shooting from the hip, and all the while they were yelling at the top of their lungs. I thought all that—rebel yells and the like—had gone out with the Civil War.

The bulllike charge seemed to unnerve the Germans. They abandoned their machine guns and stomped into the woods, with paratroopers of all three assault companies right on their heels. There in the maze of trees a confused struggle was waged.

Among those cut down was Marshall Dalton, the 27-year-old leader of A Company, who was knocked cold when a flat-trajectory shell exploded next to him. Wood Joerg, who had joined in the assault, radioed A Company: "Have you any officers there?" Replied 1st Sgt. Roy McCraw: "Negative!" Joerg said he would send Lt. Keith Harsh to take command, not knowing that Harsh had been shot in the shoulder. When Harsh arrived, McCraw could see that he was in agony. "I'll stay until I can be replaced," Harsh insisted.

Tree bursts—a special dread of foot soldiers—were taking a heavy toll. One exploded above Tims Quinn. Martin Kangas, who had been a machine-gun section leader, recalled that episode:

> Captain Quinn had chunks of shrapnel in him, I knew, for his rear end was all bloody. But he was dashing around bellowing orders like always—a .45 Colt in one hand, no helmet on. A medic tried to

get him to go back to an aid station, but Quinn yelled at him to go to hell, to take care of someone who really needed help.

Later that afternoon, Joe Cicchinelli, a scout for A Company, and a few comrades leaped behind an earthen embankment when the machine guns on a panzer spewed bullets at them. Between bursts, Cicchinelli heard a low moan and peeked cautiously over the embankment. Lying in the snow 100 feet into a field and bleeding badly was Cicchinelli's good friend, Don Thompson, the platoon sergeant. The same panzer that had been firing at Cicchinelli's group had cut down Thompson when he was leading a few men to knock out the German tank.

Capt. Tims Quinn. *(Dan Morgan)*   Lt. Col. Wood Joerg. *(Clark Archer)*

While the panzer continued to sweep the field with machine-gun fire, Cicchinelli slithered out to his badly wounded pal and tediously dragged him back to a roadside ditch. "Don't try to get up, Don," Cicchinelli said, "your left leg has been almost shot off."

After applying a tourniquet and giving a morphine shot, Cicchinelli reloaded Thompson's tommy gun and told him, "We've got to move on, but we'll try to get back to you after nightfall."

Shivering violently from the bitter cold and shock, Thompson lay alone in the blackness for perhaps four hours. Then he became aware of low voices that seemed to be coming closer. As silently as possible, he cocked his tommy gun. Moments later, he realized that comrades had returned and were calling his name.

Using an improvised stretcher of a pup-tent half and two rifles, a pair of Five-Fifty-Ones lugged their husky platoon sergeant for two miles to an aid station.[3]

Night brought mass confusion to the thick forest where Germans and Americans had become entangled in the swirl of that day's bloodletting. Roads and other landmarks were few. In the blackness and nearly impenetrable maze of trees, almost everyone lost his sense of direction. Tiny bands and lone soldiers—American and German—groped about, trying to find their units. Men shot first, asked questions later.

Pat Casanova, who had been an A Company scout, was with one wandering pack:

> It was so damned dark that we all had to join hands because we couldn't see a thing. Suddenly, the moon sneaked through an opening and we saw all these helmets lined up—German helmets. Our platoon leader, Lt. Dick Durkee—the roughest, toughest officer I ever saw—started blasting away, and the rest of us joined in. The Krauts scattered, but Durkee had bagged a couple of them.
>
> A short time later, we stumbled into a Kraut bivouac area. They were sleeping in slit trenches and on the frozen ground. Durkee took his rifle by the barrel and with the butt bashed the first German over the head.

When A Company was trying to reassemble in the darkness, Pfc. George Kane was sent back for a missing trooper in his machine-gun squad, but could find no trace of the man. On his return, Kane suddenly discerned the dim outline of an American helmet on a figure only 30 feet to his front. Detecting the figure raising his rifle, Kane belly flopped and the other emptied his eight-round clip at him. Kane felt the bullets driving chunks of ice and rock into his face. While the figure was reloading, Kane shouted the password repeatedly, and his assailant—a lost paratrooper—ceased firing.

Somewhere in the inky forest, a little knot of 551st troopers was stumbling along, bound for an aid station. Six or eight of them were wounded, and a few medics were carrying the semiconscious Capt. Marshall Dalton on a stretcher. Bringing up the rear was Pfc. Jack Westbrook, a 551st Battalion intelligence trooper, who had a German prisoner in tow.

Suddenly, a gutteral shout rang out from the front: "Halt!" As the paratroopers hit the ground, long bursts of Schmeisser fire zipped over their heads. Then silence resumed. Pfc. Thomas B. Waller and Pfc. Earl Grinstead, both of whom had been wounded a few hours earlier while manning their machine gun, convinced Captain Dalton that they were heading in the wrong direction.

So the group reversed course, with Waller out in front as lead scout. He came upon a narrow road, and his sixth sense told him it was going the right way, so he took it. A half-mile later, a German voice shouted something. Waller dived into a ditch, while the German prisoner 20 yards behind him yelled: "*Nicht schiessen! Nicht schiessen!* [Don't shoot]"

Then a shouted conversation began between the POW and the Germans hidden in the blackness. Moments later, two SS men carrying rifles edged out of the brush and came up to the band of Americans in the road. Perhaps the POW had told them that his captors were unarmed.

Thomas Waller recalled that event:

> *Our POW no doubt saved our lives. We gave the Krauts cigarettes and D-rations [chocolate bars] and promised them good treatment, hot coffee, and food if they would go with us to our aid station.*

Finally, the two Germans agreed to join in the trek to the 551st Battalion aid station, but they refused to surrender to unarmed Americans. So when the curious column trudged onward, the pair of *Feldgrau* held onto their weapons and brought up the rear as though escorting their "prisoners." Reaching an old farmhouse holding a few armed paratroopers, the Germans put down their rifles and, in turn, became POWs of the Americans.

Around midnight, Joerg's exhausted troopers in the woods tried to rest by scraping away a foot of snow and lying on the bare, frozen ground. Rest was impossible. No fires were permitted. Without overcoats and overshoes, men furiously jogged in place in a futile effort to keep warm. Sleep could mean death by freezing, so junior officers and noncoms went around shaking men who dozed off, but three 551st troopers fell asleep and froze to death.

Shortly after dawn, the badly chewed up 551st Battalion resumed its attack. Stomachs ached: The men had had nothing to
eat in 34 hours.

Carl Noble, who had been a machine-gun sergeant, recalled
that day:

> We were having a hell of a fight in a thick forest, and the fog was
> about two feet off the ground. If you wanted to see anything, you had
> to lie flat on the ground, and then you could see only feet moving
> around. One of our guys said, "Well, if you see German boots and
> keep firing, you can cut off the feet, then the legs, then the body—
> and finally you can tell if it really was a German you had just
> riddled!"

By later afternoon of January 6, Joerg's battalion, attacking
relentlessly for 96 hours, had clawed forward over a mile and a
half of Belgian territory and lost more than half of its men. Hoping for a short breather, the troopers got a jolt instead: orders
came to seize Rochelinval, a heavily defended village perched on
high ground along the Salm River.

Lt. Donald Booth, a resolute officer who had succeeded
Marshall Dalton as A Company commander, reconnoitered the
ground in front of Rochelinval, where an estimated 500 Germans
were entrenched. Seared into his being were the haunting words
"suicide mission." Not only would the freezing, exhausted, and
chopped-up battalion of paratroopers be attacking a larger force,
but German machine gunners on the ridge outside the town
would be looking down the throats of the Americans struggling
up the slope.

Booth and the other company commanders, all tough, courageous leaders, protested the mission to Wood Joerg. "Orders
came from division," Joerg replied. "We'll go in as ordered."

Before it got dark, 1st Sgt. Roy McCraw lined up A Company
to weed out those who had been concealing wounds, bronchitis
ailments, and trench-foot because they refused to "desert" their
comrades. Two truckloads of these casualties were sent to the aid
station, whittling down even farther the attacking force.

Joerg drew up an assault plan. Don Booth's A Company
would make the main effort, a frontal assault on the left; C Company would lay down heavy fire from the center, and B Company would attack from the right.

Just before daylight, Booth and his troopers, shivering from the cold, slipped into position at the bottom of the slope before Rochelinval. Faint tappings could be heard up on the ridge— Germans digging in deeper and getting their weapons ready. Sgt. Robert Hill came up to Dick Durkee, whose platoon would spearhead A Company's assault, and in even tones remarked: "Most of us will never get up there."

As H-hour drew near, a trooper called out in an angry whisper: "Where in the hell is that goddamned barrage?" Someone from on high had promised that artillery would plaster Rochelinval before the paratroopers jumped off—not a single shell would arrive.

Now a grim Don Booth arm-signaled Durkee to start up the slope, and two minutes later, the decimated platoon was raked by a torrent of machine-gun and rifle fire. Pvt. Robert Mowery, Durkee's lead scout, got it first—bullets in the stomach and one in the head. Seeing Mowery go down, Sgt. Bob Hill rushed to his side, grabbed his fallen comrade's BAR from the snow, and began firing at the Germans. He squeezed off two magazines before he, too, was killed.[4]

John "Milt" Hill, who had been executive officer of the 551st headquarters company, recalled events:

> Don Booth and his people were catching all kinds of hell. Machine guns, rifles, mortar and artillery shells. [Lt.] Phil Hand came up to me, and he had seen what was happening on the slope and was so upset he could hardly talk. Booth had just raised up to wave his men forward when he was shot and killed. Many of his men were also killed. Durkee—he was a fighter from way back—led his platoon up there, and hardly anybody was left.

On a hill just behind the assault companies, Wood Joerg picked up the radio transmitter to give orders when a salvo of shells screamed in. One exploded in a tree over Joerg's head, and a fragment tore through his helmet. A few troopers carried the semiconscious colonel to a jeep, and he was rushed to the rear.

A short time later, Reuben Tucker, a long-time close friend of Joerg's and leader of the 504th Parachute Infantry Regiment, happened to pass the aid station. With Tucker was Capt. Louis Hauptfleisch, his adjutant.

Hauptfleisch recalled his surprise over Rube Tucker's reaction:

Wood Joerg was laying on a makeshift sawbuck-and-wooden pallet in the open air outside the aid-station house. We could see he was barely breathing and had massive head wounds. Perhaps they had placed him out in the cold because there was no hope for him and the house was crammed with paratroopers whose lives might be saved.

Tucker, a hard-nosed combat commander, was emotionally upset, and I had never seen him like that. He tried to remove Colonel Joerg's West Point ring, saying, "I want to make damned certain that this gets back to his home." I reminded Tucker firmly that there were official procedures for handling the effects of a deceased soldier. So grudgingly, Tucker backed away and stood there cursing loudly at "those goddamned Krauts," as he always called them.

Maj. William N. Holm, the battalion executive officer, took command, but the troopers battling on the slope were unaware of their leader's death. Sgt. Harry Renick and a few comrades were pinned down by machine-gun bullets and exploding mortar and artillery shells.

Harry Renick recalled that hot-spot:

One guy had his arm blown off. He screamed and hollered, and the medic came and gave him a shot of morphine. After that he calmed down and said: "Well, you guys give me your girlfriends' addresses, 'cause I'm headed for the States and intend to look them up." His severed arm was laying there in the snow, but he was most happy: he had survived!

A short time later, John Pieniazek, a really tough cookie, who had been with the leading assault platoon, came back with no rifle, no helmet, no nothing—and half-crying. His entire squad had been wiped out; how he had gotten out alive, no one will ever know.

Somehow, tough Dick Durkee had reached the outskirts of Rochelinval. Just yards to his front, a German machine gun rattled angrily. Durkee looked back and was stunned: None of his men were with him. Have my boys run out on me? he thought. Then Durkee spotted Pat Casanova in a draw about 40 yards down the slope and shouted: "Get our guys to goddamned hell up here!" Casanova yelled back: "They're all dead!"

An American light tank came out of nowhere, and the desperate paratroopers put it to use. They hoped that the Germans would not know that its turret was jammed, so its cannon could not fire. On the tank's heels, grim survivors of the three assault companies hobbled into the town and face-to-face mayhem erupted. Like the Americans, the Germans at Rochelinval had nearly reached the limit of human endurance, and the roaring, disabled tank seemed to shatter their final resolve. Many of the defenders pulled back over the Salm, and large numbers poured out of houses with arms upraised.

Both sides had been bled white. A ghostly silence settled over bloody Rochelinval. Jack Affleck, who had been a battalion medic, recalled the scene, which looked like something Dante might have conceived:

> I went over to the west side of Rochelinval where Booth's A Company had been attacking. I came across several abandoned German machine guns that were sighted down the slope with perfect fields of fire. No wonder A Company had been cut to pieces.
>
> A single paratrooper, who I identified by his dog tags as Lt. Fon D. Dahl, lay dead near the first house, well out in front of other bodies in his platoon. That had been the new lieutenant's first attack, and his .45 Colt was still clutched in his frozen hand.
>
> Drained completely of the elation I felt earlier, I moved down the slope up which A Company had come, checking each group of American bodies for any sign of life. Stiffened already, their faces had a sallow, waxlike hue and were contorted with open mouths and wide, staring, sightless eyes.
>
> In one group of corpses I came across a friend I had known since jump-school days. Half his face had been shot away, and his helmet had come loose and lay beside his head. In it, badly stained by his blood, were several unopened letters which he apparently had received the night before but had not had time to read.
>
> Sprawled in the open on the slope, I found the body of the gallant Lt. Don Booth. He had nearly been cut in two by bullets. Judging from the position of his body, it looked as though the lieutenant was waving his men on forward when cut down.

Rochelinval had sounded the death knell for the proud 551st Parachute Infantry Battalion. Of the 793 officers and men who had departed from near Trois Ponts five days earlier, only about 100 remained—and many of them were suffering from minor wounds and physical ailments.

*   *   *

Since January 3, Ekman's 505th Parachute Infantry and Charles Billingslea's 325th Glider Infantry had been hacking forward steadily and absorbing heavy casualties. As soon as the 82nd Airborne attack got rolling, Tucker's 504th and Lindquist's 508th Parachute Regiments were hurled into the assault, and in a few days, the All-Americans had reached a timbered heights that was eight miles south of the line of departure. From there, the troopers could look across a wide valley to Thier-du-Mont and see large numbers of Germans feverishly digging in and setting up weapons.

Gavin was anxious to attack Thier-du-Mont before the Germans completed their defensive measures, but was ordered to hold in place until divisions on either side were on line with the 82nd Airborne.

Lindquist's 508th was given the nasty job of seizing Thier-du-Mont, and after a vicious fight, both sides had been cut down. When the Five-O-Eights had secured the village, one of its companies had only 33 men left.

Meanwhile, on the same day that Lt. Col. Wood Joerg had been killed, Ben Vandervoort's amazing good luck since Sicily had run out. During an attack, a shell exploded next to the leader of the 2nd Battalion of the 505th, and a white-hot chunk of jagged metal smashed him in the face, destroying an eye. Ben Vandervoort's long war was over.

At the command post of the 2nd Battalion of Tucker's 504th in the pulverized village of Fosse, Cpl. George Graves eagerly opened three bundles that had been sent by a SHAEF section in Paris. The packages contained items for distribution to the troops, most of whom were attacking or were shivering in icy foxholes. Graves and others in the command post turned the air blue with curses as they gazed in astonishment at a large collection of dart boards, ping-pong paddles and balls, checker and domino sets, and Monopoly games.

In six days of brutal battle, Courtney Hodges' First Army assault divisions had struggled only halfway to their goal—Houffalize—and a linkup with Patton's spearheads coming up from Bastogne.

45
Closing the
Trap

On the morning of January 3, 1945, Baron Hasso von Manteuffel held no illusions: Hitler's gamble in the Ardennes had collapsed. But the Führer, in his anger over the stubborn stand by the "Nuts!" Americans at Bastogne, now ordered the 47-year-old leader of the Fifth Panzer Army to capture the town, no matter what the cost in the blood of German boys.

Bastogne's most serious crisis loomed. Now the Wehrmacht was getting around to doing what it had not done during the siege—launching simultaneous assaults in strength at separate points of the Bastogne perimeter.

At dawn that day, four divisions of Lt. Gen. Hermann Priess' I SS Panzer Korps struck Bastogne from the north astride the road to Manhay and Liege. At the same time, the green 11th Armored and largely untested 87th Infantry divisions of Middleton's VIII Corps jumped off southwest of Bastogne toward Houffalize. The opposing assaults collided head-on, and in the savagery that ensued, the 11th Armored lost nearly one-third of its tanks and the 87th Infantry Division was badly chewed up.

Patton's drive northward to a juncture with Hodges' First Army had been halted in its tracks. That night the customarily dynamic Patton was gripped with gloom, penning in his personal diary: "We can still lose this war."[1]

Meanwhile, Max Taylor's 101st Airborne, in defensive positions in a large semicircle in front of Bastogne, had been beating off repeated efforts by Hermann Priess' SS troops to crash into the town. That night, with the issue of Bastogne still in doubt, Cpl. William Davis of the 502nd Parachute Infantry was hunkered down in a slit trench at a machine-gun outpost when a dark figure tapped him on the shoulder from behind and asked directions—in German.

Davis quickly bagged the enemy soldier and escorted him to the 101st Airborne command post. The German proved to be an intelligence gold mine. A member of the 9th SS Panzer Division, he had been sent to deliver attack orders to company command post, but had gotten lost in the darkness and thick forest.

The SS man "volunteered" the information that an all-out assault against Bastogne would hit at 4:00 A.M. One hour before that time, several American artillery barrages plastered a woods north of Longchamps, where the German force was to assemble, and the attack from that direction never came.

At dawn, Julian Ewell's 501st Parachute Infantry pushed forward to drive the Germans from murky Bois Jacques (Jack's Woods), two and a half miles northeast of Bastogne. Fighting was vicious and confused. A platoon led by Lt. James B. McKearney was pinned down by heavy fire from a German machine gun. Sgt. Desmond D. Jones jumped up to rush the enemy weapon, tripped and fell; his helmet was shot off as he went down. Jones crawled forward to within 10 yards of the machine gun (whose crewmen were now firing in another direction), took aim, and squeezed the trigger of his tommy gun. It failed to fire. Then he whipped out a pistol—it jammed.

With Jones sprawled flat, the Germans suddenly swung the muzzle around and began sending bursts of fire directly over his head. Only a small shrub concealed him.

Earlier, during a lull on another part of McKearney's platoon front, about 40 yards away, machine-gunner Pfc. John M. Fox, who could speak German, shouted for the enemy in the woods to send out someone to talk with him. (In the dense forest, actions could take place unseen and unheard by others only a short distance away.)

A German medic, wearing a white smock with large red crosses fore and aft, came forward. Fox asked if his comrades would surrender. If they did not do so, the paratrooper warned, the large force behind Fox would annihilate them. Actually, there were only 20 men in Fox's platoon.

"I'll have to go back and find out," the medic replied. A short time later, the German returned with a husky *Feldwebel* (equivalent to a platoon sergeant), who said he had many wounded men and that none of them had eaten in three days.

While John Fox breathed a deep sigh of relief, the Feldwebel called his 65 grenadiers out of their holes. Among those surrendering were the machine gunners who held Sgt. Desmond Jones' life in their hands. In the patch of woods, in addition to the prisoners, 30 German corpses were counted.

As the savage battle raged around Bastogne, a 101st Airborne staff officer was wading through the snow toward the front. Nearing the American foxhole line, he came upon a familiar scene: a long row of frozen German bodies. However, something looked different about these particular bodies. Puzzled, the officer halted momentarily. Then he knew what had caught his eye: The third finger, left hand, was missing from each corpse.

With his drive to link up with First Army at Houffalize bogged down, George Patton rushed in Bud Miley's largely green but eager 17th Airborne Division to spearhead a renewed VIII Corps assault. Because of the bad flying weather, Miley had been unable to ferry his division from England to the Continent until the day before Christmas. Landing at airfields near Rheims, Miley's troopers were hurried into defensive positions along the west bank of the Meuse, where panzer-tipped spearheads were threatening to break over the river and dash for Antwerp.

When Hitler's legions were halted after a 60-mile plunge into Belgium, the 17th Airborne men were trucked to Neufchâteau, southwest of Bastogne, from where they marched north to the battered town of Morhet, arriving late in the afternoon of January 3.

Despite its lack of battle action, the 17th Airborne was regarded as a crack unit. Col. Lou Coutts' 513th Parachute Infantry had its origins as a parachute-school troop unit at Fort Benning, and many of its junior officers and noncoms had been selected from among the best graduates. Back at Camp Forrest, Tennessee, Bud Miley had set up a jump school, and some 3,000 men of the two glider regiments had qualified as paratroopers.

Miley had hardly settled into his command post at Morhet that night when the 17th Airborne was ordered to attack at 8:15 in the morning and seize the town of Flamierge. George Patton had told Miley, "There's nothing out in front of you." Miley reflected: "Then who cut to pieces the 11th Armored and the 87th Infantry Divisions when they attacked over this same terrain a few hours earlier?"

Despite Patton's upbeat view, Miley's boys would gain their

baptism of fire under brutal conditions that would have sorely tested the mettle of experienced airborne units. Aside from the horrible weather, Miley had no time to send out probing patrols or to reconnoiter the terrain, so his troopers would be attacking blind. Because of the ammunition crunch, the preparatory artillery barrage would be limited to only 10 minutes, and a blizzard made it impossible to observe and correct the shelling.

Feverishly, Miley and his staff drew up an attack plan. Two regiments would push forward abreast: Lou Coutts' 513th Parachute Infantry on the right, Col. James R. Pierce's 194th Glider Infantry on the left. Held in reserve would be Col. Maurice G. Stubbs' 193rd Glider Infantry and the 507th Parachute Infantry, the latter having fought with distinction in Normandy. Commander of the 507th now was Edson Raff, the fiery young colonel who had led America's first combat jump during the invasion of North Africa more than two years earlier.

Supporting the 17th Airborne assault would be three artillery battalions equipped with 75-millimeter pack howitzers: Kenneth L. Booth's 466th Parachute, Paul F. Oswald's 680th Glider, and Joseph W. Keating's 681st Glider.

Promptly at H-hour, the Thunder from Heaven troopers trudged forward in a thick fog and bitter cold. Almost at once Coutts' 2nd Battalion, led by Lt. Col. Allen C. "Ace" Miller, ran into a fusillade. Screaming Meemies (multibarreled mortars) pounded the paratroopers advancing across open, snow-blanketed fields. Miller's E Company lost three commanders, one after the other, while struggling forward to the jump-off line. Lt. Samuel Calhoun, who had joined the Army after his 1939 graduation from high school, formed his F Company platoon into a skirmish line, and the troopers began advancing across a flat, open piece of ground devoid of cover. Suddenly, the Germans began raking Calhoun and his boys with murderous automatic-weapons fire.

Samuel Calhoun recalled:

> I could see my platoon being mowed down to my left and tracers were ricocheting off their bodies. My runner, Pfc. Patrick Keller, and I hit the snow. I could see the little black lines across the snow as bullets zipped past me and ripped into Keller's body. I hugged the ground and yelled at three of my boys lying nearby on the ground. All three were dead.
>
> Knowing that to move would mean certain death, I decided to

> *play dead, hoping the Germans would believe that I, laying between the three dead troopers, was also dead, and relax their firing.*
>
> *I laid there in the bitter, freezing cold for maybe 30 minutes. Then, suddenly, I leaped to my feet and made a dash to a pile of beets covered with dirt, about 75 yards to my left rear. It was the only cover in the huge field. German automatic weapons opened up on me and I could hear bullets whistling past my ears as I ran. Gasping for breath but thankful to be alive, I took a headlong plunge behind the frozen beet pile. The firing stopped.*

Lieutenant Calhoun managed to slip back to where his platoon had jumped off earlier that morning and began rounding up his men. There were only 14 of them. The remaining 24 or so troopers had been killed or wounded. Again Calhoun and his men pushed forward and spread into a skirmish line behind an embankment. Out to the front could be seen German soldiers dug in along the edge of a woods.

"Fix bayonets! Fix bayonets!" Calhoun shouted. There were clinking sounds as the pointed pieces of metal were fastened to the tips of rifles. Then a shout: "Let's get the bastards!"

Sam Calhoun recalled that rare event in modern combat, the bayonet charge:

> *Every one of my men scrambled over the embankment, and we charged, screaming and yelling, across the field of deep snow toward the line of German foxholes along the edge of the woods. As we neared them, some 28 to 30 Germans popped up from their holes, hands in the air.*

When Lieutenant Calhoun and his men came out of the thick part of the woods, they could see Lt. Richard Manning and his E Company platoon digging out Germans from their log-covered bunkers in the eastern part of the woods. What enemy soldiers survived the mad charge of Calhoun's and Manning's decimated platoons began to surrender in wholesale numbers.

Continuing the attack, E and F Companies were raked by machine-gun fire, and several men were cut down. Three medics, conspicuous with their red crosses on white fields painted on helmets, dashed to the aid of their fallen comrades and were shot and killed.

On Ace Miller's right, Lt. Col. Alton R. Taylor's 1st Battalion, after reaching Cochleval, was pinned down by heavy fusillades of machine-gun fire. Suddenly, two German tanks broke out of the fog and rumbled toward Taylor's boys, one of whom was 20-year-old Sgt. Isadore S. "Izzy" Jachman. Born in Berlin of Jewish parents, the cheerful, well-liked youngster volunteered for the paratroopers and action in Europe because he had a score to settle with the Nazis. His father, who had fought for the Fatherland in World War I, and his mother had fled with their son to the United States, but several of Jachman's relatives had been hurled into concentration camps and others were murdered.

Col. James W. "Lou" Coutts. *(Edward Siergiej)*

Sgt. Isadore S. Jachman. *(Lou Varrone)*

Now Jachman shouted for his bazooka man, and saw that he was dead. So the sergeant leaped to his feet and, crouching over, ran to the side of his fallen comrade and picked up the bazooka. Arming the rocket launcher, he put it to his shoulder, and crept toward the oncoming panzers. While bullets whistled past him, Jachman kneeled and squeezed the trigger, sending a rocket into the first tank. Reloading, he crawled forward and scored a bull's-eye on the second panzer.

Wounded several times during his duel with the belching monsters, Jachman was finally killed by a burst of machine-gun fire. Izzy had lost his life, but had at least partially settled his account with Nazi Germany, disrupted the enemy attack, and possibly saved his comrades.[2]

Meanwhile, on the left of Coutts' Five-Thirteens, Jim Pierce's glidermen advanced steadily against spotty resistance and quickly seized the hamlet of Hubremont. But Pierce's glider soldiers, along with Coutts' parachutists, had crashed into the flank of elements of four German divisions trying to break into Bastogne from the west.

Pounded heavily by artillery and mortars, assaulted by tanks and raked by machine-gun fire, Miley's two assault regiments were badly mauled and fell back almost to the line of departure.

Patton had been wrong—dead wrong. In the words of one of Coutts' officers: "The joint was lousy with Krauts!" Shaken and bruised, Miley's men would have no time to tend to their wounds. Word came from Troy Middleton: Jump off again at dawn (January 17) and seize Flamierge.

William Miley recalled the situation:

> *Nothing had changed. The Germans were still there—dug into the same positions. We had to cross the same terrain. The weather remained miserable, so there was little if any chance for fighter-bomber support. But Third Army [Patton] continued to insist that there was nothing out there in front of us.*

For the second lunge at Flamierge, three regiments would attack abreast: Pierce's glidermen on the left, Stubbs' glider soldiers on the right, and Coutts' paratroopers in the center. Almost at once the glidermen on the two flanks ran into fierce resistance and bogged down. But Coutts' parachutists slugged their way forward to within a mile of Flamierge.

Late that morning, Bud Miley went forward to the 513th Parachute Infantry command post. Lou Coutts remembered the general's visit:

> *Bud [Miley] suggested that we hold in place and wait for Pierce's and Stubbs' glidermen on our flanks to catch up. I discussed it with my battalion commanders, and we agreed that we had the Germans on the run and should keep them on the run. I wanted to grab Flamierge before the Krauts had a chance to dig in. So Miley gave me the green light to attack.*

Coutts designated his 3rd Battalion, led by Maj. Morris S. Anderson, to spearhead the assault. (The 3rd Battalion's commander, Lt. Col. Edward F. Kent, had been wounded earlier that day.)

Fanning out in skirmish lines, Anderson's boys waded across flat, open fields devoid of cover or concealment, toward Flamierge, a mile away. Overcoats and overshoes had been left behind.

When the Americans were within 200 yards of the town, an unexpected artillery barrage pummeled Flamierge. Despite the shell shortage, Lou Coutts had managed to get approval for the bombardment. Now Anderson's paratroopers charged into Flamierge, and a close fight erupted. Three German panzers were knocked out by bazookas. Within two hours, the surviving Germans withdrew to the north.

It had been a costly victory. Some 535 of Morris Anderson's battalion had launched the attack, but 152 troopers had become casualties.

Seeking to bolster his toehold in Flamierge, Lou Coutts rushed forward three more battalions: Taylor's 1st and Miller's 2nd of the 513th, and Lt. Col. John T. Davis' 3rd Battalion of Raff's 507th Regiment. Coutts' outfit was sticking out in a vulnerable salient.

In Flamierge, Anderson saw Germans moving onto the terrain his battalion had crossed, so he set up defensive position facing in all directions, much like a circled wagon train in the Old West.

Shortly after dawn, Lt. Col. Ward Ryan, executive officer of the 513th, managed to thread his way through isolated bands of Germans and reach Flamierge with a few tank destroyers to help the paratroopers handle an armored assault. But when Ryan, taking a circuitous route, arrived back at his command post, the tank destroyers had already beaten him there.

Early that morning, the Germans struck. Fifteen to 20 panzers and self-propelled guns emerged from the fog and rumbled across the fields toward Flamierge. Then German artillery shells screamed into the town. Almost at once, the telephone line to the rear was cut, and Anderson's radio balked, leaving him out of touch with any other unit or command post.

Anderson's troopers had plenty of bazooka ammo and held off the panzers by firing at them long-range. But then the tanks moved into positions from where they could hurl high-velocity shells into the town. All day, a vicious battle raged, and by nightfall, Anderson's battalion was surrounded.

On Anderson's flank, Col. Ace Miller, leader of Coutts' 2nd Battalion, had fallen asleep while seated at a kitchen table in his farmhouse command post along the Bastogne-Marche Road. Not far to Miller's front, his men were spending a miserable night, huddled in frozen foxholes, bone-tired and without a hot meal for five days. Just before 4:00 A.M. Cpl. Curtis A. Gadd climbed out of his front line hole to check on nearby troopers. Stalking through the darkness, Gadd stumbled over a comrade lying on his back in broad tank tracks.

Gadd thought the trooper was dead until he heard the man speak. Calmly and coherently, the other explained that a panzer had run over his legs 36 hours earlier and that he had been lying there in the sub-zero weather without medical treatment, food, or water since that time. No stranger to battlefield courage, Curt Gadd was astonished over this trooper's valor, and he hurried back to send up stretcher bearers.

A few minutes after 4:00 A.M., Ace Miller was rudely awakened by heavy explosions nearby. Moments later his field telephone rang and he picked it up. "Tanks?" Miller asked calmly. "Are you sure they're tanks?" Graying, blue-eyed, and old (35 years old) for a parachute battalion commander, Miller cocked an ear and heard tanks rumbling in the distance. Hurrying outside into the ice cold, Miller was startled. In the gathering dawn, he saw a swarm of panzers rolling toward him, with hundreds of white-sheeted grenadiers in their midst. Miller's battalion, with no armor or antitank guns, was in danger of being overwhelmed. Those who could navigate were pulling back before the German onslaught.

Miller dashed back across the snowy field that Lt. Sam Calhoun and his boys had won the day before in a bayonet charge, planning to set up a command post at the edge of a woods and rally his troopers for a last-ditch stand. Plunging through the snow, the battalion leader and other troopers were sniped at by 88s and raked by the machine guns of the panzers. All around, troopers dropped in the snow.

Curtis Gadd saw two lieutenants of D Company standing upright and firing madly—and futilely—into the charging panzers at point-blank range. Moments later, each officer was virtually cut in half by machine-gun bursts.

A trooper knelt and aimed his bazooka at a German tank bearing down on him and squeezed the trigger. The rock exploded in the tube, blowing off the man's head. A few feet away, Corporal Gadd felt something strike him in the chest; bloody flesh from the decapitated bazookaman. Sickened, Gadd flicked off the substance and continued hurrying back to the woods. A short distance later, Gadd saw another hideous sight: a parachutist had had both legs shot off and was painfully crawling over the snow, leaving behind two bloody trails.

Breathless and weary, Ace Miller reached his destination: the thick wood. A white Belgian bedsheet he was wearing was riddled with bullet holes. Panting, he looked back and saw many clumps in the huge field—his boys. Of some 150 men in Miller's assault company, perhaps 25 were left.

With Ace Miller's battalion already shattered and gone, Anderson's surrounded men in Flamierge were ordered to pull back that night—if they could. Anderson had to face the most agonizing period of his life: He had been told to leave his seriously wounded behind with an officer to surrender them to the Germans.

In bands of 10 or 12, Anderson's troopers, including the walking wounded, stole out of the town, its battered houses ghostly hulks in the starlit night. Exhausted and largely without sleep for 48 hours, each paratrooper reached friendly positions, bringing his weapon and most of his ammo with him. Anderson was the last man to leave Flamierge.

Lou Coutts' 513th Parachute Infantry had been hit hard, and the two glider regiments sustained heavy losses. Now the mauled 17th Airborne went over to the defensive.

On January 7, Tony McAuliffe, a folk hero back in the States after his "Nuts!" reply, got word that he had been promoted to major general and would command the 103rd Infantry Division. In a Bastogne cellar, McAuliffe was given a farewell dinner and a well-lubricated send-off by Screaming Eagle officers. In a bit of paratrooper humor, the general was presented with a parting gift—a pair of canvas leggings.[3]

While Joe Collins' and Matt Ridgway's corps in the north continued to hack their way toward Houffalize, Hitler ordered Sepp Dietrich to pull his SS troops out of Belgium. German soldiers were bitter over what seemed to be an action to save the hides of the Führer's elite. At the same time, the *Feldgrau* were ordered to fight to the death in the Ardennes.[4]

Learning of the SS pullout from POWs, Courtney Hodges decided to strengthen the XVIII Airborne Corps drive southward. On the left flank of the 82nd Airborne, Hobbs' 30th Infantry and Hasbrouck's 7th Armored Divisions were hurled into the assault from the Stavelot-Malmedy sector. Their objective was the pulverized town of St. Vith, 15 miles south of Malmedy.

Pfc. Frank Espinoza of 508th Parachute Infantry can still muster a smile. Near Anbrefontaine, Belgium. *(Pierre Gosset)*

To leaders of the 7th Armored Division, St. Vith had become a Holy Grail. For a week after *Wacht am Rein* struck, Bruce Clarke's Combat Command B of the 7th Armored, along with a few attached units, had made an epic stand in the town, taking heavy casualties but disrupting German plans and timetables.

In St. Vith, a German lieutenant, whose mauled and exhausted unit awaited the American onslaught to recapture the town, penned a note to his wife back in the Fatherland: "There are those among us who talk in terms of despair and even the ultimate loss of the war. But I do not think so. Come what may, I and others will fight on with everything we have in us."[5]

Rupert Graves' 517th Parachute Infantry was split up for the drive on St. Vith, with Don Fraser's 1st and Forest Paxton's 3rd

Battalions going to the 30th Infantry Division and Dick Seitz's 2nd Battalion being assigned to the 7th Armored Division.

Graves' paratroopers with the 30th Division were to jump off from Stavelot at 8:00 A.M. on January 13, and they would have to cross a wide, open valley in broad daylight under direct observation of the Germans in the hills to the south. There was every likelihood that the Five-Seventeens would be decimated by artillery and mortar fire before they came to grips with the Germans.

"To hell with the 8:00 A.M. jump-off," Graves told his commanders. "We're going to get across that open valley and into the woods before dawn."

Troopers of Rupert Graves' 517th Parachute Infantry advancing through Henumont, Belgium, near Malmedy. *(Pierre Gosset)*

Shortly after nightfall on January 12, a company of Paxton's battalion slipped across a broken-down stone bridge over the Ambleve River that bisects Stavelot and into the southern half of the town. No resistance was encountered. Once over, however, Sgt. Carl E. Votti was standing by a building awaiting orders when a German suddenly stuck a Schmeisser into his ribs. Votti, who had been a football player at Delaware University, wheeled around like a cat, and grabbed the gun barrel, slammed the six-foot-two, muscular German to the frozen ground, and took him prisoner.

Taken to the 517th, the captive turned out to be a platoon sergeant. After a little "persuasion," the German revealed the precise positions of enemy troops in the hills south of Stavelot, crucial information that would save many American lives.

That night, other 517th units stole over the bridge, and by daylight, both battalions were in the thick woods south of Stavelot and concealed from German view. At 8:00 A.M., Graves' men pushed forward through the deep snow and soon reached the main German defenses that were pinpointed by the captured platoon sergeant. A heavy shoot-out erupted.

Moving forward through the woods with his command-post group, Forest Paxton came to a trail, and the troopers halted to debate whether it was covered by Germans. "Well, wait a minute and I'll go see," Paxton said. A short time after he had gone forward, a German machine gun was heard clattering. Paxton came back with bullet holes in both trouser legs and said evenly, "Yes, I guess the Krauts are there."

Sgt. Carl E. Votti. *(Clark Archer)*   Lt. Col. Richard J. Seitz.
(Author's collection)

By dusk, Fraser's and Paxton's boys had broken through German defenses and were dug in on their initial objective.

Meanwhile the Bastogne region had erupted with renewed savagery. Max Taylor's 101st Airborne assaulted Noville, a short distance northeast of Bastogne, and got into a bloody fight. Among the casualties was Julian Ewell, leader of the 501st Parachute Infantry, who was hit in the foot and disabled.

West of Bastogne on January 13, Bud Miley's 17th Airborne Division jumped off for the third time in 10 days, with the objective of the Ourthe River near Houffalize. Two regiments were moving abreast: Edson Raff's 507th Parachute Infantry (veterans of Normandy) and Jim Pierce's 194th Glider Infantry. Like a tandem of spirited thoroughbreds, Raff's and Pierce's outfits lunged forward, steamrollered the Germans in Givry and Gives, and reached the Ourthe on January 15.

After suffering bloody noses in its first two battle actions, the 17th Airborne had rapidly come of age.

A patrol of the 17th Airborne Division links up with one from the 24th Cavalry near La Roche, on January 14, 1945, to help snap shut the Bulge trap. *(U. S. Army)*

A day later, on January 16, spearheads of Joe Collins' VII Corps, slugging their way southward, and leading elements of Middleton's VIII Corps (which included the 17th Airborne), linked up in "heavily liberated" Houffalize, as George Patton described the destroyed town.

A gigantic trap had been snapped shut on German units to the west.

46
St. Vith,
Herresbach,
and "Bloody
Huertgen"

In a blizzard on the morning of January 20, Hasbrouck's 7th Armored Division struck southward in the direction of St. Vith, and after hacking its way through Germans and snowdrifts for a few miles, stalled before the strongly defended village of Born, four miles north of St. Vith. The job of taking Born was given to Ed Tomasik's skeleton 509th Parachute Infantry Battalion, now whittled down to some 100 men.

Supported by four Sherman tanks, the Five-O-Nines fought their way into the edge of Born, but were raked by heavy fire. Within minutes, a lone panzer knocked out the four Shermans, and the paratroopers fell back a few hundred yards.

In the aftermath of the firefight and withdrawal, Doc Alden found himself alone with the Germans in Born. He managed to slip out of town without being spotted, and while walking back to where his battalion was regrouping, came upon two seriously wounded comrades lying motionless in the snow. Stooping, the surgeon recognized Capt. Leslie Winship, a former soldier of fortune who had fought in the Spanish Civil War, and a young sergeant named Wilson. Both men's legs had been ripped to shreds by .50-caliber machine gun bullets, and their jumpsuits were saturated with blood.

Alden knew that the two ashen-faced men were dying, but he gave each a morphine shot and remained with them, even though he was aware that he was in no-man's-land and might be captured. A short time later, a German tank clanked down the road from Born, and Alden quickly pitched his tommy gun and Luger into a snow bank before being taken prisoner for the second time in the war. While the German tankers frisked Alden, Winship and Wilson died.

Wearing his trademark red beret, Alden was marched into Born and roughly shoved down steps into a candlelit basement. To his astonishment, he was interrogated by a female German officer. Calmly, the surgeon spun a fanciful lie about an American regiment, supported by swarms of tanks, that was closing in on Born.

(Doc Alden was the "Great Escape Artist" of the paratroopers. Two weeks after being captured at Born, he escaped from deep inside Germany and was recaptured while trying to sneak back through the Siegfried Line. A few days afterward, he fled from a building holding POWs in Pruem, Germany, by sliding down an improvised rope for five floors. This time he infiltrated German lines and reached friendly forces in Belgium. Twice the previous year in Italy, Captain Alden had been captured while alone behind German lines, and he escaped both times.)

After the Five-O-Nines attacked again and seized Born, Ed Tomasik was called in by Bruce Clarke, the hulking leader of the Seventh Armored's Combat Command B. Clarke was suffering from gallstones and had to take pain killers, but he refused to be evacuated until his command had recaptured St. Vith. Clarke pointed to a map and told Tomasik that his 509th Battalion was to seize a hill overlooking St. Vith.[1]

Tomasik replied: "Sir, you should be advised that the current strength of the 509th Parachute Infantry Battalion is six officers and 57 men." Looking Tomasik in the eye, Clarke said: "Major, you will attack as ordered."

Led by Lt. Ken Shaker, the Five-O-Nines clawed their way up the targeted hill and killed or captured a large number of Germans and an 88-millimeter gun. Forty-three zombielike officers and men remained of the nearly 700 men of the 509th Battalion who had arrived in the Ardennes a month earlier.

Meanwhile, Dick Seitz's 2nd Battalion of the 517th hooked up with the 7th Armored's Combat Command A, whose leader, Col. William S. Triplet, formed the paratroopers, a company of tanks, and a platoon of tank destroyers into Task Force Seitz. In biting cold and blackness before dawn on January 21, Task Force Seitz jumped off to clear the Germans from the murky Auf der Hardt woods before St. Vith. After a swirling, day-long fight, most of the Germans had been killed or driven off.

On the following morning, Task Force Seitz struck again in an attack on Hunnange, a mile northwest of St. Vith, and by midafternoon, the parachutists and tanks were closing in on the village. Two hours later, Hunnange was nearly blown off the map by a TOT (time on target, a synchronized artillery salvo in which all shells impact simultaneously), after which the troopers climbed onto the tanks and began a wild charge. When the mechanized stampede neared Hunnange, the tankers fired the cannon and the paratroopers blasted away from the decks with the .50-caliber machine guns.

Hunnange was quickly overrun, and 126 Germans, most of them in shock from the TOT, were rooted out of the rubble. Seitz rapidly pushed on to Lorentswaidchen (three-fourths of a mile from St. Vith) and that night sent patrols into the outskirts of St. Vith.

Richard Seitz recalled subsequent events:

> Our patrols received virtually no opposition, and we could have moved on into St. Vith. But we received an order, "Hold fast in your present positions." The next day, Bruce Clarke and his CCB— together with lots of press—passed through our positions and entered St. Vith.

On January 27, Rupert Graves' 517th Parachute Combat Team was pulled out of the front lines after 37 days of continuous action as a "fire brigade" up and down the XVIII Airborne Corps sector. Graves' combat team had lost over 700 men in the Ardennes—600 of them in the rifle companies.

At Juslenville, Belgium, where the remnants of his mauled 551st Parachute Infantry Battalion were in reserve, Bill Holm and his boys received an unexpected jolt: The unit would be deactivated. Upon hearing the news, the Five-Fifty-Ones were angry and dismayed. Some of the toughest ones cried.

William Holm recalled:

I talked with General Ridgway to see if we couldn't go back to Laon [France] to get our records and close out the battalion in order. He said it couldn't be done—that our [surviving] officers and men were needed in other units at the front. Ridgway also said that he had had orders from the Pentagon earlier to break up the separate parachute and glider battalions, but had held up the action when the Ardennes fighting erupted.

Despite their protests, troopers of the 551st Parachute Infantry Battalion were distributed among 82nd Airborne regiments, with a few going to Graves' 517th Parachute Combat Team.

A short time later, the pioneer 509th Parachute Infantry Battalion also was summarily axed. William Yarborough, who had been that pioneer unit's commander, remembered:

I had been sent back to the States for a nine-week course and expected to command the 509th when I returned. On going to Washington to get my orders after finishing the course, I ran into Jim Gavin, who told me that the 509th had been decimated and disbanded.

This made me so damned angry. Nobody had even bothered to tell me this had happened, even though ostensibly I was still in command of the battalion. The thought that this great paratroop outfit had been pulled apart and its guidon and battle streamers pitched into some dirty warehouse was to me a crime of the first order.

So I charged into the War Department and tried to find out who was responsible for this. I was hostile as hell. Instead of being thrown out, as I might have been, they sympathized with me and said it had been done by order of General Ridgway.

Most of the embittered men of the 509th Parachute Infantry were integrated into the 82nd Airborne, while others were assigned to Maj. Gen. Eldridge G. Chapman's 13th Airborne Division, which had recently arrived from the United States.[2]

With the linkup at Houffalize and the recapture of St. Vith, the Americans wheeled eastward to finish deflating the Bulge. After two weeks of rest, Gavin's 82nd Airborne was sent back into the line northeast of St. Vith to spearhead an ambitious XVIII Airborne Corps offensive whose objective was Euskirchen, a German city 42 miles northeast of St. Vith. It would be a monumental task. The weather remained horrendous, snowdrifts

Eighty-second Airborne troops moving forward near Fraiture, Belgium. *(Pierre Gosset)*

were waist-high, and the icy roads were nearly impassable for tanks and vehicles.

Before dawn on January 28, the 82nd Airborne pushed off without any artillery bombardment in order to gain surprise. Julian Cook's 3rd Battalion of the 504th lunged forward, caught the *Feldgrau* still in their sleeping bags, wiped them out, and trudged onward for nearly two miles. Cook's boys had scored a clean breakthrough.

Reaching a wooded hill from which the troopers could look down on Herresbach, a village resting on the valley floor about a mile away, Cook halted the battalion and called in his company commanders. "That town down there is in [Ed] Willems's [2nd Battalion] zone," Cook explained. "But Ed's been held up far to our right rear by heavy opposition. So if your boys want to sleep in those houses tonight, we're going to have to chase the Krauts out of town." Cook radioed Rube Tucker and was given the green light to seize Herresbach.

Leading the attack would be Capt. Carl Kappel's H Company, with the platoons of Lt. Richard "Rivers" La Riviere and Lt. James "Maggie" Megellas out in front. Just before shoving off for Herresbach, La Riviere was jolted by a radio message: His air corps brother, Ronnie, had been killed fighting the Germans.

A half hour before nightfall, Cook's battalion, with three tanks accompanying the assault platoons, headed down a road that led to Herresbach. Suddenly, scouts motioned frantically for the troopers behind them to take cover. Marching up the hill four abreast in parade-ground formation directly toward the Americans was a column of some 200 Germans, who no doubt believed that they were far behind the "front lines."

Concealed in the brush along side the narrow road, Cook's men and the three tanks waited until the unsuspecting *Feldgrau* were nearly upon them, then opened a torrent of fire at point-blank range. Spitting out streams of red tracers into the gathering dusk, the machine guns on the Shermans cut down the closely packed enemy force as though a huge scythe had been wielded. Clumps of German bodies piled up in the snow. The *Feldgrau* did not try to surrender, and the troopers made no effort to take prisoners. Each time one of Dick La Riviere's men killed a German, he called out, "That one's for Ronnie!" (La Riviere's dead brother.)

Within minutes, every German had been killed.

Pushing onward, Kappel's H Company troopers blasted their way into Herresbach where a wild melee erupted in the darkness.

George Graves, who was a corporal in Rube Tucker's head-quarters company, remembered:

> After a month in the Ardennes, our old vets were punch-drunk and didn't much give a damn what happened to them. They had nothing to look forward to—except a wound that would evacuate them or a coffin. All the men [in Cook's battalion] were fighting mad after wading through waist-high snowdrifts for 12 hours to get to Herresbach. Some of our boys ran wild, shooting everything that moved in the town. The Krauts used up all their ammo shooting at our guys, then came out yelling, "Kamerad!" Our troopers would reply with "Kamerad, hell!" and a burst from a tommy gun.

By 9:00 P.M., Herresbach—and its coveted houses—had been taken over by the men in baggy pants. A total of 138 German corpses would be counted in the town, in addition to the 200 bodies sprawled along the road into Herresbach. Another 200 *Feldgrau* had been flushed out of cellars and locked in a large barn.

In the assault on Herresbach by Julian Cook's battalion, an

Artillery elements of the 82nd Airborne move forward. *(U. S. Army)*

incredible battlefield oddity had occurred: Despite the heavy fighting, not a single paratrooper had been killed or wounded or was missing.

Meanwhile, two and a half miles from Herresbach in Holzheim, C Company of Roy Lindquist's 508th Parachute Infantry was slugging it out house-to-house with the Germans. While the fighting raged, some 80 German prisoners were being guarded by four paratroopers.

At this point in the Ardennes, white camouflage clothing had been issued to American fighting units (although not nearly enough for every man), so when four Germans in "snowsuits" and carrying weapons approached the German POWs, the paratrooper guards thought that they were Americans. The startled Five-O- Eights were disarmed, and the newcomers quickly began rearming the freed POWs with abandoned weapons to attack C Company in Holzheim from the rear.

When only a few of the prisoners had weapons, 1st Sgt. Leonard Funk happened to walk around a building and directly into the midst of the group. A German major stuck the muzzle of a Schmeisser into Funk's ribs and demanded that he surrender.

Leonard Funk recalled:

All through the war, I had always said to myself and to others that I would never surrender. They'd never take me alive as long as I had ammunition and the strength to fire my weapon. So when the Kraut poked the Schmeisser in my side, I said to myself, "Well, here goes! This is it! Good-bye world!"

Slowly, Funk began to remove the tommy gun that was hanging by its strap over his shoulder, as though he were going to hand over the weapon, then gambled with odds of 1000-to-1 against him. In one sweeping motion he grabbed the tommy gun in mid-air, swung it around, and held down the trigger, riddling the German major.

A wild scramble erupted. The four disarmed paratroopers whipped out their trench knives and plunged them into the nearest Germans, then picked up discarded weapons and blasted away at the three Germans in snow suits and the armed POWs. Funk, in the meantime, reloaded twice more and joined in the shoot-out. At the height of this pier-six brawl, German shells screamed into the street, and the Americans and most of the *Feldgrau* hit the deck. Most of the German prisoners became prisoners again.

Lenny Funk didn't get a scratch, but two days later he was wounded for the third time since Normandy, and would go on to become America's most decorated paratrooper.[3]

American brass had hoped to score a major breakthrough in the current eastward drive to flatten the Bulge, believing that the battered Wehrmacht was in total disarray. Instead, the *Feldgrau* fought tenaciously for every yard of frozen turf, and after six days the 82nd Airborne had advanced only 15 miles—a herculean feat considering the arctic weather and the stiff opposition, but not fast enough for SHAEF. So General Eisenhower canceled the offensive.

Early in February, the 82nd Airborne and its attached 517th Parachute Combat Team were trucked northward to the Huertgen Forest, which had earned a sinister reputation as a man-eating monster. Since September, four American divisions had suffered 21,900 casualties while trying on four different occasions to penetrate "Bloody" Huertgen (as it was called) and seize the key town of Schmidt and the nearby Schwammenauel Dam on the Roer River, which flows parallel to the Rhine.

Men of the 17th Airborne's 513th Parachute Infantry catch a ride on an artillery piece as they push toward Siegfried Line. (*Pierre Gosset*)

Pressure to rapidly capture Schwammenauel Dam, a massive concrete structure 700 feet long, was now being exerted from on high. If the Germans blew the dam, the Roer Valley downstream (north) would be flooded, halting for at least two weeks the Allied drive to the Rhine, 20 miles to the east.

"Bloody" Huertgen, a seemingly impenetrable mass, was honeycombed with thick minefields, barbed wire, large pillboxes, and machine guns with interlocking fields of fire. Sprawled in the maze of trees were the corpses of hundreds of American soldiers, grotesque and rigid, just emerging from the deep snow under which they had been preserved all winter.

Jim Gavin's 82nd Airborne (Ekman's 505th, Lindquist's 508th, and Graves' attached 517th Regiments) were to attack toward the German stronghold of Schmidt. Graves' outfit in particular was handed a nightmarish mission. At midnight of February 5, it was to jump off southward from pulverized Bergstein (two miles north of Schmidt), negotiate the treacherous forest, cross the Kall River and its steep ravine, and seize the high ground a mile and a half from the line of departure.

Promptly at the stroke of midnight, Dick Seitz's 2nd and Forest Paxton's 3rd Battalions marched out of Bergstein. It was inky black. Fluorescent strips were stuck to the back of each man's helmet; the trooper in back was to follow the white blob.

It had been deathly still until the Five-Seventeens hit minefields and concertina wire 600 yards below Bergstein. Then the enemy opened up with machine guns, artillery, and mortars. Troopers, their faces ghostly in the glare of brilliant flares, were cut down on all sides. Throughout the night, the paratroopers tried to inch forward. Screams pierced the blackness as men were blown to pieces by *Schu* mines and "Bouncing Bettys"—especially fiendish devices that hopped upward before exploding at face level.

In the hailstorm of fire, F Company commander George Giuchici and his men tried to circle around the German force to their front. Myrle Traver, who had been a BAR man, remembered:

> We were all crawling. Machine guns and flares were keeping me scared to death. Somehow we got through a minefield and began moving up and down hilly trails. After a while I looked back —no one was with me. I ended up in a foxhole with Lieutenant Canfield. Two German officers unknowingly walked up to our hole. Canfield popped up and drilled both of them at three feet.
>
> At dawn we came on to some of our boys and started walking. Now our own artillery shelled us. Captain Giuchici told me and George Flynn to follow him, and we ran and ran. We stumbled onto a young German soldier—he looked about 13 years old. He begged us not to kill him, and Giuchici said to bring him along.
>
> We—Giuchici, the German kid, and me—hid in a large shell crater and waited for our battalion to catch up. We didn't know that the attack had been called off.

For two freezing days and nights, the two paratroopers and the German boy huddled in the crater. On the first night, a pair of German officers stood talking and smoking at the edge of the hole. George Giuchici reached up and touched one German's boot—"just for the hell of it."

Myrle Traver remembered:

> Late on the second night, Giuchici woke me and said the kid prisoner was gone. Just after daybreak, we saw some soldiers heading our way. We thought they were our fellows, but the brush

was thick and it was hard to tell. Six German helmets and six guns
came over the edge of the crater—then we knew.
  The Krauts wanted to kill Giuchici, but the kid was with them
and told them that since we hadn't killed him, then they shouldn't
kill us. He talked them out of shooting Giuchici.

In the meantime, 20-year-old Cpl. Allan R. Goodman of Oak
park, Illinois, and his comrades in the 596th Airborne Engineer
Company had been engaged in a tedious and perilous task: clearing a path through a huge minefield just south of Bergstein.
Only later would these engineers learn that it was the largest
German minefield on the Western Front.[4]
Working in shifts under steady mortar explosions and occa-
sional bursts of machine-gun fire, the 596th Engineers deacti-
vated scores of Bouncing Bettys, *Schu* and Teller mines, and laid
a white tape for several hundred yards through the cleared lane.
It was a nerve-racking task. Pine needles on the forest floor con-
cealed the buried explosives and trip-wires, adding to the danger.
Any moment an engineer might be blown sky-high.
Allan Goodman recalled:

It took us more than two days and nights to get the job done. We
were physically and mentally exhausted, but fortunately, none of our
fellows were blown to bits. That night I was called to a CP for a
briefing on the next morning's attack, and was told by a lieutenant
that he wanted us engineers to lead the way. I told him that we had
cleared the mines, but we weren't supposed to be sheep. The
lieutenant got angry, but backed off when a major backed me up.

With the path marked through the minefield, Graves' troopers
launched a new attack toward Schmidt. Morale had hit bottom.
This assault had all the earmarks of disaster. Some officers and
men had reached the limits of their endurance and had to be
evacuated. One officer refused to lead his men into what he considered to be certain death.
When the decimated regiment had snaked its way through
the minefield it was dawn, and the German 6th Parachute Regiment raked the Five-Seventeens with murderous fire. For several
hours a vicious fight raged. One battalion commander, Dick
Seitz, radioed F Company for its current strength. Came back the
reply: "Three radio operators and one machine-gun team."
That night the 517th Parachute Combat Team was relieved.

Sgt. Allan R. Goodman.
(Author's collection)

In three days in the Dante's Inferno of Bergstein, Graves's outfit had lost one-quarter of its men.

On February 8, the 78th Infantry Division captured the Schwammenauel Dam, but it was too late: The Germans had already blown the locks and flooded the Roer Valley.

The Winter War was over.

In the Pacific, momentous events were emerging—and American paratroopers were in the thick of it all.

PART VI

Final Operations

47
The "Mud Rats of Leyte"

True to the promise he had made when a woefully unprepared America was driven from the Philippines in spring 1942, Douglas MacArthur had returned to those embattled islands on October 20, 1944. In two and a half years of "shoestring warfare," MacArthur's "hit-'em-where-they-ain't" strategy had taken his forces some 2,000 miles north of Australia to an assault landing by Walter Krueger's veteran Sixth Army on Leyte.

Defending the Philippines was 59-year-old Tomoyuki Yamashita, one of Japan's most able generals and a folk hero on the homefront. Six feet, two inches tall, and husky, his bullet head completely shaved, Yamashita was known as the "Tiger of Malaya" since he had stunned the world by forcing 90,000 British Empire troops to surrender en masse on that fortress island in January 1942.

Shrewd and energetic, Yamashita had concluded that MacArthur would invade Luzon, the largest island in the Philippine chain, and concentrated most of his forces there. On Luzon were virtually all of the worthwhile military objectives in the islands: Manila, many airfields, and two major naval bases. Typically, MacArthur struck where least expected, not at Luzon, but at Leyte, a large, primitive island 300 miles southeast of Luzon in the central Philippines.

Walter Krueger's assault troops landed at Leyte Gulf on the east coast and began hacking their way westward toward Ormoc, a key Japanese-held port on the west coast. Ormoc was but 25 miles away from the landing beaches as the crow flies, but Krueger's foot-sloggers bogged down because of the treacherous central mountain range, torrents of rain, and tenacious Japanese.

Reacting with customary speed, Tomoyuki Yamashita began pouring troops into Leyte from Luzon, using small boats, barges, tramp steamers, canoes and row boats. In less than one month, Yamashita had 10,000 more soldiers on Leyte than he had had when MacArthur landed.

Krueger, meanwhile, responded to the Nipponese buildup by bringing over the Leyte Gulf beaches Joe Swing's green—but spirited and keenly trained—11th Airborne Division. Swing's troopers were not happy to be coming into action from the sea. That approach was hardly the bold "strike-and-hold" mission from the sky for which they had been honed. But Krueger, in his war of limited manpower and resources, urgently needed foot soldiers.

Swing, who had been the 82nd Airborne's artillery commander, had led the 11th Airborne since its birth at Camp Mackall, North Carolina, on February 23, 1943. At West Point, he had played on the varsity football team that included another halfback named Dwight Eisenhower.

Although he looked every inch a Hollywood scriptwriter's version of an American general—white-thatched, tall, and ruggedly handsome—the 48-year-old Swing shunned flamboyance like the plague, and he conscientiously avoided publicity. Hence, unlike the big airborne names in Europe—Matt Ridgway, Slim Jim Gavin, and Maxwell Taylor—Joe Swing was hardly a household word in the United States, and neither was the 11th Airborne Division.

Like most airborne leaders, Swing was a physical fitness addict, and he expected no less from his men. Back at Mackall and later at Camp Toccoa, Georgia, he bounced countless officers from the division because they could not keep up with him in grueling 15-mile runs he led through thick brush and swamps.

When the 11th Airborne was shipped to New Guinea and began arduous jungle training, Swing pulled strings in Washington and got a jump school established on that primitive island. His goal was to have the entire division—including glider soldiers—qualified as paratroopers. By the time the division embarked for

Leyte, some 85 percent of officers and men were jump-qualified.

On reaching Leyte in late November 1944, Joe Swing set up his command post at San Pablo, one of a complex of three primitive airstrips adjacent to the town of Burauen, some eight to ten miles west of the Leyte Gulf landing beaches, and began deploying his troops.

Col. Harry Hildebrand's 187th Glider Infantry Regiment was assigned to protect the division's rear installations in the vicinity of the beach, and Col. Robert H. "Shorty" Soule's 188th Glider Infantry was to aggressively patrol in the direction of La Paz and Bugho, flushing out Japanese bands. The 511th Parachute Infantry Regiment, led by 36-year-old Col. Orin D. "Hardrock" Haugen, got the toughest nut to crack: hacking through the towering, jungle infested Mahonag Mountains to Ormoc on the west coast.

Haugen, a career officer from Alabama, like the big boss, Joe Swing, was tough and demanding. Back at Camp Toccoa, his men had given him the nickname "Hardrock" for his penchant to lead them on 25-mile runs through the mountains. Haugen had earned a reputation as the toughest man in the regiment.

While Haugen's paratroopers began a tortuous climb into the Mahonag Mountains, Maj. Henry A. Burgess, acting G-3 (operations officer) of the 11th Airborne, was handed what was called a "crystal ball" report. Twenty-six-year-old Burgess, a rancher from Sheridan, Wyoming, had never heard of a crystal ball report. The coded message warned that the Japanese were about to launch a parachute assault against the airstrip complex—San Pablo, Buri, and Bayung.

Burgess rushed the alarming message to Joe Swing, who knew that the mysterious crystal ball reports had been remarkably accurate in the past. But only 26-year-old Lt. Col. Henry "Butch" Muller, the 11th Airborne intelligence officer, knew the source of these supersecret signals—Maj. Gen. Charles Willoughby, MacArthur's chief of intelligence.

Earlier, the hulking, six-foot-six, 250-pound Willoughby, who had been born Karl Widenback in his native Germany, had called in Butch Muller and revealed a startling fact. An American code-busting agency had cracked the Japanese code and was regularly intercepting secret enemy messages. Muller was direly warned not to disclose that crucial intelligence coup, one of America's most profound secrets, to anyone in the 11th Airborne—even to Joe Swing.

Now at San Pablo, Swing took the crystal ball report from Henry Burgess, scanned it, and frowned. The general scoffed at the notion that the Japanese had the capability to launch such a daring major airborne assault.

At San Pablo just at twilight on December 6, Capt. Kenneth A. Murphy, a husky former football player at the University of Minnesota, was lined up for supper outside a mess tent. Since San Pablo was far behind American "lines" in the mountains of central Leyte, neither the 25-year-old Murphy nor others were carrying their weapons.

Murphy gazed casually skyward at two flights of transport planes approaching the airstrip at about 700 feet. Joe Swing, who was seated nearby in a folding chair, thought they were C-47s. So did Henry Burgess. As the planes drew closer, Murphy and Burgess were startled: The aircraft were lighted and a man was standing in the doorway of each one, ready to jump.

Unknowingly, the 11th Airborne troopers were seeing the fine cutting edge of Operation *Wa*, a daring Japanese airborne and ground offensive designed to seize the initiative on Leyte. In the approaching flight were elements of the 350-man 3rd Parachute Regiment, led by a fire-eating young lieutenant colonel, Tsunehiro Shirai, who would jump from the first plane.

Shirai's paratroopers were to capture San Pablo, Buri, and Bayong airstrips, destroy large numbers of American planes based there and the facilities, and pull back into the mountains to link up with attacking Japanese ground troops.

Moments after the 11th Airborne men in the chow line had spotted the figures standing in the airplane doors, the grayish sky was awash with parachutes. Cries of, "They're Japs!" rang out. Supper was forgotten, mess kits were sent flying, and men rushed madly to their tents to retrieve weapons.

It was an extraordinary situation: paratroopers dropping on paratroopers.

Most of the Japanese landed on San Pablo, instead of on Buri as had been planned. Perhaps 50 Japanese, including Colonel Shirai, dropped on Buri. Several Nipponese were killed when their parachutes failed to open. On both San Pablo and Buri, some of the invaders torched and blew up light aircraft, gasoline dumps, and buildings. But most seemed to be confused or drunk—or both. In the shadows cast by the flickering flames, Japanese paratroopers dashed helter-skelter around San Pablo screaming *Banzai!*, shooting off flares at random, and sounding their horns, clappers, whistles, and gongs. Others, however, quickly organized into small groups.

At San Pablo pandemonium reigned: Confused 11th Airborne troopers and equally mystified Japanese parachutists, alone, in pairs, and in tiny bands, were entangled in a lethal cat-and-mouse game, stalking and being stalked. Wild shoot-outs erupted constantly; tracer streams zipped across the black terrain; grenades exploded with fiery bursts. In the darkness, no one could be certain if a shadowy figure was friend or foe.

Kenneth Murphy, the parachute captain, recalled:

Someone let loose with tracers, and I leaped into a two-man foxhole that was deep enough to stand in. A dark figure was already in it. Since there were Japs all around, I didn't speak nor did the other man. That might have drawn a shower of Jap grenades.

Just as the sky began to turn gray, I glanced at my companion's helmet. It had a strange look about it. Then it came to me—I was in a hole with a Jap paratrooper.

At the same moment, the Nipponese soldier had apparently arrived at the same conclusion with regard to Murphy, for he raised his rifle with fixed bayonet and gave the American a vicious hack on the side of the neck. Murphy tried to raise his carbine to shoot, but a split-second later another blow of the razor-sharp bayonet sliced into the captain's left shoulder. The bayonet was raised for yet another, possibly fatal, slash when Murphy fired his carbine. The bullet caught the Japanese in the head, and he crumpled in a bloody heap on the bottom of the hole.

Murphy, the victor in this duel, took a silk flag and a pistol from the dead Japanese. Bleeding and dazed, he pulled himself from the hole and joined others in organizing a defense.[1]

At daylight, Joe Swing rounded up a hodgepodge collection of 11th Airborne troopers: artillerymen, engineers, cooks, clerks, and MPs. Acting in the role of company commander and shouting orders to his skirmish lines, Swing led his men in killing or chasing off the nocturnal invaders remaining on San Pablo. But many of the Japanese paratroopers moved over to Buri airstrip, two miles away, where they joined Colonel Shirai's force and elements of the 16th Division.

By no means were Shirai's tough, resolute paratroopers finished; they still threatened the San Pablo strip and had a firm grip on the fields at Buri and Bayug. In the meantime, a 187th Glider Infantry battalion led by Lt. Col. George N. Pearson of Sheridan, Wyoming, rushed to the scene and joined in the fight at Buri. At noon on December 7, a battalion of the 38th ("Cyclone") Infantry Division reached the airfield complex and began fighting at Buri.

Far outnumbered, the Japanese parachutists held on to Buri against elements of four battalions until December 10, when one final American assault killed or drove off the sky invaders.

Still, the dogged Japanese survivors refused to quit. One group charged down the road toward Burauen and, using captured American automatic weapons, began blasting away at Maj. Gen. Ennis P. Whitehead's Fifth Air Force headquarters building. An irate air corps staff officer telephoned an 11th Airborne unit command post nearby and demanded that "this promiscuous firing by our troops cease at once." Told that it was Japanese doing the shooting, the excited air corps officer exclaimed that "bullets are coming right through the general's office."

Deeply annoyed by now, the airborne voice shouted back, "Then tell the goddamned general to get his goddamned ass down on the floor!"

Operation *Wa* had fallen apart. Not only was the paratroop force wiped out, but the Japanese 11th and 26th Divisions, which were to have attacked the three airstrips from the west, got bogged down by the treacherous terrain and then bumped into elements of the 11th Airborne Division in the Mahonag Mountains.

While Joe Swing's men were busily mopping up die-hard Japanese paratroopers around Burauen, some 10 miles to the west Hardrock Haugen's 511th Parachute Infantry had struggled over narrow, slippery trails to the tiny village of Manarawat, high in the Mahonag Mountains. Manarawat sat on a high plateau and was surrounded on three sides by sheer cliffs, accessible only by means of a steep slope from the rear.

Before resuming the overland trek toward the primary objective of Ormoc, Haugen knew that more firepower would be needed—the 511th had outdistanced the big guns positioned near the landing beaches. Ten miles to the rear were the 75-millimeter howitzers of Lt. Col. Nicholas G. Stadtheer's 457th Parachute Field Artillery Battalion, but it could take weeks to get disassembled pack howitzers, carried by sturdy beasts of burden, through the thick, tangled jungles and across deep gorges to

Manarawat. Resourceful by gift and by training, Nick Stadtheer set out to solve the unsolvable riddle.

Stadtheer knew that 13 C-47s would be needed to drop men of his A Battery, their guns, and equipment. These C-47s were not available. So, in the words of an admiring fellow officer, Stadtheer "conned" a pilot at San Pablo to use his lone battered airplane to ferry the parachute artillerymen to Manarawat. It would require 13 round trips by the carrier plane to get the job done.

Meanwhile, engineers on the small, tabletop plateau at Manarawat had scraped out what passed for a drop zone, clearing about 475 feet by 170 feet. It was a dangerously small drop zone. A sudden gust of wind could blow the descending parachutists into the treacherous jungle 150 feet below the plateau.

Even the aircraft's approach would be fraught with peril. The pilot would have to wing up a steep canyon to the plateau, make a sharp turn to drop the paratroopers and cargo, then pull up sharply and swerve to the left to avoid crashing into a mountain.

Stadtheer went along on the first flight, and five men of A Battery bailed out and landed dead-center on target. All 12 succeeding round-trip flights went off like clockwork. The disassembled howitzers—barrels, wheels, and plates—were dropped from makeshift racks attached to the bottom of the plane. Stopgap as the situation may have been, Nick Stadtheer and his cannoneers had conducted the 11th Airborne Division's first combat parachute operation.

In the meantime, the 187th Glider Infantry's 2nd Battalion, led by Lt. Col. Arthur H. Wilson, Jr., had trudged across the mountains to the Manarawat region to reinforce Haugen's 511th Parachute Infantry, and on Pearl Harbor Day (December 7) the arduous attack resumed toward Ormoc on the west coast.[2]

The fighting was savage, and both sides suffered heavy casualties. Three times the 2nd Battalion of the 511th tried to seize a hill but was driven back by fierce fire. Company E was designated to cover the battalion's third pullback.

One of the E Company paratroopers was Pfc. Elmer E. Fryar, a quiet, unassuming son of the Deep South. To the enlisted men, whose average age was 19, Fryar was positively elderly—all of 32 years. He was the unofficial company barber, and often remarked that when the war was over he hoped to return home and open his own small shop. In an outfit where profanity and hard drinking were the norms, Elmer Fryar shunned both. Had a vote been taken by E Company to choose the least likely hero, the well-liked Fryar would have won hands down.

Now, in the green hell of Leyte, E Company was suddenly attacked by a throng of Japanese screaming *Banzai! Banzai!* During the raucous shootout, Elmer Fryar saw an enemy platoon trying to slip around the company flank. Dashing forward to an exposed knoll, he was promptly knocked down by Japanese bullets. Bleeding and dazed, the aspiring barber pulled himself to a kneeling position and blazed away at the enemy platoon, killing many of them and disrupting their charge.

Moving back to rejoin E Company, Fryar came upon a seriously wounded trooper lying in the jungle. Despite his own painful wounds, Fryar somehow picked up his comrade and began carrying him. Minutes later, he met his platoon leader, who was kneeling to give first-aid to a wounded parachutist. Then the four 11th Airborne men started toward the rear together. Suddenly, a Japanese soldier leaped out into the narrow path, raised his rifle, and took aim at the platoon leader. Elmer Fryar jumped in front of the parachute officer and the bullet intended for the lieutenant tore into Fryar's body.

Fryar, blood spurting from his chest, collapsed. But by superhuman effort he managed to pull the pin from a grenade and hurl it at the Nipponese soldier, killing him. Soft-spoken Elmer Fryar would never open his small-town barber shop. Minutes later, he let out a faint gasp and died.[3]

Because of the nature of the horrendous terrain—unchanged since the Stone Age or before—there was no solid front line. Often the "front" in a given sector would be a steep, slippery, three-foot-wide path over which the paratroopers would struggle in single file. Many Japanese bands, cut off from supplies but fully armed, were bypassed, and they would ambush other American units pushing forward.

Machine guns, mortars, ammo, and other heavy accoutrements of war had to be lugged, and Joe Swing's boys were in the dual role of fighters and two-legged pack mules. They clawed their way up and down deep gorges and wrestled up the peaks. The thick jungle was hot and humid, and razor-sharp rocks cut through combat boots and slashed feet. Rot lay just beneath the lush greenery. Decaying vegetation emitted a sour, nauseating odor that caused tension-racked troopers to vomit. Dampness, thick and heavy, hovered everywhere, penetrating clothing and increasing the general misery.

Pfc. Elmer E. Fryar. *(U. S. Army)*

Torrential rains and 60-miles-per-hour winds turned the tangled jungles into quagmires. At night, the blackness was especially ominous, filling Swing's boys with a hundred fears. All the while the paratroopers were confronted by a wily, enigmatic, and tenacious foe. Always, there was the haunting specter of sudden death or mutilation.

In primitive Leyte raged the most brutal, exhausting, and rugged fighting that the 11th Airborne Division would know. Yet, the troopers clung to their grim humor: They called themselves the "Mud Rats of Leyte."

Even while Joe Swing's boys were battling in the Mahonag Mountains, Douglas MacArthur was ready to leap to Mindoro, a large island 260 miles northwest of Leyte and the final stepping-stone on the long and tortuous jungle road back to Corregidor and Bataan and Manila. The landing would be made only 190 miles from Manila, in southwestern Mindoro, where three airstrips would be used for land-based planes to support the invasion of Luzon.

MacArthur was banking on Gen. Yamashita's leaving Mindoro lightly defended and husbanding his forces on Luzon for the looming showdown that could decide the ultimate victor in the Pacific war. The forecast was remarkably accurate—there were only 1,000 rag-tag Japanese soldiers scattered throughout Mindoro.

Just past 7:00 A.M. on December 15, George "The Warden"

Jones' independent 503rd Parachute Infantry Regiment and elements of the 24th Infantry Division waded ashore on Mindoro and were contested mainly by a few notoriously ill-tempered carabao engaging in their favorite pastime—chasing and butting American soldiers. Forty- eight hours later, the captured airstrips were operational.

On December 17, two days after N-Day at Mindoro, Hardrock Haugen's weary paratroopers broke through to Leyte's west coast, and on Christmas Day, they were relieved by George Pearson's 1st Battalion of the 187th Glider Infantry and Thomas Mann's 2nd Battalion of the 188th Glider Infantry. The glider troopers promptly assaulted a pair of strongly held ridges, and in two days of brutal fighting wiped out a force of some 240 Japanese.

In the meantime, two of Haugen's paratroopers, Pfc. Charles Feuereisen of New York City and Pfc. Ralph Merisiecki of Cleveland, were sent back to 11th Airborne headquarters near Burauen on a special mission. Their company had surprised and killed a band of Japanese, and in a dead officer's briefcase was found a large military map of California on which were marked several invasion sites. Feuereisen and Merisiecki delivered the captured document, then had three days to spend before they would be able to hitch a ride on a C-47 and parachute back to their company in the Mahonag Mountains. So the two men decided to go to Tacloban, in northeast Leyte, a community of some 25,000 population and the only one on the large island that could lay a claim to any modern civilization.

Located in the center of Tacloban was Price House, a commodious, two-story mansion in which Douglas MacArthur had established his headquarters. Price House was now pockmarked with bullet and shrapnel holes, for the Japanese knew that MacArthur was there, and warplanes had been repeatedly trying to kill him.

"Ralph, we'll never get this close to General MacArthur again," the 24-year-old Feuereisen said to his comrade. "Why don't we visit him?"

"Are you crazy?" the 21-year-old Merisiecki blurted out. "We'd get pitched in the stockade!"

Feuereisen was insistent, and finally his friend agreed to the venture. Working their way through a minefield of guards and assorted functionaries, the pair of paratroopers reached Mac-

Arthur's outer office, where they were received by Lt. Col. Roger O. Egeberg, the Supreme Commander's physician and aide.
Charles Feuereisen recalled subsequent events:

> As extremely busy as he was, General MacArthur came out, greeted Ralph and me warmly, and shook hands. There were two Australian generals and three American colonels waiting to see him, but he left them sitting and courteously escorted us into his private office. We sat in cushioned chairs that I guess a lot of big brass had used. We talked friendly-like for, oh, I guess ten minutes. He called us Charlie and Ralph. We were astonished that the general knew all the details of the 11th Airborne's actions on Leyte.
>
> Finally he said, "Well, what can I do for you boys?" So being young and brash, I told him politely what had been bugging 11th Airborne paratroopers: we had been trained to strike from the sky but were being used as straight infantrymen in the mountains. Of course, he could not tell us the reason—that he was desperately short of foot soldiers.
>
> "I can understand how you paratroopers feel," the general said, puffing all the while on a corncob pipe whose stem seemed to be two feet long. "But I assure you that the 511th [Parachute Infantry] will soon be engaged in a combat jump." He meant on Luzon, we would learn later.
>
> Then General MacArthur accompanied us to the door and again graciously shook hands. The Australian generals eyed us, wondering who in the hell were these lowly GIs conferring with the Supreme Commander while they were left cooling their heels.
>
> General MacArthur's parting remark to us was: "Tell your boys that I'm real proud of the 11th Airborne."[4]

On New Year's Eve 1944, Radio Tokyo grimly told *Jinno Tanaka* (the Japanese equivalent of John Q. Public): "The battle for Luzon, in which 300,000 American soldiers are doomed to die, is about to begin."

48
On to Manila!

With the arrival of New Year's Day 1945, the climax of the war in the Pacific was at hand as Douglas MacArthur prepared to strike at the main Philippine island of Luzon, 300 miles northwest of Leyte. It would be a clash of titans. MacArthur would head the most powerful land, sea, and air force ever assembled in the Pacific, and Tomoyuki Yamashita was lying in wait on Luzon with the largest army that Americans in the Pacific had ever encountered—nearly 300,000 battle-tested warriors pledged to fight to the death for their Emperor.

MacArthur would launch three trip-hammer blows—all designed to converge on and seize Manila, Bataan, and Corregidor in southwestern Luzon. On S-Day, January 9, 1945, assault elements of Walter Krueger's veteran Sixth Army would land at Lingayen Gulf, 120 miles north of Manila, where the Japanese had invaded in December 1941. Krueger's spearheads would drive southward to the Philippine capital.

On January 29, Maj. Gen. Charles P. "Chink" Hall's XI Corps would storm ashore on the west coast of Luzon just above Subic Bay, capture Bataan (where Americans had made their epic stand three years earlier), and link up with Krueger's forces coming down from Lingayen Gulf.

Now the stage would be set for "Blow 3"—a coordinated amphibious-parachute assault by Joe Swing's 11th Airborne Division south of Manila. The scope of Swing's operation would depend upon developments. At worst, it would be a diversionary attack that would cut Japanese communications and pin down a considerable number of Luzon's defenders. At best, it could be a decisive maneuver that would hasten the capture of Manila.

The 11th Airborne plan called for a seaborne landing by elements of two glider regiments at the coastal city of Nasugbu, 55 miles south of Manila, and a rapid push inland to 3,000-foot Tagatay Ridge, 22 miles from the landing beaches and overlooking beautiful Lake Taal. Meanwhile, Orin Haugen's 511th Parachute Infantry and elements of the 457th Parachute Field Artillery Battalion and a platoon of the 221st Airborne Medical Company would jump over Tagatay Ridge and link up with the glidermen.

As the Luzon invasion time neared, two 11th Airborne paratroopers, Lt. Robert L. Dickerson and S. Sgt. Vernon W. Clark, slipped ashore from a PT boat near Nasugbu to reconnoiter the situation. They returned with sketches of Japanese defenses along the shore and with a warning from Philippine guerillas that there were 2,000 Nipponese around Nasugbu, 12,000 more with artillery and tanks back of those, and 15,000 enemy troops assembled on Tagatay Ridge.

Lt. Gen. Robert L. Eichelberger, commander of Eighth Army, who would lead the operation south of Manila, tended to discount the gloomy report, but staff officers at MacArthur's headquarters were pessimistic, concerned that Joe Swing's boys would run into a meat-grinder. A compromise was worked out. The 11th Airborne operation would be considered a reconnaissance in force. If the glidermen landing by sea at Nasugbu met with fierce resistance, Eichelberger would order their withdrawal to ships offshore. In the meantime, Haugen's paratroopers would be held on the alert at Mindoro airfields, and they would not be given airplanes until Eichelberger was satisfied with the glidermen's land advance toward Tagatay Ridge.

In other words, Bob Eichelberger would decide on the scene whether to hit or run.

Douglas MacArthur's Luzon "hit-'em-where-they-ain't" battle plan unfolded with clocklike precision. With several American divisions pressing down on Manila from the north and Chink Hall's men knifing in from the west, MacArthur was ready to plant yet another haymaker onto the forces of the burly, bullet-headed Tomoyuki Yamashita. X-Ray Day for the 11th Airborne assault at Nasugbu Bay was January 31.

X-Ray Day dawned warm and cloudless, and the sea was

calm. After a massive bombardment by warships of the invasion
fleet, the 188th Glider Infantry's 1st Battalion, led by Lt. Col.
Ernest H. LaFlamme, splashed ashore at Nasugbu against only
sporadic machine-gun fire. By 12:30 P.M., both glider regiments
and Joe Swing were on the beaches. It was quickly evident that
the Japanese were following their customary pattern—minimal
defense at the beachhead and tough defense at prepared positions in the hills.

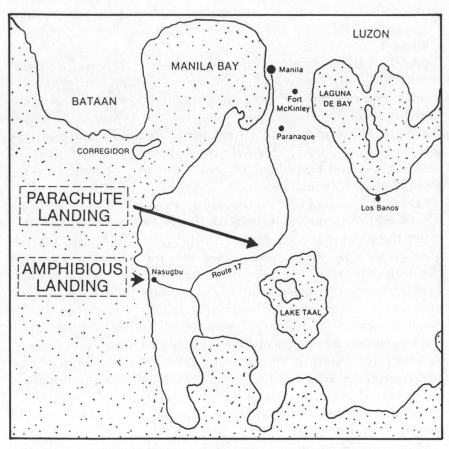

11th Airborne Landings in Manila Region

Nasugbu was almost untouched by war, and it was one of the
few towns of any consequence that Joe Swing's troopers had seen
in the Pacific. There was a tumultuous welcome. Filipinos lined
the streets as the glider soldiers marched eastward along Route
17 (which lead to Tagatay Ridge and Manila) and gave away pre-
cious and hoarded food—eggs, chickens, papayas, bananas.

There was loud cheering and excited chatter, and a native band, that compensated for a paucity of musical ability with raucous tones, gave forth from a stand on the Nasugbu square.

It was a mini-Paris-liberation extravaganza. But the glidermen (who were also trained paratroopers) marched on and reached a huge sugar warehouse and industrial plant some six miles to the east. Once there, Swing's boys found a Lilliputian railroad. It had narrow tracks, tiny locomotives, cars about the size of a living-room sofa, and it had been used in peacetime to transport sugar to the coast. The miniature railroad was immediately inducted into the United States Army and began hauling supplies and troopers inland.

Three hours after the initial Nasugbu landing, Bob Eichelberger was ashore and decided that he would hit, not run. Word was flashed to Hard Rock Haugen on Mindoro: The Tagatay Ridge jump was on as planned.

So speedy was the 11th Airborne glidermen's advance inland that the U. S. Navy had to literally chase the U. S. Army to turn over command. That afternoon, Joe Swing, covered from head to toe with dust, spotted a racing jeep approaching his command post near the Palico River bridge. Climbing out of the jeep was Rear Adm. William M. Fechteler, commander of the invasion fleet. Fechteler, also blanketed with dust, was in charge of the amphibious operation until ground troops were firmly ashore.

"Thank God I've caught you, Joe," the admiral said to Swing. "Thought I might have to chase you all the way to Manila. I'm tired of playing hare-and-hounds in a jeep. Please take over and let me get back to my ships."[1]

Palico River bridge, eight miles from the coast, was a primary reason for the 11th Airborne's speed-march. Advance elements of Robert Shorty Soule's 188th Glider Infantry reached the span, which could hold the 11th Airborne Division's heaviest loads. It was an arched, steel-trussed structure that crossed a gorge 250 feet deep. If the bridge was blown by the Japanese, the division would have to take a time-consuming detour that would delay for several days the 11th Airborne's rush to Manila.

Soule's troopers could see Japanese engineers on the far side preparing demolition charges. Taking the chance that the bridge might be blown sky-high while they were on it, a platoon of troopers raced across and pounced on the enemy engineers, who had apparently been unaware of the Americans' presence. Within minutes, the Japanese band was wiped out.

By 3:00 P.M., the entire 188th Glider Infantry and an attached battalion of the 187th Glider Infantry were across the Palico River. Then they kept going along Route 17, a two-lane road whose bed was rough and rocky all the way to Tagatay Ridge. Under a tropical moon and passing white clouds, the Mud Rats of Leyte marched—mostly uphill—throughout the night.

Tagatay Ridge was the most important military terrain feature in southern Luzon. Bleak and forbidding, the elevation guarded the approaches to Nichols Airfield, Fort William McKinley, and sprawling Manila, once known as the "Pearl of the Orient" but now frowzy and drab after three years of Japanese occupation.

Toward dawn, Shorty Soule's foot-weary troopers were approaching the Aga Pass defile leading to Tagatay Ridge. North of the pass, the broken, scrub-covered Mount Cariliao (2,100 feet) looked down on Route 17; to the south was Mount Batulao (2,700 feet). On the face of these two rugged elevations, the main body of Col. Masatoshi Fujshige's force defending the southern approaches to Manila was dug in and waiting.

For two days and nights, Soule's boys battled the entrenched Japanese on the heights before Tagatay Ridge. Fighting was furious—and to the death. No quarter asked; none given. At one point, four generals—Joe Swing, Bob Eichelberger, and a pair of brigadiers—were pinned down by Japanese machine-gun bullets hissing only inches above their heads.

Typically, Shorty Soule, a crew-cut career officer, was upfront in the thick of things. Crawling back toward his radio transmitter with Japanese fire whistling past, he was shot. Finding the transmitter damaged, Soule slithered to his jeep and gave instructions over the vehicle's radio for his executive officer, Norman E. Tipton, to take over temporarily. Before Tipton could reach the command post, Soule struggled to an exposed to an exposed knoll for observation, and by walkie-talkie continued to issue attack orders.

Bob Eichelberger watched a doctor dig the slug out of Soule and fill the hole with iodine. Then the general saw Soule take off through the high, coarse grass to cheer on his troops to the conquest of Tagatay Ridge. They renamed the spur they fought over "Shorty Ridge."[2]

On the evening of February 2, Joe Swing flashed a signal to Hardrock Haugen on Mindoro: "Jump tomorrow morning."

"Operation Shoestring," as cynical troopers called it, was aptly named. There were only 48 C-47s available, so the 511th Parachute Infantry would be ferried to Tagatay Ridge in three flights—the first at 8:15 A.M., the second at around noon, and the third at 8:00 A.M. the following day, February 4.

Haugen's first flight lifted off at dawn on the third, carried by Col. John Lackey's 317th Troop Carrier Group, with 915 paratroopers aboard. As the winged armada passed over Lake Taal, Haugen himself stood in the door of the lead C-47. At 8:14 A.M., the green light flashed on in Haugen's aircraft and he bailed out, followed closely by his stick. At the same time, 17 other C-47s dropped their paratroopers. All of them came down on the drop zone atop rugged Tagatay Ridge. That would be the last thing to go right in the parachute operation that day.

While the trailing C-47s were still more than five miles from the drop zone, someone in the first aircraft pitched out two equipment bundles. Jumpmasters standing in the doors of the other carriers interpreted this action as a signal that the flight was over the drop zone. In moments, the sky was awash with billowing white chutes of 540 paratroopers. They jolted to earth some four to five miles from Tagatay Ridge.

Then, at noon, 51 C-47s carrying the second serial of paratroopers winged toward the drop zone. Jumpmasters looked down and saw the discarded parachutes of those who had jumped nearly five miles short of the target that morning and, presuming this to be the drop zone, ordered their sticks to bail out, repeating the mistake of the previous flight.

Orin Haugen found himself standing on his objective with only about a third of his paratroopers. He was lucky: There was not a single Japanese soldier to be found on Tagatay Ridge. Early the next morning, the final flight of 511th paratroopers was dropped—this time on the correct drop zone.

Later that morning, just south of Tagatay, Bob Soule's glidermen broke through Japanese defenses on Mount Cariliao and Mount Batulao and linked up with the paratroopers. Joe Swing now had his Mud Rats of Leyte together, and they pushed on northward to the Paranaque River, three miles south of Manila's outskirts. Along the Paranaque the airborne men butted up against the Genko Line, a fortified belt of reinforced concrete pillboxes and bunkers, and the strongest defensive network in the Manila region. The Genko Line included the strongholds of

Nichols Field and old Fort William McKinley and reached all the way back to suburban Manila, where pillboxes abounded at street intersections.

Devious techniques were employed to give the Japanese guarding the southern approaches to Manila the impression that they were facing a large force. American vehicles, trailing clouds of thick dust, raced up and down Route 17. By the generous use of artillery and air strikes, by the spirited and heavy ground assaults, and by the accelerated use of radio messages (many of them phony), the Nipponese concluded that an entire field army—complete with an armored division—had invaded southern Luzon. Reinforcing that erroneous view, the American radio announced that the "United States Eighth Army" had landed at Nasugbu.

In Europe, Courtney Hodges' First and George Patton's Third Army each had between 275,000 and 400,000 men at any one time. In southern Luzon, Bob Eichelberger's attacking Eighth Army numbered some 7,800 combat troops, nearly all of them 11th Airborne troopers. So if Eichelberger was to capitalize on this gigantic bluff, the Genko Line would have to be cracked—and soon. Otherwise, the scattered Japanese would come back out of the hills, cut the American supply route, and isolate Eighth Army.

Four days after the Nasugbu landing, the 11th Airborne had a beachhead described by one trooper as being "69 miles deep and 100 yards wide."

With the 11th Airborne poised to attack the Genko Line, incredible communications breakdowns occurred. Swing and Eichelberger had been trying desperately for five days to get information about the advance of Krueger's Sixth Army on Manila from the north, but could learn nothing. Then on the morning of February 4, word seeped through that the 1st Cavalry Division (actually, regular foot soldiers) had just reached the outskirts of northern Manila and were pushing into the city against sporadic opposition.[3]

Only later would American commanders learn that General Yamashita had believed that MacArthur's *coup de main* would hit at southern Luzon, so 12,500 of the 16,000 Japanese marines and sailors guarding Manila were entrenched in a protective corridor in the area of Fort William McKinley and Nichols Field— the Genko Line.

Late on the night of February 4, at his headquarters in an

ornate structure called Garcia Mansion fronting on Manila Bay, Joe Swing ordered Haugen's 511th Parachute Infantry to launch a dawn attack against the Genko Line. Actually, the Genko Line fighting had erupted earlier that same day at an old wall-enclosed Spanish barracks where Japanese marines were holed up and resisting with customary fervor. The barracks' walls were five feet thick, and the Nipponese covered all avenues of approach with heavy mortar and machine-gun fire.

T. Sgt. Robert C. Steele, of the 511th, ordered his pinned-down platoon to cover him with fire, then advanced alone and climbed to the roof of the barracks while the Japanese tried to pick him off. With his bare hands, Steele tore a hole in the roof, poured gasoline inside, and ignited the fuel—and the Japanese—with a phosphorous hand grenade. Rushing from the building, some screaming and with their clothes on fire, the Nipponese were cut down by Steele's platoon.

A few days later, Bob Steele would be killed in action in Manila, never knowing that his feat at the Spanish barracks would be recognized with the Distinguished Service Cross.

That night of February 4, there was hard fighting at the bridge over the Paranaque River, and Col. Irwin R. Schimmelpfennig, the 11th Airborne's 36-year-old chief of staff, went forward to assess the situation prior to the dawn attack on the Genko Line. A Japanese machine gun fired from out of the blackness, and Schimmelpfennig, one of the division's most popular officers, toppled over dead.

Schimmelpfennig's death left many in the 11th Airborne stunned. Was this a harbinger of disaster for the looming assault, for which the lightly armed paratroopers would have neither the heavy guns, tanks nor heavy equipment necessary to breach a concrete and steel defensive line?

Among those devastated by Irwin Schimmelpfennig's death was Orin Haugen: The two parachute officers were the same age and had been close friends since their days as classmates at West Point. Those around Haugen overheard him muse that he might soon be sharing his friend's fate.

At first light, the 511th Parachute Infantry forced a crossing of the Paranaque River and battled northward along the shore of Manila Bay against dug-in Japanese machine gunners and riflemen. It was a savage clash. The paratroopers routed out tenacious Japanese pillbox by pillbox, house by house, with rifles, bayonets, grenades, and flame-throwers. It took two days for

Trooper of 11th Airborne Division peers northward at burning
Manila. *(Richard Hoyt)*

Haugen's boys to hack out a hole 2,000 yards deep into the
Genko Line.

On the morning of February 11, the 511th Parachute Infantry jumped off and barged on into Manila. Just before 2:00 P.M.,
Hardrock Haugen entered the command post of Lt. Col. Norman E. Tipton, leader of the 188th Glider Infantry.

Richard N. Laughrin, who was present, remembered the episode:

> *Colonel Haugen was standing at the end of a long oak table looking
> at situation maps. The Japanese were firing, and several shells
> exploded outside the building. The colonel paid no attention to them.
> Then a shell came through an open window and hit the far end of
> the table, demolishing it. A fragment hit Haugen in the chest and he
> fell to the floor. After the smoke had cleared, medics carried our
> badly wounded colonel away.*

A short time later, unaware that Haugen had been cut down,
Lt. Col. Edward H. Lahti, the 511th's executive officer, set up the
regimental command post in an abandoned building inside Manila. Lahti recalled subsequent developments:

Shortly after three o'clock that afternoon, Joe Swing burst inside the CP and came up to me. "Haugen's been hit and evacuated," the general said. "Lahti, you're in command!" That was it. Swing spun around, retraced his steps and left the building.

At only 31 years of age, Ed Lahti was a 15-year veteran of army service. Lying about his age, he had joined the Oregon National Guard and was promoted to corporal at age 16. After several years as an enlisted man, Lahti had received an appointment to and graduated from West Point, where he was a star baseball player and earned the nickname "Slugger." He was probably the Army's youngest regimental commander.

That night, Lahti was ordered to hold in place and send a patrol northward to contact a patrol of Maj. Gen. Verne D. Mudge's 1st Cavalry Division working its way southward through the sprawling metropolis. Lahti decided to go himself, and after a harrowing jeep ride during which he was fired on numerous times, the new 511th leader managed to locate the 1st Cavalry patrol.

While Joe Swing's paratroopers were hacking through the center of the Genko Line—and taking heavy casualties—Shorty Soule's 188th Glider Infantry and an attached battalion of the 187th Glider Infantry had been battling forward on the right flank in an effort to capture Nichols Field, the strongest point in the fortified enemy defenses around Manila. The flat terrain around Nichols bristled with antiaircraft guns and concrete bunkers, each holding machine gunners and riflemen and camouflaged by vegetation that had grown up around them over the years.

On the morning of February 12, American artillery unleashed a thunderous bombardment on Nichols Field, and fighter planes bombed and strafed the Japanese defenses. Then, grim glidermen, expecting to be decimated by the torrents of enemy fire, began advancing to dig out men of the 3rd Naval Battalion. Nipponese fire had lessened dramatically; the heavy barrage had done its job. By dusk, the 11th Airborne glider soldiers had nearly wiped out the Japanese marines, nearly all of whom fought to the death.

However, the new landlords of Nichols Field were being pounded by big guns from Fort William McKinley, northeast of the airfield. Until that Japanese strongpoint in the Genko Line was captured, Nichols could not be used as a badly needed base for American warplanes.

Elements of Ed Lahti's 511th Parachute Infantry were ordered to capture Fort McKinley, which was being defended by the 4th Naval Battalion. Lead scout of a platoon commanded by Lt. Ted Baughn was 21-year-old Pfc. Manuel Perez, Jr., a quiet, unassuming paratrooper who wore a perpetual smile. Lead scout was an occupation that never held out the promise of longevity.

Manny Perez had nearly washed out of the paratroopers back in Camp Mackall—he could not shoot accurately. After everyone in the company had qualified with the rifle, Ted Baughn had been assigned to tutor Perez on firing techniques and worked with him on the rifle range for a week. Perez finally qualified with a rating of marksman—the lowest of the three designations in riflery.

Now, outside Luzon's frowning old Fort McKinley, scout Manny Perez was far out in front of his advancing company. His pal Ancel Upton had been worried about Perez's blue mood of late: only that morning Perez had confided to Upton: "Ancel, I'm tired of all this fighting and killing. Today, I will be killed or wounded—one way or the other, I'm going back home."

Nearing the fort, Baughn's platoon was raked with increasingly heavy Japanese fire, and troopers were going down on all sides. Up ahead, Manny Perez spotted a concrete bunker from which two machine guns were blasting away. There was little or no cover, and the paratroopers lay flat in the open as streams of Japanese bullets hissed past. Despite the torrent of fire, Perez scrambled to his feet and, crouching and weaving, headed for the chattering machine guns while Baughn's platoon peppered the bunker with small-arms fire.

Crawling up to the concrete structure, Perez tossed a couple of grenades through the embrasure. There were loud blasts. Then Perez climbed on top and dropped two phosphorous grenades into the vent. His comrades saw the scout flatten out, and then they caught the flash from the explosion. The machine guns fell silent.

Through a cloud of smoke, Manny Perez stood up on the bunker, looked back at his comrades, and held up his hand to form a circle with his thumb and first finger. They could see that Perez was grinning broadly.

Manny's work was not finished. There were 10 more pillboxes in the string defending this approach to Fort McKinley. Returning to his platoon, Perez loaded up with grenades, then, dodging and weaving, dashed back to the bunker next to the one he had

Pfc. Manuel Perez, Jr. *(Drawing by Lou Varrone)*

knocked out. He fired his rifle four times into a port, and Japanese sailors and marines scrambled out the rear door. Perez, the "man-who-couldn't-shoot-straight," shot and killed all eight of them.

Screaming *"Banzai!"* one Japanese charged Perez and hurled his rifle with fixed bayonet toward him. The paratrooper parried the flying rifle, but the jolt knocked away his own. So the quiet trooper-turned-tiger snatched up the other man's rifle and bayoneted him with it. Four more Nipponese came out the rear door. Perez clubbed two of them to death and bayonetted the others. Then he scrambled inside the bunker where he encountered the sole survivor. A hand-to-hand struggle erupted, and Perez killed his foe with a Japanese bayonet.

Perez continued his rampage until he had knocked out 11 pillboxes in all, returning periodically for fresh grenades and rifle ammo. When the smoke had cleared, heaps of Japanese dead were sprawled in and around the concrete structures.

Perez's earlier premonition that he would be killed or wounded that day and returned to his native Chicago "one way or another" failed to come true. But a month later, Manuel Perez would be dead—killed by a sniper's bullet while out in front of his attacking company—never knowing that his Genko Line heroics would be recognized with the Medal of Honor.[4]

Meanwhile, elements of the 511th Parachute Infantry had

clawed their way to the last ridge overlooking Fort McKinley. Unbeknownst to the Americans, resolute Adm. Sanji Iwabuchi, who had pledged to defend Manila to the last brick, was inside the fort. Aware that Swing's boys would soon overrun the bastion, Iwabuchi ordered its defenders to blow up the facility and its ammunition, then pull out on the night of February 17.

Just past 3:00 P.M. on February 16, Ed Lahti, the 511th leader, and his battalion commanders, Maj. Frank "Hacksaw" Holcombe and Maj. Henry Burgess, were gathered on the final ridge to discuss the next move when explosions erupted inside Fort McKinley—the Japanese were blowing up artillery shells.

Henry Burgess recalled ensuing events:

> *Suddenly, I heard a whirring noise drawing closer and closer. Moments later Ed Lahti, standing only three feet from me, was struck a powerful blow and knocked over backwards. Lying beside him was a large chunk of iron that had catapulted from Fort McKinley. I escaped unscathed, and so did Hacksaw Holcombe.*

Dazed and bleeding, Ed Lahti glanced at his upper arm where a chunk of shell the size of a loaf of bread had struck him. Lahti recalled:

> *It didn't look too bad, from what I could see. But what I couldn't see was that I had received a deep slash reaching entirely around my arm and back to my shoulder. Burgess and Holcombe insisted that I wait for an ambulance. I replied, "Hell, no, I'll get back [to an aid station] on my own." So I located a small scooter—the type dropped from aircraft to provide paratroopers with some mobility on the battlefield—and sped away in a cloud of dust.*

Reaching a command post, Ed Lahti radioed Joe Swing: "I've got a little flesh wound. I'll have the doc sew me up and get right back on the job."

Shortly afterward, Maj. Wallace L. "Doc" Chambers, the 511th Parachute Infantry surgeon, was performing extensive embroidery work on Lahti. "A hundred years from now you'll never know you'd been hit!" Chambers said.

At age 39, Doc Chambers was eight years older than his regimental commander, Lahti. Despite horrendous conditions and a shortage of medical supplies and equipment, Chambers had operated on soldier after soldier right up near the front "lines," first on Leyte and now on Luzon. He had continued to perform surgery while *Banzai!* attacks raged only a few hundred yards away and as Japanese mortar and artillery shells exploded around his primitive "operating room," and had been wounded during one especially vicious clash.

Now Ed Lahti, as a grudging concession to the large amount of blood he had lost, rested for two hours. Then, with his arm in a black sling, the parachute leader went back to the front line—carrying with him 32 of Doc Chambers' surgical stitches.[5]

Inside Manila, savage fighting would rage for weeks—even though General MacArthur had announced to the press as early as February 7 that his troops had "secured" the capital. Finally, when the last Japanese had been rooted out, the once beautiful Manila—the fabled Pearl of the Orient—was but a gutted, blackened shell. Of all the great cities of Europe demolished during the war, only Warsaw suffered more extensively than the Philippine capital. Some 100,000 Filipinos, trapped in the metropolis, were killed by shells and bullets, or butchered by the doomed Japanese garrison.

Even while the savagery raged inside Manila, Douglas MacArthur's eyes were riveted on a huge rock perched in the mouth of Manila Bay—Corregidor. There, three years earlier, a woefully weak America had suffered a humiliating defeat. Shortly after that catastrophe, MacArthur had exclaimed that "Corregidor symbolizes within itself that priceless, deathless thing, the honor of a nation. Until we lift our flag from its dust, we stand unredeemed before mankind."

Meanwhile, in southern Mindoro, George Jones, the young colonel who commanded the independent 503rd Parachute Infantry Regiment, visited the hospital bedside of his old pal, Col. Orin Haugen, who had been badly wounded in Manila a few days earlier. After an exchange of greetings, Jones remarked in an offhand manner, "Orin, we're jumping on Corregidor in a few days."

Prior to the war, Haugen had been posted on the craggy, steep-sided rock and knew that there was no suitable drop zone, that the island was heavily fortified, and that brisk winds could carry large numbers of Jones' paratroopers plunging to their deaths in Manila Bay.

"Corregidor!" Haugen exclaimed. "Oh, no, George, they can't do *that* to you!"

George Jones would never see his good friend again. A few days later, Orin Haugen would die on a medical plane bound for the States.

49
"Attack and Seize Corregidor!"

Since Douglas MacArthur had returned to the Philippines, the Japanese high command had been growing increasingly concerned over Fortress Corregidor. Like the Americans, the Nipponese knew that the massive rock had a significance to both sides far beyond its military value in controlling shipping into Manila. MacArthur had pledged to recapture Corregidor, and if he succeeded, the Emperor and the Japanese Empire would lose enormous face in the eyes of the world.

Beginning in October 1944, with American troops on Leyte, the Japanese had begun reinforcing "The Rock" with Imperial Marines and infantry units, as well as several *Shinyo* squadrons (suicide boats packed with explosives). Imperial Navy Capt. Akira Itagaki was the commander of the Manila Bay Entrance Force, and had troops on Corregidor and three nearby tiny islands. Repeatedly, Itagaki had been warned by the Imperial high command in Tokyo to take measures against a parachute assault. Itagaki scoffed at the warnings, declaring that Corregidor, where he had his headquarters, was too small and had too many natural obstacles for the Americans to assault by parachute.

In early 1942, the Japanese warlords had considered and rejected a parachute attack against American-held Corregidor, focusing on an invasion by sea instead. Now, with the shoe on the other foot, Itagaki concentrated most of his troops and fire-power at the few available landing beaches.

Shaped like a tadpole, with its bulbous head pointing west toward the South China Sea, Fortress Corregidor is but three and a half miles long and one and a half miles across at its widest point. The tadpole's eastern "tail" is sandy, wooded, and only about 150 feet above Manila Bay at its highest point. At the cen-ter of the island, Malinta Hill rises abruptly to a height of 350 feet. In a tunnel burrowed into Malinta Hill Douglas MacArthur and later Gen. Jonathan "Skinny" Wainwright had directed the last-ditch stands at Corregidor and nearby Bataan in early 1942.

Just to the west of Malinta Hill the ground falls away sharply to a 500-yard-wide waist rising only 100 feet above the water. This low area was known as "Bottomside," and to the north and south are wide sandy beaches, suitable for amphibious assault. It was here, on the northern beaches, that the Japanese had in-vaded Corregidor nearly three years earlier.

West of Bottomside lies a gradually rising area called "Mid-dleside," giving way on the west to the steep incline leading up to "Topside," the tadpole's huge head. Rising more than 500 feet above Manila Bay, Topside drops precipitously to the bay on the north, west, and south, and was the key terrain feature on Cor-regidor. A Japanese force congregated on Topside could bring any amphibious landing beaches under murderous fire.[1]

At the time Joe Swing's 11th Airborne troopers were battling the Japanese along the Genko Line south of Manila, General MacArthur issued a terse order to Walter Krueger, the tough, 64-year-old leader of Sixth Army: *Attack and seize Corregidor.* MacArthur had been counting the minutes for over two and a half years until he could give that command.

Krueger and his staff drew up a bold plan: a combined para-chute-seaborne assault built around four battalions that were designated the "Rock Force." Col. George Jones was appointed overall commander of the operation, and Lt. Col. John "Smiling Jack" Tolson was named to be his deputy. (Tolson had gained distinction at Nadzab airfield in September 1943 as the first American paratrooper in the Pacific to bail out in a combat oper-ation.)

Carrying the ball in the Corregidor assault would be Jones' 503rd Parachute Infantry Regiment, supported by Maj. Arlis E. Kline's 462nd Parachute Field Artillery Battalion, a company of the 161st Parachute Engineer Battalion, and assorted medical, signal, antitank, and ack-ack outfits. Making a coordinated sea-borne assault on Bottomside would be Lt. Col. Edward M. Postlethwait's 3rd Battalion, 34th Infantry, of the 24th ("Taro Leaf") Infantry Division, who were veterans of heavy Pacific fighting.

Regaining Corregidor would be a very personal matter for Jones, Tolson, and Postlethwait. Several of their West Point class-mates had been captured by the Japanese in the 1942 American debacle at Corregidor and Bataan, three miles across Manila Bay.

D-Day was set for February 16, 1945. Ten days earlier, George Jones flew low over Corregidor with a regular bomber flight. He recalled that episode:

> I was encouraged by what I saw—or didn't see. There had been no
> sign of Japanese defenders, a fact that seemed to confirm Sixth
> Army's "Estimate of the Situation" that had reported there were only
> 600 to 800 troops on the fortress. We would learn soon after
> jumping that this figure was grossly inaccurate. Actually, there were
> nearly 6,000 Japs living largely underground on The Rock, a
> mixture of combat and service troops.

On returning from his reconnaissance, George Jones and his staff drew up an operational plan. At 8:30 A.M. on D-Day, approximately one-third of his paratroopers would bail out over Topside, the bulbous head of the tadpole. They would aim at two small drop zones: the golf course and the parade ground in front of Topside barracks. That afternoon and the next morning, two more of Jones' parachute battalions would jump. Meanwhile, at 10:30 A.M. on D-Day, Ed Postlethewait's 24th Infantry Division battalion would storm ashore.

Topside would be the worst conceivable locale for a mass par-achute drop. Both drop zones were tiny (each less than 1,000 feet long and 430 feet wide), and the ground was littered with boulders, deep bomb craters, scrap iron, debris, and razor-sharp sheets of tin roofing. Bordering the parade ground and golf course were bomb-splintered trees capable of impaling a de-scending paratrooper. Half-demolished barracks and other buildings presented yet another frightening peril. If the wind blew briskly—and it probably would—the parachutists stood an excellent chance of missing Topside and plunging into Manila Bay and drowning, or being pulled over the side of the cliff be-fore they could get free from their chutes.

After his reconnaissance flight, George Jones estimated that up to 50 percent of his paratroopers would suffer injuries in the jump. But the risk had to be accepted in order to rapidly establish a strong force on Topside to furnish covering fire for Ed Postlethwait's boys coming in by boat. Otherwise, the amphibious assault could result in a bloodbath.

The postage-stamp-size drop zones on Topside, the small size of the island, the concrete-hard surface, the tons of scattered debris, the tricky wind currents, and the possibly concentrated Japanese fire were all factors that meant that the paratroop operation would be the most daring and unorthodox of the war. There would be no margin for error: If the mass drop was not carried out with clockwork precision, the entire Corregidor operation could end in a monumental American debacle.

The Corregidor invaders had an ally that might help ensure their survival—B-24 bombers of the 307th Bomb Group. Since January, the four-engined heavies had been plastering The Rock, giving special attention to Topside, as well as Malinta Hill, which was the nerve center of the Japanese command. Then, starting on February 7, they doubled their tonnage. By the time Jones' boys leaped out over Topside, The Rock would have been hit by a deluge of 3,128 tons of bombs—the most concentrated pounding any invasion target would receive during the Pacific war.

Before dawn on D-Day, grim-faced warriors of the 503rd Parachute Regimental Combat Team had been awakened at their air strips in southern Mindoro to face the most trying ordeal of their young lives—a drop onto heavily defended Corregidor. Waiting tensely for the order to take off, these American paratroopers were going into battle with vengeance in their hearts. However, there were no flamboyant exhortations to "Remember Bataan!" or "Avenge Corregidor!" There was no need. All knew of the suffering starvation and humiliation endured in the Philippines by their brothers-in-arms three years earlier—at a time when a large percentage of these 503rd troopers had been attending high school proms. Rather, George Jones—The Warden—had set the tone: "The Jap wants to die for his Emperor. Do your best to accommodate him!"

Shortly before 8:30 A.M., Col. John Lackey, commander of the 317th Troop Carrier Group, was at the controls of the lead C-47 in a flight carrying Lt. Col. John L. Erickson's 3rd Battalion and support units. Lackey's sky armada would fly over the drop zone in two columns at 1,000 feet above sea level, which would permit the paratroopers to jump from 500 feet above Topside.

Standing in the door of Lackey's aircraft—"Gooney Birds," the paratroopers called them—was John Erickson, who would be the first armed American to set foot on Corregidor since the American capitulation in June 1942. Lanky and tough, Erickson was something of a medical miracle. While fighting on New Guinea, he had been so seriously wounded that doctors had doubted he would survive.

Minutes earlier, calls of "stand up and hook up" had rung through the cabins of the Gooney Birds. It took an effort to stand. The paratroopers felt awkward in their cumbersome combat gear as they staggered into position, one behind the other. The excruciating stress from waiting returned—worse than ever. Thoughts of avenging Corregidor vanished momentarily, replaced in each man's mind with the haunting question: "Will I still be alive five minutes from now?"

Now John Erickson, crouched alertly in the doorway, spotted his drop zone, the parade ground. On went the green light, and with a shout of "Let's go!" he leaped into space. On his back—almost literally—were Cpl. Arthur O. Smithback of Stoughton, Wisconsin, and Pfc. Stanley J. Grochala of Trenton, New Jersey, the first two armed American enlisted men to return to The Rock.

The death struggle for what Douglas MacArthur called the "Holy Grail of Corregidor" had erupted.

Jumping in a 25-miles-per-hour wind, Wyoming native John Erickson was carried far from his parade ground drop zone and hit with a jolt near Battery Wheeler, one of the prewar American gun positions guarding Manila Bay, southwest of his target. Cut and bruised, the battalion commander shucked his chute, climbed over the ramparts of Battery Wheeler, and trudged off toward the parade ground to assemble his men. Only later would Erickson learn that recesses under the big-gun positions had been filled with Japanese soldiers.

The smoky blue sky over Corregidor was awash with billowing white parachutes as troopers plunged through jagged roofs of bomb-wrecked concrete and steel buildings and into deep bomb craters. Others slammed into the sides of cliffs and were left dangling when their chutes caught on trees. One stick of eight men landed in front of a cave filled with Japanese, and the Americans were mowed down with grenades and automatic weapons before they could get out of their harnesses. Some

Minutes before bailout over Corregidor. *(U. S. Army)*

troopers were impaled on splintered trees and on steel reinforcement poles, suffering agonizing deaths.

Capt. Logan W. Hovis Parkersburg, West Virginia, one of two 3rd Battalion surgeons, landed in a heap in the center of the rubble-strewn golf course. Dr. Hovis recalled:

> *I weighed just over one hundred and forty pounds and lugged forty pounds of medical equipment and supplies. The wind caught my chute and dragged me across the rock ground. Fearing injury to the surgeon's hands I would need, I made no effort to collapse the chute. Eventually the chute halted when it caught in some bomb-splintered trees, but I was so twisted in cord that I was unable to move. I was pretty well cut up and bruised. Finally Lt. William Ziler happened by and cut me free.*

Dropping onto The Rock. *(Rocco Narcise)*

Logan Hovis' fellow surgeon, Capt. Robert McKnight, suffered a severe fracture of the ankle on crashing to the ground. Japanese machine gunners immediately brought the doctor under fire, and he lay in pain behind a fallen tree for 20 minutes. Much to his distress, McKnight would have to be evacuated.

When Cpl. Walter Gonko's chute popped open, he saw, to his horror, that he was descending directly toward a bombed-out barracks. Gonko recalled his feelings:

> *Just before I struck the third floor ledge a vision of my brother,*
> *Julian "Luke" Gonko, flashed before my eyes. Luke had been a*
> *marine aboard the cruiser* Nashville *and was killed by a* kamikaze.
> *"Luke, I'm joining you!" I called out. Then everything went black.*

When Walt Gonko regained consciousness, he was laying at the base of the building. Bullets were ripping against the wall overhead, and his harness was so twisted he was unable to move. Gonko lay motionless and in intense pain for what seemed to be an eternity before a comrade came by and cut him loose. Crawling arduously onto the parade ground, Gonko was found by medics who gave him a morphine shot, tagged him for a broken back, and took him to an aid station in a beat-up barracks.

Another parachutist also was plunging toward a wrecked barracks. Lt. Col. Arlis Kline, commander of the 462nd Parachute Field Artillery Battalion, slammed onto its roof, rolled off, and fell three stories into bombed rubble. Knocked unconscious, Kline suffered numerous broken bones in his face and body. His operations officer, Maj. Melvin R. Knudson, took over the battalion.

Among the first Americans to jump was Capt. Emmet R. Spicer of Goldsboro, North Carolina, surgeon of the parachute artillery battalion. Spicer had become bored with the humdrum job the Army had assigned him on being called into service, and volunteered for the paratroopers. The free-spirited Spicer found the exhilaration of leaping out of airplanes far more to his liking.

Now, on the bleak, pock-marked rock in Manila Bay, Doc Spicer had just finished treating two wounded troopers when a third dashed up to him and blurted out, "Doc, McKee's been hit bad and he's out there in Jap positions!" The surgeon rejected pleas from his medics not to go to McKee's aid, that "the Japs are popping up from holes like gophers all over the place!"

Spicer walked off toward the locale where Trooper McKee, and possibly other wounded comrades, were lying. Apparently, he was shot by a Japanese sniper as he walked alone. Although dying, Doc Spicer sat down on the ground, injected himself with a shot of morphine, and filled out his own medical tag. He wrote down his name, rank, serial number and diagnosis: "GSW [gunshot wound], perforation left chest. Severe. Corregidor. 16 February, 1945."

Later, Emmet Spicer's body was found. His open first-aid kit, an empty morphine tube, a cigarette stub, and his empty canteen lay beside the dead parachute surgeon.[2]

While Emmet Spicer's life was ebbing away, Cpl. Frank Arrigo and Pfc. Clyde I. Bates dashed across the bullet-swept parade ground with a folded American flag tucked under the arm of one of them. They shinnied up a tall flagpole as Japanese snipers tried to pick them off, attached the banner to the top, and scooted back down. For a few moments, the two paratroopers gazed proudly at their handiwork: The Stars and Stripes was fluttering majestically. It was 9:47 A.M. America had returned to Corregidor.

Capt. Probert E. Herb, Protestant chaplain of the 503rd Parachute Infantry, was writhing in agony on the golf course, unable to move and under heavy fire. Both of the chaplain's legs had been shattered on landing. Parachute medics carried Herb to an aid station on a door.

The regiment's Catholic chaplain, Capt. John Powers, was

having equally bad luck. While in midair, he had been struck in the rear upper leg by a Japanese bullet. Moments later, Powers ricocheted off an artillery piece near the edge of a cliff and struck his head on the rock surface. Dazed and bleeding, the padre stumbled around Topside in a totally disoriented state of mind.

Monsignor John Powers recalled:

My clerk, Jimmy Fraser, finally found me sitting on the ground directly in front of a cave filled with Japanese. He could hear them chattering inside. Jimmy told me later that I was showing a total lack of concern over my perilous predicament, and that I even wore a fixed grin. He pulled me to safety. Later, I told Jimmy that I was a lot more courageous out of my mind than I was in it.

Early in the parachute assault, good fortune smiled on the invaders. Several paratroopers spotted a number of Japanese dashing into a cave on the southern edge of Topside, near Breakwater Point, and hurled grenades inside. There were piercing screams from the cave, then silence. The troopers carefully probed into the cavity and found eight mangled and dead Japanese officers. Among them was Imperial Navy Capt. Akira Itagaki, commander of the Manila Bay Entrance Force, who had been convinced that a parachute assault on Corregidor was impossible. At the time the defenders needed him the most, they had been deprived of their leader.

High overhead in his circling Gooney Bird control plane, George Jones saw that the gusty winds were blowing his troopers far from the parade ground and golf course drop zones, and over the cliffs in some instances.

So the Rock Force leader radioed all pilots: "Drop remainder of paratroopers at four hundred feet." This would be a hundred feet lower than "Long John" Erickson and his first sticks had jumped from. Jones knew that his decision could add to jump injuries—parachutes would barely have time to open before troopers slammed into the ground. But it would also result in more men landing on the drop zone instead of in Manila Bay or onto Japanese positions.

Jones was one of the first to bail out from the lower altitude. A wind gust pulled him toward Wheeler Battery, where John Erickson had crashed earlier. Jones recalled:

In a split-second, I saw that I was going to miss Topside and plunge into Manila Bay, more than five hundred feet below. So I tugged desperately on the risers to change my course away from the cliff's edge. Then I slammed into a tree that had been splintered by the bombardment, and felt a stab of sharp pain. A needle-like, five-inch splinter of tree had pierced the inside of my upper thigh and lodged there. It hurt like hell, but I was able to pull out the huge splinter. Later, I told my officers that if the splinter had been an inch or two farther up, I would be talking to them a pitch or two higher.

With his leg throbbing convulsively, Jones hobbled across the parachute-strewn and fire-swept parade ground to a long, battered barracks that had been selected earlier as the Rock Force command post. Later that morning, Jones took a quick nose count. Of the 1,000 men who had jumped, 750 were in action or ready to fight. Nearly all had received broken bones, cuts, bruises, sprains, or concussions. On landing, they had been jolted with an impact roughly similar to leaping off the rear top of a railroad boxcar traveling at 35 to 40 miles per hour—onto a concrete surface littered with countless chunks of sharp-pointed debris.

For an hour and twenty minutes, John Lackey's "Goonies," each one of which had to make several passes, dropped paratroopers, then made a beeline back to the airstrips on southern Mindoro to pick up Lawrence Caskey's battalion for the second mass jump that afternoon.

Hardly had the last C-47 faded into the distance than 28-year-old Ed Postlethwait—a tall, lean officer from Bloomington, Illinois—led his 24th Infantry Division battalion ashore on the southern beaches of Bottomside. It was 10:28 A.M.—two minutes ahead of schedule. From towering Topside, Long John Erickson's paratroopers poured covering fire into Japanese positions, but after the first four waves hit Bottomside, heavy machine-gun fire raked the amphibious invaders.

Postlethwait lost a tank, a self-propelled gun, and an antitank gun to mines, but two of his rifle companies scrambled up steep Malinta Hill, and by 11:01 A.M., they had secured that key elevation.

An hour and a half later, 51 Gooney Birds were approaching The Rock with Caskey's battalion and attached units, and 10 minutes later, the smoke-filled sky was again sprinkled with blossoming white parachutes. One of those who bailed out was Smiling Jack Tolson, the deputy commander of the Rock Force. Crashing down into a shellhole, Tolson broke his foot, but medics splinted it and he limped off to the Rock Force command post.

When the C-47 carrying Lt. Edward T. Flash of Cleveland winged overhead, a stream of bullets riddled the plane and wounded three men. Despite their pain, two troopers insisted on jumping, but the third was bleeding so profusely he could not stand. On the third pass, the 24-year-old Flash bailed out, and his chute barely opened before he smashed into the ground beside a large, empty swimming pool at the edge of the golf course.

Flash was trying to shake the cobwebs from his head when he noticed a blurry object plunging from the sky: a trooper with a "streamer"—a parachute that had failed to open. With a sickening thud, the unlucky soldier splattered onto the bottom of the concrete pool, sending up small geysers of blood. Flash felt like vomiting.

Nearly all of Flash's platoon landed on the golf course, with the usual array of sprains, breaks, cuts and bruises. Rapidly assembling his men, Flash hurried the platoon to his assigned position near Wheeler Point.

Edward Flash recalled developments:

> We saw a red American roadster with a rumble seat piled high with Japs coasting from Topside down the road toward Bottomside. Apparently, they had no gasoline. It was a crazy sight, a snappy, fire-engine red sports car rolling through the middle of a battlefield. We gawked in amazement for several moments, then two of our machine guns riddled the vehicle. It crashed into a ditch, and four or five surviving Nips tried to run, but our guys picked them off.

After all of Larry Caskey's lift had jumped, George Jones again took stock of the situation. Of the 2,019 paratroopers who had jumped that day, 279 had been killed, seriously wounded, or injured. With Topside and Malinta Hill secured by the Americans, the Warden radioed Chink Hall, the XI Corps commander, and requested a change in plans. Maj. Robert H. "Pug" Woods' 1st Battalion was to jump onto Topside at 8:30 A.M. the next morning, but in order to avoid additional jump injuries, Jones recommended that Woods' parachutists land in assault boats on Bottomside. Approval was granted.

As D-Day night drew a black curtain over the Philippines, Warden Jones and his deputy, Jack Tolson, were optimistic over cleaning up the fortress island in fairly rapid fashion. After all, Sixth Army G-2 had reported that there were but 600 to 800 Japanese on The Rock, so the Americans outnumbered the defenders three or four to one. However, burrowed into countless caves, tunnels, spider holes, and crevices were nearly 6,000 Japanese soldiers and Imperial Marines ready to die for their country.

A ghostly hush had fallen over Corregidor.

50
"Sir, I Present You Fortress Corre- gidor!"

Later that night on black, eerie Corregidor, Japanese marines and soldiers, in small packs, in pairs, and alone, began stealing out of the maze of underground cavities. Soon, at scattered points on Topside and on Malinta Hill, a cacophony and fiery flashes erupted—hand-grenade explosions, rifle and machine-gun fire. Throughout the hours of darkness countless clashes raged. Then, shortly before dawn, the Japanese slipped back underground, and silence again blanketed The Rock.

At sun-up, Lt. Ed Flash and his paratrooper platoon lay exhausted after the tense night. They had been on constant alert as shadowy figures tried to slither and crawl through their positions. Suddenly, a pitiful cry for help rang out from down the cliff. But was the voice that of a wounded paratrooper, or was it an enemy trick to get Americans out into the open where they could be cut down by machine-gun fire?

Edward Flash recalled:

> I took a couple of men, and we crawled down toward the pleading voice. When we got there, we found an ashen-faced paratrooper. His jumpsuit was saturated with blood, and flies covered a ghastly wound in his stomach. I scooped off a handful of insects, but they were immediately replaced by other flies.
>
> We put the wounded man on a cot spring we had brought along and began the hard trek back up to our positions. Nip riflemen and machine-gunners were taking pot-shots at us all the while. We finally got back, and all of us were exhausted. Only after the wounded trooper had been taken on to an aid station did all four of us who had gone on the rescue mission realize that we had been hit by Jap bullets.

In the meantime, Cpl. Walt Gonko, a former coal miner, had ripped up the medical tag that stated "broken back," and hobbled off from the aid station in search of his squad in the 462nd Parachute Field Artillery. Gonko soon became lost; not a single American could be seen. Rounding a small hillock, he was greeted by a horrible sight.

Walter Gonko remembered:

> There were four Nips, all black and burned to a crisp, standing upright, just as they had been before being showered with napalm. It was sickening, but I could not take my eyes off them. Their teeth protruded against the charred black background, and they seemed to be laughing at me. I got the hell out of there—fast.

Just past 8:30 that morning of D-Day plus 1, John Lackey's Gooney Birds, hauling Pug Woods' battalion and attached units, approached Corregidor. They would drop equipment bundles on The Rock, then wing onward to the San Marcelino airstrip on nearby Bataan, from where the paratroopers would be shuttled by boat to Bottomside.

It immediately became clear that George Jones had made a prudent decision. Recovered from the massive sea and air bombardment and the surprise paratroop drop on D-Day, Japanese gunners raked the Gooney Birds with murderous fire. Of the 44 planes in the flight, 16 were hit and several men were wounded, including airmen. Had Woods' boys bailed out as initially planned, the heavy ack-ack fire would have turned on them.

But Caskey's parachutists were far from being home free. As their tiny assault boats neared Bottomside, Japanese in overlooking caves opened up on them with ravaging bursts of automatic-weapons fire. Then mortar shells exploded around the craft. In one of the first boats, Lt. Jesse B. Gandee of Winter Park, Florida, was lying flat on the deck as bullets whistled past just overhead.

Jesse Gandee recalled:

I heard a yelp when the guy in front of me was hit. I glanced backward and saw a young sailor—he must have been 17 or 18— blasting away with twin thirty-caliber machine guns. Then his guns fell silent—a bullet had caught him right between the eyes.

Moments later, a mortar round exploded, gouging a large hole in the assault craft. Flying splinters and shrapnel ripped into Gandee's back, paralyzing him (temporarily) from the waist down. The boat went dead in the water, but it was close enough to shore for the survivors to wade onto Bottomside. Gandee and another wounded man lay helpless in the riddled boat, and after an interminable period, they were rescued by a passing craft and taken to a destroyer.

All the while, enemy machine gunners in the caves were raking Caskey's paratroopers as they dashed across the beach. Scores were pinned down with their noses in the wet sand. Finally, the destroyer *Claxton* edged in close to shore and poured shells at point-blank range into the cave mouths. The Japanese machine guns fell silent. In rapid fashion, Pug Woods assembled his battalion and led them up onto Topside. Now all three of the parachute battalions were congregated on the rocky head of the tadpole.

That same afternoon of February 17, Lt. William T. Bailey's F Company of Caskey's battalion assaulted Battery Wheeler, where Long John Erickson had crunched down at H-Hour. Flamethrowers and grenades were used against the Japanese in underground ammunition magazines, but F Company was driven back and three of its six officers were casualties.

Then Lt. Joseph A. Turinsky's D Company was ordered to seize Battery Wheeler, and the Japanese greeted the attackers with murderous machine-gun fire. But Turinsky's boys reached the massive coastal battery—a minifortress in itself—and scrambled up onto its ramparts, where a hand-to-hand fight erupted. When the brawl ended, Battery Wheeler was in American hands. Sprawled about the concrete emplacement were the bodies of 64 dead Nipponese, but the Americans had also suffered—20 killed or wounded.

At the same time, a brutal fight was raging on the road leading from Topside down to Bottomside. One of Ed Postlethwait's infantry companies was attacking up the road from the east, and a company of paratroopers was fighting down the road from the west. Halfway down the steep incline, the parachutists were raked by machine-gun fire from Japanese holed up in a series of caves overlooking the road. While the parachutists took cover, a hurried call was put in for Lt. William E. Blake of Ronceverte, West Virginia, chief demolitions officer of the 503rd Parachute Infantry.[1]

Rapidly taking stock of the situation, Blake saw that there were six cave openings. While riflemen peppered the cavities with small arms fire, Blake, Cpl. Delbert L. Parsons, and Pfc. Willie J. "Andy" Anderson edged to within a few yards of the entrances. Moments later, grenades flew out of a cave and exploded, wounding Anderson in the legs.

Bill Blake pitched a WP (white phosphorous) grenade—whose particles burn into human flesh—into one cave opening, then hurled a second one that missed the target. It bounced off the cliffside and detonated near the paratroopers, showering them with phosphorous and inflicting light burns. Despite his painful wounds, Anderson snaked up to the cave mouths and hosed them down with a flamethrower.

Nine screaming Japanese, on fire from head to foot, bolted out of the caves and nearly trampled Blake, Anderson, and Parsons. Flaming napalm fell off the enemy soldiers as they ran. "Fry, you goddamned bastards, fry!" the covering paratroopers yelled as they shot down the enemy soldiers.

When the racket ceased, Blake could hear scores—perhaps a few hundred—Nipponese chattering inside the six-cave complex. But not another peep was heard from the Japanese soldiers huddled inside as Blake and his two troopers proceeded to systematically bury them alive by sealing the opening with TNT charges.

In the next few days, Corporal Parsons and a few demolitionists would seal 43 caves on that one cliffside.

By nightfall on D-Day plus 1, the pattern for the death struggle on Corregidor had been established. Because of the small size of the island fortress, the rocky terrain, and the maze of connecting tunnels, caves, and underground pillboxes and powder magazines, coordinated actions by companies and battalions would be impossible. Rather, American patrols would have to fan out from Topside at dawn and dig out the Japanese with flamethrowers, grenades, dynamite charges, and point-blank howitzer fire. There would be no such thing as a rear area—medical stations, supply dumps and command posts would be subject to surprise attack at any time, particularly at night.

At midnight, George Jones knew that the G-2 estimate of Japanese strength had been wrong—dead wrong. Already more than 800 enemy corpses were strewn around The Rock, and an untold number had been buried alive in sealed caves and other underground chambers. Each American knew that it would be a savage, no-holds-barred fight to the death. Each Japanese would resist until killed, no matter how hopeless his situation.

Troopers of 503rd Parachute Infantry digging Japanese out of Corregidor cave. *(U. S. Army)*

On the morning of D-Day plus 2, an overpowering stench hung over Corregidor—the 800 Japanese had become bloated and blackened by the rays of the boiler-hot sun. The smell of the decaying corpses made many of the Americans vomit. So bulldozers were put to work digging long, shallow trenches, then shoving hundreds of enemy corpses into the excavation and covering them with dirt. Perhaps 50 Japanese bodies were pushed over the cliffs of Topside, plunging 500 feet into Manila Bay.

Flies—by the millions—tormented Americans and Japanese alike. A GI trying to eat found it impossible to put a bite of food into his mouth without a dozen flies descending on it. Not only was the situation intolerable, but it was a threat to the Corregidor mission. So George Jones called in his S-4 (supply officer), Capt. Robert M. "Cracker" Atkins of Miami, Florida. "We've got to do something about those damn flies," the Rock Force commander declared. "Get on it!"

Jones knew that Atkins was an enterprising officer, but he had given him a tall order. How does one make tens of millions of flies, on a tiny island, half of which was held by a hostile force, vanish?

Undaunted, Cracker Atkins quickly radioed the brass at XI Corps headquarters, explained the situation, and a few hours later a C-47 with external wing tanks filled with DDT insecticide began crisscrossing Corregidor at deck level. "Hot damn," Atkins enthused to George Jones. "The flies are dropping like flies!" Each day thereafter, a DDT plane winged back and forth. The fly scourge was eliminated, much to the relief of all Americans—and no doubt to the Japanese as well.

Fighting was flaring all over Topside and on Malita Hill when George Jones set out on foot down the road leading to Bottomside. There he came upon a platoon of his paratroopers who were blasting away at a band of Japanese holed up in an old ice plant. On an overlooking hill, other enemy soldiers were pouring fire down on the 503rd men. The Rock Force commander decided that he would personally lead an assault to wipe out the Japanese band on the hill.

Rapidly, Jones collared a squad of 24th Division GIs and told them to follow him in the assault. The GIs were far from enthused; Jones wore no rank insignia and they had never seen him before. Pistol drawn, the colonel charged up the hill as bullets hissed past. Reaching the top, Jones looked back: He was alone.

Jones edged around a railroad boxcar and suddenly found himself face-to-face with a Japanese marine. Both were startled by the unexpected confrontation and stood staring at one another. Then the antagonists scrambled for cover and began a shoot-out that lasted for several minutes.

George Jones recalled:

> *I soon decided that a dead Rock Force commander would be of little value to the Corregidor operation. So I called the shootout with the Jap marine a draw and slipped back down to Bottomside. Only later would I learn that Lt. Dick Williams, a Signal Corps cameraman who had parachuted in with us, had been up on Topside recording the two-man shootout with a telescopic lens.*
>
> *On my way back up Topside to our CP, I remarked to my aide: "Well, I guess one could say that as a squad leader, I'm a flop." My aide discreetly made no reply.*

Meanwhile up on Topside, the demolitions expert, Bill Blake, had been summoned to an underground powder magazine where a Japanese band was holed up and defying efforts by Capt. Joseph M. Conway's M company to root them out. As Blake hovered over the ventilator shaft, he heard a voice from below speaking in fluent English: "I wouldn't drop anything if I were you—there's much dynamite down here."

Blake yelled down the shaft: "Hi, ya, Nip!"

"Very much dynamite down here, you will blow us all up."

"Okay, Nip."

As Blake and two men blew off the top of the ventilator to prepare to drop a charge, they could hear much Japanese chattering below. "Don't blow us all up," came the voice.

"Well, come on out then, Nip."

"I can't come out."

"Okay. How much dynamite is down there, Nip?"

"Much, much dynamite, 80,000 pounds."

"Well, Nip, if you can't come out, we'll do you a favor and send all of you to your ancestors."

"Hokay."

Bill Blake dropped a time-delay explosive charge down the shaft, and he and his men raced for cover. Then there was an enormous roar followed by a large black puff mushrooming sky-ward. The powder magazine had disintegrated, leaving a huge hole in the rock.

Turning to his men, Blake remarked dryly, "You know, the Nip was right. Eighty thousand pounds is a hell of a lot of dyna-mite."

Shortly after 2:00 A.M. on February 19—D- Day plus 3—all was quiet at Capt. William T. Bossert's A Company command post located in an old barracks near Breakwater Point, 500 yards southeast of the Rock Force command post. Bossert and his troopers were serenely unaware that they were directly on top of an underground Japanese ammunition dump. Suddenly, an enormous blast rocked Corregidor: Some 45 enemy soldiers had ignited the explosives in the chamber. An equal number of Bossert's paratroopers were killed by the blast.

George Jones and his operations officer, Maj. Ernest C. Clark, Jr., had been sleeping on the floor of their command post and were jolted awake by the explosion. Moments later, a chunk of rock the size of a football sailed into their room (the barracks was roofless) and landed within a few feet of them. The force of the explosion had catapulted it 500 yards.

A haunting silence returned. But some 600 Japanese soldiers and marines had emerged from caves below and were stealthily clawing their way up the steep cliffs along the southern sector of Topside. Shortly before daylight, a swarm of grenades flew through the darkness and exploded on and around Bill Bossert's still-stunned A Company, Turinsky's D Company, and Lt. Wil-liam T. Bailey's F Company. The first coordinated Japanese at-tack on Corregidor had been launched.

An orange signal flare burst majestically in the sky, and swarms of Japanese soldiers and marines, screaming *Banzai! Banzai!* charged the paratroopers. The attackers' bayonets gleamed in the light of the flare.

Turinsky's company received the heaviest blow. Japanese bodies piled up before the paratroopers' rifles and machine guns, but the screaming Nipponese soldiers continued to storm D Company positions. A face-to-face fight broke out, with bayonets, rifle butts, trench knives, and fists. A grenade flew into the plot-ting room of Battery Wheeler where Joe Turinsky was on the field telephone. Thirteen troopers were cut down by the blast, one of those killed being Joe Turinsky.

Along Bailey's F Company sector, an avalanche of shouting, shadowy figures bounded forward. Pvt. Lloyd G. McCarter of Tacoma, Washington, immediately began blasting away with his rifle. A free spirit whose off-duty antics had often plunged him into hot water, the 27-year-old McCarter was a terror on the battlefield. Now, in the face of a full-blooded assault, McCarter, who wore no stripes or bars, assumed a leadership role. With his company on the brink of being overrun, he shouted encouragement to his comrades, profanity at the Japanese.

Soon all the troopers around him had been killed or wounded. Picking up a tommy gun, McCarter began crawling to an exposed position, and the Nipponese concentrated their fire on him. When his tommy gun would no longer function, he grabbed a BAR from a dead comrade and continued to inflict heavy casualties on the attackers. Eventually, McCarter was seriously wounded, but not before he had killed at least 37 enemy soldiers and forced the enemy assault to waver in front of F Company. Bleeding from head to foot and unable to stand, Lloyd McCarter resisted efforts to evacuate him. Only when he lost consciousness could he be carried to an aid station.[2]

Up and down the sector being assaulted, tiny bands of Japanese broke through the outnumbered Americans' positions and headed for the command posts located in the long barracks fronting the parade ground, as well as for the nearby howitzers. A number of Japanese worked their way to a barracks and pitched grenades into the space occupied by Cracker Atkins, the regiment's supply officer, and his men. Four troopers were wounded by the explosions, but Atkins and the others, clad only in the undershorts in which they had been sleeping, began blasting away at the enemy outside.

In the same long barracks was the Rock Force command post. Bullets hissed into the building. George Jones grabbed his carbine, dashed onto a second floor balcony, and began firing at the Japanese darting about the parade ground. Shooting alongside Jones was Jack Tolson, the Rock Force deputy commander, whose broken foot did not interfere with his marksmanship.

The fight on Topside ebbed away at midmorning, although Nipponese would be rooted out of spider holes for two more days. Strewn about the landscape were perhaps 500 Japanese marines and soldiers. A rapid check disclosed a startling fact: American losses had been moderate—33 men killed and 76 wounded.

Col. George M. Jones. (*Author's collection*)

Pvt. Lloyd McCarter. (*Lou Varrone*)

The men of Rock Force were becoming increasingly nervous about being perched on top of the world's most enormous powder keg. George Jones and a few key staff officers knew that the anxieties were fully justified. A captured document disclosed that there were sufficient explosives stored underground to blow up all of Corregidor if detonated at one time. Cached in tunnels and powder magazines were some 93,000 hand grenades, 80,000 mortar shells, 2 million rounds of small-arms ammunition, 35,000 artillery and mortar shells, and hundreds of tons of dynamite.

Just past 11:00 P.M. on February 21, a stillness was shattered by a powerful explosion in the tunnels under Malinta Hill. The entire island was shaken. Flames rushed out of tunnel entrances, lighting up the horrified faces of Americans. Rocks and debris landed as far as two miles away. Hundreds of Ed Postlethwait's GIs on Malinta Hill were knocked down, and six of them were buried alive. Untold numbers of Japanese—perhaps hundreds—in the tunnel had blown themselves up by the blast. However, swarms of Nipponese survivors fled from the tunnel entrance and headed eastward into Corregidor's tail.

By midnight of February 23—D-Day plus 7—George Jones was convinced that Topside and Malinta Hill were sufficiently secure to launch operations that would wipe out Japanese in the tail. Caskey's battalion would continue to dig out enemy soldiers and tiny bands still holed up on Topside, while Pug Woods' 1st Battalion would jump off at 8:30 A.M. the next day, spearheading an attack down the narrow tail. John Erickson's 3rd Battalion would follow in Woods' wake to wipe out bypassed enemy bands.

Shortly after dawn on the twenty-fourth, Woods' battalion, with Bill Bossert's A Company out in front, pushed forward. Up on Topside, Mel Knudsen's nine pack howitzers pounded the terrain to the front of their attacking comrades. Anxious to get in their licks, PT boats and destroyers edged in close to the shore and poured point-blank fire into Japanese-held caves. Overhead, swarms of Thunderbolt fighter bombers circled menacingly, then swooped down to bomb and strafe enemy positions.

Advancing steadily, the paratroopers met only sporadic opposition. As darkness started to fall, George Jones was sitting in a large bomb crater that was serving as the command post for Pug Woods' battalion. Only 2,000 yards remained before the paratroopers reached the tip of Corregidor's tail. Jones and Woods briefly discussed plans for resuming the attack at daybreak, then the Rock Force commander said he had to return to his command post on Topside.

"Why don't you stay here tonight, colonel?" Woods suggested. "It's getting dark, and if the Japs don't shoot you, one of our own itchy-fingered guys might do it."

"Well, Pug, that's a chance I'm going to have to take," Jones replied. "General MacArthur's sending one of his aides to see me."

Jones scrambled from the frontline bomb crater and walked off toward Topside. It was a decision that would save the Rock Force commander's life.

Shortly after Jones departed, Woods summoned his company commanders to his bomb crater. Hardly had they gathered than a Japanese mortar shell exploded in the excavation, killing the boyish-faced Pug Woods and wounding severely Capt. John P. Rucker of C Company. Two communications men, Pfc. Roy E. Marston and Pfc. Glen R. Knapp, were also killed by the blast. Sitting on the crater bottom next to Woods, Sgt. Matt Dallas survived unscathed.

Maj. John N. Davis, Woods' exec, took command of the battalion. That night a force of some 600 Nipponese, screaming Banzai!, charged the Americans, and after a brutal hand-to-hand fight in the blackness, perhaps 100 survivors of the attacking force pulled back farther into the tail.

At dawn, Davis' battalion jumped off again, and by dusk had fought its way forward 1,000 yards to a craggy ridge overlooking the short airstrip known to the Americans as "Kindley Field." Few, if any, of the parachutists knew, or cared, that they had reached a terrain feature called Monkey Point. Most of the exhausted troopers, unaware that they were perched atop tons of explosives crammed into a tunnel—the largest cache on Corregidor—fell into a fitful sleep on the hard, rocky surface.[3]

Just before 10 o'clock the following morning—D- Day plus 11—S. Sgt. Andy Amaty, a former New York City stevedore and Davis' battalion communications chief, and Sgt. Matt Dallas were washing up in helmets for what Amaty quipped would be the "Corregidor Victory Parade."

Andy Amaty recalled:

> Most of us were in reasonably good spirits that morning, the Nip fire had slackened greatly, and we had only a thousand yards to go to reach the tip of the tail. Suddenly an enormous explosion under Monkey Point rocked Corregidor and, I heard later, shook Bataan, three miles away. Everything went black—I had been knocked cold.

Scores of bodies, American and Japanese, were tossed into the air like rag dolls. Boulders, dirt, concrete, chunks of metal, and bits and pieces of human bodies rained back down from the sky. All over Monkey Point surviving but shaken paratroopers were frantically digging out comrades who were covered by dirt landslides but still alive.

Bennett M. Guthrie, an Oklahoman who had been a staff sergeant and near the main force of the blast, recalled:

> One trooper was cut in half, but lived for a minute or two. I saw one man, along with a tree, blown so high into the sky that they nearly disappeared from sight. One chunk of coral landed on a destroyer two thousand yards to the south. Another bit of debris injured a trooper on Topside, a mile or so distant.

The Japanese in the Monkey Point tunnel had set off tons of dynamite in order to kill as many Americans as possible. Their handiwork had gouged out of mostly solid rock a crater nearly 150 feet long, 75 feet wide, and 32 feet deep.

A 30-ton Sherman tank firing into caves had been hurled 50

feet, and the scorching heat from the blast sealed its three-man crew inside. A surviving tanker was cut out by an acetylene torch that had been rushed to the site. Capt. Holger S. Mouritsen, surgeon of the 462nd Parachute Field Artillery Battalion, had been wounded in the explosion, but he began tending to mutilated paratroopers and saved the surviving tanker's life by amputating his leg on the spot. A short time later, ashen-faced from loss of blood and shock, "Doc" Mouritsen lapsed into unconsciousness while kneeling over a badly injured trooper.

Several hundred yards from Monkey Point, 3rd Battalion surgeon Logan Hovis had been tending to a teenaged parachutist who had been shot in the chest. When the blast occurred, a falling chunk of rock penetrated the hood of the ambulance next to which Hovis had been working.

Dr. Logan Hovis recalled ensuing events:

> Along with two of my medics, I ran to the explosion scene. I was shocked at the carnage. Butchered bodies were strewn about everywhere. Other men lay motionless, dead but with no visible marks on them. Scattered about were arms, legs, heads, and pieces of bone and flesh. It was a horrible sight.

Tending the wounded along with Hovis was Capt. William C. McLain, the 1st Battalion surgeon. McLain had been but a few feet from the edge of the blast and nearly buried by dirt and debris.

Meanwhile, George Jones, notified of the disaster by radio, rushed to Monkey Point. Gazing at the scores of dead and mangled paratroopers, Jones had to fight back tears. Those killed by concussion appeared to be sleeping peacefully and, in his anguish, the Rock Force commander felt like calling out to them, "Get up, boys, get up!"

The *Banzai* blast at Monkey Point had inflicted 196 casualties, including 52 killed, on John Davis' battalion. Perhaps 200 Japanese in the tunnel had committed hara-kiri by blowing themselves into dust.

George Jones did not let his anguish over the Monkey Point carnage influence his tactical judgment. John Erickson was ordered to pass his troopers through the remnants of the decimated battalion and continue the assault. Jumping off at once, Erickson's boys pushed to the tip of the tail at East Point, then wiped out die-hard Japanese holed up in caves on Hooker Point, a sliver of rock lying 100 yards offshore.

By darkness of February 27, organized resistance on Corregidor had ceased. Rock Force intelligence officer Capt. Francis Donovan counted 4,506 Japanese dead, but many hundreds more had been sealed into caves, and large numbers had blown themselves up in suicide explosions underground. Numerous but uncounted Nipponese corpses had been shoved over Topside cliffs by bulldozers, and perhaps 200 enemy soldiers had been killed trying to swim the three miles to Bataan. Altogether, some 6,000 Japanese had died defending Corregidor—eight to 10 times as many as Sixth Army had estimated had been manning the island fortress.[4]

At 10:00 A.M. on March 2, four PT boats edged into North Dock on Bottomside, and Douglas MacArthur and a galaxy of his high brass stepped ashore. It was MacArthur's supreme moment in the war—his triumphant return to the Holy Grail of Corregidor. Hopping into a jeep driven by paratroop Cpl. Sims H. Smith, MacArthur went first to Malinta Tunnel, his headquarters during the agony at Bataan nearly three years earlier. He promptly strolled into the entrance of the burned-out excavation.

George Jones, who had accompanied the supreme commander on his jeep tour, remembered:

Col. George Jones (facing camera) accompanies Gen. Douglas MacArthur on post-battle tour of Corregidor. *(Author's collection)*

This was an anxious period for me. I could visualize some die-hard Japanese marine popping out of a spider hole and shooting General MacArthur. In fact, armed Jap stragglers had been lurking deep in Malinta Tunnel itself. I felt a surge of relief when the supreme commander finally walked back out of the tunnel.

When MacArthur's jeep cavalcade packed with generals and admirals reached the parade ground, the supreme commander hopped out and glanced around at the white and colored para-

One of American military history's most dramatic moments. Gen. Douglas MacArthur at Corregidor flag raising. *(U. S. Army)*

chutes still dangling from trees and wrecked buildings. Bordering the parade ground stood the old Corregidor flag pole, a slightly bent, bomb-scarred ship's mast with twisted rigging and ladders hanging from its yardarm.

Douglas MacArthur walked briskly to where George Jones stood at the head of a battle-weary but proud honor guard in their soiled and torn uniforms. Some were wearing blood-stained bandages. Jones saluted smartly and said, "Sir, I present you Fortress Corregidor!"

Speaking under a brilliant blue sky, MacArthur declared that Rock Force had carried out "one of the boldest feats in military history." The supreme commander said: "I see the old flag pole still stands. Have your troops hoist the colors to the peak, and let no enemy ever haul them down."

As hundreds of American eyes—many welled with tears—watched Old Glory waving in the breeze, proud were hearts filled with grief over the heavy price paid to repurchase Corregidor: 223 men killed, 1,107 wounded or injured—nearly one-third of the entire Rock Force.

51
"Angels from Heaven" to the Rescue

Early on Sunday morning, February 16, 1945, the 511th Parachute Infantry's 1st Battalion, led by Maj. Henry Burgess, a young Wyoming rancher and Harvard University graduate, was pulled out of the Fort William McKinley fight and brought into nearby Manila for what was thought to be a rest. However, Burgess was promptly ordered to report to 11th Airborne Division headquarters in a rambling, old Spanish villa at Parañque, a few miles south of the Philippine capital. Burgess had no knowledge of the fact that he was destined to lead one of history's boldest rescue missions.

Electrifying events had originated eight days earlier, on February 8, when the 11th Airborne night duty officer, Lt. Col. Glenn "Mac" McGowan, received a top secret message from a higher headquarters: "Imperative you move on Los Baños ASAP." It was 3:02 A.M.

A short time later, Douglas MacArthur discussed the mission with Joe Swing. "Joe, I want you to rescue the American civilian prisoners at Los Baños," the supreme commander said. How the feat would be accomplished was left to Swing and his staff and battle leaders.

Burgess promptly huddled with Swing, Lt. Col. Henry "Butch" Muller, the division G-2, Lt. Col. Douglas N. Quandt, the division operations officer, and their staffs. Burgess was told that he and his battalion would conduct the rescue raid.

"Why me?" the major blurted out.

"Because Ed Lahti [the 511th Parachute Infantry leader] picked your battalion for the job," came the reply.

Los Baños internment camp was located on the grounds of the University of the Philippines agricultural college, 25 miles below Manila near the southern shore of a large lake called Laguna de Bay. In the fence-enclosed prison were some 2,200 emaciated American civilians, most of whom had been captured when Manila fell to the Japanese in January 1942.

Los Baños had been a source of concern to Douglas MacArthur since the Americans invaded Luzon the previous month. Rather than allow the inmates' liberation, would the Japanese guards commit mass murder? Chilling bits of intelligence indicated that the enemy planned to do just that.

While Doug Quandt, a soft-spoken West Pointer, outlined a super-secret plan that had been drawn up, Henry Burgess was sobered by the tremendous obstacles to the success of the rescue mission. Burgess recalled:

How could my force of 412 paratroopers slip undetected deep into Japanese-controlled territory, wipe out a large number of enemy guards at the camp before they could kill the inmates, and bring back to safety 2,200 weak men, women and children, many of whom were unable to walk?

Burgess was in for yet another jolt: Some 8,000 men of the Japanese 8th Division were assembled only eight miles southwest of the prison camp. Part of the enemy force could be rushed to Los Baños by truck in less than one hour, so total secrecy was the password. Should the Japanese get advance word of the raid, Los Baños by truck in less than one hour, so total secrecy was the password. Should the Japanese get advance word of the raid, Los Baños would run red with American blood—prisoners' as well as paratroopers'.

Butch Muller had been trying frantically to collect scraps of information about Los Baños prison camp, but there were chilling gaps. How many guards were there? Where would the guards be at the time the camp was hit? Where would the civilian prisoners probably be located? How many internees would be too sick or aged to walk? Where would these invalids be housed? When would be the best time to attack the camp?

Then at noon on Monday—L-Day (Liberation Day) minus 4—an unexpected intelligence bonanza reached 11th Airborne headquarters. Peter Miles, an engineer who had once been a snake charmer and saloon bouncer, had escaped from the Los Baños camp only the previous day. Keen-minded, meticulous, and articulate, Miles provided a wealth of information about daily life in the Los Baños camp—including the fact that only those guards actually on duty were armed.

"The Japs not on duty arise just before dawn and take calisthenics in an open area near their barracks," Miles pointed out. "At that time, precisely 7:00 A.M., their weapons are locked in a rack in a connecting room between two long barracks where the Nips are housed and sleep."[1]

Early that same morning, Henry Burgess contacted his number 2 man, 27-year-old Capt. Nathaniel "Bud" Ewing, also a Wyoming rancher, and instructed him to begin marching the battalion southward from Manila in the direction of Los Baños. Burgess and Ewing had served together in the Wyoming National Guard, and were longtime close friends.

Shorty Soule, leader of the 188th Glider Infantry, was put in overall charge of the rescue operation. L-Day was set for Friday, February 23. By Wednesday, February 21, the rescue plan was finalized. Twenty-year-old Lt. George E. Skau, a rough, tough native of Poughkeepsie, New York, and his 31-man reconnaissance platoon would paddle over Laguna de Bay in *bancas* (native boats) on the night of L-Day minus 2, slip ashore at Mayondon Point two miles north of the prison camp, and make contact with a Philippine guerilla force that would attack outlying Japanese positions.

George Skau, whose troopers called themselves the "Killer Platoon," was no stranger to Los Baños. On the dark night of February 12, he had paddled across Laguna de Bay in a *banca* to scout the camp, and since that time had made several round trips to sketch maps and terrain features and to coordinate activities with the guerrillas.[2]

In the early L-Day hours of darkness, Skau's Killer Platoon, loaded with grenades and carrying tommy guns, would crawl up to the Los Baños guard posts and pillboxes and wait for the 7:00 A.M. signal to attack. Skau's rugged troopers would then storm the camp and kill the on-duty guards.

At the moment that the Killer Platoon began shooting and grenading, Lt. John B. Ringler of suburban Buffalo, New York, and his B Company of the 511th would bail out of nine C-47s and land next to the compound. Even the jump would be especially fraught with peril.

John Ringler recalled that "our drop zone was a small field hemmed in by the barbed wire of the camp, a high voltage electric transmission line, and a railroad track. There would be no margin for error. It was a tight fit, but I never doubted but that we would land okay." As soon as Ringler's parachutists were on the ground and shucked their chutes they were to bolt into the camp and race for the weapons rack where the arms of the off-duty guards were kept. It was hoped that these guards would be engaging in calisthenics, a procedure they customarily followed at precisely 7:00 A.M. each day. No one doubted that the off-duty Japanese would run hell-bent for their weapons when Ringler's men landed, so the side that reached the arms rack first could well determine if the rescue mission had a chance to succeed or would result in a bloodbath for American civilian prisoners and paratroopers alike.

Meanwhile, Bud Ewing would have marched Burgess' battalion southward for 15 miles from Manila, and the force would bivouac on the western shore of Laguna de Bay near the town of Mamatid. Burgess would join his battalion there, and at 4:00 A.M. on L-Day, the paratroopers would load onto 54 amphibious tractors, also known as "alligators" and "amtracs," which would then slip into Laguna de Bay and "swim" to Mayondon Point, two miles north of the Los Baños camp. Going along with Burgess' infantrymen would be 100 men and four guns of Capt. Louis Burris' D Battery of the 457th Parachute Field Artillery Battalion.

The amtracs were to rumble onto the beach at 7:00 A.M., the precise time that George Skau's Killer Platoon would be attacking camp guards and John Ringler's parachutists would be jumping. While some of Burgess' amtrac-borne troopers would fan out to protect the crucial Mayondon Point beachhead, the remaining men would roll on to the prisoner encampment.

At the same time, a diversion would be launched to draw the nearby Japanese 8th Division away from Los Baños. Shorty Soule would accompany his 188th Glider Infantry's 1st Battalion, led by Ernest LaFlamme, in an attack down the road from Manila toward Nipponese positions at the east-west flowing San Juan River near Mamatid, seven miles northwest of Los Baños. In Soule's force would be a squadron of the 637th Tank Destroyer Battalion and elements of the 472nd and 675th Field Artillery Battalions.

Meanwhile, Ringler's B Company paratroopers, who would jump on Los Baños, were in jail, and had been since Monday afternoon. In dank cells inside frowning, high-walled New Bilibid Prison, Ringler's boys whiled away their time and conjectured endlessly over what grotesque twist of fate had resulted in their incarceration. Ringler could not tell them that they had been ensconced to assure security.

Late on Thursday afternoon—L-Day minus 1—John Ringler returned from 11th Airborne headquarters and broke the news to his flabbergasted paratroopers: At 7 A.M. tomorrow, they would jump onto a postage-stamp-size drop zone 25 miles deep into Japanese-controlled territory at a place called Los Baños. Briefing his men, Ringler cautioned: "Watch out in particular for the high-tension line bordering the DZ—if you hit it, you're fried!"

That night, Joe Swing, Butch Muller, and Doug Quandt huddled at the Spanish villa in Parañque. Their faces were grim. A "Black Widow" (P-61 night recon plane) had just returned with a chilling report: a large number of trucks with headlights blazing were moving toward the Los Baños camp area. What did this mean? Had the Japanese learned the secret, and were they rushing troops into position to ambush Henry Burgess' men when their amtracs crawled onto the shore north of the prison camp? Was the enemy rushing the 2,200 civilian prisoners to a distant locale? Or was the flurry of truck movements just a coincidence?

Joe Swing pondered this alarming development for only a few minutes. There was no way that the raid could be canceled. Swing could recall Henry Burgess' amtrac force and John Ringler's company, but George Skau and his Killer Platoon would strike the prison camp at 7:00 A.M., and there was no way to get word to them. For better or for worse, the die was cast.

While Joe Swing was wrestling with that crucial decision, John Ringler's "jailbirds" were sleeping under the wings of C-47s at Nichols Field, where they had been taken from New Bilibid prison. Or at least they pretended to sleep. Most tossed and turned fitfully, their tormented minds awhirl with potential dangers.

In the early morning blackness of L-Day, tension was thick in the bivouac area of Henry Burgess' battalion, which was sited along the western shore of Laguna de Bay. Fifty-four amtracs of Lt. Col. Joseph W. Biggs' 672nd Amphibious Tractor Battalion had arrived. These ponderous vehicles were awesome to the eye and ear. In movement, they were noisy, belching and spurting exhaust flames, but they were slow, thin-skinned, and lacked maneuverability. Biggs and his boys would have their work cut out for them. Their alligators would have to navigate course changes in blackness with only hand compasses, keep the column close to avoid chaos, and hit a pinpoint target at a precise time after a circuitous trek of some 20 miles.

Twelve miles to the southeast of Burgess' bivouac, sleep was coming fitfully, if at all, for inmates of the Los Baños camp. Earlier that day, they had been told that the camp's food had been exhausted and no more was coming. All day, perspiring Japanese soldiers had been digging a long, deep ditch outside the barbed-wire fence. Most prisoners were convinced that they would be buried in the excavation in the morning, after being bayonetted or machine gunned.

Shortly after dawn on L-Day, John Ringler and his 130 paratroopers at Nichols Field climbed up short ladders and into nine C-47s of the 65th Troop Carrier Squadron. With Maj. Don Anderson at the controls of the lead plane, the Gooney Birds sped down the bomb-pocked runway and lifted off, precisely on time—6:40 A.M.

Maj. Gen. Joseph M. Swing.
(U. S. Army)

Lt. John B. Ringler. *(Author's collection)*

After pitching out an equipment bundle of automatic weapons and ammo, Ringler would be the first to jump. "If the Japs shoot at the first parachute out, they'll hit the equipment bundle and not me," the lieutenant quipped.

Eighteen minutes later, in the hot, fearful prison camp, inmates heard the roar of powerful engines. Many squinted into the early morning sun and saw a low-flying formation of airplanes approaching the camp. A short time later, John Ringler and his boys bailed out.

James Bateman, who had been a 20-year-old civilian prisoner of Los Baños, remembered:

> We all thought this would be the last day of our lives, that we would all be executed. Then parachutes rained out of the sky. At first we thought they were dropping food in the camp. Then we realized they were American soldiers. We yelled and screamed and danced with joy.

Ringler's parachutists made an almost textbook-perfect landing. Only one man was injured when his head struck the railroad track bordering the tiny drop zone.

By now, George Skau and his Killer Platoon, which had been lying in wait outside the fence, pounced on the Japanese guards, hurling grenades, and shooting. Confused and panicky, the sentries surviving the first assault ran around aimlessly, and they, too, were cut down.

Meanwhile, Ringler's parachutists, moving like a well-oiled machine, rushed inside the camp, where they joined the Killer Platoon in the do-or-die race for the building holding the weapons of the off-duty Japanese. Skau and his boys ran hell-bent past the large number of guards who, stripped to the waist, were undergoing their usual morning calisthenics, as anticipated. Now the startled guards realized what was happening, and they dashed toward their weapons cache. Skau and his men won the race.

Thanks to the one-time saloon bouncer, Peter Miles, the paratroopers knew the camp layout precisely. The camp commandant's office was in the next building, and George Skau charged up the steps and barged into the first room. A Nipponese officer leaped from behind a desk and bolted through the window. Skau plugged the enemy officer in the head while the man was mid-air in his final swan dive.

Bedlam reigned. A harsh cacophony of grenade explosions and tommy-gun and rifle fire reverberated throughout the camp as paratroopers flushed out Japanese hiding inside and near the enclosure. Other guards were gunned down as they dashed about helter-skelter. Each new fusillade brought terrified screams from female internees. Most of the fearful inmates remained in their barracks to escape the violence raging outside.

Over a smuggled radio, the inmates had learned of the amphibious landing by United States Marines on Iwo Jima, a tiny patch of rock and black sand, four days earlier. So when one of Ringler's boys, ferreting out Japanese, bolted into a barracks where a group of priests and nuns was sprawled on the floor to escape flying bullets, a sister asked in a shaky voice: "Are you a Marine?" In an exasperated tone, the tall, blond teenager replied: "Hell, no, I ain't a gyrene! I'm an American paratrooper!" The inmates were puzzled. "What is a paratrooper?" they wondered.

At the same time that John Ringler and his boys had jumped, the 54 alligators carrying Henry Burgess' force crawled out of Laguna de Bay two miles to the north, and began clanking inland. Approaching the camp, the driver of the first alligator called out to Burgess: "The gate's closed—what should I do?" the major replied: "Crash through the damned thing!" Looking much like an enraged prehistoric beast, the alligator charged the barrier.

There was a loud, crunching sound, as bits and pieces of metal, wood, and wire flew in all directions. Other alligators followed.

Inside the chaotic compound, 23-year-old Lt. Tom Mesereau, a 1942 All American football lineman at West Point who stood six feet, four inches and weighed 235 pounds, quickly formed up his C Company of 80 men and prepared to rush off on a crucial mission. Mesereau and his men were to rapid-march to the southwest and to intercept leading elements of the Japanese 8th Division, which would probably be heading for the camp once word was received of the American operation.

Henry Burgess recalled his conversation with Tom Mesereau at the gate:

> *Tom was a great soldier, and if anyone could get the job done, he could. I told him that when he made contact with the Jap advance guard to shoot the hell out of them and force them to deploy. That should hold them up for at least an hour and give us a little more time to get the inmates to the beach.*

John Ringler and George Skau, their tommy guns figuratively smoking, came up to Burgess, who was busily engaged in lining up the alligators. Shaking his head in frustration, Ringler said, "My men can't get the internees to head for the loading area. Most of them are cringing in their barracks and shacks."

Burgess was also frustrated. An hour had passed since the Americans first stormed the camp, and little seemed to have been done—except for killing some 250 Japanese guards. No one had thought to bring a bullhorn, so the raid commander had no way of communicating with the milling, frightened inmates. The fire-fights had set a few shacks afire, and the blaze, fanned by a brisk wind, sent thick black clouds wafting over Burgess, Ringler, and Skau, who were standing by the amtrac loading area.

The fires proved to be a blessing. Terrorized and bewildered by the flames and the smoke rolling over the camp, the internees poured out of their structures and headed for the loading area. Paratroopers dashed into the shack that served as a hospital and tenderly carried out 130 ill and weak patients and carefully loaded them into the alligators. For a few inmates, the boys in jump boots had arrived too late: Several corpses lay on filthy hospital cots. These dead bodies were brought out as well, and they would later be given decent burials.

Alligators rumbling through Los Baños during rescue mission.
(U. S. Army)

Once the 130 ailing patients were aboard, men, women and children scrambled into the remaining alligators, and the long line of vehicles rumbled off toward Laguna de Bay. They would cross the lake, deposit their passengers, then make a return trip to pick up the remainder of the internees and paratroopers.

As the raging blazes crept closer, Henry Burgess, shouting to be heard, told the remaining inmates: "The Japs are probably closing in on us. So we want to get you out quickly. You'll have to walk the two miles to the beach. Take only essential items. The army will supply you with clothes when we get there."

Sister Patricia Marie turned to other nuns and whispered: "Oh, dear! Can't you just see us wearing khaki pants and shirts and black veils!"

Lines of dazed and weakened prisoners shuffled out of the camp. Mingled among them, for protection and to provide help, were paratroopers, who were hungry, having given away their rations to the starving inmates. Some people fell, unable to continue; they were picked up and carried by the soldiers. One trooper cradled an infant in his arms. The column was soon strung out for nearly a mile, and progress was so slow that Burgess feared it would take days to get to Laguna de Bay.

Finally reaching the shoreline at the tail of the column, Burgess was greeted with alarming news. Tom Mesereau, who had just returned from his mission of intercepting any Japanese force heading for Los Baños, said that he and his company had engaged in a shoot-out with an enemy band, and that there were indications that a much larger body of Japanese troops was approaching. If the alligators did not return soon, some 1,200 civilians and paratroopers might be trapped and wiped out.

All afternoon, the Americans waited anxiously. A few mortar shells exploded nearby, and a long distance burst of machine-gun fire zipped overhead. Suddenly, a rousing cheer split the air: Joe Biggs' alligators were coming. Rapidly, inmates and paratroopers climbed aboard. Henry Burgess was with the last group of six amtracs to shove off—just in the nick of time. Mortar shells splashed around them, but the drivers took evasive action and none of the amtracs was hit.

Sixth Army commander Gen. Walter Krueger pins Combat Legion of Merit on Maj. Henry A. Burgess for leading Los Baños rescue mission. (*Author's collection*)

When the raid leader reached the relative safety of the beach at Mamatid, from where the alligator force had departed some 15 hours earlier, everyone had been evacuated. But one man was on hand to greet Burgess: Maj. Gen. Oscar W. Griswold, commander of XIV Corps.

The Los Baños rescue raid had been an epic operation. With the aid of Filipino guerillas, Burgess and his "Angels from Heaven," as the 11th Airborne Division were called, had beaten gargantuan odds. All 2,147 internees and 412 paratroopers had been brought out from under the noses of the Japanese. The lone casualty was Irene Wightman, who had been grazed on the neck by a Japanese bullet back at Mayondon Point while she sat waiting for the alligators to return.

As the days ahead unfolded, the 11th Airborne troopers eagerly anticipated the arrival of Stateside newspapers to see the blaring headlines and the long, rousing articles that would tell the home folks of their probably unprecedented rescue feat. Their vigil would be in vain. Pictures of the dramatic Marine flag-raising on bloody Iwo Jima and related articles were splashed across front pages. Buried inside were brief items mentioning that some American civilian prisoners had been liberated from a place called Los Baños in the Philippines.[3]

52
Poised to Leap the Rhine

In early March 1945, Nazi Germany was hemmed in on all sides by hostile forces and was teetering on the brink of collapse. Powerful Soviet armies, only 42 miles from Berlin, were hammering at the gates of the Third Reich in the east American, British, Canadian, and French armies were stretched out for 450 miles along the western border of Germany from Holland to Switzerland.

General Eisenhower was ready to unleash his forces over the Rhine, a mighty barrier to be surmounted before the war could be concluded. In bomb-battered Berlin, Adolf Hitler was determined that the western Allies would fail. He intended for the Rhine to run red with American and British blood.

Since Operation Market-Garden in Holland in September 1944, Lewis Brereton's First Allied Airborne Army staff had been furiously grinding out proposed parachute and glider missions. One of these, "Operation Eclipse," was the focus of heated debate at the highest levels of the Anglo-American alliance. Eclipse was a breath-taking plan for a parachute assault by more than two divisions to capture Berlin before the Russians snared that propaganda prize.

Dwight Eisenhower was opposed to Eclipse, arguing, naively perhaps, that his was not a "political army" and that Berlin was not an important *military* target. Winston Churchill, on the other hand, along with Field Marshals Alan Brooke and Bernard Montgomery, were demanding that the Western Allies seize Berlin by any means necessary and as soon as possible—ahead of the rampaging Russians. The British pointed out that nothing would be gained if the Western Allies won the war strategically and lost it politically.

Meanwhile, "Looie" Brereton's staff issued detailed orders for Eclipse. It would be the war's most audacious operation: a lightly armed airborne force attacking hostile Berlin, a sprawling metropolis with a peacetime population of some 3,000,000 persons, located 325 miles behind German lines along the Rhine. The orders read: "Be prepared to enter Berlin, quell local disorders." Those disorders, it was implied, could come from armed German soldiers, violence-prone civilian groups—or Soviet troops bursting into the Nazi capital.

Operation Eclipse orders called for the following:

1. James Gavin's 82nd Airborne Division to seize airfields Tempelhof and Rangdor, priority Tempelhof;
2. Maxwell Taylor's 101st Airborne Division to capture airfields Gatow and Staaken, priority Gatow, but be

prepared to seize airfield Schönwald as an emergency
alternate;

3. A British brigade to capture airfield Oranienburg, with
Schönwald as an emergency alternate;
4. One Polish parachute regiment in reserve.

Meanwhile, Gavin's All-Americans and Taylor's Screaming
Eagles were conducting "dress rehearsals" for the "Big Berlin
Show" under the strictest security. Only those with an absolute
need to know were privy to details, fewer yet to the target—
Berlin. Most officers and men in the two airborne divisions
thought that they were undergoing the customary vigorous train-
ing routines. Despite the intense secrecy, Soviet dictator Josef
Stalin knew all about Eclipse.[1]
James Gavin remembered:

*It would be about two decades before I learned that the Russians had
acquired knowledge of Eclipse, apparently in some detail. Cornelius
Ryan, the author and historian, told me that he had interviewed
several World War II Russian generals in 1963, and they had told
him that Marshal Stalin had told these generals that two Allied
airborne divisions were being rapidly readied for a drop on Berlin.
Stalin then called in the commander of the two Soviet army groups
nearest to the German capital, Marshals Ivan Konev and Georgi
Zhukov, and pitted them one against the other, challenging each to
get to Berlin ahead of the other—and ahead of the Americans.*

While Eclipse was ready to go, electrifying events erupted
along the Western Front. On March 7, spearheads of Maj. Gen.
John W. Leonard's 9th Armored Division stunned the world—
and SHAEF—by unexpectedly seizing intact the huge Ludendorff railroad bridge over the Rhine at Remagen. Omar Bradley
promptly funneled five divisions over the Ludendorff to hold a
bridgehead.

Then, on the night of March 22, George Patton, in an audacious action, slipped Maj. Gen. S. LeRoy "Red" Irwin's 5th Infantry Division over the water barrier, near Mainz. That feat
cleared the way for "Sandy" Patch's Seventh Army on Patton's
right and Gen. de Lattre de Tassigny's French First Army still
farther south to get over the Rhine without great difficulty.

As a result of these spectacular coups, "Choker II," an airborne assault over the Rhine at Worms in front of Patch by the newly arrived 13th Airborne Division, was scrubbed.

Officers and men of the 13th Airborne, a tough and keenly trained outfit, would deny that its unlucky (to some) numerical designation played a role in its destiny, but the unit seemed to have been jinxed since its birth. The 13th had been the fifth and final American airborne division to be created during the war, having been activated at Camp Mackall, North Carolina, in August 1943—on Friday the 13th.

Maj. Gen. George W. Griner had been the 13th Airborne's first commander, but he was replaced the following December by Eldridge Chapman, head of the Airborne Command at Mackall. Chapman, who had seen World War I action as an infantry lieutenant, brought his division to Europe in February 1945, and settled it into billets at Auxerre, Sens, and other small towns some 70 miles southeast of Paris.

In the Auxerre region, Chapman put his men through grueling training exercises culminating in "Operation Comet," a mass jump across the Yonne River, simulating a bailout on the far side of the Rhine.

The 13th Airborne had arrived in France with only one parachute regiment, the 515th, commanded by burly Col. Harvey J. Jablonsky, a former All American football lineman at West Point. Two glider regiments filled out the division—Col. Samuel Roth's 88th and Col. William O. Poindexter's 326th. However, the division was beefed up on March 1 when Rupert Graves' independent and battle-tested 517th Parachute Regimental Combat Team, fresh from the bloody Ardennes cauldron and the Siegfried Line, was brought back and assigned as a component.

Graves' boys found it hard to adjust to their new situation— even having to rip off their coveted 517th shoulder patches and replacing them with the 13th Airborne emblem was an agonizing experience. Nor did the 517th veterans of heavy fighting in Italy, Southern France, Belgium, and Germany take kindly to being given orders by 13th Airborne officers who had never heard a shot fired in anger.[2]

Now Chapman's division was alerted for another daring mission: a jump on the large city of Stuttgart, 40 miles east of the Rhine, to capture German scientists holed up there. Detailed information was received, and squads and platoons were assigned to house, university, and laboratory addresses where each scientist could probably be nabbed. This mission would be canceled when a French division overran the 13th Airborne drop zone—Charles de Gaulle, head of the Free French, had issued orders to his unit to apprehend the same pool of scientists.

With spring—and good flying weather—rapidly approaching, it appeared that the 13th Airborne would get another chance to make its first combat jump. At its new headquarters at Maisons-Lafitte outside Paris, Brereton's staff had cooked up an audacious parachute and glider operation, one mindboggling in scope.

Code-named "Operation Arena," the plan called for dropping and landing four to six Allied airborne divisions, in multiple lifts, on high ground lying between Kassel and Paderborn, 100 miles east of the Rhine. In that locale were several Luftwaffe airfields, which would be seized and used to fly in five conventional infantry divisions.

Along with the untested 13th Airborne, Brereton's planners had earmarked for Arena's initial assault the 17th, 82nd, and 101st Airborne Divisions, and the British 1st and 6th Airborne Divisions. Once the airhead was secured, Walter Robertson's 2nd, Alex Bolling's 84th, and Tony MacAuliffe's 103rd Infantry Divisions, along with a fourth yet to be designated, would be flown in.

Arena's logistics would be gargantuan, dwarfing those of any earlier airborne operation. All of the First Triple A's huge fleet of C-47s and the new, larger C-46s would be used to fly two round trips daily from bases in France and Belgium, and Jimmy Doolittle's Eighth Air Force heavies, whose bombs had been making a greater wreck of the Greater Reich, would help fly 2,900 tons of supplies daily into the isolated airhead. D-Day for Arena was set for May 1.

Omar Bradley, who was perhaps Eisenhower's closest confidant, was not enthused by Arena. He called on the supreme commander and argued that, with Hodges, Patton, and Patch already over the Rhine, two of his armies could reach the Kassel-Paderborn region before the massive airborne operation could be launched. Eisenhower was sold, and canceled Arena.[3]

Now the airborne spotlight on the Western Front focused on "Operation Varsity," code name for a three-division parachute and glider assault in support of Bernard Montgomery's "Operation Plunder," a crossing of the Rhine by the 21st Army Group at Wesel. Ticketed to strike four to six miles east of the river barrier were Chapman's 13th, Miley's 17th, and Bols's 6th.

Great enthusiasm again saturated the 13th Airborne's camps south of Paris. Then the hard, cold reality of logistics intruded: There would be sufficient aircraft to lift only two airborne divisions at one time. One would have to be British. So it was left to Matt Ridgway, whose XVIII Corps would command Varsity, to decide which American division—the 13th or 17th—would make the mission. Based on the 17th Airborne's combat experience in the Ardennes, that outfit got Ridgway's nod.[4]

Harvey Jablonsky, wartime leader of the 515th Parachute Infantry, recalled:

It was a frustrating experience for these highly trained troops. It became embarrassing as I called the regiment together after each cancellation to inform the men and officers why we were not committed. I wore out such excuses as "we are SHAEF's strategic reserve." Another excuse, "You are soldiers of opportunity" did not sit well either after I used it several times.

The Montgomery vault over the Rhine would be awesome. Under his command would be 1 million British, American and Canadian troops, including 80,000 in the assault. In the scope of its firepower, massed ground troops, airborne—and even naval—support, Plunder would be second in magnitude only to the D-Day landings in Normandy.

Plunder/Varsity would be a reversal of all other Allied airborne operations against enemy defenses: Montgomery would send his amphibious troops over the Rhine on the night of March 23, and the 17th and 6th Airborne Divisions would jump and land after daylight.

As time neared for Montgomery's monumental Rhine crossing, Allied intelligence gathered evidence that Adolf Hitler and the German High Command knew that a prodigious airborne assault over the Rhine was imminent. A captured Wehrmacht document outlined defense measures to be taken against an assault from the sky. At secluded Bletchley Park, 40 miles north of London, supersecret Ultra intercepted a series of coded German radio messages warning that the Allied airborne onslaught would hit between Wesel and Duisburg.

Ultra intercepts also revealed that Gen. Johannes Blaskowitz, the able leader of Army Group H along the northern Rhine, had virtually stripped his air defenses in Holland and rushed down to the Wesel region 81 heavy and 252 light antiaircraft guns. Allied intelligence soon confirmed this haunting development: swarms of gun snouts, pointed skyward, showed clearly in aerial photos.

Blaskowitz would be counting on this fearful concentration of firepower to defeat the looming airborne strike by knocking from the sky large numbers of paratroop-laden transport planes and tug-glider combinations. For Ultra disclosed that Blaskowitz had but 80,000 men (11,000 of them in the Wesel locale) along a 65-mile stretch of the Rhine opposite Montgomery's powerful army group.

If the *Oberkommando der Wehrmacht* (high command) had any lingering doubt over where Plunder and Varsity would hit, such indecision vanished when Montgomery blanketed with a smoke screen a 50-mile stretch of the Rhine between Wesel and Rees.[5]

German forces east of the Rhine would be struck by an enormous thunderclap from the blue, the mightiest simultaneous airborne operation that history had known. Within a time span of about two and a half hours, 17,122 American and British paratroopers and glidermen would pounce on the Wehrmacht, bringing along 614 jeeps, 286 guns and mortars, and hundreds of tons of ammunition, fuel, food, medical supplies and assorted equipment.[6]

Never before had two entire airborne divisions been flown into battle in a single effort. Larger numbers of paratroopers and glider soldiers had been delivered in both Neptune (Normandy) and Market (Holland), but these operations had been conducted over several days and the aircraft and crews used more than once.

Miley's 17th (Thunder from Heaven) Airborne would take off from 17 airfields in the region bounded by Amiens, Orléans, and Evereux. Bols' Red Devils would depart from 11 airfields in southeastern England. Flying this combined force would be 1,572 transport planes and 1,326 gliders, escorted by 889 fighter planes. Paul Williams' veteran IX Troop Carrier Command would haul all paratroopers from both divisions and tug the 17th Airborne gliders. Two groups of Royal Air Force planes would tow the 6th Airborne gliders.

Measuring five miles deep and six miles wide, the Varsity airhead would be the most congested concentration of parachute and glider troops yet attempted, with 17,122 airborne men elbowing for space. If they did not come down on the heads of the Germans, they well might land on top of one another.

A few days before D-Day, Miley's 17th Airborne in the Châlons-sur-Marne region and Bols' 6th Airborne in southeastern England were sealed into camps to await takeoff. Tension ran high. Rumors were rampant. It was whispered that fanatical SS troops near Wesel had taken blood oaths that they would die in place fighting the sky invaders. What is more, the rumor mill had it, German old men, women, and children had been trained to kill, maim, or poison the Allied paratroopers, and glidermen. And, "authentic reports" had it, hundreds of thousands of sturdy, needle-sharp sticks had been planted on the drop zones to skewer descending paratroopers.

At midafternoon on March 23, Bernard Montgomery conferred with his battle leaders and staff at 21st Army Group headquarters in Venlo, Holland. A final-minute report from his meteorologists determined that climatic conditions would be right on the morrow for the airborne phase of the Rhine assault, so at 3:32 P.M., the code phrase to strike—"Two if by Sea"—was flashed to Bud Miley at Châlons-sur-Marne and Eric Bols at Aldershot.

Miley's Thunder from Heaven boys in north-central France and Bols's Red Devils in southeastern England had been "sealed" in camps surrounded by thick strands of barbed wire. Alert guards were posted at the few exits with orders to take whatever action was necessary to keep the airborne men penned up.

Tension heightened. In one of Miley's camps, 25-year-old Lou Varrone, a trooper in Edson Raff's 507th Parachute Infantry Regiment, had tuned in his small radio to the Berlin Bitch, the sobriquet given to a sultry-voiced propaganda virtuoso on Radio Berlin who played popular American tunes interspersed with lurid descriptions of sexual activities—a sure-fire formula for drawing and holding American GI's. To heighten her credibility, the Berlin Bitch was fed current war information by German intelligence agencies.

While Varrone and his comrades perked up their ears, the Berlin Bitch cooed: "Hi, all you good-looking guys in the 17th Airborne Division there in France. The British are getting you ready to be slaughtered for the greater glory of their King and Empire, aren't they? And how do you fellows in the 507th Parachute Infantry like being cooped up in that old French prison compound? Couldn't they have found a better place for you to spend your last night on earth?"

Varrone and his comrades exchanged grim glances. Indeed, they were "cooped up in an old French prison compound."

Officers and men of the 17th Airborne minutes before taking off for Wesel. *(U. S. Army)*

The Berlin Bitch giggled, then added: "We know you're coming tomorrow and we know where you're coming—at Wesel. Ten crack divisions from the Russian front will be a reception committee to greet you. So don't worry about your landing. Flak will be so thick you can walk down from the sky."

On the night of March 23, some 3,100 big guns, massed hub to hub on the west side of the Rhine, opened one of history's most thunderous bombardments. At 9:00 P.M., the 51st (Highland) Division crossed the wide moat at Speldrop and Rees, and an hour later, the British 1st Commando Brigade paddled over the river two miles below Wesel. Last to go over the Rhine, at 2:00 A.M., were the 15th (Scottish) Division and two American divisions, Leland Hobbs' 30th and Wyche's 79th.

Pushing ahead, the commandos ran into tenacious German paratroopers, who fought for each foot of the rubble pile known as Wesel.

53
A Thunder-
clap from
the Blue

Dawn of Varsity's D-Day burst bright and clear over Europe. In southern England, 645 aircraft hauling and towing 3,837 paratroopers and 3,383 glidermen of Eric Bols' 6th Airborne Division began speeding down runways and lifting off for the Rhine. Conforming to a fine-tuned timetable, Bols' flight took off first because it would have a longer journey than would Bud Miley's 17th Airborne taking off from airfields in north-central France.[1]

Just over an hour later—at 7:17 A.M.—a C-47 piloted by the young pathfinder pioneer, Joel Crouch, of the air corps soared skyward from an air strip outside Chartres. On board was Edson Raff, the 34-year-old colonel whose veteran 507th Parachute Infantry Regiment would spearhead the 17th Airborne assault.

Trailing Raff's C-47 in order were the 1st Battalion, commanded by Paul Smith, Charles Timmes' 2nd Battalion, and Allen Taylor's 3rd Battalion. Bringing up the rear of Raff's flight was the attached 464th Parachute Field Artillery Battalion, led by Lt. Col. Edward S. Branigan of Manhasset, New York. About to see their first combat, the cannoneers called themselves "Branigan's Bastards," because they were not an organic component of the 17th Airborne.

A total of 181 workhorse C-47s were hauling some 2,100 of Raff's regiment and about 390 of Branigan's artillerymen. Grim and largely silent, the troopers were gripped by the customary prejump jitters. However, all felt relieved about one crucial factor: After nearly three years of American airborne operations, the C-47s had finally been fitted with self-sealing fuel tanks; if hit by bullets, the tanks would not leak gallons of inflammable gasoline. The target for Raff's combat team was Drop Zone W, at the southern edge of the thick Diersfordter Wald (forest), three miles northwest of Wesel.

Next in the line of flight was Lou Coutts' 513th Parachute Infantry, making its first combat jump after seeing heavy action in the Battle of the Bulge, and its attached 466th Parachute Field Artillery Battalion, led by Lt. Col. Kenneth L. Booth of Fort Smith, Arkansas. Coutts' regiment was being carried in the new, larger C-46 Commando transport planes; Booth's artillerymen were in C-47s.

Finally, Jim Pierce's battle-tested 194th Glider Infantry, which would be launching its first glider assault, was bringing up the tail of the column. Altogether, 912 C-47s and C-46s were hauling and towing into battle 9,577 men of the 17th Airborne Division—4,964 paratroopers and 4,613 glider soldiers.

Winging majestically through the cloudless blue sky, the Thunder from Heaven armada rendezvoused with the British flight southeast of Brussels, Belgium, and the two long columns, flying roughly side by side, set a course for Wesel. It was one of warfare's most spectacular extravaganzas. In a single stream, stretching back for 100 miles, were some 1,545 aircraft and about 1,300 gliders. Hovering like mother hens over their broods, hordes of American and Royal Air Force fighter planes formed a protective cocoon around the sky armada.

Ed Raff, a hard-bitten fighting man, started to fidget in his seat when the C-47 train had been in flight for nearly two hours. Raff recalled:

> I went forward to the cockpit to talk with the pilot, Joel Crouch, whom I had known a long time and had worked with before. "I'll bet you a case of champagne that we drop you right on the button," Crouch said. Knowing the difficulties that C-47s had had finding a DZ in earlier operations, I fired back, "You're on!"[2]

At 9:51 A.M., Raff's C-47 was nearing the Rhine. Suddenly, the red light flashed on—four minutes to bailout. There was a rustling of gear as troopers struggled to their feet and hooked up static lines to the anchor cable running the length of the cabin. Knees felt like jelly, partly from the 90 pounds of weapons, ammo, and equipment each man carried, partly from the excruciating tension. Mouths went dry as cotton. Foreheads and palms perspired. A few men vomited.

Crouched in the door, his hands gripping each side, Ed Raff felt a surge of exhilaration on seeing the Rhine, a shimmering silver strip. Beyond the broad moat was a thick pall of early morning haze and the lingering clouds of smoke from Field Marshal Montgomery's generators. Raff sensed trouble. The pall had veiled the drop zones and landing zones.

Johannes Blaskowitz, the wily leader of German Army Group H, had guessed right about the Allied airborne target. When the first American and British troop-carrier aircraft winged over the Rhine, an ear-splitting din erupted from scores of ack-ack guns that Blaskowitz had brought down from Holland and hidden in the Diersfordter Wald and in the rubble of the small towns near the drop zones and landing zones. Hundreds of black puffs from exploding shells dotted the sky. It would be the heaviest flak barrage that airborne troops had encountered during the war.

Now the green light glowed in Raff's plane, and with a "Let's go!" the 507th Regiment leader leaped into space. The cabin was cleared in less than 10 seconds. Paratroopers—hundreds of them—were spilling out of planes, and in moments, the hazy sky a few miles east of the Rhine was awash with blossoming white parachutes.

Right on Raff's back—almost literally, as he went out the C-47 door—was Sgt. Harold E. Barkley, a bazooka squad leader. Barkley remembered:

> Coming down, I was aware of a large barn directly below me. Its shingles had been blown off, and all that remained of the roof were the rafters. This is it, I thought. Smacking into a sturdy rafter would split me in two. I crossed my feet, grabbed my chute risers, and offered up a silent prayer. Then I plunged unscathed through a three-foot gap between rafters and landed unhurt in the barn's mow filled with loose hay.
>
> Down below in the barn I heard a rustle. No doubt some Krauts had come after me. I gripped my rifle and peered cautiously over the edge of the mow. Staring curiously up at me were two wide-eyed cows, probably wondering who was this stranger dropping suddenly from the sky.

Peripatetic pathfinder pilot Joel Crouch would lose his case of champagne bet with Ed Raff. Because of the thick blanket of ground haze and smoke, Crouch's serial dropped Raff and 493 of his troopers miles near the small town of Diersfordt, two miles northwest of their designated Drop Zone W. However, the remainder of the 507th Regiment landed on or near to W. Ed Branigan and most of his 464th Artillery Battalion parachuted on or adjacent to W, as planned. Branigan recalled:

> We were raked by heavy machine-gun fire while we were descending in our chutes. Bullets came so close to me that, after crashing down, I found that the dispatch case I had been carrying was riddled. On landing, my artillery men began slithering over the ground under a hail of fire, and they quickly set up three .50-caliber machine guns and began firing back at the German machine gunners.

Spotting one enemy machine gun in a farmhouse, Branigan rapidly rounded up five of his artillerymen and led them in a charge. Firing their tommy guns and rifles, Branigan and the others raced over open ground. First Sgt. Edmund L. Kissinger went past the battalion commander, pitched a grenade into the house, and keeled over dead, a bullet through the head. Branigan and the other troopers bolted inside, sprayed the rooms with tommy-gun fire, and killed or captured the Germans.

Troopers of Raff's 507th Parachute Infantry after dropping near Wesel. *(Edward Page)*

By now parts of three howitzers had been collected and assembled, and their crews opened direct fire on German positions. Branigan's Bastards had achieved their goal of becoming the first airborne artillery outfit to land, fight, and fire its howitzers east of the Rhine.

Bud Miley, the 17th Airborne commander, jumped with Branigan's Bastards, hit squarely on drop zone W, and was promptly pinned down by withering bursts of machine-gun fire. A short distance away, Miley spotted three privates clinging to the ground while bullets hissed just overhead, and to one side, the general saw an equipment bundle with markings that identified it as a machine gun.

Above the raucous chatter of the German automatic weapons, Miley shouted at the three troopers, "Meet me over there." He pointed at the bundle holding the disassembled machine gun and ammo. Slithering over the ground, Miley and the others ripped open the bundle, assembled the gun, and within minutes a two-star general and three privates were blasting away at the tormenting enemy machine gun. When firing slacked off in the immediate area, Bud Miley abandoned his emergency role as a machine gunner and departed in search of his pre-selected command post.

All over the drop zone, countless small, vicious firefights had erupted. Pfc. George J. Peters, a mild-mannered native of Cranston, Rhode Island, had parachuted into a field near the town of Flüren, along with 10 other troopers. While struggling to get out of their harnesses, Peters and his comrades were raked by withering bursts of fire from a machine gun supported by a squad of riflemen 75 yards away. Caught in the open, the men of the 507th lay helpless.

Suddenly, on his own volition, George Peters leaped to his feet and, armed with only a rifle and a few grenades, charged the German stronghold. Spotting the lone man with baggy pants, the enemy gunners concentrated their fire on him.

Shooting as he ran forward, Peters was halfway to the spitting automatic weapon when a burst of bullets knocked him down. Bleeding profusely, the youth struggled to his feet and continued the charge. Again, German slugs plowed into Peters' body, and down he went for the second time. Crawling onward to within 15 feet of the enemy gun, the paratrooper summoned his remaining strength to pitch two grenades, then collapsed. The fiery ex-

Pfc. George J. Peters (U. S. Army)

Pvt. Stuart S. Stryker (U. S. Army)

plosions at the German machine gun killed its crew and caused surviving riflemen to flee. Moments later, George Peters died.

Meanwhile, Edson Raff had assembled the 493 troopers who had landed with him off-target and led them toward his regiment's drop zone two miles to the southeast. Almost at once, Raff's force bumped into a large group of hostile Germans, and after a brisk but brief shootout, captured more than 300 and killed 56 of the enemy.

Perhaps three-quarters of a mile away, the 507th Parachute Infantry commander spotted a German 155-millimeter gun battery blasting away at ground forces pouring over the Rhine five or six miles away. Instead of skirting the enemy battery, Ed Raff ordered an attack and the paratroopers stormed the enemy position and killed or scattered the crews. After spiking the gun barrels with thermite grenades, Raff and his men marched on toward the drop zone. On the way, they passed a paratrooper hanging from a tree in his parachute harness, a bullet hole in the center of his forehead. All of the grim-faced troopers recognized the dead man: the beloved Protestant chaplain of the 507th Parachute Infantry.

Raff and his force neared now Schloss Diersfordt, a thick-walled castle in the center of the Diersfordter Wald and an objective of the regiment. Paul Smith, leader of Raff's 1st Battalion, and some 200 of his troopers had dropped nearby and were shooting up Schloss Diersfordt. Raff's men joined in the siege. While some paratroopers poured fire into turrets and upper windows, other Americans bolted into the cavernous structure and for two hours battled it out room to room with the Germans.

When the shooting ceased, nearly 300 surviving *Feldgrau* were taken prisoners, along with a number of high officers on the staff of Maj. Gen. Hans Straube's LXXXVI Corps, which was using the castle as a command post. Rescued from a dungeon where they were being held were eight captured paratroopers. After their incarceration, the eight Five-O-Sevens had discovered several bottles of liquor stamped "For the Wehrmacht Only" and were well lubricated when liberated.

At the time that Ed Raff's 507th combat team was jumping, Bols' 6th Airborne Division winged over drop zones in the northern portion of the airhead. Bailing out were Brigadier S. James L. Hill's 3rd Parachute Brigade (regiment) and Brigadier J. H. Nigel Poett's 5th Parachute Brigade. Coming down near the town of Hamminkeln, the 1,917 men of Poett's brigade ran into tenacious resistance from dug-in Germans.[3]

In the wake of Raff's sky armada, 72 new C-46s of Col. William L. Filer's 313th Troop Carrier Group were approaching the haze-covered Rhine with Lou Coutts' 513th Parachute Infantry. Coutts and his staff were in the lead plane, and following were Harry Kies' 1st Battalion, "Ace" Miller's 2nd Battalion, and the 3rd Battalion, led by Morris Anderson.

Air corps designers and engineers considered the C-46 to be a vast improvement over the old C-47, having a higher cruising speed and carrying 36 parachutists instead of 18. Exit doors were on both sides of the C-46, permitting the craft to be cleared of paratroopers as quickly as a C-47 would be with its single door.

Unbeknownst to paratroopers and air crews alike, the C-46s would soon prove to be fiery death traps. Despite their improvements, the C-46s did not have self-sealing fuel tanks; when a wing fuel tank would be punctured by a bullet, it would leak gasoline that would trickle inside the wing toward the engines.

After the red light flashed on, Lou Coutts took his place in a door of the lead C-46, piloted by group commander Bill Filer. Ready to bail out right behind him was the renowned *Life* photographer, Robert Capa. As the aircraft passed over the Rhine,

Coutts heard several sharp cracks nearby—exploding ack-ack shells.

Lou Coutts recalled subsequent events:

> *A chunk of shrapnel ripped a large hole in the plane's fuselage next to my head. I glanced back and saw blood running down the floor, so I knew one or more men had been hit. Then the plane's motor burst into flame. My sergeant, not knowing the motor was on fire, had unhooked the wounded trooper's static line. I yelled to hook him up again and push him out the door, for I knew that the plane was doomed. His static line and parachute would save the wounded trooper; this was the only way he could survive. So, semiconscious, out the door he was shoved. He did survive.*

The C-46 had lost power and was down to 542 feet. The green light flashed on and Coutts and his stick rapidly bailed out the two doors. It was the lowest jump that the colonel and his regiment had ever made, but Coutts landed with a routine hard jolt amidst a hail of bullets. Hardly had the last man leaped, when the C-46 exploded.

Crashing to the ground nearby was *Life* photographer Bob Capa. A native of Hungary, the naturalized American was having difficulty in getting out of his parachute harness, and was pinned to the ground by bullets whistling just overhead. In his frustration, Capa was cursing loudly in Hungarian. "Hey, buddy," a nearby prone paratrooper shouted to Capa, "them Jewish prayers ain't gonna do you no good here in Germany!"[4]

Now the blue sky east of the Rhine was a bizarre panorama of burning C-46s and countless black puffs from exploding ack-ack shells. The C-46 hauling "Ace" Miller, leader of the 2nd Battalion, was flying so low that rifle and machine-gun bullets were zipping through the floor. A few men were hit. Now the plane caught fire. An excited crewman burst into the cabin and shouted, "The co-pilot's been hit!" Moments later, Miller and his stick bailed out into withering fusillades of automatic weapons fire, which raked them all the way to the ground.

Ace Miller crashed down in a farmer's pigpen. Swarms of bullets were hissing past as he shucked his chute and pulled out his .45 Colt. Slithering over the ground, Miller peeked around the corner of a ramshackle shed. His heart skipped a beat. Ten feet away was a machine gun manned by four *Feldgrau*. Miller squeezed the trigger four times, and a German toppled over dead each time.

Miller dashed into the farmhouse; two German machine gun crews were blasting away through open windows at Lou Coutts' boys coming down in their parachutes. The American pitched a grenade into one room, then into another, blowing up both machine-gun crews. Then he dashed out of the farmhouse.

One of those leaping from a flaming C-46 torch was Maj. Bill Moir of Stillwater, Minnesota, the 513th regimental surgeon, a veteran of the 509th Parachute Infantry Battalion's pioneer jump in North Africa in November 1942.

Dr. William Moir recalled events east of the Rhine:

> As soon as I reached the ground, I scrambled into a nearby bomb crater, for the terrain was being swept by machine-gun bursts. A short time later, Capt. "Odo" Odorizzi, the regiment's dental officer, jumped in the hole with me. Neither one of us had a weapon.
>
> We looked up and saw a horrible sight. A paratrooper was coming down near us, his suit was on fire, and he was screaming in agony. Odo and I ran to him. His clothing was still on fire, and we extinguished it. We lugged the badly burned man to a ditch, and began treating him. I was vaguely aware that two figures had jumped into the ditch right behind us. I glanced back—and into the faces of two armed Germans.
>
> We were startled by the sudden confrontation, and so were the Germans. For long seconds, the Krauts and us stared at each other. Finally, I said in passable German, "Our paratroopers are all around you. You had better surrender to us or you'll be killed." Of course, the Germans were not surrounded, but what I had to say apparently made an impression. They pitched away their rifles and helmets and became our prisoners.

Studying his map and the terrain features, Lou Coutts quickly realized that his regiment had been misdropped two to three miles northeast of its drop zone and was partially in the zone of the British 6th Airborne. So he contacted his battalion commanders and instructed them to head south to drop zone X, then to swing east and seize the bridges over the Issel River.

With his tommy gun clutched in one hand, Coutts marched off after picking up a lone trooper who was lugging one of the new 57-millimeter recoilless rifles, a sort of hand-held artillery piece.[5] Soon the colonel spotted German soldiers hastily removing the camouflage from three or four panzers. Coutts and the trooper, acting as a team, fired a rocket that exploded near one of the iron monsters. No doubt believing that they were under fire from a large force, the German tankers scrambled into their tracked vehicle, slammed the turrets shut, and clanked away.

Hard on the heels of the 513th Parachute Infantry's flight in the "Flying Coffins" (as the troopers would call them), Ken Booth's 466th artillerymen leaped from old C-47s—and onto a hornets' nest. Except for nine men who jumped prematurely west of the Rhine, 376 of Booth's cannoneers and 12 disassembled howitzers came down dead-center on their designated Drop Zone X. As soon as his chute popped open, Pfc. Harry Boyle became aware that streams of tracers were zipping past him, so he feigned being killed and hung limply in his harness until crashing in a heap onto the hard, bullet-swept terrain.

Harry Boyle recalled:

I slithered over the ground for about one hundred feet and into a gully. Then I peeked over the edge and began looking for a likely target—there were plenty of Krauts around. I saw what looked like a German helmet sticking up from a ditch, and I drew a bead on it. Just as I was ready to squeeze the trigger, my target shifted, and I saw that the figure was wearing a chartreuse scarf—which each of our 466th artillerymen had been issued for identification. That trooper would never know that his scarf kept him from getting a bullet through the head.

Jumping with Booth's cannoneers were two "visiting firemen" from the States: Brig. Gen. Josiah T. Dalbey, commander of the Airborne Training Center at Camp Mackall, and Ridgely M. Gaither, who headed the Parachute School at Fort Benning. They had made the Rhine mission to get the "feel" of combat operations.

That "feel" would be almost instantaneous. The two generals were raked by heavy machine-gun fire during their descent, then found themselves face-down on the drop zone with swarms of bullets whistling past. However, along with Booth's artillerymen, Gaither and Dalbey began returning the fire. Dalbey then collared a few paratroopers and led an attack that wiped out a German ack-ack battery.

Fifteen minutes behind the last paratroop transport came the seemingly infinite stream of tugs pulling gliders. In the lead were

441 large Horsa and Hamilcar gliders carrying Brigadier R. Hugh Bellamy's 6th Air Landing Brigade with Eric Bols and his division staff aboard. Minutes later, the sky east of the Rhine was saturated with swarms of motorless craft that had cut loose from their tugs. Most of Bellamy's gliders came down in a tight concentration on their landing zone near the town of Hamminkeln, about five miles north of Wesel.

Casualties in the 6th Air Landing Brigade were heavy, and only one in five of its gliders ran the gauntlet of German fire unscathed. Typically, glider pilots were badly mauled: 38 of them were killed and the same number wounded or seriously injured. But the British glider troops would have suffered even larger casualties had it not been for the unforeseen *chance de guerre* whereby Lou Coutts' American paratroopers misdropped onto a section of the British landing zone and had gone to work clearing the landscape of German soldiers.

Next in the line of flight came some 910 American Wacos—many double-towed by C-47 tugs—carrying Jim Pierce's 194th Glider Infantry Regiment, which included Frank L. Barnett's 1st Battalion, William S. Stewart's 2nd Battalion, and the 3rd Battalion, commanded by Robert L. Ashworth. Supporting units were Paul Oswald's 680th Field Artillery Battalion, Joseph W. Keating's 681st Glider Artillery, and John W. Paddock's 155th Antiaircraft Battalion.

Pierce's flight ran into machine-gun tracers crisscrossed the

Men of Raff's 507th Parachute Infantry escort prisoners near Wesel. *(Edward Page)*

sky, and large numbers of black smoke puffs erupted around the flimsy gliders in the wake of ack-ack explosions. Two-thirds of the Wacos were struck by the savage torrent of fire, and 12 C-47 tugs crashed in flames moments after releasing their motorless craft. An additional 147 C-47 tow-planes were hit by bullets but kept flying until their gliders had been cut loose.

On the ground, American paratroopers not actively battling the Germans looked up in horror at the holocaust in the sky. One of those was Pvt. Charles L. Worrilow of Lima, Ohio, a rifleman in Coutts' regiment, who was walking cross-country to his drop zone. Worrilow recalled:

> *A short distance away, I saw three Waco gliders swooping in for a landing. They smashed into some high powerlines, cartwheeled down, all the while flinging out glidermen, looking like rag dolls, in all directions. One man was hurled into the upper branches of a tall tree, where he remained motionless. I guess he was dead.*

All over the landing zone countless dust plumes spiraled into the sky as the Wacos crash-landed and skidded on their bellies for hundreds of yards. Edward J. Siergiej, who had been a mortar-man in the 194th Glider Infantry, recalled the terrifying experience:

> *We pancaked in at about 80 miles per hour and bumped along over the rough terrain at high speed for what seemed to be hours. All the while our flimsy craft was creaking and groaning and threatening to rip apart. We twelve glider soldiers held on for dear life and prayed that a pole or a stone wall or a tree stump would not suddenly loom up in our path.*

Scores of Wacos did smash into sturdy obstacles and crumple like accordions. Screams from the wreckages pierced the terrific din of German gunfire as glider soldiers were slashed to ribbons or pinned in the carnage with hideously broken bones. Many of Pierce's boys had their teeth knocked out. One lieutenant's foot was hacked off. From other glider ruins came only an eerie silence: Everyone aboard had been killed on impact.

Jim Pierce, who taught Sunday school when visiting his home town of Troy, Pennsylvania, and most of his troopers came down in the middle of German artillery batteries, which were firing at Montgomery's ground forces pouring across the Rhine by boat.

Startled at first, the *Feldgrau* gunners lowered their barrels and began firing flat-trajectory shells at the gliders after they landed.

Most of the able-bodied soldiers scrambled from their craft shooting, and scores of clashes broke out. Part of F Company, led by Capt. Robert Dukes, charged a German command post with such swiftness that a colonel and all of his staff were captured. In the enemy colonel's briefcase, Dukes and his boys discovered an intelligence bonanza: maps and overlays of all German defenses in the Wesel region.

Once again in Pierce's flight, the glider pilots had taken a bloody beating. These free spirits who rode in the noses of the fragile craft held that any landing in which they could walk away was a good landing. There were few good landings east of the Rhine. Thirty-two glider pilots hauling the 194th were killed, 106 were wounded or injured.

Elsewhere on the airhead, Company E of the 513th Parachute Infantry was attacking along a railroad track and had reached a point 250 yards from a large farmhouse. The sturdy structure was a German command post and defended by a large force with machine guns, rifles, and four artillery pieces. One parachute platoon headed for the house and had edged forward for only 50 yards when it was pinned down by fusillades of machine-gun fire.

Pfc. Stuart S. Stryker of Portland, Oregon, was in a relatively safe position to the rear of E Company when he saw that the exposed platoon was at the mercy of the enemy machine gunners. Stryker rushed to the head of his company and, standing upright in full view of the Germans, he brandished his carbine and shouted to his comrades: "Let's go get the bastards!"

Inspired by Stryker's exhortation and despite the machine-gun bullets lacing the air around them, troopers scrambled to their feet and followed Stryker in a charge toward the German-held house. Stryker was cut down only 25 yards from the structure. As he lay on the ground bleeding profusely, his comrades rushed past and surrounded the strongpoint. A fierce fight raged at close quarters. Then white flags fluttered from the windows of the house, and E Company took 200 prisoners and freed three American bomber crewmen who were being held in the basement. Stuart Stryker did not live to see the mass German surrender.

By 2:00 P.M.—only four and a half hours after Ed Raff had been the first American to bail out east of the Rhine—the mighty airborne thunderclap had shattered German defenses around

Wesel. All three of Bud Miley's regiments—the 507th and 513th Parachute and the 194th Glider and supporting artillery—had performed in dazzling fashion. The objectives had been seized, some 5,000 Germans were confined in makeshift POW enclosures, and scores of artillery pieces as well as eight or ten tanks had been knocked out or captured.

Eric Bols' Red Devils had also performed with great dash and elan, clearing the northern portion of the airhead, grabbing thousands of prisoners and linking up with advance elements of Montgomery's over-water troops.

As shadows began to lengthen on D-Day, B. J. McQuaid, a correspondent for the *Chicago Daily News*, caught a ride with an ambulance which was moving rapidly through the eerie Diersfordter Wald, the scene of some of the bloodiest fighting by both the 17th and 6th Airborne Divisions. There was good reason for the fast pace: The forest was full of snipers and isolated pockets of die-hard Germans.

In open spaces, the small, neatly fenced fields were filled with the carcasses of cattle, horses, sheep, goats, and the grotesque, twisted corpses of men, most of the latter in Wehrmacht uniforms. Everywhere were the skeletons of shot-up, shot-down, cracked-up, and burned-up gliders and transport planes. The putrid stench of death assaulted nostrils. McQuaid shuddered at this ghastly scene.

It was nearly dark when Matt Ridgway, who had crossed the Rhine in an amphibious vehicle a short time earlier, and Bud Miley climbed into a jeep at 17th Airborne headquarters in Flüren and drove northward to locate Eric Bols' command post. Several troopers were "riding shotgun" in two trailing jeeps. It was just past midnight when the three-jeep convoy took leave of the 6th Airborne commander and set out for the return trip to Miley's command post. The jeeps slowed to creep around the burned-out wreckage of of a vehicle just as Ridgway caught a glimpse of a shadowy figure scurrying about to the front.

"Krauts!" someone in the jeep called out. Ridgway, Miley and the others leaped out and opened fire. A loud howl rang out, and one of the dark figures fell to the ground. Ridgway, firing his trusty old Springfield rifle, was convinced that he had bagged the German. Now a shoot-out erupted under the thin rays of a pale half-moon.

Suddenly, Ridgway felt a sharp pain in his shoulder: A German potato-masher grenade had exploded only a few feet away, but a wheel of the jeep had absorbed much of the blast and shrapnel.

There was suddenly an eerie silence. Ridgway and Miley could hear men breathing in the blackness on all sides. For long minutes none in the party moved or uttered a sound. Then Ridgway called out in a stage whisper to Miley: "You okay, Bud? I think I got one of them."

Slipping back into an undamaged jeep, the two generals and their bodyguards began edging through the woods once more. Miley saw a quick movement on the dark path ahead and fired his pistol. There was no response. So the 17th Airborne commander, clutching his Colt .45, stole out of the jeep and stalked forward until he bumped onto two of his paratroopers manning a machine gun.

Spontaneously, Miley exploded: "Damn it, you've got orders to shoot at anything you can't identify! Why didn't you shoot?" The two paratroopers made no reply. Back in his jeep, Miley reflected sheepishly: If my two machine gunners had literally followed orders, I would now be dead!

Matt Ridgway, for his part, made no mention to the others that he was now carrying a small chunk of German metal in his shoulder as a result of the near-miss grenade explosion.

Varsity was a spectacular success—but the price tag had been costly. Within a few hours, Miley's 17th Airborne had suffered 159 men killed, 522 wounded, and 81 missing. Bols' 6th Airborne had 1,300 men killed, wounded, or missing (although a few hundred of the missing would turn up later). Paul Williams' IX Troop Carrier Command airmen also paid a stiff penalty: 41 killed, 153 wounded and 163 missing.[6]

Seventy-eight Allied planes (including 15 heavy bombers conducting low-level resupply missions) had been shot down, and 475 were damaged, many extensively. Nineteen of the C-46 Flying Coffins had gone down in flames, and another 38 received damage. Only 24 British Horsas and Hamilcars and 148 Wacos would be salvaged for future use. The remainder of the 1,305 motorless craft had been so badly smashed up or riddled by gunfire that they were left on the airhead—mute sentinels to the savagery that had raged there.[7]

54
Alles Kaput!

In his deep bunker under the garden of the Reich Chancellery in pulverized Berlin, Adolf Hitler flew into a rage over news that Bernard Montgomery's 21st Army Group was over the Rhine in strength. The Führer promptly ordered poison gas be unleashed against the Wesel and other Allied bridgeheads east of the Rhine and that thousands of American and British airmen who were POWs in the Third Reich be shot. Cooler heads, pointing out that the Allies could retaliate on a far more massive scale, prevailed.

Basking in the glow of the monumental Plunder-Varsity triumph, Montgomery fired off a message to his boss, Field Marshal Alan Brooke, in London: "My goal is to drive hard for the line of the Elbe [River] . . . thence via the autobahn to Berlin."

However, General Eisenhower sidetracked Monty's "Berlin Express" before it could pull out of the station. Berlin would be left to the Russians. Instead, the 21st Army Group would drive northeast and capture Hamburg, Bremen, Lubeck, and other Baltic ports to keep Joe Stalin's surging armies out of Denmark and Norway. At the same time, Hodges' First Army and Patton's Third would break out of the Remagen and Oppenheim bridgeheads and race deep into the Third Reich, while Sandy Patch's Seventh Army and Gen. de Lattre de Tassigny's First French Army farther to the south would push southeast toward Munich and the Bavarian Alps.

This would be an all-out offensive to bring Nazi Germany to its knees—and American paratroopers would be in on the kill. On March 27—Varsity D-Day plus 3—parachutists of Lou Coutts' 513th Regiment, perched on tanks of Brigadier C. I. H.

Dunbar's British 6th Guards Armoured Brigade, bolted out of the Wesel bridgehead to lead Bernard Montgomery's powerful thrust. Eric Bols' Red Devils, also piggy-back on Dunbar's tanks, jumped off on Coutts' left.

Hitler's once-vaunted Wehrmacht had begun to disintegrate, now that the Rhine, the ancient barrier to invasion from the west, had been breached at several places. Largely disconnected fragments of the German army thrashed about in isolated sectors, led by the highest-ranking officer or noncom on the scene.

Lou Coutts recalled his regiment's curious cross-country dash:

I rode on the tank of the 6th Guards Armoured Brigade's commander, Brigadier Dunbar, holding tight to my tommy gun. Sometimes it was like a jaunt through a peaceful park, then all hell would break loose. When we were halted by heavy fire, my paratroopers would jump off the tanks and dig out the enemy from foxholes and buildings in towns. Sometimes I got in on the action with my tommy gun. Then we'd all scramble back onto the tanks and, with a mighty roar, off we'd go again.

On Easter Sunday (April 1) the 513th Parachute Infantry column rolled up to the outskirts of Münster, a large city 50 miles east of the Rhine. When the local German commander refused Bud Miley's surrender demand, the paratroopers and tankers barreled into Münster, where heavy fighting erupted.

Coutts and a group of troopers were advancing along a street when a rain of mortar shells exploded around them. The parachutists wisely flopped down—the colonel remained standing, and white-hot shrapnel ripped into him.[1] Seriously wounded, Lou Coutts' war was over. Twenty-four hours later, Münster was captured.

Meanwhile, other Allied spearheads were racing at spectacular speeds, and by April 3, elements of the U.S. First, Ninth, and Fifteenth Armies had forged a ring of steel around the Ruhr, the heart of Hitler's industrial might. Trapped in the Ruhr, about half the size of New Jersey, were Field Marshal Walther Model, whose tactical genius had thwarted Bernard Montgomery at Arnhem in Holland, and remnants of 14 German divisions.

At the same time, Jim Gavin's 82nd Airborne and Max Taylor's 101st Airborne were rushed forward from north-central

France to hold the west bank of the Rhine in the Cologne-Dusseldorf region—in effect forming the west edge of the Ruhr Sack. To keep the enemy guessing and off balance, paratrooper patrols periodically paddled across the once "impregnable" Rhine to tangle with what the 504th's Rube Tucker always called "the goddamned Krauts."

On April 4, American forces began putting the squeeze on the Ruhr Sack from three sides. In the north, Bud Miley's 17th Airborne was in the thick of the action. Ed Raff's paratroopers of the 507th barged into Essen, home of the huge Krupp steelworks that had poured out big guns and shells for the Fatherland in two world wars, where they nabbed their first Nazi bigwig—Alfred Krupp von Bohlen und Halbach, boss of the arms empire. Much to Krupp's indignation, he was hustled out of his luxurious mansion by Raff's gleeful troopers and locked up in his gardener's tiny, decrepit cottage.

Not to be outdone, Jim Pierce's glidermen quickly bagged their own Nazi luminary. In his palatial home on a secluded estate outside Hirschberg, east of Essen, Franz von Papen had just sat down to supper when Pierce's boys burst inside and seized Hitler's longtime diplomat and confidant, the wiliest of all Nazis. "I wish the war was over," von Papen moaned to his captors. Snapped Sgt. Hugh G. Fredrick: "So do 11 million of our guys!"[2]

When the Ruhr Sack was flattened on April 18, some 325,000 dispirited and haggard *Feldgrau,* along with 29 generals, straggled into captivity. Their commander was not one of them. Walther Model, who felt that he had failed his Führer, had entered a woods near his headquarters, pulled out his Luger, and put a bullet through his head. Aides buried him in a secret grave near Wuppertal.[3]

All the while, Allied armies continued to plunge deeper into the Third Reich. At 7:56 P.M. on April 11, Bill Simpson's Ninth Army reached the Elbe, 100 miles west of Berlin, where it had been ordered to halt and await the arrival of the Russians. Nine days later, Hodges' First Army on Simpson's right pressed up to the Elbe.[4]

Eight days later, on April 28, Jim Gavin received orders to rush his 82nd Airborne from the Rhine at Cologne to the vicinity of Bleckede, 200 miles to the northeast on the west bank of the Elbe south of Hamburg. The All-Americans would be attached to Miles Dempsey's British Second Army.

Gavin preceded his division and set up a command post near

Bleckede. On the night of the April 29, Dempsey, an old friend from the Holland days, called on the 82nd Airborne commander.

James Gavin remembered the tense discussion:

> *General Dempsey said that he and Montgomery were most anxious for my division to establish a bridgehead across the Elbe as soon as possible. Dempsey wanted the 82nd to get over the river to cut off the advancing Russians and keep them out of Denmark and Norway. The British had already crossed the Elbe about twenty miles to our left, Dempsey said, but if we used that bridgehead, it would delay us for four or five days.*

Since Bill Ekman's 505th Parachute Infantry arrived at Bleckede first, it was chosen by Gavin to make the crossing. Ekman's boys were far from enthused—none sought the "honor" of being the last American paratrooper to be killed in the European war.

Shortly after midnight on April 30, Ekman's paratroopers, with Jim Gavin in the first wave, slipped across the Elbe in boats and amphibious vehicles. Taken by surprise, the Germans were rousted out of foxholes along the bank by bayonets; and at dawn, the veteran 505th held a firm bridgehead but was being pounded heavily by German artillery batteries bent on expending their ammunition.

At the same time the 82nd Airborne had kicked off its road and rail dash to Bleckede, Roy Lindquist's 508th Parachute Infantry had been detached from the division, and Robert J. Ballard's 501st Parachute Infantry had been detached from the 101st Airborne. Both regiments were on standby at airfields in north-central France for a mission code-named "Operation Jubilant."

Lindquist's and Ballard's paratroopers were to jump in teams onto some 23 POW camps after the German will to fight had become so weak that only token resistance would be met. When the "Go" signal would be flashed, squad-size units were to drop inside or adjacent to the camps with high-powered radios. Then the main body of parachutists would jump directly into the POW enclosures.

Hard on the heels of the Jubilant paratroopers would come 10 to 12 gliders per battalion, bringing in medicines, food, and other supplies, along with a contingent of linguists and interrogators. Jubilant was destined for a lingering death, however.

The POW camps would be overrun by advancing Allied armies.

At the same time, troopers of Eldridge Chapman's 13th Airborne Division were at airfields in the Paris region, waiting eagerly for word to launch "Operation Effective," a jump into the Bavarian Alps.

Finally, Chapman's boys would have a chance to show the world what they could do. Based on SHAEF intelligence reports, Eisenhower and Omar Bradley were convinced that the Führer and his cronies would abandon Berlin in the next two weeks and flee to a so-called National Redoubt in the Bavarian Alps. There 250,000 die-hard Nazi troops, steeled by SS outfits, would barricade themselves on the towering peaks and prolong the war indefinitely.

Morale was never higher among Chapman's men, especially after they were given lists of Hitler's bigwigs thought to be holed up in the National Redoubt and whom the parachutists were to capture. Actually, the National Redoubt was an intricate fabrication concocted by Joseph Goebbels, the Nazi propaganda genius. For months, Goebbels' National Redoubt myth had bamboozled SHAEF intelligence and may have influenced Eisenhower's crucial decision to send his armies toward the Bavarian Alps instead of on to Berlin.

Just as Harvey Jablonsky's 515th and Rupert Graves' 517th Parachute Infantry troopers were boarding C-47s for the jump into the Bavarian Alps, Operation Effective was canceled. Patch's Seventh and de Lattre's French First armies were already converging on the National Redoubt. For the fourth time, the 13th Airborne's hopes were dashed.

Jack W. Bauer, who had been a rigger in Chapman's division, recalled:

> *Many of us in the 13th Airborne felt cheated to have volunteered for an elite fighting force only to have a European vacation at the expense of the United States government. We had exceptionally fine leadership in the 13th Airborne, and could have given a good account of ourselves in any mission. We could have measured up with any of our other airborne outfits.*
>
> *I was really disappointed. My older brother, Joe, had always beaten me in everything from childhood on up, and he had been a combat paratrooper with the 509th Parachute Infantry Battalion, so he was one up on me again.*

Staff of 515th Parachute Infantry, 13th Airborne Division. Left to right: Riggs Miller, Mason Wood, Col. Harvey J. Jablonsky (commander), George Barker, George Black, Jack Tallent. *(Author's collection)*

Meanwhile, on the night of April 30, while Jim Gavin and his boys were crossing the Elbe, Russian troops were but two blocks from Adolf Hitler's bunker in Berlin. Minutes after being married to his longtime companion, Eva Braun, the Führer put a Luger's muzzle to his head and pulled the trigger. Two days later, the Soviet army had conquered all of Berlin.

At Bleckede, Jim Gavin rapidly shuttled his remaining 82nd Airborne units over the Elbe, and the 740th Tank Battalion, an old friend of the All-Americans, clanked across the river on a pontoon bridge built by engineers under a murderous shelling. At 5:30 A.M. on May 1, the 740th, with 10 paratroopers atop each Sherman, rolled forward. One tank commander, who had joined the armored battalion only six weeks earlier, radioed back to his squadron leader:

"Believe it or not, Captain, four paratroopers on bicycles just passed my tank and are now spearheading the attack!"

A few minutes later, he radioed again, "Good God, here comes a horse and buggy loaded with about eight paratroopers—and they're passing me, too!"

Then a third call: "Captain, this is the goddamnedest thing I ever saw. Over there on the left, there's about 20 paratroopers galloping around on horses and rounding up Krauts!"[5]

Radio Berlin had announced the Führer's "heroic" death, and now the Germans in front of Gavin's All-Americans were eager to surrender—before they fell into the clutches of the Russians. At precisely 8:00 P.M. on May 2, Lt. Gen. Kurt von Tippelskirch, commander of the German 21st Army Group, arrived at the 82nd Airborne command post, which was in a magnificent palace in the charming Mecklenberg town of Ludwigslust.

In a stiffly formal ceremony, Tippelskirch, still wearing his ankle-length greatcoat, surrendered to Jim Gavin and his 82nd Airborne the entire German army group, numbering some 145,000 men, along with all of their accoutrements of war. It may have been the first time in history that such a large force had surrendered to a single American division.

Going into captivity with Kurt von Tippelskirch and his staff were nine other generals. For 36 hours, German soldiers by the thousands poured into the 82nd Airborne lines, where they were disarmed and shunted along farther to the rear. Roads were jammed; one could ride for miles and not see the end of the columns of humanity. The Germans were not moving as a disciplined military body, but as refugees fleeing the scene of a disaster. With the advancing Russians on their heels, the *Feldgrau* needed no prodding.

On the following morning, Rube Tucker, leader of the 504th Parachute Infantry, and one of his staff officers, Lt. Chester A. Garrison, climbed into a command car and headed eastward. Tucker, a fiery combat leader, apparently wanted to end his war in Europe in a blaze of glory by being the first 82nd Airborne man to link up with the Russians.[6]

Chester Garrison recalled that episode:

We drove along a road cluttered with hordes of Germans moving west on foot or in decrepit vehicles. Soon, our car could no longer penetrate the flow, so Tucker and I continued on foot. We were a curiosity to the Germans we passed, the first Americans they had seen close up. Seeing us, they threw their firearms into roadside ditches. Groups of sullen SS troops stared at us smolderingly. Some of the SS officers, in a final symbol of defiance, fired their revolvers in the air before dumping them. Wary that some embittered German could

easily shoot Tucker and I without detection, I pulled and cocked my
revolver, knowing how futile that was, and strode along with my
eager leader.

We were the American point with thousands of unpredictable
Germans between us and our 82nd Airborne comrades. We marched
for about two miles. When the Russians failed to materialize and
darkness was approaching, even Colonel Tucker's ardor finally
faltered, and we reversed our long walk through hordes of
presumably "captured" Germans, many of whom were still armed.
When we were back among our own, I issued a deep sigh of relief.

A few days earlier, at the same time the 82nd Airborne departed for Bleckede, Max Taylor's 101st Airborne was pulled out
of its Rhine sector opposite Dusseldorf and rushed some 250
miles southeast to Patch's Seventh Army to assist in mopping up
the remaining armed Germans in the Bavarian Alps. SHAEF was
apparently still clinging to the National Redoubt theory.

On the night of May 3, Bob Sink's 506th Parachute Infantry
troopers were electrified. Orders came directing the regiment to
capture Berchtesgaden, the charming Alpine village indelibly
linked with Adolf Hitler and Nazism. On a towering peak overlooking Berchtesgaden was the *Adlerhorst* (Eagle's Nest), the
Führer's secluded retreat.

Berchtesgaden was thought to be loaded with fleeing Nazi
bigshots and with *souvenirs de guerre*. More significantly, the village was thought to be lightly defended.

At 6:00 A.M. the next day, truck convoys crammed with Five-
O-Sinks high-tailed it out of the Miesbach area for the 65-mile
dash southward to Berchtesgaden. At Siegdorf, some 19 miles
north of Berchtesgaden, Sink's convoy struck a snag—numerous
blown bridges and narrow roads clogged with Gen. Jacques
LeClerc's French 2nd Armored Division and Maj. Gen. John W.
"Iron Mike" O'Daniel's 3rd Infantry Division.

At XXI Corps headquarters, a harried staff officer radioed
Seventh Army: "Everybody and his brother trying to get into
Berchtesgaden."

O'Daniel's division won the race, with LeClerc's tankers right
on its heels. Then came the Bob Sink's paratroopers.

All the while, Germans had been surrendering—by companies, battalions, and even divisions—and masses of *Feldgrau*
were streaming back past the advancing Americans. But when
only a short distance from Berchtesgaden, two Screaming Eagles

lost their lives—Pvt. Nick Kozovosky and Pfc. Claude E. Rankin may have been the last American paratroopers killed in action during the war in Europe.

Max Taylor's division was ready to continue its attack southward on May 6 when a dramatic message came through: "Effective immediately all troops will stand fast . . . German Army Group B in this sector has surrendered. No firing on Germans unless fired on."

Now rumors were rampant that numerous Nazi bigshots—including Adolf Hitler—were holed up in and around Berchtesgaden. Amateur detectives wearing the Screaming Eagle shoulder patches sprang up like daisies after a spring shower.

Indeed, the ghost of the Führer did invade Berchtesgaden. Excited troopers of Steve Chappuis' 502nd Parachute Infantry were convinced that they had discovered Hitler's decomposed body in a forest near Hutte. A battalion surgeon rushed to the site, took a look at the corpse and told the dejected troopers that it was a woman.

At about the same time, Bob Sink of the 506th Parachute Infantry received a message that another Nazi bigwig, Field Marshal Albrecht Kesselring, was in the region. Smiling Al Kesselring, who had succeeded Gerd von Rundsted as *Oberfehlshaber West* (commander in chief, west) after the Remagen bridge debacle, was now comfortably ensconced in the *Brunswick,* his private nine-car train parked nearby.

Other American outfits around Berchtesgaden received similar reports, and all concerned dashed madly to the *Brunswick.* A comic-opera scenario unfolded. Within minutes, Kesselring's train was ringed by the field marshal's own German armed guard, by Bob Sink's troopers, and by soldiers from a U.S. cavalry group and an infantry division. Except for the German bodyguards, all of them were trying to coerce Smiling Al out of his private car without creating a ruckus.

While the mixed bag of armed combatants from both sides milled about in indecision, rumors surfaced that a die-hard gang of SS troops in the region was planning to launch a raid to "kidnap" Kesselring to keep him out of the clutches of the Americans.

For two days, negotiations for his surrender continued in the field marshal's coach. In between sessions, American newspaper reporters barged inside to interview the famed German. Presuming that the civilian correspondents, who were clad in American uniforms, were high-ranking officers of some kind, German MPs at Kesselring's coach door snapped to attention each time the newsmen entered or departed.

Finally, Albrecht Kesselring agreed to surrender—to Maxwell Taylor.

Now the Screaming Eagles' net hauled in another large Nazi fish. Acting on a tip from a German priest, Capt. Neil J. Sweeney, a company commander in the 502nd, and a few troopers rushed to a shoemaker's house in Schleching, where they dragged a sleeping figure from his bed on the third floor. The German protested violently. But a short time later, a local *Burgermeister* identified him as Dr. Robert Ley, a longtime Hitler crony and leader of the so-called Nazi Labor Front.[7]

A week after Ley was collared, Maj. Henry Plitt of the 502nd Parachute Infantry received an anonymous telephone tip. Plitt and a few of his men hurried to a farmhouse outside Waldring, where they found a bearded man who gave his name as Sailor. He was leisurely creating a painting on canvas.

"You're Julius Streicher, you bastard!" Plitt exploded.

Streicher had long been a close chum of the Führer and a notorious anti-Semite.

"No, no," the German protested. "I am a painter. I have never had any interest in politics."

Finally, the man admitted to being Julius Streicher. His capture was of special satisfaction to Henry Plitt, a highly decorated Jewish officer.[8]

Others rounded up by the Screaming Eagle "detectives" were the Führer's sister, Paula Hitler Wolf, who was living in Berchtesgaden; Eric Kempke, Hitler's chauffeur, who had been in the Reich Chancellery bunker and had viewed the Führer's body being burned by SS troops; and Karl Albrecht Oberg, a high-ranking SS officer who had been in charge of police activities in occupied France and was known as "The Butcher of Paris."[9]

While the Nazi hunt was in full swing in Bavaria, a monumental event was taking place in the red brick school building that served as SHAEF advance headquarters in Rheims, northeast of Paris. At 2:41 A.M. on May 7, 1945, Gen. Alfred Jodl, Adolf Hitler's closest military adviser throughout the war, signed Nazi Germany's unconditional surrender to the Allied powers.

After 68 months of relentless bloodshed and destruction, a shaky peace hovered over Europe.

55
The Last
Hurrah

Adolf Hitler's Nazi Germany and Benito Mussolini's Fascist Italy had been crushed, and now the awesome armed might of the United States was being mustered to knock out Japan, the lone survivor of what Allied media called "the Axis Gang." Some 30 veteran American divisions, along with air corps and naval units, were being rushed from Europe to bolster Supreme Commander Douglas MacArthur's forces for "Operation Downfall," a gargantuan invasion of the Japanese homeland.

One crack unit hoping to join in the assault on Japan was the green but eager 541st Parachute Infantry Regiment, led by Col. Ducat McEntee, who had formed the outfit in August 1943, at Fort Benning. Its ranks had been diluted numerous times when 541st men were sent to Europe as parachute replacements. But finally, McEntee and his boys would see action as a unit.

In mid-1945 the 541st arrived by ship in the Philippines. But before the troopers could even debark, Colonel McEntee received devastating news: the keenly disciplined 541st Parachute Infantry would be deactivated and its officers and men assigned to the 11th Airborne Division, which had suffered nearly 2,000 casualties since landing on Luzon. Yet another proud parachute outfit had vanished with the twist of a mimeograph-machine handle.

Months earlier, on July 1, 1945, a sister regiment of the 541st, the 542nd Parachute Infantry, suffered the same fate, having been deactivated at Camp Mackall. Activated at Fort Benning on September 1, 1943, with Col. Bill Ryder, "America's First Paratrooper," as its commander, the unit was constantly drained to provide replacements for paratroop units in combat overseas. In the spring of 1944, Ryder was sent to the Pacific, where he became an airborne adviser to Gen. Douglas MacArthur.

Now Bill Ryder was coordinating the airborne phase of Downfall. It was planned to use three airborne divisions in the invasion of Japan. One, Joe Swing's 11th, was already on the scene, still battling die-hard Japanese troops in the rugged mountains of Luzon. Eldridge Chapman's 13th and Maxwell Taylor's veteran 101st in Europe had been alerted for redeployment to the Pacific, once high-point men were weeded out and, as the troopers phrased it, "busted to civilians." (The Pentagon had devised a point system to decide which soldiers would return home: so many points for length of combat duty, decorations, time in service, and dependents.)

MacArthur planned a two-step assault: Kyushu on November 1, 1945 ("Operation Olympic"), and the main island of Honshu

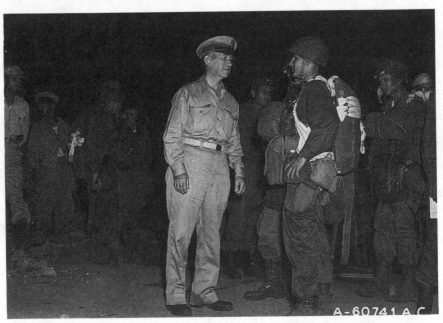

Gen. Walter Krueger chats with Lt. Stanley Orchel of the 11th Airborne Division prior to takeoff for Aparri, northern Luzon, in the Philippines, to cut off escape by sea of a large Japanese force, in June 1945. Known as "Gypsy Task Force," the assault unit, led by Lt. Col. Henry Burgess, consisted of paratroopers and glidermen. Unopposed, the landing at Aparri was the final major airborne operation of World War II. (*Richard L. Hoyt*)

on March 1, 1946 ("Operation Coronet"). Downfall would be the mightiest amphibious operation ever envisaged: 776,723 men in the initial assault, 2 million more to follow. America—and the world—stood on the brink of the most horrendous massacre of the human race since the days of the Mongol warlord Ghengis Kahn.

MacArthur notified Washington that American forces would suffer in excess of 1 million casualties, and twice as many Nipponese soldiers and millions more civilians would perish.[1] Fanatical Japanese generals and admirals were grimly preparing "Ketsu-Go" ("Operation Decision"), the last-ditch defense of every foot of the home islands that all Japanese held sacred, having fallen as drops from the sword of an ancient god.

In addition to some 2,350,000 soldiers, all deeply imbued with the warriors' *Shintoist* code that held it a sacred duty and an honor to die in battle for the emperor, there would be 32 million Japanese civilian militia (including women and children) ready and willing to fight to the death. Their weapons would include muzzle-loading rifles, ancient cannon, butcher knives, bows and arrows, ice picks, and bamboo spears. Children had been trained to strap explosives around their waists, roll under American tank treads and blow themselves up.

This was the vision of the Japanese enemy that the Pentagon—and the American fighting man in the Pacific—had learned to hate and fear. The image was of a nation of fanatics, to the Western mind, who were dedicated to hara-kiri, and pledged to slaughter at the cost of their own lives as many invaders as possible.

Meanwhile, halfway around the globe, Berlin was still in chaos when the 82nd Airborne arrived in July 1945 to take over the task of policing and patrolling the American sector of the German capital. Jim Gavin's boys retained their readiness for combat, but became "America's Honor Guard" in Berlin. White bootlaces and scarves were fashioned from parachute shrouds and silk. White gloves and chromium bayonets made the All-Americans even more spiffy.

Berlin was a magnet for VIPs. Swarms of them—congressmen, senators, ministers from European countries—descended upon the city, most of them bent on getting their pictures taken to show the folks back home that they were in the forefront of the prolonged struggle against Nazi tyranny.

*   *   *

On August 6, a lone B-29 Superfortress, piloted by Col. Paul Tibbetts, dropped what was later described to an awed world as an atom bomb on the industrial city of Hiroshima. When the Japanese high command ignored a surrender demand, a second nuclear explosion demolished Nagasaki. At noon on August 15, diminutive, myopic Emperor Hirohito, defying his generals and admirals, took to Radio Tokyo to announce the empire was capitulating.

Just past six o'clock on the morning of August 30, Col. John Lackey was at the controls of a big C-54 transport plane as it landed at Atsugi airfield just west of Tokyo. Lackey and his C-47 pilots had carried the 11th Airborne on all of its combat missions. Seated behind Lackey in the C-54 was Joe Swing, whose division had been selected by Douglas MacArthur for occupation duty in Japan.

White-haired Swing walked first down the ramp and was greeted with outstretched hand by a bowing three-star Japanese general. Scowling, Swing refused the man's gesture and instead barked at the other to remove his samurai sword, a Japanese symbol of authority.

In the wake of Swing's C-54 was a stream of troop carriers and commercial transports stretching all the way back to Okinawa, some 300 miles to the south: The largest single airlift in history was bringing the entire 11th Airborne Division to Atsugi. In one of the first aircraft was 20-year-old paratroop Cpl. George Doherty of Riverside, California.

Doherty recalled that episode:

> I hadn't been on the ground very long at Atsugi when word rapidly spread that the Bataan—General MacArthur's C-54—was arriving. All of us paratroopers were excited, to say the least. When the Bataan landed, nearly all of the American brass in the Pacific advanced to the aircraft ramp, and after what seemed an interminable time, the door of the Bataan opened and there stood the great general, corncob pipe in mouth. Wow! I thought—this is the hour the minute, of one of history's most momentous occasions.
>
> I also thought that if Japan was ever going to pull a second Pearl Harbor, this was the time and place to do it. There were untold thousands of fanatical Japanese still under arms in the Atsugi region, and only a few hundred of us paratroopers. Had they

The Philadelphia Inquirer
PUBLIC ✦ LEDGER
An Independent Newspaper for All the People
FINAL
CITY EDITION

Atomic Bomb, World's Most Deadly, Blasts Japan; New Era in Warfare Is Opened by U. S. Secret Weapon

Bong Killed
Testing New

Terrific Missile
Unleashes B──
Force

been so inclined, the Japs could have wiped out General MacArthur, all the Pacific brass, and us paratroopers in one blow.

On the other side of the world in early November, Jim Gavin of the 82nd Airborne Division and a few of his officers were flying back to Berlin after a trip to London. Rain, fog, and thick clouds gripped the Continent and Gavin's C-47 had to set down in Schweinfurt. The young general promptly telephoned his chief of staff, Col. Robert H. Wienecke, in Berlin to advise him of his whereabouts.

Wienecke dropped a bombshell: The 101st had been selected by the War Department to be the Regular Army's only postwar airborne division, to be stationed at Fort Bragg. Because of peacetime budget limitations, the 82nd Airborne would be deactivated, its guidon, heavy with battle streamers, put in mothballs. Gavin was devastated by the shocking news.

At the 101st Airborne command post at Auxerre, south of Paris, Brig. Gen. Stuart Cutler, commander of the Screaming Eagles, and his staff popped champagne corks on getting the good word. (Max Taylor had returned to the States to be superintendent of the United States Military Academy at West Point.)[2] Cutler's troopers also rejoiced. They were to sail from France on December 5, 1945, and debark to a wild celebration in New York City.

Back in Berlin, the 82nd Airborne was numb. Then Lt. Col. Barney Oldfield, who had been a newspaperman, radio commentator, and a press agent at Warner Brothers Studio in Hollywood, went to work behind the scenes to "save" the All-American Division. Oldfield, after qualifying as a paratrooper in mid-1942, had been the third man to report to then-Lt. Col. Gavin when the 505th Parachute Infantry was activated at Fort Benning.

Oldfield's "covert action" was directed from a command post in the Berlin Press Club, which he had established a few months earlier in the former home of Hitler's Reichsminister for Economics, Dr. Walther Funk. Oldfield rounded up 12 German stenographers with a reasonable understanding of English, and he and others began writing a "home-town story" on each officer and trooper in the 82nd Airborne. All the while, a passel of photographers labored around the clock on regional photos, Jim Gavin each time pointing on a large wall map to a particular state to where an All-American would go home.

Barney Oldfield recalled:

> There were a lot of correspondents hanging around the bars in the Berlin and Paris Press Clubs with nothing to write about, so we encouraged any and everybody to send home to their newspapers "why" stories—specifically, why not the 82nd as the surviving United States airborne division? If one of the correspondent's head was throbbing from the previous night's excesses, we had someone write his "why not the 82nd Airborne?" story for him. As one of them, leaning against the bar, told me, "Hell, I'll put my byline on any good writing!"

Under Barney Oldfield's watchful eye, a GI truck carrying 36 bulging mailbags slipped off from the Berlin Press Club in the dead of night, bound for the Army Post Office. The bags contained envelopes with photos and hometown-boy stories going to every newspaper in America with 10,000 or more circulation and to all radio stations.

In Washington, the Pentagon was inundated with clippings from the subtly generated "why" stories, and the homefolks bombarded members of Congress with newspaper clippings about their 82nd Airborne sons, brothers, husbands or nephews. Clearly, this was a spontaneous grassroots plea to save the 82nd Airborne.

Then the War Department did an about-face: Because of its much longer record in combat, it announced, the 82nd Airborne would remain on postwar active duty, and the 101st Airborne

Gen. James Gavin (left) of the 82nd Airborne and Lt. Col. Barney Oldfield, Berlin, fall 1945. *(Author's collection)*

would be deactivated. Again champagne corks popped—this time at Jim Gavin's headquarters in Berlin.

At the tented Camp Lucky Strike outside the port of Le Havre, France, the 82nd Airborne was awaiting orders to sail for home. It was December 1945. Electrifying news came over the teleprinter at the division command post. The 82nd Airborne had been elected for a victory march in New York City, representing all the men and women who served in the armed forces during the war.

Shortly after noon on January 12, 1946, Jim Gavin was at the Washington Arch in New York. Stretched out for blocks behind him were his All-Americans, wearing jump helmets, boots and dress uniforms. Precisely at 1:00 P.M., Gavin called out "Forward!" and stepped off to lead his legion as they swung up Fifth Avenue past frenzied throngs that rocked the concrete jungle with thunderous cheers and applause.

Marching along with the 82nd Airborne troopers, visible only to those with the knowing eye, were thousands of gray ghosts from all of the United States parachute outfits. Proud, standing tall with cheerful, boyish faces beaming, these noble apparitions had made the supreme sacrifice on far-flung battlefields of the world in defense of principles that most Americans hold sacred. Now they were in lock-step with their jump-booted comrades.

The New York victory parade was the last hurrah for World War II paratroopers. Most had already returned to civilian life; others would soon follow. However, only their physical beings would be absent. Left behind for future generations of daring young Americans accepting the challenge to "stand up and hook up" was a legacy of exceptional courage, unswerving devotion to duty, and a fierce will to win.

Principal
Participant
Interviews
and
Contacts

Teddy M. Abrams, Col. John F. R. Akehurst (Ret.), Dr. Robert Akers, Col. Carlos C. Alden (Ret.), Col. Mark J. Alexander (Ret.), John A. Alicki, Andrew J. Amatay, Orville A. Amarose, Joseph J. Anslow, Col. Joseph C. Antrim (Ret.), Clark Archer, Fielding J. Armstrong, Col. Robert M. Atkins (Ret.), Harry Bailey, Clyde Baker, Fred J. Baldino, Robert M. Baldwin, Harold E. Barkley, John E. Bartlett, Jack Bauer, Joseph E. Bauer, Eugene G. Bennett.

William H. Berndt, Col. John T. Berry (Ret.), Lt. Col. Bradley Biggs (Ret.), Lt. Col. Archie G. Birkner (Ret.), John Bishop, Edward J. Bisso, Lloyd Bjelland, Maj. Gen. William E. Blake (Ret.), Rocco Botti, Frank Boyd, Dr. Frederic D. Boyle, Frank Boyle, Harry Boyle, Col. William J. Boyle (Ret.), Brig. Gen. Edward S. Branigan, Jr. (Ret.), Eugene B. Brewer, Leonard Broderick, Paul Brown, George Brownstein, Richard L. Bryan, William J. Bryan, Col. Henry A. Burgess (Ret.), David Burlison, Ralph Burrell, Ray J. Butler.

Ray C. Cagle, Maj. Samuel Calhoun (Ret.), Jesse C. Campbell, Buffalo Boy Canoe, John Canziani, Roger G. Carquerville, Virgil

F. Carmichael, Levi Carter, Pat Casanova, Victor Castillo, Dr. Judson I. Chalkley, Billy J. Chandler, Joe M. Cicchinelli, Gen. Mark W. Clark (Ret.), Ralph K. Clink, James W. Collins, John C. Cooley, Frank P. Costa, Kenneth E. Cordry, Brig. Gen. James W. "Lou" Coutts (Ret.), William Cowan, Col. Thomas R. Cross (Ret.), Cleo Crouch.

Lt. Col. Jack M. Darden (Ret.), Sam DeCrenzo, Nicholas De-Gaeta, Dan DeLeo, Thomas J. Dellaca, Max Demuth, Col. Douglas Dillard (Ret.), Lt. Col. Eugene A. Doerfler (Ret.), George Doherty, Virgil Dorr, Charles H. Doyle, John K. Doyle, Haynes Dunlap, Donald B. Ellis, Charles S. Fairlamb, Cliff Faulkner, Charles Feuereisen, Ted Fina, Richard D. Fisco., Lt. Gen. Edward Flanagan (Ret.), Edward T. Flash, Willard R. "Bill" Follmer, George Fontanesi, Alex France.

John N. Frazier, Maj. Gen. John D. Frost (Ret.), Adolph Fuessel, Leonard A. Funk, Martin Galuskin, Jesse B. Gandee, Donald Garrigues, Col. Robert W. Garrett (Ret.), Chester A. Garrison, Lt. Gen. James M. Gavin (Ret.), Stanley Gerk, Col. Henry W. Gibson (Ret.), John M. Gibson, Sr., Walter Gonko, Allan R. Goodman, Benny Goodman, Thomas W. Graham, Ed Gramza, George D. Graves, Jr., Col. Rupert D. Graves (Ret.), Col. James A. Gray (Ret.), Ken Gridley.

Frank Guild, Jr., Bennett M. Guthrie, Bart Hagerman, Gordon R. Hahn, Dr. Robert Halloran, Phil Hand, Maj. Gen. Joseph W. Harper (Ret.), Col. Edward Hartman (Ret.), Louis A. Hauptfleisch, James A. Haynie, Jim Heffernan, R. E. Hendrickson, William Herb, Joe Hernandez, Pat Herr, Col. Ray "Pappy" Herrman (Ret.), Eugene Herrman, John "Milt" Hill, O. B. Hill, Joseph Hoban, Park A. Hodak, Hugh G. Hogan, Tom Holland, Roy Hollingsworth.

Col. William Holm (Ret.), Dr. Logan Hovis, Richard L. Hoyt, Milo C. Huempfner, Clarence Hughart, Park A. Hughart, Col. Alfred W. Ireland (Ret.), Maj. Gen. Harvey J. Jablonsky (Ret.), James W. Jacobus, Lt. Col. G. Wilfred Jaubert (Ret.), Brig. Gen. George M. Jones (Ret.), Col. John T. Joseph (Ret.), Frank P. Juliano, George H. Kane, Martin Kangas, Stanley Kargol, Col. Morton N. Katz (Ret.), John Kessler, William E. King, Jr., William "Red" King.

Lt. Gen. Harry W. O. Kinnard (Ret.), James Klingman, Milton V. Knight, George Koskimaki, Joseph Kosowski, Lt. Col. Walter B. Kroener (Ret.), Rev. Delbert A. Kuehl, Col. Charles LaChaussee (Ret.), Col. Edward H. Lahti (Ret.), Karl H. Landes,

Donald Lassen, Dr. Daniel McIlvoy, Maurice W. Leland, Hoyt Livingston, Dr. Ralph E. Llewellyn, William W. Lumsden, Donald Lundy, Leon Maenhout, John F. Magill, Jr., Roman W. Maire, Walter Marcum, Gordon Marjala.

Will Marks, Lt. Col. John R. Martin (Ret.), Richard Mascuch, Duffield W. Matson, Jr., Royal W. Maynard, Justin T. McCarthy, James H. McNamara, Maj. Gen. William M. Miley (Ret.), Leon Mims, Col. Harris T. Mitchell (Ret.), Dr. William W. Moir, Dan Morgan, Truesdell "Pat" Moser, James M. Moses, Col. Kenneth Murphy (Ret.), Gordon L. Nagel, Maj. Rocco Narcise (Ret.), Col. Francis E. Naughton (Ret.), Carl Noble, Maj. G. G. Norton (Ret.), Bernard M. O'Boyle, Maj. Keith O'Kelley (Ret.).

Col. Barney Oldfield (Ret.), Maj. John J. O'Malley (Ret.), Donald M. Orcutt, Frank O'Rourke, Edward Page, William Pahl, William L. Pandak, Edward W. Pawloski, Maj. Gen. George Pearson (Ret.), Alexander Peters, Charles A. Place, Jack Pogue, Max Polick, Edmund C. Pollack, Nolan L. Powell, Monsignor John J. Powers, Dr. Charles E. Pugh, Joe Quade, Thomas J. Quatro, Tims A. Quinn, Col. Edson D. Raff (Ret.), Col. Hewlett E. "Reb" Rainer (Ret.), Charles B. Rawls, Jr.

Lt. Col. Ercel R. "Pip" Reed (Ret.), James Reith, Harry Renick, Samuel M. Richards, Col. John B. Ringler (Ret.), Hugh Roberts, Arnie Robinson, Leo Rodrigues, Roland W. Rondeau, Maj. Gen. Ward Ryan (Ret.), Brig. Gen. William T. Ryder (Ret.), Carl Salisbury, Charles Sammon, Monsignor (Maj. Gen., Ret.) Francis L. Sampson, Otis L. Sampson, Elmer Sandeen, Col. Edward M. Sayre (Ret.), Howard Scanlon, Maj. George R. Schnurr (Ret.), Erwin "Bud" Schroeder, John J. Schwartz, Lt. Gen. Richard J. Seitz (Ret.).

Michael Sembrat, Kenneth R. Shaker, Lt. Col. Mack C. Shelley (Ret.), Richard Sibio, Ernest R. Siegel, Edward J. Siergiej, Joe Silver, Glenn Slucter, Thomas J. Smith, George W. Stenger, Paul W. Stephenson, Dr. Harry Stone, William S. Story, William W. Sullivan, Ellery Sweat, Billy J. Tackett, Gen. Maxwell D. Taylor (Ret.), Brig. Gen. David E. Thomas (Ret.), Brig. Gen Edward H. Thomas (Ret.), Donald M. Thompson, John H. "Beaver" Thompson.

Maj. Andrew Titko (Ret.), Lt. Gen. John J. Tolson, III (Ret.), Leroy Tolson, Col. Edmund J. Tomasik (Ret.), Hugh A. Tracy, Leon L. Tracy, Myrle Traver, Paul Troth, Leo Turco, Seymour H. Tuttle, Dr. William Vandenberg, Col. Benjamin H. Vandervoort (Ret.), Frank Varelli, Lou Varrone, James B. Vignola,

Jerard Vlaminck, Richard Wagner, Ted Wallace, Thomas B. Waller, Sol Weber, John Webster, Sgt./Maj. Benny Weeks (Ret.), Otto D. Weer, James P. Welsh.

Ralph Wenthold, L. P. Wess, William F. Whipps, Col. Warren R. Williams (Ret.), Lloyd Willis, Lloyd G. Wilson, Jim Wittenmeyer, Rev. George B. Wood, Charles L. Worrilow, Lt. Gen. William P. Yarborough (Ret.), Harvey J. Zeigler.

Notes and Sources

INTRODUCTION

1. Col. William P. "Billy" Mitchell was court-martialed for defiance of his superiors in 1925. He had consistently called for more air power with which to fight future wars. Mitchell resigned from the Army rather than accept a five-year suspension. Early in World War II, when events confirmed many of Mitchell's predictions, Congress condemned the court-martial and erased the sentence from his record. However, the controversial figure had died several years earlier, in 1935.
2. Gen. Kurt Student became recognized as the "Father of the German Airborne," and numerous of his innovations were copied by American and British airborne leaders, who were striving desperately to catch up with the Germans.
3. In World War II, George Kenney would be Gen. Douglas MacArthur's air chief in the Southwest Pacific.
4. Paratroop volunteers had to be unmarried, be between 5 feet 6 inches and 6 feet 2 inches in height, weigh no more than 185 pounds, and be aged 21 to 32 years. Paratroop recruiters often winked at the height and weight restrictions.
5. A few years later, William T. Ryder would be General MacArthur's airborne advisor.
6. Paratrooping was (and is) a young man's game. During World War II, parachute battalion commanders ranged in age from 25 to 29 (there were exceptions).

CHAPTER 1. FIRST TO FIGHT

1. Henderson Field was named after Maj. Lofton Henderson, a Marine pilot, killed in the sea battle at Midway.
2. Later, Lt. Col. Frank Goettge was killed in action.
3. There was no stigma to be washed out of flight school. James M. Gavin, the famed wartime leader of the 82nd Airborne Division, and the legendary navy skipper John D. Bulkeley (a Medal of Honor awardee who had rescued General MacArthur from surrounded Corregidor in a PT boat) also washed out.
4. Gavutu was headquarters of Burns-Philp Company, a large copra firm operating in the British Solomons. Employees had been evacuated the previous February.
5. Robert E. Lee, *Victory at Guadalcanal*. Novato, California: Presidio, 1982, p. 17.
6. Richard Tregaskis, *Guadalcanal Diary*. New York: Random House, 1943, p. 91.
7. Edson, of Chester, Vermont, and Bailey, of Danville, Illinois, were awarded the Medal of Honor for actions on Guadalcanal.

CHAPTER 2. MISSION IMPOSSIBLE

1. During the war, the 509th Parachute Infantry Battalion had three different numerical designations: the 504th Parachute Infantry Battalion; 2nd Battalion, 503rd Parachute Infantry Regiment; and finally, the 509th Parachute Infantry Battalion. To avoid reader confusion, this outfit is referred to throughout these pages by the latter designation, by which it is best known.
2. William Yarborough's jumpsuits were worn throughout the war by parachute units in Europe and the Mediterranean, and in 1945 they were replaced by standard combat fatigues worn by all Army troops. Although made of lightweight fabric, the jumpsuits were found to be too hot by some parachute units in the Pacific, and they adopted regular fatigues for combat operations.
3. Officers and men of the 509th Battalion were tutored for many hours by demolition experts on techniques for disabling French aircraft on the ground.
4. The estate belonged to Lady Ward, an American married to a titled Englishman.
5. Rumors ran wild, and many Five-O-Niners swore that Airfields A and B were in Berlin.

CHAPTER 3. "ADVANCE ALEXIS"

1. After the war, aged Marshal Henri Pétain was tried as a traitor by the French, was found guilty, and was sentenced to death. Later, the sentence was commuted to life imprisonment.
2. Aircraft radios were tuned to 440 kilocycles, the *Alynbank* was broadcasting on a frequency of 460 kilocycles.
3. Lt. Col. John K. Waters was the son-in-law of Gen. George S. Patton, Jr. Later, Waters was captured, spent the remainder of the war in a POW camp in Germany, and was liberated by advancing American troops shortly before the conflict ended.
4. The 509th Parachute Infantry Battalion named its North African bivouac "Camp Kunkle" after Lt. Dave Kunkle.

CHAPTER 4. RAFF'S RUFFIANS

1. Five months after Tommy Mackall's death, a new paratroop training center in North Carolina, Camp Mackall, was named in his honor.
2. Col. William Bentley was released a few days later when the French and the Allies reached an armistice.
3. Because of political conditions necessary to get the French to fight on the Allied side, General Eisenhower appointed Admiral Jean Darlan head of the government in northwest Africa. Darlan was shot and killed on Christmas Eve 1942 by a 20-year-old Frenchman.
4. John Berry recovered from his broken leg, returned to duty with the 82nd Airborne, and ended the war as a battalion commander.
5. In his postwar memoirs, General Eisenhower said of Edson Raff: "His boldness and aggressiveness kept the enemy confused during a period of weeks."

CHAPTER 5. "BLOW UP ROMMEL'S RAILROAD!"

1. Anthony Cave Brown, *Bodyguard of Lies*. New York: Harper and Row, 1975, p. 287.
2. Col. Philip Cochran was the role model for the hero in "Terry and the Pirates," a popular comic strip of the era. In the strip, his name was Flip Corkin.

3. Dan DeLeo had enlisted as a private in the Illinois National Guard in 1937, and received his commission through the army Officer Candidate School in 1942.
4. Later, Roland Rondeau was seriously wounded in the Battle of the Bulge.
5. Frank Romero was subsequently killed in Italy, and John Betters was wounded and captured during a jump behind German lines at Salerno. DeLeo would be hurt in Italy, and seriously wounded in the Battle of the Bulge.
6. In addition to those who emerged safely from the raid, 15 others would eventually return during or after the war, either from escaping POW camps or being liberated by Allied troops.
7. A parallel situation occurred on the American side in March 1942: Gen. Douglas MacArthur was trapped on Corregidor in the Philippines. President Roosevelt ordered MacArthur to break through the Japanese blockade in a PT boat and go to Australia, 2,000 miles to the south, in order to fight another day.
8. The Combined Chiefs of Staff consisted of the top military officers of the United States and Great Britain. The Combined Chiefs decided global strategy during the war.

CHAPTER 6. FEUDS AND A CRUCIAL SECRET

1. Dr. John C. Warren, *Airborne Missions in the Mediterranean*. Washington: Department of the Air Force, 1955, p. 21.
2. Maj. Gen. G. F. "Hoppy" Hopkinson was later killed in Italy by a sniper's bullet.
3. Maj. Gen. Maxwell D. Taylor much later became the army chief of staff and ambassador to South Vietnam.
4. John C. Warren, *Airborne Missions*, pp. 22–29.
5. Gen. Matt Ridgway apparently had mellowed by the time he penned his memoirs some twelve years later. He described Boy Browning as "a man of great gallantry with a keen mind."
6. Matthew B. Ridgway, *Soldier*. New York: Harper, 1956. p. 68.
7. The first night parachute operation had been carried out in the early hours of February 11, 1941, when a force of 38 British paratroopers under Maj. T. A. Pritchard jumped to blow up the Tragino acqueduct in southern Italy. All of the paratroopers were captured.
8. Edson Raff was promoted to colonel at 31 years of age and reassigned to the Airborne Command at Fort Bragg, North Carolina.
9. An 82nd Airborne veteran told the author: "Jim Gavin was introduced as the new commander of our 505th Parachute Infantry Regiment in mid-1942. He appeared to be so frail and his face was so youthful that I whispered to a trooper next to me in the formation: "Good God! Are we going to be led into battle by a choirboy?"
10. Reuben Henry Tucker retired as a major general, became commandant of cadets at The Citadel, a private military college in Charleston, South Carolina. President of the college was Gen. Mark W. Clark (Ret.).
11. Field Marshal Albrecht Kesselring got his "Smiling Al" moniker because of the toothy grin he invariably was flashing when his photograph appeared in German newspapers.
12. It was not until just before the Battle of the Bulge, in December 1944, that Hitler apparently became suspicious that the Allies had cracked the Enigma code, and he ceased using it for a few months.
13. James Maurice Gavin told the author in 1987 that it was not until 25 years later that he learned that the Allied high command had held back from him the Ultra revelation. In the late 1950s, Gavin retired at three-star rank, and in the early 1960s he was President Kennedy's ambassador to France.
14. John Hall "Beaver" Thompson covered the remainder of the war, mostly from the frontlines, and later reported on the Korean War. In the mid-1970s Thompson retired as military editor of the *Chicago Tribune*.

CHAPTER 7. PARACHUTE ASSAULT ON FORTRESS EUROPE

1. *U. S. Army in World War II, Mediterranean Theater of Operations.* Washington, D.C.: 1955, p. 317.
2. A "stick" is an arbitrary number of men, usually 15 to 18, who jumped out of one airplane.
3. The password and countersign for the night came from the name of Gen. George C. Marshall, U. S. Army Chief of Staff.
4. After Sicily had been secured by the Allies, a British warship patrolling off the southeast tip of the island recovered the floating body of Capt. Robert G. Kaufman.
5. Pvt. William N. "Red" King followed Ryder out of the door and is recognized as America's first enlisted paratrooper.
6. Maj. Mark Alexander would be wounded severely in the Normandy campaign, injuries that would later force his early retirement at the rank of colonel.
7. John Norton later rose to general rank and commanded the 1st Cavalry Division in Vietnam, as well as NATO's southern command headquartered in Naples.
8. Capt. Willard Follmer's bad luck continued. His leg mended in time to parachute into Normandy on D-Day, where he again tore it up.
9. The surrender of 250 Italians to 14 American paratroopers would be typical of the Sicily campaign. Although individual soldiers were not lacking in courage, the Italian army's morale—especially on Sicily—had hit rock bottom.
10. Later promoted to major, James McGinity was killed during the Normandy invasion in June 1944.

CHAPTER 8. "ALL MISSIONS ACCOMPLISHED!"

1. Panic created by a mass parachute drop behind their lines was not limited to Italians and Germans. In December 1944, the Germans dropped a few hundred paratroopers behind American lines in the Battle of the Bulge, and panic infected the rear areas and some commanders and troops.
2. Samuel E. Morison, *Sicily and Salerno.* Boston: Little Brown, 1954, p. 126.
3. Correspondent Martha Gellhorn's story reprinted in the 82nd Airborne Division history, 1945.
4. Lt. Gen. James M. Gavin (Ret.) told the author that the performance by Lt. Col. Arthur Gorham and his men on Piano Lupo was a feat unparalleled at any time later in the war. However, Gorham received only the Distinguished Service Cross (posthumously), the nation's second-highest decoration.
5. "Amis" was a derogatory name for Americans, used in a similar manner to the use of "Krauts" by Americans.

CHAPTER 9. CRISIS ON BIAZZA RIDGE

1. Charles Billingslea was promoted to colonel and given command of the 325th Glider Infantry Regiment of the 82nd Airborne in the European campaigns. After the war, he rose to two-star rank.
2. Until this desperate point, Colonel Gavin had been wary about calling for naval gunfire because he felt the warships' gunnery officers might not know the precise location of Biazza Ridge and would drop shells on the Americans.
3. Capt. (later Maj.) George B. Wood was only American chaplain to make four combat jumps—Sicily, Salerno, Normandy, and Holland. After the war, he served as rector of the Episcopal Church of Fort Wayne, Indiana, for 24 years.
4. Lt. Col. Charles W. Kouns was later captured.
5. The serial number of Lt. John M. Gibson's plane was D-42-68708.

CHAPTER 10. HOLOCAUST IN THE SKY

1. Matthew Bunker Ridgway, who became Army chief of staff in the 1950s, has always maintained that no one knows who fired the first shot. "A few opened fire at the C-47 flight and the firing was contagious," Ridgway explained.
2. When Colonel Tucker's C-47 returned to Tunisia, the air crew counted more than 1,000 holes in it.
3. Albert N. Garland and Howard McG. Smyth, *Sicily and the Surrender of Italy*. Washington: Office of the Chief of Military History, 1965, p. 187.
4. Curiously, after a perilous 25-mile trek through enemy territory to American positions on the southern coast, the first person Yarborough and his troopers encountered was Charles Billingslea, an old friend and West Point classmate of Yarborough's.
5. Since World War II, the U. S. Army has thought that General Keerans had been killed when his plane crashed that night. But the author contacted the pilot of his C-47, John Gibson, and was shown statements from two crew members that Keerans was alive and well on the following morning.
6. T. B. Ketterson, "Official History of the 82nd Airborne Division," Ridgway Papers, U. S. Army Military History Institute, Carlisle Barracks, Pennsylvania.
7. Lt. Ivan F. Woods, a 505th Parachute Infantry officer from Humble, Texas, scored an impressive feat after Trapani fell. Taking 28 of his paratroopers in an old leaking fishing boat, Woods sailed to three offshore islands held by 437 Italian soldiers and talked them into surrendering without a shot being fired.
8. The German grenade had a handle on it and was shaped like a potato-masher, hence its name.
9. The author asked Mack Shelley why he went AWOL while seriously wounded to fight the Germans. He softly replied: "Because I was mad."
10. After the war, Dr. Carlos C. Alden, who had emerged as a highly decorated and legendary paratrooper, was considered by the army to be unqualified physically to be a peacetime paratrooper. So he transferred to the Air Force, later became its chief of psychiatry, retiring in 1964 at the rank of colonel.
11. General Eisenhower appointed a board to determine who was to blame for the friendly fire disaster. Testimony was so conflicting that no person nor unit was held responsible.

CHAPTER 11. MACARTHUR'S "KIDS" STRIKE IN THE PACIFIC

1. George C. Kenney, *General Kenney Reports*. New York: Duell, Sloan and Pearce, 1949, pp. 289–292.
2. MacArthur was prone to motion sickness. When he escaped from Japanese-surrounded Corregidor in March 1942 by means of a 560-mile PT boat trek, the general was below and stretched out on a bunk violently ill during most of the bold trip.
3. George C. Kennedy, *General Kenney Reports*, p. 292.
4. Nadzab was built into one of the largest United States airfields in New Guinea.
5. Throughout the war, Douglas MacArthur's casualty rate was incredibly low, as compared with Marine casualty percentages and those of American commanders in Europe.
6. John J. Tolson, III, rose to three-star rank long after the war and was commander of the XVIII Airborne Corps in the States.
7. New Guinea is the world's fourth-largest island.
8. John Powers returned to civilian life after the war and eventually was elevated to monsignor.
9. MacArthur's famed gold-braided cap was the one that had been designed for him when he was appointed a field marshal in the Philippines army after his retirement from U. S. service.
10. William Manchester, *American Caesar*. Boston: Little, Brown, 1978, p. 333.

11. Bennett M. Guthrie, *Three Winds of Death*. Chicago: Adams Press, 1985, p. 58.
12. John R. Galvin, *Air Assault*. New York: Hawthorn, 1969, p. 116.

CHAPTER 12. GIANT 2: SUICIDE MISSION

1. Albrecht Kesselring, *A Soldier's Record*. New York: William Morrow, 1954, p. 172.
2. When the 82nd Airborne men learned that the Hermann Goering Panzer Division, their foe on Sicily, was in the Rome region, some of the "All-Americans" were eager to "wipe out whatever remains" of that unit.
3. The behind-the-scenes maneuvering between Allied Force headquarters and the Italian government was stitched together from the following sources: Mark W. Clark, *Calculated Risk*, New York: Harper, 1951; Dwight D. Eisenhower, *Crusade in Europe*, New York: Doubleday, 1948; Maxwell D. Taylor, *Swords and Plowshares*, New York: Norton, 1972; A. N. Garland, *Sicily and the Surrender of Italy;* John C. Warren, *Airborne Operations-Mediterranean*, Maxwell Air Force Base: Air Force, 1956. Also 1985 correspondence with Gen. Maxwell D. Taylor and Lt. Gen. James M. Gavin.
4. Richard Tregaskis, *Invasion Diary*. New York: Random House, 1944. p. 47.
5. Ibid., p. 49.
6. Lyman L. Lemnitzer eventually rose to four-star rank after the war and was chairman of the Joint Chiefs of Staff, 1960–1962, and NATO supreme commander, 1963–1969.
7. In 1950, when Lt. Gen. James Gavin was chief of staff of Allied Forces, Southern Command, in Naples, he studied the airfields and terrain around Rome where the 82nd Airborne was to have landed. "There was no doubt in my mind that the decision to cancel was the proper one," Gavin wrote.

CHAPTER 13. DOOMSDAY LOOMS AT SALERNO

1. Contrary to the views of some history theorists, Mark Clark never panicked under the pressure at Salerno. Lt. Gen. William P. Yarborough (Ret.) and Gen. Alfred M. Gruenther (Ret.), who were with Clark most of the time, told the author that the Fifth Army commander remained calm, cool, and collected.
2. Mark Clark and Bill Yarborough had had a number of casual conversations in recent days on possible missions for the 82nd Airborne and its attached 509th Parachute Infantry Battalion.
3. Mark W. Clark, *Calculated Risk*, p. 137.
4. A number of musicians were dispatched to hold a small hill. Wags promptly dubbed the elevation "Piccolo Peak."
5. Ralph P. Eaton had served overseas in World War I, and in his youth he had been a good semipro baseball pitcher and maintained an avid interest in the sport.
6. Maj. Dan Danielson had been appointed battalion commander after General Ridgway relieved William Yarborough for protesting circumstances surrounding the shooting down of 23 troop carriers in Sicily.
7. Lt. Col. Joel L. Crouch had long taken a deep interest in developing pathfinder techniques. He certainly may be regarded as being at least one of the "fathers" of the pathfinders.

CHAPTER 14. BAILOUTS TO SAVE AN ARMY

1. A drop zone (DZ) is any relatively flat piece of ground, largely free of boulders, trees, or other obstacles, and of a sufficiently large size to accommodate landing of a unit (platoon, company, battalion, or regiment).

2. A jerry can is a narrow, flat-sided five-gallon liquid container of German design. The Americans used them by the tens of thousands, to hold water, gasoline, coffee—and, on occasion, alcoholic drinks.
3. Americans were not supposed to carry diaries in combat situations, because the journal might be of value to enemy intelligence officers.
4. Risers are the straps that connect a parachutist's harness to the shroud lines. *Blood on the Risers* was (and is) sung to the tune of the *Battle Hymn of the Republic.*

CHAPTER 15. THE LOST BATTALION OF AVELLINO

1. William W. Sullivan, one of the more rugged, easy-going types in the battalion, later received a battlefield commission. Much to the astonishment of his wartime comrades, Sullivan became a school teacher after his army discharge.
2. A few days after the 509th jump, George Fontanesi donned civilian clothing and made a perilous entry into a German-occupied village, bringing back food to his hungry band of comrades.
3. Sgt. Walter Cherry's hideous wound became infected. Lt. Dan DeLeo slipped into a nearby town crawling with Germans and brought back an Italian civilian doctor, who treated the wounded American.
4. After the Allies broke out of the Salerno bridgehead, Capt. Doc Alden searched the region for the treacherous Roger, but was never able to locate him.
5. Lt. Jack Pogue and Lt. Col. Doyle Yardley spent the remainder of the war as POWs.
6. "Doc" Alden later made a daring escape from captivity. He would be captured three more times later in Europe, always while far out in front of friendly lines or behind German lines.
7. Capt. Archie Birkner survived the war as a POW.
8. Gen. Mark W. Clark in letter to author, Dec. 8, 1983.
9. In his postwar memoirs, Gen. Jim Gavin said of the 509th Parachute Infantry's Avellino mission: "The battalion accomplished what Gen. Mark Clark had had in mind. It disrupted German communications and partly blocked the Germans' supplies and reserves. It also caused the Germans to keep units on antiparachute missions that otherwise could have been used at the point of their main effort at Salerno."

CHAPTER 16. ON TO ROME!

1. William Yarborough, while in Naples, conceived a unit patch for the 509th Parachute Infantry, which was drawn by a paratrooper artist, Bud Pardieck. The battalion men wore the patch throughout the remainder of the war, even though Army regulations prohibited insignia patches below the division level.
2. One of famed war cartoonist Bill Mauldin's most enduring drawings was that of a pair of nonjumper brass strolling past a paratrooper while wearing jump boots.
3. Martin Blumenson, *Salerno to Casino.* Washington: United States Army, 1969, pp. 154–156.
4. John C. Warren, *Airborne Operations-Mediterranean,* p. 70.
5. Chester G. Starr, *From Salerno to the Alps.* Washington: Infantry Journal Press, 1948, pp. 40–41.
6. Many officers in the 82nd Airborne had been surprised that Brig. Gen. Maxwell D. Taylor, the division artillery commander, did not get the post of assistant division commander.
7. A rigger was a paratrooper whose job was to keep parachutes and related equipment in working condition.
8. Mark Alexander told the author that his 504th battalion was the first Allied unit to cross the Volturno.

9. Letter Matthew Ridgway to Mark Clark, 11/5/43, U. S. Military History Institute.
10. *Time,* November 1, 1943, p. 35.

CHAPTER 17. MOUNTAINS, MUD, AND MULES

1. Dr. William Engleman confounded the prognosis of his army physicians and returned to practicing surgery after the war.
2. Trench foot is a swelling and discoloration of the member which, on occasion, resulted in amputation.
3. Capt. Charles C. W. Howland, one of the more popular officers in the 509th Parachute Infantry Battalion, was later killed by a mortar shell in the Battle of the Bulge.
4. A. E. "Ernie" Milloy eventually rose to two-star rank after the war.

CHAPTER 18. DEVIL'S CAULDRON

1. C. L. Sulzburger, *Picture History of World War II.* New York: American Heritage, 1966, p. 385.
2. Mark W. Clark, *Calculated Risk,* p. 179.
3. Source of high level views: Maj. Gen. Edwin J. House of the Air Support Command in postaction report, U. S. Military History Institute.
4. Albrecht Kesselring, *A Soldier's Record, p. 213.*
5. C. L. Sulzburger, *Picture History of World War II,* p. 387.
6. Many troops also called the big railroad guns (there were two of them, not one) "Anzio Annie."

CHAPTER 19. DEATH STRUGGLE

1. Sgt. Alvin C. York single-handedly killed more than 20 Germans and forced 132 others to surrender, October 8, 1918. York was a member of a patrol sent to silence German machine-gun nests. A member of the 82nd Division (forebearer of the 82nd Airborne), York was awarded the Congressional Medal of Honor.
2. Paul B. Huff became the first American paratrooper to receive the Medal of Honor for his action on Anzio. After the war, he went into civilian life, rejoined the army in 1949, spent two years in the Vietnam conflict (1967–1968).
3. Despite his legendary wartime deeds, Ted Bachenheimer's highest award was the Distinguished Service Cross. Comrades say that was because there were no eyewitnesses—except for the Germans—to his feats behind enemy lines.
4. The mine was called *Schu* after the name of its inventor. American GIs thought it was a "shoe" mine, so named, they believed, because it blew off a victim's foot.
5. Until today, and no doubt forever more, the 504th Parachute Infantry is known as the "Devils in Baggy Pants."
6. John R. Martin survived his serious wounds and the war as a POW.

CHAPTER 20. THRESHOLD OF OVERLORD

1. Gen. F. A. M. Browning was married to acclaimed authoress Daphne du Maurier.
2. James Gavin was orphaned at an early age and was raised by relatives in Mount Carmel, Pennsylvania.
3. In July 1942, the Allies—mainly some 5,000 Canadians—conducted what was billed as

a reconnaissance in force against the French Channel port of Dieppe. The operation was a bloody failure.
4. Chaplain Francis L. Sampson also saw heavy action in the Korean War, later rose to two-star rank as the army's chief of chaplains. In the 1980s, long after his retirement, he served as assistant to the president of Notre Dame University, and he became a monsignor. He also earned the gold wings of a Century Jumper (one who has made 100 or more jumps).
5. William Carey Lee would never regain good health, but he lived long enough to see large American airborne forces play decisive roles in winning the war in Europe.

CHAPTER 21. FORECAST: AIRBORNE BLOODBATH

1. The code-name Overlord was adopted at the suggestion of Winston Churchill.
2. Col. Joel Crouch's executive officer at the Pathfinder School was Lt. Col. James T. Blair, who became governor of Missouri in the late 1950s.
3. Omar Bradley, *A Soldier's Story*, p. 184.
4. Ibid., p. 186.
5. Ibid.
6. Dwight D. Eisenhower, *Crusade in Europe*, pp. 246–247.
7. Until his death, Dwight Eisenhower would declare that his decision over whether to call off the American airborne attack in Normandy was one of his most difficult decisions of the war.

CHAPTER 22. BLAZING THE TRAIL

1. Gordon A. Harrison, *Cross-Channel Attack*. Washington: Department of the Army, 1951, p. 179.
2. "Cover and Deceptions for Air Force Operations, European Theater of Operations" (also known as the Harris Report).
3. Ironically, Greenham Common, where American boys lifted off to fight Hitler was the site of large anti-American demonstrations by British "peace" groups in the 1980s.
4. Maxwell D. Taylor, *Swords and Plowshares*, p. 147.
5. There were 18 men in Capt. Frank Lillyman's lead pathfinder plane. Long after the war, Lillyman would quip that he had heard so many boasts from paratroopers who claimed to have jumped from his C-47 that he calculated at least 1,000 men must have been shoe-horned into his plane.
6. American paratroopers jumped with unloaded weapons, a measure that theoretically would prevent them from shooting comrades on landing.

CHAPTER 23. DARK INTRUDERS

1. Col. George Van Horn Moseley was hospitalized in England, and never returned to the 101st Airborne.
2. Charles R. Ryan carried the German major's pistol home after the war.
3. Paul Carell, *Invasion—They're Coming!* Boston: Little, Brown, 1964, p. 30.
4. Ibid., p. 35.
5. Ibid.
6. The Centurie underground network plotted nearly all German defenses along the Atlantic Wall and smuggled them to London in map form.

7. Col. Robert Sink, who most regarded as an exceptional officer, never was promoted during the war. However, years later he rose to three-star rank.

CHAPTER 24. SWAMPS AND MORE SWAMPS

1. Since World War II, Robert Murphy, a Boston lawyer, returns to Normandy on the D-Day anniversary each year and makes a parachute jump, his most recent one being in 1988.
2. After the war, William Walton became a good friend of a future president, John F. Kennedy, and his wife Jacqueline.
3. In the mid-1980s, citizens of Leonard Funk's hometown, McKeesport, Pennsylvania, erected a monument to him. In 1988, Funk was married for the first time, at age 71.
4. Paul Carell, *Invasion,* p. 51.

CHAPTER 25. DEATH STALKS THE HEDGEROWS

1. *Utah Beach to Cherbourg,* Department of the Army, 1954, p. 72.
2. Ibid. Six weeks later, Gen. Teddy Roosevelt died of a heart attack, never knowing that he had been promoted to two-star rank.
3. Dwight Eisenhower, *Crusade in Europe,* p. 247. Later that year Air Marshal Trafford Leigh-Mallory was killed in a plane crash.
4. Harrison Summers's incredible feat was recognized with "only" a Distinguished Service Cross, after a Medal of Honor recommendation was rejected. Summers would be seriously wounded in Holland and unable to walk for seven months.

CHAPTER 26. "FLUID" SITUATIONS

1. Lt. Turner Turnbull was killed in action later that day.
2. Lt. Waverly Wray would be killed later in Holland. All the while he was in the Army, beginning in January 1941, Wray contributed to his Shiloh (Mississippi) Methodist Church. When young Wray learned that the church's building fund was stalemated, he offered to match (from his Army pay) dollar for dollar all other contributions. Over a two-year period Wray matched some $2,300, and arranged for his father to carry out his commitments should he be killed. In 1948, the new Shiloh Methodist Church building was dedicated to Waverly Wray.
3. On D-Day James Van Fleet, as a 52-year-old colonel, led his 4th Infantry Division regiment in the assault of Utah Beach. He would finish the war with three stars and a corps command. Later in Korea, Van Fleet would receive his fourth star.
4. Col. Howard Johnson would say that the calm composure of Runge and Lenz bolstered his own confidence and caused him to continue with the surrender mission.
5. Omar Bradley, *A Soldier's Story,* p. 147.

CHAPTER 27. CARNAGE AT LA FIÈRE CAUSEWAY

1. Gen. Matthew Ridgway would say in later years that the La Fière causeway was the "hottest spot" he had been in during World War II and later in Korea.
2. Capt. John Sauls was wounded that night but recovered.
3. On later reflection, Gen. James Gavin concluded that this was an old military map

from Hitler's looming invasion of England ("Operation Sea Lion") in 1940 and that the circled region was an objective of a Wehrmacht unit.
4. Lt. Col. Charles J. Timmes, soft-spoken and low key, proved to be an outstanding combat commander, much to the surprise of fellow officers in the 82nd Airborne. General Gavin told the author that Timmes proved that one didn't have to be "loud and profane and act tough" in order to be a successful combat leader.
5. The Gammon grenade was named after a British sergeant who discovered the enormous explosive properties in Composition C.
6. Col. George V. "Zip" Millett survived the war in a German POW camp.

CHAPTER 28. DEATH ALLEY AT CARENTAN

1. Lt. Col. Robert Cole's postaction recollections.
2. Ibid.
3. For leading the bayonet charge, Lt. Col. Robert Cole would receive the Congressional Medal of Honor posthumously.

CHAPTER 29. MASS MURDER AT GRAIGNES

1. Paratroopers who escaped from Graignes would never learn the fate of the two 29th Infantry Division soldiers, the glider pilot, or the C-47 pilot.
2. In a July 6, 1986 ceremony at Graignes, presided over by Secretary of the Army John Marsh, 70 townspeople were presented Department of Defense commendations for helping the American paratroopers 42 years earlier. Walking with a cane and supported by her two daughters, Madame Boursier, age 90, moved forward to receive the Distinguished Civilian Service medal, the highest award that the military can bestow upon a foreigner.
3. Three days later, Lt. Lowell Maxwell was killed in Graignes.
4. Names of these 12 murdered paratroopers were furnished and spellings verified by Clarence Hughart, executive secretary of the 507th Parachute Infantry Association, and by Frank P. Juliano, president of the Allied Airborne Association, who was a Graignes participant.
5. Mayor Alphonse Voydie lived to a ripe old age and died in 1980.
6. Graignes townspeople converted the church ruins into a lasting memorial to neighbors who were killed by enemy action or were executed and to the American paratroopers who perished there.
7. The author is indebted to the following who, along with several participants, furnished information that allowed the Graignes massacre to be pieced together: Clarence Hughart, Lt. Col. Ercle R. "Pip" Reed (Ret.), Col. Francis E. Naughton (Ret.), and Frank P. Juliano.
8. Complications set in for Clarence Hughart's wounds, and he was shipped back to the States and hospitalized for a year.

CHAPTER 30. JUNGLE WAR ON NOEMFOOR

1. Vogelkop is Dutch for "bird's head." New Guinea is shaped like a turkey.
2. Gen. George Jones told the author that Col. Harris T. Mitchell (Ret.) was "one of the finest and most courageous officers" he had served with during the war.
3. Sgt. Ray E. Eubanks received the Congressional Medal of Honor posthumously.

CHAPTER 31. THE WAR'S WORST-KEPT SECRET

1. It has been frequently published that the First Special Service Force was the antecedent of today's United States Special Forces, or "Green Berets." Gen. William Yarborough, who commanded the Green Berets in the early 1960s, told the author that OSS units in World War II were the forerunners of today's Green Berets.
2. At age 43, Rupert Graves was the oldest U. S. paratroop regiment commander in the war.

CHAPTER 32. THUNDER ALONG THE RIVIERA

1. Rupert Graves, in his early 50s, led a regiment in heavy actions in the Korean conflict. In 1988, Graves was still attending the annual reunions of the 517th Parachute Infantry Association.
2. At the end of the war, Melvin Zais became commander of the 517th Parachute Infantry and brought it back to the States. He served two tours in Vietnam, including one as leader of the 101st Airborne Division. He retired in 1976 as a four-star general.
3. Today (1988) a main street in Draguignan bears the name of Albert W. Robinson.
4. Duffield W. Matson, Jr., the 20-year-old incorrigible (his description) did an about face. He graduated from the University of Miami, and today (1988) is a millionaire and respected Miami businessman.
5. Robert W. Frederick completed the war as commander of the 45th "Thunderbird" Infantry Division after his southern France airborne force was disbanded.

CHAPTER 33. OBJECTIVES SECURED

1. Andy Titko's "Dear John" letter had a happy ending. In 1948, he married the young lady, an Army nurse.
2. Some 20 glider pilots received broken legs and a few others were badly injured.
3. Col. Rupert Graves told the author in 1986: "The curious attitude of the British led us to conclude that Brigadier Pritchard had secret orders from Jumbo Wilson (the British general who was Allied supreme commander in the Mediterranean) to conserve the parachute brigade's strength. Apparently it was to go to the Balkans soon in support of British interests there." After five years of war, Great Britain was running short of manpower.
4. Richard J. Seitz became a general during nearly two years of combat command in Vietnam. Later, he attained three-star rank as leader of the XVIII Airborne Corps at Fort Bragg.
5. In 1988, Joe Cicchinelli still had the Nazi flag, and it adorns the wall in his Arizona home.

CHAPTER 34. WAR AMONG THE WINDMILLS

1. After the war, General Eisenhower wrote: "Had the pious, teetotaling Monty have staggered into SHAEF with a hangover" he could not have been more astonished than he had been by the boldness of the normally cautious field marshal's Market-Garden plan.
2. Lewis H. Brereton had been a United States Naval Academy graduate, class of 1911, who switched to flying prior to World War I.
3. James Gavin was one week younger than Robert Frederick.
4. In 1989, the Dutch people were still observing September 17 (D-Day for Market-Garden) as Holland Liberation Day.

CHAPTER 35. HELL'S HIGHWAY

1. Ted Bachenheimer's ventures with the Nijemgen underground came from a magazine story by war correspondent Martha Gelhorn and were verified to the author by many of Bachenheimer's 504th comrades.
2. After the war, Arie D. Bestebreurtje came to the United States and was naturalized. The former Dutch Olympic speed skater turned to the ministry and for many years was pastor of the First Presbyterian Church in Charlottesville, Virginia. Bestebreurtje died at age 66 in 1983 when he fell through thin ice while skating on the Rivanna River.
3. Gen. Kurt Student's First Parachute Army was in name only. It consisted of his headquarters staff and the resolute 6th Parachute Regiment.
4. Maj. John Stopka was killed in action during the Battle of the Bulge by American fighter-bombers.
5. James Gavin, *On to Berlin*, p. 164.

CHAPTER 36. EPIC CROSSING OF THE WAAL

1. James Gavin, *On to Berlin*, p. 170.
2. Several 504th Parachute Infantry participants in the Waal crossing told the author that Chaplain Delbert Kuehl toted a tommy gun over the river because two parachute medics had been hired on a day earlier. They added that they did not know if the padre had to use the weapon to protect himself.

CHAPTER 37. TRIUMPH AT NIJMEGEN

1. James Gavin, *On to Berlin*, pp. 180–81.
2. The multibarreled *Nebelwerfers* were called "Screaming Meemies" by the Americans because of the eerie screech emitted when the shells flew out of the muzzles. The Brits called the mortars "Moaning Minnies."
3. John D. Frost was held a prisoner for the rest of the war, and eventually reached two-star rank.
4. James Gavin, *On to Berlin*, pp. 181–82.
5. Pvt. John R. Towle was awarded posthumously the Congressional Medal of Honor.
6. John H. Michaelis recovered from his wounds and before the end of the war became chief of staff of the 101st Airborne. He gained wide fame as a regimental commander in the Korean War, and later rose to four-star rank.
7. *Time* magazine, October 9, 1944.
8. In the weeks ahead, some 280 more Red Devils escaped to the south bank after having been hidden by Arnhem region civilians at great peril.
9. Julian Ewell later became a battle leader in Korea and in Vietnam, and later became a three-star general.
10. After the war, Ted Bachenheimer was eventually buried in Hollywood, California. As of 1989, old comrades in the 504th Parachute Infantry were still visiting his grave.
11. Howard R. "Jumpy" Johnson's wife has remarried, but in 1988 she was still attending an occasional reunion of 501st Parachute Infantry veterans.

CHAPTER 38. AMERICA'S FIRST BLACK PARATROOPERS

1. Years later, Benjamin O. Davis's son, Benjamin O. Davis, Jr., would also wear general's stars.
2. The six lieutenants who received parachute wings were: Bradley Biggs, Jasper E. Ross, Clifford Allen, Edward D. Baker, Warren C. Cornelius, and Edwin H. Wills.
3. Lt. Col. Harvey J. Jablonsky, later a regimental commander in the 13th Airborne Division, after the war rose to two-star rank.
4. Lt. Warren C. Cornelius' hand was blown off.
5. James H. Porter continued with army service after the war and eventually retired as a lieutenant colonel.
6. Bradley Biggs distinguished himself in Korea in the then-integrated United States Army. As commander of an assault rifle company, he led his unit in the capture of Yechon, one of the first American victories in the conflict.

CHAPTER 39. A MAD RUSH TO BELGIUM

1. *Wacht am Rein* was Adolf Hitler's scheme, not that of Field Marshal Gerd von Rundstedt, as has popularly been presumed. The Fuehrer approved each detail, down to the boots to be worn by assault infantrymen.
2. James Gavin may have been the youngest officer since the Civil War to function as an acting corps commander.
3. Robert E. Merriam, *Dark December*. Chicago: Ziff-Davis, 1947, p. 87.
4. Hitler had sternly decreed that any Wehrmacht commander who used another unit's roads would be shot. Clearly, that did not apply to Jochen Peiper.

CHAPTER 40. COLLISION WITH *KAMPFGRUPPE* PEIPER

1. Penicillin was fairly new in the treatment of battle wounds to prevent infection.
2. William Walsh survived.
3. In 1988 and for many years prior to that, Donald Lassen was publisher of the national airborne newspaper *The Static Line,* at Atlanta, Georgia.

CHAPTER 41. ARDENNES MEAT GRINDER

1. In 1963, Milo Huempfner returned to Leignon for the wedding of Victor DeVeille's youngest son, Willy.
2. Harry W. O. Kinnard was commander of the 1st Cavalry Division in Vietnam in 1965–1966, and later retired at three-star rank.
3. After the war, Joseph Harper reached major general's rank.
4. John Toland, *Battle: The Story of the Bulge.* New York: Random House, 1959, p. 210.
5. Gen. Heinz Lammerding's 2nd SS Panzer Division had received notoriety shortly after the Normandy landings at the French village of Oradour-sur-Glane. According to testimony at a 1946 Nueremberg trial, the SS troopers murdered 652 Oradour civilians—men, women, and children.
6. Melvin Biddle escaped unscathed from this venture, but was wounded two days later. Shortly after the war, President Harry Truman, in a White House ceremony, pinned the Congressional Medal of Honor on Biddle.
7. John S. D. Eisenhower, *Bitter Woods,* New York: Putnam, 1969, p. 356.

CHAPTER 42. A VIOLENT CHRISTMAS EVE

1. On July 11, 1946, Jochen Peiper and 42 others in his *Kampfgruppe* were sentenced to death by an Allied court for their alleged roles in the Malmedy massacre in which some 100 unarmed prisoners were shot, even though testimony disclosed that Peiper knew nothing about the episode until later. In 1954, Peiper's sentence was reduced to 35 years in prison, and in 1956 he was freed. Soon, he took his family to live on a secluded farm in French Alsace, and in 1976 a French Communist newspaper article disclosed his whereabouts. Two weeks later, Jochen Peiper was killed when his house was firebombed.
2. Joss Heintz, "In the Perimeter of Bastogne," *Kiwanis* magazine, August 1975, p. 67.
3. John Toland, *Battle*, p. 237.
4. It could have been that the Germans had not deliberately withheld food from the famished POWs. The Reich's rail system was in ruins from repeated bombings, and the Wehrmacht found it almost impossible to distribute food and supplies even to its own soldiers.
5. Chaplain Francis Sampson made himself a pain in the neck to the guards at his permanent POW camp as he battled for the rights of his fellow prisoners. The Germans threatened to shoot him several times.
6. Hugh M. Cole, *The Ardennes*. Washington: Office of the Chief of Military History, U. S. Army, pp. 585–589.

CHAPTER 43. THE FLOODTIDE EBBS

1. The 2nd Panzer Division (army) had often been confused in Allied order of battle reports with the 2nd SS Panzer Division.
2. Leonard Rapport and Arthur Norwood, Jr., *Rendezvous with Destiny*. Privately printed, 1948.
3. John Toland, *Battle*, p. 264.
4. The author was a platoon sergeant in B Company, 87th Mortar Battalion, which was virtually destroyed within an hour.
5. Only half of Louise Fisco's haunting dream had come true. Surgeons saved Richard Fisco's arm.
6. It would be 35 years before author would learn the identity of the American paratroop outfit that counterattacked and drove the SS troops out of Sadzot.
7. Leonard Rapport and Arthur Norwood, Jr., *Rendezvous with Destiny*, p. 598.

CHAPTER 44. BATTLE OF THE BILLETS

1. Thomas J. Cross recovered and eventually retired as a colonel.
2. After the war, Col. William J. Boyle was visited at Halloran hospital in the States by Dr. Ben Sullivan, surgeon of the 517th Parachute Infantry, who had treated the seriously wounded battalion commander at the aid station. Sullivan told Boyle that he had thought that the wounded officer would not live long enough to reach a field hospital. In the Korean War, "Wild Bill" Boyle made two combat jumps with the 187th Airborne Regimental Combat Team.
3. A few days later, Donald Thompson was captured when SS troops overran an aid station. "Even though I was badly wounded, the SS guys beat the hell out of me because I was a paratrooper," Thompson told the author in 1988.
4. Sgt. Robert Hill was put in for a posthumous Distinguished Service Cross. But being from a "bastard" unit, the 551st, the recommendation disappeared in the bureaucratic maze.

CHAPTER 45. CLOSING THE TRAP

1. Ladislas Farago, *Patton*. New York: Obolensky, 1964, p. 313.
2. Sgt. Isadore S. "Izzy" Jachman was awarded posthumously the Congressional Medal of Honor.
3. Anthony J. McAuliffe eventually rose to four-star rank after the war, and forever would be known as the man who said "Nuts!"
4. These SS divisions were rushed to the Eastern Front to try to stem the Red Army's threat to overrun the Third Reich.
5. Letter found on dead German lieutenant by American intelligence officers.

CHAPTER 46. ST. VITH, HERRESBACH, AND "BLOODY HUERTGEN"

1. Two weeks later Gen. Bruce Clarke underwent surgery and did not return to the 7th Armored. After the war, Clarke eventually reached four-star rank.
2. The 509th Parachute Infantry Battalion veterans were still angry in 1989 over what they considered to be the callous way in which their pioneer outfit had been deactivated.
3. Leonard Funk received the Congressional Medal of Honor for this action in a postwar ceremony at the White House. President Harry Truman presented the decoration to Funk.
4. Source for the Bergstein minefield being the largest: *Stars and Stripes*, March 26, 1945.

CHAPTER 47. THE "MUD RATS OF LEYTE"

1. Kenneth Murphy saw heavy action in Korea as a battalion commander. Yet he would say that that night at the Leyte airfield was the most confusing that he had been involved with in two wars.
2. Lt. Col. Arthur H. Wilson's father, Arthur Senior (West Point 1904) had been awarded the Congressional Medal of Honor in 1909 while fighting the Moros in the Philippines.
3. Elmer E. Fryar was awarded posthumously the Congressional Medal of Honor.
4. In 1968, Charles Feuereisen was elected National Commander of the Jewish War Veterans of the USA.

CHAPTER 48. ON TO MANILA!

1. Robert L. Eichelberger, *Our Jungle Road to Tokyo*. New York: Viking, 1950, p. 190.
2. A month later Robert "Shorty" Soule was promoted to brigadier general and become assistant commander of the 38th Infantry Division.
3. Men of the 11th Airborne Division were unhappy over the massive publicity that the 1st Cavalry Division received for liberating large numbers of civilian prisoners in Manila. The 11th Airborne should have gotten at least partial credit for these liberations, its veterans claim, because the 11th Airborne was fighting against the bulk of the Japanese forces defending Manila.
4. Max Polick, who had been a squad leader in Manuel Perez's platoon, said in recent times: "Manny's Medal of Honor citation said he killed 18 Japs. Hell, Manny killed at least 75 Nips and knocked out all 11 bunkers."
5. In 1988, Col. Edward Lahti still had the loaf-of-bread-sized chunk of metal that had wounded him. It had been recovered by his troopers and later presented to him.

CHAPTER 49. "ATTACK AND SEIZE CORREGIDOR!"

1. Today (1989), as it has been for many years, Corregidor is a mecca for tourists from all over the world. Excursion boats leave Mariveles on Bataan and circle "The Rock." From Corregidor Inn on "Bottomside," tour buses run daily.
2. Capt. Frederick Pope, Jr., battery commander in the 462nd Parachute Field Artillery Battalion, and Emmet Spicer's close friend, recovered the medical tag that the parachute doctor had filled out on himself as he was dying. In 1989, the tag remained a part of a memorial set up for Dr. Spicer after the war at the University of North Carolina School of Medicine, which Spicer had attended.

CHAPTER 50. "SIR, I PRESENT YOU FORTRESS CORREGIDOR!"

1. From 1957 to 1961, William E. Blake was adjutant general of the state of West Virginia.
2. One of Lloyd McCarter's wounds was a bullet imbedded close to his heart. For the remainder of his life, this caused him great agony. His wife died in 1952 and, despondent over this loss and his increasing physical pain, McCarter took his own life.
3. Before Corregidor was captured by the Japanese in early 1942, the tunnel under Monkey Point was used by the U. S. Army as a wireless center to intercept enemy radio messages.
4. On New Year's Day of 1946, nearly 10 months after the Americans recaptured Corregidor, 18 or 20 bedraggled Japanese soldiers emerged from a cave and surrendered to an astonished soldier in an American Graves Registration Company posted on "The Rock."

CHAPTER 51. "ANGELS FROM HEAVEN" TO THE RESCUE

1. Henry A. Burgess told the author that Peter Miles contributed more than any other intelligence source to the success of the Los Baños rescue mission. Burgess has practiced law for many years in Sheridan, Wyoming.
2. Shortly after the war in the Pacific ended, Lt. George Skau was killed in an airplane crash on Okinawa.
3. Gen. Masaharu Homma, who led the Japanese invasion of Luzon in 1942, and General Yamashita, who commanded in the Philippines in 1944–1945, were tried by a tribunal of American army officers in Manila in 1946. The enemy generals were found guilty of "war crimes" and executed at Los Baños in February 1946.

CHAPTER 52. POISED TO LEAP THE RHINE

1. Lt. Gen. James M. Gavin (Ret.) told the author many details of his involvement with "Operation Eclipse." Other details were supplied by Col. Barney Oldfield (Ret.), who had been scheduled to bring war correspondents into Berlin in a specially equipped heavy bomber.
2. A veteran 517th Parachute Infantry officer told the author that the 13th Airborne's staff, fresh from the States, was still operating "by the book" and demanded that the 517th submit its S-3 journals for the time it had been in combat. None—or only

sketchy ones—had been kept, so a 517th officer spent weeks "inventing" and back-dating the journals, which were more or less daily diaries of events.
3. In his postwar memoirs, Omar Bradley told of recommending that Dwight Eisenhower call off "Operation Arena."
4. Gen. Matt Ridgway was the apparent victor in his long-running feud with Gen. "Boy" Browning. After the Holland operation, Browning was shipped off by the British to a post in Ceylon, halfway around the world.
5. Bernard Montgomery's smoke screen caused extensive bronchial discomfort, not only to the Germans but also to the British and American troops along the west bank of the Rhine.
6. All troop and aircraft figures and statistics in the Rhine chapters are from John Warren's official American airborne operations' books, produced by the army's Chief of Military History office.

CHAPTER 53. A THUNDERCLAP FROM THE BLUE

1. Gen. Bud Miley told author in 1984 that he was opposed to a daylight airborne assault, but so many complex factors were involved that he finally agreed to it.
2. Many years later, Edson Raff bumped into Joel Crouch for the first time since Varsity and demanded payment of the case of champagne. After a friendly argument, Crouch agreed to paying for half a case.
3. Brigadier Nigel Poett used a fox-hunting horn to assemble his 5th Parachute Brigade.
4. Much to the astonishment of colleagues, the daring Robert Capa survived the war. A few years later, he was killed while covering a war in Indochina.
5. The new 57-millimeter recoilless rifle was shoulder-held and weighed 45 pounds. It was designed to replace the ineffective 2.36-inch bazooka, which had been bouncing off German tanks since North Africa in late 1942.
6. Dwight Eisenhower wrote in his postwar memoirs: "Varsity was the most successful airborne operation we carried out during the war." Many knowledgeable sources would say over the years that Rugby, the airborne strike against southern France, was at least equally successful.
7. Gen. Matt Ridgway ordered that the C-46 "Flying Coffins" were never to be used again to carry paratroopers into battle.

CHAPTER 54. *ALLES KAPUT!*

1. Brig. Gen. Lou Coutts quipped to the author: "The reason I remained standing was that I didn't want to get my uniform muddy!"
2. Franz von Papen was a highly successful spy for the Kaiser in the United States during World War I.
3. It would be four months before Allied intelligence learned of what had become of Field Marshal Model and found his grave.
4. Gen. William Simpson had established a bridgehead over the Elbe and was convinced that there was little opposition to his front and that he could dash on to Berlin. However, he was ordered to pull back over the Elbe and await the Russians.
5. Radio conversation overheard by Lt. Col. G. K. Rubel, commander of the 740th Tank Battalion.
6. Lt. Chester A. Garrison had been badly wounded as a line officer with the 82nd Airborne in Sicily.
7. While a defendant in the so-called war crimes trials in Nuremberg the next year, Dr. Robert Ley hanged himself in his cell.
8. Julius Streicher was tried, convicted, and hanged at Nuremberg. None of his 23 code-

fendants, except for Robert Ley, would even speak with Streicher before and during the trial.
9. Paula Hitler Wolf was placed under house arrest, but later released.

CHAPTER 55. THE LAST HURRAH

1. The expected 1 million American casualties to subdue Japan would be as many as U.S. forces in all branches had sustained throughout World War II.
2. Brig. Gen. William Nelson Gillmore, who had come to the 101st Airborne in February 1945 as division artillery commander, replaced Maxwell Taylor. Gillmore was succeeded on September 25 by Brig. Gen. Gerald St. Clair Mickle, formerly commander of the 75th Infantry Division. Two weeks later, Mickle was replaced by Brig. Gen. Stuart Cutler, a veteran of the 1916 Mexican Border campaign and of World War I, and among a number of World War II positions had been that of deputy chief of staff of the First Allied Airborne Army.

Index